D1806963

Regards,
Larry

The History of Basque

Basque is the sole survivor of the very ancient languages of western Europe. Due to its unusual structure and its seeming lack of relatives, the language has long been the object of curiosity and speculation.

More than a century of specialist work has succeeded in shedding a great deal of light on the history and especially the prehistory of Basque, but this work has up until now been almost entirely confined to the specialist literature, and has not been available to general historical linguists. This book, written by an internationally renowned specialist in Basque, finally rectifies the problem. It provides a comprehensive survey of all that is known about the prehistory of the language, including pronunciation, the grammar and the vocabulary. It also provides a long critical evaluation of the search for relatives, as well as a thumbnail sketch of the language, a summary of its typological features, an external history and an extensive bibliography.

This book will be of particular interest to undergraduate and graduate students of Historical Linguistics and to specialists in Romance Languages.

R. L. Trask is currently lecturer in linguistics at the University of Sussex and is author of *A Dictionary of Grammatical Terms in Linguistics* (1993), *Language Change* (1994), *Language: the Basics* (1995) and *A Dictionary of Phonetics and Phonology* (1996).

The History of Basque

R. L. Trask

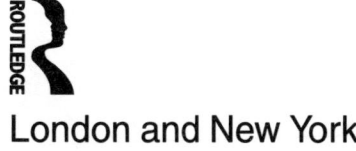

London and New York

First published 1997
by Routledge
11 New Fetter Lane, London EC4P 4EE

Simultaneously published in the USA and Canada
by Routledge
29 West 35th Street, New York, NY 10001

© 1997 R. L. Trask

The author has asserted his moral rights in accordance with the
Copyright, Designs and Patent Act 1988.

Typeset in Times by
RefineCatch Limited, Bungay, Suffolk
Printed and bound in Great Britain by
Mackays of Chatham, PLC, Chatham, Kent

All rights reserved. No part of this book may be reprinted or
reproduced or utilized in any form or by any electronic,
mechanical, or other means, now known or hereafter
invented, including photocopying and recording, or in any
information storage or retrieval system, without permission in
writing from the publishers.

British Library Cataloguing in Publication Data
A catalogue record for this book is available from the British Library

Library of Congress Cataloguing in Publication Data
Trask, R. L. (Robert Lawrence), 1944–
The History of Basque / R. L. Trask.
Includes bibliographical references and index.
1. Basque language–History. I. Title.
PH5024.T73 1997
499'.92'09–dc20   96–15702

ISBN 0–415–13116–2 (hbk)

Estherri,
aspaldikoari

Contents

Figures

Tables

Preface

Few languages have exercised so much fascination upon the collective
linguistic consciousness as Basque, and at the same time few European
languages are so little known to professional linguists. The only non-
Indo-European language in western Europe, Basque has long been an object
of speculation and wonder. Regrettably, it has also often been an object of
misunderstanding, confusion and ignorance. Not only irresponsible popular
books on language, but also the books and monographs of professional
linguists, constantly assert and perpetuate the most absurd errors and mis-
conceptions about the language.

Nowhere is this lack of understanding more profound than in the history
and prehistory of the language. All too often, one encounters in the linguistic literature a remark to the effect that 'nothing is known about the history
of Basque'. This is not remotely true. Scholarly work on the prehistory of
Basque has been underway for more than a century, and we now know a
good deal about the unattested earlier stages of this enigmatic language,
going back to the time of the Roman settlement of Gaul and Spain in the
first century BC. An ancestral form of Basque is actually attested at this
time, and it has been identified with certainty as an ancient form of the
language. At the same time, the ceaseless claims that Basque is related to this
or that other language, living or dead, have been shown to be without foundation. The phonological system has been reconstructed in great detail for a
period of perhaps 2,000 years ago, and the subsequent phonological development is very well understood. Layers of loan words dating back perhaps
more than two millennia have been identified and separated out from the
truly indigenous vocabulary, and many hundreds of secure etymologies have
been put forward. Understandably, perhaps, the prehistory of the morphology and syntax is much less well understood, but we have still managed to
discover important things about the origins of both nominal and verbal
morphology.

That this work is so little known to historical linguists in general is perhaps the fault of us vasconists (specialists in Basque). With rare exceptions,
all of our results are buried deep in the specialist literature, often in obscure

or defunct journals or in books long out of print and hard to find. The information available in the general literature is sparse, often linguistically uninformed and frequently inaccurate, out of date or just plain fantastic.

This book is an attempt to put that right. It might better have been called *The Prehistory of Basque*, since by far the greater part of it deals with the prehistory of the language, the long centuries during which Basque is attested only in fragments. Within the limits of the space available, I have tried to present everything we know, believe and suspect about the origins and development of this famous but little-known language. At the same time I have been at pains to identify the numerous errors, misunderstandings, unsubstantiated hypotheses and outright fantasies which have grown up around Basque and to demonstrate why they must be dismissed.

Naturally, most of the work presented here is not my own. Work of a sort on Basque goes back to the sixteenth century; serious descriptive work dates from the middle of the nineteenth century; with a few minor exceptions, scholarly work on the prehistory of the language dates from the 1880s, and it has continued ever since. All of this work is summarized and evaluated here, including some important work which is so recent that it remains unpublished at the time of writing. At the same time, I have not hesitated to include my own ideas where they are relevant: I include my own published work, of course, but I also present some of my recent work which has not previously been published and which has therefore not yet had the benefit of scrutiny by my colleagues.

The book is organized as follows. Chapter 1 is an introduction, including an external history of the language (and of the Basque people) and a history of linguistic work on Basque. Chapter 2 provides a brief sketch of the language, and it draws particular attention to the most frequent untruths and misunderstandings found both in popular books and in the linguistic literature; it also provides a typological checklist. Chapter 3 gives an account of the phonological prehistory of the language. Chapter 4 describes the work that has been done on the prehistory of Baque morphology and syntax. Chapter 5 describes the sources of the Basque vocabulary; it includes descriptions of structured parts of the lexicon, with etymologies, and it explains what is known about the origins of place names and personal names. Finally, Chapter 6 deals with possible connections between Basque and other languages; it focuses on the attempts at finding relatives for the language. Hundreds of references are provided to the original literature, and the most important reference works are critically described.

The history of Basque offers a number of fascinating phenomena and engaging problems: a unique phonological system which has undergone a striking transformation in structure, a remarkable apparent case of reversal of merger, the development of an extraordinarily rich and elaborate verbal system unparallelled in Europe, and the presence of the most thoroughgoing morphological ergativity on the planet, to cite just a few. It would be satisfying

to see enlightened discussions of some of these issues in the general literature, in place of the ignorant misunderstandings which have so far been the
norm.

The book is aimed primarily at historical linguists who would like to learn
enough about Basque to take it into account in their own work and to
evaluate proposals in their field which involve Basque. But I hope it will also
prove useful to aspiring specialists in the language who require a good
introduction to its prehistory.

Acknowledgements

First of all, I am indebted to my Basque teachers, particularly Esther Barrutia, Yvan Labéguerie and Joxe Mari Ibarguren. Next, I am indebted to all those other people who spoke Basque to me and made me feel welcome in the Basque Country: Itxaso Barrutia, Alejandro Barrutia, Carmen Azula, Tía Paula, all the clan Azula, Jon Madinabeitia (and Esti), Rosa Madinabeitia, Jesús Acha, Mari Asun Acha, José María Zabala and Kata, Julián and José Maritxu, Javi Ayala, all the clan Labéguerie, the people of Elorrio and of Milafranga (not forgetting *ma cousine* Françoise), Arantza Etxeberria, Txillardegi, Karmele Rotaetxe, and dozens of others too numerous to mention.

Third, I am grateful to the members of Euskaltzaindia, the Royal Basque Language Academy, for inviting me to their congresses (at their own expense) and for providing some splendid discussion. Fourth, I am grateful to the public libraries of Donostia and of Elorrio, to the British Library and to the Interlibrary Loan office at the University of Sussex Library, for their assistance in allowing me to consult specialist works.

Fifth, I am indebted to a number of colleagues for stimulating discussions of various problems, most especially to José Ignacio Hualde, Joseba Lakarra, Georges Rebuschi, Roger Wright, Bill Jacobsen, Richard Coates, Theo Vennemann and Xabier Zabaltza. Sixth, I am indebted to all of the following for bringing relevant work to my attention or for assisting me in obtaining it: José Ignacio Hualde, Joseba Lakarra, Esther Barrutia, Itxaso Barrutia, Arantza Diez de Tuesta, John Bengtson, Paul Sidwell, Marc Picard, Roslyn Frank, Jon Patrick, Roger Wright, Alexis Manaster-Ramer, Theo Vennemann and Xabier Zabaltza.

Finally, it will be immediately obvious than I am indebted above all to the generations of vasconists whose labours have provided the great bulk of the material assembled in this book, and particularly to that greatest member of our tribe, the late Luis Michelena.

None of these people necessarily shares any of the views expressed in this book, and all shortcomings are my own responsibility.

The writing of this book was made possible by a leave of absence funded by the British Academy and by the University of Sussex. I am deeply grateful to both institutions, and also to the colleagues who covered for me during my leave.

Euskara bizi bedi!

Abbreviations

Abl	ablative (case)
Abs	absolutive (case)
adj.	adjective
adv.	adverb
Aezk	Aezkoan dialect
All	allative (case)
Aq	Aquitanian
Ara	Araba (province)
Aux	auxiliary
B	Bizkaian dialect
Biz	Bizkaia (province)
Bq	Basque
Cast	Castilian Spanish
Com	comitative
Dat	dative (case)
Def	definite
Det	determiner
dimin.	diminutive
Erg	ergative (case)
F	female
Fr	French
Fut	future
G	Gipuzkoan dialect
Gen	genitive (case)
Gip	Gipuzkoa (province)
HN	High Navarrese dialect
Ib	Iberian
IE	Indo-European
Imperf	imperfective aspect
Indef	indefinite
Instr	instrumental (case)
inst.	instinctive

L	Lapurdian dialect
Lap	Lapurdi (province)
Lat	Latin
LN	Low Navarrese dialect
LNav	Nafarroa Beherea (Low Navarre) (province)
Loc	locative (case)
M	male
n.	noun
Nav	Navarre (province)
NFS	noun-forming suffix
NP	noun phrase
Occ	Occitan
Perf	perfective aspect
PIE	Proto-Indo-European
Pl	plural
postp.	postposition
Pres	present tense
R	Roncalese dialect
Rel	relative clause marker
Rom	Romance
Sal	Salazarese dialect
Sg	singular
Skt	Sanskrit
Sout	Southern dialect (extinct)
Sp	Spanish
Tns	tense
tr.	transitive
v.	verb
VFS	verb-forming suffix
Z	Zuberoan dialect
Zub	Zuberoa (province)

A note on citation forms

In this book, as is usual in linguistic work on Basque, nouns and adjectives are cited as their free forms, the form called the 'absolute indefinite' by Basque grammarians. Thus, the words for 'man' and 'new' are cited as *gizon* and *berri*, respectively. Most native speakers, however, differ in that they cite such words with the article attached: hence *gizona* and *berria*. A few older dictionaries and other works follow the practice of native speakers.

Again following common practice, verbs are cited as their perfective participles, the morphologically most central form and the one from which all other forms can usually be predicted: hence *ikusi* 'see', *joan* 'go' and *hartu* 'take'. Most native speakers do the same, but some eastern Basques use either the radical or the gerund as their citation form, and hence they would cite 'see' as *ikus* or as *ikustea*. A few dictionaries also use the radical.

Grammatical particles, having only a single form, present no difficulties for citation.

Whenever dialect variation is not at issue, words are cited in the modern standard orthography. The reader should bear in mind that the ⟨h⟩ written in words like *harri* 'stone' represents [h] only in the French Basque varieties; elsewhere it represents phonetic zero. I adopt this policy merely to avoid the constant writing of things like (*h*)*arri*. When dialect variants are relevant, these are cited in the manner adopted by the Basque linguist Luis Michelena in all his works. The standard orthography is used as far as possible to represent local forms. The aspiration [h], where present, is written ⟨h⟩, and the aspirated plosives of the northern varieties are represented as ⟨ph th kh⟩. The front rounded vowel of the Zuberoan dialect is written ⟨ü⟩, and the distinctively nasalized vowels of Zuberoan and Roncalese are marked with a tilde: ⟨ã õ⟩ and so on. The conspicuous stress accent of Zuberoan is marked with an acute accent. The contrastive voiced sibilants of Zuberoan are usually not marked, since they rarely figure in any discussion; when necessary, they are marked with an underline: ⟨s̲ z̲⟩. When the phonetic character of the diaphone [j] is at issue, an IPA symbol in brackets is used; thus *jan* 'eat' may be written as [j]*an* or as [x]*an* or in some other way. Any other phonetic details which need to be expressed are represented with IPA symbols in square brackets.

The phonemes reconstructed for Pre-Basque (around 2,000 years ago) are cited in boldface, in order to avoid a profusion of asterisks. But all unattested and reconstructed words and forms are cited in italics with an asterisk. Words cited from Latin are presented in small capitals according to the convention of romanists: hence FLORE 'flower'. Words from all other languages are cited in italics.

Words cited from twentieth-century texts are silently converted into modern orthography unless there is some reason to do otherwise. Words cited from earlier texts are, of course, presented in their original orthography, with an annotation where necessary, except in a few (identified) instances in which only the syntax is at issue.

Personal names present special problems. For centuries, most Basques have been given Spanish or French forenames, but each such name commonly has at least one Basque equivalent, and sometimes more, especially when a Basque diminutive is in use. An individual may be known sometimes by one form of the given name and at other times by another, and moreover the form used by the owner of the name may not necessarily be the one used by later writers to refer to him or her. On top of this, Spanish Basque writers often adopt the curious Spanish custom of translating all French names into Spanish. So, for example, a French Basque called *François* in French will usually be *Pantxo* or *Pantxoa* or *Patxi* in Basque, or any of several other local forms, and a Spanish Basque writing in Spanish will probably call him *Francisco*. A Spanish Basque named *José María* in Spanish will be either *Joxe Mari* or *Txema* in Basque. A woman named *María del Mar* in Spanish is *Itxaso* in Basque, and one called *María Teresa* will usually be *Maite* (this last is not even a translation equivalent, but it is traditional). A Spanish *Pedro* will be a Basque *Kepa* or *Pello*; a French *Françoise* will be *Pantxika*; a French *Jean* may well be *Manex* or *Joanes*.

Surnames likewise present difficulties, since, at the very least, they are most often spelled differently in Basque and in the other two languages, and sometimes there are additional complications. And all names, though most especially surnames, may be spelled differently in Basque according to the orthographic customs obtaining at different times and in different places.

The very first Basque writer to be published displays all of these problems very well. His first name was *Bernard* in French, but he is often known as *Beñat*, the Basque equivalent, and Spanish Basque writers call him *Bernardo* in Spanish. Worse, his surname is *Etchepare* in both French and Basque, according to the prevailing orthography of his day, but this name is today often written *Etxepare*, in accordance with the modern standard orthography, while Spanish Basques spell his name *Echepare* when writing in Spanish. Further, the French particle *de* is often fused to his name, producing all of *Detchepare*, *Detxepare* and *Dechepare*. As if that were not enough, some writers translate the French particle into Basque, producing *Etxeparekoa*. The resulting variation is a bibliographer's nightmare.

The two Basque linguists who write their names *Luis Michelena* and *Alfonso Irigoyen* in Spanish sign themselves *Koldo Mitxelena* and *Alfontso Irigoien* when writing in Basque.

Yet another complication is the Basque tradition of using pen names, so that, for example, the Basque linguist *José Luis Alvarez Enparantza* writes under the name *Txillardegi* – though his earlier works are signed *Larresoro*.

One final complication is the quaint practice, introduced in the late nineteenth century, of signing one's name surname first, with the ethnonymic suffix -*tar* attached. The instigator of this practice was christened *Sabino de Arana y Goiri*, or *Sabino Arana* for short, but he signed himself *Arana'tar Sabin*. Fortunately, this practice is now all but obsolete.

I have found no principled solution to this problem. In practice, I have chosen whichever seems to be the most widely used form of a person's name, if such exists. Otherwise, I have arbitrarily selected one widely used form and tried to use that consistently.

The major Basque cities of Bilbao, San Sebastián, Bayonne and Pamplona are generally cited in these familiar Spanish and French forms, though their Basque forms are also given at first mention. The city of Vitoria is usually cited as *Vitoria-Gasteiz*, its official form. Other towns are cited by their Basque names.

The seven Basque provinces are cited by their Basque names, except for Navarre, whose English name is familiar. The recognized dialects of Basque are cited as far as possible by names derived from the Basque names of the provinces and valleys after which they are named.

Chapter 1

Introduction

1.1 THE BASQUE LANGUAGE: TERRITORY, SPEAKERS, DIALECTS

The Basque language (self-designation *euskara*; dialect variants *euskera* and *eskuara*) is spoken today by about 660,000 people (according to the 1991 census) at the western end of the Pyrenees, along the coast of the Bay of Biscay. The Franco-Spanish frontier runs through the middle of the Basque-speaking territory, leaving rather fewer than 80,000 speakers on the French side, and the remaining half million or so on the Spanish side. The Basque-speaking region extends from just outside the cathedral city of Bayonne (Basque *Baiona*) in the north to the outskirts of the huge industrial port of Bilbao (Basque *Bilbo*) in the west; these two cities, and the ancient city of Pamplona (Basque *Iruñea*), all lie just outside the territory, though all three cities contain significant numbers of Basque-speakers. The beautiful resort city of San Sebastián (Basque *Donostia*) lies squarely in the middle of the region. As a result of emigrations at various times and for various reasons, Basque-speakers are also to be found in the major cities of Spain and France, in Belgium, in England, in the western United States (mostly in Nevada, Idaho and California), in many parts of Latin America and in Australia. The number of these expatriate speakers is not known, but is probably no more than several tens of thousands.

Like other minority languages, Basque is often perceived primarily as a language of the rural countryside, but this is a misconception: as a result of the heavy industrialization of the two principal Basque provinces of Bizkaia and Gipuzkoa, more than half of all Basque-speakers now live in cities and towns. Moreover, since the creation of the Basque Autonomous Region in 1979, Basque has been co-official with Spanish in the three provinces of the Autonomous Region: Bizkaia, Gipuzkoa and Araba. In the autonomous province of Navarre, Basque also has a degree of official standing. In the French Basque Country, the language has no official status.

The Basque-speaking territory extends for about 100 miles (160 kilometres) from west to east, and for about 30 miles (50 kilometres) from north

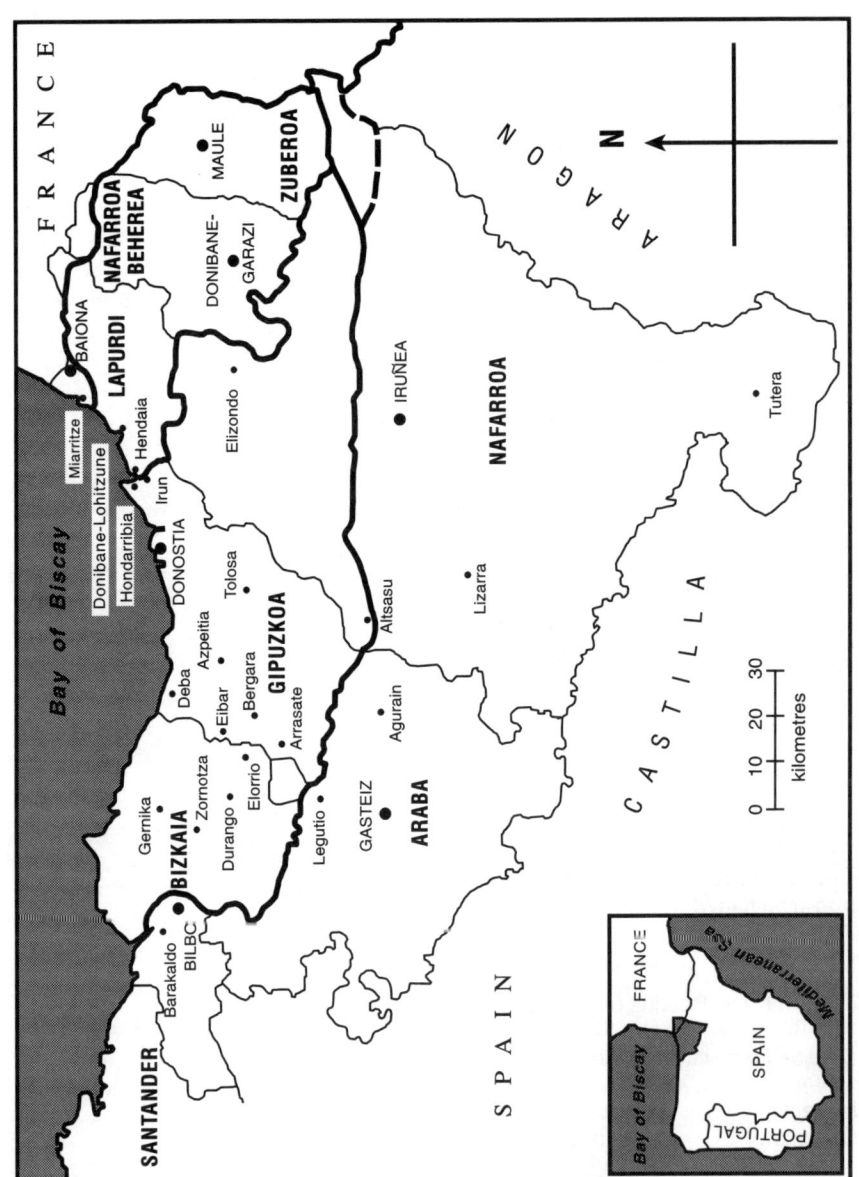

Figure 1.1 The extent of the language

to south (see Figure 1.1). The language now occupies less than half of the territory of the Basque Country (Basque *Euskal Herria*), the region which is historically, ethnically and culturally Basque. Basque-speakers make up about 20 per cent of the roughly 3 million people who live in the Basque Country, more than a million of whom are Spanish immigrants who came to find work in the industrial cities of Bizkaia and Gipuzkoa; few of these immigrants learn Basque. For centuries, Basque has been losing territory to Spanish in the south (see Figure 1.2, which illustrates our best guesses on the basis of the often scanty information available, but note that it is not possible to ascertain the boundaries of the language with precision at any time before the nineteenth century), while the boundary between Basque and Gascon in the north has been largely stable. Apart from small children, probably all Basque-speakers under the age of seventy are now bilingual in Spanish or French, though a number of elderly monoglot speakers remain, particularly in the centre of Gipuzkoa. With the political freedom that followed the death of the Spanish dictator General Franco in 1975, however, there have been determined efforts to reassert the importance of the Basque language in the south, and today, for perhaps the first time in its history, Basque has a sizeable number of speakers who speak it as a second language: *euskaldun berriak* (literally, 'new Basques'), as they are called in Basque (the word *euskaldun* means 'Basque-speaker').

The Basque Country is traditionally divided into seven provinces, whose names are given in Table 1.1 both in Basque and in Spanish or French. Nafarroa has a conventional English form Navarre; Bizkaia was formerly known in English as Biscay, but today that name is largely confined to the bay and to the abyssal plain which lies off it. In this book I shall use the Basque forms, except that I shall use 'Navarre' for Nafarroa.

The four Spanish provinces retain their identity today as provinces of Spain; the first three (Bizkaia, Gipuzkoa, Araba) are united in the Basque Autonomous Region, while Navarre constitutes its own autonomous region. The three French provinces lost their political identity after the French Revolution, when they were merged with the non-Basque region of Béarn in a

Table 1.1 The Basque provinces

Basque form	Spanish/French form
Bizkaia	Vizcaya
Gipuzkoa	Guipúzcoa
Araba	Alava
Nafarroa	Navarra
Lapurdi	Labourd
Nafarroa Beherea	Basse-Navarre
Zuberoa	Soule

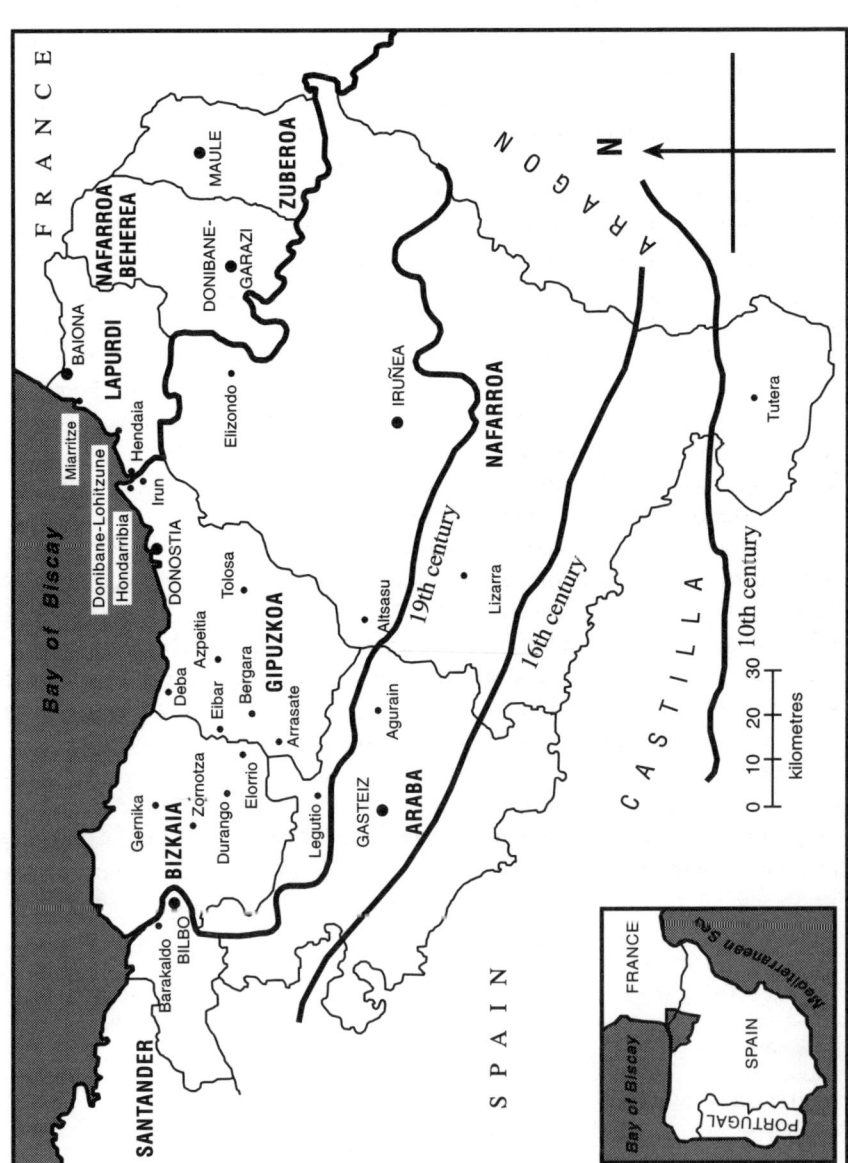

Figure 1.2 The recession of the language

département originally called *Basses-Pyrénées*, but now called *Pyrénées-Atlantique*.

The mountainous terrain of the Basque Country, combined with the long-standing low prestige of the language, has produced some considerable diversification into dialects. This diversification is great enough that speakers from different areas may have significant difficulty in understanding one another if they use their vernacular forms of Basque. None the less, this diversification should not be exaggerated, as has often been done in the literature: the dialects are overwhelmingly congruent in their fundamentals, and differ chiefly in vocabulary and in a few rather low-level phonological rules. There is a popular perception that the Bizkaian dialect in the west of the country is the single most divergent variety, but this perception is not supported by linguistic evidence. In the middle of the nineteenth century, the French linguist L. L. Bonaparte proposed a classification of Basque into eight dialects; half a century later, his system was somewhat reorganized by the Basque linguist R. M. de Azkue into seven dialects; in the 1950s, the Basque linguist Luis Michelena further elaborated the system into nine dialects, and it is Michelena's classification which I shall follow in this book. These dialects are listed in Table 1.2, while Figure 1.3 shows their conventional boundaries. The Roncalese dialect has for years been on the very brink of extinction, and now appears to be actually extinct. In addition, one other distinctive dialect, long extinct, is attested in a single book compiled in 1562; this dialect, apparently spoken in Araba, is called *meridional* by Michelena, and I shall call it *Southern* (Sout). The province of Gipuzkoa has the largest number of Basque-speakers, but, because the speech of much of western Gipuzkoa is classified as Bizkaian, it is probably the Bizkaian dialect which has the most speakers of any dialect.

Speaking very broadly, it appears that the central dialects have been the most innovative and the peripheral dialects the most conservative. But this is no more than a vague impression: at present, our knowledge of the histories

Table 1.2 The dialects of Basque

Dialect	Abbreviation	Spanish/French form
Bizkaian	B	vizcaíno
Gipuzkoan	G	guipuzcoano
High Navarrese	HN	alto-navarro
Aezkoan	Aezk	aezcoano
Salazarese	Sal	salacenco
Roncalese	R	roncalés
Lapurdian	L	labourdin
Low Navarrese	LN	bas-navarrais
Zuberoan	Z	souletin

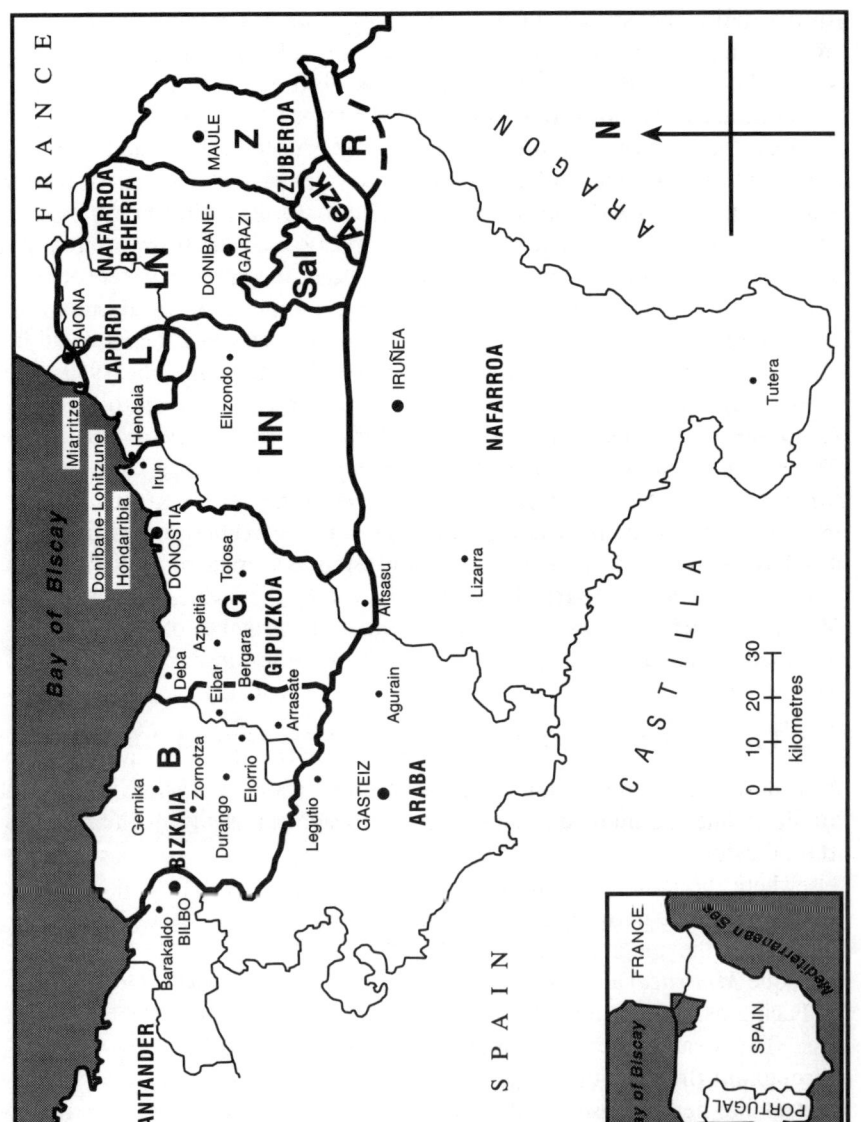

Figure 1.3 The dialects

of the several dialects is still in its infancy, apart from the phonological history, of which we know a good deal. But it would be a trivial matter to list apparent innovations which are confined either to the eastern varieties or to Bizkaian in the west, and it may be that our vague impression will be substantially altered by further work. In any case, it is often next to impossible to decide whether particular regional features, such as the dative flag -ts- of Bizkaian, or the words ler 'pine tree' and aizto 'knife' of Roncalese, are archaisms or innovations.

Since the 1960s the Basques have been gradually developing a standard form of the language, called *euskara batua*, or Unified Basque, under the leadership of *Euskaltzaindia*, the Royal Basque Language Academy. A standard orthography was promulgated in 1964, followed by a standard morphology, standard forms of all place names, and a basic vocabulary for schools; this standard is largely based on the central dialect of Gipuzkoan, with significant input from Lapurdian and Low Navarrese. More recently, the programme has been continued by others, particularly by the educational organization UZEI, which has published a large number of technical dictionaries, as a result of which it is now possible to write in standard Basque on virtually any subject. Most younger speakers of Basque can now write in *batua*, and can adjust their speech to *batua* norms when speaking to people from outside their own area. Neither the pronunciation nor the syntax has yet received any standardization, however, and considerable lexical differences remain, particularly between French Basques and Spanish Basques. A brief history of the standardization of Basque can be found in Rebuschi (1983/1984).

1.2 THE COUNTRY, THE PEOPLE AND THEIR HISTORY

The Basque-speaking region is overwhelmingly mountainous: this is a land of limestone mountains, separated by narrow V-shaped valleys, with only the occasional broader valley. In the north there is a narrow coastal plain; elsewhere the mountains run right down to the sea. The seacoast is blessed with several fine natural harbours and with the great estuary of Bilbao, and of course the magnificent sandy beaches of San Sebastián and Biarritz (Basque *Miarritze*) are world-famous.

Facing as it does onto the Bay of Biscay, the Basque-speaking region is wet. The weather comes from the sea and drenches the country almost throughout the year: the steady drizzle the Basques call *zirimiri* is a familiar fact of life here. Consequently, the land is green: except where bare mountaintops rise whitely above the tree line, a dark green carpet of deciduous forest covers the hills: beech, birch, ash, oak, with the occasional stand of fir or wild pine. Or at least this used to be so: today a huge area of the Spanish Basque Country has seen its indigenous forest stripped away and replaced by cultivated pine trees grown for timber. Summers are warm rather than hot; winters are mild but very wet, and snow is not common in the valleys. Overall, the climate is reminiscent of that of England.

Very different is the southern half of the Basque Country, the area in which the language has been lost. Much of this region is a high plateau, flatter and drier than the north, hotter in summer and colder in winter. Here the dominant colours are yellow and brown, all the way down to the narrow green ribbon which outlines the course of the Ebro, the great river which marks the southern edge of the Basque Country. The far south is wine country: it forms part of the Rioja, Spain's most famous wine-producing region. Today you are unlikely to hear a word of Basque spoken in the vineyards, but the names on the bottles are still unmistakably Basque: Ardanza, Olite, Murrieta, Ochoa, Olarra, Amezaga, Arana, Alberdi, Muga, Sarria and many others.

The Basque Country has been more or less continuously inhabited since palaeolithic times, though evidence from the lower palaeolithic period is sparse, and it may be that only the final retreat of the ice around 10,000 years ago allowed the country to become permanently habitable. From the upper palaeolithic period we begin finding extensive testimony of human habitation, the most striking being, of course, the cave art preserved in the region's numerous limestone caves; the most important of these caves are Otsozelaia (French *Oxocelaya*) in the French Basque Country, Ekain in Gipuzkoa and Santimamiñe in Bizkaia.

During the neolithic period (roughly 4,000–2,000 BC), the evidence for habitation becomes very much more abundant, possibly because of a steadily improving climate. In this period, pottery and agriculture make their first appearance, as do open-air settlements, though all these are largely confined to the south of the country; again, it may well have been a harsher climate which obliged the mountain dwellers in the north to retain their pastoral economy and their cave dwellings. Only in the Bronze Age (*ca.* 2000–900 BC) do we begin to find clear evidence of a settled agrarian economy in the mountains. A further striking difference between the two regions consists of megaliths: megalithic structures, and above all dolmens, are common in this period in the mountainous north, but unknown in the south. Archaeologists are divided as to whether this difference represents two distinct populations, with their own economies and cultures, or whether it should be interpreted as indicating a single population practising both agriculture and seasonal transhumance. If the dolmens are interpreted as tombs, it is hard to deny the presence of two distinct cultures, but if, as some have suggested, they were merely seasonal shelters for shepherds, a single population becomes entirely plausible.

On the whole, in spite of the regional differences, archaeologists are satisfied that the record of occupation in the Basque Country from the palaeolithic to the end of the Bronze Age is one of continuity: everything points to the uninterrupted presence of the same people, with their culture evolving in place and receiving influences, but not invasions, from elsewhere in Europe. Consequently, many people have somewhat enthusiastically declared the Basques to be the direct descendants of the original human settlers of Europe, the Cro-Magnon people of some 35,000 years ago. While by no means totally out of the question, such speculations have until recently been supported by little more than negative evidence – the absence of evidence for new populations – and, as we shall see in the next section, they run into difficulty with the linguistic evidence.

On the other hand, the geneticist Luigi Luca Cavalli-Sforza and his colleagues have recently been constructing a genetic map of Europe, and they conclude that the Basques are, genetically speaking, strikingly different from their neighbours (Cavalli-Sforza 1988; Bertranpetit and Cavalli-Sforza 1991; Cavalli-Sforza et al. 1994). These workers find a sharply defined genetic gradient separating the population of the Basque Country from the other inhabitants of the Iberian Peninsula, and a somewhat more diffuse gradient separating them from the other people of France, with the southwest of France showing marked affinities with the Basque Country, an observation which is strongly in harmony with the linguistic evidence discussed below.

Bertranpetit and Cavalli-Sforza (1991) draw the following bold conclusions:

> [T]he major difference in the Iberian Peninsula is that between people originally of Basque and non-Basque descent. The recession in time of the boundaries of the Basque-speaking area seems correlated with the progressive genetic dilution of the Basque genotype in modern populations. . . . Most probably, Basques represent descendants of Paleolithic and/or Mesolithic populations and non-Basques later arrivals, beginning with the Neolithic.
>
> (p. 51)

> [Our results suggest] that, in Iberia, the Basques were less changed by subsequent admixture with later arrivals, while in other areas of Mesolithic development, this dilution has largely altered the initial genetic pattern.
>
> (p. 60)

The Iron Age (about 900–200 BC) is significantly different: here we find signs of what can plausibly be taken as evidence for invaders, in the form of a small number of fortified settlements quite different from anything seen earlier in the region but rather similar to those associated with the Iron Age culture of the Celts across much of Europe. These settlements persist until the Roman invasion of Spain, and, since we have certain evidence for Celtic-speakers in Spain before the Romans, and (as we shall see) clear evidence for Indo-European-speakers, most likely Celts, in much of the Basque Country, it is not excessively rash to conclude that it was during the Iron Age that the Indo-Europeans moved into the Basque Country.

In the second century BC the Romans began their slow conquest of the

Iberian Peninsula, which was finally completed late in the first century BC. In the process, the Romans conquered the Celtiberian (i.e., peninsular Celtic) city of Calagurris (modern Calahorra) in the Ebro valley, and the Roman general Pompey founded the city of Pompeiopolis (modern Pamplona) in Navarre in about 75 BC; Pamplona was, so far as we know, the first city ever built in the Basque Country.

In about AD 7, the Greek geographer and historian Strabo completed his *Geography*, much of which was devoted to Spain. Drawing upon the now lost works of earlier travellers, Strabo (who had probably not visited Spain himself) devotes only a few pages to the north of Spain, and especially to the western Pyrenees. Fascinatingly, he declares that the western Pyrenees, all the way down to the sea, are inhabited by a people he calls the Ουασκωνους (*Ouaskōnous*), a name usually rendered into English as 'Vasconians'. These people have generally been identified with the people later called the *Vascones* by the Romans, and who, according to Roman sources, inhabited part of the modern Basque Country (see the next section). Strabo also declares that the chief cities of the Vasconians are Calahorra, Pamplona and a certain 'Oiasona'. This last, like the later Roman name Oeasso, has usually been identified with the modern town of Oiartzun in Gipuzkoa; though this identification has long been debated, it is now generally accepted. Very likely this was another Roman settlement, since there is no evidence that the Basques were building cities at this time. (On all this, see Michelena 1956a.)

The classical writer Ptolemy also mentions several towns in the Basque Country: Δηουα (modern *Deba* (Gip), Sp *Deva*), Γεβαλα (modern *Gebara* (Ara), Sp *Guevara*), (Τριτιον) Τουβορικον (sometimes identified with modern *Mutriku* (Gip), Sp *Motrico*; the proposal is *Tuboricum* > **But(o)ricum* > *Mutriku*). Ptolemy also mentions the puzzling Ιτουρισσα on the Mediterranean coast, which looks just like *Iturritza*, a conspicuously Basque place name attested for a locality in the Basque Country itself. The Roman writer Pliny mentions the *Ilu(m)beritani*, the people of the town which is modern Basque *Irunberri* (Nav; Sp *Lumbier*), and the *Alabanenses*, the people of the province of *Araba* (Sp *Álava*).

Strabo's few remarks about the culture of the mountain people are probably not very trustworthy, but it is interesting that he declares the sacrifice of rams to be an important part of their religion, since there is evidence that the sacrifice of rams or he-goats was a central part of Basque religion until the (very late) arrival of Christianity in the region.

Unlike their neighbours, several of whom fought bloody wars of rebellion against Roman dominion, the Basques appear to have accepted Roman overlordship without demur. There are no records of any fighting in the Basque Country, and indeed relations appear to have been good, as witnessed by the extensive presence in Basque of Latin loan words from a very early period (see Chapter 5). On the other hand, Roman authority appears to have been wielded in the Basque Country with a very light hand: few Romans settled in the territory, and the degree of romanization appears to have been minimal, except in the Ebro valley, the *Ager Vasconum*, where romanization was intense. (The unromanized north of Navarre was called in contrast the *Saltus Vasconum*, while the territory north of the Pyrenees, formerly called *Aquitania*, was renamed *Novempopulania*.) The historian Roger Collins (1986: 55) suggests that the Roman army traded with the Basques, buying grain, meat, furs and hides for its troops, but that the Romans never regarded the Basques as a threat and otherwise left them in peace. Indeed, several historians have suggested that the region was scarcely romanized at all until some time around the beginning of the second millennium AD. This lack of Roman interest undoubtedly resulted from a perception that the mountainous Basque terrain, with little agricultural land, no cities, few obvious resources, and harbours that faced uselessly (from the Roman point of view) onto the Atlantic, was simply too insignificant to be worth the trouble of colonization. And the same lack of Roman interest is very largely what guaranteed the unique survival of the Basque language. See Echenique (1987: Ch. 3) for a summary with references on the romanization of the Basque Country.

The famous bronze inscription found at Ascoli in Italy records the gratitude of the Roman commander Pompeius Strabo for the assistance in capturing that town of some unidentified soldiers from north of the Ebro, most likely Vascones. Later, perhaps because of P. Strabo's friendly relations with the Vascones, the Vascones fought on the side of his son Pompey during the Sertorian war of 87–72 BC, and this is when the Vascones appear in Roman records for the first time. According to the historians Sallust and Strabo, some of the fighting took place in or near the territory of the Vascones, in which Pompey founded the city of Pamplona.

Roman interest in the Basque Country was chiefly military. The Romans built a number of roads across the Pyrenees in order to link the Ebro valley to the south of France; the most important of these crossed the mountains at the pass of Roncesvaux (in French; in Spanish, *Roncesvalles*; in Basque, *Orreaga*). At the mouth of the river Adour, in the modern French Basque Country, they built the fort of Lapurdum, which eventually became the city of Bayonne. Like other inhabitants of the empire, the peoples of the Basque Country provided Rome with soldiers. Fragmentary Roman records attest to the existence of a unit called Cohors II Vasconum Civium Romanorum or Cohors II Vasconum Equitata, whose name shows that it was drawn from the Vascones. Much better documented is another unit, Cohors I Fida Vardullorum Equitata, obviously drawn from the Varduli, the people who inhabited much of Gipuzkoa in Roman times. This unit apparently distinguished itself: it was awarded first the epithet 'Fida' for some unknown display of loyalty and later the epithet 'Antoniniana' by its apparently grateful general Marcus Aurelius Antoninus (Caracalla). Interestingly, the Vardulian unit is known to have been stationed for much of its time in Britain, particularly at High Rochester in Northumberland.

Remarkably, after the collapse of Roman power in northern Spain, the Basques resisted bitterly the attempts of the Visigoths and the Franks to establish their authority in the area. From the sixth to the ninth centuries, the Basques, finding themselves wedged between the two rival kingdoms, engaged in a series of raids, ambushes and pitched battles against both Germanic kingdoms (and also against the Arabs, when these invaders reached the Ebro). In 581 the Frankish duke Bladast led what was apparently a punitive expedition into Vasconia, only to see most of his army destroyed. In 587, according to Gregory of Tours, the Vascones came down from their mountains and pillaged the plains of southern Aquitaine, laying waste the countryside and carrying off livestock and captives. In 635, during a gigantic Frankish military operation intended to subdue the Basques, a force led by Duke Arnebert was annihilated in the valley of 'Subola', thought to have been in the modern Zuberoa. In 755 Yusuf al-Fihri, the Arab governor of Al-Andalus, launched another apparent punitive expedition against the Basques of Pamplona, only to be defeated. Visigothic campaigns by King Suinthila in 625, King Wamba in 673 and King Roderic in 711 met with no greater success: the Basques fought stoutly, yielded briefly when they had to, and then rebelled again. One of these battles has passed into European legend: in 778, the Basques ambushed and destroyed a retreating Frankish army at the Pyrenean pass of Roncesvalles, thus inflicting upon Charlemagne the only major military defeat of his long career. Appalled and scandalized by this crushing defeat at the hands of an unregarded mountain people, Charlemagne's bards embroidered the story into the magnificent *Chanson de Roland*, greatest of all medieval romances, in which the defeat is ascribed to a vast Muslim army aided by demons from hell. (Interestingly, a second Frankish army was crushed at Roncesvalles in 824.) As a result of these efforts, the Basques were never effectively subdued by Franks or Visigoths, and they eventually formed their own autonomous states, the same states which now constitute the provinces of the Basque Country. Indeed, there is every reason to believe that, during this period, the Basques succeeded in imposing themselves upon, and settling, sizeable areas of Visigothic and Frankish territory which they had not previously inhabited: this was probably the time when the modern boundaries of the Basque Country were at least approximately delineated. None the less, the city of Pamplona was frequently in the hands of the Visigoths or the Franks, and for a while even of the Arabs.

It was during these largely unsuccessful military operations that the Visigothic king Leovigild, in 581, reportedly occupied part of southern Vasconia and founded a city called Victoriacum. It has been widely assumed that this is the modern Basque city of Vitoria in Araba, but only for lack of a better candidate: there is no evidence to support this identification. Indeed, the *fuero* (charter) granted to Vitoria by King Sancho the Wise in 1181 specifically declares that 'Vitoria' is a name being *newly* conferred upon the city, which is said to have been known previously by its Basque name of Gasteiz.

A particularly vexed question throughout this period is that of religion. It is clear that there was a significant Christian presence in the Ebro valley from the fourth century onwards, and a bishopric is attested in Pamplona from 589. On the other hand, the Basque heartland in the mountains is devoid of any trace of Christianity before the tenth century: even the bishopric of Bayonne is not attested earlier than this date. In the words of Roger Collins (1986: 66), 'From the land between Pamplona and the river Adour, and between Pamplona and the Bay of Biscay, there exists no evidence for the person of a single Christian in this period.' What evidence we have of Basque religion is evidence for continued paganism and hostility to Christianity. Around 630 or 640 the missionary bishop Amandus (later Saint Amandus) made an attempt to convert the Basques, but his mission met nothing but opposition and failure. The famous cemetery of Argiñeta in Elorrio (Bizkaia), generally dated to 883, shows discoidal tombstones (sunsigns?) with no trace of a cross, and is thought to represent pre-Christian burial practices. Arab writers not infrequently referred to the Basques as *maǧūs* 'wizards, pagans'. Consequently, most historians other than Christian apologists have concluded that the Basques of Bizkaia, Gipuzkoa and the French Basque Country did not accept Christianity before the tenth century, and in some cases later than that.

Unfortunately, the eventual Basque embrace of the Church of Rome was so thoroughgoing that information about their earlier religion has been all but obliterated. The Aquitanian inscriptions of the Roman period (which preserve an ancestral form of Basque; see below) record a number of divine names, one of which, Ilurberrixus Anderexus, is particularly frequent and may represent a deity of outstanding importance (see Chapter 6). Apart from Strabo's remark that the Basques sacrificed rams to their gods, attempts at reconstructing the ancient Basque religion have been frustrated by a near-total lack of reliable information, and anthropologists have been forced to extract what little they can from Basque folklore, which may or may not preserve fragments of earlier religious belief. The enigmatic figure of Mari, the lady of the mountains, is thought by some to represent a continuation of an ancient goddess, though one doubtless overlaid by the Christian Virgin. Sugaar, the serpent, may perhaps be the descendant of another deity, but Basajaun, the Old Man of the Woods, seems to be strictly a character of folklore, as does Herensuge, a monstrous serpent, while the Lamiak, or Lamiñak, beautiful but malevolent women with animal feet, are found far and wide in the folklore of southern Europe. (See Chapter 5 for some discussion of these names.) The *lauburu*, a rounded swastika resembling four commas joined at their points, is found everywhere in the country as a decorative emblem, but is of unknown origin.

Christian or pagan, the Basques by the ninth century were beginning to form states of their own. First to appear was the territory of Araba, which was quickly, if briefly, absorbed into the Kingdom of Asturias. By the tenth century, the *señorío* (seigneury) of Bizkaia was in existence, and Gipuzkoa followed a century later; both these last two had successfully fought off repeated attempts at annexation by the crowns of Asturias and León. By contrast, the French Basques were throughout this period subjects of the powerful Duchy of Gascony, a nominal vassal state of the Frankish kingdom.

But the most significant developments were occurring in Pamplona. After centuries of Visigothic, Frankish and Arab squabbling over the city, it had passed into the hands of the Banu Qasi, the descendants of a Visigothic lord called Cassius who had converted to Islam in 714 and whose descendants had controlled the upper Ebro valley ever since. The Banu Qasi governor was driven out by the pro-Frankish party, but Frankish influence did not last for long. In about 824 a certain Iñigo Arista in turn overthrew the last trappings of Frankish hegemony and founded the tiny Kingdom of Pamplona. Iñigo, like most of the population of Navarre, was a Basque. He was probably a Christian; his wife Queen Oneca certainly was, as she founded the monastery of Leire, on the eastern frontier of Navarre. The tiny kingdom survived, but at first it did not prosper: Iñigo's son King García somehow contrived to be captured by Viking raiders in 861 and had to be expensively ransomed (this in a kingdom with no coastline); moreover, García suffered repeated disastrous defeats at the hands of the Arab Ummayad armies, and his son and heir Fortún was captured and imprisoned in Córdoba.

Though Fortún eventually acceded to the throne, the history of the little kingdom at this period becomes complex and obscure. There appear to have been some remarkably tortuous political manoeuvrings on all sides, including a few betrayals and judicious marriages. The result was that Fortún's line was overthrown, and he was succeeded on the throne in 925 by Sancho Garcés I, who cemented his position by marrying his predecessor's granddaughter. As a result of some earlier political realignments, the new king found himself in possession of a large piece of Aragón, to the east; ambitiously he set out to expand his realm southwards. In spite of some setbacks, during one of which his capital was sacked by the Arabs, he persevered, and eventually, just before his death, he took control of a large part of the Ebro valley.

He was succeeded by a series of kings called alternately García Sánchez and Sancho Garcés, most of whom proved to be capable and successful at a time when the kingdom's two most influential neighbours, the Kingdom of León and the Duchy of Gascony, were on the wane. By the death of King Sancho Garcés III 'the Great' in 1035, the Kingdom of Pamplona, now renamed the Kingdom of Navarre, had become by far the most powerful Christian state in Spain. By a combination of marriage, inherit-ance, diplomacy and combat, including the novel tactic of heavy armoured cavalry, the Navarrese rulers had taken control of the entire modern Basque Country, both north and south of the Pyrenees, as well as Castile (to which large numbers of Basque settlers made their way), most of León, part of Aragón, and (briefly) all of Gascony up to the Garonne. This is the one and only time in post-Roman history when all Basques have been united in a single political entity. However, although almost the entire population of Navarre itself was Basque, and although its kings were Basques, the Kingdom of Navarre was never avowedly a Basque polity, but a Spanish one: the speech of polite society was at first Occitan and then the local Navarrese form of Romance; Latin was used for impor-tant documents; and Basque remained only the everyday language of the people.

The decline of Navarre was even faster than its rise. On the death of Sancho the Great, his kingdom was divided among his three sons, and before long it was the realms of Castile and Aragón which were expanding at the expense of Navarre: Aragón took control of much of the Ebro valley, blocking off any Navarrese ambitions to the south, while Castile detached the Basque provinces of Araba, Bizkaia and Gipuzkoa and brought them into its own orbit. North of the Pyrenees, Navarrese possessions were lost first to the rising Duchy of Aquitaine and then to the Angevin kings of England. Bayonne, which had become a rich and important port, was retaken, but only briefly, and before long Navarre still held only a tiny sliver of the French Basque Country, which came to be known as Basse-Navarre. Within a few decades, the rich and mighty Kingdom of Navarre had dwindled into insignificance, and it would never again play a leading part in political events in Spain.

The early Middle Ages were a time of urbanization and economic growth in the Basque Country. This was partly due to French influence. On the one hand, French pilgrims were flocking to the newly important shrine of San-tiago de Compostela, the routes to which all led through the Basque Country, and bringing with them all sorts of new ideas. On the other, the Navarrese kings actively encouraged French settlers to move in and found cities, few of which yet existed in the Basque mountains. The most impor-tant consequence of these developments was the founding of San Sebastián (Gipuzkoa) in 1180 and of Bilbao (Bizkaia) in 1300; these two cities and Bayonne were the only important Basque ports, and they were destined to play a major role in Basque history later, especially Bilbao. But the twelfth century in particular saw the founding of dozens of towns through-out the Basque territories; the *fueros*, or charters of foundation, of these municipalities, many of which still survive, provide us with our most impor-tant source of information about Basque society at the time.

That information is none too plentiful, but we can still form a picture of a mixed economy: pastoralism was perhaps the backbone, but small-scale agriculture was practised wherever the terrain would allow it, and there was considerable fishing along the coast. (Fishing villages had doubtless existed for centuries, but we have no records.) By the twelfth century, if not earlier, whaling was already a regular feature of Basque maritime activity; indeed, the Basques seem to have invented the practice of whaling and to have taught it to the English, Dutch and Danes. From the late twelfth century, Basque ships from Bayonne and San Sebastián (and later from Bilbao) were trading all over western and northern Europe, with a substantial effect upon the economy of the formerly remote and backward coastal region. The passage of Aquitaine, and hence of the French Basque Country, into the hands of the kings of England in the late twelfth century brought particular prosperity to Bayonne, whose fleet dominated the trade in wine and other goods between England and Aquitaine. This trade is abundantly documented, but even the much sparser surviving documentation from south of the Pyrenees points to extensive dealings of the southern Basques both with their northern cousins and with England, and later also with the Low Countries, where Basque traders became exceedingly prominent.

From about 1200 Bizkaia and Gipuzkoa were nominally incorporated into the Kingdom of Castile, though in practice they retained a great deal of local autonomy. Localities and municipalities were granted *fueros*, or charters, by the Crown or by local magnates of standing; in the Basque Country, unusually, *fueros* were also granted to entire provinces. A complex system of checks and balances was set up, developing eventually into a (to our eyes) strange arrangement whereby the provincial assemblies had the right to review and even to reject royal legislation (the *pase foral*), subject to the control imposed by the king's representative, the *corregidor*. Tax demands were negotiated with the Crown and were then imposed and collected as the Basques saw fit; the Basques were always successful in keeping their taxes below those in the rest of Castile. In exchange for economic concessions, the Basques frequently also obtained exemption from the military levies imposed upon the rest of the Castilian realm. At regular intervals, the Spanish sovereign was obliged to travel to the Basque town of Gernika (Spanish *Guernica*), site of the assembly of Bizkaia, and there to swear under the sacred oak tree to uphold Basque liberties. On the whole, the Bizkaians and Gipuzkoans prospered under the arrangements, though friction was of course far from rare. In an amusing adumbration of twentieth-century developments, in 1453 King Enrique IV flew into a rage upon discovering that the Bizkaians had placed the coat of arms of Bizkaia above the royal arms in the chapel which they had built in the Flemish city of Bruges; with a display of diplomatic skills for which the Basques have not commonly been noted, the Bizkaians succeeded in persuading the king to leave their arms in place.

From about 1300 we find abundant evidence of well-developed local democracy in the Basque provinces, with the partial exception of Navarre, with its regal and feudal traditions. Heads of households met regularly in front of their local church in order to debate issues and make decisions; such meetings were called *anteiglesias*. Local representatives were elected and sent to the *juntas*, or assemblies, which governed larger districts or entire provinces; the most famous of these councils were the *juntas generales* of Bizkaia, which met at Gernika. Many Basque historians have proudly declared these democratic institutions to have been an ancient feature of Basque society; this is possible, and perhaps even likely, but we lack any earlier documentation.

In spite of the odd incident of violence, the French Basques remained generally content with English rule, from which they were deriving considerable commercial benefit; when English rule finally came to an end in Gascony, Bayonne was the last place to yield to the French reconquest, in 1453.

In the southern provinces, increased prosperity made the chief Basque ports powerful cities; at times they signed naval pacts with England, one of their major trading partners. Basque fishermen and whalers were ranging far and wide over the North Atlantic; they appear to have reached Iceland no later than 1412, and they may well have reached North America before Columbus. But the steady growth in prosperity brought with it an unexpected and unpleasant consequence: clan warfare. Already by the early fourteenth century there were outbreaks of family feuds and factional violence, but these were usually quickly suppressed by the authorities. However, an effective collapse in the power of the Castilian crown in 1370, together with a weakening of provincial authority in the face of the new urban prosperity, permitted an outbreak of factional violence which lasted for much of the next century: the so-called 'War of the Bands'. Ancient grudges were revived (if there is one stereotypical Basque vice, it's a long memory), and quarrels quickly escalated into blood feuds; marriages automatically dragged into the vendettas families who had not previously been involved, and before long assassinations and pitched battles were a dominant feature of life in most of the Basque provinces. The belligerents were chiefly the local aristocrats, or *jaunchos*, but the violence affected everyone.

Taking their names from some of the families most prominent in the feuds, the chief warring parties were known in Navarre as the *Beaumonteses* and the *Agramonteses*, and elsewhere as the *Oñacinos* and the *Gamboínos*, but these neat labels oversimplify what was in reality a confused and bloody situation. Outlying farmhouses were devastated (few houses today survive from before the clan wars), and those who could afford to built *dorretxeak*, or 'tower-houses', grim but practical fortified living quarters; a few of these can still be seen today. Entire towns were burned, the most famous such occasion being the burning of Mondragón (Basque *Arrasate*) in Gipuzkoa in 1448. Eventually, in the face of official powerlessness to put down the fighting and destruction, the angry citizens formed themselves into *hermandades*, or 'brotherhoods', a kind of local militia, and these brotherhoods, with the aid of the royal *corregidores*, finally succeeded in defeating and expelling the most persistent troublemakers. From about 1460, conditions became much more peaceful, but it was only the accession to power of those capable and determined monarchs Ferdinand and Isabella in 1474 that finally put an end to the last vestiges of the violence.

The restoration of order by the Crown naturally entailed a certain tightening of royal authority in the Basque provinces, an outcome which was perhaps resented by few at the time, but the ensuing peace also allowed an upturn in prosperity. During the fifteenth century, Basque merchants and sailors were handling most of Spain's trade with western Europe, and the Basques had developed major fishing and whaling industries. Iron production, long established but formerly only on a small scale, began to expand into another major industry. In Bizkaia, the troublesome *jaunchos* settled down and moved into manufacturing and commerce. And this new-found prosperity received a boost from an unexpected quarter: the voyages of discovery.

With their well-honed maritime skills and their hard-headed administrative abilities, the Basques were involved early in these voyages. For example, both Columbus and Magellan had Basque lieutenants in charge of their ships and crews, and, after Magellan was killed in the Philippines, it was his lieutenant Elkano who brought the expedition safely home. In the Spanish-speaking world, it is Elkano, and not Magellan, who is the 'Circumnavigator'.

But it was the establishment of the Spanish empire in the Americas that transformed the Basque Country. The empire needed seamen, soldiers, settlers, craftsmen, administrators and priests, and the Basques flocked in numbers to fill these roles: it was a situation tailor-made for the Basques, among whom a farm was always inherited by a single child, with the other offspring having to find their own way in the world. From the Mexican city of Durango to the largely Basque-named vineyards of Chile, the frequency of Basque surnames and Basque place names in Spanish America bears quiet testimony to the efforts of those *amerikanuak*, who, for the next 400 years or so, would say good-bye to their homeland and spend their lives making their fortunes in the New World.

There were, however, more direct benefits. The Basque ports were ideally placed to service trans-Atlantic shipping, and both Bilbao and San Sebastián quickly acquired monopolies over large chunks of the trade with the Americas, to the consternation of other Spanish ports. Basque whalers and cod fishermen began spending their summers around Iceland, Newfoundland and the Gulf of St Lawrence, and occasionally they wintered in North America. Shipbuilding became a major industry in Bilbao, and the Basque ports were bustling and wealthy. But the returning galleons brought back something which, in its way, would be even more important than their gold and silver: maize. Maize proved to be an ideal crop for Basque conditions, both more productive and more reliable than the traditional wheat and millet in the damp Basque climate, and the introduction of maize as a staple crop over the next couple of centuries largely put an end to the periodic famines which had formerly reduced many of the people to eating acorns. For centuries the roasted maize cakes called *taloak* were consumed everywhere in the country, and the long-handled pans used for roasting them can still be seen today hanging by Basque hearths. Eventually, however, maize was shifted from human food to animal fodder, a development which, according to Gómez-Ibáñez (1975: 38), revolutionized animal husbandry in the Pyrenees and permitted a great advance in the standard of living.

In 1514 the Kingdom of Navarre, greatly reduced in territory and power, was quietly absorbed by the Crown of Castile, bringing to an end history's one great Basque political entity. Probably few people noticed when the now backward, impoverished, agricultural and essentially feudal Navarre, largely untouched by the industrialization and urbanization that had transformed the Basque provinces of the coast, ceased to exist as an independent state. Five centuries had utterly reversed the relation between progressive, dynamic, powerful Navarre and the impoverished backwater along the coast. This divergence between coast and interior would persist for several centuries more, and would lead ultimately to the shedding of blood between Basque and Basque and finally to a political split which would cut off a rejuvenated Basque political entity from its traditional capital.

The sixteenth century brought continuing prosperity and great social emancipation to the two main Basque provinces. At this time Bizkaia and Gipuzkoa were among the wealthiest regions of Spain, and they were absolutely the freest and most egalitarian. A prosperous and independent peasantry were free of the crushing taxes which were grinding down most areas of the kingdom and free, too, of the depredations of an autocratic and rapacious nobility. Indeed, the Crown granted to both provinces the recognition that *all* of their native inhabitants were of 'noble' status – though this was merely a legal device for granting the Bizkaians and Gipuzkoans freedom from most taxes and equality before the law. The system of *fueros* continued to be vigorous, and the system satisfied everybody. Inland, of course, the prosperity and emancipation were much diluted, but, even so, the population in both Araba and Navarre were better-off than most Spanish subjects.

A small but interesting piece of linguistic evidence for Basque prosperity at the time is the English word *bilbo* for a sword of outstanding quality, which occurs in Shakespeare. The word derives from the name of Bilbao, called *Bilbo* in Basque and formerly called *Bilboa* in English.

The French Basque Country did not, on the whole, share in the prosperity of Bizkaia and Gipuzkoa. The three French Basque provinces all had their own quite distinctive political systems, often featuring charters (*fors*) and representative assemblies, as in the south, and they were largely able to retain these after their incorporation into the French crown in the sixteenth century, though political interference and fiscal pressures mounted steadily in the succeeding two centuries. But, with no industrialization and no urbanization outside Bayonne, the north remained a comparatively poor and backward agricultural region, profiting scarcely at all from the prosperity transforming the lives of their cousins to the south of the line which the two Crowns eventually found it convenient to draw through the middle of the Basque Country in 1659, by the Treaty of the Pyrenees. Nevertheless, the great flowering of Basque literature which took place in the north in the sixteenth century, and more especially in the seventeenth century, is testimony to the existence of a prosperous and confident Basque bourgeoisie in the French Basque provinces (see the next section).

Deep in the mountains, however, the economic differences between French and Spanish Basques were minimal. The valley communities on both sides of the frontier co-operated extensively, regularly drawing up agreements regulating the use of land, guaranteeing the free movement of persons and goods and enjoining the valleys to assist their neighbours in times of emergency; marriages frequently took place across the divide. During the Franco-Spanish wars of the eighteenth and early nineteenth centuries, the valley people often refused to serve in the armies or to offer the slightest assistance to the troops on 'their' side; instead, they warned their neighbours across the mountains of the approach of hostile troops. Indeed, it has been said that these Pyrenean valley communities constituted 'nearly autonomous republics', engaging in free trade oblivious of French and Spanish tariffs and duties, until the nineteenth century; when Paris and Madrid finally attempted to interfere, the Basques in the valleys turned unhesitatingly to smuggling.

The eventual decline of the Spanish empire in the seventeenth century had adverse consequences for the Basque provinces, though these were less severe than in most parts of Spain, and recovery was quicker. In the War of the Spanish Succession (1702–1714), all four Basque provinces backed the winning Bourbon side, with the result that the strongly centralist Bourbon monarchy, while ruthlessly suppressing the traditional rights and privileges in Catalonia and Aragón (which had backed the losing side), left intact the whole panoply of traditional Basque usages.

However, it soon became apparent that this preservation was to be more nominal than real: while all the formal procedures remained in place, in practice the king increasingly dictated terms. Rights, privileges and exemptions were steadily reduced or abolished; fiscal pressures mounted; and the Crown even intervened in the choice of representatives to the *juntas*. The last straw, though, was the removal of the customs boundary from the Ebro, where its presence had long made the Basque provinces in effect a duty-free zone for foreign goods, to the Spanish frontier. These policies brought about a widespread fiscal revolt in Bizkaia and Gipuzkoa in 1717, the *matxinada*, which was bloodily suppressed, though the customs boundary was again returned to the Ebro, where it remained, with one brief interruption, until 1876.

Economically, the Basques suffered at this time from the loss of their long-held monopolies on trans-Atlantic trade, but the economy none the less grew markedly during the second half of the eighteenth century. Shipping, iron production and even agricultural output grew substantially, aided to some extent by the steady flow of new ideas across the border from the France of the Enlightenment. Like the Catalans further east, the Basques were ideally placed to receive and absorb new technologies from generally more progressive northern Europe, and they did so with enthusiasm. An enlightened upper-middle class of landowners, merchants and industrialists emerged, and civic consciousness blossomed. In 1764, in Azkoitia (Gipuzkoa), under the leadership of the Basque nobleman Francisco Xabier María de Munibe, Count of Peñaflorida, the Real Sociedad Vascongada de Amigos del País was formed, the first such organization in Spain, and it quickly set about the business of promoting new techniques in agriculture, education and technology, with some considerable success. Its technical academy in Azkoitia was the first private secular school in Spain, and literacy rates in the Basque Country reached levels that were almost phenomenal by Spanish standards – though only in Spanish, of course.

Paradoxically, these substantial advances were accompanied by a remarkably tenacious conservatism. The historian Stanley Payne comments (1975: 27) upon the Basques' 'remarkable ability to accept technical improvements from the outside world without completely altering the foundations of their own culture'. Basque traditions of inheritance, of household organization and management, of family loyalties, of local democracy and of devout Catholicism were little touched by the economic and political developments. True, there was a noticeable and growing division between the more progressive towns and the more traditionalist countryside, but this dichotomy oversimplifies what was a wide-ranging and pervasive Basque conservatism.

In the north, the French Revolution of 1789 at first attracted little more than idle curiosity and a hope that the excesses of the aristocracy might be curbed. But stubborn Basque Catholicism and hostility to revolutionary innovations soon attracted the ire of the Republican authorities, and many Basques became victims of the Terror. The three provinces themselves were abolished, and the French Basque Country was merged with non-Basque Béarn into a single new *département*. The new language laws, prohibiting the use of regional languages, gradually came to have a strongly adverse effect upon the use of Basque, which was reduced from its formerly considerable prestige to the status of an insignificant patois. Perhaps the most profound disturbance, however, was the imposition of the inheritance laws of the Code Napoléon, by which a household could not be passed on intact to a single heir but must be divided among all children. Though the Basques did not lack for ingenuity in finding ways round this requirement, and succeeded more often than they failed, a number of barely sustainable farms were none the less brought to ruin by being chopped up into absurdly uneconomic plots, thus accelerating that forced emigration which has ever since been such a prominent feature of the French Basque Country.

In 1795, invading French forces occupied the Spanish Basque provinces, as they had done before in 1720, and Gipuzkoa took advantage of the occasion to declare itself a self-governing protectorate of the French Republic. On the withdrawal of the French forces, the Spanish authorities, in reprisal, came close to abolishing Basque liberties altogether, but the prime minister, Godoy, finally drew back for fear of upsetting the now important Basque bourgeoisie. This hesitation would not last long.

During Napoleon's invasion of Spain (1808–1814), the Spanish Basques fought alongside their neighbours against the French, a patriotic stance that would gain them little credit in post-Napoleonic Spain. The chief consequence of the Peninsular War in Spain was the new liberal constitution of 1812, which sought to establish a strong centralized regime and to eliminate all the differences in rights and privileges which had accumulated over the centuries. The new Liberal government accordingly attacked such targets as the Church, with its tax-free lands, and the foral privileges of the Basque provinces; the government pressed hard to extend taxation and military service to these provinces, which had for centuries been largely exempt. The Basques naturally resisted, and the course was set for conflict.

In spite of the new taxes, Madrid's encouragement of industry and commerce won the support of the Basque bourgeoisie in the cities and towns, and its disenfranchisement of both Church lands and communal lands resulted in a new class of large landowners who were eager to see the traditional agricultural practices swept away in favour of agrarian capitalism. The Basque farmers of the countryside rallied under the banner of Carlism, a vague collection of rather hazy and inconsistent doctrines clustered around demands for a return to traditionalism and Catholicism, and in 1833 war broke out: the First Carlist War. Above all, the Carlist flame burned fiercely in unindustrialized Navarre, and Navarre it was that provided the most numerous and effective troops to the anti-Liberal cause. Under the brilliant Basque general Tomás Zumalacárregui, the Carlists at first won a series of impressive victories, but Zumalacárregui's sudden death turned the tables, and in 1839 the war ended in a Liberal victory. Many of the ancient foral rights were brusquely stripped away by Madrid, and the rural Basques of Navarre harboured a burning resentment against the urban Basques of the coastal provinces for having betrayed their foral heritage and supported the other side during the struggle.

In the succeeding decades, the Basques largely concentrated on passive resistance to the demands from Madrid, dragging their feet in every way possible, though there were again brief outbursts of armed rebellion. Political disappointment reinforced the long tradition of emigration for economic reasons, and a growing number of Basques emigrated to the New World, first to Spanish America and then, increasingly, to the western United States, where Basque sheepherders became legendary for their skills (and eventually came into conflict with cattlemen in the famous range wars).

The single most famous emigrant was José María Iparraguirre (1820–1881), a guitar-playing bard from Gipuzkoa who at first placed himself in voluntary exile. His fiercely republican and Basque nationalist ideals got him into constant trouble with the authorities. He was arrested and deported from France, where the newly restored monarchy of Napoleon III objected to his defiant singing of the *Marseillaise*. Returning to the Spanish Basque Country in 1851, he began stirring up Basque feeling with his songs. In 1853, he performed for the first time (in a Basque café in Madrid, of all places) his new hymn *Gernikako arbola* (*The Tree of Gernika*), a celebration of Basque liberties which has ever since been the Basque national anthem. The anthem quickly became a great favourite in the Basque Country, and Iparraguirre's unsubtle attempts at stimulating Basque nationalism soon led to his forced expulsion from Spain. Much of the rest of his life was spent in wandering, particularly in Spanish America, where expatriate Basques wept at his songs about the homeland most of them would never see again. Eventually allowed to return to France, he made his way to the French Basque Country, where he stared across the frontier at his home province and composed his other most famous song, *Ara nun diran* (*Look Where They Are*). Late in life, he was finally permitted to return home, where the admiring Basque authorities granted him a pension and numerous honours. Today his guitar is enshrined in the Casa de Juntas in Gernika.

In 1873 war broke out again in earnest. This Second Carlist War saw the same divisions among the Basques as the first, and the same result: a Liberal victory in 1876. This time almost every remaining trace of the *fueros* was obliterated, and the customs boundary was moved once and for all to the Spanish frontier. With a surprising amount of sense, however, Madrid followed this demolition by agreeing to a series of *conciertos económicos* with the Basque provinces, by which Basque industry and mining were assisted by protective tariffs, taxes on industry were slight, and the Basques were responsible for levying and collecting their own taxes. Very significantly, the age-old provision in the *fuero* of Bizkaia prohibiting the export of the natural resources of the province was annulled, and the Bizkaians were soon exporting millions of tons of iron ore every year, most of it to Britain; British capital in turn funded the expansion of the local iron and steel industry and the associated enterprises of railroads and shipbuilding. The result was a rapid and spectacular growth of industry and prosperity in Bizkaia and Gipuzkoa, which once again became the wealthiest areas in Spain. The new economic elite was inclined to see the old Basque cultural traditions as outdated and reactionary, and hence an observer might have been forgiven for assuming that the 'Basque problem' had been solved – but such a conclusion would have been hopelessly, catastrophically wrong. Conflict and tragedy had yet to visit their most severe attentions upon the Basque Country, and the seeds were being sown in, of all places, wealthy and liberal Bilbao.

Sabino Arana (1865–1903) was born in a village which has since been swallowed up by metropolitan Bilbao, to Basque-speaking parents who had done well out of the new industrial development and who refused to speak any language but Spanish to their children. Learning Basque (imperfectly) only in adolescence, young Sabino proved to be a remarkable individual of great and lasting influence. Galvanized by a long stay in Barcelona, where he was impressed by the nationalist feeling of the Catalans, he returned to Bilbao in 1888 and devoted the rest of his short life to bringing his message to his countrymen. Primarily a journalist who wrote for several Basque magazines and himself founded a couple, Arana also threw himself into both politics and the Basque language with the fervour of a messiah and the simplistic doctrines of a dilettante. In an age when governments frowned upon such activities, he devoted himself publicly and noisily to what we would now call 'consciousness-raising': he wrote and lectured ceaselessly on the need for the Basques to reassert their identity in the face of Spanish oppression. Traditionalist and Catholic in outlook, he descended at times into what looks uncomfortably like racism, but his dogged efforts had far-reaching consequences for the future of the Basque Country, extending down to our own day. For his pains, he was constantly in trouble with the Spanish authorities, and on two occasions he was imprisoned.

It was Arana who designed the flag which has ever since been the national flag of the Basques, the red, white and green *ikurriña* under which Basque soldiers fought in the Spanish Civil War and which flies everywhere in the Basque Country today. It was Arana who made a number of eccentric and colourful attempts at reforming the Basque language, attempts which are discussed elsewhere in this book. It was Arana who founded and led what later became the Basque Nationalist Party, or PNV, the party which would lead the short-lived Basque Government during the Spanish Civil War and which is still a major political force today. And it is Arana who is known to all as the father of Basque nationalism.

Arana's journalistic and political efforts were prodigious and tireless. Those who listened were primarily the members of the petty bourgeoisie: lawyers, architects, journalists and the like, people who were doing well enough under the new arrangements but whose stubborn Basque streak of

Catholic conservatism was uneasy with the dramatic transformation of their country, and particularly with the increasingly important forces of anarchism, socialism and anticlericalism.

Organizing politically from 1895, the Basque nationalists scored some early successes in local elections. Thereafter, their fortunes waxed and waned: years of electoral success alternated with years of failure and virtual bankruptcy. After Arana's early death in 1903, a more pragmatic leadership took control, and the nationalists made slow but steady progress. Growing disputes over policies and tactics, however, produced a split in the nationalist ranks, from which the newly named Partido Nacionalista Vasco emerged in 1920 as the dominant nationalist political force, though it was not without rivals.

In 1923 the Spanish prime minister Primo de Rivera declared martial law. Abrogating the constitution and dissolving the Cortes (Parliament), he installed a ruthless right-wing dictatorship which was extremely hostile to the slightest trace of regional identity. The PNV was forced to go underground; its newspaper was closed and all overt political activity was prohibited. For more than six years the Basques were obliged to take cover and to confine their political aspirations to clandestine discussions; these often took place on mountaintops, as the long-popular mountaineering clubs (the *mendigoizaleak*) were largely turned into political discussion groups which could meet far from the prying eyes and ears of the Spanish police.

In 1930 the dictatorship collapsed. Municipal elections were held, in which the right-wing parties performed poorly throughout Spain; the right-wing King Alfonso XIII abdicated, and the Second Spanish Republic was proclaimed. Like all the other suppressed political parties, the PNV returned to the political arena with energy and determination, their agenda now headed by a demand for autonomy. In this campaign, however, they made little progress: their pro-Church stance alienated the left-wing parties in the Cortes, while their sympathy for the rights of industrial workers upset the right, which in any case had little enthusiasm for any kind of regional autonomy. Consequently, in spite of endless political manoeuvres and deals (which sometimes upset its own supporters), the PNV made no headway, even though the Republic's constitution explicitly guaranteed the right of autonomy to any region with 'common historical, cultural and economic characteristics'. Dominated by Spanish and Catalan left-wingers, the government in Madrid looked with suspicion and mistrust upon Basque aspirations, and its sometimes strident left-wing rhetoric won it few friends in the Basque Country. The Catalans soon won a statute of autonomy; the Basques got nothing.

At least, however, the Basques were again free to declare their nationalist feelings. Public displays of Basque identity once again became the norm, and the Basque national day of *Aberri Eguna* ('Fatherland Day'), another of

Arana's inventions, became an annual event of importance. Basque-language publication once again flourished.

This uneasy state of affairs lasted until 1936. In that year, a group of right-wing army officers, dismayed by the left-wing noises coming out of Madrid (which in fact were matched by few policies), unleashed a carefully planned coup against the government, which, preoccupied with its own squabbling, was caught entirely unawares. The rebels declared a conservative and Catholic crusade to rid Spain of the supposedly 'communistic' and certainly anticlerical elements who were running the country, and they looked to conservative parts of Spain, such as the Basque Country, for support.

The response in the Basque Country was complex. The military governor of Araba was in on the plot, and his troops occupied the province before anyone knew there was a coup. In Carlist Navarre, the traditionalists rallied to the rebel cause with enthusiasm, and their red-bereted *requetés* proved to be some of the most reliable and effective troops on the rebel side, officially called the Nationalists, but soon known to its Republican opponents as the Fascists. Though he had joined the coup only at the very last minute, General Francisco Franco showed a flair for achieving media coverage, and he eventually assumed leadership of the Fascist side after two other generals were killed in plane crashes.

Bizkaia and Gipuzkoa, however, reacted differently. While some of the industrialists were tired of what they saw as the reactionary and obstructive nature of Basque nationalism, and were prepared to welcome the rebels, the PNV realized quickly that Basque nationalism would have little future under Fascism. They therefore at once declared their support for the Republic, but continued to demand their autonomy statute. Desperate for support from any quarter, Madrid granted the statute in October of 1936, by which time the Basques were already deep in war.

Their first job was to establish authority in the face of widespread panic and sectarian violence; after some initial violence and even atrocities, the PNV leaders finally took control and restored order. To the end of the war, the PNV leaders distinguished themselves by their refusal to permit the atrocities which were taking place almost everywhere else in Spain, on both sides. An effective administration was quickly established, and, in the words of Robert Clark (1979: 62), 'the Basque Nationalist Party performed minor miracles in these early days of the war'.

In late July, Carlist troops under the rebel general Mola attacked Gipuzkoa, with the intention of closing the frontier with France and hence of cutting off the Basques from any contact with Republicans in the rest of Spain. Though the Basques resisted stoutly, they had no real army and no weapons to speak of, and Mola's tanks and artillery steadily drove them back. The border town of Irun was taken on 3 September, and, on 13 September, San Sebastián fell, and thousands of Basques streamed westward to the comparative safety of Bizkaia.

Utterly without an army in July, the Basques in Bizkaia had by September somehow managed to put nearly forty infantry battalions into the field, though these had little training and practically no weapons. The Basque Defence Minister, Telésforo Monzón, tried to buy arms in Barcelona, but was told the Republic had none to spare; he tried Paris, only to be told that France was remaining scrupulously neutral. Eventually he got his weapons in Germany, of all places; these were shipped back to the waiting soldiers on the frontier of Bizkaia. They arrived and were distributed in early October; the next morning, Mola's Carlists attacked and were repulsed.

Several days later, the prominent nationalist and former football star José Antonio Aguirre was elected *lendakari*, or president, of the Government of Euzkadi, as the autonomous government chose to style itself, adopting the first two of many of Sabino Arana's coinages. A coalition government was sworn in under PNV leadership.

For the next few months, the Fascists turned their attention elsewhere, as winter and the Basque mountains made further progress difficult against tolerably well-organized resistance, and Republican resistance elsewhere, especially in Madrid, claimed the attention of Franco and Mola. The Basques therefore concentrated their attention on looking after the hundreds of thousands of refugees now in Bilbao, and on reinforcing the city for the expected attack. The main problem was a critical shortage of food, since the Fascist navy was blockading the Basque ports. For a while, the British government refused to respect the blockade and sent warships to escort British merchant ships supplying Bilbao, thus keeping the population alive. Eventually, however, the British opted for strict neutrality and withdrew their protection, thereby virtually sealing the city's fate. The Basques could now only run the gauntlet of Fascist cruisers with lightly armed fishing trawlers to guard their supply ships. One of these attempts led to a now celebrated conflict.

On 5 March 1937, several Basque trawlers were escorting the cargo ship *Galdames* from Bayonne to Bilbao when they ran into the Fascist cruiser *Canarias* trying to seize a neutral merchant ship. While one trawler took the merchant vessel into Bilbao, the other three, with their tiny guns, opened fire on the *Canarias*, the most modern warship in the Spanish navy. Two of them were soon so badly damaged they were forced to withdraw, but the remaining trawler, the *Nabarra*, fought on all day, until her guns ran out of ammunition, the ship was sinking, and only fourteen of her crew of fifty-two were still alive, all of them seriously wounded. These fourteen managed to lower the lifeboat into the water; as the cruiser closed in, they continued to fight, throwing hand grenades at the cruiser. Captured at last, the surviving crewmen were jailed, but spared execution on account of their heroism. This would be the first and last act of magnanimity by the Fascists in the Basque Country until long after the war was over. When word of the *Nabarra*'s heroism got out, the English poet C. Day Lewis was moved to write a poem about it; his poem, 'The Nabarra', opens with the line 'Freedom is more than a word . . . '.

The steadfast neutrality of the European democracies deprived the Republic, and the Basques in particular, of any military assistance beyond the few obsolescent tanks and planes contributed by Stalin's Russia, none of which reached the Basques. In contrast, Fascist Italy and Nazi Germany were sending troops, tanks, guns, planes and pilots to assist the rebels. Eager to gain some combat experience for his air force, Hitler sent his entire Condor Legion, 120 modern planes and pilots, into the war on Franco's side. It was the Basque Country which felt the force of the German planes, as the rebels, whose advances were being stymied elsewhere, decided to make a major effort to capture Bilbao.

On the last day of March 1937 the Condor Legion launched a terrorist air attack on the Bizkaian market town of Durango, a target of no military significance. In the attack, 127 people were killed, and the town was largely razed to the ground. This was the first use of air power in history purely for the purpose of terrorizing civilians. This attack received little publicity in the wider world. But, less than a month later, the Condor Legion made another terrorist attack on the Basque holy city of Gernika, which again had little military significance. Deliberately choosing a market day, when the town was crowded with visiting farmers, the Legion launched its attack on Monday, 26 April; its planes bombed the town into oblivion, and then machine-gunned terrified people trying to flee the devastation. Virtually nothing was left standing, except, miraculously, the Casa de Juntas, the traditional home of Basque democracy, and the aged oak tree in front of it, the Tree of Gernika, under which Spanish sovereigns had centuries before sworn to respect Basque liberties.

This time the attack was widely reported by foreign correspondents, leading to revulsion against Franco's Fascists in much of Europe. Franco, ever conscious of public relations, realized the damage to opinion abroad, and dealt with it by means of a classic instance of the Big Lie: he declared that the Basques themselves had destroyed the town to keep its (non-existent) military capacity out of Fascist hands. So successful was this lie that it was widely accepted in the west for decades, and it was only in the 1970s that the American historian Herbert Southworth finally established the truth by tracing German pilots who had participated in the attack.

The Basques were meanwhile expending all their limited resources in constructing fortifications around Bilbao, the so-called 'Band of Iron'. But then a certain Captain Goicoechea, who had designed these defences and supervised their building, deserted to the Fascist side, taking the plans with him. As a result, when the attack on Bilbao finally came, in June 1937, the Fascists had little difficulty in overrunning the city. Basque officials and their families fled into exile in those few European countries which would accept them, chiefly France and Britain. Some of those children evacuated are still living in Britain today.

Elsewhere in Spain, the war dragged on for another two years. Meanwhile, the Basques began at once to suffer Franco's hostility: feeling aggrieved that the Catholic Basques had declined to support his 'crusade', he declared Bizkaia and Gipuzkoa to be 'traitor provinces', and he set about punishing the Basques with what one right-wing American commentator has called 'a disappointing lack of magnanimity', but what most people would call savagery. Not content with winning, he shipped the surrendered Basque soldiers and anyone else who caught his attention off to prison, where they faced long terms of captivity, concentration camps and forced labour; many were tortured and many others shot, in a bloody orgy of mindless vengeance. All outward signs of Basque identity were prohibited by law; even the very speaking of Basque was declared illegal. Their cities shattered and their once-flourishing economy ruined, the Basques were obliged to struggle for years just to find enough to eat. All contact was prohibited with the French Basques (who in any case were soon to find themselves under Nazi occupation), and the Basque Country entered the blackest period in its long history.

After 1945, Fascist Spain found itself isolated and snubbed by the western democracies, and the Basque government in exile, established in Paris, continued to press for international assistance in recovering civil rights in the Basque Country. For a time things seemed encouraging, but the outbreak of the Cold War led to a rapid change: the United States suddenly began to see Franco as a steadfast ally against Communism; breaking with their European allies, the Americans signed a deal with Franco to permit American military bases in Spain, and the Basques were forgotten.

Meanwhile, as a semblance of normality returned to the country, the Basques began a clandestine resistance. A radio station was set up in France, and there were occasional protest strikes in Bizkaia and Gipuzkoa; the largest of these strikes, in 1951, spread to Araba and even to Navarre, where Franco's former supporters were rapidly becoming disillusioned with the Fascist regime they had fought for. To every sign of resistance, Franco's police reacted ferociously, arresting and torturing hundreds of people. Meanwhile, the PNV re-formed itself in secret and began operating as a clandestine political force, fostering a sense of Basque identity but declining to get involved in anything resembling violent opposition.

The most significant development, though, occurred at the University of Deusto in Bilbao, when, in 1953, a group of students formed a discussion and pressure group originally called Ekin (from the Basque for 'get busy'); this group grew rapidly by taking in young people from all over the country. Associated for a while with the PNV, Ekin soon grew restless with the patient, non-confrontational style of the older organization; in 1959 it broke away and gave itself a new name: Euskadi Ta Askatasuna 'Basque Homeland and Liberty'. ETA had been born.

At first ETA was in no way revolutionary or violent in its actions, and it undertook little beyond circulating calls for action and displaying the Basque flag in public places. As usual, Franco's police reacted savagely, and the members of the organization felt more and more pressured to respond in kind. The decisive step was taken in 1961, when ETA attempted to derail some trains carrying Fascist veterans to an anniversary of the coup. So careful were they to avoid injury that none of the trains was in fact derailed, but the police once again swooped, arresting and torturing over a hundred Basques, most of whom were sent to prison for anything up to twenty years. Finally deciding that nothing could be achieved by passive resistance, ETA therefore decided, in 1962, to turn instead to armed resistance. This decision led to repeated fragmentation of the organization over the next few years, but ETA was there to stay. For a while ETA's violence was more theoretical than real, but not so that of the Spanish authorities: the Spanish police stepped up their brutality, making indiscriminate attacks on Basque towns and cities, beating and arresting people at random, and systematically torturing anyone they arrested. Checkpoints were set up at arbitrary points on Basque roads, and drivers failing to stop were machine-gunned, even though many of these were just innocent passers-by who had failed to notice the tiny signs used by the police.

After several years of this increasingly violent police terrorism, ETA finally took the plunge into violence of its own. Financing itself largely by bank robberies, the organization turned its attentions at first to known torturers and killers in the Spanish police, most famously the sadistic police chief of San Sebastián, Melitón Manzanas, who was assassinated in 1968. Violence escalated on both sides, but ETA continued to take great pains to attack only specific targets and to avoid injuring innocent people, a policy of no interest to the Spanish police, who all but declared war on the Basques.

Meanwhile the Spanish authorities were clamping down with equal ferocity. All Basques charged with political offences were tried in the military court in Burgos, and a string of Basques, including a number of priests, were sentenced to jail terms of anything up to sixteen years for such offences as 'attending illegal meetings' and 'distributing illegal propaganda'. But it was the assassination of Melitón Manzanas that produced the best-known trial. Not for the last time, Madrid declared a 'state of exception' – effectively martial law – in the Basque provinces and began arresting people in numbers. One of those arrested, a pregnant woman, was tortured until she miscarried; she was later absolved of all responsibility in the crime. Eventually, sixteen Basques were brought to trial in Burgos for the killing. Aware of the bad publicity it was getting abroad for its abuses, the Spanish government resolved to hold the trial in public, with foreign journalists allowed to be present, an innovation intended to reassure the world about the quality of Spanish justice.

The effect was exactly the opposite. It rapidly became clear that the evidence against the accused was flimsy in the extreme and appeared to have been manufactured; the defendant charged with the shooting did not match the description of the assailant provided by eyewitnesses and was not identified by them in court; defence lawyers were barred from presenting evidence for their clients; all of the accused declared that they had been tortured, and few onlookers doubted them. The foreign journalists' reports caused an uproar abroad, particularly in France.

At the height of the commotion, ETA kidnapped the West German consul in San Sebastián, Eugen Biehl, and offered to release him unharmed in return for lenient treatment of the defendants, in particular for the commutation of any death sentences. A secret agreement was reached, and Biehl was released. The court then handed down its verdicts: six defendants were sentenced to death, and all but one of the others to jail terms of up to sixty-two years. Two days later, Franco commuted all the death sentences to thirty years' imprisonment.

(Incidentally, Biehl was held during his captivity in a farmhouse in Montory, in the French Basque Country. According to a story which I have been unable to confirm with certainty, but which I have heard from many sources, he once managed to escape in his socks and to make his way into a café in town. Quickly putting two and two together, the local French Basques immediately handed him back to his captors and said not one word to anyone. They might not have been intimately familiar with the goings-on in Burgos, but they knew that Basques were being persecuted, and they didn't like it.)

After this trial, there was no further attempt to try Basques in public. Mounting police violence in the Basque Country, ranging from routine beatings and torture to outbursts described by foreign observers as 'police riots', led to widespread support for ETA. ETA became less selective in its targets, and began gunning for any policemen or army officers they could get at. Aging and increasingly feeble, Franco allowed his police to run loose while he busied himself with choosing a successor who would maintain his hard-line policies. His choice was his old chum Admiral Luis Carrero Blanco, who he felt he could rely upon to keep the lid on the growing pressure all over Spain for democratic reforms.

In December 1973, while on his usual route to church, Carrero Blanco was assassinated by an ETA unit which had laboriously tunnelled under the road and installed a huge bomb. The admiral's car was blown entirely over an adjoining building, and he died in hospital shortly after. This technically expert assassination was to have profound consequences for the whole succeeding development of Spanish politics, though not for a further two years. Few tears were shed in the Basque Country, and in fact the Basques composed a boisterous song about the event which, at the crucial moment, involved tossing into the air whatever the singers were carrying.

The violence in the Basque Country grew steadily worse, and it reached a peak in 1975, as Franco was finally dying. By this time the police were almost entirely out of control: the depredations of the police in uniform were supplemented by death squads composed of off-duty policemen, who carried out murders with impunity. In one particularly awful incident, an 18-year-old schoolboy celebrating the passing of his baccalaureate exams was arrested by the police for singing a Basque song, dragged into the police station and shot dead. Towards the end of the year, the old dictator finally passed away, and there was a huge sigh of relief.

With Carrero Blanco out of the way, there was no one in Franco's circle with sufficient authority to maintain the iron grip Franco had wanted to continue. The new king, Juan Carlos I, assumed the throne, and a pragmatic government set out to wash away the stains of nearly forty years of brutal dictatorship and to start on the job of turning Spain into a modern European democracy. Political parties were legalized, and in 1977 the first democratic elections since the Civil War were held. In the Basque Country, a startlingly large number of new parties appeared, many of them espousing Basque nationalism with varying degrees of militancy, from the hard-line Herri Batasuna to the traditionalist and authoritarian (but now nominally socialist!) Carlist Party. There were also various left-wing parties with few nationalist sympathies; these drew a significant Basque membership but were chiefly composed of Spanish immigrants drawn to the industrial Basque region. Nevertheless, it was the PNV which once again emerged as the single strongest party in the Basque heartland, though, in the elections, it was fractionally pipped by the new socialist party in the Basque Country as a whole.

For the Basques, there were two items on the agenda: amnesty for their political prisoners and a statute of autonomy. The king in fact quickly granted an amnesty for all those prisoners convicted of non-violent offences (about three-quarters of the total), but it took years of further haggling and protest before the remaining prisoners finally came out of jail, one way or another. Meanwhile, the lengthy process of granting autonomy got underway, and finally, in 1979, the long-sought-after statute was finally approved by the Spanish Cortes for the three provinces of Bizkaia, Gipuzkoa and Araba. In a previous referendum, the people of Navarre had voted against joining the new Basque autonomous government, with the result that that new government was deprived not only of much of the traditional Basque territory but also of the traditional Basque capital city, Pamplona.

Before and during this period, there were both unofficial and official efforts to improve the status of the language. The first avowedly nationalist Basque music appeared in the 1960s; like Basque literature centuries earlier, this began in the north, with the French Basque singer Michel Labéguerie, but the southerners quickly followed suit with the pioneering group called Ez Dok Amairu and a number of outstanding individual singers like Mikel Laboa and Xabier Lete. Basque-language magazines and radio stations appeared in some numbers, and Basque-language books of all kinds were published in steadily increasing numbers. More and more parents sent their children to the still unofficial Basque-language schools, the *ikastolas*. The new standard form of the language began to be constructed and publicized by the Basque Language Academy in the 1960s and 1970s; in spite of a good deal of opposition, this gradually succeeded in establishing itself.

Further elections in the new autonomous region produced a government dominated by Basque nationalists, particularly the PNV. Establishing its capital in Vitoria-Gasteiz (Araba), the new authority moved quickly to deal with the Basques' numerous grievances. Basque-language education was a major goal, and the *ikastolas*, which had been struggling for years outside the state system, were made official and given funding from the new tax revenues. A Basque university was established in Vitoria-Gasteiz. A new Basque police force, trained in Britain, was set up and took over most of the everyday policing jobs in the country (though the Spanish police were not withdrawn by Madrid and would continue to constitute a menace for years to come). Improvements were made to the badly neglected road system, and a vigorous building programme got underway, especially in and around the new capital. A new television station was set up and began broadcasting entirely in Basque. Almost as though Franco had never lived, the Basques had achieved most of what they wanted, and they could settle down to grumbling about politicians and taxes like everybody else in Europe.

The violence, however, did not go away. While many members of ETA left the organization to resume a normal life, a hard core of left-wing fanatics continued with shootings and bombings; these became increasingly indiscriminate, and bombs began to be placed in crowded public places in large cities all over Spain and in popular tourist resorts. The new governments in both Madrid and Vitoria made vigorous attempts to persuade the remaining members of ETA to give up their campaign, but with limited success. In response, a shadowy organization called GAL appeared and began killing suspected members of ETA, particularly in the French Basque Country; this would eventually lead to a scandal, when evidence appeared that GAL, which had murdered a number of innocent people, was closely linked to parts of the Spanish government, and possibly also to parts of the French government.

Today, however, the Basque Country is generally as peaceful as any other part of western Europe. Like everyone else, the Basques have their economic problems. In particular, their heavy industry is now struggling, hampered by antiquated plant and by fierce competition from elsewhere, such as the Pacific rim. Unemployment is high, and a significant drug problem has emerged in the major cities. On the whole, though, Bizkaia and Gipuzkoa remain prosperous, and prosperity is spreading to the traditionally backward provinces of Araba and Navarre (the second of which has finally obtained an autonomous government of its own). Spain's accession to the

European Union has brought some benefits, not least in bringing Spanish and French Basques closer together. The economic decline of the French Basque Country has been somewhat stabilized, though there are still few jobs in the north, and many French Basques are even now obliged to leave the country to find work. Still and all, Euskadi, the Basque state, a mere concept for all but a few months of the last century, is now a reality, even if there are still tens of thousands of Basques outside its official borders.

Today the Basques remain physically somewhat distinct from their neighbours. They are typically broad-shouldered and heavily built, with distinctive triangular faces, and they have light brown or medium brown hair and often blue or grey eyes. As is well known, they have the highest proportion of rhesus-negative blood in Europe (25 per cent) and one of the highest percentages of type-O blood (55 per cent). Many have interpreted these data, together with the recent genetic data discussed above, as evidence that the Basques genuinely do represent a continuation of an ancient European population, comparatively little affected by millennia of the movement of peoples from east to west across Europe, just as their language indisputably represents the last survival of the pre–Indo-European languages of Europe.

As the preceding pages may have suggested, the Basques are a practical people *par excellence*. They excel at business and commerce and they have produced notable industrialists and bankers. The estuary of Bilbao is lined with blast furnaces and shipyards, and every city and town in Bizkaia and Gipuzkoa is crammed with industrial concerns, large and small, though the recent economic recession has hit the country hard. Increasingly there are signs that economic activity is moving from the crowded coastal provinces to the more spacious and comparatively undeveloped expanses of Araba and Navarre. The French Basque Country has not shared in this industrial development: designated by the centralist government in Paris as an area set aside for tourism, it offers little employment apart from that available in the garish strip clubs and casinos of Biarritz and the rest of the coast. Two miles from Biarritz, the quiet Basque farmhouses look much as they looked a hundred years ago, though more and more of them are being abandoned as uneconomic, and the region is suffering depopulation as younger Basques leave to look for work elsewhere. It remains to be seen whether Spain's accession to the European Union will help to reverse this depressing trend by providing more opportunities for French Basques just across the border.

On the whole, the Basques are not well known for their achievements in arts and letters or in music – which is a little surprising in the last case, since the Basques' devotion to their musical traditions is such that they are called by the French *le peuple qui chant*. There are, however, some significant exceptions. The composer Juan Crisóstomo de Arriaga achieved considerable acclaim in his day, but he died at the early age of twenty. The French composer Maurice Ravel was Basque on his mother's side, but seems to have shown little musical interest in his Basque origins. The composer Jesús

Guridi has achieved local prominence in Spain with his *zarzuelas* (operettas), of which *El Caserío*, set in the Basque Country, is an enduring favourite. The great Basque writer Pío Baroja wrote all his novels and stories in Spanish, but many of them are set in the Basque Country and feature Basque themes and traditions. And Bernardo Atxaga's delightful book *Obabakoak* has recently become the first Basque-language novel to be translated into English, to general acclaim.

The distinctive metal blocks of the Basque sculptor Eduardo Txillida are world-famous, and Txillida has enjoyed the honour of being appointed artist-in-residence at Harvard University.

In sport, the Basques have traditionally pursued exhausting pastimes like weight-lifting, wood-chopping and rowing. Their fast and colourful national game of *pilota*, a relative of squash, called *jai alai* in English (though not in Basque), has established itself in the United States and in Latin America, though not yet elsewhere. The late tennis player Jean Borotra, the 'Bouncing Basque', was one of the famous 'Musketeers' in the days when France was a dominant tennis-playing nation. More recently, the golfer José María Olazábal, whose name is perpetually unpronounceable to British television commentators, has achieved the world number one ranking. The French Basques play rugby, and the French national rugby team always has a few Basques in it. The Spanish Basques prefer football (soccer), a game which was introduced into the Basque Country from England; the Spanish national team is typically almost half Basque, and the goalkeeper is always a Basque. Most recently, the repeated victories in the Tour de France by the cyclist Miguel Induráin have made cycling such a popular sport in the Basque Country that the roads often seem to have more bikes than cars.

1.3 AN EXTERNAL HISTORY OF THE LANGUAGE

Basque is a genetically isolated language: there is not the slightest shred of evidence that it is related to any other living language, and the frequent assertions to the contrary in the literature may be safely disregarded. On the other hand, the fragmentary remains of the ancient Aquitanian language of southwestern Gaul are so transparently Basque that we may safely regard Aquitanian as an ancestral form of Basque. Consequently, Basque is beyond dispute the sole surviving pre-Indo-European language of western Europe. (All this is discussed in more detail in Chapter 6.)

Our historical knowledge of the Basque Country and of the Basque language begins only with the arrival of the Romans in Spain and Gaul in the second and first centuries BC. Though writing had already been known in much of Spain for several centuries before the Roman arrival, there is not a single text, word or name recorded from before the Roman period which can be safely regarded as Basque. As is well known, the Romans found most of Gaul to be inhabited by Celts, with the single major exception of the southwest, where they reported a quite distinct people whom they called the Aquitanians (*Aquitani*), the people whom we now know to have spoken an ancestral form of Basque. In Spain, the position was altogether more complex. Much of the east and south of the Peninsula was occupied by the Iberians, a mysterious people of unknown origin who have left us a substantial number of texts in their Iberian language, most of them written in an indigenous script. That script has finally been deciphered, but we still can't read the texts, and all that can be concluded is that Iberian was neither Indo-European nor Basque (see Chapter 6). Much of the north and centre of Spain was inhabited by Indo-European speakers, at least some of whom (the Celtiberians) indisputably spoke a variety of Celtic; it is by no means clear, however, that all the Indo-Europeans in Spain were Celts. Both Greek and the Semitic language Punic were spoken in a number of colonies established by the Greeks and by the Carthaginians. In the south of Spain and Portugal, we have a few texts in the mysterious Tartessian, which does not appear to be related to anything else at all. Much of the west is a blank, with no texts and only a handful of tribal names; as a result, we know nothing of the languages that might have been spoken there. (See Tovar (1961) or Anderson (1988) for an account of the ancient languages of Spain.)

South of the Pyrenees, the Romans recorded the existence of several tribes of people in the approximate area of the present-day Basque Country: the Vascones, the Varduli, the Verones, the Caristii and the Autrigones (the very approximate distribution of these peoples is shown in Figure 1.4; note that some scholars prefer to put the Caristii into eastern Araba, rather than the Varduli). It is probable that at least some of these peoples were Basque-speaking, but the direct evidence for this supposition is scanty: only two inscriptions from the Roman period, both of them in eastern Navarre, record what appear to be unmistakably Basque personal names. Note, however, that the name *Vascones* is the source of Spanish *vasco*, French *basque* and English *Basque* (see Chapter 5 for a discussion of the name of the language, and for a possible etymology of the name *Vascones*). The entire territory of the modern province of Gipuzkoa is nearly devoid of any texts at all from this period; we may take this as evidence that Gipuzkoa was a backwater of little interest to the Romans, a factor which probably encouraged the survival of Basque in the region. To the west and south, in the territory of the modern Araba, in much of Navarre, and to a smaller extent in Bizkaia, personal names are frequently recorded but are clearly non-Basque. Indeed, many of them appear to be Indo-European: *Ablonius*, *Ambatus* and *Ambata*, *Betunus*, *Boutia*, *Buturra*, *Calaetus*, *Doitena*, *Equesus*, *Rectunus*, *Segontius*, *Viriatus*, and so on. (For the evidence, see Schulten (1927), Ybarra (1955) and especially Gómez Moreno (1925).) This implies that the Caristii, the Verones and the Autrigones, at least, and perhaps also the Varduli, were not Basque-speaking, and indeed there is some evidence to suggest that the Caristii and the Varduli were close kin to their western

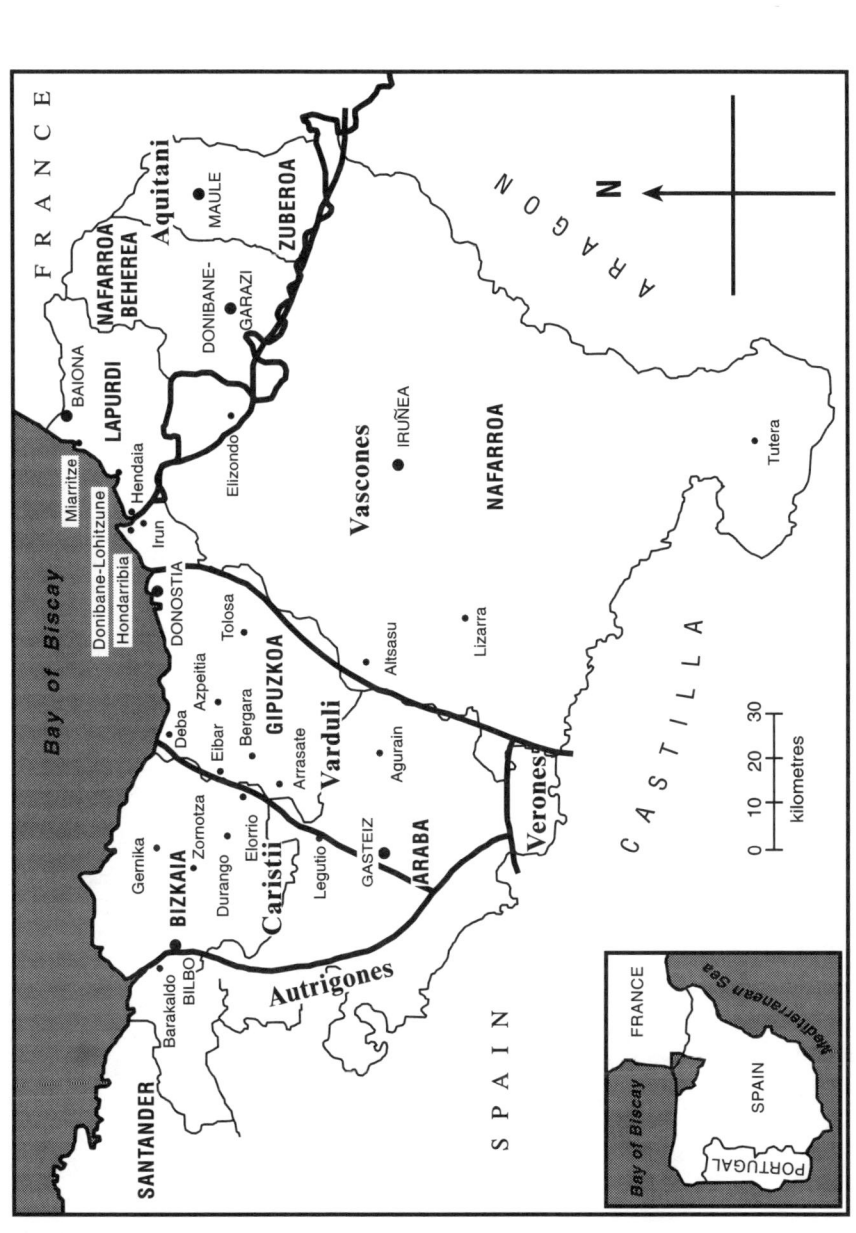

Figure 1.4 The Basque Country in the Roman era

neighbours the Cantabrians, who are widely regarded as Indo-European-speakers. Of course, personal names are not an infallible guide to the vernacular language. It is conceivable that Basque-speakers might have chosen Indo-European personal names for reasons of fashion or prestige, in roughly the same way that, many centuries later, generations of monoglot Basques used nothing but Spanish or French personal names. But the evidence from personal names is backed up by the evidence from place names.

As we shall see in Chapter 5, there are very many place names in the Spanish Basque Country which are certainly not of Basque origin and which in many cases appear to be Indo-European. This is further evidence that much of the modern Basque Country was not Basque-speaking, or at least not predominantly Basque-speaking, in the Roman era. But note that qualification 'not predominantly'. Many modern scholars have tended to assume that the peoples identified by the Romans in Spain were nothing more than 'tribes' or 'clans', with a minimal degree of social or political organization and a high degree of ethnic and linguistic homogeneity in each case. There is no evidence, however, for such assumptions. It is perfectly possible that many of these peoples had already created organized states before the arrival of the Romans, and, more importantly, there is no reason to exclude the possibility that these peoples may have consisted of mixtures of Basques with Indo-Europeans or others. Hence it is best to refrain from jumping to any rash conclusions about the identity of any of these peoples, even the Vascones, who have the strongest case for being considered Basques. Indeed, Michelena (1961–1962: 447) declares flatly that it is beyond dispute that both Aquitanian (i.e., Basque) and an Indo-European language were spoken in the territory of the Vascones at the time of the Roman settlement, and sees no reason to suppose that the linguistic position had been less complex in the preceding centuries; in the same vein, Echenique (1987: 47–48) sees Basque as one of several languages spoken side by side in the ancient Basque Country, and suggests that bilingualism may have been common. Nevertheless, most specialists are satisfied that the Basque language was introduced into much of the Basque Country in post-Roman times, most likely during the Visigothic period discussed above. Consequently, the traditional view that Basque is a language of Spain which has extended itself to the north of the Pyrenees has had to be revised: we now see Basque as a language of Gaul which has spread south and west.

Even today, there is a debate about the likely frontiers of Aquitanian south of the Pyrenees. Some scholars would like to see the city of Calagurris in the Ebro valley, described by Roman sources as lying within the territory of the Vascones, as Basque-speaking, and some would place Basque-speakers in much of modern Aragón. Here I merely note that the evidence for such views is sparse in the extreme, and most specialists, I think, would be reluctant to posit Basque speech so far south and east.

In what is now Granada, in the far south of Spain, the Romans reported the presence of a city called *Iliberris* (modern *Elvira*), and a second city of the same name is attested in Roussillon in the eastern Pyrenees (modern *Elne*). Fascinatingly, this name looks to be transparently Basque, since **ili berri* is straightforwardly the reconstructed form of the modern *hiri berri* 'new city'. There was also a city called *Iturissa* on the Mediterranean coast, deep inside Iberian territory, and this has been interpreted as a derivative of Basque *iturri* 'spring, fountain'. There are, however, no other traces of the language at so far a remove from the historical Basque Country as Granada or the Mediterranean, and these names may be sheer coincidence, or they may perhaps even represent settlements founded by expatriate Basques. (Roussillon, though, probably was Basque-speaking; see below.)

Like the Celtic languages of Gaul, Aquitanian was probably displaced by Latin at an early date, though it may have lingered longer in the far south-west, where the name of the modern inhabitants, the Gascons, is thought by most scholars to represent a continuation of the Latin *Vascones*. South of the Pyrenees, the language not only survived but apparently extended its domain. At some early stage the language spread into the entire territory of the modern Basque Country, and, at some time after the fourth century, probably earlier rather than later, Basque-speakers expanded into the Rioja and Burgos to the southwest. Medieval Basque toponyms in Burgos and the Rioja are similar to those of Araba and Bizkaia, notably in the frequent presence of the final element *-uri*, the Bizkaian variant of common *(h)iri* 'town', as in *Zufiuri* 'bridge-town' and *Guipuzauri* 'town of the Gipuz-koan(s)'. Burgos has also a number of Romance toponyms like *Báscones*, *Basconcillos*, *Villabáscones* and *Bascuñana*, all of which point to a substantial Basque presence. (See Merino Urrutia (1978) for a treatment of Basque toponyms in this region.) The Spanish of Araba until recently (at least) featured respectful terms of address derived from Basque kinship terms: *eita* ~ *egga* (< *aita* 'father'), *eigiga* (< *aitita* 'grandfather'), *anderazo* (< *andere atso* 'grandmother') and *ama* (< *ama* 'mother'), among others.

Some scholars are inclined to think that it was probably also at this time that the language was reintroduced north of the Pyrenees, but there is little hard evidence on this point one way or the other, and the majority view is that Basque survived without interruption in the French Basque Country. Moreover, the work of the German linguist Gerhard Rohlfs and of the Catalan linguist Juan Corominas (or Joan Coromines) has demonstrated to general satisfaction, chiefly on the basis of place names, that Basque was once spoken on both side of the Pyrenees, as far east as the valley of Arán, in territory which has been Catalan-speaking in historical times (see especially Rohlfs 1935, 1952 and Corominas 1965). For example, the frequent place names ending in *-ós* and *-ués* in this area are sometimes interpreted as representing Basque *(h)otz* 'cold' (though the frequency of this ending makes such an interpretation dubious), and are commonly interpreted as testimony of earlier Aquitanian or Basque speech. See Figure 1.5, which displays the distribution of toponyms with this ending and of toponyms with Latin -ANUM and -ACUM. Most likely this extension represents a survival of Aquitanian south of the mountains, rather than a later spread: there is abundant evidence that the Pyrenees have long been a linguistic bridge between north and south, rather than a barrier.

Indeed, we have documentary evidence that Basque was spoken around the city of Huesca in the fourteenth century. The bylaws of Huesca in 1349 prohibited the use of Basque in the city's marketplace: 'Item nuyl corredor nonsia usado que faga mercadería ninguna que compre nin venda entre ningunas personas, faulando en algaravia ni en abrach nin en basquençe' ('Let no merchant be employed who buys or sells with anybody speaking in Arabic, Hebrew or Basque') (Arco 1993: 433).

Conspicuously Basque place names are found today throughout the area of the seven provinces, and in small areas lying just outside, particularly to the east, and, as I have just remarked, apparently Basque names occur throughout much of the Pyrenees. Further afield, however, there is little or no clear toponymic evidence of Basque speech, apart from the cases of *Iliberris* and *Iturissa* cited above. There is, of course, no shortage of problematic place names in the Iberian peninsula, many of which appear clearly to contain elements of non-Romance origin, but strenuous attempts to interpret some of these names as Basque have been generally unsuccessful and often rather fanciful. A case in point is the town of *Iria Flavia* in Galicia, which generations of scholars have tried to relate to modern Basque *hiri* 'city', but we would have expected **ili*, not the phonologically and morphologically incomprehensible *iria*, and the identification is rejected by specialists today. South of the Pyrenees, then, there is no real evidence that Basque was ever spoken much outside the territory of the present-day Basque Country, except in the Pyrenees themselves and, briefly, in the Rioja and parts of Burgos.

Immediately to the west of the Basque Country lie the Cantabrian Mountains, which in Roman and early medieval times were inhabited by a people whom their neighbours called Cantabrians. There is no evidence that the Cantabrians were Basque-speaking, and indeed many specialists are satisfied that they spoke an Indo-European language, but the Cantabrians have sometimes been confused with the Basques in historical writing, and occasionally one finds the term 'Cantabrians' used, very confusingly, as a Latinate label for the Basques.

Apart from the Aquitanian materials, possibly the single earliest record of Basque is a set of lead tablets, dating from the Roman period, pertaining to a medicinal spring in Roussillon, in which the local nymphs are invoked with the word *NESCAS* or *NISCAS*, which appears transparently to represent Basque *neska* 'girl' (attested in Aquitanian) (Coromins 1975). Otherwise, the earliest records of Basque are personal names recorded in early medieval manuscripts and inscriptions, first in Latin, later in Spanish. The single

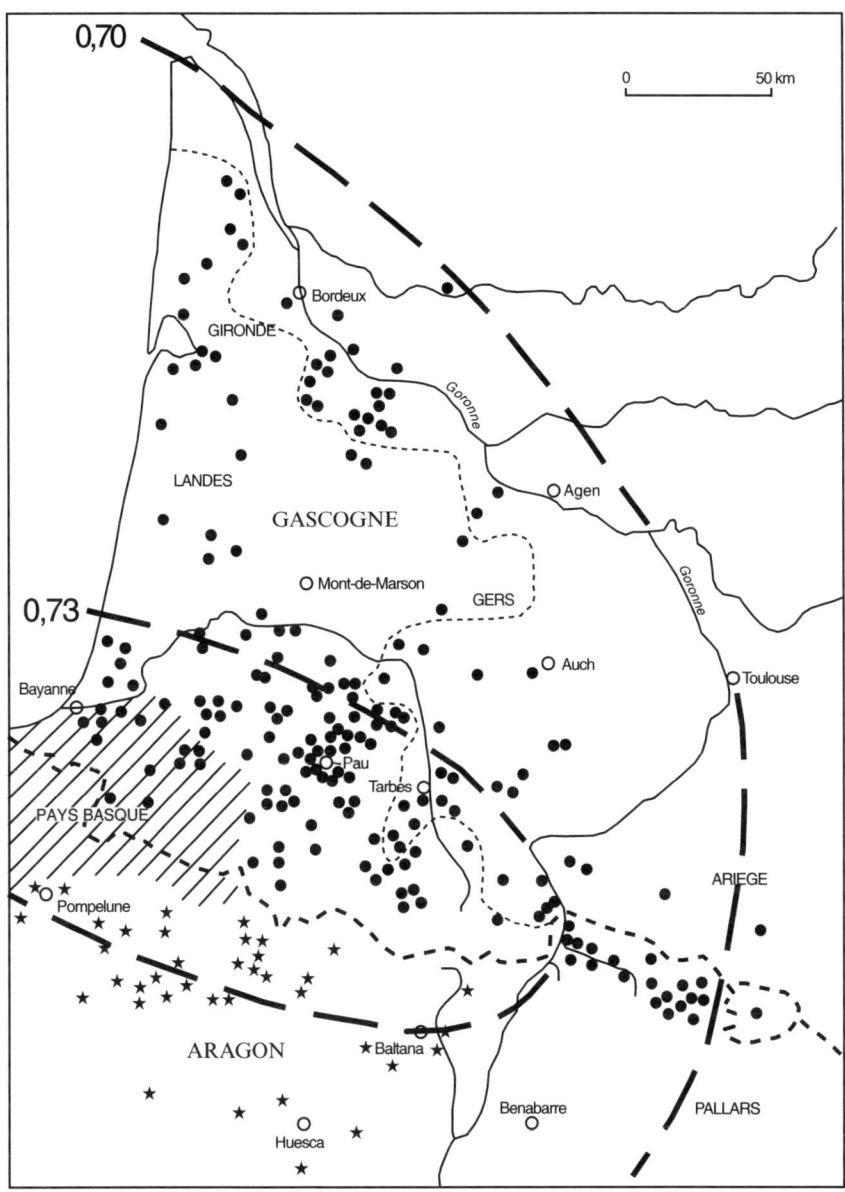

Figure 1.5 Place names in -os

Source: Roger Collins (1986) *The Basques*, Oxford: Basil Blackwell, p. 105.

earliest such name is *Momus*, a latinized form of *Mome*, a name no longer in use but well attested in medieval Bizkaia, which occurs in a Latin inscription in the famous (apparently pre-Christian) cemetery of Argiñeta in Elorrio (Bizkaia); this inscription is conventionally dated to the year 883. Michelena (1964a) provides a complete catalogue of these texts.

The earliest known connected phrases are the well-known Emilian Glosses, two glosses in Basque added to a Latin manuscript found at the monastery of San Millán in the Rioja, the wine-producing territory at the southwestern edge of the modern Basque Country, which is known to have been Basque-speaking in early medieval times. The manuscript is usually dated to around 950, though a few scholars have argued for a date as much as a century later. The relevant passages are as follows; the Basque glosses are italicized, and the second passage also contains a gloss in Spanish:

> Gaudeamus fratres karissimi et Deo gratias agimus, quia uos, secundum desideria nostra, jncolomes (sanos et salbos) jnueniri meruimur (*jzioqui dugu*) . . .
>
> . . . timeo ne quando boni christiani cum angelis acceperint uitam eternam nos, quod absit, precipitemur (*guec ajutuezdugu*) (nos nonkaigamus) ingeenna.

The first phrase is *jzioqui dugu*, where *dugu* is transparently the auxiliary verb-form *dugu* 'we have (it)', while *jzioqui* (in modern orthography *izioki*) is entirely obscure, even with the help of the Latin text: it is probably the perfective participle of a verb, which would fit perfectly with the following auxiliary, but it could equally be an adverb. The second gloss is *guec ajutu-ezdugu*, where *guec* is obviously the modern *guk*, ergative of the pronoun *gu* 'we' (or possibly its intensive form *geuk* 'we ourselves'), and the last part is equally obviously *ez dugu* 'we don't have (it)', but *ajutu* is again obscure, though it too is most likely the participle of a verb. (Both -*ki* and -*tu* are common endings for participles of verbs.) Michelena (1964a: 41–44) discusses the various attempts at interpreting these two puzzling words without reaching any firm conclusions. Other such glosses exist, and are listed in Michelena (1964a).

It is from the tenth century that we begin to find documents recording Basque personal names and place names in significant numbers. Most of these are recordings of bequests, tithes or donations of some sort, or the founding charters of religious establishments. Interestingly, the earliest of these come from Araba, the Rioja and Burgos, areas from which Basque was soon to disappear, and are also preserved at the monastery of San Millán. One of the most important is the *Reja de San Millán*, a copy of a document of 1025 listing the expected annual contributions to the monastery from the towns and villages of Araba lying within its district. Some of the 200-odd names listed are Romance, but the overwhelming majority are Basque, and these names exhibit a degree of archaism unmatched in any other document. Names are frequently much longer than their modern forms, and the aspiration is exceedingly frequent in all positions. The well-known topo-nymic suffixes *-eta* and *-tza* occur repeatedly, the second in its archaic form *-zaha* ~ *-zahea*. Some examples: *Bahaheztu* (modern *Maeztu*), *Uhulla* (*Ula*), *Kerrianu* (*Gerriau*), *Mizquina* (*Mezkia*), *Elhorzahea* (*Elortza*), **Betollazaha* (emendation for the clearly erroneous *Betellogaha*) (*Betolaza*), *Huriuarri* (*Uribarri*), *Hurizahar* (*Urizar*), *Elhorriaga* (*Elorriaga*), *Harizavalleta* (*Arrizabaleta*), *Helkeguren* (unknown, but would be **Elgeguren*). Since so many of the villages have known locations, we can for once draw a fairly sharp line on a map to represent the Basque–Romance boundary in Araba at the time, though there was doubtless a zone of bilingualism along this line.

Also decidedly archaic are the personal names and place names in the first significant document from Bizkaia, the charter founding the monastery of Varria (San Agustín de Echebarria) in Elorrio, dating from 1053, though only a later copy survives. Examples: *Olhabeeçahar* (modern *Olabezar*), *Çumelhegi* (*Zumelegi*), *Harhegi* (*Arregi*), *Acenari* (*Azeari*), *Laçkanu* (*Laz-kao*), *Turanko* (*Durango*). Several of the personal names appear to contain the ancient diminutive suffixes *-so*, *-to*, *-ko* attested in Aquitanian and found later throughout the medieval Basque Country: *Nunuto*, *Nunnuso*, *Uitaco*. Since *Miota* is known to have been a *barrio* (district) of Elorrio, the form *Miotaco* probably represents one of the earliest attestations of the relational suffix *-ko*.

On the whole, documentation of any kind is much scantier in Gipuzkoa than elsewhere from the Roman period up to the eleventh century, but one of the earliest Gipuzkoan documents is quite extraordinary. This is a record of a donation made in 1055 by the *senior* García Azenáriz and his wife Gayla of the monastery of Ollazabal near Azpeitia, together with all of its possessions. Though the body of the document, as was customary, is in Latin, the all-important description of the boundaries of the bequest is in Basque, presumably because this is what the owners and the witnesses would have understood. The text is hard to understand in places; possibly the Basque has been garbled by copyists ignorant of the language. Here is the text, from Arocena (1948):

> Gaharraga Orer urte Alvizt urre, super Lascurende, alia parte inferiorem vel de Ainarte, de Areiz nabar sub Arzagicorin usque vera sibia in finem manzaneto de senior Garcia Azenariz, haralarre Heziza zaval, alia Hezi caray cum arrandari Sanzoiz, manzaneto de Ugarte Zuhaz nabar cum ossavio de medio manzaneto, ipsos tradimus.

We might read *urre* as western *urre* 'near', but it seems more likely that *Alvizt urre* is intended as *Alviz-turre* 'tower of Alviz'. We can safely read *zaval* as *zabal* 'wide', and *caray* as *garai* 'high place', and possibly *zuhaz* as *zuhaitz* 'tree'. But for *urte*, neither *urte* 'year' nor *urte* 'flood' makes any sense, and this word has probably been garbled. The word *nabar* occurs twice and looks like *nabar* 'dark-coloured, grey', though the point of such an adjective is far from clear. The words *haralarre* and *arrandari* certainly look Basque enough, but are hard to interpret. The first probably contains *larre* 'pasture, meadow', which fits the sense, and may contain the same first element as *Aralar*, the name of a mountain range in Gipuzkoa and Navarre. For *arrandari*, the best guess is *arrandari* 'tenant', which appears to make a certain amount of sense, though this word is otherwise attested only scantily and only in the French Basque Country.

This document is unique of its kind: no other such text is known, though doubtless many others existed once. The widespread destruction visited upon the Basque Country by the clan warfare of the late Middle Ages, by the Carlist Wars of the nineteenth century and by the Spanish Civil War has undoubtedly removed from our grasp a huge number of what would otherwise have been priceless testimony to the Basque Country of the early medieval period.

The Basque that is recorded in these early documents already shows traces of dialectal diversification, but these appear to be modest (though the absence of finite verb-forms no doubt conceals some rather greater differences, as does the paucity of material from the French Basque Country). So far as we can judge from the scanty material at our disposal, the language was much more uniform in the tenth and eleventh centuries than it was when publication began in the sixteenth century. Indeed, so great is the uniformity among all varieties of the language down to the sixteenth century that many vasconists are convinced that a pan-Basque koiné must have have existed not many centuries earlier: the distinctive characteristics of the modern dialects appear to be very recent indeed.

The earliest known glossary of Basque is that provided by the twelfth-century French pilgrim Aimery (or Aymeric) Picaud, who stopped in the Basque Country on his journey to the shrine at Santiago de Compostela and recorded a handful of Basque words in his journal, which is still extant. All of them are transparent, though some are recorded with the article *-a* or another affix attached. He records *Urcia* 'God', a fascinating word discussed in Chapter 5 under the names of the days of the week; *Andrea Maria* 'the mother of God' (modern *Andre Mari(a)*; the extra article is puzzling); *ogui* 'bread' (modern *ogi*; Picaud was using a French-style orthography); *ardum* 'wine' (modern *ardo*, from **ardano*; the spelling probably represents *ardũ*, with a nasalized vowel, a dialect variant found today in the east); *aragui* 'meat' (modern *haragi*); *araign* 'fish' (modern *arrai(n)* ~ *arraiñ* (from **arrani*); *echea* 'house' (modern *etxe*); *iaona* 'master of the house' (modern *jaun*); *andrea* 'lady of the house' (modern *andre*); *elicera* 'church' (modern *eliza*; Picaud's form is possibly the allative *elizara* 'to church', but more likely the unusual definite form which still occurs as *elizara* in modern Salazarese); *belaterra* 'priest' (modern *beretter* 'sacristan', a loan from Romance); *gari* 'wheat' (modern *gari*); *uric* 'water' (modern *ur*; *urik* is the partitive: 'some water'); *ereguia* 'king' (modern *errege*); *Iaona domne Iacue* 'Saint James' (here the first element is again *jaun* 'lord; sir', while *domne* is a loan from

Latin which, in the form *don(e)*, is still used in saints' names today). Finally, Picaud records the puzzling word *aucona* 'dart', a word which is widespread in the neighbouring Romance languages but which occurs in modern Basque only in the rather different form *azkon*.

From the early twelfth century onwards we find an increasing number of Latin and Romance texts containing Basque personal names, place names, words and phrases. These include the *fueros* (the charters granted by the Crown to provinces, cities and towns) and many other legal documents of various kinds, as well as a few personal letters.

A figure of note is Gonzalo de Berceo (?1195–?1264), the 'father of Castilian poetry'. Born in the village of Berceo in the Rioja, he was educated at the monastery of San Millán in Araba, close to what was then the Basque–Castilian frontier. He became a celebrated poet and bard, the first poet whose name we know to write in Castilian, which was then considered a rustic patois. Strikingly, however, he spattered his poems with vasconisms, such as *don Bildur* (a personification of *bildur* 'fear'), *zatico* (a derivative of western *zati* 'period of time') and *gabe* 'without'.

The earliest known connected Basque text longer than a couple of words is a prayer, or perhaps rather a magical charm, recorded in a manuscript in the cathedral of Pamplona and usually dated to the late fourteenth century, but discovered only in 1957 by the British vasconist Douglas Gifford. Little more than seven lines long, and partly damaged, this passage is almost entirely transparent; it is published with an interpretation in Gifford and Michelena (1958) and in Michelena (1964a: 57–59); its significance is discussed in Gifford (1964). Because of its historical priority, I reproduce it here, together with the best interpretation we have; the punctuation and the capital letters have been silently inserted into the text, as have the line numbers:

1 Vyrguo clemens, Vyrguo pia, Vyrguo dulçis al[. . .
2 todauja. Pater noster chjcia, Deus peretençia lur<r>ac dac[a]r og[. . .
3 çoçoc ardan bustia, baradiçu menda uerde macu onac ard[. . .
4 liburuetan iracurten, arguiçagui eraiçeten çerua[. . .
5 dauilça Jangoicoaren apostru maestru jaun d[. . .
6 Agnus Dei qui tollis peccata mundi egunean
7 telo meo guaradela çure guomendatu gura jruretan d[. . .
8 arima saluatu.

1 Virgo clemens, Virgo pia, Virgo dulcis, al . . .
2 still. Little pater noster, God penitence, the earth bears bread . . .
3 Twigs, wet wine, paradise, green mint, good *maku*s, ? sheep . . .
4 Reading in the books, lighting candles, heaven . . .
5 The apostles of God go about, master lord d . . .
6 Agnus Dei qui tollis peccata mundi every day
7 Telo meo that we may be commended of you, that one three times d . . .
8 To save the soul.

Very similar verses are well attested in Navarre in more recent times, though the wine is usually characterized as 'red' or 'white', rather than as the unexpected 'wet'. The word *maku* is otherwise unattested in Basque, but in medieval Navarre *Maku* was very common as an epithet or surname.

At the very end of the fifteenth century the German pilgrim Arnold von Harff recorded another Basque glossary, consisting of the numerals from one to ten, a further nine words, and four complete sentences. Von Harff's transcriptions are far less accurate than Picaud's had been, but all except one of the individual words are immediately recognizable, as are two of the sentences and, with a little more charity, the third sentence. His final sentence is the engaging *schatuwa ne tu so gausa moissa*, which he glosses as 'Beautiful young lady, come and sleep with me'. The first word is clearly *neskato(a)* 'young lady', and *ne tu so* is a garbled rendering of *nahi duzu* 'do you want?', but the remainder is puzzling. Several generations of highly embarrassed commentators have seen *gausa* as representing *gauza* 'thing' and *moissa* as representing *motz(a)* 'cunt', but the syntax is impossible; Michelena (1964a: 64–65) suggests that *gausa m-* is a missegmented version of the subjunctive *gautzan* 'that we go to bed' or possibly of *goazen* 'that we go', but this still leaves -*oissa* hard to interpret.

In the early sixteenth century the Italian humanist who called himself Lucius Marineus Siculus made a tour of Spain and published an account of his observations; this volume includes a list of several dozen Basque words which the author had collected from an unidentified source. His words are clearly western in form, and must have been collected in Bizkaia or Araba, but what is particularly noteworthy is that he marks the position of the word-accent in nearly all of them: *améa* 'mother', *echéa* 'house', *cerúa* 'sky', *alauéa* 'daughter', *irarguía* 'moon', *ardáoa* 'wine', *çorçí* 'eight', *vedraçí* 'nine', *gorpuçá* 'body', *edatendót* 'I drink it', and so on. (See Michelena 1957–1958: 225; Urquijo 1925: 477ff.)

From the sixteenth century onwards we find increasing numbers of Basque texts: songs, poems, prayers, epitaphs and personal letters. The songs and poems are particularly prominent, and it is noteworthy that many of these were clearly composed one or two centuries before their first attestation in writing. The brief *Song of the Battle of Beotibar*, for example, recounts the events of a battle that took place in 1321 between the forces of Gipuzkoa and Navarre, while the famous group of verses known collectively as *The Burning of Mondragón* recounts the destruction by fire of the city of Mondragón (Basque *Arrasate*) in Gipuzkoa in the year 1448 during the violent clan warfare that was afflicting the Basque Country at the time. (On these, see Michelena and Rodríguez Herrero 1959, Michelena 1964a: 81–88.)

It is noteworthy that the medieval Basque recorded in all these sources is strikingly similar to modern Basque. The vast majority of the vocabulary consists of words in use today, though naturally there are a number of words recorded which are now unknown. The inflectional and derivational morphology are almost indistinguishable in most respects from the morphology of the modern language, and the differences in syntax are not much greater. Phonologically, it appears that most of the phonological developments which we know to have occurred since Roman times had already occurred before our earliest texts were written down, though there are some possible exceptions, as we shall see in Chapter 3. Basque in the last thousand years appears to have been an astonishingly conservative language, much more conservative than, say, English.

By far the longest text preserved from the period before publication began is a lengthy personal letter written in 1537 by Fray Juan de Zumárraga, the first Bishop of Mexico, who, in spite of his name, was a native of Durango in Bizkaia. The letter is published in Otte (1979) and discussed in Michelena, Tovar and Otte (1981).

From about 1550 to 1650 a pidginized form of Basque was in use as a trading language in the North Atlantic; a few words from this pidgin found their way into indigenous languages from Labrador to Maine, but particularly around the mouth of the St Lawrence River. The explorer Jacques Cartier reported in 1542 that the local 'Indians' understood some form of Basque. A history of New France dating from 1617 contains a list of 'Souriquois' words used in the local Algonquian languages; some of these words are clearly Basque, and 'Souriquois' is thought by some specialists to be a French spelling of Basque *zurikoa* 'the [language] of the whites'. As late as 1710 the indigenous peoples of the Gulf of St Lawrence were found to be using a lingua franca containing a number of Basque words. See Bakker (1987) for an account of this North American Basque pidgin. (Another Basque-based pidgin was in use by Icelanders in the seventeenth century; the Icelanders compiled lists of words and sentences in this pidgin and these have been published by Deen (1937).)

The year 1545 saw the appearance of the first book ever published in Basque: a collection of poems, entitled *Linguae vasconum primitiae*, by the French Basque Bernard (or Beñat) Dechepare (Etxepare). This was followed in 1571 by a Basque translation of the New Testament by the French Basque Ioannes Leizarraga, who also wrote a couple of other minor religious works in Basque. The first Basque book published in the south was an anonymous collection of proverbs entitled *Refranes y sentencias*, written in the Bizkaian dialect but published in Pamplona in 1596. The sole known copy of this work was discovered by the Dutch vasconist van Eys in 1894 and taken to Germany, where it disappeared in the Second World War. At around the same time, the historian Esteban de Garibay of Mondragón compiled two collections of proverbs, also in Bizkaian, which, however, were not published until several centuries after his death.

The modern dialectal differences are already detectable in these sixteenth-century texts, but were less prominent than today, and the Bizkaian of the time was markedly similar to Lapurdian.

During the early seventeenth century, a number of minor devotional works appeared in Basque. These were inconsequential in comparison with the next major work to be published: the *Gero* of Pedro de Axular, published in 1643. This is a substantial volume of Christian devotion; its title, which means 'later', represents the procrastination which is the book's main theme. Axular was born in the village of Urdazubi (Spanish *Urdax*) in Navarre, near the top of the pass which crosses the Pyrenees at that point; his name Axular, in typical Basque fashion, is the name of his family house, and not his surname (see Chapter 5). Axular spent his life as the parish priest of Sara, on the French side of the frontier, and he wrote his only book in an elegant and carefully cultivated version of the French Basque dialect of Lapurdi. Still today he is regarded as one of the finest stylists ever to write in Basque.

The success of Axular's book (it was reprinted several times) is testimony to the high status of Basque in the French Basque Country at the time, a high status which is supported by other evidence. The Zuberoan lawyer and historian Arnaut Oihenart, the first non-cleric to write in Basque, produced poetry and an important collection of proverbs; his elegant and elaborate style and his large vocabulary make him one of our most important sources of information about the language of the time. Practical handbooks were written in Basque, such as Martin de Hoyarzabal and Piarres Detcheverry's book on marine navigation (1677) and Mongongo Dessança's volume on farming techniques (1692). Non-Basques from the coast of Lapurdi learned Basque, and at least two of them wrote in the language: Estève Materre and Silvain Pouvreau, the second of whom compiled an unpublished dictionary which is still extant. It was thus the French Basques – Etxepare, Axular, Leizarraga and those who followed them – who were chiefly responsible for initiating Basque literature.

Since the seventeenth century there has been a steady flow of publications in Basque. Naturally, most of these are written in the author's own dialect, but gradually there emerged moderately standardized versions of the four dialects that were chiefly used for publication: Bizkaian, Gipuzkoan, Lapurdian and, to a smaller extent, Zuberoan; these four dialects were accordingly once known as the 'literary dialects' of Basque. As a consequence of this steady publication, we have abundant textual evidence for Basque during the last four centuries or so. For linguistic purposes, however, it is worth bearing in mind that some dialects of Basque are attested both earlier and more copiously than others. The earliest texts in Bizkaian, consisting as they do of proverbs and transcriptions of medieval poems, are particularly valuable in that they record a number of archaisms unattested elsewhere.

Publication in the south was, on the whole, much slower to develop than in the north. The eighteenth-century writers in Bizkaia and Gipuzkoa were largely apologists rather than literary figures, and they mostly wrote in

Spanish; their work is accordingly discussed in the next section. An outstanding exception was the Gipuzkoan Agustín Cardaberaz, whose 1761 book *Eusqueraren berri onac*, an essay on Basque rhetoric, was written in Basque, an unusual decision in the south at the time. Otherwise, literary output in the south was largely confined to mediocre translations of religious texts.

From about the time of the French Revolution, however, the literary centre of gravity of the language began shifting rapidly from the north to the south. On the one hand, French Republican persecution weakened the position of Basque in the north; on the other, the growing prosperity of Bizkaia and Gipuzkoa favoured increasing interest in the use of the language.

Publication in Basque was interrupted during times of oppression, most notably in the aftermath of the Spanish Civil War, when for some years almost the only publications in Basque were those produced by exiles in the Americas. Eventually, and very gradually, publication resumed in the Basque Country, first on the French side, where Franco's writ did not run, and then on the Spanish side.

During these centuries of publication, the language was slowly losing territory in the south. Bilbao was still largely Basque-speaking in the sixteenth century; by the seventeenth century the inhabitants were bilingual, and their Basque was heavily romanized, as we know from a little textbook compiled by Rafael de Micoleta in 1653, though the local speech also preserved a number of archaisms. Not long after this date, the language had retreated to the eastern shore of the estuary. As Figure 1.2 shows, the southern frontier of the Basque-speaking area, which in the sixteenth century still lay in the Ebro valley, has been steadily retreating northwards across Araba and Navarre, until today only the northernmost part of Navarre, and one small corner of Araba, still retain the language. Just in the last few years, Basque has disappeared entirely in the valley of Roncal. The northern boundary with Gascon has remained stable for centuries, but Gascon itself has now largely given way to French, and the French Basque varieties are now probably under more intense pressure than the southern dialects.

On the other hand, the number of speakers of Basque has actually increased in the last several decades, from below 600,000 to about 660,000 in 1991. This total includes a significant number of people who have learned it as a second language. It remains to be seen, however, just how successfully the language will resist the pressures which are everywhere threatening minority languages with extinction.

1.4 LINGUISTIC WORK ON BASQUE

The Basques were writing about their language for centuries before any outsiders took an interest in it, but their early attempts at contemplating the language consisted of little more than fantasies punctuated by preposterous etymologies. A few of these etymological proposals were for Basque words, including such derivations as *gizon* 'man' from *gauza on* 'good thing' and *emakume* 'woman' from *eman* 'give' and *ume* 'child'. The great majority, however, were strictly fantastic attempts at finding Basque sources for words and names in Spanish, Latin, Greek and other languages. Here is a modest sample: *Asturias* (name of a Spanish province) from Bizkaian Basque *aztu* 'forget' and *uri* 'town' (apparently on the assumption that Asturias is full of ghost towns); *Celtiberia* (an ancient Celtic region of Spain) from *zaldi* 'horse' and *ibar* 'valley'; Spanish *ancho* 'wide' from *handi* 'big' plus the diminutive suffix *-txo*; Spanish *borujón* 'lump, bump' (on the body) from *buru* 'head' plus *jo* 'hit'; *Ebro* (a river) from *ur bero* 'hot water'; Spanish *vasco* 'Basque' from *baso* 'wilderness' plus the relational suffix *-ko*; late Latin *labarum* (the Christian banner carried by Constantine) from *lauburu* 'Basque swastika', itself from *lau* 'four' and *buru* 'head'; Spanish *asco* 'disgust' from *asko* 'much, many'. Readers will no doubt be familiar with this sort of thing in other domains.

Some of these etymologies are the work of Andrés de Poza (†1595), a Bizkaian lawyer of prodigious erudition, who, like his more famous successor J. J. Scaliger, classified the languages of Europe into families. Poza argued that Basque had anciently been the language of the entire Iberian Peninsula, and that it had been one of the seventy-two languages created by God at the Tower of Babel.

The earliest known attempt at providing any kind of description of Basque was a dictionary completed in 1562 by an Italian called Niccolò Landucci, often known by the Spanish form of his name, Nicolás Landuchio. Landucci had lived for many years in the Basque Country, though it appears that he had not himself learned Basque, but merely collected his words from Basque-speaking acquaintances. What is particularly striking is that the dialect represented in his *Dictionarium linguae cantabricae* is clearly distinct from all the modern dialects, and appears to have been a variety which is long since extinct. This is the dialect that I shall be calling 'Southern'; the best guess is that it was spoken in Araba, where Basque was almost completely supplanted by Castilian centuries ago, most likely in or around the capital city of Gasteiz (Spanish *Vitoria*). Unsurprisingly, the Basque represented here is strongly castilianized, but the work none the less records a number of words unattested elsewhere, such as the curious *errexala* 'tree'. The dictionary somehow found its way into the Royal Library in Madrid, where its existence was known to at least a few interested scholars from the early eighteenth century, but it was only finally published in a version edited by Agud and Michelena in 1958. Michelena's illuminating introduction is reprinted in Michelena (1988a: II, 762–782).

Sometime in the seventeenth century, a Frenchman called Sylvain Pouvreau, who had learned Basque as a second language, compiled a small Basque dictionary; this dictionary long remained unknown, but it can be found today in the National Library in Paris, though it has never been published. Some of Pouvreau's entries are unusually interesting, such as his striking citation of *ur ibaia* for 'ford, fordable river', in which the word *ibai*, today the nearly universal noun meaning 'river', is apparently used as an adjective modifying *ur* 'water'.

Also in the seventeenth century, the Zuberoan Jacques de Bela, the Lapurdian Joanes Etcheberry of Ziburu and the Low Navarrese Dominique Bidegaray produced a number of brief grammars and dictionaries, none of which was published until much later and some of which are now lost. The Zuberoan Arnaut Oihenart, mentioned in the last section, included in his volume of history *Notitia utriusque vasconiae* (1638) a brief sketch of Basque grammar, the first such work which has come down to us. A unique publication was a guide to Basque conversation published in Bayonne in 1642 under the name Voltoire, a figure otherwise unknown to us; this little book was a great success and went through several editions. See Oyharçabal (1992b) for an account of all this work.

Apart from these comparatively minor figures, the first efforts at providing a linguistic account of Basque were offered by the engaging figure of Padre Manuel Larramendi (1690–1766) in the eighteenth century. In 1729 he published the first ever grammar of Basque, rather colourfully entitled *El imposible vencido* ('The Impossible Vanquished'). Written entirely within the confines of traditional Latin grammar, this volume is by no means easy to read. For example, the luxuriant ergative-based case system of Basque is crammed absurdly into the six Latin cases, leading to two 'nominatives' and rather a lot of 'ablatives'. None the less, Larramendi was a sharp observer, and his descriptions of pronunciation and usage are taken with great seriousness today. Larramendi followed his grammar in 1745 with the first published dictionary of Basque. This took the form of a Spanish–Basque bilingual dictionary, with each Spanish word rendered by its supposed Basque equivalent. Unfortunately, whenever the author failed to find a native Basque equivalent for a Spanish word, he simply invented one, with no clue to the reader that he was doing so, and his dictionary is therefore stuffed with his own inventions, greatly reducing its value as a scholarly document. Larramendi's style of word creation was, it has to be said, admirably direct, if not always in keeping with the more usual patterns of the language: for example, *sutumpa* 'fire-bang' for 'artillery piece' and *surrauts* 'nose-powder' for 'snuff'. In other cases, though, he seems to have constructed his words out of thin air, as with *godaria* 'chocolate', which is vaguely reminiscent of *gozo* 'sweet' but otherwise has no identifiable Basque source. Because of this dictionary, Larramendi is regarded, perhaps a little unfairly, as more of an eccentric than a scholar. (It should be pointed out that Larramendi, by his own account, had access to an unpublished Basque dictionary compiled a few years earlier by Joannes d'Etcheberri of Sara; Etcheberri's dictionary was never published and is apparently lost.)

Larramendi was followed by the Bizkaian Pedro Antonio de Añibarro

(1748–1830), whose substantial literary and linguistic output included a dictionary in which regional words were explicitly identified as Bizkaian, Gipuzkoan or Navarrese, and a comparative grammar listing the morphological forms typical of each of these three dialects. Neither of these pioneering works was published until the 1960s.

In 1773 Pedro Rodríguez de Campomanes proposed to the Real Sociedad Vascongada a comprehensive dictionary of Basque; though the proposal seems to have been well received, nothing came of it.

The late eighteenth and early nineteenth century witnessed a flowering of interest in the Basque language within the Basque Country. During this period Basque literature experienced one of its most brilliant periods, and several writers undertook essays on the language itself. Unfortunately, all of these were apologias rather than serious descriptive works. The best-known of them is Pablo Pedro de Astarloa's 1803 volume, whose (abbreviated) title is *Apología de la Lengua Vascongada o ensayo crítico filosófico de su perfección y antigüedad sobre todas las que se conocen*; the title describes the content of the book very well, since the author was primarily concerned to demonstrate that Basque had anciently been the language of all Spain, and that it best preserved the 'perfect' state of the ancestral human language. Astarloa, a native of Durango in Bizkaia, was not entirely devoid of analytical abilities. For example, he was the first person to point out that the Basque verb distinguishes more moods than do the Romance languages. But he was, in the words of Antonio Tovar, 'incorrigibly ethnocentric': all his life, he stoutly maintained that the five vowels of Basque (and of Castilian) were the only five vowels which the human mouth was capable of producing; after studying French, with its fifteen or so vowels, he concluded stubbornly that the French were pronouncing their vowels 'imperfectly'. He also completed a bulky volume which he called a 'philosophical grammar' of Basque, but this book, published only in 1883, long after the author's death, is little more than a mystical treatise on the supposed original significance of each of the letters of the alphabet in the primordial stage of the language.

Inevitably, Astarloa and the other apologists continued the tradition of proposing fantastic etymologies: Greek *iesis* 'going' from *ihes* 'flight'; Greek *kínesis* 'motion' from *zin* 'oath' plus *ihesi* 'flee'; Greek *eros* 'sexual love' from *ero* 'crazy'; the name of Sweden (in Spanish *Suecia*) from *su* 'fire', on the ground that Sweden is so cold that fire is a constant necessity; Spanish *España* 'Spain' from *ezpain* 'lip'; Latin URBE 'in the city' from *ur be* 'below the water'; *Astarte* (name of a Near Eastern goddess) from *astearte* 'Tuesday'; Latin MILES 'soldier' from *hil* 'kill'; and (my particular favourite) *euskara* (the Basque name of the Basque language) from *asko gara* 'there are quite a lot of us'. Recognizing the influence of Astarloa in these exercises, Basque historiographers sometimes refer to such screwball etymologies as 'astarloisms'. An engaging review of all this activity can be found in Tovar (1980).

A considerably more clear-headed apologist was Joseph-Dominique Garat of Ustaritz (Lapurdi), who actively campaigned against the obfuscations and *a priori* declarations which were so much in fashion in the study of language in his day. In 1785 Garat published an article on the Basque language in the *Encyclopédie méthodique*, which brought him to the attention of the scholar who was soon to begin the first serious linguistic work on Basque.

This was the great German linguist and philosopher of language Wilhelm von Humboldt (1767–1835), who, during an exceptionally full and busy career as a statesman, diplomat, politician and educationalist, somehow found the time to study an astounding range of European, Asian and North American languages and to produce an impressive series of descriptive and comparative studies and, more particularly, his famous treatises on the relation between language, mind and culture.

Humboldt made two visits to the Basque Country in 1799 and 1801, during which he made strenuous attempts to learn as much Basque as he could and collected such sparse materials as he could find. He met both Astarloa, who gave unstintingly of his time and handed over his as yet unpublished work, and Garat, whose ideas had a notable influence on the German scholar. Between his visits, Humboldt worked on his material in Paris, where he was stationed at the time, and combed the Royal Library for works on Basque. He even attempted to revise Larramendi's dictionary into a Basque–Spanish format, an unfortunate undertaking.

Humboldt made frequent references to Basque in his voluminous published works, and gradually gained a reputation as the leading specialist in the language. Unfortunately, he published very little in the way of explicit descriptive or analytical work on the language. Like so many of his other ambitious projects, his planned major work on Basque was never completed, and only two substantial fragments ever appeared. His 1821 book on the original inhabitants of Spain makes frequent references to Basque but contains little in the way of valuable information – though it does contain his famous proposal that Basque is the modern continuation of the ancient Iberian language of Spain, a proposal which Humboldt had taken over from Astarloa and which I shall consider in Chapter 6; in pursuit of this idea, he attempted to interpret a number of ancient toponyms by means of modern Basque words. Amazingly, he failed to recognize the obvious and numerous Latin loan words in Basque, and pursued a fantastic connection with Greek, for reasons best known to himself. Apart from such speculations, he had no interest in historical matters and attempted no contributions to the history of Basque; indeed, from our standpoint, his ideas about language history were very backward. This is hardly surprising, since in his day the very field of historical linguistics was only beginning to take shape, and the pioneering work of Rask, Bopp and Grimm had yet to appear.

Though Humboldt was clearly fascinated by Basque, he was interested in it primarily as a vehicle for developing his rather sweeping ideas about the philosophy of language: for him, Basque was primarily a specimen. His descriptive work on the language is disappointingly modest and severely limited in importance when regarded from the point of view of Basque linguistics *per se*. His command of the language was limited, and he worked almost entirely from written materials, as a result of which he was frequently guilty of what has been called 'eye philology' – the manipulation of written letters without regard for the speech which those letters imperfectly represent. Inevitably, he was the first European linguist to find himself mystified by the ergative morphology of Basque: in one of his papers, he complains in apparent puzzlement that Basque does 'not always distinguish in sound between nominative and accusative'. Humboldt was also an early practitioner of what would later become almost a disease among European linguists working on Basque: the approach I shall call 'analysis by translation'. This technique consists of translating a Basque sentence morpheme by morpheme into one's mother tongue, always using the same translation for each Basque morpheme, then examining the structure of the resulting translation and finally announcing as a result the structure of the original Basque sentence. Noting, for example, that the Basque rendering of 'I eat bread' is *Ogia jaten dut*, in which the word *ogi* 'bread' requires the article *-a*, and having already decided that this article must always be translated as 'the', Humboldt declares that, in Basque, one cannot say 'I eat bread', but only 'I eat it, the bread'. This kind of approach constantly defaces later work on Basque by European linguists, and it is largely responsible for many of the absurd myths which have sprung up about the language.

Humboldt did not, however, put forward anything comparable to the wild interpretations of Basque grammar which characterize the work of so many of his successors. He deserves full credit for being the first scholar to bring Basque to the attention of European linguists, but his name is hardly ever mentioned by vasconists today, and he is not usually regarded as the founder of the continuous tradition of Basque linguistics.

That honour belongs to a Frenchman, Prince Louis Lucien Bonaparte (1813–1891), nephew of Napoleon and, it is said, the spitting image of his illustrious uncle. Born in England, raised in the Papal States, much travelled in Europe and the United States, the polyglot Bonaparte dabbled in chemistry and mineralogy before settling on a career in linguistics. After the breakup of his first marriage, he married a native Basque-speaker with the unusual name of Clemencia Richard, and he then devoted all the rest of his life to the study of Basque. He produced a long series of treatises on the language; the majority of these were descriptive studies of particular regional dialects, but he also wrote some more general studies on aspects of Basque grammar, the most important being his book *Le Verbe basque*, published in 1869, a comparative study of the verb-forms in the several dialects. And, though it was hardly among his central concerns, he was the first linguist ever to attempt any work on the historical linguistics of Basque: here and there, he proposed a number of *ad hoc* and rather speculative reconstructions of particular words and forms. These proposals have not stood up, and I shall not discuss them here, except to note that he was, so far as I can determine, the originator of the notion that Basque possesses a number of tool names built on the stem *haitz* 'stone', a proposal which is examined in Chapter 5.

As a linguist, Bonaparte was strictly an amateur. He had no training in the discipline, and his work was unscientific in every way. He had little taste for generalization and synthesis, but preferred to concentrate on the accumulation of details – indeed, Michelena has said of the Frenchman that he had 'a horror of general questions'. However, Bonaparte deserves credit for two contributions to Basque linguistics of the first magnitude. First, he classified the language into dialects (and subdialects) with speci- fied boundaries. He was working a couple of decades before the great pioneers of dialectology began their work in France and Germany, and his methods were somewhat unsystematic and his criteria usually inexplicit – for example, he identified virtually no isoglosses for particular regional differences, and he largely ignored phonetics and phonology in favour of morphology and lexis. Nevertheless, the famous map which he published in 1869 is still today the basis of our classification of Basque dialects, though both Azkue and Michelena later made some minor amendments to it. Sec- ond, Bonaparte encouraged and inspired the Basques to take their lan- guage seriously, to write in it and to construct linguistic descriptions of it. In these efforts he was spectacularly successful, and Luis Villasante, past President of the Royal Basque Language Academy, has written (1979: 174) that 'The Basque people owe eternal gratitude to Prince Louis Lucien Bonaparte.'

The single most important consequence of Bonaparte's encouragement was the publication in 1858, by his longtime teacher and collaborator, Emmanuel Inchauspé, of *Le Verbe basque*. Preceding and eclipsing Bona- parte's own efforts in this area, this was the first attempt ever at presenting a comprehensive account of the entire verbal system of Basque, or rather of one dialect, the author's own Zuberoan. In spite of its dramatic opening sentence, 'The Basque language has only one verb', which need not be taken too seriously, this is a sober and careful study. Like most of its successors, it is rather long on lists of forms and rather short on analysis, but this is the book which set the tone and provided much of the vocabulary for what was later to become something of a national pastime in the Basque Country: producing lists of verb-forms. Villasante (1979: 179) describes Inchauspé's book as 'a revelation in its time', and the distinguished vasconist René Lafon has called it 'a work of the first order'.

Since the efforts of Bonaparte and Inchauspé, there has been an uninter- rupted tradition of work on Basque. The last several decades of the nineteenth century saw the publication of a number of complete grammars, the most notable of which was Arturo Campión's monumental 1884 volume, which treats all four of the so-called 'literary' dialects. A traditional but substantial grammar of Lapurdian Basque was published in fascicles from 1894 to 1907 by the Lapurdian Jean Ithurry. The first truly scholarly dictionary of Basque was compiled in the final decades of the century by Maurice Harriet, a native of Lapurdi who had gained extensive knowledge of the southern dialects of Basque during his career in the Church; this magnificent manuscript of over 3,500 pages the author flatly refused to publish, and it resides today in the seminary of Ustaritz, where it has been regularly consulted by linguists and lexicographers ever since.

At the same time, the conclusion in 1876 of the long series of rather puzzling conflicts known as the Carlist Wars, in which the Basques had largely fought on the losing side against the growing centralism of the government in Madrid, led to the flowering of the cultural movement which the Basques call the *Berpizkundea*, literally 'Rekindling', but usually known in English as the Basque Renaissance. Frustrated in their political ambitions, the Basques turned with growing enthusiasm to the examination, maintenance and recording of their traditions. A body of dedicated amateur scholars collected and published songs, verses, stories and folktales, and hence preserved a good deal of material that might otherwise have been lost to scholarship.

Of course, outsiders continued to take an interest in Basque. The Dutch linguist W. J. van Eys, who discovered Landucci's dictionary, published a comparative grammar of the dialects; he also published (in 1883) the first grammar of Basque to appear in English. Van Eys proposed a number of what appear to be intended as reconstructions of inflected and derived forms (he is not very explicit), but he unfortunately belonged to that school of etymology in which consonants and vowels are to be inserted or deleted arbitrarily, according to the result required by the analyst, and none of his proposals can be taken seriously.

Two English amateurs, Wentworth Webster and Edward Spencer Dodgson, devoted themselves to the advancement of Basque language studies and literature, in particular by republishing a number of classical literary works; Dodgson's rescue and publication of the 200-year-old manuscript of a Basque translation of Genesis by Pierre d'Urte was particularly noteworthy, since d'Urte, almost uniquely among Basque authors, made a practice of marking the word-accent.

In the late 1870s the French romanist Achille Luchaire undertook the first serious historical work on Basque. He made a study of the ancient Aquitanian texts and put forward the idea that Aquitanian was an ancestral form of Basque, and he also carried out pioneering studies in medieval Basque onomastics, both personal names and place names. Regrettably, however, his attempts to introduce a historical dimension to Basque linguistics were, with only minor exceptions, not picked up by others until well into the twentieth century.

In the 1880s there was a flowering of interest in Basque studies in Germany; a *Baskische Gesellschaft* was formed in Berlin in 1886, and it published a journal, *Euskara*, from 1886 to 1896.

The German Victor Stempf, a minor figure in Basque studies in most respects, published in 1889 a small pamphlet arguing for a startling interpretation of the Basque verb; a modified version of his thesis rapidly gained popularity as the 'passive' theory of the Basque verb, according to which all transitive verbs in Basque are 'really' passives. Within a very few years this surprising view, induced almost entirely by the ergative morphology of Basque, had become the orthodox position among foreign vasconists (though never among native speakers, who have uniformly rejected it).

Around the same time there appeared on the scene an extraordinary individual who seemed poised to turn the study of Basque into a scientific discipline but who then abruptly turned his back on the language: the enigmatic Miguel de Unamuno (1864–1936). Born in Bilbao, Unamuno was not a native speaker of Basque, but he learned the language in adolescence and, according to some reports, became fluent in it. In 1884, at the tender age of nineteen, he submitted to the University of Madrid a doctoral thesis on the origin and prehistory of the Basques, for which he was awarded his doctorate with distinction. Well-read in general linguistics, Unamuno was a believer in the stadial ideas of linguistic evolution which were fashionable in his day, but he turned his formidable intelligence upon his chosen subject and began what was nearly a revolution. With withering contempt he dismissed the fantastic fables of the Basque apologists, their mythical histories, their absurd etymologies; in the same manner he waved away the currently popular notions that Basque was an aberrant Celtic language, a bastardized form of Latin or Germanic, or a remnant of Etruscan. These preposterous conceptions he replaced with a clear-headed recognition that Basque was an ancient and distinct language which had been heavily influenced by Latin and its Romance descendants. He launched himself into an ambitious project to identify and separate the various levels of Latino-Romance incrustations which had overlaid the original language during 2,000 years, a project which, if ever carried through, would have earned him full credit for being the founder of Basque linguistics as a serious professional discipline.

But Unamuno's attitude towards the language was always ambiguous: on the one hand, he took a deeply sentimental view of the language of his ancestors and countrymen; on the other, however, he could never bring himself to believe that Basque was really a 'proper' language as deserving of respect as any other. Famously, he denied that Basque possessed any words denoting abstractions or generalizations; flying in the face of the plainest evidence to the contrary, for example, he heatedly denied that there were any Basque words for such concepts as 'spirit' or even 'tree'. When, in 1888, he lost out in a competition for a new chair of Basque in Bilbao (to R. M. de Azkue, on whom see below), this negative side of his character exploded to the fore. He dropped his project and, for the rest of his life, he did no further work on Basque. Indeed, he almost never spoke of the language again, except in bitter and abusive terms, most famously in his article of 1902 (published in 1916), in which he argued that Basque was too crude and backward to become a language of culture and must therefore die. (See Ugalde (1979) for a study of Unamuno's ideas.) The world remembers Unamuno as a philosopher, as a writer and as the distinguished rector of Spain's prestigious University of Salamanca, but his bizarre behaviour deprived us of the chance to remember him as the real founder of scientific Basque linguistics.

That honour belongs to a scholar who was twenty years older than Unamuno, but who came to Basque late in his career: the exasperating but highly original German linguist Hugo Schuchardt (1842–1927), who was born in the engagingly named town of Batman. Schuchardt, of course, is a prominent figure in historical linguistics generally: apart from his work on Romance languages, his celebrated opposition to the doctrines of the Neogrammarians brought him a large measure of notoriety, and, after the triumph of the Neogrammarians, he was virtually declared an unperson for several decades, until changing ideas in the field led to his rehabilitation.

Though best known as a romanist and a creolist, Schuchardt took a restless interest in the languages surrounding the Romance area. He finally came to Basque, and, after reading several books on the language, he paid a visit to the Basque town of Sara in 1887, at the age of forty-five. Thereafter, he worked on Basque at intervals throughout the remainder of his career. Aside from a number of minor but illuminating monographs, he produced the lengthy 1893 paper 'Baskische Studien' and four short books: *Baskisch und Romanisch* (1906), *Zur Kenntnis des Baskischen von Sara* (1922), *Primitiae linguae vasconum: Einführung ins Baskische* (1923) and *Das Baskisch und die Sprachwissenschaft* (1925).

Schuchardt's work on Basque is almost a monument to disorganization. He seems to have jotted things down just as they occurred to him, and then never to have revised anything. His 1893 paper, consisting of eighty-one very large pages, is divided into no sections, though mysterious unlabelled enumerations do pop up from time to time. A typical paragraph is six to eight pages long, and shows no discernible structure. For example, the fourth paragraph begins by considering the past-tense forms of Basque, leaps abruptly into a comparison of Basque verb-forms with those of an Italian dialect and of Arabic, introduces some non-finite verb-forms, proposes several reconstructions, returns to the past-tense forms with a survey of dialect variants, proposes some more reconstructions, and then resumes the survey of dialect variants – and this is one of the shortest paragraphs. The writing style is crabbed and dense, stuffed with multiple parentheticals and with cryptic abbreviations and formulae, ranging from simple things like 'F 7' and 'VB XV' to nightmarish stuff like '$P_3{}^s p^s \rho p^s p_3{}^u$'. Finally, Schuchardt was a proponent of (indeed, he was one of the most influential disseminators of) the 'passive' theory of the Basque verb, and hence he conscientiously glosses his verb-forms with things like 'ich könnte gehabt werden ^{dir} [von ihm]' and 'von uns wurden gehabt sie ^{dir}' (the superscript elements represent the presence of a so-called 'allocutive', a second person which is coded in the verb but which represents no argument). In short, Schuchardt is not much fun to read.

Moreover, his historical work suffered from certain handicaps. He was working at a time when nothing was known about the phonological history of Basque, and he himself made no contribution in that area, apart from a single paper demonstrating that the word-initial /p/ of Basque must be a recent innovation (Schuchardt 1887); otherwise, he worked exclusively on morphology and lexicon. Furthermore, the notoriously hypochondriac Schuchardt hated travelling, and he seems never to have made a second visit to the Basque Country, relying for his materials on published works, together with what he could obtain by post from other scholars. These limitations show up clearly in his writings, as, for example, when he proposes to derive Basque *bazkari* 'lunch' from an unattested Latin *pascuarium, not realizing that the earliest texts uniformly show *barazkari*, of which *bazkari* can only be a contraction, rendering his proposal immediately untenable.

He also made enthusiastic if typically unsystematic attempts at connecting Basque with other languages. His pages are spattered with miscellaneous and ill-considered parallels between Basque and a wide range of European, African and Asian languages: Finnish, the Caucasian languages, Arabic, Hebrew, Maasai, Dinka and others. He was particularly taken with the Berber languages, and he repeatedly tried to identify Basque words, morphemes and mere morphs with similar-looking elements in Berber, an implausible enterprise in which it has to be said he enjoyed no success whatever (see Chapter 6). At times he allowed this obsession to obscure his vast command of Romance, as when he proposed a North African origin for Basque *haizkora* 'axe', overlooking the straightforward derivation from Latin ASCIOLA, which is now almost universally accepted.

Nevertheless, Schuchardt's achievements were considerable. His prodigious knowledge of Basque, both spoken and written, was superior to that of any of his predecessors. In his disorganized way, he made a number of shrewd suggestions about the history of nominal and (especially) verbal morphology in Basque, and what understanding we have today of the history of finite verb-forms is very largely due to his efforts. He brought his considerable knowledge of Romance languages to bear on the question of the sources of the Basque vocabulary, and his was the first sustained attempt to identify systematically the layers of Latin and Romance loan words in the language; very many of his etymologies are still accepted today, though a number of others have admittedly been dismissed as untenable. Above all, he put the study of Basque onto a more secure scholarly footing than it had ever known before. It is not too much to assert that Schuchardt found Basque linguistics an amateur pastime and left it a scholarly discipline. Anyone who wants to become versed in Basque historical linguistics is obliged to read Schuchardt, but a new reader might be advised to begin with the 1923 book, which takes the form of a series of annotations on Leizarraga's Basque translation of the parable of the prodigal son. It's no better organized than his other work, but at least the paragraphs are short.

In total contrast to Schuchardt's scholarship were the excesses of Sabino Arana (1865–1903), who was introduced above. Though born to Basque-speaking parents, he did not himself learn Basque until adulthood, and reportedly never mastered it completely; interestingly, his first Basque teacher was the Dutch vasconist van Eys.

Arana attempted to re-form the Basque language of his day into something more to his liking. Unfortunately, his imperfect grasp of the language, combined with his near-total lack of linguistic training, led him constantly into bizarre and fantastic excesses. At an early stage, he devised a completely new orthography for Basque, stuffed with pointless and highly inconvenient diacritics, apparently in the confused belief that the language required a bit of *Abstand* to set it apart visually from its Romance neighbours. (In fact, of course, Basque needs *Abstand* like a fish needs a bicycle.) This orthography was presented in the form of a new alphabet with a completely original order of letters; its name, the *agaka*, derives from its first three letters, A G K. This orthography could not be printed without special type and could not be typewritten at all, but it was none the less widely used for several decades; a slightly modified version was used by the distinguished vasconist Azkue (see below) in all his works, including his great dictionary, and was approved by the Basque Language Academy, though almost no one followed Arana in his proposed new alphabetical order. Perhaps the only appealing outcome of the Spanish Civil War is that it effectively put paid to the use of this diabolical orthography (though a handful of diehard Aranistas continued to use it as late as 1960, often especially in books published in exile in places like Guatemala).

Brushing aside the scholarship of Schuchardt, Arana sought his inspiration in the fantasies of the eighteenth-century apologists, which he developed and extended to new depths. The Oscans, the Etruscans, any ancient people whose name contained an /sk/ cluster, all were declared to have been *vascos*. (If Arana had come across my family, no doubt we would have found ourselves added to the list.) The standard of his etymological theorizing is well represented by such gems as *Africa* from *alferrik* 'uselessly, in vain', *Barcelona* from *Bart ze(r) lo ona!* 'What a good sleep last night!' and *Castilla* from *ke* 'smoke' plus *asto* 'donkey' plus *illa* 'dead' (dialect variant of *hila*); the motivation for calling a region 'smoke dead donkey' is frankly far from clear.

But Arana's greatest linguistic efforts were directed towards the coining of neologisms and the reform of personal names; these efforts are considered in some detail in Chapter 5.

The Frenchman Julien Vinson (1843–1916), a forestry official assigned to the Basque Country, published a stream of books and monographs on various aspects of the country and the language. One of nature's antagonists, he took issue with everybody on everything, and his writings are characterized by a hostility that borders on violence. He conducted public arguments with van Eys, with Stempf and, in spite of his almost berserk hostility to Neogrammarian ideas, even with Schuchardt. So strange were Vinson's ideas that Michelena (1973c) has described him as 'a sort of living anachronism'. Yet he was able to produce a number of valuable works, the most important of which is his superb *Bibliographie de la langue basque*, published in 1891, with a supplement in 1898. This was the first such bibliography ever compiled. Vinson is also noteworthy for his staunch rejection of the 'passive' theory, which at the time was rapidly becoming a dogma among foreign vasconists.

The new century saw a brief *Congrès basque* held in 1906 in Hondarribia (Gipuzkoa); here the idea of a Basque Language Academy was first mooted.

The turn of the century also witnessed the appearance on the scene of one of the titans of Basque linguistics, Resurrección María de Azkue (1864–1951), a native of Lekeitio in Bizkaia. A native speaker of Basque, Azkue had a phenomenal capacity for work. He was the driving force behind the organization of the first real congress of Basque studies, held in Oñati (Gip) (Spanish *Oñate*) in 1918; it was largely Azkue's efforts at that congress that led to the founding of the Sociedad de Estudios Vascos (and its *Boletín*) in the same year and of the Basque Language Academy (Euskaltzaindia) in the following year, and he served as the Academy's first president until his death. Except when interrupted by war and suppression, the Academy's journal, *Euskera*, has been a major vehicle of Basque linguistics ever since. Again at that same conference, Azkue put forward a proposal to construct a standard form of Basque, and himself defended his *Gipuzkera Osotua* ('Completed Gipuzkoan') as the basis of that standard. He published an unremarkable grammar of Basque and a vast four-volume collection of folktales, as well as a number of lesser works, including a much-neglected essay on the history of the language. He also devised the famous *Triple Questionnaire* (*Erizkizundi Irukoitza*), designed to elicit information about the pronunciation, morphology and vocabulary used in all corners of the Basque Country. But he is best known for his two great works: his magnificent dictionary and his volume on morphology.

His *Diccionario vasco–español–francés*, published in 1905, is still the finest dictionary that Basque has ever received, and it will remain so at least until the completion of the Academy's new dictionary, which does not appear to be imminent. Covering all dialects and making extensive use of published and unpublished materials, as well as of the author's own observations, the great dictionary is an incomparable source of information about the lexicon of Basque, including dialect variants and localized and archaic words. Since its appearance, no vasconist has been able to do without it. But see section 1.5.2 below for some observations on the use of the dictionary.

Azkue's other major work was his *Morfología vasca*, a long book originally published in 1923–1925 as the entire content of consecutive issues of *Euskera*, the journal recently set up by the Academy, and finally published in book format only in 1969, under the misleading title *Gramática vasca* (the 1969 edition includes a long commentary on the work published in 1934 by Severo Altube, of whom more below). This is a wide-ranging, if rather quaintly organized, survey of virtually all aspects of the morphology of Basque, of which the most valuable part is a catalogue of almost the entire set of bound morphemes in the language. The book requires a certain amount of care to use. For one thing, Azkue was at pains to promote his own individual theories about the nature of Basque. For another, he does not distinguish between inflectional and derivational affixes, but groups affixes largely on semantic grounds; though he includes a section dealing with phonological rules, he none the less often lists the two or three variant forms of an affix in different places. But the index is good, and the author's tireless collection of archaic and dialectal forms, most of them with provenances supplied, makes this a fascinating and exceptionally valuable secondary source for the student of historical morphology.

Azkue's occasional attempts at descriptive studies of regional varieties are somewhat less successful. That same delight in collecting archaic and anomalous forms which helps to make his dictionary so valuable proved to be a severe handicap in compiling his descriptions, which stress such picturesque curiosities at the expense of normal everyday use and which rarely recognize the important influence of Romance. As a result, his accounts are unbalanced and incomplete.

Azkue's younger contemporary Julio de Urquijo (1871–1950) deserves a mention here, even though he was not strictly a linguist. Above all, Urquijo was an organizer and administrator. Distressed by what he saw as the amateurish state of Basque studies, he turned his considerable energies to the task of promoting serious scholarly study and of weeding out the enthusiastic but often incompetent amateurs who seemed to outnumber the scholars. To this end, he founded in 1907 the journal *Revista Internacional de los Estudios Vascos* (*RIEV*), also known by its French title, *Revue International des Etudes Basques* (*RIEB*). Until killed off by the Spanish Civil War in 1936, this was the premier journal of Basque studies generally and of Basque linguistics in particular; its pages were graced by contributions from all of the most distinguished scholars who worked on Basque during the following three decades, from Schuchardt to Meyer-Lübke. The present-day Seminario de Filología Vasca 'Julio de Urquijo', a prominent publisher of important work in Basque linguistics, is named in Urquijo's honour.

According to Villasante (1979: 103), it was Urquijo who stumbled across some previously lost works of the eighteenth-century writer Etxeberri of Sara gathering dust in a monastery in Zarautz (Gipuzkoa), though Echenique (1987: 111) credits this discovery to the British scholars Wentworth Webster and Llewelyn Thomas.

Also contemporary with Azkue and Urquijo was the talented Dutch linguist C. C. Uhlenbeck (1866–1950). Uhlenbeck was attracted to Basque by its ergative morphology; he was a passionate defender of the 'passive' theory, not just for Basque, but for ergative languages generally (see his famous 1916 paper). Over several decades he turned out a number of articles on almost every aspect of the language, but particularly on comparative phonology and morphology; he was the first linguist to approach the study of Basque from a rigorously Neogrammarian point of view (Schuchardt, of course, was anything but Neogrammarian in his approach), and he was the only vasconist to show any interest in structuralist ideas before the 1940s. In one of these articles (1927), Uhlenbeck originated the celebrated proposal (celebrated among vasconists, at least) of the 'body-part prefix' *be-, which I shall examine in Chapter 5. Uhlenbeck was also an enthusiastic proponent of the Basque–Caucasian genetic link discussed in Chapter 6.

Mention must be made of the Zuberoan Pierre Lhande, whose 1926 dictionary, while largely based upon Azkue's, provides much more extensive coverage of the French Basque dialects. Particularly useful are its illustrations of household objects and agricultural implements. Unlike Azkue, Lhande attempts etymologies for many of his entries, but the great majority of these are too fanciful to be taken seriously. Lhande died before the book was finished, and it was completed and published by several younger collaborators.

Another Zuberoan, Jean Larrasquet, pioneered the application of instrumental phonetics to Basque and carried out important descriptive work on his native Zuberoan dialect (Larrasquet 1928, 1934, 1939).

Never was a linguist more aptly named than Severo Altube (1879–1963), born in Mondragón (Gipuzkoa). Severo was his name and severe was his outlook on language and on life. By profession he was the manager of an arms factory; by preference he was a fiercely devout Catholic, a musician, a minor politician and a vasconist. If the Basque language was never more than a hobby for him, it was a consuming one. Like many others, he found his career cut short by the Spanish Civil War and the subsequent Fascist repression; forced into decades of exile, he published in 1957 a tract entitled *La Fonction de la douleur*, in which he argued that pain is the essence of human existence and that a successful life can be achieved only by the maximization of pain. His views on language were not entirely unrelated.

His several works on Basque stand out in several respects. First, some of the minor ones were written in Basque: Altube was the first vasconist who saw fit to use his mother tongue as a medium for linguistic work, even if his major works were all written in Spanish. Second, much of his work was given over to the study of the syntax of Basque, a topic which had hardly been approached by earlier investigators. Altube was the first linguist to point out explicitly the importance of word order in Basque in reflecting the thematic structure of sentences. Finally, and perhaps unsurprisingly, Altube brought to his studies a fierce flame of purism and prescriptivism – not so much in vocabulary, but in syntax. Well-read in the classics, he was dismayed by what he saw as the increasing tendency for Romance sentence structures to be calqued into Basque. His most famous book, *Erderismos* (the name means, roughly, 'Foreignisms in Basque'), published in 1929, is at the same time a clear-headed exposition of sentence structure and a passionate demand for Basque-speakers to reject the insidious effects of their Spanish and to return to the unsullied speech patterns of their ancestors. Of course, he went too far, and some of the constructions he recommends as 'genuine' Basque had probably never been normal in the language. The book is none the less indispensable reading as the first serious attempt at describing the syntax of Basque.

After the death of Schuchardt in 1927, the acknowledged doyen of Basque linguistics was the French scholar Henri Gavel (1878–1959), born in Normandy; Gavel, having started as a romanist, married a Basque wife and took up the study of Basque with some fervour. His major works were *Eléments de phonétique basque* (1920), the first serious description of Basque phonetics, and the first volume of a Basque grammar (1929); only a fragment of the second volume was ever published, in 1937, with the co-authorship of Georges Lacombe. These works, particularly the first, contain a great deal of information which is of considerable value for historical phonology. Unfortunately, the author, like his predecessors, was untouched by the structuralist ideas which had been gathering strength in European linguistics, and his otherwise often insightful volumes are characterized by a failure to distinguish phonetics from phonology, phonology from morphology, or synchrony from diachrony. On the other hand, his several descriptive studies are gems: free of puristic biases and of excessive concern for the idiosyncratic, these studies are distinguished by their precision and explicitness. Gavel records exactly what he finds, and, like Azkue but unlike most of the lesser figures who were essaying descriptive studies in the early decades of this century, he is scrupulous about identifying the provenance of every one of his words and forms.

Gavel's advances in descriptive work were not matched by progress in historical linguistics. Indeed, Basque historical studies went through something of a lull around this time: many outsiders, such as Uhlenbeck, Trombetti, Dumézil and Lafon, were increasingly turning their attention to the vexed question of finding relatives for Basque, an issue which I reserve for Chapter 6, while Basque linguists were either concentrating on purely descriptive work or debating the new issue of a standard form of Basque, the project proposed at that 1918 congress.

One exception was the German romanist Gerhard Rohlfs, a specialist in Gascon who contributed some important work to the study of the influence upon Basque of the Romance languages, particularly Gascon, and who also helped to demonstrate the existence of ancient Basque place names in and around the Pyrenees. Another might have been the very unusual vasconist Gerhard Bähr (1900–1945), born into a German family in Legazpia (Gipuzkoa), where his father was the manager of a mine. He learned Basque in childhood, and then returned to Germany for his education. Obtaining a series of academic posts in Germany, he too published several articles of very high quality on Basque–Romance connections. Drafted into the German army in 1939 as an interpreter, he none the less managed to gain his doctorate from the University of Göttingen in 1940 with a thesis on Basque and Iberian. Soon after, he was dispatched to the Russian front with the infamous Blue Division, where he remained until 1944. Released from the army, he obtained a teaching post in Berlin, where he was apparently killed in the Russian capture of the city in 1945. Universally admired and respected, both personally and professionally, he might have made an outstanding career if circumstances had been kinder to him.

The outbreak of the Spanish Civil War in 1936 had catastrophic consequences for the Basques, who fought on the losing Republican side. The brutal repression installed by the victorious General Franco was applied to the Basques with particular savagery: exile, imprisonment and execution were the fate of large numbers of prominent figures; the very speaking of Basque was outlawed, and work on Basque language and culture was ruthlessly suppressed. Moreover, only a year after Franco's victory, the fall of France to the invading Germans meant that the French Basques now found themselves under Nazi occupation.

Curiously, it was during this very occupation that there appeared perhaps the most important work in Basque historical linguistics since Schuchardt's 'Baskische Studien': René Lafon's *Le Système du verbe basque au XVIe siècle*, published in 1944. Lafon (1899–1974) was a quiet French scholar who, aside from his long preoccupation with a Basque–Caucasian genetic link, had immersed himself in the study of the earliest Basque texts. His one and only book is a magisterial examination of the verbal system illustrated in those texts, in which he dissects and lays bare the structure of the system with a clarity and scrupulousness that had never before been achieved in any area of Basque linguistics. For the remaining decades of his life he continued to publish a long sequence of papers on Basque morphology, most of them with a strong historical orientation, and nearly all of them dealing with his beloved verbal system. Cautious almost to a fault, he none the less offered a number of proposals about the prehistory of the Basque verb, many of which will be considered in Chapter 4.

Interestingly, the same year, 1944, also saw the publication of Pierre Lafitte's *Grammaire basque (navarro-labourdin littéraire)*, which, in spite of the limited focus expressed in its subtitle, was far and away the most comprehensive, detailed and illuminating grammar of the language ever written. The revised third edition is still in print, and, in spite of its very traditional orientation, it has still not been surpassed as a reference grammar of the language. Generations of foreign linguists, including me, have learned much of their Basque from the pages of this splendid book.

By the late 1940s Basque studies were beginning to recover from the ravages of two major wars. The Franco government tacitly lifted a few of its restrictions, and it even allowed the Basque Language Academy to begin functioning again after a fashion, though Spanish Basques were still officially forbidden to talk to their French Basque cousins until quite a few years later. Things began to move again. The Basque anthropologist Julio Caro Baroja, who had already managed to publish two books dealing with the prehistory of the Basque Country and of the language, resumed his investigations of the Basque vocabulary, and produced a number of studies dealing with such topics as tool names, names of household objects and the names of the months, as well as personal names and place names; his was the first work in this area since Luchaire's. Some of his proposals will be considered in Chapter 5.

Soon after, Basque-language periodicals started to appear, beginning with the literary review *Egan* in 1954 and the cultural journal *Jakin* in 1956.

Also around 1950, the distinguished French linguist André Martinet turned his attention to Basque. Martinet's grammatical work on the language is decidedly odd: he has proposed an analysis in which Basque sentences have no subjects or predicates, in which verbs are 'neutral' (voiceless), and in which a sentence consists merely of a series of predications of existence. Thus, the Basque equivalent of 'The dog bit the man' is literally, for Martinet, 'There is a dog (agent) and a man (patient) and a biting (past)'. Except in France, no one has taken these ideas seriously. Much more interesting, however, is Martinet's work on the historical phonology of Basque; in several publications, but most notably in his famous 1955 book *Economie des changements phonétiques*, he has proposed a striking hypothesis about the prehistory of the Basque phonological system, which I shall consider in Chapter 3. But Martinet's most signal contribution to Basque historical linguistics was not his own work but his encouragement of an obscure student.

Luis Michelena (in Basque, Koldo Mitxelena) (1915–1987) is, beyond any comparison, the greatest figure in the whole history of Basque linguistics. Born in Rentería (Gipuzkoa), he fought in the Basque army during the Civil War and, like many others, he was condemned to death by Franco after the war. By some miracle he was pardoned and released, but he was unable to find a job. Thanks to the kindly intervention of the Spanish linguist Antonio Tovar, who had managed to maintain good relations with the Franco regime, Michelena was eventually able to obtain the newly created chair of Indo-European at the University of Salamanca, the oldest and most prestigious university in Spain. There, although he did not entirely neglect his nominal subject, he began his illustrious career as a specialist in Basque, during which he would utterly transform our understanding of the history and prehistory of the language.

It is impossible to do justice here to the breadth and depth of Michelena's contributions. His knowledge of Basque, ranging from the most ancient and obscure texts to the vagaries of the present-day dialects, has never been equalled or approached by anyone else. To this he added a substantial command of Latin and of a number of Romance languages, as well as a broad familiarity with many other languages of Europe. Crucially, however, he possessed a solid understanding of the principles of linguistic theory: Michelena was the first person ever to place the study of the history of Basque firmly within the framework of structural linguistics. To cite just one important example, he was the first vasconist ever to understand clearly the concept of a phonological system, the lack of which had previously prevented any success in understanding the phonological history of the language.

The bibliography of Michelena's vast output occupies thirty-one pages of fine print in his posthumous Festschrift. If there had been research selectivity exercises in his day, he would have had little fear of the outcome, though doubtless there would have been some snide bureaucratic comments about his failure to form a 'group' with a designated 'research strategy': until his somewhat reluctant move to the new University of the Basque Country in Vitoria, late in life, he was the only vasconist at his university, and he usually worked alone. Only a handful of his articles and editions were produced in collaboration.

Michelena worked on everything: historical phonology, the verbal system, place names, personal names, etymology, syntax, genetic relations, Romance influences, dialectology, literary criticism, the word-accent and so on. The list is endless, though by far the great bulk of his major work is historical. He was the first to demonstrate that the ancient Aquitanian language was an ancestral form of Basque. At the same time as Tovar, but working independently, he destroyed the proposed Basque–Iberian link, and he later did the same to the Basque–Caucasian proposals. His 1964a book is an annotated catalogue of virtually the entire corpus of Basque words and texts from the Aquitanian period to the beginning of publication in the sixteenth century. He produced a book-length study of Basque surnames, a history of Basque literature, a monograph on place names, a brief history of the language, an enormous number of etymological studies dealing with particular words, a study of the sources of Azkue's dictionary, innumerable studies of particular Basque authors, critical editions of previously unpublished manuscripts, hundreds of perceptive book reviews, dozens of pieces of literary criticism and several contributions to linguistic theory. And he was the single most influential figure in the construction of the new standard form of Basque in the 1960s.

But there is no dispute about his greatest single contribution. Encouraged by Martinet to make a study of the historical phonology of Basque, he devoted more than ten years to the project. Taking advantage of his unmatched knowledge of ancient and medieval documents and of modern dialect variants, he applied his sure command of phonological theory to produce, in 1961, his *magnum opus*: the anachronistically titled *Fonética histórica vasca* (*FHV*), cited here in the expanded edition of 1977. In this masterpiece of historical work, Michelena traces the history and prehistory of Basque phonology back some 2,000 years; he reconstructs the phonological system of the language at around the time of the Roman invasion of the Basque Country, even down to the word-accent; and he explicitly identifies the various phonological changes which have led to the modern language, including the major dialectal variants. Before Michelena, nothing of significance was known about Basque historical phonology; since Michelena, little remains beyond tidying up the details. *FHV* is the single most important publication in Basque linguistics, and it is a work that can be read with profit by anyone who wants to see how historical phonology is done. Michelena's work on historical phonology will make up the largest portion of my Chapter 3, but his influence will be everywhere visible in the remaining chapters of this book.

Quite apart from his rescue of Michelena's career, the Spanish linguist Antonio Tovar deserves attention for his own work on Basque. At the same time as Michelena, but independently of him, he too succeeded in demolishing Humboldt's proposal that Iberian had been an ancestral form of Basque. He published a number of papers on Basque, as well as three books: a general survey, a volume on the search for relatives, and a fascinating little treatise on the long history of mythographic writing on the language. He also argued in several papers for a prehistoric *Sprachbund* involving Basque and Indo-European, a proposal examined in Chapter 6.

The Basque historian and archivist Jon Bilbao (1914–) was born in Puerto Rico to parents from Getxo (Bizkaia). A specialist in the activities of the Basques in the New World, he deserves mention here as the editor of an eight-volume bibliography of books and other materials dealing with the Basques, the Basque Country and the Basque language (Bilbao 1970–).

The last figure whom I shall single out for individual attention is Alfonso Irigoyen, one of the rare Basque-speakers born in Bilbao. Irigoyen might prefer to be called a philologist, rather than a linguist, since his chosen specialty is the histories of particular words and names, in the pursuit of which he has made a number of striking discoveries and proposals, some of which will figure later in this book. Perhaps the most important of these is his proposed etymology of the name of the language, discussed in Chapter 5.

Since the 1960s the field of Basque linguistics has grown enormously. Where formerly the field was the preserve of a handful of specialists most of whom were personally acquainted with one another, today it is more than I can do even just to list the names of all those who are working on the language. Two more major specialist journals of Basque linguistics have appeared: *Anuario del Seminario de Filología Vasca 'Julio de Urquijo'* (*ASJU*; founded 1967) and *Fontes Linguae Vasconum* (*FLV*; founded 1969). The proceedings of the several conferences organized by Euskaltzaindia, and the two Festschrifts for Michelena (Melena 1985 and Lakarra 1991), contain contributions from well over 200 scholars, local and foreign. Still, it is worth citing the names of some of the more prominent figures, many of whom are actively investigating the history and prehistory of the language: Basque historical linguistics is currently undergoing a vigorous revival.

In the Basque Country, we have Joseba Abaitua (syntax and computational linguistics), Lino Akesolo (syntax and lexicography), Jabier Alberdi (historical linguistics), Patxi Altuna (critical editions), José Luis Alvarez Enparantza ('Txillardegi') (phonetics and grammar), Adolfo Arejita (syntax), Gotzon Aurrekoetxea (dialectology), Miren Azkarate (syntax), María José Azurmendi (sociolinguistics), Piarres Charritton (philology), Andolin Eguzkitza (syntax), María Teresa Echenique Elizondo (historical linguistics), Ana María Etxaide (sociolinguistics), Patxi Goenaga (syntax), Ricardo Gómez (historical linguistics), Joaquín Gorrochategui (historical linguistics), Jean Haritschelhar (poetics), Xabier Kintana (lexicography and historical linguistics), Endrike Knörr (philology), Itziar Laka (syntax), Joseba Lakarra (historical linguistics), Luis Mari Mujika (historical linguistics and morphology), Miren Lourdes Oñederra (phonology), Patxi Oroz Arizcuren (philology), Jean-Baptiste Orpustan (onomastics), Jon Ortiz de Urbina (syntax), Beñat Oyharçabal (syntax), Rosa Miren Pagola (dialectology), Txomin Peillen (morphology and philology), Karmele Rotaetxe (descriptive linguistics and sociolinguistics), Koldo Sainz (historical linguistics), Pello Salaburu (phonology and syntax), José María Sánchez Carrión (historical linguistics), Juan San Martín (onomastics), Ibon Sarasola (philology and lexicography), José María Satrústegui (philology), Patri Urkizo (philology), Charles Videgain (dialectology), Luis Villasante (descriptive linguistics), Pedro de Yrizar (morphology) and Koldo Zuazo (historical linguistics), among many others. Many of these, especially the historical linguists, are based at the University of the Basque Country in Vitoria-Gasteiz. A few Basque-born linguists work abroad, such as José Ignacio Hualde (phonology and historical linguistics) at the University of Illinois and Juan Uriagareka (syntax) at Amherst.

Among the foreign scholars working on Basque, I might cite Jacques

Allières (general linguistics and dialectology), Catherine Paris (typology) and Georges Rebuschi (syntax and historical linguistics) in France, Manuel Agud (etymology) and Javier de Hoz (ancient languages of Spain) in Spain, Rudolf P. G. de Rijk (grammar and historical linguistics) and Peter Bakker (Basque pidgins and Basque abroad) in the Netherlands, Gunter Brettschneider (general linguistics), Bernhard Hurch (historical linguistics), Jürgen Untermann (ancient languages of Spain) and Ulrich J. Lüders (morphology) in Germany, Nils Holmer (historical linguistics) in Sweden, Jan Braun (genetic affiliations) in Poland, Natela Sturua (syntax) in Georgia, Tadao Shimomiya (syntax) in Japan, Alan King (applied linguistics) in Britain, and William H. Jacobsen (syntax and historical linguistics), Terence H. Wilbur (general linguistics) and Roslyn Frank (sociolinguistics) in the United States, and the British-based American R. L. Trask (historical linguistics and grammar). And these lists are very far from exhaustive.

Major international congresses are held in the Basque Country at frequent intervals, attracting specialists in Basque from Spain, France, the Netherlands, Germany, Poland, Russia, Georgia, Japan, the United States and a dozen other countries; the proceedings of these are published by the Academy in the *IKER* series. Two festschrifts for Michelena, Melena (1985) and Lakarra (1991), provide a reasonable sample of recent specialist work, including a good deal of historical work, and Michelena's own historical writings, apart from his big book, have been collected as Michelena (1988a). Hualde *et al.* (1995) provides a splendid collection of recent work on the history and prehistory of Basque. The new University of the Basque Country has established a Faculty of Basque Philology, which has already trained dozens of young linguists to add to those Basque linguists who received their training at places ranging from Salamanca to Paris to Tübingen to Nevada to MIT. Four specialist journals are currently devoted to Basque linguistics: *Euskera* (Bilbao), *Fontes Linguae Vasconum* (Pamplona), the *Anuario del Seminario de Filología Vasca 'Julio de Urquijo'* (San Sebastián) and the *Journal of Basque Studies* (Iowa).

1.5 REFERENCE BOOKS

Good reference works on Basque are scarce, on the historical side as elsewhere. None the less, there are a few works which the reader should be aware of, or which (in one or two cases) he or she should be warned about.

1.5.1 Reference grammars

At present there is no really satisfactory reference grammar of Basque. That gap should, however, soon be filled, since the Dutch vasconist Rudolf P. G. de Rijk is currently writing just such a book; the volume is well advanced, and it may actually be in print by the time you are reading this. Given the quality of the author's other work on Basque, one may reasonably expect that the reference grammar will be of great value. A larger reference grammar is currently at the planning stage; this is to be written by a team of specialists under the general editorship of José Ignacio Hualde.

Already in print is Saltarelli (1988). This is one in a well-known series of descriptive grammars, and it shares the virtues and shortcomings of its companion volumes. On the plus side, it contains a great deal of valuable information, particularly on syntax, which is difficult to find elsewhere. On the other hand, it is organized in a rigid way which sometimes separates related topics; there is no index, so that it can be almost impossible to find the information you're looking for; and some topics seem to have slipped through the net of the questionnaire and vanished altogether. (For example, the syntactically central and exceedingly frequent relational suffix -ko, which does not fit anything in the questionnaire, receives no more than incidental mention.) Moreover, it describes only the speech of a single (Gipuzkoan) informant, with no mention of important phenomena found in other varieties of the language.

There is one other valuable reference grammar: Lafitte (1944). The author was a Basque priest, well trained in Latin grammar but with no knowledge of linguistics, and it consequently has the expected shortcomings: it says little that is useful about phonetics or phonology; it treats morphology in the Latinate word-based model, which is quite inappropriate to Basque, with consequent confusions and misanalyses; it sometimes confuses functionally distinct morphs which happen to have identical forms; and it lacks any conception of constituent structure. Moreover, it deals exclusively with conservative literary varieties of Lapurdian and Low Navarrese, with no mention of other varieties. In spite of its limitations, however, this book is a fine piece of work: the coverage is remarkably comprehensive, with an attention to detail which is quite outstanding; the organization is excellent; and there is a good index. This is still by far the best account we have of French Basque.

One other reference grammar exists. This is the series of volumes published at intervals by the Academy, Euskaltzaindia (1985 *et seq.*). These volumes are of minimal utility to the readers of the present book, however, since they are written in Basque and since their purpose is primarily to promulgate those forms which have been recognized by the Academy as part of the standard language. Regional variants are sometimes given, especially in syntax, where there has so far been little standardization, but usually with no indication of provenance.

I am aware of no other reference grammars. Innumerable textbooks exist, mostly in Spanish or French, a few of them organized roughly along the lines of a reference grammar, but none of them is really usable in that capacity. The best textbooks of Basque are King (1994) and King and Olaizola Elordi (1996).

1.5.2 Dictionaries

As was mentioned above, there were a number of dictionaries compiled by scholars between the sixteenth and nineteenth centuries, all of which except Larramendi's remained unpublished at the time, and some of which are still unpublished today. (One or two of them have, unfortunately, been lost.) The first substantial dictionary to be published was Azkue's great *Diccionario vasco–español–francés* of 1905, in which all definitions and comments are given in both Spanish and French. (There is a 1969 reprint containing a long addendum compiled by Lino de Aquesolo, and a 1984 reprint further containing Luis Michelena's 1970a monograph on Azkue's sources.) This is still the finest general-purpose dictionary the language has ever received: it covers all varieties of the language, including both the spoken language of Azkue's day and words which are confined to older literary texts or proverbs (though it is by no means comprehensive in this last respect, and Azkue ostentatiously refused to include any words at all from Larramendi's dictionary, even the genuine ones). Azkue is usually scrupulous about recording sources and provenances, though he never gives any information about dates beyond occasionally labelling an entry 'archaic'. Obviously distinct words which happen to have identical forms are treated in a single entry, while variant forms of a single word receive separate entries, usually without cross-references. Parts of speech are not labelled or distinguished. All of this is linguistically highly inconvenient, but fortunately not fatal. In spite of its idiosyncrasies, this is still the dictionary of choice for historical linguists.

Of course, the book has its flaws. Working alone, with no collaborator or editor, Azkue occasionally made mistakes or leapt to unwarranted conclusions, and hence the appearance of a word in the dictionary with no supporting quotation is not an ironclad guarantee of its existence. A vasconist using the dictionary would do well to consult Michelena's 1970a essay and several of the papers collected in Michelena (1988a), which identify a number of these errors, especially Michelena (1966). But the errors are few and mostly of no great consequence.

Like all of Azkue's works, this one is printed in a slightly modified version of Sabino Arana's eccentric orthography (see section 1.6), which takes a little getting used to. Like many Basque dictionaries, it treats *I* and *J* as variants of a single letter. And, like many others, it ignores the letter *H* altogether in determining alphabetical order, a policy which is in fact very useful for linguistic work. The reader will note that some headwords are printed in capital letters; these are the words which, in Azkue's view, are not derived from any other words by any type of compounding or derivation.

There is one other thing that a user of the dictionary should be aware of. Azkue, who was fond of proposing etymologies of varying degrees of plausibility, could not resist the temptation of including in his dictionary some of the hypothetical words which he had proposed for Pre-Basque, such as the alleged *iz 'water' and *gor 'flesh', which I shall consider in Chapter 5. These items are not marked with an asterisk, but are usually identifiable by some annotation along the lines of 'not used in isolation' or 'now reduced to a radical'. More than one European or American linguist has been misled into citing these things in print as though they were attested forms, rather than mere speculations. Aside from these odd speculations, however, Azkue makes no attempt in his dictionary to propose etymologies for his entries.

Next in importance to Azkue's dictionary is that of Pierre Lhande, whose 1926 *Dictionnaire basque–français*, while largely based upon Azkue's, provides much more extensive coverage of the French Basque dialects. This work (which is written in French) uses the traditional French Basque orthography, including *h*, *ph*, *th* and *kh*, except that it curiously uses *ŕ* in place of *rr*; moreover, the editor claims a distinction between *r* and *ŕ* even in positions in which they are neutralized, with *r* preceding alphabetically. Hence, for example, the entries *par*, *paŕ* and *phara* are all widely separated in the dictionary, and a user looking for a particular word may have to check as many as four different places. The editor provides sources and provenances for most of his entries, and he also gives synonyms and often variant forms. Compounds and derivatives are treated in an exceptionally thorough and well-organized manner, but there are no part-of-speech labels. Words which the editor considers (rightly or wrongly) to be obvious loans from Latin or Romance are marked with an asterisk. A particularly useful characteristic of the dictionary is its illustrations of household objects and agricultural implements. Unlike Azkue, Lhande attempts etymologies for many of his entries, but the great majority of these are too fanciful to be taken seriously.

Another important dictionary is that compiled by Ibon Sarasola, which has been appearing as a series of fascicles since 1984 and is not yet complete. This dictionary contains all the words found in more than a hundred written works selected by the author from all periods, including all the major literary works in Basque, all the significant earlier dictionaries, and the medieval fragments collected in Michelena's (1964a) book *Textos arcaicos vascos*. The editor is fastidious about part-of-speech labels, a glaring weakness of most other dictionaries of Basque, and this dictionary has the great virtue of recording the date of the first attestation of each word found by the editor, and (in most cases) the work in which that attestation is found. Identifications of provenance are otherwise vague or non-existent, however, being confined to occasional labels such as 'northern'. All words are spelled in the modern standard orthography, regardless of their spellings in the texts; this includes the introduction of *h*. Variant forms are sometimes noted under the corresponding main entries, but receive no entries of their own. The dictionary is written in Basque, but it needs only a very minimal grasp of Basque to read everything apart from the definitions themselves.

At the present time the Basque Language Academy is editing and publishing a huge multi-volume dictionary of the language which is intended to include every word attested in writing from the earliest days up to several decades ago, with supporting quotations. Several volumes have so far appeared at lengthy intervals, but it will clearly be a long time before the dictionary is completed. Editing of the dictionary was begun by Luis Michelena and the work is therefore commonly cited as Michelena (1987–); since Michelena's death, Ibon Sarasola has been overseeing the editing.

Apart from the earlier published and unpublished dictionaries recorded in section 1.4 above, these are the only dictionaries of Basque which are useful for scholarly historical work on the language. There are, of course, many other more recent general-purpose dictionaries of varying sizes, but these are of little or no linguistic value: they are compiled by enthusiastic amateurs, rather than by scholars or by professional lexicographers; they are practical works aimed at language learners; they mostly lack even such basic apparatus as part-of-speech labels, and they routinely incorporate neologisms which are not identified as such. The only Basque–English dictionary is Aulestia (1989).

1.5.3 Etymological dictionaries

In 1968 the German linguist Martin Löpelmann published a thick volume entitled *Etymologisches Wörterbuch der Baskischen Sprache*. Dealing exclusively with words found in the French Basque dialects, this work is unreliable and downright fanciful. On the one hand, its author shows a peculiar inclination to derive Basque words from Portuguese; on the other, he frequently suggests absurd connections with Sumerian and other improbably remote languages. His fantasies are punctuated by the odd plausible etymology, but the author provides no sources for any of his etymologies, rendering the work almost useless even when it is sober. In short, this volume, in spite of its reassuring title, cannot be trusted and should not be taken seriously.

Naturally, the most important work in Basque etymology was carried out by Luis Michelena. Michelena's etymological observations are scattered across the whole body of his published work. Fortunately, however, Juan José Arbelaiz undertook some years ago to read through all of Michelena's publications and to extract every single remark on etymology to be found there. The result was published as Arbelaiz (1978), which is an indispensable guide to Michelena's work.

Towards the end of his life, Antonio Tovar began compiling a comprehensive etymological dictionary of Basque; regrettably, he died before completing it, but the work has finally been completed by Manuel Agud. The result is an annotated dictionary including all the serious and fanciful etymological proposals which have ever appeared; this book has been published in fascicles in the journal *ASJU* since volume 22, number 1, in 1988, and also in separate fascicles by the same journal. At the time of writing, publication is still not complete, but this is already the most valuable work we have on Basque etymology.

1.5.4 Other works

Azkue's other major work was his *Morfología vasca*, a long book originally published in 1923–1925 as the entire content of consecutive issues of *Euskera*, the journal recently set up by the Academy, and finally published in book format only in 1969 (the 1969 edition includes a long commentary on the work published in 1934 by Severo Altube). This is a wide-ranging, if rather quaintly organized, survey of virtually all aspects of the morphology of Basque, of which the most valuable part is a catalogue of almost the entire set of bound morphemes in the language. The book requires a certain amount of care to use: Azkue does not distinguish between inflectional and derivational affixes, but groups affixes largely on semantic grounds; though he includes a section dealing with phonological rules, he none the less often lists the two or three variant forms of an affix in different places. But the index is good, and the author's tireless collection of archaic and dialectal forms, most of them with provenances supplied, makes this a fascinating and exceptionally valuable secondary source for the student of historical morphology.

The single most important work in Basque historical linguistics is, of course, Luis Michelena's magisterial reconstruction of Pre-Basque phonology, *Fonética histórica vasca*, published in 1961, with an expanded edition in 1977 and further reprints in 1985 and 1990. This 600-page tome incorporates a simply colossal amount of information on the history and prehistory of the language, and it is essential reading for anyone interested in the history of the language. Most of the remainder of Michelena's voluminous historical writings are assembled in three collections, Michelena (1985, 1987, 1988a); his Basque-language writings are collected in Michelena (1988b).

The most detailed treatment of Basque phonology available is Hualde (1991). A number of other descriptions of Basque phonology, syntax and especially morphology exist, but these are written in Basque.

There are two general introductions to Basque language and linguistics, both of them somewhat miscellaneous in their coverage: the brief Lafon (1968b) and the much longer Allières (1979).

1.6 BASQUE ORTHOGRAPHY

The modern standard Basque orthography was promulgated by Euskaltzaindia, the Royal Basque Language Academy, in 1964; the linguist Luis Michelena was the most influential figure in designing it. The new orthography was in no way a radical departure from what had gone before; every single one of its features had earlier been widely used, and the standard orthography represents merely a definitive choice from among competing forms. None the less, the new orthography at first met considerable hostility, particularly among elderly and conservative individuals who objected strongly to making any changes in the particular orthographic conventions with which they were most familiar. The most vigorous objections were raised by conservative Spanish Basques against the decision to incorporate the letter *h* into the new standard, since this letter had never been used by Spanish Basques, the aspiration [h] being entirely absent from all Spanish varieties of Basque since our earliest published texts. In spite of the opposition, the new standard gradually won acceptance, and today it is almost universally used for writing the language; only a handful of elderly diehards continue to use other orthographic conventions.

The Basque alphabet consists of the following twenty-two letters: *a b d e f g h i j k l m n ñ o p r s t u x z*. The letters *c q v w y* are not considered part of the alphabet, but are, of course, sometimes used in writing foreign names and words; when necessary, these letters are inserted into the alphabetical order in their familiar positions. The digraphs *dd ll rr ts tt tx tz* all represent single segments, but they are considered to be sequences of letters rather than single letters. This decision was not made clear in 1964, and hence some dictionaries and other works exist in which all of these digraphs (usually excepting *rr*) are treated as single letters with their own places in the alphabet, following *d, l* or *t*. The phonological values of the letters are for the most part about what one would expect, except for *h j s x z* and the digraphs, which are less obvious. A full account is provided in Chapter 2. Here I note merely that *z s x* represent three contrasting voiceless fricatives and *tz ts tx* the corresponding affricates, while *tt* and *dd* represent palatal plosives and *r* and *rr* contrasting rhotics; *h* and *j* have values which vary according to region.

When Basque first began to be written, it was usually written with Spanish or French spelling conventions as far as possible, with various additional devices introduced to handle sounds not found in the Romance languages. Hence in very many older texts, the syllables now spelled *ke, ki, ge* and *gi* are spelled, Romance-fashion, as *que, qui, gue* and *gui*, respectively. Otherwise, the letter *c* is often found in place of the modern *k*. Likewise, the syllables now spelled *za ze zi zo zu* were formerly often spelled *ça ce ci ço çu*, and *ç* was often used instead of *z* in non-prevocalic positions. Table 1.3 shows some examples.

Especially on the French side, older texts often show *s* for the modern *z* and *ss* for the modern *s*, the latter usually only in intervocalic position, and we occasionally also find *ss* for *z*, as in the surname *Elissalt* (= *Elizalde*). The modern fricative *x* is commonly represented as *ch* on the French side. The affricate *tz* is often written *tç*, or sometimes just *ç*, while *tx* is very commonly represented as *ch* on the Spanish side and as *tch* on the French side; on the

Table 1.3 Examples of the older orthography

Older spelling	Modern spelling	Gloss
deçaquet	dezaket	Auxiliary verb-form
eguin	egin	'make, do'
guiçonac	gizonak	'men'
cer	zer	'what?'

Table 1.4 Further examples of the older orthography

Older French	Older Spanish	Modern	Gloss
etche	eche	etxe	'house'
ikussi	ikusi	ikusi	'see'
ichuri	ixuri	ixuri	'pour'
atço	atço	atzo	'yesterday'
oxo	otso	otso	'wolf'

French side, *ts* is often rather bewilderingly written *x*. Table 1.4 provides some examples.

On the whole, the representation of the six Basque sibilants, for which Romance orthographic conventions are quite inadequate, presented the greatest difficulties, and older texts are sometimes characterized by vacillation, confusion and ambiguity. The problem was made more acute by the fact that, in the seventeenth century, the sibilants represented as *z* and *s* fell together in pronunciation in the west, as did *tz* and *ts*; the resulting orthographic confusion produced a number of unetymological spellings, and these 'ghost forms' have occasionally misled lexicographers ever since.

In regions in which modern *j* represents [j] or something similar, older texts sometimes show *y* or *i* in place of *j*, and hence one may find such spellings as *yan* or *ian* for modern *jan* 'eat'. But perhaps the most visually striking characteristic of earlier texts is the distribution of the letter *h*. The French Basques have traditionally represented their aspirated plosives as *ph th kh*, and they have traditionally written *h* in all positions in which the aspiration [h] is present. The Spanish Basques, lacking aspiration altogether, have traditionally never used the letter *h* at all, except sometimes in the digraph *ch* (= modern *tx*). The Academy's delicate compromise, the one which upset so many conservatives, was to write *h* wherever the French Basques have the aspiration [h] word-initially or intervocalically, but not to write *h* elsewhere. Table 1.5 provides some examples.

In a number of cases, phonological developments occurring after the loss of the aspiration on the Spanish side resulted in much larger differences in the traditional spellings; Table 1.6 shows a few examples.

Naturally, older texts often use a more phonetic style of spelling than

Table 1.5 Aspiration and the orthography

Older French	Older Spanish	Modern	Gloss
iphar	ipar	ipar	'north'
ethorri	etorri	etorri	'come'
khe	ke	ke	'smoke'
alhaba	alaba	alaba	'daughter'
senhar	senar	senar	'husband'
erhi	eri	eri	'finger'
urhe	urre	urre	'gold'
hau	au	hau	'this'
nahi	nai	nahi	'desire'
aho	ao	aho	'mouth'

Table 1.6 Some further traditional spellings

Older French	Older Spanish	Modern	Gloss
zahar	zar	zahar	'old'
uhalde	ugalde	uhalde	'flood'
eihar	igar	both used	'dry'

does the modern standard. For example, modern *denbora* 'time' and *kanpo* 'outside' are sometimes spelled *dembora* and *kampo*. The automatic palatalization of coronals after *i* which is found in many dialects is often represented explicitly: hence, for modern *oina* 'the foot', *hila* 'dead' and *ditu* (an auxiliary verb-form), older texts often have *oiña* (or *oña*), *illa* and *dittu*. But the biggest differences from the standard spelling arise in the representation of vowel sequences, which are subject to a variety of processes in various parts of the country. Standard *astoa* 'the donkey' and *lorea* 'the flower' are often written as *astua* and *loria* in areas in which such spellings represent the local pronunciations; *gaua* 'the night' and *ahoa* 'the mouth' may appear as *gaba* and *aba*; and *zaldia* 'the horse' may be written as *zaldiya* or *zaldiye*.

The front rounded vowel of the Zuberoan dialect is usually written *ü*, but in older works one often finds *u* and *ou* used, French-fashion, for *u* and *u*.

Finally, I must comment on the bizarre orthography devised by Sabino Arana in the late nineteenth century. This daft system puts a tilde over each of the letters *t d s n l* to represent the palatal counterparts now written as *tt dd x ñ ll*, and it uses *ŕ* in place of *rr*. Impossibly cumbersome for printing and typing, this orthography was used by Azkue in all of his publications (except that Azkue used *rr* in place of *ŕ*), and it was very widely employed before the Spanish Civil War. Thankfully, it is now extinct, but scholars consulting Azkue's writings and other materials of the period must still get used to it.

Note that a number of Basque dictionaries treat *i* and *j* (and sometimes also *y*, when this is used) as variant forms of a single letter for purposes of alphabetical order, and that many dictionaries of a scholarly nature ignore the letter *h* altogether in assigning alphabetical order; this second policy is highly convenient for linguistic purposes.

1.7 THE STANDARD LANGUAGE

As soon as the Basques were reasonably free to consider the issue, after the years of Francoist repression, they returned to the question of devising a standard form of the language. Inevitably, opinion was divided. The polemicist Federico Krutwig argued for the classical Lapurdian literature of the seventeenth century as the basis of the new standard, and he found support: for example, Gabriel Aresti (1933–1975), undoubtedly the finest poet the Basques have ever produced, in spite of being *euskaldun berri*, exhibited considerable classical influence in his poems. In the end, however, the Basque Language Academy took upon itself the onus of making the hard decisions, and, under the considerable influence of Luis Michelena, it opted for a standard as close as reasonably possible to contemporary speech.

After the promulgation of its orthography in 1964, the Academy turned its attention to morphology, and by the early 1970s it had completed a standard set of nominal and verbal inflected forms. These forms were chiefly based upon the central dialects, especially Gipuzkoan. The most obvious characteristic of the standard nominal forms is that they are morphemic in nature. That is, the combination of *zaldi* 'horse' and article *-a* is written *zaldia*, even though many Basques actually pronounce [saldije], [saldiʒe] or [saldiʃa]; likewise, the definite form of *buru* 'head' is *burua*, though phoneti- cally this form is variously [buruwa], [buruβa], [buruja] or something else. Otherwise, the guiding principles seem to have been to make the nominal paradigms as regular as possible and to distinguish in form those inflections which are functionally different wherever possible. So, for example, since the ablative ending is normally *-tik*, the southern ablative plural form *-etatik* was preferred to the northern *-etarik*; since the diphthong *au* is normally fol- lowed by *e* when a consonant-initial suffix follows, the absolutive plural of *hau* 'this' is western *hauek* instead of eastern *hauk*. But the absolutive and ergative plural suffixes chosen were eastern *-ak* and *-ek*, respectively; western dialects have *-ak* in both instances.

The Academy then turned its attention to place names, and produced a definitive list of the official Basque forms of the names of all the cities, towns and villages in the country. The choices were based upon a combina- tion of early documentary evidence and modern popular usage. Not all the choices were uniformly popular: for example, some of the inhabitants of the town of Rentería in Gipuzkoa campaigned for years to have the official choice of popular *Errenteria* deposed in favour of *Orereta*, an old name for the town attested in a single medieval document.

Standardization of word forms has not proceeded at all systematically. The Academy did publish a few small dictionaries: one for use in schools, another containing business terms, and so on. But the Academy's stately progress in these manoeuvres was rapidly overtaken by more impatient language planners. Both Xabier Kintana and Luix Mari Muxika published substantial dictionaries of the new standard language in the 1970s; both of them stuffed their volumes with thousands of neologisms which they themselves had coined. These early dictionaries ran into the problem of alphabetical order mentioned above, with the digraphs being listed as distinct letters. They also exposed a few other gaps in the earlier decisions. One of these concerns words of Greek origin: should the Basques write *thermometro* and *psykhologia*, more or less in the French fashion, or should they write *termometro* and *sikologia*, in the Spanish fashion? The Academy eventually went for the second option, though not before some dictionaries had been published using the first. Similarly, it was eventually decided that the word for 'sex' should be written *seksu*, rather than *sexu*, which suggests the wrong pronunciation altogether, or *setsu* or *sesu*, which accurately represent popular pronunciations conforming better to Basque phonotactics.

On the other hand, spellings like *geologia* have now become standard, even though most Basques use various pronunciations which would be more accurately represented by the rejected spelling *jeolojia* (Spanish Basques have [χ], French Basques [ʝ]). Very early on, though, the Academy had determined to use the international spellings in words like *sozialista*; the French Basque practice of writing *zozializta*, reflecting their (French-derived) pronunciation, was rejected.

Before long, almost every writer was setting up shop as a language planner, and neologisms of varying quality were (and are) being produced in vast numbers. Most prominent here was UZEI, a private organization devoted to compiling technical dictionaries; before eventually running out of funding, UZEI produced more than a dozen large dictionaries in fields as diverse as linguistics, politics, printing and physics. The resulting confusion has still not settled down, but there now appears to be at least one coinage to match every existing Spanish or French word, and doubtless we can now expect a period of consolidation and selection.

Syntax is an area in which there has been almost no standardization. Most Basques still speak and write with the syntax of their local variety, with perhaps a few minor adjustments away from local forms which are not used in most of the country. In its recent grammar of the standard language (Euskaltzaindia 1985 *et seq.*), the Academy simply recognizes all those syntactic forms which are recorded as in use in some part of the country, with little or no attempt at prescriptivism, apart from a refusal to recognize certain patterns which blatantly result from the imposition of alien Romance norms upon Basque sentence structure, such as the practice of putting a focused item at the end of a sentence, instead of immediately before the verb.

Pronunciation has likewise received no standardization, and almost all speakers cling to their native pronunciation with at most a few adjustments in the direction of the standard orthography, such as pronouncing *zaldia* as [saldia] instead of using a local form like [saldije]. It is noteworthy, though, that a few speakers for whom the diaphone |j| is natively [χ] have self-consciously rejected this pronunciation as a castilianism, and tried to replace it with one of the voiced palatal pronunciations (on this, see Chapter 3).

Chapter 2

A thumbnail sketch of the language

2.1 PRELIMINARIES

This book does not attempt to be a reference grammar of Basque. However, I am aware that a reader who knows nothing about the structure of the language may at times find it difficult to follow the discussion in the later parts of the book, especially in Chapter 4, which deals with historical grammar. This chapter will therefore present a very brief summary of the major structural features of Basque in sufficient detail to allow a reader to follow the remaining chapters comfortably. A reader who already has this background may choose to skip this chapter.

Naturally, I have had to be very selective in deciding what information to include here, and a reader cannot be sure of finding detailed information about any particular topic. One thing I have tried very explicitly to do, however, is to clear up some serious misunderstandings about the phonology and grammar of Basque which have propagated themselves through the literature. For example, it has been very commonly asserted that Basque *b d g* represent 'voiced fricatives', that Basque has 'retroflex' consonants, that Basque nouns can be inflected according to three different patterns, that the suffix *-ko* is a 'locative genitive' case-marker, that Basque permits 'superdeclension' – the stringing together of sequences of case-endings – and that Basque has a passive-with-agent construction. All of these statements are quite false, and I will be at some pains to explain the truth.

Other books exist for the reader who wants to learn more about the structure of Basque. There are dozens of traditional grammars of varying quality, all of them written by people with absolutely no knowledge of linguistics; from these books it is typically very difficult to extract even the most elementary information. By far the best of them is Lafitte (1944), which is remarkably comprehensive, detailed, orderly and well indexed; a reader of this book should be aware, however, that it confines its attention to conservative literary varieties of the Lapurdian and Low Navarrese dialects, ignoring otherwise widespread phenomena not present in these varieties, that it is linguistically unsophisticated, and that it consequently contains some serious errors of analysis. Vastly more sophisticated is Saltarelli (1988), a questionnaire-based description of a variety of the Gipuzkoan dialect; this volume contains a wealth of valuable information, but it has no index, and looking up any particular topic can be next to impossible. The best textbook of Basque in English is King (1994), which treats the Gipuzkoan variety of Donostia/San Sebastián.

A few general remarks may be in order here. Basque has a remarkably simple phonology for a European language, and there is little motivation for positing underlying forms which are significantly different from surface forms. The morphology is strongly agglutinating, and the individual morphemes are generally easy to segment; the few exceptions to this statement are mostly confined to the morphology of finite verbs and auxiliaries. Both case-marking and verbal agreement (which is unusually extensive) are overwhelmingly ergative, with accusative morphology confined to agreement in certain past-tense verb-forms, though a semantically arbitrary subset of intransitive verbs requires transitive morphology. At the same time, the syntax of the language is exclusively accusative, with no trace of ergativity; on this point, see Heath (1974), Anderson (1976), Rotaetxe (1978), Ortiz de Urbina (1989: Ch. 1) and especially Trask (1989).

2.2 PHONOLOGY

There is no standard pronunciation of Basque, and the phonological differences among dialects are far from insignificant. I shall attempt to describe the principal characteristics of all the major varieties of the language; naturally, my remarks about the particular regions in which individual features are found will necessarily be somewhat broad and rough. I lack the space to provide detailed information about isogloss boundaries, and such information is rarely available anyway.

2.2.1 Phoneme inventory

So far as possible, I represent segmental phonemes by the symbols of the standard orthography, resorting to the IPA only when necessary.

Plosives. All varieties have unaspirated voiceless plosives *p*, *t* (dental) and *k*. Many eastern varieties add a voiceless palatal plosive, notated *tt*; in some western varieties, the same sound occurs only as an allophone of *t* (after *i*). Almost all northern varieties also have a set of aspirated voiceless plosives, traditionally notated *ph*, *th* and *kh* (the modern standard orthography does not distinguish these from *p t k*). In the northern varieties L and LN, the phonological status of the aspirated plosives is anomalous: aspiration appears to be neither predictable nor contrastive. Thus, a northerner says *ethorri* 'come', but unaspirated *etorri* is regarded merely as an unusual or faulty pronunciation, and minimal pairs are generally unknown and perhaps impossible. In Z, however, the aspirated plosives are clearly contrastive, and a few minimal pairs can be found, such as *ókher* 'twisted' vs. *óker* 'belch'. None the less, the functional load of the aspiration contrast in Z is close to nil. All varieties have voiced plosives *b d* (dental) *g*. These are in fact realized phonetically as plosives only after a pause, after a nasal or (*d* only) after *l*; elsewhere they are realized as voiced continuants (approximants with no audible friction). (They are frequently described in the literature as 'voiced fricatives', but this is inaccurate.) Phonologically, however, they behave like plosives. Some varieties add a (very rare) voiced palatal plosive, notated *dd* and sometimes realized as an affricate [dʒ]; see also under the diaphone |j| below.

Fricatives. Most varieties have three voiceless sibilants: lamino-alveolar *z*, apico-alveolar *s* (apico-post-alveolar for most French Basques), and palato-alveolar *x*. The first of these resembles English /s/, while the second resembles Castilian Spanish /s/ and is not well described as 'retroflex', a label often encountered in the literature. In many western varieties the *z/s* contrast has been lost fairly recently in favour of an apical sibilant, but the distinction continues to be made in writing. Almost all varieties have labio-dental *f*, though some varieties of G lack this, generally having *p* instead. Some varieties have a voiceless velar or uvular fricative [x] or [χ]; see below under the diaphone |j|. Almost all northern varieties have an aspiration *h*, which is clearly a phoneme initially (*hura* 'that one' vs. *ura* 'the water') and between vowels which could form a recognized diphthong (*sehi* 'boy, servant' vs. *sei* 'six'); elsewhere the presence of the aspiration is generally predictable: it occurs at the onset of the second syllable, between vowels which do not form a recognized diphthong, as in *liho* 'flax', *behar* 'need', *aho* 'mouth', *zahar* 'old'. All southern varieties lack the aspiration, though *h* is written in certain positions in the standard orthography. Z alone has contrastive voiced fricatives, represented in linguistic work by *z s ž*. The functional load of the voicing contrast in Z is exceedingly small. For *ž*, see below under the diaphone |j|.

Affricates. Most varieties have three voiceless affricates *tz*, *ts* and *tx*, corresponding exactly to the three sibilants. In many western dialects the *tz/ts* contrast has been lost fairly recently in favour of a laminal affricate, but the distinction continues to be made in writing. A few western varieties have a voiced lamino-alveolar affricate *dz*; this is entirely confined to onomatopoeic items like *dzast!* 'bang!', and is not found in lexical items. See also under the diaphone |j| below.

Nasals. All varieties have three nasals: bilabial *m*, alveolar *n* and palatal *ñ*, contrasting only before a vowel. Exception: Z contrasts *n* and *ñ* word-finally.

Laterals. All varieties have two laterals: alveolar *l* and palatal *ll*, contrasting only before a vowel.

Rhotics. All southern varieties have two rhotics: an alveolar tap *r* and an alveolar trill *rr*. These contrast only intervocalically, as in *ere* 'also' and *erre* 'burn'; elswhere the contrast is neutralized, usually in favour of the trill, and the orthography writes only a single ⟨r⟩. In Z, r has been almost entirely lost in ordinary speech, and only the trill rr exists. In L and LN, rr is invariably realized as a voiced uvular with noticeable friction noise. The same pronunciation is increasingly, but not invariably, heard for r, and the contrast is therefore variable.

The diaphone [j]. Basque exhibits an extraordinary case of a diaphone. The segment in question is almost always notated j, but its phonetic realization varies regionally in a dramatic fashion. Six different pronunciations can be distinguished:

1 voiced palatal glide [j];
2 voiced palatal plosive [ɟ] (thus merging with the existing but very rare dd);
3 voiced palato-alveolar affricate [dʒ];
4 voiced palato-alveolar fricative [ʒ] (perhaps better 'alveolo-palatal': the sound is more strongly palatalized than the similar English and French consonants);
5 voiceless palato-alveolar fricative [ʃ] (thus merging with the existing x);
6 voiceless velar or uvular fricative [x] or [χ].

Figure 2.1 shows the approximate distribution of these in about 1960. Since then, the velar/uvular fricative has been moving westward: Durango, for example, is shown as having [dʒ], and older speakers do indeed have this realization, but younger speakers have [χ] or [x].

Approximants. While phonetic glides are common enough in resolving certain cases of hiatus, phonemic glides are absent except in those varieties in which the diaphone [j] is a palatal glide. There are no other approximants.

Vowels. All varieties have the five vowels a e i o u, and most varieties have only those. Z has additionally a front rounded vowel, notated ü, which is phonetically [y], as in German fünf. Both R and Z additionally have a complete set of corresponding (and contrastive) nasal vowels, except that some varieties of Z have no nasal counterpart to o.

Diphthongs. Most varieties have the six diphthongs ai ei oi ui au eu; all are diminuendo diphthongs except for ui, which is a crescendo diphthong. A few varieties lack ui or eu or both. B has an additional diphthong ao, which phonologically behaves differently from au. These diphthongs are never distinct from the corresponding sequences of simple vowels; they are singled out merely because they behave as single syllables phonologically and because they are always pronounced as single syllables, even in careful speech; other vowel sequences constitute separate syllables in careful speech, though they may be realized as diphthongs in rapid speech, and they always count as two syllables for phonological purposes.

See Moutard (1975a, 1975b, 1976) for presentations of the phoneme systems in all the major varieties of Basque.

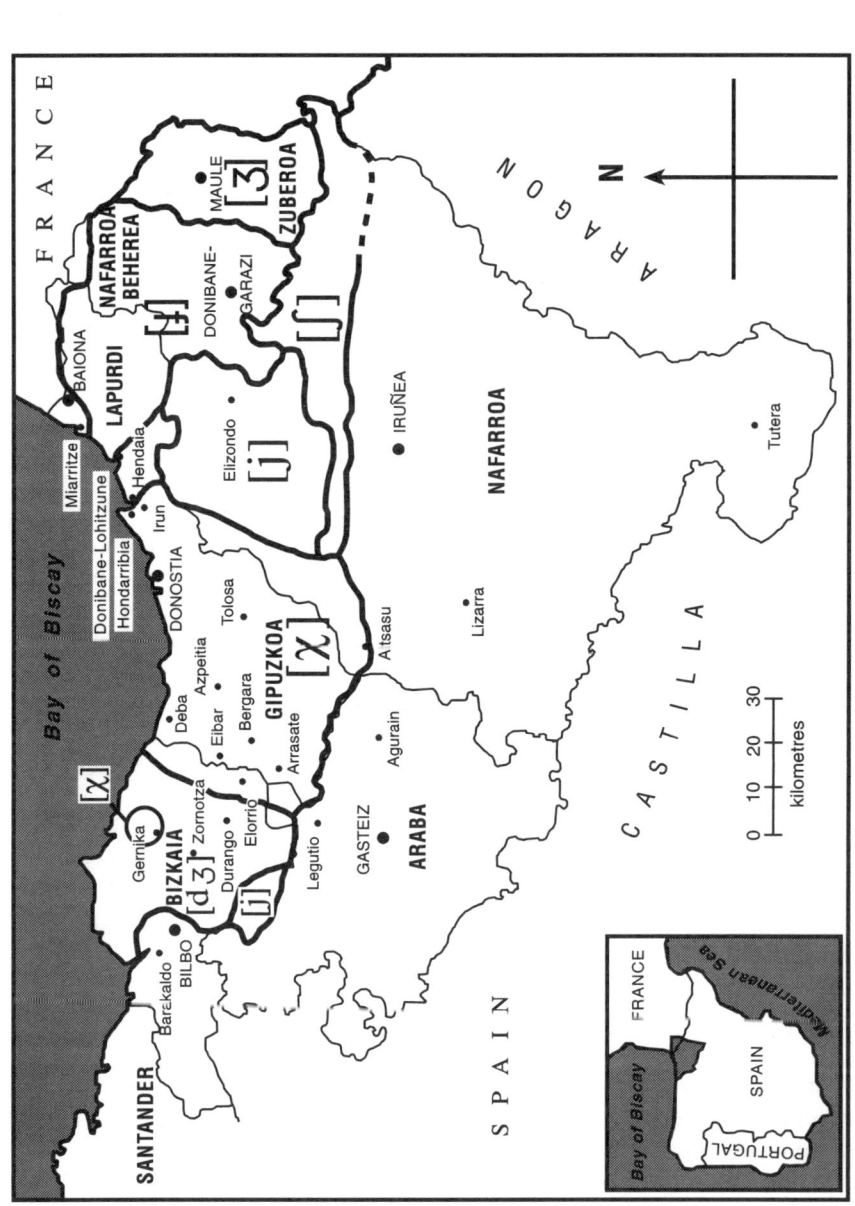

Figure 2.1 The diaphone |j|

2.2.2 Word-accent

Most varieties of Basque possess a prominent word-accent, but both the nature and the position of that accent vary considerably across the country. The word-accent has not been well studied; the principal summaries are Michelena (1957–1958, 1972a), from which the following summary is chiefly drawn.

Type I: pitch-accent.   Nouns fall into two classes: unmarked (characterized by a sustained pitch) and marked (characterized by a pitch fall at some point). The marked class includes all plurals and a scattered collection of non-plurals. This type is found in most varieties of B and G, and in western varieties of HN.

Type II: stress-accent.   This falls on the historical penult. In cases in which the last two syllables have merged into one for any reason, stress is final. This system is well preserved in Z, while R has innovated by moving the stress to the first syllable in most singular forms.

Type III: stress-accent.   Stress most often falls upon the modern penult, but there are numerous exceptions. This is found in southern varieties of HN.

Type IV: stress-accent.   Stress falls on a monosyllabic stem but on the second syllable of most other stems. Stressed syllables are loud and have lengthened vowels; post-tonic syllables are often lost. This type is found on the southern bank of the Bidasoa, in northern varieties of HN.

Type V: extinct and recorded only in writing; probably a stress accent. Position as in Type IV, except that the accent cannot occur earlier than the antepenult. This type was formerly found in western L and perhaps near the mouth of the Bidasoa generally.

Type VI: no word-accent.   All syllables have equal prominence. This type is typical of modern L and LN.

In a more recent survey, Hualde (1995) reports that some southern varieties of the area classified as Type I now have a Type IV accent, and I can confirm this from my own observations; the Type IV accent appears to be a recent innovation here.

2.2.3 Phonotactics

There are virtually no significant differences in phonotactics among the dialects. Basque phonotactics is characterized by extensive neutralization.

Word-initially, all consonants, vowels and diphthongs are permitted, except for the following: (1) the two rhotics, neither of which can ever begin a Basque word, excepting only very recent loans like *radar*, and then only in the speech of those younger speakers who have spoken Spanish or French since early childhood; exceptional are some of the Pyrenean dialects, in which there exist Romance loans in *r-*; (2) the affricates, which do not occur initially as a rule, though most western and some eastern varieties regularly have initial *tx-* where other varieties have *x-*, and some eastern varieties have the unique word *tzar* 'bad', plus a handful of 'expressive' formations with initial affricates. The only consonant clusters which can begin words are those shown in Table 2.1; these clusters occur only in recent loan words.

Table 2.1 Initial clusters in modern Basque

pl-	pr-	tr-	kl-	kr-
bl-	br-	dr-	gl-	gr-
fl-	fr-			

Intervocalically, all consonants can appear except *j*, which is strictly word-initial except in a few loan words and compounds.

Word-finally, all vowels and diphthongs are permitted, but only the following consonants can appear: *t k* (both largely confined to inflected word-forms, and rare in lexical items), the affricates (very frequent), the three sibilants (rare and largely confined to inflections, loan words and verb-stems used as free forms), the nasal *n* (representing the neutralization of all three nasals; very frequent), a single neutralized rhotic (notated *r*, but usually pronounced as a trill; fairly frequent), and a single neutralized lateral *l* (less frequent than the others). The only common final cluster is *-rtz*; *-ltz* and *-ntz* are less common, and a handful of others occur very occasionally: *-st*, *-rt* and one or two others.

The possible medial clusters are shown in Table 2.2; some are much more frequent than others.

Table 2.2 Medial clusters in modern Basque

-np-	-nt-	-nk-	-lp-	-lt-	-lk-	-rp-	-rt-	-rk-
-nb-	-nd-	-ng-	-lb-	-ld-	-lg-	-rb-	-rd-	-rg-
-ntz-	-nts-	-ntx-	-ltz-	-lts-	-ltx-	-rtz-	-rts-	-rtx-
-zp-	-zt-	-zk-	-sp-	-st-	-sk-	-xp-	-xt-	-xk-

Note that only affricates can normally appear after *n*, *l* or *r*. Some eastern varieties, however, also permit sibilant fricatives in this position. A handful of other miscellaneous clusters occur in one or two words: *-rl-*, *-rn-*, *-rm-*, *-lf-*, *-sn-*, *-sm-* and *-xm-*. In loan words, most of the clusters listed above as occurring initially can also occur medially. Finally, there are a few three-consonant clusters in medial position: *-ndr-*, *-rst-* and a few others.

Basque has sibilant harmony: a lexical item may contain only the laminal sibilants *z* and *tz*, or only the apical sibilants *s* and *ts*: *zezen* 'bull', *izotz* 'ice', *sasi* 'bramble', *itsusi* 'ugly' and so on. Compounds and loan words tend to undergo harmonization, usually in favour of the apical: *zin* 'truth' + *-etsi* 'consider' yields archaic *zinetsi*, modern *sinetsi* 'believe'. Spanish *francés* 'French', originally borrowed as *frantzes*, is now usually *frantses*.

2.3 NOUN PHRASES, THE CASE SYSTEM AND POSTPOSITIONS

2.3.1 The structure of noun phrases

Almost without exception, the existing grammars of Basque present a hopelessly confused picture of noun phrases, the existence of which they most often do not even recognize. Their central failing is a dependence upon the traditional latinate model in which the basis of description is the single phonological (or orthographic) word, with no recognition of constituent structure; as a result, they present a bewildering mishmash of confused and erroneous claims, typically involving such notions as 'three classes of inflection for nouns' and 'the inflection of adjectives'. In fact, neither nouns nor adjectives are inflected at all in Basque: *it is noun phrases, and only noun phrases, which are inflected in Basque*. Recognition of this vital fact permits a simple and insightful account.

The canonical structure of the noun phrase is as follows:

complex modifier – Det1 – noun – adjective – Det2 – number – case

The only obligatory item is a determiner; I use 'determiner' in the broadest possible sense, to include articles, demonstratives, a variety of indefinite determiners, quantifiers and numerals. With certain minor exceptions, an NP always contains a determiner; with just one major exception, an NP contains only one determiner. There are two possible positions for a determiner, Det1 and Det2; some determiners occupy the first, others the second, as follows:

Det1
all numerals except *bat* 'one' (and, in B alone, *bi* 'two');
some quantifiers (e.g., (*h*)*anitz* 'many, much', *zenbat* 'how many?', 'how much?');
some indefinite determiners (e.g., *zenbait* 'some, several', *zein* 'which?').

Det2
definite and indefinite articles;
demonstratives;
the numeral *bat* 'one' (and, in B alone, *bi* 'two');
some quantifiers (e.g., *asko* 'many, much');
some indefinite determiners (e.g., *batzu*(*k*) 'some, several');
the partitive.

Determiners may be conveniently divided into 'definite' and 'indefinite' determiners. There are only four definite determiners: the so-called 'definite article' -*a* (whose use is much broader than the label would suggest) and the three demonstratives. *Only the definite determiners distinguish number* (singular and plural), and hence only a noun phrase bearing a definite determiner can be marked for number (e.g., *gizona* 'the man' vs. *gizonak* 'the men'; *gizon hau* 'this man' vs. *gizon hauek* 'these men'). NPs with indefinite determiners do not distinguish number, and hence, for example, *zein gizon?* can mean either 'which man?' or 'which men?', indifferently.

The only case in which two determiners can co-occur is the combination of a numeral with a definite determiner. Consider these examples, which illustrate the normal use of numerals (*bi* = 'two'; *lau* = 'four'):

bi gizon 'two men' (B *gizon bi*)
bi gizonak 'the two men', 'both men' (B *gizon biak*)
lau gizon 'four men'
lau gizonak 'the four men', 'all four men'
lau gizon hauek 'these four men'

The partitive affix *-ik* is a unique item: it may not co-occur with any other determiner or with any other case-ending. Existing grammars invariably treat it as a case-ending; here I shall treat it as a determiner, an analysis first suggested by Alan King (p.c.). The use of this affix is described below.

There are three types of complex modifier: (1) genitives; (2) relative clauses; (3) *-ko* phrases. A *-ko* phrase is a modifier constructed from virtually any type of adverbial by the addition of the relational suffix *-ko*, which occupies a central place in Basque syntax; see section 2.5.

Here are some typical examples of NPs:

Kepa-(r)en lagun-a-k
Peter-Gen companion-Det-Pl
'Peter's companions'

Bilbo-ko   kale   zahar hori-ek
Bilbao-[Loc]-*ko*   street old   that-Pl
'those old streets in Bilbao'

lau   atso-(r)ekin
four old.lady-Com
'with four old ladies'

zenbait liburu zahar
several book   old
'several old books'

Multiple adjectives can occur; the order is precisely the opposite of the English order (or it's identical, if you think in terms of distance from the noun):

etxe   zuri   txiki polit bat
house white little   pretty a
'a pretty little white house'

A noun phrase need not contain a noun:

gorri-a-k	gizon-a-ren-a
red-Det-Pl	man-Det-Gen-Det
'the red ones'	'the man's (one)'

hori	ikusi d-u-gu-n-a
that	saw it-Aux-we-Rel-Det
'that one'	'what we saw', 'the one we saw'

mendi-e-ta-ko   handi haiek
mountain-Pl-Loc-*ko* big   those
'those big ones in the mountains'

Multiple complex modifiers can occur:

hemen-go gu-re   mendi-a-k
here-*ko*   we-Gen mountain-Det-Pl
'our mountains here'

The genitive case-ending -*en* is, of course, added to a noun phrase, and the relational suffix -*ko* may be used to construct a complex modifier from a case-inflected NP. It is possible to build up fairly complex NPs containing smaller NPs within them:

mendi-e-ta-ko   gizon-a-(r)en alab[a]-a-(r)i
mountain-Pl-Loc-*ko* man-Det-Gen daughter-Det-Dat
'to the daughter of the man in the mountains'

As with any NP, the smaller and larger NPs in such constructions may have no lexical heads:

mendi-e-ta-ko-∅-a-ren-∅-a-ri
mountain-Pl-Loc-*ko*-∅-Det-Gen-∅-Det-Dat
'to the one of the one in the mountains'

Such NPs are perfectly normal in context. Imagine, for example, that you are discussing the three unmarried daughters of three men, only one of whom lives in the mountains, and you want to say that you intend to give a present to the daughter of the one who lives in the mountains: you could perfectly well say *Mendietakoarenari emango diot* 'I'm going to give it to the [daughter] of the [man] in the mountains.' The existence of such NPs, combined with the mistaken belief that -*ko* was a case-ending (see below) and the failure to realize that the bound morpheme -*a* was a determiner, led to the erroneous conclusion among Basque grammarians that Basque permitted 'superdeclension', the addition to a single noun phrase of a sequence of case-suffixes. They (wrongly) analysed a form like *mendietakoarenari* as a single NP with four consecutive case-endings: locative, -*ko*, genitive, dative.

2.3.2 The cases

There are about a dozen cases in Basque, the precise number depending both upon the variety and upon the analysis. All cases are marked by agglutinated suffixes. With just a few exceptions and complications, all but one of them utterly trivial, *all noun phrases in Basque are case-marked identically*. Basque has no grammatical gender and no noun classes, and the same case suffixes are attached to all NPs, regardless of whether the NPs are definite or indefinite, singular or plural. The only significant exception is a difference in the forms of the local cases between animate and inanimate NPs. Here is a summary of the cases; note that case-marking is ergative. The locative, ablative and allative cases, and the compound cases derived from the allative, are the 'local cases'; these have some distinctive morphological characteristics.

Absolutive: -∅. Some older books call this the 'nominative', a label which is not appropriate. The absolutive case is used (1) for the subject of an intransitive verb; (2) for the direct object of a transitive verb; (3) for the complement of a copular verb; (4) as a vocative. Some postpositions govern the absolutive; see below.

Ergative: -k. Many grammars call this the 'active' or 'agentive' case. The ergative case is used for the subject of a transitive verb. It has no other function. Some books claim that it marks the agent of a passive, but this is a serious misanalysis.

Dative: -i. The dative case marks indirect objects and ethic datives, and generally serves to indicate an entity affected by an action. A number of transitive and intransitive verbs may or must govern dative objects. A few postpositions govern the dative; see below.

Instrumental: -z. Called the 'mediative' by French Basque grammarians, the instrumental case primarily expresses instruments, but it also has a number of miscellaneous and idiosyncratic uses. This is the 'dustbin' case, used when no case appears to be obviously appropriate. One or two verbs govern instrumental objects.

Comitative: -ekin. The comitative case (called the 'sociative' or 'unitive' by Basque grammarians) expresses accompaniment and corresponds to English 'with, in the company of'. Some younger speakers also use it to express an instrument, but this usage is widely regarded as substandard. Some northern varieties have a variant -ekila; many varieties of B have -gaz (plural -kaz).

Genitive: -en. The genitive case marks a possessor NP. Most personal pronouns have -e instead of -en. Many postpositions govern the genitive; see below.

Locative: -n. This case is called the 'inessive' by most Basque grammarians, a label which is not appropriate. It expresses position in space or time, and variously corresponds to English 'in', 'on' or 'at'. In some circumstances it can also express (motion) 'into'. Finer distinctions are expressed by the use of postpositions; see below. One or two postpositions govern the locative.

Ablative: -tik. Called the 'elative' by French Basque grammarians, the ablative case primarily expresses the source of motion, and it corresponds to English 'out of', 'from' or 'away from', but it can also serve as a partitive when attached to an identified whole. Northern varieties have a variant *-rik* in certain circumstances.

Allative: -(r)a. The ending is *-ra* in most circumstances but *-a* in a few circumstances, notably with place names. Often called the 'lative', this case expresses the goal of motion, and it corresponds to English 'to' in that sense. Some northern varieties have *-rat* and/or *-la(t)*.

The remaining case-endings are compound in form: each is constructed from either the genitive or the allative by the addition of a further morph. The compound cases naturally exhibit all the morphological idiosyncrasies of the simple cases from which they are derived.

Benefactive: -entzat. Called the 'prolative' by French Basque grammarians, this case expresses the person for whom something is done, and it corresponds to English 'for' in that sense. In some northern varieties, it also handles the functions of the destinative case (see below). It is constructed from the genitive by the addition of *-tzat.*

Destinative: -(r)ako. This case expresses the inanimate entity towards which some action is directed, and it corresponds to English 'for' in that sense. Some northern varieties have *-(r)akotz*, while in others its functions are handled by the benefactive. It is formed from the allative by the addition of *-ko(tz).*

Terminative: -(r)aino. Also called the 'approximative', this case expresses the meanings 'as far as, up to, until'. Some northern varieties have *-(r)adino*. It is formed from the allative by the addition of *-ino.*

Directional: -(r)antz. This case expresses the direction of motion and corresponds to English 'towards'. It has the regional variants *-(r)ontz* and *-(r)untz*. It is formed from the allative by the addition of *-ntz.*

These are the only cases which I recognize in this book. Most Basque grammars, however, recognize a further three or four cases. Here I shall call these the 'pseudo-cases'; I discuss each in turn with an explanation of my reasons for not considering it a true case.

Partitive: -ik. The partitive is not properly a case, since it cannot be added to a full NP containing a determiner. Instead, it is added to an N-bar, just like a determiner, and hence I prefer to regard it as a determiner. An NP bearing the partitive is a negative polarity item, and it occurs only in contexts in which the absolutive would otherwise be used. The partitive marks the direct object of a negated transitive verb, and it also serves in negative existential sentences to mark the entity whose non-existence is asserted. In northern varieties (only), it also occurs in non-negative questions like *Ba da ogirik?* 'Is there any bread?'; southern varieties use the ordinary absolutive here with the definite article: *Ogia (al) dago?*

Locative genitive: -ko. All other grammars of Basque treat this as a distinct case, a special type of genitive expressing a connection with a location and translatable roughly as 'who/which is in/on/at'. I regard this as a serious error of analysis: the 'locative genitive' is nothing more than an ordinary *-ko* phrase constructed by adding *-ko* to a noun phrase in the locative case. For details, see section 2.5 on the relational suffix *-ko*.

Essive/translative: -tzat. Called the 'prolative' by many Basque grammarians, the essive/translative expresses the capacity in which someone performs an act, the manner in which someone is regarded or the capacity into which someone is translated; it corresponds to English 'as, for' or zero in such senses. Examples: *Semetzat daukat* 'I consider him *my son*'; *Emaztetzat nahi zaitut* 'I want you *for my wife.*' This is not a true case-form, because the morph *-tzat* cannot be added to a full NP with a determiner, but only to an N-bar.

Causal: -engatik. Some grammars recognize this as a case expressing the meaning 'because of'. This analysis is unnecessary: what we have here is merely the postposition *gatik* 'because of', which, like many postpositions, governs the genitive.

Table 2.3 shows the paradigms for *mendia* 'the mountain', *mendiak* 'the mountains' and *zein mendi?* 'which mountain?'; the compound cases can be obtained by adding the requisite morphs to the genitive or the allative. Observe that the plural form of the article is *-e-* in all oblique cases and that an *-r-* appears to separate vowels in hiatus in non-plural forms. The local cases exhibit a few idiosyncrasies: the singular article *-a* vanishes and a morph *-ta* appears in non-singular forms.

Table 2.4 shows the comparable paradigms for the noun *hitz* 'word';

Table 2.3 Nominal morphology: vowel-final nouns

	Singular	Plural	Indefinite
Absolutive	mendia	mendiak	zein mendi?
Ergative	mendiak	mendiek	zein mendik?
Dative	mendiari	mendiei	zein mendiri?
Instrumental	mendiaz	mendiez	zein mendiz?
Comitative	mendiarekin	mendiekin	zein mendirekin?
Genitive	mendiaren	mendien	zein mendiren?
Locative	mendian	mendietan	zein menditan?
Ablative	menditik	mendietatik	zein menditatik?
Allative	mendira	mendietara	zein menditara?

Table 2.4 Nominal morphology: consonant-final nouns

	Singular	Plural	Indefinite
Absolutive	hitza	hitzak	zein hitz
Ergative	hitzak	hitzek	zein hitzek
Dative	hitzari	hitzei	zein hitzi
Instrumental	hitzaz	hitzez	zein hitzez
Comitative	hitzarekin	hitzekin	zein hitzekin
Genitive	hitzaren	hitzen	zein hitzen
Locative	hitzean	hitzetan	zein hitzetan
Ablative	hitzetik	hitzetatik	zein hitzetatik
Allative	hitzera	hitzetara	zein hitzetara

observe that an -*e*- is inserted to break up consonant clusters, and note the curious form of the locative singular.

Animate NPs are inflected identically except in the formation of their local cases. Western varieties add a morph -*gan* to the genitive (which can optionally be dropped in the definite singular), while eastern varieties use a morph *baita*- instead; the case-ending follows this, and there are a few idiosyncrasies. Table 2.5 shows the local cases of *gizona* 'the man', *gizonak* 'the men' and *zein gizon?* 'which man?'

Finally, note that an animate plural NP can take the inanimate form of the locative to denote 'among': *alabengan* 'in/on the daughters', but *alabetan* 'among the daughters'.

Proper names are in no way unusual, except that place names take allative -*a*. Table 2.6 shows the paradigms for the female personal names *Esther* and *Itxaso* and the place names *Elorrio* and *Gasteiz*.

Western varieties (only) have a distinct proximate plural: next to *gizonak* 'the men', we find *gizonok*, translatable as 'we men' or 'you men' according

Table 2.5 Local cases of animate NPs

	Singular	Plural	Indefinite
Loc	gizona(ren)gan	gizonengan	zein gizonengan?
Abl	gizona(ren)gandik	gizonengandik	zein gizonengandik?
All	gizona(ren)gana	gizonengana	zein gizonengana?
Loc	gizona(ren) baitan	gizonen baitan	zein gizonen baitan?
Abl	gizona(ren) baitarik	gizonen baitarik	zein gizonen baitarik?
All	gizona(ren) baitara	gizonen baitara	zein gizonen baitara?

Table 2.6 Morphology of proper names

Abs	Esther	Itxaso	Elorrio	Gasteiz
Erg	Estherrek	Itxasok	Elorriok	Gasteizek
Dat	Estherri	Itxasori	Elorriori	Gasteizi
Instr	Estherrez	Itxasoz	Elorrioz	Gasteizez
Com	Estherrekin	Itxasorekin	Elorriorekin	Gasteizekin
Gen	Estherren	Itxasoren	Elorrioren	Gasteizen
Loc	Estherrengan	Itxasorengan	Elorrion	Gasteizen
Abl	Estherrengandik	Itxasorengandik	Elorriotik	Gasteizetik
All	Estherrengana	Itxasorengana	Elorriora	Gasteiza

to context. In the oblique cases, the *o* replaces the *e* of the ordinary plural forms.

2.3.3 Pronouns and demonstratives

Table 2.7 shows the Basque personal pronouns. The western dialects alone have third-person pronouns: *bera* 'he/she', *berak* or *eurak* 'they'. Other dialects use demonstratives when third-person pronouns are required.

The use of the intimate pronoun *hi* is extraordinarily restricted. It is normally used between siblings and between close friends of the same sex and roughly the same age. It may optionally be used in addressing children. It may be used when teasing or abusing someone. It is not used in addressing animals, except when abusing them, and it is never used in addressing God. Except between siblings, it is never used between adults of opposite sex, not even between man and wife. It is almost never used in addressing a significantly older person, though it may be used in addressing a younger one, particularly if that usage was established when the younger person was a child: it is not usual in Basque to change from one pronoun to the other for any reason at all. Usage varies in a way which is perhaps more individual than regional. Some younger speakers, especially in Gipuzkoa, use *hi* as freely as they use *tú* in Spanish; other Basques are often considerably annoyed by this. This eccentric usage does not appear to be spreading.

A few eastern varieties have a distinctive second-person pronoun *xu*, a palatalized form of *zu* and intermediate in familiarity between *hi* and *zu*.

Table 2.7 The personal pronouns

ni	(first-person singular)
hi	(second-person singular intimate)
zu	(second-person singular unmarked)
gu	(first-person plural)
zuek	(second-person plural)

Some southern varieties have a highly respectful pronoun of address, *berori*, from *ber-* 'self' + *hori* 'that'; this is used only in addressing a person of markedly superior status.

The personal pronouns show some idiosyncrasies of inflection, most prominently in forming the genitive: *ni* (*ene* ~ *nere* ~ *nire*); *hi* (*hire*); *zu* (*zure*); *gu* (*gure*); *zuek* (*zuen*).

A few varieties also have dative *eni* for *ni*. Otherwise the personal pronouns inflect like ordinary animate NPs, except in the instrumental: Abs *ni*, Erg *nik*, Dat *niri* (or *eni*), Instr *nitaz*, Com *nirekin*, Loc *ni(re)gan*, Abl *ni(re)gandik*, All *ni(re)gana*.

The intensive pronouns are constructed by adding the proximal demonstrative *(h)au(r)* to the personal pronouns, or to the genitive forms of these pronouns. There is considerable regional variation: the intensive of *ni* is *nihaur*, *neu* or *nerau* 'I myself', and the others show comparable variation. In some varieties the intensive pronouns have genitive forms distinct from those of the ordinary personal pronouns: *neure*, *heure*, *zeure*, *geure*, *zeuen*. Elsewhere, these intensive genitives do not exist, and only the ordinary genitives are found. The third-person intensive pronouns are singular *bera*, plural *berak*; these are the forms which function as ordinary third-person pronouns in western dialects.

The reflexive pronouns are constructed by combining the intensive genitives (where these exist; otherwise the ordinary genitives) with the noun *buru* 'head' plus the article *-a*; these are shown in Table 2.8. They take normal case inflections, but can never stand in subject position.

The reciprocal pronoun is *elkar* (variants: *elgar*, *alkar*) 'each other, one another'. This takes normal case inflections but can never stand in subject position.

Interrogatives are formed from the two stems *no-* and *ze-*; the principal forms are listed in Table 2.9.

Three series of indefinite pronouns exist, all of them formed from the interrogatives. The first series is generally formed by suffixing *-bait* to the corresponding interrogative; it corresponds to English indefinites in 'some-', such as 'somebody' and 'something': *norbait* 'somebody', *zerbait*

Table 2.8 The reflexive pronouns

neure burua	'myself'
heure burua	'yourself'
zeure burua	'yourself'
bere burua	'himself/herself'
geure burua	'ourselves'
zeuen burua	'yourselves'
beren burua	'themselves'

Table 2.9 The interrogatives

nor	'who?'	*zer*	'what?'
noiz	'when?'	*zein*	'which?'
non ~ nun	'where?'	*zelan*	'how?'
nola	'how?'	*zerga(i)tik*	'why?'
nolako	'what kind of?'	*zerta(ra)ko*	'what for?'
nondik	'where from?'	*zertaz*	'what about?'
nora	'where to?'		

'something', *noizbait* 'sometimes', *nonbait* 'somewhere', *nolabait* 'somehow' and so on.

The second series is generally formed by prefixing a vowel to the interrogative, but there are complications; these correspond to the English negative polarity items in *any-*, such as *anyone* and *anything* in negative and interrogative contexts. Northern varieties have some alternative forms borrowed from Romance: *inor ~ nehor* 'anybody', *ezer ~ deus* 'anything', *inoiz ~ sekulan* 'ever', *inon* 'anywhere' and so on.

The third series is constructed in either of two ways: (1) by reduplicating the interrogative around the item *edo* 'or'; the result is very frequently reduced or contracted in some way; (2) by suffixing *-nahi* 'want' to the interrogative. These items correspond to the English indefinites in *any-* when these are *not* negative polarity items, that is, when they mean *anyone at all, anyone you like*. With the first pattern, we have *nor-edo-nor ~ edonor* 'anybody (at all)', *zer-edo-zer ~ edozer ~ zeozer* 'anything (at all)', *non-edo-non ~ edonon* 'anywhere (at all)' and so on. With the second, we have *nornahi* 'anybody (you like)' *zernahi* 'anything (you like)', *nonnahi* 'anywhere (you like)', and so on.

Basque has no negative pronouns or adverbs; these are rendered by combining the items in the second series with *ez* 'not': *inor ez* 'nobody', *ezer ez* or *deus ez* 'nothing', *inoiz ez* 'never' and so on.

There are three demonstratives, all of which show stem suppletion: proximal *hau ~ hon- ~ haue-* 'this'/'these'; mesial *hori ~ horr- ~ ho(r)ie-* 'that'/ 'those' (not far from the speaker); distal *hura ~ har- ~ haie-* 'that'/'those' (far from the speaker). The position of the addressee does not appear to be important in deciding between the last two; nevertheless, *hori* is commonly used in direct address in certain special circumstances, as in abuse: *Alu hori!* 'You jerk!'

2.3.4 Postpositions

Basque is exclusively postpositional; most, but not all, postpositions are case-inflected nouns. Most postpositions govern the genitive case, with the absolutive as a frequent alternative; a few postpositions govern other cases.

The biggest group is based on a set of spatial nouns: *aurre* or *ai(n)tzin* 'front', *atze*, *gibel* or *oste* 'back', *gain* 'top', *azpi* 'bottom', *alde* or *ondo* 'side', *inguru* 'vicinity', *erdi* 'middle, centre', *kanpo* 'outside', *barru* or *barne* 'inside'. These can take any of the local case-suffixes to form postpositions of appropriate meaning; such postpositions govern the genitive, but, when the governed NP is both inanimate and singular, both the determiner and the genitive ending are optionally dropped. Examples:

gizonaren atzean 'behind the man'
mahai(aren) gainean 'on top of the table'
eliza(ren) aldean 'beside the church'
aulki(aren) azpitik 'out from under the chair'
mendien erdira 'to the middle of the mountains'

The item *kanpo* exceptionally often governs the ablative, and often takes no case-ending itself: *etxetik kanpo* 'outside the house'.

Other postpositions govern various cases. With the genitive, we have *gatik* 'because of', *aurka* and *kontra*, both 'against', and *alde* 'on behalf of, in favour of'. With the dative, we have *buruz* 'about'. With the locative, we have *zehar* 'across'. With the absolutive, we have *gabe* ~ *baga(rik)* 'without' (which often takes the partitive affix on the governed NP), *baino lehen* 'before', *ondoren* 'after', *bezala*, *legez*, *gisa* and *moduan*, all 'like, as'.

There is some variation in the case governed by some of these; the last six in particular will usually take the case logically required by their object: *Zuk bezala egingo dut* 'I'll do it like you', in which *bezala* has an ergative object *zuk*, since the sense is 'I'll do it the way you [did it].'

2.4 ADJECTIVES AND ADVERBS

Basque has a large and open class of adjectives, many of them lexically simple, like *handi* 'big' and *agor* 'dry', others derived from other words by means of word-forming suffixes, like *harritsu* 'stony' (*harri* 'stone') and *emankor* 'fertile' (*eman* 'give'). Some adjectives are identical in form to nouns (or less commonly verbs) of related meaning. Thus *bero* 'hot' and *ilun* 'dark' can also be nouns meaning 'heat' and 'darkness', while *busti* 'moist' and *hil* 'dead' are also verbs meaning 'moisten' and 'die, kill'. Generally speaking, though, adjectives are distinct from all other parts of speech.

As explained above, an adjective may occur inside an NP, in which case it follows its noun: *etxe zuria* 'the white house', *gizon handi haiek* 'those big men'. Certain adjectives and adjective-like items, however, commonly precede the noun, or may do so. These include (1) adjectives formed with the suffix *-dun* 'having' (a reduced relative verb-form), as in *haurdun emakumeak* 'pregnant women' (*haur* 'child'); (2) adjectives formed with the ethnonymic suffix *-(t)ar*, as in *donostiar ikasleak* 'the students from San Sebastián' (*Donostia*); (3) adjectival modifiers formed with the relational suffix *-ko*, as in *gaurko egunkaria* 'today's newspaper' (*gaur* 'today'; these are not true adjectives); (4) adjectives of nationality, however formed, as in *Frantses Bidea* 'the Milky Way' ('the French Road'); (5) the unique item *bertze* ~ *beste* 'other'.

As in Romance languages, any adjective can be nominalized: *gorria* 'the red one', *zaharrak* 'the old ones', *haurdunak* 'the pregnant ones'.

In most dialects, an adjective in predicate position takes a determiner which agrees in number with the subject; so, with *on* 'good', we have *Liburu hau ona da* 'This book is good', but *Liburu hauek onak dira* 'These books are good.' The Zuberoan dialect alone is different: it distinguishes *Liburu haur hun da* 'This book is good', with no determiner, from *Liburu haur huna da* 'This book is the good one.'

There are a number of lexically simple adverbs like *bihar* 'tomorrow' and *la(i)ster* 'soon, quickly', and there are others derived from other words, like *hala(n)* 'thus' (from *har-*, oblique stem of *hura* 'that') and *hemen* 'here', from *hau* 'this'. Adverbs of manner are derived from adjectives by the addition of a suffix. This suffix is usually *-ki* in most dialects but *-to* in B; in a few cases we find *-ro* or the compound suffix *-kiro*. Thus, *on* 'good' forms *ondo* 'well' in B but *ongi* in most other varieties; some northern varieties have *ontsa*, with a suffix found only in this one word.

Both adjectives and adverbs may be compared; the suffixes used are positive zero, comparative *-ago*, superlative *-en* and excessive *-egi*. Thus, for example: *Etxea handia da* 'The house is big'; *Etxea handiagoa da* 'The house is bigger'; *Etxea handiena da* 'The house is the biggest (one)'; *Etxea handiegia da* 'The house is too big.' The word *on* 'good' uniquely forms an irregular comparative *hobe* 'better'; its superlative is usually the regular *onen*, but a few varieties have *hoberen* or *hoben*. A comparative suffix follows a manner suffix in an adverb: *txarto* 'badly', *txartoago* 'worse'.

In comparative phrases, the order is standard–pivot–comparative, where the pivot is *baino* 'than': *zu baino handiagoa* 'bigger than you'. The standard takes any case-marking required: *Jonek zuk baino hobeki egiten du* 'John does it better than you', where *zu* 'you' takes the ergative, since it is the subject of an understood transitive verb. Equative phrases are formed identically with pivot *bezain* 'as … as': *zu bezain handia* 'as big as you'. In superlative phrases, the standard appears most often in the ablative, though the partitive is found if the standard is indefinite: *gizonetatik handiena* 'the biggest of the men', but *gizonik handiena* 'the biggest of men'.

2.5 THE SUFFIX -*ko*

The 'relational' or 'adnominal' suffix *-ko* is of central importance in the grammar of Basque, but it has often been misdescribed in grammar books. Briefly, *-ko* can be added to virtually any kind of adverbial phrase, regardless of its syntactic structure, to produce a complex adjectival modifier which can appear within a noun phrase. The adverbial phrase can be a lexical adverb, an adverb derived from an N-bar, a case-inflected NP, a postpositional phrase, a participial phrase involving an adverbial participle, an adverbial clause, or even a complement clause. The only adverbials which cannot take -*ko* are adverbs of manner derived from lexical adjectives (for which a -*ko* derivative would carry no meaning beyond that of the lexical adjective itself) and those for which a -*ko* derivative would be senseless. The final -*n* of the locative and comitative cases is usually lost before -*ko*, as is the -*a* of the locative singular. Examples:

atzo 'yesterday'
atzoko egunkaria 'yesterday's newspaper'

hemen 'here'
hemengo jendea 'the people here'

esku huts 'bare hand' (N̄)
esku-huska 'bare-handed' (adv.)
esku-huskako pilota partida bat 'a game of bare-handed pilota'

mendian 'on the mountain'
mendiko etxeak 'the houses on the mountain'

mendietan 'in the mountains'
mendietako haitzuloak 'the caves in the mountains'

Bilbon 'in Bilbao'
Bilboko kaleak 'the streets of Bilbao'

mendira 'to the mountain'
mendirako bidea 'the road to the mountain'

gurekin 'with us'
gurekiko neskak 'the girls who are/were with us'

dirurik gabe 'without money'
dirurik gabeko ikasleak 'students without money'

zu bezala 'like you'
zu bezalako pertsona bat 'a person like you'

mahai gainean 'on top of the table'
mahai gaineko liburuak 'the books on top of the table'

trumoiak adituta 'having heard the thunder'
trumoiak aditutako umeak 'the children who had heard the thunder'

guk ikusita '(having been) seen by us'
guk ikusitako jendea 'the people seen by us'

izarra agertu zitzaienean 'when the star appeared to them'

izarra agertu zitzaieneko garaian 'at the time when the star appeared to
   them'

idi bat hegan ikusi zuela 'that he had seen an ox flying'
idi bat hegan ikusi zuelako kontua 'the story that he had seen an ox flying'

All of these are normal, but the addition of *-ko* to an NP in the locative is
particularly frequent. Note the difference in sense between a genitive and a
locative plus *-ko*: *etxearen kolorea* 'the colour of the house', *etxearen izena*
'the name of the house', *etxearen historia* 'the history of the house', but
etxeko atea 'the door of the house', *etxeko andrea* 'the mistress of the
house', *etxeko gelak* 'the rooms in the house'. The *-ko* phrase is used to
mark something which is physically present in the house or which forms a
physical part of the house or a person who lives in the house.

This frequent addition of *-ko* to an NP in the locative, combined with the
loss of the locative case-ending before *-ko*, is what led many earlier investigators into concluding (wrongly) that Basque had a distinctive 'locative genitive'
case in *-ko*, a special genitive case expressing a relation of location. It does not.

The suffix *-ko* has a second function, formally quite distinct. In certain
circumstances it can be added to an N-bar to produce a modifier. Examples:

hortz bi 'two teeth'
hortz biko sardea 'a two-pronged pitchfork'

bihotz on 'good heart'
bihotz oneko neska bat 'a good-hearted girl'

hiru urte 'three years'
hiru urteko ume bat 'a three-year-old child'

beso eder 'beautiful arm'
beso ederreko pilotaria 'a pilota player with a great arm'

The N-bar involved must be at least two words long, and there are some ill-
defined semantic restrictions.

There are a few other miscellaneous occurrences of *-ko*, a striking one
being the word *balizko* 'hypothetical', derived from the finite verb-form
balitz 'if it were', as in the old proverb *Balizko olak burdinarik ez* 'A hypothetical forge doesn't produce any iron.'

2.6 NON-FINITE VERB-FORMS

Basque is rich in non-finite verb-forms; these are numerous and frequent.
The most central of these are the so-called 'radical' (the stem functioning as
a free form), the perfective participle, the gerund and the imperfective participle. The radical is the morphologically simplest form; for example, *ikusi*
'see' has radical *ikus*. The perfective participle is usually formed by adding a
suffix: hence *ikusi*. The gerund is formed by adding a different suffix: hence

ikuste. (In fact, the form is *ikustea*, because the gerund always takes the article, but it is linguistically convenient to cite the gerund without the article.) The imperfective participle is formed by adding the locative case-ending *-n* to the gerund: hence *ikusten*.

Verbs may be classified according to the form of the perfective participle. One class takes *-i*: *ikusi* 'see', *ekarri* 'bring', *jalgi* 'go out', *ipini* 'put' and so on. A second class takes *-tu*: *hartu* 'take', *saldu* 'sell', *lortu* 'succeed', *aberastu* 'get rich' and so on. A third class takes no suffix, and hence the perfective participle is identical to the radical: *ito* 'drown', *bota* 'throw', *ebaki* 'cut', *hil* 'die, kill' and so on. Finally, there is a fourth, anomalous class of verbs in *-n*, such as *joan* 'go', *egin* 'do, make', *esan ~ erran* 'say' and *eman* 'give'. In these verbs, the perfective participle is identical to the radical, but the final *-n* disappears in certain other contexts, and these verbs show a number of morphological peculiarities.

The gerund is formed with either *-te* or *-tze*; there is some regional variation in the choice: *ikuste* 'seeing', *ekartze* 'bringing' (B *ekarte*), *saltze* 'selling' (B *saldute*), *ebakitze* 'cutting'. The *-n* class verbs behave oddly: the *-n* is lost, and northern varieties further insert an *i* before the ending: *joate* 'going' (northern *joaite*), *emate* 'giving' (northern *emaite*) and so on. Eastern varieties of B use *-keta* to form all gerunds: *ikusketa* 'seeing', *ekarketa* 'bringing' and so on. In all cases, the addition of *-n* to the gerund yields the imperfective participle.

There is also a future participle, or perhaps better a prospective participle, which is formed by adding *-ko* or *-en* to the perfective participle. Western dialects use *-ko* exclusively; eastern ones use *-en* exclusively; central ones use *-ko* after a vowel but *-en* after a consonant. Thus, *ikusi* 'see' forms *ikusiko* or *ikusiren*; *hartu* 'take' forms *hartuko* or *harturen*; *joan* 'go' forms *joango* or *joanen*; *hil* 'die' forms *hilgo* or *hilen*.

All remaining non-finite forms are obtained by adding a further suffix (most often an ordinary case-suffix) to either the perfective participle or the gerund, occasionally with a postposition as well. Thus, with *ikusi* 'see', we have western *ikusita*, eastern *ikusirik* 'having (been) seen', *ikusiz gero* 'having seen' (in the sense of 'since NP has seen' (causal, not temporal)), *ikustean* 'on seeing', *ikustekotan* 'in the event of seeing', *ikustearren* 'because of seeing', *ikustera* 'in order to see' (adverbial), *ikusteko* 'in order to see' (adnominal) and so on; there are very many of these. Non-finite forms are intrinsically unmarked for voice, and they can take case-marked NP arguments.

Of great importance in western varieties is the adverbial *-ta* participle, formed by adding *-ta* to the perfective participle; see Rebuschi (1978, 1983) for a discussion of this and related participles.

2.7 FINITE VERB-FORMS

Basque verbal morphology is overwhelmingly periphrastic. All verbs have mostly periphrastic forms, and all but a handful of verbs have only periphrastic forms. Each periphrastic form consists of a non-finite form followed by a finite auxiliary. The non-finite form is marked at most for aspect; the finite auxiliary is marked for tense (past or non-past) and mood and carries all agreement markers.

All transitive verbs take as auxiliary the defective verb *edun 'have', whose non-finite forms are supplied where necessary by ukan 'have' in eastern dialects and izan 'be' in the west; most textbooks use one of these as the citation form for the auxiliary. For non-indicative forms, the defective verb *ezan (or, in B, egin 'do') is used suppletively in place of *edun. Intransitive verbs take the auxiliary izan 'be', with non-indicative forms using the defective verb *edin suppletively. The subclass of intransitive verbs which require transitive morphology, of course, take *edun.

Basque distinguishes a large number of periphrastic forms differing in tense and mood. The forms listed in Table 2.10, all except the imperative, cited here in the minimal third-person singular intransitive forms of the verb etorri 'come', without datives, are recognized by the Academy; some of these are now purely literary, especially in southern varieties.

Here I have space to illustrate in some detail only the six indicative forms. In the indicative mood, each of the perfective, imperfective, or future participles may combine with past or non-past ('present') auxiliaries to produce six possible combinations:

1 perfective + present   recent past or perfect
2 imperfective + present   present habitual
3 future + present   future
4 perfective + past   remote past or pluperfect
5 imperfective + past   past habitual
6 future + past   future-in-the-past or unreal conditional

Examples with the simplest possible auxiliary forms, using hartu 'take' and joan 'go':

1 hartu dut   'I took it' (earlier today) or 'I have taken it'
   joan naiz   'I went' (earlier today) or 'I have gone'
2 hartzen dut   'I take it' (regularly)
   joaten naiz   'I go' (regularly)
3 hartuko dut   'I'll take it', 'I'm going to take it'
   joango naiz   'I'll go', 'I'm going to go'
4 hartu nuen   'I took it' (before today) or 'I had taken it'
   joan nintzen   'I went' (before today) or 'I had gone'
5 hartzen nuen   'I used to take it'
   joaten nintzen   'I used to go'
6 hartuko nuen   'I was going to take it' or 'I would have taken it'
   joango nintzen   'I was going to go' or 'I would have gone'

Note the clear difference between recent and remote past tenses 1 and 4. The

Table 2.10 Tense and mood distinctions in Basque

Indicative

Recent past/perfect	*etorri da* 'he/she has come', 'he/she came' (earlier today)
Present habitual	*etortzen da* 'he/she comes'
Future	*etorriko da* 'he/she will come'
Remote past	*etorri zen* 'he/she came'
Past habitual	*etortzen zen* 'he/she used to come'
Future-in-the-past:	*etorriko zen* 'he/she was going to come' (also 'he/she would have come')

Irrealis

Past protasis	*etorri balitz* 'if he/she had come'
Present protasis	*etortzen balitz* 'if he/she came' (now)
Future protasis	*etorriko balitz* 'if he/she came' (later)
Past apodosis [1]	*etorri litzateke* 'he/she would have come'
Pres apodosis [1]	*etortzen litzateke* 'he/she would come' (now)
Future apodosis [1]	*etorriko litzateke* 'he/she would come' (later)
Past apodosis [2]	*etorri zatekeen* 'he/she would have come'
Pres apodosis [2]	*etortzen zatekeen* 'he/she would come' (now)
Future apodosis [2]	*etorriko zatekeen* 'he/she would come' (later)

Epistemic indicative

Past	*etorri dateke* 'he/she will have come' (I suppose)
Present	*etortzen dateke* 'he/she will be coming' (I suppose)
Future	*etorriko dateke* 'he/she will be going to come' (I suppose)

Subjunctive

Past	*etor zedin* 'that he/she come'
Present	*etor dadin* 'that he/she come'

Realis conditional

Past	*etor baledi* 'if he/she should have come'
Present	*etor badadi* 'if he/she should come'

Potential

Past	*etor zitekeen* 'he/she could have come'
Present	*etor daiteke* 'he/she can come' (now)
Future	*etor liteke* 'he/she could come' (later)

Jussive	*etor bedi* 'let him/her come'
Imperative	*etor hadi, etor zaitez* 'come!'

habitual sense of 2 and 5 is quite marked, but not unavoidable; particularly with verbs which don't easily take a progressive aspect, other English translations are possible: thus, *ikusten dut* can mean 'I see it' (now) as well as 'I see it' (regularly). The conditional use of 6 is condemned by some prescriptive grammarians, but is very widespread.

An indicative form involving a perfective participle may take the participle of *izan* 'be' to express further distinctions, but the function of these forms varies regionally. In northern varieties, it adds remoteness in time, so that *hartu izan dut* means 'I took it' (a very long time ago), while *hartu izan nuen* is virtually unusable with a first-person subject: third-person *hartu izan zuen* means 'he took it' (in the remote past). In southern varieties these forms have a perfect sense, and most typically correspond to an English pluperfect: 'I had taken it'.

Agreement in Basque is extensive: the finite auxiliary agrees in person and number with its subject, with its direct object (if any) and with its indirect object (if any). There may thus be as many as three agreement markers. There is one restriction: in a three-person form, the direct object must be third-person; English sentences like *I'll introduce you to her* cannot be expressed in the ordinary way, and require other constructions. Agreement is in most circumstances ergative; the general form of an auxiliary is as follows:

Abs – tense – (*n*) – root – (flag – Dat) – (Erg) – (tense)

The term 'flag' denotes an extra morph which almost always precedes a dative agreement-marker. Present tense is usually marked by *a* in the first tense slot. Past tense is marked by *e* or *i* in this same slot, sometimes followed by *n*, and always by a final -(*e*)*n*. The root itself may vanish in some cases, as may the tense-marker or the flag. Plurality is usually marked by an overt morph, but this morph is quite variable in its form and position. Examples:

joan-go n-a-iz
go-Fut 1SgAbs-Pres-Root
'I'll go'

joan-∅ g-i-n-∅-en
go-Perf 1PlAbs-Past-*n*-Root-Past
'we went'

joan-go n-a-tza-i-o
go-Fut 1SgAbs-Pres-Root-Flag-3SgDat
'I'll go to him/her'

ikus-ten   z-a-it-u-t
see-Imperf 2Sg-Pres-Pl-Root-1SgErg
'I see you'

(The reason for the plural marker is that the pronoun *zu*, now singular, was formerly plural.)

ikus-i   z-i-n-du-da-n
see-Perf 2Sg-Past-*n*-Root-1SgErg-Past
'I saw you'

In the present tense, when the absolute is third person, a morph *d*-occupies the absolutive slot. This is not a true agreement marker, as is commonly asserted in textbooks; it is discussed in Chapter 4.

ikus-i   d-∅-u-gu
see-Perf *d*-Pres-Root-1PlErg
'we see him/her/it'

etorr-i   d-∅-a
come-Perf *d*-Pres-Root
'he/she/it came/has come'

eman-go d-i-z-ki-zu-t
give-Fut *d*-Pres-Pl-Flag-2SgDat-1SgErg
'I'll give them to you'

(In this case the tense-marker (if that's what it is) appears as *i*.)

In the past tense, we don't find this *d*-. Instead, we usually find *z*- (B zero). Examples:

ikus-i   z-∅-u-te-n
see-Perf *z*-Past-Root-3PlErg-Past
'they saw him/her/it'

eman-∅   z-∅-∅-i-gu-∅-n
give-Perf *z*-Past-Root-Flag-1PlDat-3SgErg-Past
'he/she gave it to us'

However, in a past-tense transitive form, when the direct object is third person and the subject is first or second person, something very odd happens: the *z*- does not appear, and the (ergative) subject marker appears in the absolutive slot:

ikus-i   n-∅-u-en
see-Perf 1SgErg-Past-Root-Past
'I saw him/her/it'

eman-go n-∅-∅-i-o-n
give-Fut 1SgErg-Past-Root-Flag-3SgDat-Past
'I was going to give it to him/her'

In this circumstance, then, the ordinary ergative pattern of agreement is disrupted, and transitive subjects (ergatives) are marked just like intransitive subjects (absolutives).

When the addressee is addressed with the intimate singular pronoun *hi*, there exists a special set of finite forms in which the second person is overtly marked even though there is no second-person argument in the sentence;

Table 2.11 Some synthetic verb-forms

nator	'I'm coming'	*dakit*	'I know it'
hator	'you're coming'	*dakik, -n*	'you know it'
dator	'he/she's coming'	*daki*	'he/she knows it'
gatoz	'we're coming'	*dakigu*	'we know it'
zatoz	'you're coming'	*dakizu*	'you know it'
zatozte	'you're coming'	*dakizue*	'you know it'
datoz	'they're coming'	*dakite*	'they know it'
nentorren	'I was coming'	*nekien*	'I knew it'
hentorren	'you were coming'	*hekien*	'you knew it'
zetorren	'he/she was coming'	*zekien*	'he/she knew it'
gentozen	'we were coming'	*genekien*	'we knew it'
zentozen	'you were coming'	*zenekien*	'you knew it'
zentozten	'you were coming'	*zenekiten*	'you knew it'
zetozen	'they were coming'	*zekiten*	'they knew it'

these are called *allocutive* forms. Thus, *etorri da* 'he has come' has allocutive forms *etorri duk* (male addressee) and *etorri dun* (female addressee); *joango naiz* 'I'll go' has *joango nauk/naun*; *hemen nago* 'I'm here' has *hemen niagok/ niagon*; *nator* 'I'm coming' has *niatorrek/niatorren*; *datorkit* 'he's coming to me' has *zetorkidak/-dan*; *emango diot* 'I'll give it to him' has *emango zioat/ zionat*; *ikusi dut* 'I saw him' has *ikusi diat/dinat*. Allocutive forms occur only in main clauses, but are obligatory there. They show enormous regional variation in form.

A modest number of verbs can be inflected synthetically, without auxiliaries. Though the Academy recognizes synthetic forms of more than three dozen verbs, scarcely a dozen of these (including the auxiliaries themselves) have any synthetic forms in ordinary speech, usually only the present and past indicative and sometimes the imperative. These are inflected along the same lines as the auxiliaries, with a few minor idiosyncrasies. As a rule, the synthetic forms differ from the corresponding periphrastic ones in being explicitly progressive in aspect, or at least imperfective. Thus, for example, the periphrastic forms of *etorri* and *jakin* mean 'come' and 'find out', while their synthetic forms mean 'be coming' and 'know (a fact)'. Table 2.11 lists the present and past indicative forms of these two verbs.

These synthetic forms take datives and plural objects normally: *natorkizu* 'I'm coming to you', *dakizkit* 'I know them' (this verb takes an unusual plural object marker).

Any good grammar of Basque will provide a more or less comprehensive list of periphrastic and synthetic verb-forms; Euskaltzaindia (1979) is recommended for an orderly presentation of the forms recognized as standard.

Further auxiliaries are used to express additional distinctions of aspect and modality: *hasi* 'begin', *jarrain* 'continue', *nahi *edun* or *gura *edun* 'want to', *behar *edun* 'have to, must', *ahal izan* or *ahal *edun* 'be able to, can', *ari izan* 'be . . .ing', *ohi *edun* 'be in the habit of . . .ing'. Some of these are always construed intransitively, others always transitively, while *ahal izan* varies in this respect according to region. Here are some typical examples:

irakur-tzen hasi n-in-tz-en
read-Imperf start 1SgAbs-Past-Aux-Past
'I started to read (it)'

ikus-i   nahi d-∅-it-u-t
see-Perf want Pres-Pres-Pl-Aux-1SgErg
'I want to see them'

joan-∅ behar-ko d-∅-u-gu
go-Perf must-Fut Pres-Pres-Aux-1PlErg
'we'll have to go'

eman-∅   behar n-∅-∅-i-o-n
give-Perf must 1SgErg-Past-Aux-Flag-3SgDat-Past
'I had to give it to him/her'

bizi-tzen   ahal d-∅-ira   *or* bizi-∅   ahal d-∅-u-te
live-Imperf can Pres-Aux-3PlAbs   live-Perf can Pres-Pres-Aux-3PlErg
'they can live'

bidal-tzen   ari n-a-iz
send-Imperf Prog 1SgAbs-Pres-Aux
'I'm sending it/them'

2.8 SENTENCE STRUCTURE

Basic word order (better: phrase order) is SOV (de Rijk 1969), but this order is far from rigid, and all orders may occur, though the verb-initial ones are decidedly uncommon. The order of elements within major phrases is rigid. A non-periphrastic finite form absolutely cannot be the first element in a sentence. A constituent in focus occurs immediately before the verb. Examples:

Jonek Kepa jo zuen.
'John hit Peter.'
Kepa Jonek jo zuen.
'It was John who hit Peter.'
Kepa jo zuen Jonek.
'It was Peter who John hit.'
Jo zuen Jonek Kepa.
'John *hit* Peter.'

There are various devices for putting the verb in focus, with regional differences.

One common device is to use *egin* 'do' as a 'dummy' verb, with the real verb preceding it:

Jonek jo egin zuen Kepa.
'John *hit* Peter.'

Negation is expressed with the particle *ez* 'not', which immediately precedes the finite auxiliary or verb, and the order changes. So, *Kepak Ana ikusi zuen atzo* 'Peter saw Ana yesterday' has the corresponding negative *Kepak ez zuen Ana ikusi atzo* 'Peter didn't see Ana yesterday', and *Etxera noa* 'I'm going home' has the negative *Ez noa etxera* 'I'm not going home.'

In a wh-question, the question word or phrase must immediately precede the verb, and it is normally also sentence-initial:

Nork   egin   du   hau?
who-Erg do-Perf Aux this
'Who did this?'

Zer   ordutan   helduko   dira?
what hour-Loc   arrive-Fut Aux
'At what time are they going to arrive?'

Nola aurkitu   du   hau Kepak?
how find-Perf Aux this Peter-Erg
'How did Peter find this?'

Nork   ez du   Ana ikusi?
who-Erg not Aux Ana see-Perf
'Who didn't see Ana?'

Yes–no questions are formed in several ways: (1) by rising intonation alone; (2) by placing the question particle *al* between the main verb and the auxiliary; (3) by suffixing *-a* to the auxiliary (this causes various phonological changes). So, corresponding to *Jonek ikusi du* 'John saw it', the question 'Did John see it?' may be expressed as *Jonek ikusi du?* (with rising intonation), as *Jonek ikusi al du?* (also usually with rising intonation), or as *Jonek ikusi duia?* (usually with falling intonation). The second pattern is primarily Gipuzkoan; the third is strictly northern. When both are present, *ez* precedes *al*: *Ez al duzu ikusi?* 'Didn't you see it?'

A synthetic (non-periphrastic) verb-form may in no circumstances come first in a sentence; when necessary, the affirmative morph *ba* precedes the verb: *Ardoa al dago?* 'Is there any wine?', *Ba dago* 'There is' (also commonly written *Badago*).

A topicalized constituent is set off by comma intonation: *Atzo ikusi nuen* 'I saw him *yesterday*' (with *atzo* 'yesterday' in focus), but *Atzo, ikusi nuen* 'Yesterday, I saw him' (with *atzo* topicalized). Note also *Gaur datoz* 'They're coming *today*', but *Gaur, ba datoz* 'Today, they're coming', in which the second requires *ba* before the synthetic verb-form.

The order of major phrases within a Basque sentence is quite free, and this freedom has often been interpreted in recent years as evidence that Basque is best regarded as a non-configurational language. A non-configurational analysis of Basque was first suggested, on typological grounds, by Jelinek (1984), but the most prominent advocate of such an analysis has been Georges Rebuschi (Rebuschi 1985a, 1985b, 1985c, 1986, 1989). Taking the opposite view, that Basque is a configurational language, are Eguzkitza (1986), Salaburu (1986) and Ortiz de Urbina (1989). A discussion of this topic is beyond the scope of this book, and the interested reader is invited to consult the literature; note that most of this is embedded within the Government-and-Binding framework.

2.9 VALENCY AND VOICE

Some verbs are exclusively intransitive: *etorri* 'come', *iduri* 'seem', *erori* 'fall down', *ibili* 'go about, be active', *jarraiki* 'follow' (which takes a dative complement), *hasi* 'start' (in most varieties; it takes a locative complement), *ari izan* 'be busy at, be . . . -ing', *joan* 'go' (in most varieties), *jario* 'flow', *jaio* 'be born' and many others. A semantically arbitrary subclass of syntactically intransitive verbs requires transitive morphology, including an ergative subject: *amets egin* 'dream', *lo egin* 'sleep', *musu eman* 'kiss' (which takes a dative complement), *irakin* 'boil', *iraun* 'last, endure', *argitu* 'shine' (e.g., of the sun), and dozens of others. A few intransitive verbs take intransitive morphology in the east but transitive morphology in the west: *igan* ~ *igo(n)* 'go up', *irten* ~ *urten* 'go out', *afaldu* 'eat dinner', *dantzatu* 'dance' and some others.

A number of verbs can be construed either intransitively or transitively, with a more or less predictable difference of meaning: *hil* 'die' or 'kill', *sartu* 'enter' or 'insert', *galdu* 'get lost' or 'lose', *sortu* 'be born' or 'create', *jarri* and *eseri* 'sit down' or 'put', and a number of others.

A very few intransitive verbs require a dative complement: *gustatu* and *laket* 'be pleasing' (i.e., 'like'), *jarraikitu* 'follow', and one or two others. The person pleased or followed is marked with the dative; the thing which pleases or the person who follows stands in the absolutive. Examples: *Liburu hauek gustatzen zaizkit* 'These books are pleasing to me', 'I like these books'; *Kepari jarraiki natzaio* 'I followed [to] Peter.' A somewhat larger group of verbs requires transitive morphology but permits only a dative object: *eutsi* 'grab, seize, grasp', *musu eman* 'kiss' and a number of others. Examples: *Pistolari eutsi diot* 'I grabbed [to] the pistol', *Kepak Edurneri musu eman dio* 'Peter kissed [to] Edurne.'

The majority of verbs are primarily transitive, and all these require transitive morphology: *ikusi* 'see', *eman* 'give', *jo* 'hit', *maite *edun* 'love', *ipini* 'put', **edun* and *eduki* 'have', *ekarri* 'bring', *hartu* 'take' and hundreds of others. However, almost every one of these can be construed intransitively in a construction called the *mediopassive*; this is functionally equivalent to an English passive without agent:

Sagarr-a-k   bil-du   d-it-u-gu.
apple-Det-Pl-Abs gather-Perf Pres-Pl-Aux-1PlErg
'We gathered the apples.'

Sagarr-a-k bil-du d-ir-a.
                Pres-Pl-Aux
'The apples were gathered.'

Ibai-a   leiho-tik   ikus-ten   d-∅-u-t.
river-Det-Abs window-Abl see-Imperf Pres-Pres-Aux-1SgErg
'I [can] see the river from the window.'

Ibai-a leiho-tik ikus-ten d-∅-a.
                Pres-Pres-Aux
'The river is seen from the window', 'The river is visible from the window.'

The mediopassive does not allow an overt agent to be expressed.

A less common alternative is the use of a transitive construction with an impersonal third-plural subject. Thus, *Poliziek Kepa ikusi dute* 'The police saw Peter' (earlier today) has a corresponding mediopassive *Kepa ikusi da* 'Peter was seen', but also possible is *Kepa ikusi dute* 'They saw Peter', 'Peter was seen.' This second construction is usual with the verb *hil*, which means both 'die' and 'kill': in opposition to *Poliziek Kepa hil zuten* 'The police killed Peter' (before today), *Kepa hil zen* would normally be interpreted as 'Peter died', and so 'Peter was killed' is rendered as *Kepa hil zuten* 'They killed Peter.'

All periphrastic forms constructed with the three ordinary participles are explicitly eventive. Stative forms are obtained by using the perfective participle with further suffixes together with the ordinary copula; both transitive and intransitive verbs may occur. There are regional differences: eastern varieties do this by adding the ordinary definite article to the participle, effectively converting it to an adjective:

Lan hori egina   da. Ibaiak kutsatuak   dira.
work that do-Perf-Det is   rivers pollute-Perf-Det-Pl are
'That job is done.'   'The rivers are polluted.'

Note the difference between *Garia heldu zen* 'The wheat ripened' (periphrastic verb, eventive) and *Garia heldua zen* 'The wheat was ripe' (participial complement, stative), or between *Leihoa hautsi da* 'The window got broken' (this morning) and *Leihoa hautsia da* 'The window is broken.'

Western varieties add to the perfective participle the adverbial suffix *-ta* plus the relational suffix *-ko*, which turns adverbials into adjectivals; the article is then added:

Lan hori egindakoa   da. Ibaiak kutsatutakoak   dira.
    do-Perf-*ta-ko*-Det   pollute-Perf-*ta-ko*-Det-Pl
'That job is done.'   'The rivers are polluted.'

The point of these constructions is that the verb is the copula alone; the suffixed participle is not part of the verb, but rather a predicate complement. In such constructions, as in most participial constructions, the participle may take case-marked NP arguments normally, including an ergative subject:

Etxe   hori aitak   egina   da (*or*: egindakoa da).
house   that father-Erg build-Perf-Det is
'That house was built by [my] father', lit. 'That house is father-built.'

This construction is functionally equivalent to a passive-with-agent, but it is not passive in form. Here *aitak* 'father' is an argument only of the participle *egina* ~ *egindakoa*; *aitak egina* or *aitak egindakoa* forms a constituent and cannot be broken up; and the verb is *da* alone.

Western varieties can also use the *-ta* participle alone, with no further suffixes; in this case, the verb is usually not the ordinary copula *izan*, but rather *egon*, which is preferred with adverbial complements:

Lan hori eginda   dago. Moxkortuta   nago.
    do-Perf-*ta* is   get.drunk-Perf-*ta* I-am
'That job is done.'   'I am drunk.'

As usual, note the difference between *moxkortu naiz* 'I got drunk' (a little while ago) (eventive, with *izan*) and *moxkortuta nago* 'I'm drunk' (stative, with *egon*).

Basque has a fully productive causative suffix *-erazi* ~ *-arazi* (B *-erazo* ~ *-arazo*); this can be added to the stem of virtually any verb, transitive or intransitive, to obtain the corresponding causative, which is always transitive. The causer becomes the 'new' subject; the 'old' subject of an intransitive verb becomes a direct object; the 'old' subject of a transitive verb becomes an indirect object. Examples:

Kepa etxera etorri da.
'Peter came home.'

Edurnek Kepa etxera etorrerazi du.
'Edurne made Peter come home.'

Kepak eskutitza idatzi du.
'Peter wrote a letter.'

Edurnek Kepari eskutitza idatzarazi dio.
'Edurne made Peter write a letter.'

It is not normally possible to form a causative from a verb-form that already has an indirect object.

A few verbs exhibit an ancient causative prefix *-ra-*: *joan* 'go', *eroan* ~ *eraman* 'take away', *ibili* 'be active', *erabili* 'put into motion, use' and a few others. Some such pairs are now semantically anomalous: *ekarri* 'bring', *erakarri* 'attract'; *jantzi* 'get dressed', *erantzi* 'get undressed'.

2.10 SUBORDINATE CLAUSES

Unless it is very long, a subordinate clause quite commonly precedes a main clause. The majority of subordinate clauses involve the addition of a suffixed complementizer to the finite verb or auxiliary: either -*(e)la*, which is [–WH], or -*(e)n*, which is [+WH]. These suffixes produce a few phonological complications; among other things, underlying forms of agreement suffixes show up overtly. The verb bearing the complementizer typically comes last in its clause, but need not do so, except in a relative clause, in which this is obligatory.

A complement clause is formed by adding -*(e)la* to the finite clause. Examples:

Etorriko da.
'She's going to come.'
Etorriko dela esan dit.
'She told me she's going to come.'

Kotxe berria erosiko dut.
'I'm going to buy a new car.'
Uste dut kotxe berria erosiko dudala.
'I think I'm going to buy a new car.'

If the matrix verb is negated, then instead of -*(e)la* we find -*(e)nik*, consisting of the partitive affix -*ik* added to the complementizer -*(e)n*:

Ez dut uste kotxe berria erosiko dudanik.
'I don't think I'm going to buy a new car.'

(Some speakers would require *kotxe berrırık*, with a partitive ending on the direct object as well.)

A 'whether' clause takes the complementizer -*(e)n*, with optional reinforcement by -*etz* or by *ala ez* 'or not', depending on variety:

Joango naiz.
'I'm going to go.'
Ez dakit joango naizen / joango naizenetz / joango naizen ala ez.
'I don't know whether I'm going to go (or not).'

Other embedded questions just take -*(e)n*:

Nork egin du hori?
'Who did that?'
Ba al dakizu nork egin duen hori?
'Do you know who did that?'

A relative clause takes -(e)n; the relative clause precedes its head, the relativized NP is represented within the relative clause by a gap, and there is no relative pronoun. The verb in the relative clause agrees normally with the gapped NP:

Bihar hiria ikusiko dugu.
'Tomorrow we're going to see the city.'
[Bihar e ikusiko dugun] hiria oso zaharra da.
'The city we're going to see tomorrow is very old.'
Neskari musu bat eman diot.
'I gave the girl a kiss.'
Ez dakit [e musu bat eman diodan] neska nor den.
'I don't know who the girl I gave a kiss to is.'

Note that both *diot* and its relativized form *diodan* show agreement with a third-singular indirect object.

Subjects (transitive and intransitive), direct objects and indirect objects can all be relativized with complete freedom; these are the three arguments with which the finite verb agrees. Genitives and objects of comparison cannot be relativized. With oblique objects, the position is complex. Speakers differ in whether they accept constructions like this:

[Bizi naizen] herria polita da.
'The town I live in is pretty.'

Here the locative ending has vanished entirely. But all speakers find the next case perfectly normal.

[Bizi naizen] herrian ibaia dago.
'In the town I live in there is a river.'

The difference is that this time the 'missing' locative ending is present on the head noun. Relativization on an oblique NP is always possible if the head noun bears a case-ending identical to the one it would logically bear inside the relative clause. For further details, see de Rijk (1972).

Finite adverbial clauses are formed in a variety of ways, but most commonly by adding both one of the complementizers and a further suffix or postposition to the verb in the subordinate clause; one or two types additionally take a clause-initial particle, and 'if' clauses take the prefix *ba-* on the finite verb. Table 2.12 shows a few examples, based on *ikusten dut* 'I see it'.

Basque also has a large number of non-finite subordinate clauses built on

Table 2.12 Some finite adverbial clauses

ikusten dudanean	'when I see it'
ikusten dudanetan	'whenever I see it'
ikusten dudan baino lehen	'before I see it'
ikusten dudan ondoren	'after I see it'
ikusten dudanez gero	'since I see it' (= 'because')
ikusten dudalako(tz)	'because I see it'
ikusten dudalarik	'while I see it'
nahiz (eta) ikusten dudan	'although I see it'
ikusten (baldin) badut	'if I see it'

either the perfective participle or the gerund, though northern varieties use the radical instead of the participle with a postposition. Table 2.13 shows a brief sample.

Arejita (1978) and Goenaga (1980), both writing in Basque, present convenient summaries of both finite and non-finite subordinate clauses. Such information is often difficult to extract from general textbooks and grammars of Basque.

Table 2.13 Some non-finite adverbial clauses

ikustean	'on seeing it'
ikustekotan	'in the event of seeing it'
ikustearekin	'at the moment of seeing it'
ikusteagatik	'because of seeing it'
ikusiz gero	'having seen it', 'since NP has seen it'
ikusita (gero)	'having seen it', 'after seeing it'
ikusi ondoren	'after seeing it'
ikusi arte or *ikus arte*	'until seeing it'

2.11 A TYPOLOGICAL CHECKLIST

The idea that typological features might be important in determining historical connections among languages was popular in the centuries before the rise of scholarly historical linguistics in the early nineteenth century. With the success of the comparative method, however, typology was increasingly relegated to the outer darkness of historical investigations, and for generations typological characteristics have been generally regarded as of little or no significance in historical work, except, of course, that typological shifts have themselves sometimes been the object of examination. In recent years, though, typological characteristics have once again come to be viewed by some historical linguists as worthy of attention in their own right. Many linguists have argued that typological features tend to cluster in consistent patterns, and that it is possible therefore to classify languages into a small number of structural types. Moreover, some linguists have recently revived the old notion that languages tend to develop historically from one structural type to another; this stadial view has been developed especially in the former Soviet Union, and most prominently by the Russian linguist G. A. Klimov. Building on Klimov's work, the American linguist Johanna Nichols has, in a recent and highly controversial book (Nichols 1992), argued that plotting typological features on a map can shed light on the prehistory of languages and particularly on the ancient spread of languages.

Here I shall take no position on the validity of Klimov's and Nichols's ideas. But, in an effort to make this handbook as maximally useful as possible, I present below a checklist of typological characteristics and their manifestations, if any, in Basque. The checklist is based primarily upon the list in Nichols (1992: 9–10), itself derived from Klimov (1977), but I have added to it all those characteristics which I have found cited elsewhere in the literature as being possibly important for classification. Most of the points summarized here are described in more detail earlier in this chapter, or else later in the book.

2.11.1 Phonological properties

P1: Phoneme inventory.   The set of phonemes is rather small. Most varieties have only the five canonical vowels, though eastern varieties add a set of contrastive nasal vowels or a front rounded vowel or both. Most varieties have fewer than two dozen consonants, though some have slightly more. Voicing is contrastive only for plosives. There are six contrasting voiceless sibilants (three fricatives, three affricates), with the apical/laminal contrast being particularly noteworthy. There is no dental fricative. The Zuberoan dialect alone has a (recently acquired) set of contrasting voiced fricatives, but the functional load of the voicing contrast for fricatives is almost nil. Most varieties have two contrasting rhotics. There is a full set of palatal and palato-alveolar consonants, though these occupy a somewhat special position in the system. There are no 'exotic' segments.

P2: Suprasegmentals.   There are no lexical tones and no contrasts of length. Most varieties have a word-accent, but there is considerable regional variation in its nature. Many western varieties have a pitch-accent: words are divided into accented and unaccented classes, and an accented word is marked by a fall in pitch at some point. Eastern varieties have a stress-accent which is often largely, but perhaps never completely, predictable; the rules for assigning stress vary considerably among regional varieties. A few central varieties have no word-accent.

P3: Phonotactics.   Consonant clusters are few and simple, though common in medial position; three-consonant clusters are uncommon. Native words never contain either initial clusters or clusters beginning with plosives, though all these are found in well-integrated loan words. Vowel sequences occur, but (except for diphthongs) are not favoured. Nearly half of native nouns and adjectives begin with vowels.

P4: Morpheme structure. Roots are distinguished from stems only for ancient verbs. Monosyllabic stems are not rare, but the great majority of native nominal stems are bisyllabic, and a significant number are trisyllabic; ancient verbal roots are frequently monosyllabic. There are notable constraints on the possible combinations of consonants within roots.

P5: Morphophonology. Alternations are few, simple and in most cases phonologically transparent. The most elaborate cases are almost entirely confined to word-formation, which exhibits alternations not found elsewhere. Vowel harmony is absent, apart from some very rudimentary manifestations in a few varieties. Sibilant harmony is present.

2.11.2 Lexical properties

L1: Noun classification. Basque has no noun classes, no well-developed classifiers and no grammatical gender of any kind. Sex-marking is weak and inconsistent; when present, it is conveyed by lexical differences or (rarely) by the use of sex-marking suffixes, both male and female. Nouns are not divided into active and inactive classes. Animate and inanimate noun phrases differ only in the way they form their local cases, and in no other respect. (In Basque, it is only NPs which are inflected, and not nouns.) There is no lexical suppletion for number.

L2: Verb classification. Basque verbs may be classified morphologically according to the suffix found in the perfective participle, but this classification is of historical interest only, and has no grammatical consequences. Only a tiny handful of common verbs can be directly inflected, without auxiliaries. Transitive verbs differ from intransitive verbs in taking different auxiliaries and different morphology generally. Every transitive verb can be construed intransitively (the mediopassive), but some verbs are exclusively intransitive. A semantically arbitrary subclass of intransitive verbs requires transitive morphology, apparently as a result of various historical accidents. Some morphologically transitive verbs take only a dative object. Otherwise, verbs are not classified, and all verbs behave identically. There is no verb suppletion for number, for animacy of subject or object, or for any other semantic property.

L3: Auxiliaries. A small number of auxiliaries are used to conjugate all other verbs periphrastically. There are also some auxiliaries used in making finer overt distinctions of tense, aspect and mood. Some of these auxiliaries also occur as independent lexical verbs and some do not, and some are compound verbs in form, but all auxiliaries are completely verbal in their morphology and syntax, except that some are compound verbs consisting of a noun plus a simple verb.

L4: Non-finite verb-forms.   Basque is very rich in non-finite forms, and these are frequently used. There is a gerund, or verbal noun, which approximates in function to the infinitive of Indo-European languages; this is exceedingly frequent.

L5: Adjectives.   There is a large and open class of lexical adjectives. Adjectives are sharply distinct from verbs and recognizably distinct from nouns. The class of adjectives is not subdivided in any way. Adjectives distinguish positive, comparative, superlative and excessive forms, all but the first marked by suffixes. With a single exception, comparative morphology is absolutely regular.

L6: Copula.   All varieties have a copula, used both in equational sentences and in predications of class membership. Southern varieties distinguish two copulas, the second being roughly confined to expressing temporary states or conditions and location (temporary or permanent).

L7: Personal pronouns.   There are first- and second-person pronouns, singular and plural, all unrelated in form. Pronouns do not show stem suppletion. In the second-person singular, an intimate pronoun of extraordinarily restricted use contrasts with an unmarked pronoun. The inclusive/exclusive distinction is absent. There are no third-person pronouns, except in western varieties, where these have been recently created from the intensive pronouns.

L8: Body parts.   Names of certain body parts are often used metaphorically, but otherwise body-part names are entirely distinct from all other sections of the lexicon.

L9: Word-formation.   Compounding is very well developed for forming both nouns and verbs. Compounds are almost exclusively head-final, except for nouns formed with the noun–adjective pattern. Basque is exceedingly rich in derivational suffixes, but prefixes are virtually absent.

2.11.3 Morphological properties

M1: General.   The language is strongly agglutinating and overwhelmingly suffixing. The few prefixes are nearly all loans or calques, except for those used in verbal morphology, which are ancient. Umlaut and ablaut are absent. The degree of morphological complexity is rather high in finite verbs and auxiliaries, but otherwise moderate. Basque also has a high degree of analytical character.

M2: Number.   Definite noun phrases consistently distinguish singular number from plural; the distinction is borne by the determiner, since nouns themselves are not directly inflected. Indefinite NPs never distinguish number at all, except that a handful of indefinite pronouns have overt plural forms in western dialects only, and except that western varieties show 'semantic' number agreement with indefinite NPs in the verb. Number is marked in finite verbs only via agreement. Lexical suppletion for number is absolutely unattested in all parts of speech. There is no trace of a dual.

M3: Possessive phrases.   Possession is expressed by the presence of an invariable genitive case-marker on the possessor NP; the possessed NP bears no overt mark of possession. The genitive marker is not related to any verbal affix, except perhaps to the [+WH] complementizer used in forming relative clauses and embedded questions. Alienable and inalienable possession are not distinguished.

M4: Case system.   Noun phrases are inflected for case; there are about a dozen distinct cases, all marked by agglutinated suffixes. These include distinct cases for marking core grammatical relations (absolutive, ergative and dative); with minor qualifications for the dative, these three cases have no other function, except that the absolutive also serves as the complement of a copular verb and as a vocative, and that both the absolutive and the dative are governed by certain postpositions. The absolutive case is marked by zero. Animate and inanimate NPs form their local cases slightly differently; otherwise, apart from a few trivial phonological complications, all NPs are inflected identically.

M5: Agreement.   A finite verb or auxiliary agrees in person and number with its subject, with its direct object (if any) and with its indirect object (if any). Agreement is ergative: an absolutive (intransitive subject or direct object) is marked by a prefix, while an ergative (transitive subject) is marked by a suffix, except that non-present-tense transitive verbs with third-person direct objects exceptionally mark the ergative with a prefix. A dative is marked by a suffix, which precedes an ergative suffix (if present) and which is usually preceded by an overt morph flagging it as a dative. Third person is marked by zero, except in the dative, where overt third-singular and third-plural morphs are used. Except in dative agreement, plural number is marked by a distinct and overt morph; usually, distinct morphs are used for pluralizing absolutives and for pluralizing ergatives. Most, but not all, of the first- and second-person agreement markers are clearly related to the corresponding free pronouns. In the case of agreement with an intimate second-person singular pronoun, the sex of the addressee is marked whenever the agreement morph is a suffix. Apart from the transitivity difference just described, all verbs show the same agreement pattern.

M6: Other verbal morphology.   Apart from agreement, a finite form is inflected for tense (past versus non-past) and for mood (indicative/subjunctive/potential/irrealis/imperative), but not for aspect or Aktionsart. Further distinctions of tense and aspect are made by periphrastic means, using various auxiliaries and non-finite forms. There is a special set of finite forms used when addressing someone with the intimate pronoun; these include an overt marker of second person even when there is no second-person argument. When no agreement prefix is present, a finite form takes one of a set of rather mysterious prefixes which are perhaps best regarded as redundant markers of tense or mood. There is no other verbal morphology.

M7: Voice.   Non-finite verb-forms are unmarked for voice. Voice distinctions are expressed with auxiliaries: a transitive verb can be construed with an intransitive auxiliary (and with all the associated intransitive morphology) to form a mediopassive. A mediopassive may not take an overt agent. There is no true passive-with-agent, but there is a functionally equivalent copula-with-participle construction, in which the agent can be overtly expressed as the subject of the participle; with or without an overt agent, this construction is explicitly stative. There are no other distinctions of voice. Intransitive verbs make no distinctions of voice, and cannot be passivized in any way, except that those few intransitives which take 'dative experiencers' can be construed without a dative NP to form a kind of passive.

M8: Valency.   A few weather expressions permit no overt subject. Otherwise, every finite verb requires a subject, and every finite transitive verb requires a direct object, unless it is construed in the mediopassive. A semantically arbitrary subclass of intransitive verbs require transitive morphology. A number of verbs take ergative subjects (and hence transitive morphology), but take only dative objects. Most verbs permit optional indirect objects or ethic datives, and a few intransitive verbs almost always take datives representing experiencers. There is a productive causative suffix, which increases the valency of a verb (transitive or intransitive) by one; the 'old' subject of an intransitive verb becomes a direct object, while the 'old' subject of a transitive verb becomes an indirect object. A causative cannot be formed from a verb which has an indirect object to start with. There are no other ways of changing valency.

2.11.4 Syntactic properties

S1: Word order.   Basic word order is SOV. The order of major phrases, including the verb, is quite free, and variation is used for thematic purposes. The order of elements within major phrases is rigid.

S2: Heads.   Modifiers overwhelmingly precede their heads, except that lexical adjectives follow the nouns they modify. Genitives, relative clauses, complex modifiers, most numerals and a few determiners precede their nouns; most determiners and the lowest numerals follow. Auxiliaries follow main verbs, and primary auxiliaries follow modals.

S3: Head- vs. dependent-marking.   Basque is predominantly dependent-marking. However, arguments of verbs are marked both by case-marking of NPs and (in finite forms only) by agreement. In a postpositional phrase, the postposition takes a case-suffix determined by the phrase's function in the sentence, while the object NP usually takes a case-suffix governed by the postposition.

S4: Orientation.   Though the morphology is uniformly ergative, the syntax is strictly accusative: transitive and intransitive subjects behave identically in all non-morphological respects, while direct objects sometimes behave differently.

S5: Predications of possession.   All varieties have a transitive verb meaning 'have', obligatory in expressing predications of possession, though northern and southern varieties use different verbs for this purpose.

S6: Objects.   Direct objects and indirect objects are rather rigorously distinguished, in case-marking, in verbal agreement and in capacity to be mediopassivized. Such distinctions as primary/secondary objects or nearer/further objects are of no significance in Basque.

S7: Incorporation.   There is no incorporation of NPs (of any kind) into the verb, though the frequent compound verbs might be regarded as a very marginal kind of incorporation.

S8: Inverse constructions.   Basque has no inverse constructions of any kind, except that a tiny handful of verbs of perception are expressed with intransitives taking datives as experiencers (most verbs of perception do not do this).

S9: Adpositions.   Basque is exclusively postpositional. Most, but not all, postpositions are case-inflected nouns.

S10: Relative clauses.   Canonical relative clauses are finite and obligatorily verb-final; the relativized NP is represented by a gap in the relative clause and (where possible) by an agreement-marker in the verb. The verb bears an invariant marker of subordination. The relative clause immediately precedes its head, and there is no relative pronoun. Subjects, direct objects and indirect objects can be relativized freely; oblique objects can be relativized fairly freely by many speakers but only in restricted circumstances by others. Genitives and objects of comparison cannot be relativized at all. Headless relatives are common. A relative clause may be extraposed, but only by turning it into a headless relative functioning as an appositive. Basque also has participial constructions functioning as reduced relative clauses.

S11: Complement clauses.   Complement clauses are finite and bear an overt mark of subordination on the finite verb.

S12: Pro-*drop.*   Basque has extended *pro*-drop: subjects, direct objects and indirect objects, all of which are marked in the verb, need not be expressed as overt NPs. Pronominal arguments of finite verbs are not normally realized by overt pronouns except when these are required for thematic or discourse purposes.

S13: Co-ordination.   There is a common co-ordinating conjunction, which can be used to co-ordinate like constituents of virtually any category. Finite clauses may be freely co-ordinated, though there is a marked tendency to prefer a non-finite participial construction for the first of two clauses representing sequential events.

Chapter 3

Phonology

3.1 PRELIMINARIES

The phonological history of Basque during the last 2,000 years or so is very well understood. That understanding is due almost entirely to the efforts of one man, the great Basque linguist Luis Michelena. Before Michelena's work, virtually nothing of significance had been done on the historical phonology of Basque, apart from Schuchardt's (1887) demonstration that word-initial *p*- must be of recent origin.

Michelena summarized his conclusions about the history of the consonant system in his 1957 paper, but the entire body of his work is presented in his book *Fonética histórica vasca* (*FHV*), first published in 1961. A second and considerably expanded edition followed in 1977, and a third edition in 1985. Most of what follows in this chapter is explicated in much greater detail in that book, though I also include some further observations and suggestions from my own more recent work and from that of others. Here I cite *FHV* in its 1977 edition.

Many of the linguists who preceded Michelena were in fact deeply pessimistic about the possibility of recovering any useful information about the prehistory of Basque on the ground that, since Basque is a genetically isolated language, there are no other languages to compare it with, and hence no possibility of applying the comparative method, our principal instrument in historical phonology. Saussure himself remarks, in his celebrated *Cours* (Saussure 1916): 'On ne peut rien tirer du basque parce que, étant isolé, il ne se prête à aucune comparaison.' And the distinguished comparativist Meillet declares in his 1925 book:

> Entre l'état du basque au xvr^e siècle et l'état du basque aujourd'hui, il y a des différences, mais les changements ne sont pas essentiels; en substance, la langue est restée la même. Si donc on ne trouvait pas le moyen de rapprocher le basque de telle ou telle autre langue, il n'y aurait aucun espoir d'en faire jamais l'histoire.

It was Michelena's achievement to show that such pessimism was completely unfounded. To begin with, he brought to the study of Basque an unprecedented command of linguistic theory. Almost all earlier investigators had operated with a deeply atomistic and prestructuralist view of phonology, in which absolute sounds were held to be the primitive units, and there was no conception of a phonological system. This shortcoming naturally induced a great deal of confusion. For example, the observation that Latin loans like PACE, TEMPORA and CASTELLU appear in Basque as *bake*, *denbora* and *gaztelu* had led to the positing of a 'voicing' process for initial plosives. In fact, as Michelena demonstrated, Pre-Basque simply had no word-initial voiceless plosives, and further had no voicing contrasts at all, and the attested forms merely reflect the best available rendering in terms of the phonological system of Basque in Roman times.

Furthermore, Michelena was able to take advantage of a great deal of evidence whose significance had not previously been recognized. This evidence includes

the existence of systematic phonological differences among the various dialects of Basque;

the presence in all dialects of a number of systematic alternations;

the presence in Basque of a large number of loan words from Latin and from its Romance descendants;

the presence of numerous Basque personal names and place names in medieval texts;

the existence in medieval documents of a not insignificant number of individual Basque words, phrases, glosses, glossaries, verses and other items, including a fair number of connected texts.

Michelena brought to his investigations a magisterial and unprecedented command of all this material, and by applying to it his understanding of synchronic and diachronic phonology he was able to work out in stunning detail just what has happened to the phonology of Basque during the last two millennia.

In his book, Michelena proceeds by reasoning backwards from the evidence until he finally arrives at a reconstructed phonological system for the Basque of around 2,000 years ago. Here I find it more convenient to begin simply by stating that reconstructed system and then describing the various developments which have led to the modern language.

3.2 THE PRE-BASQUE PHONOLOGICAL SYSTEM

In this book I shall use the term *Pre-Basque* for the stage of the language to which Michelena's reconstruction applies. This is the time when Basque began to borrow words from Latin, and must therefore represent a period roughly 2,000 years before our own era.

For Pre-Basque Michelena reconstructs a rather sparse phonological system of just sixteen consonants and five vowels. The consonants are divided into two groups of eight, called *fortis* and *lenis* by Michelena, with each fortis consonant having a lenis counterpart. These are shown in Table 3.1. Note that the evidence for **p** in Pre-Basque is decidedly scanty. The symbols for the consonants are chosen for orthographic convenience, and as a mnemonic guide to the modern reflexes of these segments; note that Pre-Basque emphatically did *not* have contrastive voicing. In Michelena's interpretation, the fortis consonants were distinguished from their lenis counterparts by greater tension and energy of articulation. He does not elaborate much on this view, but it seems clear that the two series were distinguished at the phonetic level by at least three characteristics:

1 *Duration.* The fortis consonants were longer than the lenis ones. The nasals and liquids were probably distinguished chiefly by duration (though note that **R** was a trill, **r** a tap).
2 *Degree of occlusion.* The fortis obstruents were completely occluded; the lenis obstruents typically were not, except in certain environments, notably after nasals.
3 *Voicing.* The fortis plosives were voiceless; the lenis plosives were typically voiced, though perhaps not exceptionlessly so.

Table 3.1 The phonemes of Pre-Basque

Fortis:	(p)	t	k	tz	ts	N	L	R
Lenis:	b	d	g	z	s	n	l	r
Vowels:	i	e	a	o	u			

Moreover, this fortis/lenis contrast was entirely confined to intervocalic position, being neutralized everywhere else, except that the two series of obstruents also contrasted word-medially after a nasal or a liquid. Word-initially, only lenis consonants occurred, and not all of those: a lexical item in Pre-Basque could begin only with a vowel or with one of **b g z s n l**. Note that no lexical item could begin with **d** or **r**, or with any fortis consonant. Word-finally, only fortis consonants occurred, and again not all of them: word-final **p** was absolutely impossible, and it is highly probable that no lexical item (and possibly no affix) could end in any plosive.

Note also that Pre-Basque had no *m*, no *f*, no *j* and no phonemic *h*; the sources of these modern consonants will be discussed below.

The absence of an **m** in Michelena's reconstruction has occasionally provoked sceptical comment from non-specialists, but see section 3.3 below for the evidence.

The fact that the fortis/lenis contrast was entirely confined to medial position led me to propose, in Trask (1985), that the fortis consonants were nothing more than geminates of the lenis ones. This interpretation, if accepted, would reduce the Pre-Basque consonant system to the surprisingly small number of only eight consonants. As will be seen below, such a reinterpretation is supported by the fact that sequences of lenis consonants arising in word-formation and inflection always develop into fortis consonants, and further by the fact that the geminate sequences of Latin are invariably borrowed into Basque as fortis consonants. The reinterpretation is not, however, without problems; Hurch (1991) provides a critical view, and I am told that Michelena himself was planning to write a reply, but died before he could do so. In any case, nothing of what follows is affected by the reinterpretation, and I shall use Michelena's notation throughout the remainder of this book.

Consonant clusters were few and simple. Absolutely no clusters were permitted in word-initial position. Word-finally, a (neutralized) nasal or liquid could be followed by a fortis sibilant (an affricate), producing clusters like -*ntz*, -*rtz* and -*ltz*, but it is highly doubtful that the other final clusters of the modern language (like -*st* and -*rt*) were possible at the time, and even some of the instances of these three clusters appear clearly to result from syncope, such as *beltz* 'black' < *beletz*. Word-medially, the two-consonant clusters described in Chapter 2 (like -*st*-, -*rd*-, -*ng*-, -*nt*-, -*rl*-) were mostly present, and medial liquid–sibilant clusters like -*rz*- were also possible. Medial three-consonant clusters like -*rst*- and -*ndr*- were probably rather more frequent than they are in the modern language. There is ample evidence that a number of medial three-consonant clusters formerly present have been reduced. For example, R has *arsto* for common *asto* 'donkey'; common (*h*)*osto* 'leaf', a derivative of *orri* 'leaf', is attested in the seventeenth-century writer Tartas as *orsto*; northern *ozpin* 'lightning bolt', a compound of *ortzi* 'sky' and *bini* 'tongue', is attested in the sixteenth-century writer Sauguis as *orzpin*; western *aztu* 'forget' is *anztu* in old Bizkaian.

We simply don't know whether the modern series of palatal consonants (*tt dd tx x ñ ll*) was present in Pre-Basque. Most probably these segments were already present, but they never occurred in lexical items, but only in 'expressive' forms derived from ordinary lexical items or affixes by the replacement of another consonant with a palatal.

The vowel system of Pre-Basque is identical to that found in all modern varieties except Z and R, though, as we shall see below, there is clear evidence that the vowel system has not remained unchanged for 2,000 years but that it has rather first expanded and then contracted again.

In Michelena's interpretation, the word-accent in Pre-Basque fell most usually on the second syllable of a lexical item of two or more syllables. This accent was frequently accompanied by the presence of a phonetic aspiration [h] which had no phonological value, though in a number of cases this aspiration occurred on, or was later transferred to, the initial syllable. It was not possible for two aspirations to occur in a single word, or for any aspiration to occur later than the onset of the second syllable. (Michelena's view of the word-accent has recently been challenged by Hualde (1992, 1995), discussed below, but Hualde does not question Michelena's account of the aspiration.)

In the remainder of this chapter, we shall examine the development of this ancestral system into the modern phonological system. For the moment, though, I shall point out that this secure reconstruction has direct consequences for the possible forms of lexical items in Pre-Basque, and hence immediately renders impossible many of the suggestions which have been made by non-specialists about alleged ancient loans from Basque into other languages, or about possible cognates in putative genetic relations.

Absolutely no native Basque lexical item of any antiquity can begin with any of *p*, *t*, *d* or *r*; all modern Basque words beginning with *p*, *t* or *d* are loan words or phonaesthetic formations (initial *r* is still impossible today). (For the special case of a few words like *talde* 'group' see section 3.19 below.) The evidence for word-initial *k* in Pre-Basque is scanty and doubtful. The monosyllable *ke* 'smoke' has everywhere a voiceless initial, as do a very few other words which look plausibly ancient, such as *koipe* 'oil' and *kirats* 'stench'. Indigenous formations with initial *k* are now common, especially in northern varieties, but virtually all such items postdate the Roman period and hence cannot be projected back into Pre-Basque. We may also note one or two regional variants such as *kar* 'flame', a variant of the more usual *gar*. Probably no word beginning with *m* existed in Pre-Basque with this initial, apart perhaps from one or two loans from Celtic, such as *mando* 'mule': most words with initial *m* today are loan words or recent formations, often 'expressive' in nature, while the rest had initial **b** in Pre-Basque (see below). Native words can begin with any vowel (or with *h* in the aspirating varieties), or with any of the consonants *b g z* (very common), *s l* (less common) or *n* (uncommon). No native word can begin with any consonant cluster at all.

Consider the consequences of these observations. Such words as *tutur* 'crest', *trikatu* 'rest', *kosko* 'acorn cap' and *muga* 'boundary', found also in neighbouring Romance languages, have often been regarded as loans from Basque. But the first two of these words would have been absolutely impossible in Pre-Basque, while the other two could only have existed in different forms (such as **gosko* and **buga*) which later underwent identical changes in both Basque and Romance. It has been an exceedingly common practice in some quarters to extract words from a modern Basque dictionary and to project them unhesitatingly back to the pre-Roman period, in the same form, often on the indefensible ground that 'nothing is known about the history of Basque'. One of the goals of this book is to put a stop to such practices.

3.3 PLOSIVES

At some stage after the Pre-Basque period, the contrasting fortis and lenis plosives, with their predictable voicing difference, came to be reinterpreted as contrastively voiceless and voiced plosives, respectively; the difference in duration was accordingly lost, though the difference in degree of occlusion has remained down to the present day: in modern Basque, *b d g* are usually incompletely occluded, except for some French Basque speakers, for whom the introduction of fully occluded realizations of these segments seems to have been a very recent development, since descriptions from a generation or two ago report incomplete occlusion even in French Basque, and indeed the incomplete occlusion of *b* is clearly described by Oihenart in the seventeenth century. It is likely, of course, that the voicing contrast found in all the neighbouring Romance languages was an important influence in the introduction of a voicing contrast into Basque. The most important consequence of this reinterpretation was that the voicing contrast could be introduced into word-initial position. Hence previously impossible contrasts like *kai* 'wharf, quay' (a Romance loan) and *gai* 'material' (a native word) became part of the language, though the functional load of this contrast is still exceedingly low in initial position today. Many words show regional variation in voicing (*kar ~ gar* 'flame'; *pake ~ bake* 'peace'), and recent borrowings from Romance sometimes fail to respect the voicing of the lending language (for example, Michelena (1957) reports that, in the Basque of his native Rentería, Spanish *corbata* 'necktie' is borrowed as *gorbata*, while Spanish *gabarra* 'barge' is borrowed as *kabarra*). Nevertheless, it is not true, as some commentators have asserted, that the voicing contrast in Basque is weak or variable: the contrast is fully established, and seemingly has been at least since the time of our earliest texts.

In native words, of course, the reinterpretation left only voiced plosives in initial position. Hence we find plenty of ancient native words throughout the country with forms like *bizi* 'alive', *buru* 'head', *gogo* 'soul' and *gatz* 'salt', but practically no non-loan words with initial voiceless plosives except those of more recent origin and mostly severely localized distribution (initial *d-* is not found in native words, of course, except in finite verb-forms, in which the prefix *d-* is common; see Chapter 4). Early loans from Latin and Romance show the same pattern, reflecting the fact that Pre-Basque had only its single series of lenis plosives to render both voiced and voiceless plosives in the lending language: hence *bake* 'peace' (< PACE), *bike* 'pitch' (< PICE), *Bortu(ak)* 'the Pyrenees' (< PORTU), *berna* 'calf, leg' (< PERNA), *bekatu* 'sin' (< PECCATU), *barkatu* 'forgive' (< PARCERE), *bazkatu* 'feed' (< PASCERE), *dorre* 'tower' (< TURRE or Spanish *torre*), *denbora* 'time' (< TEMPORA), *gela* 'chamber, room' (< CELLA), *gauza* 'thing' (< CAUSA), *gerezi* 'cherry' (< CERESEA), *garden* 'clear' (of liquids) (< CARDINU 'bluish'), *ganbara* 'room' (< CAMERA), *gertu* 'certain; prepared' (< CERTU), *gorputz* 'body' (< CORPUS); *balea* 'whale' (< BALLAENA), *bedeinkatu* 'bless' (< BENEDICERE), *done* 'saint' (< DOMINE), *diru* 'money' (Z *diharü*) (< DENARIU), R Aezk *dekuma* 'tithe' (< *DECUMA), *damu* 'regret' (< DAMNU), B *domeka* 'Sunday' (< (DIES) DOMINICA), *garau* 'grain' (< GRANU), *gura* 'desire' (< GULA), *gisu* 'plaster' (< GYPSU).

In a number of cases, however, we find an initial voiceless plosive either as a regional variant or as the most usual form. Thus, for *bake* 'peace' (< PACE) some areas have *pake*; beside common *gorputz* 'body', Z and R have *khorpitz* and *korpiz*, respectively; next to *bike* 'pitch' (< PICE), *pike* is about equally common; *titare* ~ *titara* 'thimble' is perhaps more widespread than *ditare* (< DIGITALE); *katea* ~ *katiña* 'chain' (< CATENA) is much more usual than *gate*(*a*); *katu* 'cat' (< CATTU) is likewise more widespread than *gatu*; and *kaiku* 'wooden bowl' (< CAUCU 'drinking vessel') is the only attested form of this word. There are two reasons for this. First, Basque shows a sporadic but notable tendency to devoice the initial plosive if the following syllable contains a voiceless plosive (this observation would apply to all five of the examples just cited). Note that the native words *bihi* 'grain', *behi* 'cow' and *gurdi* 'cart' are nowhere attested with voiceless plosives, while their compounds *bikain* 'excellent' (< *bihi-gain*), *bekorotz* 'cow dung' (< *behi-korotz*) and *gurpil* 'cartwheel' (< *gurdi-bil*) are attested in places as *pikain*, *pekorotz* and *kurpil*, showing exactly such voicing assimilation. Second, the continuing influence of the neighbouring Romance languages, all of which generally retain the initial voiceless plosives of Latin, may have induced bilingual speakers to re-form the Basque words accordingly.

(Note: This is the position taken by the majority of vasconists, including Michelena and me, on the origin of initial voiceless plosives in some loans from Latin and early Romance. Other views are possible, however, and are preferred by some specialists: some speakers may have borrowed Latin words with initial voiceless plosives from the beginning, or there may have been a later period when Basque-speakers consistently borrowed Latin words with initial voiceless plosives regardless of the voicing in Latin. But the testimony of the native vocabulary, with its nearly categorical voicing of initial plosives, makes it impossible to entertain the view that Pre-Basque actually had a voicing contrast for initial plosives.)

Only a handful of apparently indigenous lexical items exhibit initial voiceless plosives: the items *ke* 'smoke', *kirats* (and variants) 'stench' (possibly a compound of *ke*) and *koipe* 'oil, grease' have everywhere a voiceless initial; the verb *kendu* 'remove' has a voiceless initial everywhere but in R, which has *gentu*; for 'bramble', *kapar* is more widespread than *gapar*, and for 'ignite' *piztu* is more widespread than *biztu* (this is a derivative of *bizi* 'alive'). A rare instance with *t* is *tu* 'saliva, spit', but the imitative origin of this item hardly needs pointing out. One more item is the extraordinary but virtually universal *kalte* 'injury, harm', a seeming derivative of *galdu* 'lose', doubly anomalous with its -*lt*- cluster; only R has *galte*, but the word means 'loss' in R. All of these words normally have aspirated plosives in the aspirating dialects. The reason for this handful of anomalous items is not known, though some of them may represent nothing more than voicing assimilation between plosives. (For the special case of words like *talde* 'group' and *toki* 'place', see section 3.19.2.)

Since the reinterpretation of fortis and lenis plosives as voiceless and voiced, before our earliest substantial texts, Romance words have most often been borrowed with retention of the original voicing, though, as the examples above illustrate, this is not invariably the case.

Consider first voiceless plosives: Occitan *coma* ~ *como* ~ *coumo* 'mane, horsehair' is borrowed into Basque as *kuma*; the Romance preposition *contra* 'against' is borrowed as a postposition *kontra*; a Romance form allied to Old Castilian *cocote* and Occitan *cogòt* 'nape' is borrowed as *kokot(e)*; Castilian *casco* 'skull' is borrowed as *kasko*; a Romance development of Latin PALU 'pole' is borrowed as *paru*; Castilian *pino* 'pine' or a related word is borrowed as *pinu* ~ *piñu*; a Romance word lying between Latin PUTEU and Spanish *pozo* 'well' is borrowed as *putzu*; some Romance form connected with Castilian *tosco* 'rough, crude, coarse' (of Latin origin) is borrowed as *toska* 'kaolin' (Z *toxka* 'clod'); Castilian *tabla* or Gascon *taule* 'plank, board' is borrowed as *taula*. (A few of these seem to have been borrowed very early, such as *porru* 'leek', whose vocalism suggests a source very close to Latin PORRU: cf. Castilian *puerro*, with Romance diphthongization.)

With initial voiced plosives: *bainu* 'bath' < Sp *baño*, *dantza* 'dance' < Sp *danza*, Fr *dance*, *gerra* ~ *gerla* 'war' < Sp *guerra*, Fr *guerre*.

The Romance voicing is not respected in cases like *pintza* 'membrane' (< Aragonese *binza*) and the two words cited above.

Word-medially, of course, the fortis and lenis plosives merely became voiceless and voiced, respectively. Hence words like *lepo* 'neck', *ate* 'door', *zoko* 'corner', *gabe* 'without', *sudur* 'nose' and *hagin* 'molar' simply continue the ancient plosives.

In loans from Latin, word-medial voiceless plosives, both simplex and geminate, were rendered by Pre-Basque fortis plosives and hence appear in modern Basque as voiceless plosives: *ipizpiku* 'bishop' < EPISCOPU, B *erripa* 'slope' < RIPA, *errota* 'wheel; mill' < ROTA, *aditu* 'hear, understand' < AUDITU, *nekatu* 'exhausted' < NECATU 'killed', *bake* 'peace' < PACE, *laket* 'be pleasing' < PLACET, *barkatu* 'forgive' < PARCERE, *apario* 'meal' < *APPARIU, *katu* 'cat' < CATTU, *bekatu* 'sin' < PECCATU, *zaku* 'sack, bag' < SACCU, *okela* 'morsel, meat' < BUCCELLA 'mouthful'; *zuku* 'juice, soup' < SUCCU.

In the same position, Latin simplex voiced plosives were borrowed as lenis plosives and have become voiced plosives: old G *zabau* 'tablecloth' < SABANU, *abere* 'large animal' < HABERE 'have' (or from a Romance development of this), *judu* 'Jew' < IUDAEU, *bago* 'beech' < FAGU, *lege* 'law' < LEGE, *errege* 'king' < REGE, *magi(ñ)a* 'sheath' < VAGINA. The rare Latin voiced geminates presented problems, but, being both long and completely occluded, they were most typically taken over as Pre-Basque fortis plosives:

apaez ~ *apaiz* ~ *apez* 'priest' (< ABBAS); B *zapatu* 'Saturday' (< SABBATU); the common element *Ap(h)at(a)-* (< ABBATE 'abbot') in toponyms like *Apatamonasterio* (Biz). The same occurs in the odd loan from Arabic: *atorra* 'shirt' < Arabic *ad-durrāʔa* 'type of woollen shirt' (cf. Old Spanish *adorra* 'button-up tunic', which cannot be the source of the Basque word). (And R *repat(t)an* 'shepherd boy' reflects an Arabic source with two voiced geminates, but this may be merely a loan from Aragonese.) The general rule seems to be that each of the four types of medial plosive in Latin was rendered by the Basque plosive which matched it in at least two of the three properties of duration, degree of occlusion and voicing. Note also the interesting treatment of the clusters in *apal* 'humble' (< AD VALLE) and *gutizia* 'desire' (< Old Sp *cobdicia*); on this, see section 3.19.

In Pre-Basque, the contrast between the two series of plosives was maintained after nasals and liquids, but, in all dialects except Z and R, all plosives eventually came to be voiced after *n* or *l* (though not after *r*). Thus we have common *denbora* 'time' but eastern *t(h)enp(o)ra* < TEMPORA 'times' and common *aldare* 'altar' but eastern *alt(h)are* < ALTARE. Native words show the same developments: common *ongi* 'well' (adv.) is R *onki*, Z *hunki*, and common *alde* 'side' is eastern *alte*. Very occasionally B fails to show this voicing, as in B *denpora* 'time'; the reason for this is not known.

The history of Pre-Basque **b** requires special attention. In a number of cases **b** has developed into *f*, and this represents a major source of *f* in modern Basque. This process is sporadic, unpredictable and somewhat surprising, since Pre-Basque **p** does not normally yield *f*, but it no doubt reflects the facts that **b**, like the other lenis plosives, was usually incompletely occluded, and that voicing was genuinely non-distinctive in Pre-Basque. This development occurs most often intervocalically, but rarely also initially: *kabia* 'nest' (< CAVEA) is *kafia* in some regions; the verb *ibeni* ~ *ipini* (and other variants) is *ifini* in places; common *barre* 'smile, laugh' has a variant *farre* (rarely also *parre*). The word *zubi* 'bridge' is sometimes written as *Zufi* or *Zuffi* in medieval toponyms, and one medieval document mentions a certain *Nunno-falzahuri*, 'the town of Nuño the Black', in which *falza* represents *baltza* 'the black'. Particularly striking is the name of the province of Navarre: all the evidence suggests that *Nafarroa* 'Navarre' and *nafar* 'Navarrese' were the usual medieval forms in all areas, and the town of Nafarrate in Araba is recorded as *Naffarrate* as early as 1025.

(The very rare instances of *p* > *f* are confined to names: *Fadura*, a variant of *Padura* (and *Madura*) (< PADULE 'water-meadow') and *Fradu* and *Fradue*, house names (Biz) (< Sp *prado* 'meadow').)

The other peculiarity of **b** is that, in word-initial position, it often develops into *m*, and this is the principal source of initial *m* in native Basque words. This process too is highly sporadic, but it is clearly favoured by a following nasal in the same word: *mihi* ~ *min* 'tongue' (< *mini* < *bini*); *mahats* 'grapes' (< *banats*); *min* 'pain' (< *bin*). Very occasionally, the same things happens in medial position: *zamau* 'tablecloth' (< SABANU), *zumel* 'holm oak' (< *zubel* < *zur-bel*), and possibly also in *ametz* 'gall-oak' and *amets* 'dream', for which the attested variants *amentx* and *aments* suggest original *abentz* and *abents*, respectively.

These developments suggest that Pre-Basque **b** had rather a wide range of phonetic realizations, with [m] perhaps being particularly frequent initially and [f] medially. (The suggestion of Martinet 1950, 1955 that Pre-Basque might have had a distinct phoneme /m^b/ (and also /n^d/) has found no support among vasconists.)

A third feature of **b** is that it is almost always lost in word-initial position before **o**, and very rarely before **u**. Thus, we have *ollo* ~ *oilo* 'hen' (< *bollo*, from a Romance development of PULLU 'chicken'), *ondo* 'bottom, side' (< *bondo*, from a Romance development of FUNDU 'bottom'), *okela* 'morsel, meat' (< *bokela*, from a Romance development of BUCCELLA 'mouthful'), *ostiko* 'heel; kick' (< *bostiko* < POSTICU 'posterior'), *otu* 'request, supplication' (< *botu* < VOTU), *horma* 'wall; ice' (< *borma*, attested in the seventeenth-century writer Oihenart in both senses, < FORMA). It is rarely possible to detect this development in native words, though the universal *on* 'good' may be an instance, if the Aquitanian *Bon(n)-* is the same item. Rare exceptions to this development are *bortz* ~ *bost* 'five' and *bortitz* 'strong, violent' < FORTIS. Before **u**, we have *urki* 'birch' alongside the less common *burki*, probably from Indo-European, though the rare B variant *turki* and old G *epurki* muddy the waters considerably, and the less common *buztarri* 'yoke' alongside the more widespread *uztarri*.

There is no trace of evidence that medieval Basque ever distinguished [b] from [v], in contrast to Old Spanish, which did.

In a number of cases, an original medial cluster **nb** has yielded modern *m*. Thus, *seme* 'son' surely derives from *senbe* (the form *Sembe* is attested in Aquitanian; see Chapter 6). It is probable that a number of other cases of medial *m* have a similar origin, such as *hamar* 'ten', *amu* 'hook' and possibly *ama* 'mother', if this is not merely a nursery word. There are even seemingly recent instances of this: northern *zonbat* 'how many?', a compound of *zoin* 'which?' and *bat* 'one', has a widespread variant *zomat*. The case of *ume* 'child' is particularly interesting, since both *Ombe* and *Vmme* are attested in Aquitanian, with the second looking very much like an intermediate form between an original *unbe* and modern *ume*. In one or two cases Basque *nb* continues Latin M, as in *ganbara* ~ *k(h)anbara* ~ *k(h)anbera* 'room' (< CAMERA), though this development might simply reflect a Romance development *cambra* (cf. French *chambre*).

The absence of an *m* from the Pre-Basque phonological system has sometimes attracted comment from non-specialists. But consider the evidence:

1 In modern Basque, the very frequent *m* is overwhelmingly confined to obvious loan words and to phonaesthetic formations of no great antiquity.

There are scarcely two dozen words with *m* which appear genuinely to date back to the pre-Roman period.

2 We have a large number of loan words in which modern *m* has indisputably developed from Latin or Romance *b* (or another labial borrowed into Basque as **b**): *magi(ñ)a* 'sheath' (< VAGINA), *mutil* 'boy' (< PUTILLU), *makila* 'stick' (< BACILLA), *muxika* 'peach' (< (MALA) PERSICA), *mendekatu* 'avenge oneself' (< VINDICARE), *zamau* 'tablecloth' (< SABANU), eastern *Mendekoste* 'Pentecost' (< PENTECOSTE), *mimen* ~ *mihimen* 'osier willow' (< VIMEN), Z *mühüllü*, R *mullu*, B G *millu* 'fennel' (< FENICULU), B G *mika* 'magpie' (< PICA), Z *mezpera* 'eve' (< VESPER), western *bañu*, central *mainu* 'bath' (< Sp *baño*), and many others. Some of these are attested only with *m*; others have *m* in some areas but *b* or *p* elsewhere.

3 A number of native words which normally have *b* appear with *m* in some varieties: common *biga(i)* 'two-year-old heifer' but HN LN *miga*, common *baneki* 'if I knew' (with the universal *ba-*'if') but old B *manequi*, LN *mantx-ut* 'what did you say?' but common *badantzut* 'I hear', and so on. There are also cases in which *m* is common but *b* is attested locally, such as common *me(h)ar* 'narrow' (< *benar*) but B *berar*, with nasal dissimilation.

4 Ancient items with *m* behave in word-formation as though they had *b* instead. For example, *arpin* 'plantain' may be securely derived from *ardi-bini* 'sheep-tongue'; the development of this form to *arpin* would be absolutely regular in Basque (compare *bepuru* 'eyebrow', from *begi* 'eye' plus *buru* 'head', or *okin* 'baker', from *ogi* 'bread' plus *-gin* 'who makes', or *arpigae* 'young ewe', from *ardi* 'sheep' plus *bigae* 'heifer' (< *bigana*), or *abatei* 'knell', from *abade* 'priest' plus *dei* 'call'). Similarly, *ope* 'slender bread roll' is from *ogi* 'bread' plus *mehe* 'slender' (< *bene*); northern *o(r)zpin* 'lightning bolt' derives from *ortzi-bini* 'sky-tongue'; and *ozpin* 'vinegar' is from an unidentified first element plus the common second element *-min* 'spicy, hot', related to *min* 'pain', from *bin*, all three words showing the regular devoicing of a plosive after a voiceless sibilant. This confirms that *mihi* ~ *min* 'tongue' derives from *bini*, *mehe* 'slender' from *bene*, and *min* 'pain' from *bin*.

5 In the dialects retaining the aspiration, *h* can follow any liquid or *n*: *alhaba* 'daughter', *ilhun* 'dark', *erhi* 'finger', *urrhe* 'gold', *senhar* 'husband', *anhitz* 'many', *inhurri* 'ant' and so on. But there is not a single instance of *h* after *m*, just as there is no instance of *h* after *b* (or after any other voiced plosive).

6 While most of the other Basque consonants make an appearance somewhere in the rich inflectional morphology of the language, and *n* in particular is very frequent indeed, *m* is categorically absent from inflectional affixes.

7 Likewise, *m* is categorically absent from grammatical words like pronouns, conjunctions, subordinators, determiners, question words and postpositions.

8 Among the dozens of word-forming suffixes in Basque, *m* is absolutely lacking, save only in the abstract-noun-forming suffix *-men* ~ *-mendu*, a transparent loan from Latin -MENTU.

In sum, then, the evidence is overwhelming that *m* was absent from Pre-Basque and that modern *m* has developed from earlier *b* (or *nb*) where it has not been borrowed. (See also section 5.5 for a treatment of the use of *m* in expressive formations.)

In word-final position, it seems unlikely that Pre-Basque permitted any plosives at all, at least in lexical items, though a few inflectional suffixes may perhaps have ended in fortis plosives. The modern language has several very common inflectional suffixes ending in *-t* or *-k*. The evidence from alternations shows clearly that the first-person singular agreement-marker *-t* and the second-person singular agreement-marker *-k* derive from *-da and *-ga, respectively, while the absolute plural-marker *-k* quite possibly derives from *-ge (on all this, see Chapter 4). The ergative case-suffix *-k* and the essive suffix *-tzat*, which can never be followed by any other material, exhibit no alternations, and there is no way to tell if they have a similar origin. A few lexical items have acquired final plosives by various phonological developments. Western *bart* 'last night' is *barda* in the east, and clearly results from loss of the final vowel; the universal *bat* 'one' has an apparent combining form *bede-*, pointing to original *bade or *bada. The universal *bort* 'bastard' may have a similar origin. Western *bost* 'five' is derived from *bortz*, retained in the east, by the process described in section 3.12. A modest number of loan words from Occitan or Old Spanish show final plosives, such as *kokot* 'nape' (Occitan *cogòt*), *agot* 'leper' (Old Spanish *agot*), *kok* 'coke' (Spanish *coque*). Z *topet* 'flask' doubtless has a similar source. Today final plosives are most frequent in interjections and words of imitative origin: *karrak* 'crack!', *dzast* 'bang!', *dzart* 'smack!', *(k)ok* 'vomit, indigestion', *tak* 'tick, tap', and probably also B G *txit* 'very' and also '(a single) word'. Final *-p* is absolutely unattested except in one or two interjections like B *eup*, used in mockery.

In word-medial position, the ancient **p/b** contrast has generally been continued as *p/b*. There are, however, a few items in which both voiceless and voiced plosives are attested medially. The widespread *ebaki* 'cut' (B *ebagi*) appears in some eastern and western varieties as *ep(h)ai*, and such derivatives as *epaiki* 'shears for cutting iron' and *epaile* 'cutter' are found throughout the country. (See Chapter 4 for the variation *-ki/-gi* in participles.) The verb *igan* ~ *igo(n)* 'ascend' is attested as *ikai* in the seventeenth-century writer Oihenart. The word *ipar* 'north', Michelena suggests, is identical to *ibar* 'valley' and originates in the compound *ipar-haize* 'valley wind, north wind'. Common *eduki* 'hold' (B *edugi*) has an old B participle *ituten*. The verb *egotzi* 'throw' appears to be the source of the derivatives *ekoizpen*, *ekoizte* 'product, fruit'. Moreover, the first-plural marker *-gu* sometimes appears as *-ku*, as in northern *zauku* ~ *zaiku* and B *jaku* ~ *yaku* 'it is to us', in contrast to central forms like *zaigu*, and the postposition *behe* 'under' often appears as *-pe* when suffixed, as in *lurpean* 'under ground'. The reason for such variation is not known.

Words with medial *d* in some varieties often have *r* elsewhere: *ideki* ~ *ireki* 'close', *edan* ~ *eran* 'drink', *eduki* ~ *eroki* 'hold' and others. Most of these seem to have had *d* originally, though a few may have had *r*.

Very occasionally, a Latin or Romance coronal plosive in initial position appears as *l*: *leka* 'pod' (< THECA) (but Z *theka*); eastern *lizifrina* 'discipline', *lanjer* 'danger', R *lantzatu* 'dance' (common *dantzatu*). And the modern town of *Larraga* (Nav) appears to be the town called *Tárraga* by Ptolemy.

In very rare and sporadic cases, a word-initial plosive, most often a velar, has been lost or added in post-Roman times, sometimes very recently. Examples: *kabia* 'nest' (< CAVEA) is (*h*)*abia* in places; *kamuts* 'blunted' (< Occ *camus* 'blunt') is *amuts* in places; *kokots* 'chin' is *okotz* in places; *kupa* 'barrel' is more commonly *upa*; B *tarro* 'gully' is *arro* in places; *putz* 'puff of breath, fart' is often *utz*; *poker* 'belch' is more commonly *oker*; Lat CUNA 'cradle' yields Sal *ua*. The Romance loan *kamaña* 'shepherd's bed' has a putative variant *amaña* listed in Azkue, but there is no independent confirmation of this form. Sp *carlinga* 'cabin, cockpit' appears to be the source of localized G *arlinga* 'place for the fireman/stoker on a train'. On the other hand, Sp *acero* 'steel' appears in some varieties as *galtzairu* (with an extra *l* as well). Another one is possibly *epel* 'lukewarm', if this derives from Latin TEPIDU, but this etymology is far from certain.

For the aspirated plosives of the northern dialects, see section 3.11.

In sum, Pre-Basque plosives were distributed as shown in Table 3.2. Note that **d-** was apparently not found outside of finite verb-forms and loan words.

Table 3.2 The Pre-Basque plosives

	-b-		-d-		-g-
b-		(d-)		g-	
	-p-		-t-		-k-

3.4 SIBILANTS

Generally speaking, fortis and lenis sibilants contrasted only intervocalically in Pre-Basque, except that the contrast was also maintained word-medially after a neutralized rhotic, a neutralized lateral or a neutralized nasal. Initially, only lenis sibilants occurred; finally, only fortis ones. It seems likely that the phonetic realizations of the sibilants in Pre-Basque were not very different from their modern descendants: affricates for the fortis ones, fricatives for the lenis ones. The Pre-Basque distribution is still strongly represented in the modern language. Initially, only fricatives are usual: *su* 'fire', *zu* 'you', *sortu* 'be born', *zahar* 'old', *sai* 'vulture', *zaio* (an auxiliary verb-form). Some northern varieties, however, have the unique item *tzar* 'bad'; this is thought to be a specialized and anomalous development of *zahar* 'old', resulting from the reinterpretation of a postposed form as a free form (see section 3.19). Northern varieties also have a few 'expressive' items in *tz-*, such as L *tzurruntzuntzun* '(travelling) in an old cart', Z *tzüsto* 'rotten wood', LN *tzut* 'methodical, orderly', Z *tzipi-tzapa* '(walking) in small steps' and a few others in this vein. Moreover, both the western dialects and certain eastern varieties have almost completely replaced initial *x* by *tx*, so that *xirula* 'Basque flute' and *ximista* 'lightning' appear as *txirula* and *tximista* in these varieties, and similarly for other words. Word-finally, affricates are still the norm: *hotz* 'cold', *hots* 'shout', *beltz* 'black', eastern *bortz* 'five', *mahats* 'grape(s)'. Here, however, a number of exceptions have been introduced. Verb-stems ending in a sibilant may show a fricative in the radical: hence *ikusi* 'see' has radical *ikus*. The very common instrumental case-suffix is invariably -*z*, never *-*tz*. A few imitative items end in fricatives, such as *piz* ~ *pix* 'piss' in some varieties. R, uniquely, has final *z* in a few ancient lexical items, such as *korpiz* 'body' (common *gorputz*). And recent loan words generally preserve final fricatives: hence *arroz* 'rice' (a loan from Spanish) now forms a minimal pair with native *arrotz* 'foreigner'.

In loans from Latin and early Romance, Latin s is almost invariably represented by Basque *z*: *ezpata* 'sword' < SPATHA, eastern *zamari* 'horse' < SAG-MARIU 'pack-horse', *zela* 'saddle' < SELLA, *ziape* 'mustard' < SENAPE, *bazkatu* 'feed' < PASCERE, *zigilu* ~ *zigulu* 'seal' < SIGILLU, *zoru* 'soil' < SOLU, *zabau* ~ *zamau* 'tablecloth' < SABANU, *azeri* 'fox' < ASENARIU (a personal name), *meza* '(Catholic) mass' < MISSA, *gauza* 'thing' < CAUSA, *ozte* 'host, troop' < HOSTE, *iztupa* 'hemp, oakum' < STUPPA, *gerezi* 'cherry' < CERESEA, and very many others. After a nasal or a liquid, the outcome of Latin s is *tz*: *antzara* 'goose' < ANSERE. (The eastern dialects, however, which retain the ancient contrast between fricatives and affricates after a nasal, have *anzera*.) We might have expected the Latin geminate -ss- to yield Basque -*tz*-, but there are no certain cases of this; one possible example is G *pitzatu* 'crack' (v.), which may derive from an unattested *FISSARE, but the etymology is not certain. In final position, we normally find -*tz*, as in *bortitz* 'strong, violent' < FORTIS and *gorputz* 'body' < CORPUS, but note the exceptional *apaez* (etc.) 'priest' < ABBAS and *maiz* 'often' < MAGIS 'more'. Only in a handful of seemingly ancient loans do we find Basque *s* for Latin s: *soka* 'rope' < SOCA, western *siku* 'dry' (eastern *ziku*) < SICCU, *gisu* ~ *kisu* 'plaster' < GYPSU, and a very few others. In an important article, Michelena (1965) concludes from this evidence that Latin s must therefore have been laminal, like English and French *s*, and not apical, like the *s* of the modern Iberian Peninsula. This is the single respect in which the evidence from Basque sheds otherwise una-vailable light on the pronunciation of Latin.

Our earliest written records of Basque, however, show Spanish *s* being borrowed as Basque *s*, while Basque *z* is reserved for the sibilant written *z* in Spanish; the Spanish consonant has been an interdental fricative since about the sixteenth century, at least in the north, but was earlier something differ-ent. It is difficult to tell just when Romance *s* acquired its apical pronuncia-tion, but it was probably earlier rather than later, at least in the north, and the apical was certainly present by the time of the Arab occupation of Spain. Note for example eastern Basque *deus* ~ *jeus* 'anything', from a Romance development of GENUS 'kind'; this word was clearly borrowed after the palatalization of velars before front vowels had occurred in Romance, but before the Basque loss of intervocalic *n*. Note also the interesting case of *soro* ~ *solo* 'field, meadow', borrowed from a Romance development of SOLU (cf. Castilian *suelo* 'ground'); this is the same Latin word that was earlier borrowed directly as *zoru* 'soil'.

Recall from Chapter 2 that Basque has sibilant harmony: a word may contain only laminal sibilants or only apical ones: *zezen* 'bull', *izotz* 'frost', *itsaso* 'sea', *sasi* 'bramble'. This harmony has continued to apply to com-pounds and loan words down to fairly recent times: the compound of *zin* 'truth, oath' with *-etsi* 'consider' is attested as *zinetsi*, but today the form *sinetsi* ~ *sinitsi* is universal. The Spanish word *francés* 'French' was bor-rowed as *fran(t)zes*, but since the eighteenth century the usual form has been *fran(t)ses*.

In Bizkaian, we find textual evidence for confusion between *z* and *s* beginning to appear in the early seventeenth century; today this contrast has been totally lost (in favour of the apical) throughout Bizkaian and in much of Gipuzkoan. The spread of the merger across Gipuzkoan appears to involve leaps from town to town across intervening countryside; in Azpeitia, for example, older speakers born in the town lack the contrast, while those born in the surrounding farmhouses retain it (Joxe Mari Ibarguren, p.c.). The *tz*/*ts* contrast is lost (in favour of the laminal) in the same region.

There is a detectable tendency for *z* to develop into *s* before a stop conso-nant, especially a coronal. Many of the Araba toponyms recorded in 1025 with *z* have *s* today: *Hazteguieta* (*Astegieta*), *Bahaheztu* (*Maestu*), *Eztarrona* (*Estarrona*) and so on. This is probably the reason for the regional variation observed in a few words like *ezne* ~ *esne* 'milk'. The word *adiskide* 'friend' may be another example, if Lafon's celebrated etymology is correct: he pro-poses **adinez-kide* (*adin* 'age', -(e)z Instr, *-kide* 'fellow').

Very rarely and sporadically, an initial sibilant is lost by dissimilation, as in *Anso* 'Sancho' (< *Sanso*) and the toponym *Estabe* in Araba, Spanish *Cestafe*, recorded in 871 as *Zeztave*. The common imperative verb-forms *zatoz* and *zatozte*, both 'come!', with initial *z*- marking second person, appear in G as *atoz* and *atozte*.

Such dissimilation occasionally occurs internally. B has a word *gortaits* 'manure', apparently from *gorta* 'courtyard' and *sits* 'dung', parallel to *perusits* 'guano' (*Peru* 'Peru'). Common *isats* 'broom' (both senses) has an eastern variant *jats* (< *iats*).

Very occasionally an epenthetic sibilant is inserted before a plosive, as in B *plauta* ~ *plausta* 'popgun' (< FLAUTA) and B *mutur* ~ *mustur* 'snout'.

Z, uniquely, has acquired contrasting voiced sibilants partnering *z s x*. Its /ʒ/ is the regular Z development of |j|. Otherwise, *z* and *s* acquired voiced allophones in voiced environments, and then the variety borrowed some Romance words with initial voiced sibilants, thus introducing a voicing contrast whose functional load is close to nil.

In sum, Pre-Basque sibilants were distributed as shown in Table 3.3.

Table 3.3 The Pre-Basque sibilants

	-z-			-s-	
z-		-tz	s-		-ts
	-tz-			-ts-	

3.5 NASALS

Pre-Basque had the fortis and lenis nasals **N** and **n**; these contrasted only intervocalically. Initially, only **n** appeared, and finally only **N** (see below). At some time before the appearance of our first substantial texts, intervocalic **n** was categorically lost from all varieties (apart from two special cases, discussed below). The evidence from eleventh-century toponyms suggests that this loss must have occurred before AD 1000. The fortis **N**, no longer having a lenis counterpart, was then reduced to **n**. These processes are well illustrated by the Latin word ANNONA 'provisions', which was borrowed as *aNona, but which appears in modern Basque as *anoa*.

In native words, intervocalic *n* generally continues Pre-Basque **N**: *anaia* (and variants) 'brother (of a man)' < *aNa-, *ainara* 'swallow' (bird) < *aiNala, *ene* 'my' < *eNe, *arrano* 'eagle' < *aRaNo. This fortis (or geminate) nasal is directly represented in medieval documents in a few instances, notably in the name *Annaya* (*anaia* 'brother').

A number of words, both native and borrowed, now exhibit stem alternations resulting from the fact that an original **n** was lost intervocalically but retained elsewhere. Thus, for example, *ardano* 'wine' appears as *ardao* ~ *ardo* (and other variants) today, but its combining form is *ardan-*, as in *ardandu* 'ferment' (*-tu* verb-forming suffix) and *ardantza* 'vineyard' (*-tza* noun-forming suffix), while Latin CATENA 'chain' appears as *katea* today but as *katen-* in word-formation, as in *katenbegi* 'link of a chain' (*begi* 'eye'). This shows clearly that the loss of final vowels in the first elements of compounds and derivatives (see section 3.19) predates the loss of intervocalic **n**.

In some cases in which intervocalic *n* was preceded by *i*, or by an *e* which was raised to *i*, the nasal underwent the usual palatalization to *ñ* (see section 3.8), and hence remained when *n* was lost: thus, for example, *magia* 'pod' (< VAGINA 'sheath') has a regional variant *magiña*, and *katea* 'chain' (< CATENA) has a variant *katiña*.

In a very few cases in which intervocalic *n* was preceded by *u*, the *n* developed into *m* by labial assimilation: thus, for example, the widespread *kuma* 'cradle' (< CUNA). The same occurs in the native word for 'elm', which is *zumar* in the west but *zu(h)ar ~ zugar* in the east, from **zunar*. The word *artizkuna* 'place for milking sheep', which contains the common suffix *-(g)une*, appears as *artizkuma* in G. The town in Bizkaia called *Luno* in Spanish is popularly *Lumo* in Basque.

The loss of intervocalic **n** left behind nasalization of the adjacent vowels. That nasalization in most (not all) cases remains today in the eastern dialects Z and (more regularly) R, which therefore still have a full set of distinctive nasal vowels. (R shows the peculiarity that it normally retains the nasal vowels only in nouns and verbal nouns, but not in adjectives or other verb-forms.) In B, we have the explicit testimony of two sixteenth-century writers (Garibay and Madariaga) that nasalized vowels were still present in that dialect, even though they were not overtly represented in the earliest Bizkaian texts. At some later time, probably not much later, nasalization was simply lost in B. In all the remaining dialects, nasalization was apparently lost too early to be recorded at all. Thus, for example, 'prudent' is *zu(h)ur* in most dialects but *zũhũr* (with front rounded vowels) in Z (< **zunur*), and 'slender, thin' is *me(h)e* in most dialects but *mẽhẽ* in Z (< **mene* < **bene*). A particularly good example is **zene* 'small, insignificant'. This is *zẽhẽ* in Z, *zehe* in L LN, and *ze* elsewhere; its palatalized form **xene* yields Z *xẽhẽ*, R *xẽ*, L LN *xehe*, elsewhere *(t)xe*. Sporadically, but very frequently, however, something different happened: nasalization of a vowel or diphthong was reinterpreted as representing a following *n*. Hence, for example, **zani* 'watchful, hopeful, expectant' yielded *zãĩ*, which remains today in the east, while the other varieties variously show *zai* by denasalization or *zain* by reinterpretation. This sort of variation is very common: *arrain ~ arrai* 'fish' (< **arrani*), *sehi ~ sein ~ sẽĩ* 'boy, servant' (< **seni*), *garau ~ garaun* 'grain' (< GRANU), *ihitz ~ ihintz ~ intz* 'dew' (< **initz* or possibly **inintz*).

Even R occasionally loses the nasalization. Thus Z *ãhãbe* 'bilberry' (< **anabe*) appears as *abi* in R; common (and Z) *mahats* 'grapes' (< **banats*) is *mats* in R. Some R words reported with nasal vowels by Bonaparte and Azkue had lost the nasalization by the 1950s. In a couple of words, R shows metathesis of the nasalization: *ãre* 'sand' < **arẽ* < ARENA; *gãzta* 'cheese' < **gaztã* < **gaztane*.

The twelfth-century pilgrim Picaud appears to record a nasal vowel when he writes *ardum* for 'wine': this must represent *ardũ*, a form attested today in the east.

A handful of words show an unexpected nasal vowel in R: *õla* 'hut' (Z *olha*), *õre* 'dough' (Z *orhe*), *ũr* 'hazelnut' (Z *hür*), *ũrzo* 'pigeon' (Z *urzo*). Some of these may result from contamination by near-homophones in which nasalization is normal; others are simply mysterious.

Occasionally the resolution of nasal vowels was affected by other regular or irregular processes. The word **ardano* 'wine', for example, developed to **ardãõ*. This merely becomes *ardao* in modern B, but all other dialects have reduced the unusual sequence *ao* to *o*, giving *ardo* in the central dialects. In Z, the same reduction occurred, followed by the usual raising of *o* to *u* in final syllables (see section 3.9), but the nasalization was not lost, and the Z form is *ardũ* (with final stress). In L and LN, the nasalization was exceptionally transferred to the preceding consonant, yielding *arno*. The Latin word BENEDICERE 'bless' was borrowed as **benedikatu*, which apparently underwent an early metathesis to **bedenikatu*. This in turn developed to **bedeĩkatu*, which by reinterpretation became modern *bedeinkatu* (this reinterpretation clearly happened too late for the newly introduced *n* to cause voicing of the following plosive; see section 3.3).

Very often the vowels flanking the lost nasal were protected from hiatus by the presence of the aspiration, or possibly sometimes by the insertion of an aspiration. Thus **bini* 'tongue' became first **mini* by the nasal assimilation discussed above and then **mĩĩ*. This gives *mĩhĩ* today in Z and *mihi* in the other northern dialects. Loss of the aspiration elsewhere has variously led to *mii* or (by vowel coalescence) *mi* or (most frequently, by reinterpretation) *min*. Not infrequently the dialects which have lost the aspiration have broken up the hiatus by inserting *g*, the consonant favoured for this purpose: hence the word for 'fleeing, flight' is *ies* ~ *ihes* elsewhere but *iges* in the west (< **ines*, with an unusual final fricative). Very occasionally, in the vicinity of the rounded vowel *u*, the consonant inserted is *b* rather than *g*, and even less frequently we find *d* or *r* inserted instead.

Latin N and NN were borrowed as **n** and **N**, respectively, with the same consequences as in native words: *ahate* ~ *ate* 'duck' (Z *ãhãte*, B *agate*) < ANATE, *azeri* ~ *azari* 'fox' (medieval *Azeari*, a surname) < ASENARIU, *balea* 'whale' < BALLAENA, *bilau(n)* 'peasant' < VILLANU, old G, Sout *zabau* 'tablecloth' < SABANU, *ohore* ~ *oore* ~ *ore* 'honour' (Z *õhõre*) < HONORE, *li(h)o* 'flax' < LINU, *anoa* 'provisions' < ANNONA, *mo(e)ta* 'kind, sort' < MONETA 'coin'.

Very occasionally an early dissimilation leads to a different result, as in *arima* 'soul' < ANIMA.

Basque *ba(h)e* 'sieve' cannot derive directly from Latin VANNU; it must reflect a Romance development **vane* (note French and Occitan *van*).

Initial **n** and final **N** both yield *n* in modern Basque: *neska* 'girl', *nabar* 'multicoloured; grey', *ni* 'I', *neke* 'fatigue' (< NECE 'death'), *nota* 'stain'

(< NOTA 'mark'), *min* 'pain' (< **bin*), *lan* 'work', *astun* 'heavy', *gizon* 'man', *on* 'good'. The neutralized nasal which preceded a consonant also comes down as *n*: *mendi* 'mountain', *handi* 'big', *antzare* (and variants) 'goose' (< ANSERE), *landa* 'heath' (< Rom), *ongi* 'well' (adv.) (< **onki*).

Medieval toponyms often show ⟨*-nn-*⟩ for final **N** when the article follows: *Hurigurenna* (Araba 1025; the second element is modern *guren* 'edge'), *Urrenguenna* (Bizkaia 1070; same second element). The same graphy occurs elsewhere, for example in the suffix *-no*: toponyms *Egganno* (Bizkaia 1082; modern *Echano*) and *Helcanno* (Gipuzkoa 1025; modern *Elkano*); personal names *Enneco* (modern *Eneko*), *Amunna* (*amona* 'grandmother'), *Annaya* (*anaia* 'brother'). This suggests that original **N** was still pronounced long in the eleventh century, and did not merge with **n** until later. Aquitanian stems ending in a nasal show the same phenomenon: *Belexenn-is*, *Bihoscinn-is*, *Sembetenn-is*, *Seniponn-is*, (*Herculi*) *Ilunn-o* (*Andose*), all with Latin genitive *-is* or dative *-o*. Vowel-final stems do not show this: *Andere*, dative *Andereni*, and so on.

The Latin cluster MN was resolved in two different ways. On the one hand, we have *damu* 'regret' < DAMNU, showing simplification of the cluster. On the other, we have *done* 'saint' < **DOMNE* < DOMINE and B *autono* 'September' < AUTUMNU; these last two may represent loans from a stage in which Latin MN had already become Romance **nn*.

On occasion *n* has been lost before a cluster or an affricate: *aintzin* 'front' has a common variant *aitzin*, and old B G *anztu* 'forget' is *aztu* today (cf. northern *ahantzi*). In some such cases it may be difficult to determine if the *n* is conservative or epenthetic: *ikatz* ~ *inkatz* 'charcoal', *itze* ~ *untze* (and also *iltze*, *ultze*) 'nail'.

Very occasionally, a final *n* is lost. Such words as *orain* 'now', *egun* 'today' and *ondoren* 'consequence' occur locally as *orai*, *egu*, *ondore*. The *-n* which marks past tense is systematically lost in certain eastern varieties, and old B sometimes loses the *-n* which marks the hortative use of the subjunctive. The loss of *-n* before the relational suffix *-ko* is discussed in Chapter 4.

In sum, Pre-Basque nasals were distributed as shown in Table 3.4.

Table 3.4 The Pre-Basque nasals

	-n-	
n-		-N
	-N-	

3.6 LATERALS

Pre-Basque had fortis and lenis laterals **L** and **l**, which contrasted only intervocalically; initially, only **l** occurred, and finally, only **L**. At some stage intervocalic l was converted to the tap *r*, merging with the existing **r**. This change was categorical in most dialects, but sometimes fails to occur in Z, which has, for example, *solo* 'field', *olio* 'oil' and *zelü* 'sky' for common *soro* (< SOLU), *orio* (< OLEU), *zeru* (< CAELU). The disappearance of intervocalic l left **L** without a lenis counterpart, and **L** was then reduced to *l*. Consequently, intervocalic *l* in native words must in most cases continue Pre-Basque **L**: *alu* 'vulva, vagina' < *aLu*, *alor* 'cultivated field' < *aLor*, *ola* 'forge, foundry; hut, cabin' < *oLa*, *ilun* 'dark' < *iLun*, and so on.

The fortis nature of a final lateral is indicated by the common spelling of *zabal* 'wide' as *zaball* or *zavall* in medieval toponyms: *Monnio Zaballa* (1062), *Zaballa* (monastery, 1087), *super S. Johannem de Zavalla* (945), *Harizavalleta* and *Harrizavallaga* (1025), *Lacizaballa* (1067). The same occurs with other words, such as with *apal* 'humble': *Domna Apalla* (1079). Particularly striking is the stream name *Larçabaig* in Béarn, which can only continue the common Basque toponym **Larzabal* (*larre* 'pasture'), with the usual Gascon treatment of final geminate -*ll*.

Latin intervocalic -L- and -LL- were borrowed as Pre-Basque l and **L**, respectively, and develop in the same way: *begiratu* 'watch, look at' < VIGILIARE (with a folk etymology from *begi* 'eye'), *borondate* 'will' < VOLUNTATE, (*h*)*aizkora* 'axe' < ASCIOLA, *gura* 'desire' < GULA, *gereta* 'rustic gate, enclosure' < Pre-Basque **geleta* < **CLETA*; *balea* 'whale' < BALLAENA, *makila* 'stick' < BACILLA, plural of BACILLUM, *bilau*(*n*) 'peasant' < VILLANU, *gaztelu* 'castle' < CASTELLU, *angelu* 'soil' < ANGELLU, *zela* 'saddle' < SELLA.

Initial l and final **L** have both come down into modern Basque as *l*: *lan* 'work', *lau*(*r*) 'four', *lasai* 'calm', *laket* 'be pleasing' (< PLACET), *lapitz* 'slate' (< LAPIS 'stone'), *lore* 'flower' (< FLORE), *lege* 'law' (< LEGE), *argal* 'slender', *ohol* 'plank' (< **onol*), *epel* 'lukewarm', *mutil* 'boy' (< PUTILLU), *apal* 'humble' (< AD VALLE). The neutralized lateral which occurred before a consonant also comes down as *l*: *alde* 'side' (< *alte*, preserved in the east), *elge* 'cultivated field', *albo* 'side', *giltza* 'key'.

The development of intervocalic l to *r* again produced some striking alternations: *euskara* 'Basque language', combining form *euskal-*, as in *euskaldun* 'Basque-speaker' and *Euskal Herria* 'Basque Country'; *gari* 'wheat', combining form *gal-*, as in *galgorri* 'variety of wheat' and *galbae* 'sieve for wheat'. With loans from Latin, such as *haizkora* 'axe' (< ASCIOLA), combining form *haizkol-*, it is easy to be sure of an original lateral. With native words, this is far more difficult, because there has been rule inversion; for example, Latin SAGMARIU 'pack-horse' is the source of eastern *zamari* 'horse', whose combining form is *zamal-*, as in *zamaldun* 'horseman'. (Such rule inversion must be distinguished from cases of dissimilation like that found in *txolarre* 'sparrow', from *txori* 'bird' plus *arre* 'grey'.) Hence, even when intervocalic *r* alternates with *l*, we cannot be sure that *l* was the original segment without independent testimony. Only occasionally is this available, as with *hiri* 'town', which everyone is happy to identify with the element *Ili-* found in so many town names in the Roman period.

With toponyms, we are sometimes more fortunate: *Gebara* (Ara) is Ptolemy's *Gébala*; *Padura* (Ara) is *Padule* in 1025; *Zuberoa* (the province) is apparently the medieval *Subola*; *Erronkari* (the valley) is *Roncali* in 1085; *Eskaroz* (Nav) is documented in the medieval period as *Escaloce* and *Escaloz(e)*.

In sum, Pre-Basque laterals were distributed as shown in Table 3.5.

Table 3.5 The Pre-Basque laterals

	-l-	
l-		-L
	-L-	

3.7 RHOTICS

In all likelihood, Pre-Basque **R** and **r** were a trill and a tap, respectively, and they probably contrasted only between vowels. Elsewhere the contrast was neutralized (though old Z exhibited a contrast between the two rhotics before another consonant). In modern varieties, the result of the neutralization is usually a trill, at least in careful speech, even in Romance loans like *brontze* 'bronze' and *krabelin* 'carnation', but there is evidence, as we shall see, that this may not always have been so.

The ancient contrast survives today, in the form of trilled *rr* and tapped *r*, in all Spanish Basque varieties. Minimal pairs are abundant: *ere* 'also' and *erre* 'burn', *gori* 'fiery' and *gorri* 'red' (these words are not related), *zori* 'luck' and *zorri* 'louse', *gora* 'up' and *gorra* 'deaf' (definite form), *hura* 'that one' and *hurra* 'hazelnut' (definite form) (⟨h⟩ = zero in these varieties).

In word-final position, a rhotic is almost always a trill in modern Basque, but there is a handful of words in which a final rhotic surfaces as a tap when a vowel-initial suffix is added: *zer* 'what?', *nor* 'who?', *ur* 'water', *zur* 'wood', *or* 'dog', the stem *ber-* 'self, same', the northern forms *haur* 'this', *hirur* 'three' and *laur* 'four' (which have lost their final rhotic south of the Pyrenees), and a handful of loan words, such as *plazer* 'pleasure', *tirader* 'drawer' and *erretor* 'parish priest'. Thus, the more typical *hur* 'hazelnut' has the definite form *hurra*, but *ur* 'water' has *ura*.

In Z, the tapped *r* has been almost entirely lost in ordinary speech, though it is sporadically retained by at least some speakers. Hence spoken Z has *büü* 'head' (common *buru*), *dia* 'they are' (common *dira*), *hie* 'your' (familiar) (common *hire*) and so on. The sole exception is the definite form of 'water', which is *ura* elsewhere but *hurra* in Z. The *r* is none the less usually written in Z. Note that the aspiration in Z forms like *erho* 'kill' does not prevent this loss: the modern form is *eho*.

In L and LN, something interesting has been happening. First, the former trill has become everywhere a voiced uvular fricative, somewhat resembling French /r/ but noticeably scrapier. Hence words like *erre* 'burn' and *hurra* 'the hazelnut' are invariably pronounced with a uvular, as are words like *zahar* 'old' and *zakur* 'dog', with their neutralized final rhotics. This uvular realization is spreading to the tapped *r*, and hence words like *hura* 'that one' and *hari* 'thread' are now also frequently heard with uvulars, though not invariably so. Though little research has been done on this, we appear to have a clear case here of lexical diffusion, with the uvular spreading to ever more words and with ever greater frequency. It is notable, for example, that *hura* 'that one' is far more frequently pronounced with a uvular than *ura* 'the water', and the purely anecdotal evidence at my disposal strongly suggests that the frequency of the uvular realization is increasing steadily (Yvan Labéguerie, p.c.). If this change goes to completion, then the contrast between the two rhotics will be lost, but this has not happened yet, in spite of some statements to the contrary in the literature (though it may have happened for some speakers).

The reason it is not certain that the result of the neutralization has always been a trill is the evidence from word-formation. For example, *bihar* 'tomorrow' is of course pronounced with a trill today, and this trill is retained in formations like *biharretik biharrera* 'from tomorrow to tomorrow' (i.e., 'forever', a phrase found in the seventeenth-century writer Axular). However, this word forms a seemingly ancient derivative *biharamun* ~ *biharamon* 'the next day' (probably *bihar* + *egun* 'day'), in which the rhotic shows up as a tap, suggesting that the neutralized rhotic was anciently a tap, or perhaps even that the rhotic contrast was anciently maintained in word-final position (though such a conclusion would be entirely at odds with all other fortis–lenis contrasts).

The presence of rhotics in consecutive syllables is tolerated if both are taps: *erori* 'fall', *hirurak* 'all three', B *arerio* 'enemy'. Trill–trill and trill–tap sequences do not appear to occur within single morphemes. But the case of tap–trill sequences is interesting: there is clear evidence that the tap in this case has generally been dissimilated, most often to /l/. The word for 'ear' is *belarri* in the west, *beharri* or *begarri* elsewhere, and Michelena reconstructs **berarri*. Likewise, 'snow' is commonly *elur* but appears as *edur* or *erur* in places, chiefly in B, and Michelena reconstructs **erur*. And 'breast, chest' is usually *bular*, but R has *burar* or *budar*, suggesting **burar*. Another case is 'grass', commonly *belar*, but *berar* or *bedar* in B, pointing to **berar*, and still another is *ilar* 'pea', B *idar*, suggesting **irar*. Particularly interesting is 'silver'. This is commonly *zilar* or *zillar*, but *zildar* is attested, suggesting **ziLar*. But both *zidar* and *zirar* are found in the east and in B, pointing instead to **zirar*.

Very occasionally a rhotic is lost by dissimilation, as in *adore* 'courage' < ARDORE.

R, uniquely, has acquired word-initial *r* in loans from Romance, such as *rezibi* 'receive', *reina* 'queen', *repat(t)an* 'shepherd boy'. But most such words show a prothetic vowel in R, as elsewhere.

In sum, Pre-Basque rhotics were distributed as shown in Table 3.6.

Table 3.6 The Pre-Basque rhotics

-r-	
	-R
-R-	

3.8 PALATALIZATION

The six segments *tt dd x tx ll ñ* occupy a place apart in the Basque phonological system, even though their distinctive status is no longer quite so sharply marked as it was some centuries ago. In all likelihood, these 'palatal' segments (as I shall call them) were already present in Pre-Basque, but we cannot be sure of that, since they never appeared in ordinary lexical items, except possibly as allophones of other coronal segments in predictable circumstances. They were certainly present in the language by the medieval period, and the Basque personal names recorded as early as the fifteenth century demonstrate both their presence and their distinctive role as clearly as one could hope for (Valle Lersundi 1933–1934). The byname *Gutia*, probably 'the Small', is occasionally written as *Guchia* as early as the thirteenth century; this clearly represents either *tx* or *tt*.

Broadly speaking, the palatal segments arise in two very different circumstances:

1 'Automatic' or 'phonological' palatalization occurs when an ordinary coronal consonant is preceded by the high front vowel *i*.
2 'Expressive' palatalization occurs when an ordinary segment is deliberately replaced by a palatal consonant, or, vastly less frequently, when a palatal consonant is added to the beginning of a vowel-initial word.

These two processes have nothing at all in common except the introduction of palatal segments. I begin with automatic palatalization.

It seems clear that, at some ancient stage of the language, some (but not all) ordinary coronal consonants underwent simple palatalization when preceded by the vowel *i* (possibly with additional conditions; see below). The process was automatic, and the resulting palatal segments were effectively mere allophones of the ordinary coronals. This process produced the following results: $t \rightarrow tt$, $z \rightarrow x$, $s \rightarrow x$, $tz \rightarrow tx$, $ts \rightarrow tx$, $l \rightarrow ll$, $n \rightarrow ñ$.

Note that the other coronal consonants, *d*, *r* and *rr*, apparently did *not* undergo automatic palatalization, thus posing an interesting little phono-

Table 3.7 Automatic palatalization

	Central	B, G, Z
	ditu (Aux verb-form)	B G *dittu*
	gizon 'man'	B (regional) *gixon*
	isil 'silent'	B G *ixil*
	itsaso 'sea'	B G *itxaso*
	(h)ila 'dead'	B G *illa*
	baino 'than'	B G *baiño* ~ *baño*
	oin 'foot'	B G *oin,* Z *huiñ*
	oina 'the foot'	B G *oiña* ~ *oña,* Z *huiña*
But:	*iduri* 'seem'	B G *iduri,* Z *üdürü*
	dira 'they are'	B G *dira,* Z *di(r)a*
	irrintzi 'mountain cry'	B G Z *irrintzi*

logical problem. The results of this process are still plainly evident today in B and G in the west and in Z in the east; the central dialects for the most part do not exhibit such palatalization, for reasons which I shall discuss below. Table 3.7 shows some examples; the first column gives the usual forms in the central dialects, which largely correspond to the written forms in the standard orthography. As some of these examples show, the *i* which induces the palatalization is often absorbed into the following palatal consonant if it is preceded by a vowel. In modern B and G, palatalization usually occurs only if the consonant in question is also followed by another vowel; in Z, it often occurs even in the absence of such a following vowel. Generally speaking, a coronal does not undergo palatalization if it is followed by another consonant:

izter 'thigh'   B G *izter* ~ *iztar*
gaizki 'badly'   G *gaizki*
ispilu 'mirror'   B G *ispillu*

Both B and G, however, exhibit a striking extension of this type of palatalization:

e(g)in da 'it has been done'   B G *eiñ dda*
indaba 'string bean'   B G *iñddaba*
(h)il da 'he has died'   B G *illa*

That is, if a preceding *n* or *l* undergoes automatic palatalization, then *d* also becomes palatalized, even though *d* is never palatalized directly by a preceding *i*; moreover, the sequence *ll dd* merges to *ll*.

Automatic palatalization is still productive today in B and G, and apparently also in some eastern varieties, but there are two or three clearly ancient words which sometimes or always fail to undergo it, notably *aita* 'father' and *maite* 'beloved'. It seems very odd having lexical exceptions to a productive process, especially when those exceptions are not recent loans.

The central dialects today lack such automatic palatalization (as does R), but there are grounds for believing that these varieties formerly had it as well. Such Romance loans as *ollo* 'hen' (< Sp *pollo* or something related), *muño* 'hill' (from a Romance development of **bunno*) and *bañu* 'bath' (< Sp *baño*) appear in the central dialects as *oilo, muino* and *bainu ~ mainu* (which in fact represent the modern standard orthography). Since it is difficult to avoid the conclusion that such words were borrowed with Romance palatal consonants, most specialists believe that the central dialects must have undergone depalatalization, with the earlier palatal segment being unpacked into a sequence of *i* plus a coronal consonant, and the same analysis is applied to indigenous words like central *baino*, peripheral *baño*, 'but'.

Such unpacking is occasionally attested directly. I have heard the recent Spanish loan *pañuelo* 'handkerchief' pronounced in B as *painuelo*. Some vasconists think that the universal *aita* 'father', which often fails to undergo automatic palatalization, may result from earlier **atta*, with a palatal plosive.

Expressive palatalization involves the replacement of another consonant by a palatal or the addition of a palatal to the front of a vowel-initial word. The consonant so replaced is most often a coronal, but not invariably so. Examples: *zezen* 'bull', expressive form *xexen*; *zakur* 'dog' and *(t)xakur*; *zoko* 'corner' and *(t)xoko*; *gozo* 'sweet, delicious' and *goxo*; *hezur* 'bone' and *hexur*; *labur* 'short' and *llabur ~ txabur*; *bero* 'hot' and *bello*; *Peru* 'Peter' and *Pello* (and *Txeru*); *nabar* 'many-coloured' and *ñabar*; *nabo* 'turnip' and *ñabo*; *tapa* 'step' and *ttapa*; *zuri* 'white' and *(t)xuri*; *guti* 'not much' and *gutti ~ gutxi*; *tipi ~ tiki* 'small' and *ttipi ~ txiki*; *tente* 'erect' and *ttentte*; *tu* 'saliva' and *ttu ~ txu*; *popa* 'poop (of a boat)' and *(t)xopa*; *maingu* 'lame' and Z *txainkü*; *inurri* 'ant' and *txinurri*; *onil* 'funnel' and *txonil*; *ingude* 'anvil' and *txingure ~ xinguri*; *Domiku* 'Dominic' and *Txomin*; *Martin* 'Martin' and *Txartin ~ Matxin*; *Madalen* 'Madeleine' and *Maddalen ~ Matxalen*; *Santiago* 'James' and *Xanti*; and many, many others. (See Chapter 5 for a discussion of this process in personal names.)

It seems clear that the original function of this process was to create a diminutive or affectionate form, and this function still survives in many pairs today. In a number of instances, however, the palatalized version has become the unmarked form, and the original form either has been lost or survives as either an augmentative or a pejorative variant. For example, *zakur* remains as the unmarked word for 'dog' in places, with *(t)xakur* meaning 'little dog' (but never 'puppy'); elsewhere, though, *(t)xakur* is the unmarked form, and *zakur* means only 'big dog' or is absent altogether. The word for 'calf' is everywhere *(t)xahal*, and we can't even tell what the original sibilant was. An unusually striking case of differentiation involves the word *zori*, which formerly meant 'omen'. The original form survives today as *zori* 'luck' (as in the all-purpose greeting *Zorionak!* 'Best wishes!', 'Merry

Christmas!' and so on), while its diminutive (*t*)*xori* is now the universal word for 'bird' (from the former practice of seeing omens in the flight of birds). In words with intrinsically diminutive meanings, the palatalized form has often displaced the original form more or less entirely, so that *ttipi* ~ *txiki* 'small', *gutti* ~ *gutxi* 'not much' and *xehe* ~ *txe* 'small' have all but driven *tipi* ~ *tiki*, *guti* and *zehe* ~ *ze* out of the language, except in formal styles. The same has happened with *etxe* 'house', whose earlier form *etze* or *etse* (both are attested) survives in only a few localities. It is reported that, in the Basque spoken in the United States, the force of palatalization has been lost altogether, and so, for example, 'corner' is *zoko* or *xoko* indifferently.

Today such expressive palatalization seems to be no longer productive, or at best only weakly productive. The productive manner of forming diminutives is by the addition of a diminutive suffix like *-txo* ~ *-txu*, *-tto*, *-xka* or *-ño*: *ama* 'mother', *amatxo* 'mummy, mommy'; *Jon* 'John', *Jontxu* 'Johnny'; *liburu* 'book', *liburuxka* 'booklet'; *iturri* 'spring', *iturriño* 'small spring'. Such use of diminutive suffixes is itself old in Basque, and the modern ones clearly derive from the palatalization of earlier diminutive suffixes like *-ko*, *-to*, *-so* and *-no*, all attested in the medieval period and some of them apparently attested in Aquitanian.

In the western and eastern dialects, the segment *tx* in particular is so frequent in non-expressive formations that its expressive function is now minimal.

Naturally, loan words are sometimes borrowed with palatal consonants present in the donor language: southern *Txina* 'China' (< Sp *China*), northern *Otrixia* 'Austria' (< Fr *Autriche*), southern *muñeka* 'doll, dummy' (spelled *muineka* in the standard orthography) (< Sp *muñeca*) and so on. Such loans reinforce the new status of the palatal consonants among the ordinary phonemes of the language.

3.9 VOWELS

Pre-Basque had just the five vowels **i e a o u**. So far as we can judge, it probably also had the modern set of diphthongs, **ai ei oi ui au eu**. These diphthongs were not distinguished from sequences of the corresponding vowels, but the point is that they counted as single syllables for such processes as aspiration assignment (see section 3.11), whereas other vowel sequences counted as two syllables.

Any vowel or diphthong could occur in any position in a word, as is still the case today. However, a monomorphemic word normally contained a maximum of one diphthong. At least some modern instances of diphthongs derive from the loss of intervocalic consonants. For example, *hodei* 'cloud' has final stress in Z and must therefore derive from a trisyllable **odeCe* or **odeCi*, and the same is true of *izei* ~ *izai* 'fir' and a few other words. (Word-stress in Z falls on the ancient penult.)

The Pre-Basque vowels have been astonishingly stable; indeed, for the most part they have remained unchanged for some 2,000 years, as witnessed by loans from Latin like *lege* 'law' (< LEGE), *putzu* 'well' (< PUTEU), *merkatu* 'market' (< MERCATU), *garau* 'grain' (< GRANU), *erika* 'heather' (< ERICA), B *zapatu* 'Saturday' (< SABBATU) and *ohore* 'honour' (< HONORE). Even the Aquitanian forms agree in vocalism with the modern forms, as in *NES-CATO, ANDERE* and *CISON* (modern *neskato* 'little girl', *andere* 'lady' and *gizon* 'man'). Only a few developments have disturbed the Pre-Basque vowels, almost all of them either sporadic or confined to particular varieties.

In a first syllable, *e* is usually raised to *i* if the second syllable contains a high vowel and a third syllable exists. Above all, this raising affects non-finite forms of verbs, which regularly contain the prefix **e-*. Thus: *ibili* 'go about, be active' (< *ebili* (attested)), *ikusi* 'see' (< *ekusi* (attested)), *ipini* (and variants) 'put' (< *epeini* (attested)), *ikuzi* 'wash' (< *ekuzi* (attested)). (Cf. *ekarri* 'bring', *egosi* 'cook', *edeki* 'open', *egin* 'do, make', *ekin* 'continue', *edan* 'drink', etc.) The unraised forms are more frequent in the earliest texts than they are now, and still exist today in some varieties, above all in R, suggesting that this raising was a fairly recent process. It must have been recent if, as proposed in Chapter 4, *-n* class verbs like *egin, ekin* and *edan* are derived from earlier **egini, *ekini* and **edani*.

An extremely rare process is 'vowel-doubling'. Latin VIMEN 'osier willow' and Romance *saco* 'sack' appear in the aspirating dialects as *mihimen* and *xahako* 'leather bag for wine'. There are no other certain examples of this: the oft-cited *ahaire* 'air, melody' can be explained as a compound of *aho* 'mouth' and the loan *aire* 'air'. The common cases like *zahar* 'old' appear to continue genuine ancient disyllables; the form *SA.HAR* is actually attested on the Lerga stele (see Chapter 6).

In Z, original *u* is fronted to *ü* [y] in most circumstances: *düt* 'I have it', *lagün* 'companion', *lüze* 'long', *zü* 'you', *güzi* 'all' and so on, all of which retain *u* in other varieties. This fronting is prevented by a following tapped *r* or a following fricative *s*, but not by a following trill *rr* or by a following *ts, z* or *tz*. Hence Z has *gü* 'we' but *gure* 'our' (now usually *gue*, by the recent loss of intervocalic *r*), *hür* 'hazelnut' but *hur* 'water', *güzi* 'all' and *hüts* 'empty' but *uste* 'opinion', *ikhusi* 'see' and *busti* 'moist'. The fronting is also blocked by a following cluster of *r* plus coronal plosive: hence *urde* 'pig', *urthe* 'year', but *bürkhi* 'birch', *khürlo* 'crane', *ürzo* 'pigeon', *ürpo* 'pile of dung'.

This regular pattern has been considerably disturbed by mutual assimilations among *i, ü* and *u*. So, for expected **burü*, we find *bü(r)ü* 'head'; for expected **burdiña* we find *bürdüña* 'iron'; for expected **itsü* we find *ütsü* 'blind'; and there are many other such cases.

Before another vowel, this *ü* is unrounded to *i*. Thus, *ütsü* 'blind' plus the article yields *ütsia*. In R, *u* is fronted to *i* in the same circumstances: *buru* 'head', definite form *buria*.

In Z and R, original *au* becomes *ai* except before one of *r rr s ts*. Hence common *gau* 'night' and *gauza* 'thing' are *gai*, *gaiza* in these varieties.

Assimilations involving high vowels, especially of *i* to *u*, are found sporadically, especially in B in the west and Z and (most notably) R in the east. Thus, common *ikuzi* 'wash' appears as *ukuzi* in all these varieties, while R has *urun* and *uturri* for common *irun* 'spin' and *iturri* 'spring'.

The vowel *u* is sporadically fronted to *i* in all varieties. Thus, common *umore* 'humour' appears as *imore* in some varieties of HN and LN; *kuma* 'mane' is *kima* in varieties of G; *errun* 'lay (eggs)' and *gorputz* 'body' are *errin* and *korpiz* in R; *muku* 'mucus' (< MUCCU) has a widespread variant *muki*.

In Z, original *o* is often raised to *u* in circumstances which are far from clear, but especially before *n*: Z *gizun* 'man', *hun* 'good', *huñ* 'foot', in the face of common *gizon*, *on*, *oin*. This raising does not feed the fronting of *u* and must be more recent than fronting.

In a number of words B has *u* for common *i*: B *ule* 'hair', *uri* 'town', *uger* 'swimming', *ultze* 'nail', *urten* 'go out', *uzen* 'name' and so on, in the face of common *ile*, *(h)iri*, *igeri*, *iltze*, *irten*, *izen*. The reason for this is not known, but in most cases the *u* appears to be an innovation. It is not clear whether B G *izu* 'trembling', in the face of central and eastern *izi*, represents an instance of this or whether the eastern form derives from the fronting of *u* mentioned above.

B also exhibits some peculiarities involving the vowels *a* and *e*. The final *e* of the other dialects often appears as *a* in B: *lora* 'flower' (common *lore*), *ota* 'gorse' (common *ote*), *andra* 'woman' (common *and(e)re* 'lady'). And many varieties of B have a kind of rudimentary vowel harmony, in which *a* is raised to *e* after a high vowel in the preceding syllable of a phonological word: *zaldi*[j]e 'the horse' (common *zaldia*, with the article -*a*), *egune* 'the day' (common *eguna*), *erri bet* 'a village' (common *(h)erri bat*, with the indefinite article *bat*), *etorri de* 'he/she has come' (common *etorri da*, with auxiliary *da*). Finally, a few words which elsewhere have internal *e* followed by a liquid have *a* in B: B *barri* 'new', *baltz* 'black', *garri* 'waist', in the face of common *berri*, *beltz*, *gerri*.

The Pyrenean dialects, especially Sal and R, exhibit extensive syncope of vowels, and syncope is also attested in some eastern varieties of HN, especially in the writings of Joaquín Lizarraga, a native of Elkano. Examples: Sal *aingru* 'angel' (common *aingeru*); R *bedratzu* Sal Aezk Lizarraga *bedratzi* 'nine' (common *bederatzi*); Sal *denbra* R *tenpra* 'time' (common *denbora*); R *tupla* 'onion' (common *tipula*); Lizarraga *atra* 'go out' (common *atera*); Sal R Lizarraga *abre* 'animal' (common *abere*). Forms of auxiliary verbs are affected, so that, for example, the present-tense plural forms of *izan* 'be' appear locally as *gra*, *zra*, *dra*, the second showing a unique initial cluster.

Vowels in hiatus require particular attention. When the vowels in hiatus occur in the first and second syllables of a word, various processes have applied to resolve the hiatus, and these processes are not everywhere the same. The aspirating dialects place an *h* between the vowels: *zahar* 'old', *zuhur* 'prudent', *mahats* 'grapes' (< **banats*), *ahal* 'ability', *ohore* 'honour' (< HONORE), *ihintz* 'dew' (< **ini(n)tz*), *aho* 'mouth', *behar* 'necessity', *bihar* 'tomorrow', *ziho* 'tallow' (< **zino*), *oihan* 'forest', *eihar* 'dry', *uh(a)in* 'wave' and so on. In the dialects which have lost the aspiration, things are more complex. Sometimes, particularly when the vowels are identical or both non-high, the hiatus is simply retained, or else the two vowels coalesce into one: hence *zahar* 'old' is *zaar* or *zar*; *ahal* 'ability' is *aal* or *al*; *ahate* 'duck' (< **ANATE*) is *aate* or *ate*; *ihintz* 'dew' is *intz*; *behar* 'necessity' is *bear*; *bihar* 'tomorrow' is *biar*; *aho* 'mouth' is *ao*; and so on. Frequently, however, a consonant is inserted to break up the hiatus. This consonant is most often *g*, particularly in the west, but instead we sometimes find *b* (especially next to *u* or less commonly *o*), *d* or *r*. Thus, *ohe* 'bed' is often *oge*; *bihar* 'tomorrow' is often *bigar*; *uharte* 'land between rivers' is *ugarte*; *zuhur* 'prudent' is *zugur*; *uhalde* 'riverbank, river' is *ugalde* or *ubalde*; *aho* 'mouth' is *ago* or *abo*; *zahar* 'old' is *zagar*; Spanish *bahía* 'bay' is borrowed as B *baida*; *ahate* 'duck' appears as *agate* or *arate* in some varieties of B; common *me(h)ar* 'narrow' appears as *medar* in some varieties of HN and LN; *sahats* 'willow' (probably < **sanats*) is *sagats* or *sarats* in places; and so on.

Vowels which can form recognized diphthongs usually do so: *lau* 'flat' (< PLANU), *maiz* 'often' (< MAGIS 'more'), *maizter* ~ *maister* 'tenant' (and 'master shepherd') (< MAGISTER 'master'), *deus* 'anything' (< GENUS 'kind'). The sequences *ae* and *oe* often become *ai* and *oi*, as in *haitz* 'crag' (< **anetz*), *arratoi* 'rat' (< RATONE), but note the unusual case of *moeta* ~ *mota* 'kind, sort' (< MONEDA 'coin').

The word for 'dinner' is exceptionally interesting. The most conservative form is *auhari*, preserved in LN, and, with the usual fronting of *au*, as *aihá(r)i* in Z. R has *aigari*. Sal and some western varieties have *abari*, apparently with strengthening of intervocalic *u* to *b*, and a few varieties of G have strengthened this further to *apari*. Most other varieties, however, have *afari*; here the unusual *f* is usually thought to result from a coalescence of *u* and *h* at an ancient stage, though it might simply derive from *b* in the familiar way.

Another unusual case is Latin MANICA 'sleeve'; instead of the expected **mai(n)ka*, we find *mahanka* ~ *mahanga* in the north and *mauka* in the south.

If the hiatus occurs later in a word, *h* cannot occur, of course, and the hiatus must be resolved in another way or retained. So, for example, **azenari* 'fox' (< ASENARIU) is *azeri* in most of the country today, but B has (or formerly had) all of *azegari*, *azagari*, *azeari* and *azari*. The word for 'elbow', a compound of *uko* 'forearm' and *ondo* 'bottom', appears in old B as the regular *ukaondo*, but the form *ukondo* is nearly universal today.

An important diagnostic is the treatment of the sequence **ae*, which arises in a number of circumstances in Basque morphology. Broadly speaking, this sequence is resolved to *a* in the west but to *e* in the east, as in the ergative plural affix *-aek*, which gives western *-ak* and eastern *-ek*.

When the article *-a* is suffixed to a vowel-final word, the outcome varies with region. After *i*, most dialects do nothing. In the Pyrenean dialects, the *i* is reduced to a glide, so that *zaldia* 'the horse' is [saldja]. After the *i*, B and G insert a glide [j], which often undergoes some kind of strengthening. Thus *zaldia* 'the horse' is variously [saldija], [saldiʒa] or even [saldiʃa] in these varieties, or sometimes [saldije], etc., with the raising of *a* after a high vowel. After *u*, B and G often insert a labial glide which falls together with *b* (an approximant intervocalically, recall), and so *burua* 'the head' may be *buruba* in these varieties. L and LN insert [j] in this position, and hence the local pronunciation is *buru*[j]*a*. The Pyrenean varieties have variously *bur*[jw]*a* or *bur*[j]*a*.

If the vowel is *e* or *o*, this is raised in B and in some varieties of G. Hence *lorea* 'the flower' and *astoa* 'the donkey' are realized as *loria* and *astua* (three syllables) in these varieties. L and LN do something surprising: they convert the mid vowel to a glide, and so they have *lor*[j]*a* and *ast*[w]*a*. Observe that only mid vowels become glides, and not high vowels. This pronunciation was recorded by Gavel (1920) and is still current. The Pyrenean varieties do the same, but recall that they also reduce high vowels to glides.

If the vowel is *a*, the result in most varieties is coalescence, and so *neska* 'girl' has the definite form *neska*. In Z, in which the stress-accent marks the ancient penult, these are distinguished as *néska* and *neská*, respectively. But B is very different: some varieties have the definite form *neskea*, with raising to *e*, while others have *neskia*, with raising all the way to *i*. This last form can readily be interpreted as a case of rule reordering, with the raising of *a* to *e*, formerly later than the raising of *e* to *i* in the same context, now reordered to feed the earlier raising rule. On this, see Jacobsen (1971), de Rijk (1970).

Interestingly, this raising does not affect plurals, and the plural of *neska* is *neskak* in B as elsewhere. Moreover, the lowering of final *e* to *a* in B, discussed above, has led to reanalysis, and the plurals of *lora* 'flower', *ota* 'gorse' and *andra* 'woman' in B are *lorak*, *otak* and *andrak*, in place of the expected *loriak*, *otiak* and *andriak*, and in contrast to common *loreak*, *oteak* and *and(e)reak*.

Since the stress-accent of Z and R regularly falls on the ancient penult, the oxytone words of these varieties must continue forms in which vowels anciently in hiatus have coalesced. Above I mentioned cases like Z *elíza* church' and *elizá* 'the church', but there are other cases in which an ancient intervocalic consonant has seemingly been lost: *odéi* 'cloud', *izéi* 'fir', *etsái* 'enemy', *eztéi* 'wedding' and so on. These must derive from forms like *odeCe*; the identity of the lost consonant is unknown, though it might have been *h*, especially if these words are ancient compounds or derivatives, since the language anciently allowed the aspiration in the third syllable in such formations. Such cases are parallel to others like R *artzái* 'shepherd' (< *artzani*) and recent Z *aihái* 'dinner' (< earlier *aihari*). The word *ibai* 'river' may be another of these, but the word has not survived in the east.

All ancient participles (and other non-finite verb-forms) contain a prefix *e-*. This prefix has developed variously. Before a following *a* or *o*, it becomes *j*, and this is the sole source of *j* in the native lexicon: *jarri* 'put' (< *earri*), *jan* 'eat' (< *ean*), *jautsi* 'go down' (< *eautsi*), *jo* 'hit' (< *eo*), *joan* 'go' (< *eoan*), *josi* 'sew' (< *eosi*). Before *i* or *u*, *e-* is lost: *izan* 'be' (< *eizan*; inflected forms like *naiz* 'I am' show that the *i* is part of the root), *ukan* 'have' (< *eukan* < *edukan*), *utzi* 'leave' (< *eutzi*, an attested form). There is no certain case of *e-* before *e*, but a plausible candidate is the verb meaning 'go out', for which the forms *jalgi* and *elki* are in complementary distribution, suggesting *eelki*, with mutual dissimilation in one case and coalescence in the other.

If *e-* is followed by a consonant, then, if the second syllable contains a high vowel and there is a third syllable, *e-* is raised to *i-*, as described above: *ikusi* 'see' (< *ekusi*), *ibili* 'go about' (< *ebili*), *iduri* 'seem' (< *eduri*), *iritzi* 'opine' (< *eritzi*), *ikuzi* 'wash' (< *ekuzi*); note that some of the ancestral forms are attested, and indeed some are still in regional use today. (This same development is widely attested in nouns: *ipizpiku* 'bishop' (< EPISCIPU), *tipula* (and variants) 'onion' (< CEPULLA), regional *iguzki* 'sun' for common *eguzki*, and so on.)

Otherwise, *e-* generally remains today: *egin* 'do, make', *eman* 'give', *ekarri* 'bring', *etzan* ~ *etzun* 'lie down, recline', *errun* 'lay (eggs)', *entzun* 'hear', *egosi* 'boil, cook', *ebaki* 'cut' and so on.

These are the most widespread and regular developments, but in practice there is a good deal of regional variation in the forms of these verbs. There are a few problematic forms, like *irauli* 'turn over' and *ikasi* 'learn, study', which may have acquired their *i-* by analogy, and *irun* 'spin (yarn)', which may derive from *eirun*.

The diphthongs have mostly remained stable, but there is considerable fluctuation between *ei* and *ai*: *izai* ~ *izei* 'fir', *gai* ~ *gei* 'material', *bait-* ~ *beit-* (verbal prefix), *eztai* ~ *eztei* 'wedding'. There are sporadic cases of diphthongs being levelled or reduced, especially before clusters: regional *alki* for common *aulki* 'chair', regional *arroltza* for *arraultza* 'egg', regional *ardiki* and *urthiki* for *aurdiki* 'throw'. In B, *ai* is regularly reduced to *a* in a final syllable before *n*: B *ezpan* 'lip', *gan* 'top', in the face of common *ezpain*, *gain*, etc.

Very occasionally a vowel appears to have undergone spontaneous diphthongization. The word *laster* 'quick' is attested in this form from the thirteenth century, but today it is *laister* ~ *laixter* in the central dialects, and a variant *lauster* is recorded in the north. Common (*h*)*andi* 'big' is recorded in this form since the medieval period, but modern B has *aundi*, a form attested no earlier than the late eighteenth century. (See also section 3.15 for further instances of such unetymological diphthongs in loan words.) Disliking a vague appeal to 'expressive' or 'augmentative' diphthongization, Michelena (1977a: 488–489) suggests a possible origin. He notes that, at some earlier stage of the language, diphthongs were often reduced before clusters, so that, for example, the noun *itaun* 'confession' (and other senses) forms a verb *itaundu* 'confess', which is widely attested as *itandu* in early texts. This process effectively neutralized pairs like *au/a* and *ai/a* before a cluster. This reduction was then lost, and the etymological diphthong was restored before clusters, so that the verb just cited, for example, is again *itaundu* in the modern language. Cases like *aundi* may therefore represent an overgeneralization of the restored diphthongs.

See Chapter 4 for the unusually radical reductions of diphthongs which have occurred in finite verb-forms.

3.10 GLIDES

Pre-Basque had no phonemic glides, but, at an early stage, it acquired the palatal glide [j] in certain circumstances. This [j] arose from word-initial **e** followed by **a** or **o** (or perhaps rarely by **e**). This circumstance arose chiefly, and perhaps solely, in non-finite verb-forms, in which the prefix **e-* occurs in all ancient verbs, and hence the resulting segment (orthographic ⟨j⟩) occurs only in non-finite verb-forms among native words in the modern language. (There are three exceptional nouns (*jaun* 'lord', *jabe* 'owner', *jai* 'festival'), but these are perhaps derived from ancient participles.) Examples include *jo* 'hit', *joan* 'go', *jan* 'eat' and *jakin* 'know'; the only case in which *j* is followed by any segment other than *a* or *o* is the eastern *jin* 'come', an irregular contraction of *jaugin*. The eastern verb meaning 'go out', which appears variously as *elki* or as *jalgi*, may represent two different resolutions of an original **eelki*; no other case is known of a possible initial **ee-*.

Loan words like *joko* 'game' (< IOCU) and *jende* 'people' (< Sp *gente*) have provided additional instances of this glide.

This palatal glide has had a colourful development in Basque, and that development provides a remarkable instance of a diaphone. In two widely separated areas, the coast of Lapurdi and the south of Bizkaia, the diaphone |j| is still today a palatal glide [j]. In all the rest of the country, however, it has undergone strengthening to some kind of consonant. In most of Lapurdi and Low Navarre, it has become a voiced palatal plosive [ɟ]. In the larger part of Bizkaia, it has developed into a voiced palato-alveolar affricate [dʒ], somewhat resembling the English consonant of *judge*, but slightly more palatalized. In all of Zuberoa, |j| has become instead a voiced palatal-alveolar fricative [ʒ], somewhat resembling the French consonant of *juge* 'judge', but markedly more palatalized: it is perhaps best described as an alveolo-palatal. In the southern part of the Basque-speaking region of Navarre, and in a small part of Gipuzkoa, it is likely that the same thing happened, but we have no direct record of [ʒ]: instead, what we find is the *voiceless* fricative [ʃ]. In this region, and only in this region, the diaphone |j| ceases to be a separate phoneme, for here it has merged with the existing fricative /ʃ/, notated ⟨x⟩, and, while all other Basques write *jan* for the verb meaning 'eat', regardless of their pronunciation, the Navarrese have traditionally written *xan*.

That leaves a large area right in the centre of the country, including virtually all of Gipuzkoa and the eastern part of Bizkaia, and here something truly remarkable has happened. In this region, the diaphone has also developed into a voiceless fricative, but one which is velar or uvular: [x] or [χ]. Hence, in this region, *jan* is [xan] or [χan], a pronunciation which is startlingly at odds with the voiced palatals heard in most of the rest of the country, and a surprising destiny for a segment which started out (recall) as [e].

The developments in Navarre and Gipuzkoa are, of course, strongly reminiscent of developments in late medieval Castilian, in which /ʒ/ devoiced to [ʃ], thereby merging with the existing /ʃ/, and then the resulting /ʃ/ moved to the back of the mouth to become the famous Spanish *jota*, pronounced [x] or [χ], in such words as *rojo* 'red' and *jarra* 'jar' (not to mention *Jérez*, the name which is the source of English *sherry*; the English word preserves the older Castilian pronunciation). It is therefore usually thought that we are looking at an example of a borrowed sound change, since such a shift in pronunciation is decidedly rare in languages generally and seemingly somewhat unnatural. If this is so, however, it is surprising to find the backing only in the centre of the Basque-speaking area, in an area surrounded by varieties of Basque which have not undergone the same shift, rather than in the west and south of Bizkaia and Araba, an area which has been in direct contact with Castile itself for centuries.

Be that as it may, we now come to the feature of the Gipuzkoan shift which is truly astounding. Recall that, in Navarre, |j| has simply merged with *x*. For reasons which I shall explain in a moment, it seems clear that the same merger occurred in Gipuzkoa. However, when |j| was later shifted to the back of the mouth, *original x remained palato-alveolar and did not shift!* In other words, we appear to have a case of *reversal of merger*: instances of original *x* did not shift, while instances of *x* derived from original |j| did shift. Thus, for example, *jo* 'hit' and *jan* 'eat' now have back fricatives, while original *ximist* 'lightning' and *xistu* 'saliva' are *tximist* and *txistu* in modern G.

Reversal of merger is supposed to be impossible, and the reader might be inclined to suspect that no merger ever took place at all in Gipuzkoa: that the two voiceless fricatives somehow always remained phonetically distinct. But there is evidence against this. The loan words *xaboi* 'soap' and *baxera* 'dishes' have become *jaboi* and *bajera* in modern G; *axola* 'attention, care' has become *ajola*, all with back fricatives, even though it is certain that they formerly had instances of *x* not derived from |j|. Interestingly, *gixaxo* 'poor fellow' has become *gixajo*, in which only one of the sibilants has been backed, though this retains an expressive variant *gixaxo*, and there are a few other such cases in which original *x* has exceptionally been backed.

Michelena therefore proposes that the merger genuinely took place, but that instances of original *x* mostly retained the expressive function typical of palatal segments and thus resisted the backing process, while instances of *x* derived from |j| and those found in loan words lacked this expressive function and were hence subject to backing. In a few cases, as with *axola* and the second *x* of *gixaxo*, the expressive force of the segment was no longer strongly felt, and hence these too underwent backing. If this explanation is correct, it represents an extraordinary instance of a phonological change obstructed by functional factors.

The word *joan* 'go' has in places undergone striking developments. In part of the area where |j| is [ɟ], this verb has become *gan*, while in part of the area in which |j| is [x], it has become *fan*, both forms resulting from the coalescence of the initial segment with the following *o*, probably pronounced as a glide [w].

In the preceding section we examined the strengthening in B and G of glides arising at morpheme boundaries. Something similar happens morpheme-internally in R, which has *lexo* 'window' and *batixatu* 'baptize' for common *leiho* and *bateiatu*, and similarly for other such words.

3.11 ASPIRATION

Pre-Basque had a phonetic aspiration which was both frequent and prominent. The occurrence of that aspiration within words was subject to severe constraints which are largely, but not entirely, understood. In the Aquitanian materials at our disposal, the aspiration is regularly written (as *H*) in approximately the same positions in which it occurs today in those dialects of Basque which retain the aspiration.

The history of the aspiration since the Pre-Basque period has essentially been one of loss. It appears that such loss began first in the central dialects: our earliest records from Gipuzkoa and Navarre show no trace of it. In Bizkaia and Araba, the aspiration is still written throughout most of the medieval period in Basque personal names and place names recorded in Spanish texts, and it is exceedingly abundant in the place names listed in the *Reja de San Millán*, compiled in Araba in 1025. It is generally believed that Castilian itself still retained its /h/ at this time, and hence it seems safe to conclude that orthographic ⟨h⟩ in these Basque names genuinely represents an aspiration. By the time the Bizkaian dialect came to be written down in the late sixteenth century, however, the aspiration had disappeared from this variety, and the same is true of our single document recording the southern dialect of Araba.

North of the Pyrenees, in contrast, the aspiration has survived down to the present day, except that it has been very recently lost from ordinary speech along the coast of Lapurdi. The frequency of the aspiration is not everywhere the same: it is today exceedingly frequent in Z but noticeably less frequent in LN and L.

The occurrence of the aspiration is subject to the following constraints:

1 The aspiration can occur no later than the onset of the second syllable.
2 There can be no more than one aspiration in a word, even in a compound both of whose members bear an aspiration in isolation.
3 The aspiration can occur word-initially only on a syllable which otherwise begins with a vowel or a voiceless plosive followed by a vowel; in the second syllable, it can occur only if the syllable otherwise begins with a vowel, a voiceless plosive (not preceded by a sibilant), a liquid or a nasal (but never /m/).

Note that the aspiration never falls on a syllable otherwise beginning with a voiced plosive, a fricative, an affricate or /m/, nor does it fall on a voiceless plosive preceded by a sibilant. For purposes of syllable-counting, a diphthong in the initial syllable counts as one syllable, as shown by such northern forms as *aiher* 'propensity', *gauherdi* 'midnight', *oihan* 'forest' and eastern *auhari* 'dinner'.

Constraints 1 and 2 above do not apply either to the Aquitanian materials or to the place names from Araba recorded in the *Reja de San Millán*; all these materials involve exclusively proper names, and the difference appears to be that both elements of a compound name can bear the aspiration independently, something which is impossible today. This suggests that the two elements of a compound retained their individual identity in the earlier language to a greater degree than is the case today. Otherwise, the medieval materials generally show the aspiration in the same positions in which it is found in the northern dialects today. Our earliest connected texts show essentially the modern state of affairs: all the constraints are obeyed.

Modern Z has a tiny number of exceptions to constraint 1, all of them compounds or derivatives. Z *artolha* 'shepherd's hut' and *sarjalkhi* 'entry and exit' reflect the aspiration of the independent words *olha* 'hut' and *jalkhi* 'exit', and *a(r)akhói* 'carnivorous' contains the suffix -*k(h)oi* 'fond of', which, exceptionally, is stressed in Z. But the localized Z form *baranthailla* 'February' is absolutely extraordinary and has no known explanation. Other such cases sometimes found in print are usually purely etymological spellings or out-and-out errors.

With just a tiny handful of possible exceptions, the Basque aspiration is not etymological – that is, *h* does not continue an earlier segment, and the aspirated plosives are not distinct in origin from the unaspirated voiceless plosives. Instead, the aspiration originated as a suprasegmental feature, possibly one correlated with the position of the word-accent in Pre-Basque. It is this suprasegmental origin which is chiefly responsible for the restricted distribution of the aspiration.

A simple demonstration of the non-etymological origin of the aspiration is provided by the treatment of loans from Latin, which regularly acquire aspirations reflecting nothing in Latin but required by the phonology of Basque. Table 3.8 lists some examples from the dialects retaining the aspiration:

Table 3.8 Aspiration in loan words

ARENA > *harea* 'sand'	ARMA > *harma* 'weapon'
HONORE > *ohore* 'honour'	ANATE > *ahate* 'duck'
APTARE > *hautatu* 'choose'	ASCIOLA > *haizkora* 'axe'
LEONE > *lehoin* 'lion'	SOLU > *sorho* 'field'
ANNONA > Z *anhua* 'provisions'	PIPER > Z *phiper* 'pepper'
BACILLA > *makhila* 'stick'	CERTU > *gerthu* 'certain'

As a rule, the position of the aspiration in loan words is rather consistent, but there are exceptions. Latin COLPU 'bay, gulf' is borrowed variously as *golko* ~ *golkho* ~ *kolko* ~ *kholko*, but variation to this extent is unusual. (The Basque word means also 'space between one's chest and one's clothes'.)

Note in particular the regularity with which an aspiration represents the former position of a lost intervocalic *n*.

In both native words and loan words, there are clear rules for the placement of the aspiration. Broadly speaking, these rules are as follows; they are presented in apparent order of priority, from highest to lowest priority:

1 With only a tiny handful of exceptions in older texts, a finite verb-form never bears an aspiration, save only for the presence of the prefix *h-* which marks the intimate second-person singular, as in *haiz* 'you are'. This probably reflects the lack of stress on these items.
2 The definite article *-a* is never preceded by the aspiration, nor indeed is any vowel-initial suffix.

Examples: *khe* 'smoke', def. *khea*; *hil* 'dead', def. *hila*; *lo* 'sleep', def. *loa*; *ur* 'water', def. *ura*; *hur* 'hazelnut', def. *hurra*.

3 An /h/ must appear at the onset of the second syllable to separate two vowels in hiatus if these vowels cannot form one of the six recognized diphthongs *ai ei oi ui au eu*.

Examples: *behar* 'necessity', *aho* 'mouth', *ihintz* 'dew', *ohol* 'plank', *liho* 'flax', *xehe* 'small', *iharduki* 'argue', *ihes* 'flight', *eho* 'grind', *ohoin* 'thief', *uholde* 'torrent', *ahal* 'ability', *behor* 'mare', *ohe* 'bed', *ohar* 'notice', *zuhur* 'prudent', *zuhaitz* 'tree', *lehoin* 'lion', *ahate* 'duck', *ohore* 'honour', *puhullu* 'fennel', *kaholla* 'provisions', *kaheka* 'owl'. (A virtually unique exception is *joan* 'go'.)

4 If the first two syllables begin with voiceless plosives which could in principle be aspirated, the first one usually gets the aspiration. (Virtually all of these are loan words, of course.)

Examples: *khako* 'hook', Z *khorpuz* 'body' (< CORPUS), *pharkatu* 'forgive' (< PARCERE), Z *phike* 'pitch' (< PICE), *phiper* 'pepper' (< PIPER), Z *thiti* 'breast', *khate* 'chain' (< CATEA).

But: *kanpo* 'outside', *kantu* 'song' (< CANTU), *pitika* 'kid', *tapa* 'step', *kaka* 'shit', *kalte* 'injury'.

Note that the pattern *kakha*, in which the second of two voiceless plosives is aspirated, is virtually unattested.

5 Otherwise, a voiceless plosive at the onset of the second syllable is normally aspirated, so long as it is not preceded by a sibilant:

Examples: *bethe* 'full', *bethi* 'always', *urthe* 'year', *lekhu* 'place' (< LOCU), *zathi* 'piece', *dithi* 'breast', *aphal* 'humble' (< AD VALLEM), *gathu* 'cat' (< CATTU), *artho* 'millet, maize', *aurthen* 'this year', *ethorri* 'come', *okher* 'twisted', *muthil* 'boy' (< PUTILLU), *bothere* 'power' (< POTERE), *berthute* 'virtue' (< VIRTUTE), Z *inkhatz* 'charcoal'.

But: *bake* 'peace' (< PACE), *zutik* ~ *xutik* 'standing up', *miko* 'crumb' (< Occ), *lapa* 'limpet, burdock' (< LAPPA).

The exceptional participles like *hartu* 'take' and Z *heltü* 'arrive' (common *heldu*) probably represent late formations.
Some bisyllabic participles in -*tu* and -*ki* fail to take the aspiration, doubtless by analogy with the very much larger group of participles with three or more syllables, in which these endings cannot possibly be aspirated.

6 If none of the above applies, an initial voiceless plosive is usually aspirated. (Virtually all of these are loan words, and this rule has a large number of exceptions.)

Examples: *khako* 'hook', *khe* 'smoke', *khide* 'companion', *phesta* 'fiesta', *phutzu* 'well', *phixka* 'small amount', *phiko* 'fig', *theina* 'ringworm', *thema* 'obstinacy', *thiti* 'breast', *thona* 'stain', *thu* 'spit'.

But: *kaiola* 'cage', *kontra* 'against', *korapilo* 'knot', *portu* 'harbour', *porru* 'leek', *taula* 'plank', *tamal* 'misfortune'.

7 If none of the above applies, a liquid or nasal (other than /m/) at the onset of the second syllable is aspirated if the word is not vowel-initial. (This rule has so many exceptions it is barely worth stating.)

Examples: *senhar* 'husband', *zilhar* 'silver', *berhatu* 'augment', *belhar* 'grass', *belhaun* 'knee', *gurhi* 'fat, butter', *lanho* 'mist', *zorhi* 'ripe', *zelhai* 'plain' (geog.), *sorho* 'field', *urrhe* 'gold', Z *uñhũ* 'onion' (< Fr *oignon*)

Such forms, which are very numerous, suggest that an intervocalic liquid anciently formed part of the preceding syllable, and not of the following syllable.

But: *sare* 'net', *sari* 'prize', *larre* 'pasture', *galant* 'elegant', *bele* 'crow', *gona* 'skirt', *bainan* 'but'.

8 In all remaining circumstances, the aspiration /h/ is potentially contrastive, and may occur or not. Minimal pairs are possible. The /h/ is fully contrastive word-initially or between two vowels which can form a recognized diphthong; after a liquid or a nasal it may or may not occur but has little or no contrastive value.

Examples: *ari* 'busy', *hari* 'thread', *sehi* 'boy, child', *sei* 'six', *haur* 'child', *ahur* 'palm of the hand', *gai* 'material', *nahi* 'desire', *hur* 'hazelnut', *ur* 'water', *erhi* 'finger', *eri* 'illness', *hala* 'thus', *ala* 'or', *alhaba* 'daughter', *urrhe* 'gold', *hurren* 'nearest', *gorri* 'red', *inhurri* 'ant'.

In loan words, a prothetic vowel counts as a syllable for purposes of assigning aspiration, and hence words like *errota* 'wheel' (< ROTA), *arropa* 'clothing' (< Sp *ropa*) and *ezpata* 'sword' (< SPATHA) never contain aspirated plosives.

When a compound is formed from two words, each of which is aspirated in isolation, the results are variable. For example, the word for 'cemetery' is a compound of *hil* 'dead' and *herri* 'town', but *hilherri* is impossible, and the compound is variously *hilerri* or *ilherri*. The very rare spellings like *hilebethe* 'month', found in a few early authors, are almost certainly etymological only; in the example, the second element is *bethe* 'full'.

A compound does not necessarily respect the position of the aspiration in its elements. The word for 'siblings', a compound of *haur* 'child' and *-ide* 'fellow' is *haurride* in L but *aurhide* in Z, by rule 7. The word for 'moon', a compound of *hilV-* 'moon' and *argi* 'light', may appear either as *hilargi* or (more usually) as *ilhargi*, again by rule 7. (Cf. *hilabete* 'month', with *bethe* 'full'.)

The two words *aita* 'father' and *maite* 'beloved' never have aspirated plosives. Since these two words also fail to undergo automatic palatalization, they must have an unusual history. A favourite suggestion is that they continue original geminates: *atta*, *matte*. (This proposal is due to Nils Holmer, cited in Michelena 1951.)

The participle *jakin* 'know' never has an aspirated plosive, but of course this derives from *eakin*, in which the plosive was in the third syllable.

Interjections and phonaesthetic items are exempt from the ordinary rules governing aspiration, except for the ban on multiple aspirations: Z *hupa!* 'let's go!', *hapataka* 'galloping noise'.

A crucial issue is the phonological status of the aspiration. In Z, it is indisputably contrastive: there are a number of minimal pairs with and without the aspiration, or with the aspiration in different places. Table 3.9 lists some examples from that dialect; the distinctive stress-accent of Z is written except in cases in which it is not clearly recorded, and some of these examples are taken from seventeenth-century texts but appear to be no longer current.

Table 3.9 Aspiration and minimal pairs in Zuberoan

har 'worm', *har* 'take' (radical) vs. *ar* 'male'
há(r̄)i 'to that one' (Dat) vs. *á(r̄)i* (progressive auxiliary)
hézi 'raise, domesticate' vs. *ézi* 'because, for'
auhen 'lamentation' vs. *auen* 'who has you' (relative)
hála 'thus' vs. *álha* 'eat' vs. *ála* 'or'
ha(r̄)an 'valley' vs. *a(r̄)hán* 'plum'
belhar 'grass' vs. *belar* 'forehead'
é(r̄)hi 'finger' vs. *é(r̄)i* 'sick'
ókher 'twisted' vs. *óker* 'belch'
húrte 'rainy spell' vs. *úrthe* 'year'

Observe that the contrastive value of the aspiration extends to voiceless plosives in this variety. Nevertheless, the functional load of the aspiration is not great, particularly on voiceless plosives: much more typical are cases like *khána* and *kána*, which are merely variants of the word meaning 'stick, cane' (a loan from Romance).

In LN and L, the contrastive value of the aspiration is much more marginal, with only a small number of minimal pairs, almost all of them listed in rule 8 above. In these varieties, the aspiration or lack of it on plosives is never contrastive, and using the 'wrong' value for the aspiration merely produces an atypical pronunciation. Even *h* is not infrequently facultative in LN and L: for example, *horri* and *orri* merely represent variant pronunciations of the word for 'leaf', and *anhitz* and *hanitz* are alternative pronunciations of the word for 'lots of'.

The absolute frequency of the aspiration (both *h* and the plosives) is much greater in Z than in LN or L, and, even though this variety has more minimal pairs than the others, it follows my eight rules far more consistently than do LN and L. Vasconists have often assumed that Z is conservative, that it retains the ancient state of affairs more reliably than LN or L, but this is open to question. There seems every reason to suppose that Z has in some cases extended the aspiration to words which did not historically have it. In particular, Z seems to have extended the aspiration to virtually every single monosyllable which can bear it. Hence Z forms like *hur* 'water', *hor* 'dog', *hun* 'good' and *huñ* 'foot', in the face of common *ur, or, on* and *oin*, very likely represent innovations.

Among the very few cases in which *h* may continue an earlier velar plosive are *harri* 'stone', which may be related to the substrate element **karr-* 'rock, crag' attested in Romance and Celtic, and the three demonstratives *hau(r), hori, hura*, which appear as *kaur, kori, kura* or as *gau(r), gori, gura* in the Pyrenean dialects. No one is quite sure what to make of these cases.

For further discussion of the aspiration, see Michelena (1950c, 1951, 1977a: Ch. 11).

3.12 CONSONANT CLUSTERS

Native words of any antiquity never contain initial clusters. Medial clusters in indigenous words are chiefly of the types (1) sibilant + plosive or (2) liquid or *n* + plosive, affricate or sibilant. The rare final clusters are mostly of the type liquid or *n* + affricate; at least some of these clearly derive from syncope, as with *beltz* 'black' < **beletz*. A handful of other types occur in words of some seeming antiquity: *rl* in *arlo* 'field' and *erle* 'bee' (both probably bimorphemic in origin), *rn* in *ernai* 'alert', *sn* in *esne* 'milk' (a contraction of earlier *esene*), and the extraordinary *sm* in *asmo* 'idea', an ancient loan from Romance. All these clusters generally survive today, with only three developments of note.

First, most western and central varieties have lost the affricate/fricative contrast after a liquid or *n*. Many eastern varieties still permit the seemingly ancient distinction between *rz* (as in *arzulo* 'cave') and *rtz* (as in *artzain* 'shepherd'); other varieties permit only *rtz*, and similarly for other such sequences.

A second, and particularly striking, development in Basque is the change of *rz* into *s* and the associated change of *rtz* into *st*. These two changes are most frequent in the west and least frequent in the east, but nowhere are they either categorial or unattested. Thus, eastern *urzo* 'pigeon, dove' = western *uso*; eastern *bortz* 'five' = western *bost*; eastern *-tarzun* '-ness' (a combination of *-tar* and *-zun*) = western *-tasun*; eastern *ortzegun* 'Thursday' = western *ostegun*; eastern *(h)ertze* 'intestine' = western *este*; eastern *bertze* 'other' = western *beste*. (But some of these 'western' forms are also found in varieties of Z and R.) Note also western *mesede* 'grace, favour' < Sp *merced*. The toponym *Satrústegui* (Nav) is attested in the fourteenth century as *Santurcegui* and clearly derives from *sancti Georgi* 'Saint George'; cf. modern *Santurtzi* (Sp *Santurce*) in Bizkaia. The toponym *Elosu* (Ara) derives from *elorri* 'hawthorn' + *-zu* 'full of'. The development is categorial if an apical *s* is nearby. Thus Sal has *-(t)arzun* for most abstract nouns but *osasun* 'health'. The widespread modern *sasi* 'bramble', attested as '*çarci* vel *sassi*' in the seventeenth-century writer Oihenart, probably derives from **zarzi* or **sarzi*.

The third development is the voicing of plosives after *l* or *n* (but not after *r*). This voicing applies categorically in all varieties except Z and R in the east, which fail to undergo it. Thus, as explained in section 3.3, we have common *denbora* 'time' but eastern *t(h)enp(o)ra* < TEMPORA 'times' and common *aldare* 'altar' but eastern *alt(h)are* < ALTARE. Native words show the same developments: common *ongi* 'well' (adv.) is R *onki*, Z *hunki*, and common *alde* 'side' is eastern *alte*. One or two word-forming suffixes usually fail to undergo this voicing, notably -*kizun* 'future action', -*koi* 'fond of' and -*kor* 'tending to': *eginkizun* 'task' (*egin* 'do'), *ibilkoi* 'restless' (*ibili* 'go about'), *emankor* 'fertile' (*eman* 'give'). A couple of words in B exceptionally fail to undergo the voicing: B *denpora* 'time', *ilinti* 'firebrand'. Otherwise, the occurrence of a voiceless plosive after *l* or *n* is generally a reliable indication that the word containing it is of late origin in Basque.

The unique variation found in the verb 'say', western *esan* but eastern *erran*, perhaps derives from an unusual cluster, possibly **esran*.

A handful of medial three-consonant clusters exists: *andre* 'lady' (< *andere*), *baldres* 'slovenly' (a loan from Old Spanish), old B G *anztu* 'forget' (now reduced to *aztu*), R *arska* 'crib, manger' (common *aska*), R *arsto* 'donkey' (common *asto*), R *ainzto* ~ *aizto* 'knife'. Most of these derive either from word-formation or from syncope, and they tend strongly to be reduced, with R being notably conservative in retaining a number of them unreduced.

Place names of non-Basque origin and containing clusters not usual in Basque sometimes have local pronunciations in which the clusters have been metathesized to produce more familiar clusters. Thus, the Bizkaian cities of *Gernika* and *Zornotza* have localized versions *Gerrinke* and *Zorrontza*, and *Afrika* is often *Apirka* for older speakers.

For the treatment of impermissible clusters in loan words, see section 3.15.

3.13 WORD-ACCENT

The history of the word-accent is complex and controversial, and its study has been obstructed by the fact that, until very recently, we had little in the way of reliable information on the subject for the majority of varieties. Even some of the best descriptions of regional varieties fail to note the presence of the word-accent, and more than a few have gone so far as to deny the existence of the word-accent, a position which is remote from the truth. A further complication is that, in connected speech, the word-accents are largely overridden by the phrase-accent, so that words lose their individuality; this is true of all but the eastern dialects, in which the stress-accent of a word generally remains intact.

Earlier vasconists were inclined to think that the eastern accent-type represented the most direct continuation of the ancient state of affairs, largely because of the different development of initial and medial consonants in Basque, but few would accept such a view these days. Today, it is agreed by probably all scholars that the stress-accents of the eastern varieties are late innovations, but there is no consensus on the western pitch-accent. In an important paper which has unfortunately never been published, Jacobsen (1975) argues that this pitch-accent is also an innovation, deriving chiefly from the coalescence of vowels in hiatus and then extended analogically in certain circumstances. This attractive idea accounts rather well for a striking fact about the western word-accent: while only a minority of non-plural forms are accented, all plurals are accented. Since many specialists believe that the plural endings generally result from the reduction of longer sequences, such as ergative plural -ek ~ -ak from something like *-agek (see Chapter 4), and since it is well established that pitch-accents can arise from vowel coalescence, Jacobsen's analysis is a very economical one which deserves more attention than it has so far received, no doubt because of its unpublished status. It has, however, been further developed by Grundt (1977, 1980).

Martinet (1950, 1955), as part of his account of the frequent word-initial vowels of Basque, has proposed that some ancient stage of Basque, possibly the Pre-Basque of Michelena's reconstruction, must have had a stress-accent which fell on the initial syllable of a word. This proposal has attracted little support. It does, however, have the advantage of explaining why, in loan words in which the first two syllables have voiceless plosives, it is normally the first one which receives the aspiration in those dialects retaining it: we find the type *khaka*, but not the type *kakha*.

Michelena (1957–1958, 1972a, 1977a) does not reject Martinet's idea outright, but he suggests that, if valid at all, it must have applied to a stage of the language much earlier than the Pre-Basque of his own phonological reconstruction. Michelena, in contrast, argues that Pre-Basque had a word-accent, of unstated nature but most likely a stress-accent, which regularly fell on the second syllable of a polysyllabic word, except in compounds. In this analysis, the presence of the aspiration was closely associated with the location of this word-accent; recall that the aspiration most commonly falls on the second syllable of a word when that syllable is capable of bearing the aspiration. This view has the obvious advantage of explaining why the aspiration does not normally fall later than the second syllable and why there is normally only one aspiration per word. On the other hand, it has some difficulty with the word-initial aspiration found in a substantial number of cases, and it provides no basis for understanding the western pitch-accent. An interesting consequence is that the Type IV accentual system described above must be an almost undisturbed continuation of the Pre-Basque accent, while all other accentual systems must be innovations. Michelena goes on to propose that the penultimate stress accent of some eastern varieties results from the reanalysis of three-syllable forms, in which the accent, lying on the second syllable, could be equally regarded as occurring on the second syllable from the beginning or on the second syllable from the end.

In spite of some difficulties, Michelena's account is still perhaps the majority view among vasconists.

In two recent examinations, Hualde (1992, 1995) rejects all these interpretations in favour of a very different view. Dismissing the various appeals to aspiration, initial vowels and vowel coalescence as either irrelevant or of only minor significance, he notes that the western varieties exhibiting the pitch-accent system called Type I frequently retain unchanged the word-accent of Latin and early Romance; for example, the B variety of Getxo has *dénpora* 'time' (< TEMPORA), *ántzar* 'goose' (< ANSER), *sékula* 'never' (< SAE-CULA), but *autóno* 'September' (< AUTUMNU), *doméka* 'Sunday' (< DOMINICA) and *makílla* 'stick' (< BACCILLA). All these words belong to the accented class today, which is understandable for the first group but mysterious for the second: with an accent on the second syllable, they would have been regular in Michelena's system, and hence they should have developed into unaccented words today. (In a Type I accentual system, monomorphemic words are normally unaccented unless they are loan words retaining the marked accentual position of the source language.)

Examining a range of data, including some that have only recently been made available by published descriptions, Hualde finally concludes that Pre-Basque must have had a regular word-final accent. On this basis, he is able to interpret the western systems as resulting from the retraction of the accent towards the beginning of the word.

That is the state of play today. Each proposal has certain advantages and certain drawbacks, and there is no consensus. The word-accent remains the one aspect of Pre-Basque phonology on which we are still in the dark.

One final observation: Basque versification utterly ignores the word-accent in all varieties, even in Z, with its strong stress-accent. (A treatment of versification is beyond the scope of this book; see the various writings of Jean Haritschelhar, most notably Haritschelhar (1969).)

3.14 SUMMARY OF PHONOLOGICAL CHANGES

Here I present a brief summary of the principal phonological changes leading from Pre-Basque to the modern Basque dialects. With only a few exceptions, it is not possible to determine the order in which the various changes occurred, and I therefore group them by the same categories used above. The Pre-Basque system which underwent the changes was as shown in Table 3.10. The aspiration was phonetically present but not phonemic. Initial **d-** occurred only in finite verb-forms; **p** was rare at best; final **-t** and **-k** may perhaps have occurred in suffixes (only). The vowels were **i e a o u**, and the recognized diphthongs were probably, as today, **ai ei oi ui au eu**.

Plosives. The contrasting fortis and lenis plosives were reinterpreted as distinctively voiceless and voiced, respectively. The new voicing contrast was

Table 3.10 The Pre-Basque phonological system

	-b-, -d-, -g-	
	-z-, -s-	
b-, (d-), g-	-n-, -l-, -r-	
z-, s-		-tz, -ts
n-, l-	-p-, -t-, -k-	-N, -L, -R
	-tz-, -ts-	
	-N-, -L-, -R-	

i, e, a, o, u

extended to word-initial position, and initial *t* and *d* became possible. Except in the eastern dialects, all plosives were voiced after *n* or *l*. The consonant *b* sometimes became *m* in initial position and sometimes developed to *f*, especially in medial position; initial *b* was very frequently lost before *o* and occasionally before *u*. At some stage, final *t* and *k* became possible.

Sibilants.   The contrasting fortis and lenis sibilants became affricates and fricatives, respectively, which is quite possibly what they had always been anyway. In western and central dialects the affricate/fricative contrast was lost after a nasal or a liquid. Final sibilants became possible, so that the affricate/ fricative contrast was extended to final position. In B, the *s/z* and *ts/tz* contrasts were lost in very recent times.

Nasals.   Pre-Basque **n** was lost intervocalically, and then **N** was reduced to *n*, merging with the surviving instances of **n**. This loss of **n** led to the introduction of nasal vowels, which survive today only in the eastern dialects. Elsewhere nasalization was either lost or reinterpreted as a following *n*. The hiatus resulting from the loss of **n** was often resolved by the introduction of *h* or another consonant. Initial **b** frequently became *m*, especially before another nasal, and medial **nb** was frequently reduced to *m*; these developments, together with loans from Latin, led to the introduction of *m* into Basque.

Liquids.   Lenis **l**, when intervocalic, developed to *r*, merging with existing **r**; then fortis **L** was reduced to *l*, merging with surviving instances of **l**. Fortis **R** and lenis **r** have generally survived as a trill *rr* and a tap *r* down to the present day in most varieties. In Z, however, intervocalic *r* has recently been lost, leaving Z with only one rhotic; in L and LN, *rr* has developed into a uvular fricative, and this uvular is now in the process of being extended to *r* by lexical diffusion.

Palatalization.   Most coronals were formerly palatalized automatically after

i and before a following vowel; this palatalization remains today in the peripheral dialects but has been lost in the central ones. Otherwise, the palatal
segments did not anciently occur in lexical items, but were found only in
expressive variants of lexical items, a function which is still prominent but no
longer productive. With the loss of some of the earlier unmarked forms, and
with the effect of loan words, the palatal segments must now be regarded as
ordinary consonant phonemes.

Vowels.   The ancient five-vowel system is retained in most modern varieties;
the contrastive nasalization introduced by the loss of intervocalic *n* has been
lost everywhere except in Z and R, which retain distinctive nasal vowels. In Z,
most instances of original *u* have developed into a front rounded vowel *ü*,
with some consequent mutual assimilation of *i*, *ü* and *u* within words, and *o*
has often been raised to *u*. In certain circumstances, mid vowels have been
raised or lowered, and diphthongs have occasionally been levelled or reduced,
especially before clusters.

Glides.   Word-initial *e* became *j* [j] initially before *a* or *o*; this [j] has in most
varieties been strengthened to some kind of consonant. Prevocalic *i* and *u*
(and sometimes also *e* and *o*) have in some varieties been converted into glides
[j] and [w], which in places have been strengthened to consonants.

Aspiration.   The ancient aspiration was never either segmental or contrastive. It has been retained only in the northern varieties, and has probably been
extended in Z; elsewhere, the aspiration has been lost, though it is attested in
personal names and place names in medieval Bizkaia and Araba.

Word-accent.   There is as yet no consensus on this. Martinet's word-initial
accent has found no support; Michelena's second-syllable accent is perhaps
the favourite interpretation; Hualde's final accent is still awaiting judgement.

Consonant clusters.   Little has happened to the Pre-Basque clusters apart
from the voicing of plosives after *n* and *l* in all but the eastern varieties.
Medial three-consonant clusters have usually been reduced to two-consonant
clusters. Loan words have introduced new clusters not formerly possible,
especially in initial position.

Metatheses.   Instances of metathesis, while always sporadic, are by no
means rare in the history of Basque. Latin BENEDICERE 'bless' should have
been borrowed as **benedikatu*, but this must have metathesized to
*bedenikatu to yield the attested *bedeinkatu*. Basque *mukuru* ~ *mukurru*
'height' is apparently borrowed from Latin CUMULU, with metathesis of the
earlier **kumuru*. The verb meaning 'seem, appear' occurs both as *iduri* and
irudi in various parts of the country, and no one is sure which is the more

conservative form. The western word for 'butterfly' is given only as *mitxeleta* in Azkue's dictionary, but the usual form today is *tximeleta*. Many other such cases could be adduced. An extraordinary case is the word for 'swallow' (the bird). This is *ainara ~ enara* in much of the country, but *elae* in some varieties of B. The first of these implies an original **aiNala ~ *eNala*, but the second equally implies **eLana*. One form or the other, then, must result from a metathesis of the nasal and the lateral accompanied by an exchange of fortis and lenis character between these two segments.

Compound verbs. Compound verbs are common in Basque at all periods, and they have frequently undergone complex and irregular developments leading to substantial regional variation in form. A verb meaning 'wait for' appears variously as *itxeden, itxedan, itxedon, itxadon, itxaron, itxaran, itxodon, itxogon, itxon* and *itxoin* (at least), and this is thought to be an ancient compound of *hitz* 'word' and **edun* 'have'. The widespread verb *eskaini ~ eskeini* 'offer' looks very much like a compound of *esku* 'hand' and *ipini ~ ibeni* 'put'. Another verb for 'wait for' is *iguriki ~ iguruki ~ eguriki ~ eguruki*, which is probably a compound of *egun* 'day' and *eduki* 'hold'.

3.15 TREATMENT OF LOAN WORDS FROM LATIN AND EARLY ROMANCE

Latin nouns are usually borrowed in their accusative forms: *ahate* 'duck' < ANATE, *ohore* 'honour' < HONORE, *bake* 'peace' < PACE, *ingude* 'anvil' < INCUDE, *errege* 'king' < REGE, *lore* 'flower' < FLORE. But there are a few instances of borrowed nominatives: *gorputz* 'body' < CORPUS, *lapitz* 'slate' < LAPIS 'stone', *maizter* 'master shepherd' < MAGISTER, *apaez* (and variants) 'priest' < ABBAS 'abbot'. Adjectives are borrowed in the accusative singular masculine/neuter: *ziku* 'dry' < SICCU, *xahu* 'clean' < SANU 'healthy'. A rare nominative is *bortitz* 'strong, violent' < FORTIS.

Verbs are normally borrowed as the past participle, the result being a Basque perfective participle, commonly used as a citation form: *okupatu* 'occupy' < OCCUPATU, *perekatu* 'caress' < FRICATU, *aditu* 'hear' < AUDITU, *goitatu* 'look after, pay attention to' < COGITATU. Occasionally the Basque participle is built upon the Latin or Romance infinitive, particularly when the original participle is irregular: *eskiribatu ~ iskiribatu ~ izkiriatu* 'write', from SCRIBERE, not from SCRIPTU. A unique instance of a borrowed finite verb-form is the eastern participle *laket* 'be pleasing' < PLACET (re-formed as *laketu* in places). The Latin infinitive HABERE 'have' is the source of *abere* 'animal, cattle', but this merely reflects a widespread Romance development.

Latin /a e i o u/, both long and short, are borrowed as Basque *a e i o u*, as shown in Table 3.11.

As can be seen, Basque does not diphthongize Latin short /e/, /o/. In loans from Romance after the Romance diphthongization of these vowels, the

Table 3.11 The Latin vowels in Basque

FĀGU > *bago* 'beech'	LACU > *laku* 'lake'
LĒGE > *lege* 'law'	CERTU > *gertu* 'certain'
LĪNU > *liho* 'flax'	PICE > *bike* 'pitch'
FLŌRE > *lore* 'flower'	ROTA > *errota* 'wheel'
PLŪMA > *luma* 'feather'	LUCRU > *lukuru* 'avarice'

diphthong is usually reduced: *erregu* 'request' (< *ROGU; cf. Sp *ruego*), *leku* 'place' (< LOCU). Medieval documents, notably the *Reja de San Millán* (1025), reveal that diphthongized Romance forms and non-diphthongized Basque forms of toponyms often existed side by side along the boundary between the languages. However, the Basque vowel sequences *uo* and *oe*, arising in word-formation, were taken into Romance as the diphthong /ue/: for example, the medieval toponyms *Zalduhondo* (Ara) and *Zuloeta* (Nav) are modern Spanish *Zalduendo* and *Zulueta*.

We occasionally find an unexpected *ai* in place of *a* in a first syllable: *maingu* 'lame' (< MANCU), *haizkora* 'axe' (< ASCIOLA), *maindire* 'sheet' (< MANTILE), *aingeru* 'angel' (< ANGELU), *saindu* 'saint, holy' (< SANCTU).

The Latin diphthong /au/ is borrowed as *au*: *gauza* 'thing' < CAUSA, B *autono* 'September' < AUTUMNU 'autumn'. This *au* regularly develops to *ai* in eastern dialects (Z *gaiza* 'thing' (< CAUSA)), and the same development occurs sporadically in all dialects before a following *u*: common *kaiku* 'wooden bowl' < CAUCU 'drinking vessel'. The case of *aditu* 'hear' < AUDITU is exceptional. There is no trace of Latin /ae/ in Basque: *balea* 'whale' < BALLAENA, old Z *zekuru* 'century' < SAECULU.

Latin word-initial plosives are usually borrowed as Basque *b d g*: *balea* 'whale' < BALLAENA, *diru* (Z *diharü*) 'money' < DENARIU, *garau(n)* 'grain' < GRANU, *bake* 'peace' < PACE, *dorre* 'tower' < TURRE or Sp *torre*, *gela* 'room' < CELLA. Initial /w/ and Romance /v/ are borrowed as *b*: *begiratu* 'look at, watch' < VIGILIARE, *berde* 'green' < VERDE. Initial /f/ is borrowed as *b* or lost: *baba* 'bean' < FABA, *biko* ~ *iku* 'fig' < FICU. At some later stage, probably under continuing Romance influence, we often find Latin initial voiceless plosives rendered as voiceless plosives in Basque, and some earlier loans were seemingly re-formed: *gatu* ~ *katu* 'cat' < CATTU, *gatea* ~ *katea* 'chain' < CATENA, *gerezi* ~ *kerexa* 'cherry' < CERESEA, *biper* ~ *piper* 'pepper' < PIPER. Occasionally, by apparent hypercorrection, we find Basque voiceless plosives which are not etymological: *pintza* 'membrane' < Aragonese *binza*, regional *perde* 'green' for common *berde* < Rom *verde*.

Word-medial voiceless plosives, simplex or geminate, and geminate voiced plosives are borrowed as Basque *p t k*: *ziape* 'mustard' < SENAPE, Sout *lupu* 'wolf' < LUPU, *zeta* 'silk' < SETA, *ahate* 'duck' < ANATE, *biko* 'fig' < FICU, *lapa* 'burdock' < LAPPA, *gatu* 'cat' < CATTU, *zuku* 'juice, soup' < SUCCU, *ziku* 'dry' < SICCU, *okela* 'morsel, meat' < BUCCELLA 'mouthful', B *zapatu* 'Saturday'

< SABBATU, *apaez* 'priest' < ABBAS 'abbot'. Word-medial simplex voiced plosives are borrowed as *b d g*: *baba* 'bean' < FABA, *abere* 'cattle' < HABERE 'have', *padura* 'water meadow' < PADULE, *zigulu* 'seal' < SIGILLU, *bago* 'beech' < FAGU.

The Latin sibilant /s/ is almost always borrowed as *z*: *zeta* 'silk' (< SETA), *zapore* 'taste' (< SAPORE), *zigilu* 'seal' (< SIGILLU), *ziape* 'mustard' (< SENAPE), *azeri* 'fox' (< ASENARIU), *meza* 'mass' (< MISSA), *izkribatu* 'write' (< SCRIBERE), *gerezi* 'cherry' (< CERESEA). In final position we usually find *tz*: *bortitz* 'strong' (< FORTIS), *gorputz* 'body' (< CORPUS), but note *apaez* 'priest' (< ABBAS). A very few words show *s* instead, such as *soka* 'rope' (< SOCA) and *gisu* 'plaster' (< GYPSU).

Initial clusters are always broken up in some way. Most usually, an epenthetic vowel is inserted: *boronde* 'forehead' < FRONTE, *garau(n)* 'grain' < GRANU, *gereta* 'rustic gate' < *CLETA. If the initial consonant is a labial, however, it is often lost: *lama* 'flame' < FLAMMA, *lore* 'flower' < FLORE, *luma* 'feather' < PLUMA, *lau* 'flat' < PLANU, *laket* 'be pleasing' < PLACET. (And note also B *laru* 'yellow' < CLARU 'clear'.) If the initial consonant is a sibilant, a prothetic vowel is added: *ezpata* 'sword' < SPATHA, *iztupa* 'hemp, oakum' < STUPPA. An initial /r/ always acquires a prothetic vowel: *arrosa* 'rose' < ROSA, *errege* 'king' < REGE, *Erroma* 'Rome' < ROMA.

Medial clusters existing in Pre-Basque are retained, apart from the usual voicing of plosives after *n* or *l*: *denbora* 'time' < TEMPORA 'times', *aldare* 'altar' < ALTARE, *ingude* 'anvil' < INCUDE, *maizter* 'master shepherd' < MAGISTER.

Impermissible clusters, particularly those beginning with a plosive, are broken up or reduced: *pundu* 'point' < PUNCTU, *liburu* 'book' < LIBRU, *lukuru* 'avarice, usury' < LUCRU, *zinu* 'sign' < SIGNU, B *autono* 'September' < AUTUMNU 'autumn', *eskiribatu* ~ *iskiribatu* ~ *izkiriatu* 'write' < SCRIBERE, *abendu* 'December' < ADVENTU, *ifernu* 'hell' < INFERNU, *el(e)iza* 'church' < ECCLESIA, *gisu* 'plaster' < GYPSU.

As can be seen from the examples above, Latin velars remain velars in Basque before front vowels. In later loans, the palatalization of velars before front vowels is sometimes visible in the forms of loans in Basque. Lat CEPULLA 'onion' appears variously as *kipula* ~ *tipula* ~ *dipula*, the last two variants perhaps reflecting Romance palatals. Lat GENUS 'kind' appears to be the source of French Basque *deus* ~ *jeus* 'anything'. Lat GENTE 'people' appears as *gente* in R but as *jente* ~ *jende* in the rest of the country. Lat ARCHIATER 'doctor' gives archaic *atxeter* ~ *altxeter*.

A few loans show the loss of an initial syllable: *sendo* 'robust, strong' (< EXEMPTU), *saiatu* 'try' (< Fr *ensayer*), *txertatu* 'insert' (< Sp *injertar*), *txukatu* 'wipe off, dry' (< Sp *enjugar*). Another possible case is *debekatu* 'prohibit', if this derives from Lat IMPEDICARE 'obstruct', but Michelena prefers to invoke Old Spanish *deviedo* 'prohibited'.

A few individual loan words exhibit unusually complex phonological developments. B *bi(x)ao* 'siesta' derives from MERIDIANU 'of midday'. Common *poz* 'happiness' is thought to derive from GAUDIU 'joy'. Common *bedeinkatu* 'bless', from BENEDICERE, must continue a metathesized form **bedenikatu*.

Folk-etymology has affected the forms of a few loans. Lat VIGILIARE gives Basque *begiratu* 'watch, look at', whose form has been influenced by *begi* 'eye'. Sp *zanahoria* 'carrot', of Arabic origin, yields Basque *zainhori*, literally 'yellow-root', with the final *-a* interpreted as the Basque article. The Romance loan *estable* 'shed, shelter' (cognate with English *stable*), with its alien cluster, has been re-formed as *estalpe*, from *estali* 'cover' and *-pe* 'under'. Another possible case is *buztarin(a)* ~ *uzterina* ~ *uztare* ~ *uztain* ~ Z *üztari(a)* 'crupper; hindquarters', which surely continues Lat POSTILENA 'crupper'; the Basque form suggests an unattested Lat **POSTELINA, but we may simply be seeing interference from *buztan* 'tail'.

As far as we can tell, the position of the Latin word-accent was generally retained in Basque.

3.16 THE PHONOTACTICS OF PRE-BASQUE

There has been no systematic study of the phonotactics of native Basque words of any antiquity, nor do we even have at present an agreed list of words which were certainly or probably in the language 2,000 years ago. There are, however, a few points which stand out upon even a casual inspection. Most prominent among these is the remarkable frequency of word-initial vowels.

It is obvious that vowel-initial lexical items are extraordinarily frequent in Basque. While I have seen no reliable figures, I would hazard a guess that close to 50 per cent of native nouns and adjectives begin with vowels (this includes those items which begin with *h* in the aspirating dialects). Just to provide some very rough confirmation, Table 3.12 shows the numbers of pages of entries beginning with particular letters in Azkue's 1905 dictionary, which excludes the most recent loans from Romance; the dictionary includes affixes as well as lexical items, a policy which noticeably inflates certain of the shorter sections.

The five vowels represent altogether 404 pages out of a total of 1,029 pages, or about 40 per cent (the dictionary actually contains 1,042 pages, but the 'missing' pages are devoted to C, H, J, Q, V, W and Y, for which there are no entries). The E and I sections are significantly inflated by the inclusion of a large number of verbs whose participles bear the prefix *e-* or *i-* (see Chapter 4), and the I section is further inflated by Azkue's practice of not distinguishing J from I. Still, the overall pattern is clear. Note that A, with 120 pages, is far and away the most frequent initial segment, followed by E, with 96. By comparison, the most frequent initial consonant, Z, occupies only 87 pages. Moreover, recall that *none* of the 160 pages devoted

Table 3.12 Initial segments in Azkue's dictionary

A:	120	T:	43
E:	96	N:	37
Z:	87	P:	36
I:	79	TX:	36
B:	73	D:	16
O:	62	R:	7 (affixes only)
G:	62	F:	5
M:	58	TZ:	5
K:	58	TT:	4
L:	48	Ñ:	3
U:	47	LL:	1
S:	46	TS:	0

to P, T, K, D and R can represent ancient lexical items, suggesting that the proportion of vowel-initial words in Pre-Basque was probably much closer to 50 than to 40 per cent.

The seemingly extraordinary frequency of initial vowels is the only issue in the phonotactics of Pre-Basque which has attracted any significant comment, but this topic has in fact attracted so much attention that I shall devote a separate section to it below (section 3.18). There is no point in trying to illustrate the vast frequency of initial vowels here; look at any page of this book containing words other than loan words.

Apart from the very frequent word-initial vowels, recall that lexical items in Pre-Basque could begin with one of only six consonants: **b g z s l n**. These are not of equal frequency. First, **b g z** are all exceedingly frequent in native words, and it would be easy to list hundreds of native words beginning with each. A modest sample: *buru* 'head', *begi* 'eye', *bihotz* 'heart', *beso* 'arm', *belar* 'grass', *behi* 'cow', *baso* 'woods', *burdina* 'iron', *berun* 'lead' (metal), *beltz* 'black', *berri* 'new', *bat* 'one', *bi(ga)* 'two', *bortz* 'five', *bai* 'yes', *baina(n)* 'but', *bezala* 'like, as'; *gerri* 'waist', *gibel* 'liver', *gizon* 'man', *giltza* 'key', *gar* 'flame', *gain* 'top', *gurdi* 'cart', *gudu* 'combat', *goroldio* 'moss', *gari* 'wheat', *goi* and *garai* 'high place', *gaitz* 'bad', *garbi* 'clean', *gizen* 'fat', *gorri* 'red', *gor* 'deaf', *gero* 'after, later', *gu* 'we'; *zubi* 'bridge', *zur* 'wood', *zakur* 'dog', *zaldi* 'horse', *zulo* 'hole', *zezen* 'bull', *zati* 'piece', *zabal* 'wide', *zikin* 'dirty', *zahar* 'old', *zuzen* 'straight', *zuri* 'white', *zazpi* 'seven', *zortzi* 'eight', *zehar* 'across', *zer* 'what?', *zu* 'you'.

In contrast, **s** and **l** are substantially less common, though still not rare, and one could easily find at least some dozens of native words with these initial segments. A sample: *sudur* 'nose', *sabel* 'belly', *soin* 'shoulder; body', *su* 'fire', *sagar* 'apple', *seme* 'son', *senar* 'husband', *suge* 'snake', *sarde* 'pitchfork', *sakon* 'deep', *sei* 'six'; *lepo* 'neck', *larru* 'skin', *larre* 'pasture', *lan* 'work', *lagun* 'friend', *lo* 'sleep', *leiho* 'window', *lur* 'earth', *luze* 'long', *labur* 'short', *latz* 'rough', *leun* 'smooth', *lehen* 'first', *lau(r)* 'four'. Finally, initial **n** is not common at all; I can here give something close to an exhaustive list of native words beginning with this segment: *neska* 'girl', *neba* 'brother (of a woman)', *negar* 'tears', *negu* 'winter', *neurri* 'measure', *nahi* 'desire', *naba* 'high plain', *nagi* 'idleness', *nabar* 'multicoloured, dun', *nahasi* 'mixed', *nagusi* 'chief, principal', *nor* 'who?', *ni* 'I'. There are very few others.

The very few native words with initial *m-* all derive from earlier **b**. Thus, *mihi* ~ *min* 'tongue' is from **bini*; *mendi* 'mountain' must be from **bendi* (if this is not a loan word); *mahats* 'grapes' is undoubtedly from **banats*; *mahai(n)* 'table' is probably from **banane* or something similar. The great frequency of initial *m-* in modern Basque results chiefly from borrowing, but also from the tendency to use *m-* in coining onomatopoeic and phonaesthetic items.

In word-final position, native lexical items can again have any vowel, and again vowels are exceedingly frequent here. It appears that the only word-final consonants in Pre-Basque were the fortis sibilants **tz** and **ts**, plus **N** (the neutralization of the two nasals), **R** (the neutralization of the two rhotics) and **L** (the neutralization of the two laterals).

Examples of the affricates (the laminal one is far commoner): *hitz* 'word', *gatz* 'salt', *ihi(n)tz* (< **initz*) 'dew', *hotz* 'cold', *latz* 'rough', *hots* 'shout, cry', *mahats* 'grapes', *sits* ~ *sats* 'moth; ordure'. The affricate could apparently be preceded by a nasal or a liquid, though such forms are rare and almost always involve -*tz*: *zuntz* 'strand of wool' (this word may not be ancient), *bortz* 'five', *zurtz* 'orphan', *beltz* 'black' (probably from earlier **beletz*), *hartz* 'bear' (possibly a loan from Indo-European).

Of the resonants, **N** and **R** are fairly frequent in this position, while **L** is positively uncommon: *lan* 'work', *ozpin* 'vinegar', *gurin* 'animal fat, butter', *gizon* 'man', *min* 'pain', *haran* 'valley', *ezpain* 'lip', *oin* 'foot', *ozen* 'sonorous', *gizen* 'fat', *astun* 'heavy'; *zakur* 'dog', *hezur* 'bone', *abar* 'branch', *elur* 'snow', *ibar* 'water meadow, valley', *izar* 'star', *gogor* 'hard', *eder* 'beautiful', *hiru(r)* 'three', *lau(r)* 'four' (the *r* is original in both of these), *hamar* 'ten', *agur* 'good-bye'; *ahal* 'ability', *hil* 'dead', *zabal* 'wide'. It is possible that some of those in final -*n* derive from intervocalic **n**, just as *arrain* 'fish' derives from **arrani*.

There were absolutely no word-initial clusters in Pre-Basque, and probably no final clusters other than the resonant-plus-affricate clusters just described. The word-medial clusters were discussed in section 3.12.

It is interesting to consider the possible constraints upon consonants in successive syllables. (In what follows, I omit verbs from consideration.) To begin with, the sibilant harmony described in section 3.4 for the modern language was almost certainly present in Pre-Basque, since native words other than compounds never mix laminal and apical sibilants in a single word, and we find only forms like *zezen* 'bull', *izotz* 'frost', *zurtz* 'orphan', *itsaso* 'sea', *sats* ~ *sits* 'moth; ordure' and *itsusi* 'ugly'.

A striking fact is that, in monomorphemic native words of the pattern CVCV-, it is extremely rare for both consonants to be plosives (as noted by Lakarra 1995); in the few that exist, both plosives are usually voiced: *begi* 'eye', *bide* 'road', *biga* 'two', *bigun* 'soft', *bider* 'time, occasion', *bat* 'one' (< *bade* or *bada*), *gabe* ~ *baga* 'without', *gudu* 'combat' (suspected by some of being a loan word), *gogo* 'mind, soul' (possibly a reduplication), *gibel* 'liver' (a compound) and *gogor* 'hard' (almost certainly a reduplication). Exceptional are *beti* 'always' and *guti* 'not much'; it is highly probable that these are bimorphemic and contain the ancient adjective-forming suffix -*ti*. The highly anomalous *tipi* ~ *tiki* 'small', with its initial *t*, is undoubtedly an expressive formation; José Ignacio Hualde has suggested (p.c.) that this might represent a metathesis of an original *piti*, possibly also involving the suffix -*ti* and conceivably partly of Romance origin. It appears that Pre-Basque strongly disfavoured this pattern.

Words of this form, then, including those with initial *m*, are almost invariably loan words or expressive formations of no great antiquity. Consequently, it is generally safe to regard words like *beko* 'forehead; beak', eastern *moto* 'headscarf; hair bun' (and other senses), *kako* ~ *gako* 'hook' and *mutur* 'snout; extremity' as loan words, even though no Romance source has yet been securely identified for some of them, except in those cases in which an 'expressive' origin seems more likely, as perhaps with *mutur*.

Indeed, even CVCV- words in which only the second consonant is a plosive are not exactly abundant, though they are certainly more numerous than the last group: *lapur* 'thief', *labur* 'short', *zakur* 'dog', *negu* 'winter', *lepo* 'neck', *suge* 'snake', *zoko* 'corner', *labe* 'oven'. The same goes for VCV-words, though these are probably more frequent still: *hagin* 'molar', *idi* 'ox', *hego* 'south wind', *agur* 'good-bye', *eder* 'beautiful', *ikara* 'trembling', *ugatz* '(female) breast', *hegal* 'wing', *egun* 'day', *ugari* 'numerous', *aker* 'he-goat', *odol* 'blood', *oker* 'twisted', *ipurdi* 'buttocks', *hegi* 'ridge', *abar* 'branch', *ibar* 'water-meadow, valley' and quite a few others.

Overwhelmingly, though, a plosive at the beginning of the second syllable is preceded by a resonant or a sibilant. This pattern is so exceedingly frequent as to constitute virtually the stereotype for a Basque word. Here is just a tiny sample of what is really a very large number of words. First, with a resonant: *ardi* 'sheep', *argi* 'light, bright', *erdi* 'half, middle', *zaldi* 'horse', *barda* 'last night', *alte* ~ *alde* 'side', *urde* 'hog', *sarde* 'pitchfork', *galte* ~ *galde* 'question', *garbi* 'clean', *gurdi* 'cart', *oldar* 'moment', *urte* 'year', *arte* 'interval, until', *albo* 'side', *murgil* 'dive', *arto* 'millet, maize', *handi* 'big', *enda* 'breed, race', *indar* 'power, force', *mendi* 'mountain', *ondar* 'sand, beach', *andere* 'lady', *sendo* 'strong, vigorous'. With a sibilant: *aste* 'week', *azti* 'fortune-teller', *la(i)ster* 'quick, soon', *asto* 'donkey', *ezti* 'honey', *gazte* 'young', *listu* 'saliva', *aski* 'enough', *aska* 'cradle', *esku* 'hand', *ezpain* 'lip', *ozpin* 'vinegar', *azpi* 'below', *neska* 'girl', *izter* 'thigh', *asko* 'lots of; some', *azkar* 'strong, vigorous', *azken* 'last', *oskol* 'shell', *oste* 'back', *oztopo* 'obstacle', *esker* 'thanks', *ezker* 'left (hand)', *uztarri* 'yoke' and so on – there are really very many of these.

Note, however, the following further observation. In a word of the form PVRPV-, where P is a plosive and R is a resonant, both plosives are voiced. We find plenty of words like *gurdi* 'cart' and *barda* 'last night', but seemingly none with a voiceless plosive, even after *r*, a position in which plosives have not undergone voicing. Hence there are no certain native words of the forms *$bVrtV$-, *$gVrkV$- and so on. The rare exceptions are almost certainly loan words, like eastern *barta* ~ *parta* 'mud, muddy place, swamp', which is also found throughout western Romance, and *burki* 'birch', a rare variant of *urki*, and often thought to be a loan from Germanic.

3.17 MORPHEME STRUCTURE

Monomorphemic Basque nouns and adjectives of any antiquity are overwhelmingly disyllabic; monosyllables and trisyllables, while by no means rare, are much less common. (The special case of verbs is discussed separately below.) Moreover, these ancient nouns and adjectives conform strongly to certain severe constraints on their structure. It is worth looking at these patterns in some detail; if for no other reason, recognition of these patterns can help in deciding whether a given lexical item is genuinely ancient in the language or not. It is convenient to begin with the most frequent disyllabic pattern. Ancient disyllables generally conform to the following canonical form:

$$(C_1)V(C_2)C_3V(C_4)$$

As explained above, C_1, when present, is one of *b g z s l n*, or occasionally *m*, when this derives from original *b. C_4, when present, is one of *n l r tz ts*. If C_2 is absent, C_3 can be any consonant except *j*; if C_2 is present, then C_3 must be either a plosive (most often a coronal one) or an affricate; if C_3 is a plosive, C_2 must be one of *l r n z s*; if C_3 is an affricate, C_2 must be one of *l r n*. Either vowel may be a recognized diphthong, but not both. Here are some typical examples of each possible variant of this canonical form:

VC₃V

ate 'door', *euli* 'fly', *izu* 'trembling, fear', *atzo* 'yesterday', *atso* 'old woman', *idi* 'ox', *izai* 'fir', *ogi* 'bread', *ele* 'word, conversation', *alu* 'vulva', *ira* 'fern', *orri* 'leaf', *uda* 'summer', *urre* 'gold', *aita* 'father'

With *h* as C_3: *aho* 'mouth', *ohe* 'bed', *ihi* 'reed' (< *ini)

VC₃VC₄

izar 'star', *izen* 'name', *adar* 'horn, branch', *ilar* 'pea', *itzal* 'shade, shadow', *abar* 'branch', *igel* 'frog', *elur* 'snow', *ibar* 'valley', *irin* 'flour', *ikatz* 'charcoal', *orein* 'deer', *usain* 'odour', *aker* 'male goat', *arotz* 'carpenter'

With *h* as C_3: *ahal* 'ability' (< **anal*), *ahur* 'palm', *ohoin* 'thief' (< **ono-*), *oihan* 'forest', *ohol* 'wooden plank' (< **onol*), *eihar* 'dry', *ehun* 'hundred'

VC_2C_3V

aste 'week', *asto* 'donkey', *alde* 'side', *enda* 'race, breed', *arto* 'millet', *azpi* 'below', *osto* 'side', *erbi* 'hare', *argi* 'light', *azti* 'fortune-teller', *albo* 'side', *esku* 'hand', *ezki* 'linden', *erdi* 'half', *untzi* 'vessel, container', *ardi* 'sheep', *arte* 'holm-oak', *ortzi* 'sky', *urde* 'pig'

$VC_2C_3VC_4$

izter 'thigh', *astun* 'heavy', *argal* 'thin', *ozpin* 'vinegar', *indar* 'force', *ezker* 'left (hand)', *esker* 'thanks', *ezpain* 'lip'

C_1VC_3V

gerri 'waist', *zuri* 'white', *gari* 'wheat', *zulo* 'hole', *neba* 'brother (of a woman)', *bero* 'hot', *negu* 'winter', *garai* 'height', *berri* 'new', *lasai* 'calm'

With *h* as C_1 or C_3: *hori* 'yellow', *harri* 'stone', *herri* 'country', *hego* 'south', *mihi* 'tongue' (< **bini*), *sehi* 'child, boy' (< **seni*), *lohi* 'mud', *nahi* 'desire', *behi* 'cow', *ziho* 'tallow' (< **zino*)

Note that, in this pattern, it is extremely rare for both consonants to be plosives; in the few such cases, both plosives are voiced, as in *bide* 'road' and *gogo* 'mind'. In fact, it is uncommon even for C_3 to be plosive here, and almost unheard-of for it to be a voiceless plosive, *lepo* 'neck' and *zati* 'piece' being rare exceptions.

$C_1VC_3VC_4$

berun 'lead', *nabar* 'mottled, dark', *zilar* 'silver', *sabel* 'stomach', *gibel* 'liver', *gurin* 'animal fat', *gizen* 'fat', *lizun* 'lascivious', *leizar* 'ash tree', *zezen* 'bull', *zakur* 'dog'

With *h* as C_1 or C_3: *higuin* 'disgust', *haran* 'valley', *hegal* 'wing', *mahats* 'grapes' (< **banats*), *zahar* 'old', *lehor* 'dry', *lehen* 'first', *bihotz* 'heart'

$C_1VC_2C_3V$

garbi 'clean', *sarde* 'pitchfork', *gurdi* 'cart', *zaldi* 'horse', *salda* 'broth', *gazte* 'young', *mendi* 'mountain' (< **bendi?*), *giltza* 'key', *sendo* 'robust', *galde* 'question', *bertze* 'other'

With *h* as C_1: *handi* 'big', *hertze* 'intestine', *hontza* 'barn owl'

Recall that, in this pattern, if C_3 is a plosive, it must be voiced, except after a sibilant, when it must be voiceless, or after *r*, when it may be either.

$C_1VC_2C_3VC_4$

sorgin 'witch', *laster* 'quick', *ziztor* 'icicle', *bazter* 'edge', *bizkar* 'back'

With *h* as C$_1$: *hondar* 'sand', *harbel* 'slate'

A few of these, like *astun*, *ozpin* and *harbel*, are certainly or probably compounds, but very ancient ones.

This, then, is what native Basque words look like. The much smaller group of monosyllables follows the usual rules for initial and final consonants, except that initial *b* is curiously almost absent:

> *su* 'fire', *hotz* 'cold', *hots* 'cry, noise', *hitz* 'word', *lo* 'sleep', *lur* 'earth', *goi* 'height', *gau* 'night', *lan* 'work', *zin* 'oath', *gor* 'deaf', *sits* 'moth', *ar* 'male', *ur* 'water', *or* 'dog', *hur* 'hazelnut', *hil* 'dead', *latz* 'rough', *so* 'glance', *gar* 'flame', *soil* 'lone', *soin* 'body', *zur* 'wood', *haitz* 'oak', *gatz* 'salt'

A few monosyllables have final clusters: *hartz* 'bear', *beltz* 'black' (< **beletz*), *bortz* ~ *bost* 'five', *zurtz* 'orphan', *antz* 'resemblance', *bort* 'bastard', western *bart* 'last night' (< *barda*, preserved in the east). As can be seen, some of these clusters are secondary and very likely all of them are.

Trisyllables mostly look like disyllables with an extra vowel added at the end:

> *ardo* 'wine' (< **ardano*), *itsaso* 'sea', *hodei* 'cloud' (< **odeCe*), *belarri* 'ear', *mahai(n)* 'table' (< **banane*), *udare* 'pear', *ugari* 'numerous', *uztarri* 'yoke', but *hezur* 'bone' (< **enazur*), *erreka* 'ravine', *ipurdi* 'buttocks' (possibly bimorphemic)

Four-syllable stems arc all but unknown: *goroldio* 'moss' (possibly bimorphemic) and B *arerio* 'enemy' are virtually the only examples.

Verbal roots are very different in structure. For one thing, ancient verbal roots are very frequently monosyllabic; for another, they can begin with virtually any consonant, including a rhotic or a coronal plosive. Here is a sample; the ancient prefix **e-* and the participial suffix *-i* are segmented out:

> *e-karr-i* 'bring', *j-arr-i* 'put', *e-ser-i* 'sit down', *e-ror-i* 'fall', *i-pin-i* 'put', *i-dur-i* ~ *i-rud-i* 'seem', *e-dan* 'drink', *i-zek-i* 'burn', *i-bil-i* 'go about', *e-man* 'give', *j-oan* 'go', *e-torr-i* 'come', *e-gin* 'do, make', *e-ntzun* 'hear' (< **e-nezun*), *e-kin* 'get busy', *i-raun* 'last', *j-aus-i* 'fall', *e-ba-i* 'cut', *(e)-utz-i* 'leave', *e-rrun* 'lay eggs', *i-tzul-i* 'turn'

This preponderance of monosyllabic verbal roots raises severe questions, as does the fact that any consonant at all can occur in root-initial position. It is possible, of course, that verbal roots in Pre-Basque were simply subject to different morpheme-structure rules from nouns and adjectives; after all, verbal roots are never found in isolation, but only combined with other morphemes in finite and non-finite forms. But Michclcna, in several places, suggests that verbal roots preserve a more ancient phonotactics in which word-initial coronal plosives, at least, were possible in Basque. And Lakarra (1995) has chosen to attach still more weight to the verbal facts: he suggests that, at some exceedingly remote stage of the language, *all* lexical morphemes were monosyllabic, and that the dominant polysyllabic form of nouns and adjectives results from extensive compounding aided by a certain amount of reduplication. He has enjoyed a certain amount of success in identifying some ancient morphs with perhaps recognizable meanings, but it is too early to evaluate his research programme. If there ever was such a stage, it must have been long, long before the Pre-Basque of some 2,000 years ago reconstructed by Michelena.

For the rather distinctive phonology of 'expressive' formations, see section 5.5.

3.18 THE PROBLEM OF THE INITIAL VOWELS

This very great frequency of word-initial vowels has attracted a certain amount of comment and speculation. Broadly speaking, three views may be distinguished.

The null hypothesis.   The frequent initial vowels result neither from an ancient addition of vowels nor from an ancient loss of initial consonants. Instead, they represent nothing more than a phonotactic preference among ancient speakers, and there is nothing to be explained. Though rarely or never defended explicitly, this is probably the *de facto* view of most vasconists. Interestingly, there are two striking pieces of evidence in favour of this view. First, as we saw in section 3.11, the presence of the aspiration in words like *senhar* 'husband' and *alhaba* 'daughter' suggests that intervocalic consonants in Pre-Basque, or some of them, were apparently assigned to the preceding syllable, leaving the following syllable vowel-initial; this suggests that Pre-Basque had a strong phonotactic preference for vowel-initial syllables. Second, recall from section 3.8 that coronal consonants were palatalized by a preceding high front vowel, but not by a following one, again suggesting that such consonants were more tightly bound to the preceding vowel and hence again that an intervocalic consonant was assigned to the preceding syllable. None of this is decisive, of course, but it is certainly suggestive.

The vowel-addition hypothesis.   The initial vowels result from the ancient addition of vowels to lexical items which earlier began with consonants. The several defenders of this view have not generally favoured a merely phonological process of prothesis; instead, they have seen the vowels as fossilizations of ancient prefixes. Schuchardt (1893), for example, proposes that initial *e-* and *i-* in nouns often represent a fossilized ancient article. Bengtson (1991c, 1993) interprets almost all initial vowels instead as fossilized noun-class prefixes dating from a time when Basque had noun classes (see section 6.9). At present, there appears to be absolutely no direct evidence in favour of any such interpretation, but there is one point that should be noted. In ancient verbs, in which there is no doubt at all that the prefix *e- is uniformly present in non-finite forms (see Chapter Four), the majority of roots begin with consonants, and moreover a number of such verbs exhibit roots beginning with consonants which absolutely cannot occur initially in nouns or adjectives: *etorri* 'come', *eten* 'break, interrupt', *eduki* 'hold, have', *edan* 'drink', *iduri* ~ *irudi* 'seem' (it is not clear which of these is the earlier form), *irun* 'spin', *erein* 'sow', *ipini* 'put', *ekarri* 'bring', *ekin* 'get busy', and others. However, one should not make too much of this: the verbal prefix *e- is easily reconstructible for Pre-Basque, while not a single vocalic prefix can be sensibly reconstructed for nouns or adjectives. (Schuchardt's proposal is probably accepted by no one today, and Bengtson has been unable to identify any semantic correlations for his putative prefixes.)

The consonant-loss hypothesis.   The initial vowels are the result of a wholesale loss of certain initial consonants at some ancient stage of the language. Now the fact that Michelena's reconstruction of Pre-Basque sets up the surprisingly small figure of only six word-initial consonants might be taken as providing some considerable plausibility for the idea that the language had earlier lost some initial consonants, and scholars have not been slow to explore this possibility. Two versions of this hypothesis have been presented.

One version is the view of Theo Vennemann (1994a), who suggests that an ancestral form of Basque possessed a series of 'weak' consonants which, following the Indo-European tradition, he terms *laryngeals*. These consonants, he suggests, might have been [h], [ʔ] and various non-sibilant fricatives such as [x], [χ] and [f]. In Vennemann's account, all of these weak consonants were simply lost in initial position, leaving the language with a substantial number of newly vowel-initial words; he further proposes that, as in Indo-European, certain of these consonants, such as [χ], might have altered a following vowel to *a* before disappearing, thus accounting for the enormous frequency of initial *a* in Basque.

Vennemann's proposal, it seems to me, suffers from massive difficulties. For one thing, there is not the slightest shred of direct evidence for the earlier existence of these putative lost consonants. For another, these consonants, if they ever existed, would surely also have occurred in other than initial position, but there is no trace of them in medial or final position; hence Vennemann's account would apparently require that all these consonants were lost without trace in *all* positions, a view which involves a great deal of special pleading.

The other version has been defended most vigorously by the French linguist André Martinet in several publications, most notably in his 1955 book. (A somewhat similar view has recently been independently put forward by John Bengtson (p.c.), but Bengtson has so far neither developed nor published his ideas, and so I shall not consider them here.) Martinet's central thesis is simple. He proposes that the fortis (voiceless) plosives, confined to non-initial positions in Michelena's reconstruction of Pre-Basque, were, at some earlier stage, very frequent in word-initial position. In this position, he argues, they were always aspirated, and these aspirated initial plosives underwent weakening, first to fricatives, then to *h*. This *h* has at least sometimes remained in the aspirating dialects, but otherwise it has simply been lost.

There is no doubting the intrinsic phonetic plausibility of Martinet's idea: comparable developments are well attested in a number of other languages. Against Martinet's proposal, of course, is the fact that it would destroy the perfect symmetry of Michelena's reconstruction, since the fortis/lenis contrast would be extended to initial position for plosives and only for plosives. But an argument from symmetry can hardly be decisive, especially since it is clear from the evidence of Latin loans, in which initial plosives are almost invariably retained, that the lenition process posited by Martinet, if it ever occurred, must have occurred at a time before the stage reconstructed by Michelena. The question, of course, is whether there is any evidence for the loss of ancient initial plosives.

Interestingly, the answer appears to be 'yes – but not much'. There are four pieces of evidence, all of them very sparse and fragmentary, which might be interpreted as providing some kind of support for Martinet's proposal.

The first and most striking evidence comes from the three demonstratives and their derivatives. In the aspirating dialects, these invariably show initial *h*: *hau* ~ *hon-* 'this', *hori* ~ *horr-* 'that', *hura* ~ *har-* 'that (over there)', *hemen* 'here', *hor* 'there', *han* '(over) there' and so on. The remaining dialects overwhelmingly have vowel-initial items: *au* ~ *on-*, *ori* ~ *orr-*, *ura* ~ *ar-*, *emen, or, an* and so on. But some of the Pyrenean dialects show initial plosives. R has *kau* 'this', *kori* 'that', *kura* 'that (over there)', *keben* 'here' and so on throughout all the forms. And Aezk similarly has *gau, gori, gura, geben* and so on. It is very difficult to explain these plosives except by assuming that they are original: it looks very much as though these three stems anciently began with *k*, which has everywhere been reduced to *h* or lost, except in R and Aezk, in which *k* has either been exceptionally retained or voiced to *g*. In several publications Michelena has expressed the view that the initial plosive is indeed original in these stems, and has therefore been weakened or lost in all other dialects – though not everyone agrees with him in this interpretation, and note that the article is -*a* in the Pyrenean dialects as elsewhere (this derives from the distal demonstrative).

Of course, the obvious question at this point is whether the Pyrenean dialects exhibit other examples of initial plosives which are elsewhere absent. But this time the answer is 'no': all the other words which begin with vowels in the other dialects also begin with vowels in the Pyrenees. This is not encouraging.

Second, there are one or two items which are attested in Romance with an initial plosive but which lack that plosive in Basque. Notable is the case of the universal (h)*arri* 'rock'. A stem **karr-* 'rock, crag' is widely attested in western Romance; this has no Latin source, and is generally believed to be pre-Latin, possibly from Celtic, in which the stem is also attested. (See Corominas and Pascual (1980) under *alcarrila*.) There seems every reason to suppose that the Basque word is of the same origin, and hence that it too represents an instance of the lenition of an initial voiceless plosive. Moreover, the word for 'maple tree', which is *astigar* in most of the country and *aztigar* in G, appears as *gaztigar* in some eastern varieties. This leads Michelena (1959: 525; 1973a: 60; 1977a: 253) to suggest that this word is a compound whose second element is the obscure but securely attested *ihar* 'maple' (*Acer hispanicum*) and whose first element is **kast-*, attested in tree names in Latin and Romance and apparently of substrate origin.

Third, Basque exhibits a few morphemes which have variant forms with and without initial voiceless plosives. Most strikingly, there are a couple which function both as independent words and as derivational suffixes, and which show an initial voiceless plosive when they are suffixes, but not when they occur as free forms. Thus, for example, we have *ume* 'child', but -*kume* 'offspring' in such compounds as *katakume* 'kitten' (*katu* 'cat'), *arkume* 'lamb' (*ardi* 'sheep'), and probably also *emakume* 'woman', but 'girl' in Sal (*eme* 'female'). Similarly, we have *alde* 'side', but -*kalde* in a few derivatives like *sukalde* 'kitchen' (*su* 'fire'), and *ohi* 'habit, custom' but -*koi* 'fond of', as in *ardankoi* 'fond of wine' (*ard*(*a*)*o* 'wine'). In addition, there are quite a few derivational suffixes which have two forms, the one with the initial plosive being usually found after a consonant, the other after a vowel: -*tar* ~ -*ar* (ethnonymic), -*tasun* ~ -*asun* (abstract-noun suffix), -*tegi* ~ -*egi* 'place', -*kara* ~ -*ara* 'manner', -*kide* ~ -*ide* 'fellow' and a few others.

Finally, we have some tantalizing evidence from Aquitanian. As we shall see in section 6.9, the ancient Aquitanian language is the more-or-less direct ancestor of Basque. It is noteworthy that the Aquitanian names recorded in the northern part of Aquitania frequently show an initial *t-*, while names recorded in the south (near the Basque Country) do not. Moreover, there are one or two instances in which otherwise identical morphs are attested with *t-* in the north but with *h-* in the south: northern *Talsco-*, southern *Halsco-*. This could perhaps be taken as evidence that initial *t-*, while remaining in the extinct northern varieties of Aquitanian, had been lenited to *h-* in the southern varieties ancestral to Basque.

I am not aware of any further evidence for the ancient loss of initial plosives. Of course, it is entirely possible that Martinet is right, and that, with the few exceptions just noted, the loss of initial voiceless plosives was so early and so complete that no trace of them now remains. This is exactly the sort of problem on which we might reasonably expect some light to be shed if we could ever locate any distant relatives of Basque. Unfortunately, as we shall see in Chapter 6, the innumerable attempts to identify just such relatives, quite apart from their many other shortcomings, fail on precisely this point: they *never* shed such light, and they never offer any fruitful hypotheses about the prehistory of Basque before the Roman period. As Michelena has often stressed, this fact alone is enough to render valueless all the conjectured relationships. In all probability, we will never know anything about the origin of the vowel-initial words of Basque.

(Interestingly, I am aware of no explicit attempts to test Martinet's hypothesis by the dedicated seekers after genetic connections whose work is discussed in Chapter 6. Indeed, very many of these scholars quite explicitly segment the inconvenient initial vowels of Basque into oblivion in their search for cognates, thereby effectively adopting the vowel-addition hypothesis mentioned above. Since this policy has manifestly led to no interesting results, perhaps one or two of these investigators might like to redirect their efforts with Martinet's thesis in mind.)

3.19 DISTINCTIVE PHONOLOGY OF WORD-FORMATION

Words obtained by compounding and derivation are, of course, subject to the same phonological constraints and processes as other words. In addition, however, such formations show the effects of certain additional processes not exhibited elsewhere, except occasionally in verbal morphology. Some of these additional processes involve the most complex phonological developments in the language, and, taken together with the ordinary phonological changes that have affected Basque, they produce some interesting alternations between free forms and combining forms.

Generally speaking, both compounds and derivatives formed by suffixation behave in exactly the same way, and I shall not distinguish the two types of word-formation here (recall that prefixes are not used in word-formation, apart from a handful of late calques and loans from Romance). There are, however, significant differences in the treatment of a lexical stem which occurs as the first element in a compound or a derivative and of a lexical stem which occurs as the final element in a compound, and there are further certain peculiarities exhibited by some word-forming suffixes. I shall discuss each of these in turn. Throughout this discussion, recall that Basque *h* is not a true consonant and does not behave like one; in Pre-Basque it was purely a suprasegmental, and its presence generally had (and has) no effect upon word-formation. The abbreviations *NFS* and *VFS* stand for 'noun-forming suffix' and 'verb-forming suffix', respectively.

There is one general point to be made. Haplology is the norm in Basque; it usually occurs whenever it can possibly do so. Thus, for example, *sagar* 'apple' plus *ardo* ~ *arno* 'wine' ought to yield **sagarrardo* ~ **sagarrarno* by the usual rules, but the word is *sagardo* ~ *sagarno* 'cider'. The compound of *eme* 'female' and *magiña* 'sheath' ought to yield **emamagiña*, but the word is *emagiña* 'vagina'. Syllable loss may occur even when the consecutive syllables are not quite identical: *ume* 'offspring' plus *berri* 'new' yields *umerri* 'lamb'; *beko* 'forehead' plus *gorri* 'red' yields LN Z *bekorri* 'red mark on an animal's forehead'.

3.19.1 First elements

It is first elements which exhibit the most complex behaviour. These complexities derive from the action of a sizeable number of phonological changes, both language-wide and specific to word-formation; only in a few instances is it possible to determine the order in which these developments must have occurred, and here I shall adopt an order of presentation which, I hope, will be maximally illuminating. I begin with final vowels.

A final vowel in a first element behaves differently depending on which syllable it is in. If it occurs in the first syllable (that is, if the first element is a monosyllable), the vowel is unaffected. Since monosyllables are not common in Basque, there are only a few such cases. Examples:

ke 'smoke' + *zulo* 'hole' → *kezulo* 'chimney'
lo 'sleep' + *gela* 'room' → *logela* 'bedroom'
hi 'you' (intimate) + *-keta* Activity NFS → *hiketa* 'use of the intimate pronoun'
su 'fire' + *-gai* 'suitable for' → *sugai* 'fuel'
jo 'hit' + *aldi* 'occasion' → *joaldi* '(a) blow'
su 'fire' + *harri* 'stone' → *suarri* 'flint'

A final vowel in a third or later syllable is lost:

itsaso 'sea' + *gizon* 'man' → *itsasgizon* 'sailor' (*g* = [k])
iturri 'spring' + *buru* 'head' → *iturburu* 'fountainhead'
txapela 'beret' + *-dun* 'having' → *txapeldun* 'champion'
eliza 'church' + *-koi* 'fond of' → *elizkoi* 'pious'
pilota 'jai alai' + *-ari* Professional NFS → *pilotari* 'jai alai player'
itsaso 'sea' + *untzi* 'vessel' → *itsasuntzi* 'ship'

Recent formations are often exceptions:

pilota 'jai alai' + *leku* 'place' → *pilotaleku* 'jai alai court'
euskara 'Basque language' + *-tu* VFS → *euskaratu* 'translate into Basque'

An earlier formation would have yielded **euskaldu* for the second (see below for the complications).

In a second syllable, a final vowel is usually lost before a following vowel:

baso 'woods' + *urde* 'hog' → *basurde* 'wild boar'
erre 'burn' + *hauts* 'dust' → *errauts* 'ash'
baso 'woods' + *herri* 'habitation' → *baserri* 'farmhouse'
aita 'father' + *on* 'good' → *aiton* 'grandfather'

gerra 'war' + *aldi* 'time' → *gerraldi* 'wartime'
otso 'wolf' + *eme* 'female' → *otseme* 'she-wolf'
buru 'head' + *hezur* 'bone' → *burhezur* 'skull'
oilo 'hen' + *ar* 'male' → *oilar* 'cock, rooster'
aita 'father' + *ama* 'mother' + *-k* Pl → *aitamak* '(one's) parents'

But compare

seme 'son' + *alaba* 'daughter' + *-k* Pl → *seme-alabak* '(one's) children'

Recent formations often fail to observe this rule:

gero 'later' + *aldi* 'time' → *geroaldi* 'future tense' (grammar)

Otherwise, in a second syllable, a final vowel *i* is lost:

harri 'stone' + *-gin* 'maker' → *hargin* 'stonecutter'
herri 'country' + *beste* 'other' → *herbeste* 'foreign country'
harri 'stone' + **bel* 'black' → *harbel* 'slate'

It will become clear below that such loss of *i* was anciently a pervasive process. None the less, exceptions are not wanting:

harri 'stone' + *-tu* VFS → *harritu* 'surprise' (originally 'petrify'?)

Here there is an obvious functional explanation: the expected **hartu* would be homophonous with the common verb *hartu* 'take'. In fact, however, *harri* 'stone' forms a large number of derivatives in which the *i* is not lost, such as *harrikada* 'blow with a stone' and *harriola* 'stony place'; many of these are severely localized and may be late formations. But a number of other common words, such as *berri* 'new', *gorri* 'red' and *zuri* 'white' absolutely never lose their *i*. It is hard to know what to make of this. Moreover, *i* is not normally lost after a labial: *zubi* 'bridge' + *-gin*, *-gile* 'who makes' yields *zubigin*, *zubigile* 'bridge-builder'.

In a second syllable, final *-a*, *-o* and *-e* are all neutralized as *-a*:

lore 'flower' + *-tu* VFS → *loratu* 'bloom, blossom'
zulo 'hole' + *-tu* VFS → *zulatu* 'dig'
gona 'skirt' + *-dun* 'having' → *gonadun* '(one) who is wearing a skirt'
baso 'woods' + *jaun* 'lord' → *basajaun* 'Old Man of the Woods'
golde 'plough' + *-tu* VFS → *goldatu* 'plough' (v.)
otso 'wolf' + *porru* 'leek' → *otsaporru* 'wild leek'
sendo 'healthy' + *-garri* Instr NFS → *sendagarri* 'remedy'
etxe 'house' + *gain* 'top' → *etxagain* 'roof'
maite 'beloved' + *-tu* VFS → *maitatu* 'love' (v.)
beso 'arm' + *-pe* 'under' → *besape* 'armpit'
kanta 'song' + *-tu* VFS → *kantatu* 'sing'
aza- 'cabbage' + *lore* 'flower' → *azalore* 'cauliflower'

(The noun *azak* 'cabbage' is always plural in Basque.)

The treatment of *u* in this position is complex. Sometimes it is lost (like *i*), sometimes it is neutralized to *a* and sometimes it remains unaffected. Broadly speaking, loss of *u* is most frequent in the east (especially in Z) but becomes less common as we move towards the west, while lowering to *a* is most frequent in the west, but all three outcomes are widely attested. Here are a few examples:

gatu 'cat' + *belar* 'grass' → *gatubelar* 'catnip' (L)
katu 'cat' + *-kume* 'offspring' → *katakume* 'kitten' (B G)
katu 'cat' + *narru* 'skin' → *katanarru* 'catskin' (B)
buru 'head' + *-kide* '-fellow' → *burkide* 'comrade, colleague' (Z R LN, but attested in old B)
buru 'head' + *-ko* NFS → *buruko* 'cap' (Z LN HN), 'pillow' (G), but *burko* 'pillow' (B)
esku 'hand' + *zabal* 'wide' → *eskuzabal* 'generous' (common)

Several further instances of apparent lowering merely reflect the Romance origins of the words involved: *gertu* 'certain, ready' and *gertatu* 'prepare', *kantu* 'song' and *kantatu* 'sing', and so on.

Very few lexical items end in plosives, but the cases of vowel loss just discussed often bring plosives into final position in a first element. The treatment of such final plosives is complex. If such a plosive is followed by a vowel, then the plosive is usually converted to *t*:

begi 'eye' + *ile* 'hair' → *betile* 'eyelash'
begi 'eye' + *azal* 'skin' → *betazal* 'eyelid'
gurdi 'cart' + *abere* 'animal' → *gurtabere* 'draught animal'
ardi 'sheep' + *ile* 'hair' → *artile* 'wool'
argi 'light, bright' + *izar* 'star' → *artizar* 'morning star'
sagu 'mouse' + *itsu* 'blind' → *satitsu* 'shrew'
sagu 'mouse' + *and(e)re* ~ *and(e)ra* 'lady' → *satandre* ~ *satandera* 'weasel'
erdi 'half' + *hordi* 'drunk' → *ertordi* 'tipsy' (Z)

If a sibilant follows, the combination of *t* plus sibilant yields an affricate:

begi 'eye' + *sein* 'boy' → *betsein* 'pupil' (of the eye)
ogi 'bread' + *zare* 'basket' → B *otzara* 'basket'
bat 'one' + *-zu* Indef Pl → *batzu* 'several, some'
ardi 'sheep' + *-zai(n)* 'guardian' → *artzai(n)* 'shepherd'
ogi 'bread' + *sein* 'boy' → *otsein* 'servant'
errege 'king' + *zubi* 'bridge' → *Erretzubi* (habitation name)

Before a sonorant, the plosive is lost:

bat 'one' + *-na* Distributive → *bana* 'one apiece'
bait- Verbal prefix + *naiz* 'I am' → *bainaiz* 'since I am, I who am'

If the plosive is followed by another plosive, the cluster is resolved as follows: the cluster is reduced to a single plosive which has the place of articulation of the second original plosive and which is invariably voiceless:

begi 'eye' + *buru* 'head' → *bepuru* 'eyebrow'
begi 'eye' + *gain* 'top' → *bekain* 'eyebrow'
idi 'ox' + *-tegi* 'place' → *itegi* 'stable for oxen'
errege 'king' + *bide* 'road' → *errepide* 'highway' (this one is attested as *erret bide* in the Fuero General of Navarre)
gurdi 'cart' + *bide* 'road' → *gurpide* 'cartpath'
ogi 'bread' + *-gin* 'maker' → *okin* 'baker'
ogi 'bread' + *-bil* 'round' → *opil* 'bread roll'
ogi 'bread' + *mehe* 'slender' (< **bene*) → *ope* 'slender cake'
bat 'one' + *-tu* VFS → *batu* 'unite, unify'
lot- 'tie, fasten' + *-garri* Instr NFS → *lokarri* 'link'
polit 'pretty' + *-ki* adv. → *poliki* 'slowly, gently'
ardi 'sheep' + *-kume* 'offspring' → *arkume* 'lamb'
ardi 'sheep' + *mihi* ~ *min* 'tongue' (< **bini*) → *arpin* 'plantain'
Lapurdi (a province) + *-tar* 'who is from' → *lapurtar* 'person from Lapurdi'

Oddly, this process seems rarely or never to occur when the first element contains a voiceless plosive with a following vowel: for example, *erreka* 'stream' + *bide* 'road' does not yield **errepide*, but rather *errekabide* 'riverbed' (compare *errege* + *bide* above). And, as explained above, it also fails to occur if vowel loss would expose a labial: compare *zubigin* 'bridge-builder' with *okin* 'baker'.

These developments are attested in medieval toponyms – hence *Eleizpe*, *Elexpe*, *Elizpea*, *Elizpuru*, etc., all from *el(e)iza* 'church' plus *-pe* 'below' or *buru* 'head', and *Erret Ihera* and *Erret Zubi*, from *errege* 'king' plus *ihera* 'mill' and *zubi* 'bridge'. They are not, however, attested in Aquitanian, in which we find names like *Senitennis* and *Cissonbonis*, with the combining forms *seni-* 'boy' and *gizon-* 'man', in place of the expected *sen-* and *giza-*.

Michelena (1951) proposes the following explanation for these reductions. The first element of a compound bore the primary stress (leading to reduction of the second element: see the next section). This would, in isolation, have fallen on the second syllable (section 3.13), but, in a compound, the stress would have been retracted to the first syllable by a process not unlike the familiar 'thirteen-men rule' of English. And the resulting initial stress in the first element would have led to the observed reductions.

In certain cases, the first element in a formation exhibits an unexpected *t*, or a devoicing of a following plosive, even though there is no plosive to act as a source. Examples:

su 'fire' + *argi* 'light' → *sutargi* 'firelight'

behi 'cow' + -*zai(n)* 'guardian' → *betzai(n)* 'cowherd'
zohi 'sod' + *erdi* 'half, middle' → *zoterdi* 'fallow land'
eri 'finger' + *gain* 'top' → *erkain* 'fingertip'
harri 'rock' + *gaitz* 'big' → *harkaitz* 'boulder'
bihi 'vintage, fruit, grain' + *gain* 'top' → *bikain* 'cream; excellent'
oin 'foot' + *huts* 'bare' → *ortuts* 'barefoot'

(The unexpected *r* in the word for 'barefoot' is discussed below.) It is not clear what to make of this, but Michelena (1977a: 224) is inclined to see this merely as an overgeneralization of *t*-formation in first elements, and not as a direct continuation of some earlier phonological development.

Historically, all such cases of final vowel loss clearly preceded the loss of intervocalic -*n*-. As a result, we find some striking alternations:

ardao ~ *ardo* 'wine' (< **ardano*) + -*tza* NFS → *ardantza* 'vineyard'
katea 'chain' (< **katena*) + *begi* 'eye' → *katenbegi* 'link of a chain'
harea 'sand' (< **harena*) + *erloju* 'clock' → *haren erloju* 'hourglass'
mihi ~ *min* 'tongue' (< **mini*) + -*tzo* NFS → *mintzo* 'conversation'
artzai(n) 'shepherd' (< **artzani*) + -*tza* NFS → *artzantza* 'shepherding'
balea 'whale' (< **balena*) + *bizar* 'beard' → *balenbizar* 'whalebone'
bigai ~ *biga* 'heifer' (< **bigane*) + -*txa* Dimin → *bigantxa* 'young heifer'

You will recognize here the loans from Latin CATENA 'chain', ARENA 'sand' and BALLAENA 'whale'.

Very commonly, a final *n* in the first element remains even when it is intervocalic:

sehi 'boy' (< **seni*) + *ar* 'male' → *senar* 'husband'
on 'good' + -*etsi* 'consider' → *onetsi* 'approve of'
zin 'truth' + -*etsi* 'consider' → *sinetsi* 'believe' (archaic *zinetsi*)

Such words commonly bear the aspiration in northern dialects (*senhar*, *onhetsi*, *sinhetsi*). It appears that the morpheme boundary was enough to prevent the regular loss of intervocalic *n*. But sometimes the *n* is lost:

sehi 'child' (< **seni*) + *aska* 'cradle' → *seaska* 'cradle'
on 'good' + -*asun* '-ness' → old B *o(g)asun* 'goodness'
zezen 'bull' + -*aga* → *Zezeaga* (house name in Gip)

The regular change of intervocalic *l* into *r* has led to comparable alternations:

euskara 'Basque language' (< **euskala*) + -*dun* 'having' → *euskaldun* 'Basque-speaker'
gari 'wheat' (< **gali*) + *buru* 'head' → *galburu* 'head of wheat'
haizkora 'axe' (< **haizkola*) + -*ari* Professional NFS → *haizkolari* 'woodcutter'
joare 'bell' (< **joale*) + -*dun* 'having' → *joaldun* 'bellwether'

eri 'illness' (< *eli) + *gaitz* 'bad' → *elgaitz* 'fever'
bazkari 'lunch' (< *bazkali) + -*tu* VFS → *bazkaldu* 'eat lunch'

The word for 'axe' is of course a loan from Latin ASCIOLA.
  It is clear that this second alternation has sometimes undergone inversion:

zamari 'horse' (< Lat SAGMARIU 'pack-horse') + -*dun* 'having' → *zamaldun* 'horseman'
merkatari 'merchant' (< Lat MERCATU 'market' + Lat -ARIU Professional NFS) + -*goa* Collective NFS → *merkatalgoa* 'commerce'
amore 'love' (< Lat AMORE) + -*tsu* 'full of' → *amoltsu* 'affectionate'

Naturally, it is possible that a few of the cases cited earlier might also represent instances of such inversion, rather than an original intervocalic lateral, but we have no way of knowing in the case of native words.
  First elements which end in -*n* to begin with often show unexpected behaviour. On the one hand, the nasal is sometimes simply lost; on the other, it occasionally develops into -*r*. The first of these may trigger some of the other developments we have already seen. Examples:

egun 'day' + *erdi* 'middle' → *eguerdi* 'noon'
egun 'day' + -*zki* NFS → *eguzki* 'sun' (western)
egun 'day' + -*ki* NFS → *eki* 'sun' (eastern)
egun 'day' + *aldi* 'time' → *eguraldi* 'weather'
gizon 'man' + *bide* 'way' → *gizabide* 'conduct; gentlemanly behaviour'
gizon 'man' + -*koi* 'fond of' → *gizakoi* 'man-chasing woman'
gizon 'man' + *aldi* 'time' → *gizaldi* '(a) generation'
jaun 'lord' + -*egi* 'place' → *jauregi* 'palace'
jaun 'lord' + -*etsi* 'consider' → *jauretsi* 'adore' (archaic)
jaun 'lord' + -*goa* Collective NFS → *jaurgoa* 'seigneury' (archaic)
belaun 'knee' + -*ik* adv. + -*ko* Adjectival → *belauriko* 'on one's knees'
oin 'foot' + *huts* 'bare' → *ortuts* 'barefoot'
oihan 'forest' + *zabal* 'wide' → *Oyarzabal* (surname)

The frequency of these curious developments varies according to item. For *gizon*, the combining form *giza-* is categorical and appears in dozens of derivatives; for *egun*, we most often find *egu-* before a consonant and *egur-* before a vowel, but there are exceptions, though we almost always find one or the other in ancient formations. For *jaun*, we nearly always find *jaur-* in its few derivatives; *jaun-* appears in the diminutive *jauntxo* 'local political big-wig' (a very common word in the medieval period), but diminutives often fail to undergo otherwise regular processes. For the other words cited, the combining form in -*r* is uncommon and appears only occasionally; more usually, the -*n* is retained in word-formation. (The unexpected *t* in the word for 'barefoot' was discussed above.)
  First elements which end in -*r* to begin with often lose the rhotic in

word-formation; this is most obviously the case with words which end underlyingly in the tapped rhotic, but the trilled rhotic is also lost in certain circumstances. First, examples with the tapped rhotic (*ur* 'water', Definite *ura*, and *zur* 'wood', Definite *zura*):

ur 'water' + *bide* 'road' → *ubide* 'irrigation canal'
ur 'water' + *alde* 'side' → *uhalde* ~ *ugalde* 'riverbank'
zur 'wood' + *haitz* 'oak' → *zuhaitz* ~ *zu(g)a(i)tz* 'tree'
zur 'wood' + *bihotz* 'heart' → *zubihotz* 'heart of oak'

There are very few Basque words ending in a rhotic which surfaces as a tap in intervocalic position, but these two very common ones almost always lose the rhotic in word-formation in formations of any antiquity. Formations which retain the *r*, like *urgain* 'surface of the water' (*gain* 'top') may in most cases be safely regarded as of recent origin (compare *uhain* 'wave', probably of identical formation).

Many frequent words ending in a trilled rhotic behave in the same way (*lur* 'earth', Definite *lurra*), and so on:

lur 'earth' + *bizi* 'living' → *lubizi* 'landslide'
lur 'earth' + *hartz* 'bear' → *luhartz* 'scorpion'
lur 'earth' + *gorri* 'red' → *lugorri* 'cultivated land'
adar 'branch' + *begi* 'eye' → *adabegi* 'knot' (in a tree)
hamar 'ten' + *bi* 'two' → *hamabi* 'twelve'
behor 'mare' + *-ka* Dimin → *behoka* 'filly'
izter 'thigh' + *-egi* NFS → *izte(g)i* 'groin'

This puzzling process is clearly ancient: it is generally believed that *ibai* 'river' is derived from *ibar* 'water meadow, valley' by the addition of a suffix, and that the province name *Bizkai(a)* is derived in the same way from *bizkar* 'elevation' (both *ibar* and *bizkar* have trilled rhotics). It is, however, dead: more recent formations do not show the loss of a rhotic, and we find instead forms like B *urtxakur* 'otter' (*ur* 'water' + *txakur* 'dog') and *lurrikara* 'earthquake' (*lur* 'earth' + *ikara* 'trembling').

More dramatic reductions may occur. The verb *egin* 'do, make' has a combining form *egi-* which is frequently reduced, as in the combination of its verbal noun *egite* 'deed' with the suffix *-une*; this should have yielded **egita-une*, but the attested forms in B are *itaune* ~ *itauna* ~ *itun* 'question; advice; confession'. B *egiune* 'agreement' appears to represent *egi-* plus *-une* directly.

3.19.2 Second elements

We have already seen that the initial segment of a second element is sometimes modified by the influence of the preceding first element. Beyond this, however, there are certain types of reduction which may affect a second element, particularly in the oldest compounds. Such reductions chiefly affect disyllables which have a medial aspiration in the aspirating dialects, such as *zahar* 'old': when such an item stands in second position, it must lose its aspiration, because *h*, recall, cannot occur later in a word than the onset of the second syllable. Thus:

zahar 'old' → *-zar*
behe 'below' → *-be, -pe*
mehe 'thin, slender' → *-me*
bahe 'sieve' → *-be*
gehi 'quantity, material' → *-gei, -gai*
ohi 'habit' → *-(k)oi*

Examples:

ardi 'sheep' + *zahar* 'old' → *artzar* 'old sheep' (Z LN)
or 'dog' + *zahar* 'old' → *ozar* 'big dog' (L)
zur 'wood' + *mehe* 'slender' → *zume* 'osier' (common)
zeta 'silk' + *bahe* 'sieve' → *zetabe* 'fine sieve' (Z)

The frequent noun-forming suffix *-tza* appears many times in the eleventh-century *Reja da San Millán* as *-zaha*, and even today *-tza* appears in places as *-tzai-* when followed by the article *-a*. We may reconstruct *(t)zaha + -a > *-tzaea > -tzaia.*

Various other reductions take place in this position:

luze 'long' → *-luz*
gabe ~ *bage* 'without' → *-ga, -ge, -ke*
duen 'who has' → *-dun*

Examples:

egi 'hill' + *luze* 'long' → *Egiluz* (toponym in Araba)
indar 'force' + *bage* 'without' → *indarga* 'feeble' (B)
bizar 'beard' + *duen* 'who has' → *bizardun* 'bearded (person)'

In a number of cases, it is clear, the form of a word occurring in second position has been generalized as an autonomous word. The anomalous eastern word *tzar* 'bad' (western *txar*) is derived from *zahar* 'old' used as a second element, as in *artzar* 'old sheep' above. The original *gehi* 'quantity, material' is now little used except in derivatives like *gehiago* 'more'; the form *gai* ~ *gei* has been generalized as the ordinary word for 'material, topic'. The now nearly universal *bi* 'two' doubtless results from a reduction of earlier *biga* in second position; we have clear textual evidence that this numeral was formerly postposed, as it still is in B today. The word *beltz* 'black' is a derivative of the familiar element **bel-* 'dark'; it is probably a generalization of a reduced form of **beletz*, which appears to be attested in Aquitanian. The word *ertz* 'edge' has an attested variant *eretz* which is doubtless original, *ertz* resulting from compounds like *itsas-ertz* 'seaside'. The suffix *-koi* 'fond of' has yielded in Z an independent adjective *khoi* 'inclined (to do something)', and the suffix *-kume* 'offspring' has in B given rise to a word *kume* 'offspring (of an animal)' which now contrasts with the historically related *ume* 'child'. Since the eighteenth century, the very common suffix *-tasun* '-ness' has been used as a noun *tasun* 'quality'; in the modern language this even forms derivatives like *tasunezko* 'qualitative'. The anomalously formed words *talde* 'group', *toki* 'place' and one or two others in this vein, with their initial voiceless plosives, likewise result from the generalization of what were originally bound second elements. This is a topic which needs further investigation.

3.20 PHONOLOGICAL PECULIARITIES OF PROPER NAMES

The formation of surnames and of place names is discussed in some detail in Chapter 5. A few phonological points are, however, more appropriately discussed here.

Proper names formed by compounding and derivation are, in general, subject to the usual rules of word-formation discussed in the last section. In addition, however, they sometimes exhibit two further peculiarities which are not shared by other instances of word-formation.

The first peculiarity is confined to habitation names and to the French Basque Country, but within these limits it is categorical: any name which would otherwise end in a consonant automatically acquires a final *-e*. Thus, for example, the village whose name derives from *ur* 'water' and *epel* 'warm' is *Urepele*, with the final vowel apparently added merely to prevent the occurrence of a final consonant. Likewise, the famous resort known in French and in English as *Biarritz* (an obviously Basque name) is locally known as *Miarritze*, showing the final *-e* as well as a slightly unusual instance of the development of initial *b-* to *m-*. The same final vowel appears in *Azkaine* and *Berrogañe*, two villages whose names obviously include the final element *gain* 'top', and indeed in every single other such case north of the Pyrenees. It may well be that this final *-e* results from the renalysis of inflected forms in which the *e* is required for phonological reasons.

It appears that toponyms other than habitation names are not subject to this rule. In fact, the overwhelming majority of river names and mountain names in the north also end in vowels, but in almost every case the final vowel appears to be organic or (often in the case of mountain names) to be the article *-a*. None the less, there is a river called *Aran* and a small but famous mountain called *Larrun*, so I assume that vowel addition has not in general applied to such names. Nor is there any sign of the process south of the Pyrenees, where such habitation names as *Zarautz, Lemoiz, Ipazter, Laukiz, Andoain, Oiartzun, Eibar, Elgoibar* and *Ituren* are exceedingly common.

The second peculiarity affects both habitation names and (more especially, perhaps) surnames on both sides of the Pyrenees, but it is sporadic and far from categorical. This is the loss of an *initial* vowel. For example, the northern city and town called *Baiona* and *Baigorri* appear to be transparently from **ibai ona* 'the good river' and **ibai gorri* 'red river'. These etymologies are widely accepted (though see Chapter 5 for a different view), and they appear to show a loss of an initial vowel which is virtually unknown in ordinary instances of word-formation, except in a few cases of unusual length, such as B *bariku(a)* 'Friday', from **abari-baga-ko(-a)* 'dinner-without-*ko*(-*a*)' '(day) without dinner'. In the south, we have examples like *Zeanuri*, from **azenari-uri* 'fox-city', via the loss of intervocalic *-n-* and dissimilation of the first *-r-* to *-n-*: **Azenaruri > *Azearuri > *Azeanuri > Zeanuri*. (Alternatively, the **a-* might have been lost early, when the name was still six syllables long.) Several towns, such as *Barkoxe, Bardoze* and *Barrundia*, have names whose first element looks like *ibar* 'water meadow, valley', but the etymologies are not certain. There are, however, no more than a handful of certain or probable instances of such vowel loss in habitation names, and perhaps no case among other types of toponym.

Such vowel loss is noticeably more frequent in surnames. The exceedingly common element *etxe* 'house', whose combining form as a first element is variously *etxe-* or *etxa-*, not infrequently loses its initial vowel. Hence, the surname *Etxaberri* 'new house' has a variant *Txaberri*; *Etxaide* 'house-road' (*bide* 'road') is sometimes *Txaide*; and there are other similar cases. (The male given name *Xabier* (= Spanish *Javier*, English *Xavier*) is thought to be a development of *Etxaberri*, with Romance mediation to explain the vocalism.) A few such cases produce the startling result of creating a surname with initial *r-*, something which is otherwise absolutely prohibited in Basque. Thus, *Errekalde* 'beside the stream' has a common variant *Rekalde*, and *Errotaetxe* 'mill-house' has a very common variant *Rotaetxe*, and there are quite a few others.

Given the phonological impossibility of this last group, and given the generally highly sporadic nature of the process, it seems difficult to avoid the conclusion that, at least with the surnames, we are here not looking at a true Basque development at all, but only at a process which has sometimes applied in Romance to names of Basque origin to produce forms which have then been taken back into Basque. There is certainly some evidence for such vowel loss in Romance: for example, the Spanish surname *Chávez* is thought by many to derive from the common Basque surname *Etxabeste* 'other-house', but no such form as **Txabeste* or anything similar appears to be attested in Basque. On the other hand, there seems less reason to suspect Romance intervention in the toponyms.

3.21 PHONOLOGICAL TREATMENT OF RECENT LOANS

The phonology of Basque has been much disturbed by the influx of loan words over the last 2,000 years, and it is now far more similar to the phonologies of the surrounding Romance languages, especially Castilian, than was formerly the case. Consequently, recent loans typically adhere very closely in form to their Romance models.

Romance plosives are usually taken over unchanged, even after a nasal; final *t* and *k* are now tolerated, and plosive–liquid clusters are tolerated in both initial and medial position. Examples: *kobre* 'copper' (< Sp *cobre*), *ganibet* 'knife' (< Occ *ganibet*), *preso* 'prisoner' (< Sp *preso*), *truk* 'exchange' (< Fr *troc*), *pinta* 'pint' (< Sp *pinta*).

Castilian ⟨s⟩ (apical /s/) and ⟨z⟩ (/θ/) are borrowed as *s* and *z* respectively: *sozialista* 'socialist' (< Sp *socialista*). French laminal /s/ is conventionally borrowed as *z*, and hence French Basques have traditionally said, and written, *zozializta* for the same word, but this policy has been rejected by the Academy in favour of the southern usage. French /z/ is also borrowed as *z*: *zinga* 'zinc' (< *zinc*). Final sibilants are now accepted: *arroz* 'rice' (< Sp *arroz*), which now forms a minimal pair with native *arrotz* 'foreigner'. After *n* or *l*, a Romance sibilant is borrowed as an affricate: *garbantzu* 'chick-pea' (< Sp *garbanzo*), *boltsa* 'bag' (< Sp *bolsa*). Spanish ⟨ch⟩ and French ⟨tch⟩ are borrowed as *tx*: *Txina* 'China' (< Sp *China*). French ⟨ch⟩ is usually borrowed as *x*: *Xina* 'China' (< Fr *Chine*). Both French ⟨j⟩ and Castilian ⟨j⟩ are commonly borrowed as *j*: *jeneral* 'general' (< Sp *general*, Fr *général*). The fricative *f* is now accepted both initially and medially: *falta* 'error, fault' (< Sp *falta*), *Afrika* 'Africa' (< Sp *Africa*, Fr *Afrique*). But ⟨v⟩ is borrowed as *b*: *greba* 'strike' (< Fr *grève*).

A curiosity is that the final /d/ of Spanish, which is phonetically [θ], is borrowed as [θ] by some Spanish Basques, as in *UNE*[θ]*eko* 'of UNED' (Universidad Nacional de Educación a Distancia). Such a Spanish [θ] is never borrowed as *z*, while Spanish /θ/ is invariably borrowed as *z*, and never as [θ].

Romance nasals pose few problems. The palatal nasal is usually taken over as *ñ*: *koñak* 'cognac' (< Fr *cognac*, Sp *coñac*). Some speakers, however, unpack the palatal: *kotnak*. Final *m* is not tolerated: *uraniuma* (< Fr *uranium*).

Liquids likewise pose few problems, but word-initial *r* is still not tolerated by most speakers, and a prothetic vowel must be added: *erradio* 'radium' (< Sp *radio*), *arropa* 'clothes' (< Sp *ropa*).

The five Spanish vowels are generally taken over without change, except that final /o/ is not infrequently borrowed as *u*: *banku* 'bank' (< Sp *banco*). The additional vowels and diphthongs of French pose problems. French ⟨u⟩ (/y/) is borrowed as *u*, while the other front rounded vowels are rendered variously, and the diphthongs are converted into Basque diphthongs according to their French spelling: *boitura* 'car' (< Fr *voiture*). The final schwa of Fench (which is pronounced in the south) is borrowed as *a*, as in the last example. A French nasal vowel is usually rendered with a following *n*: *trein* 'train' (< Fr *train*).

Particularly interesting is the treatment of Spanish final *-ón*, which is consistently borrowed as Basque *-oi*: *kamioi* 'truck, lorry' (< *camión*), *abioi* 'airplane' (< *avión*), *patroi* 'boss' (< *patrón*). The equivalent treatment does not apply to other vowels: *atun* 'tuna' (< *atún*), *delfin* 'dolphin' (< *delfín*), *afan* 'zeal' (< *afán*). And it happens even though final *-on* is perfectly possible in Basque: *gizon* 'man', *gabon* 'Christmas', *inon* 'anywhere'. The reason for this is a historical one. The Romance ending was originally *-one*, and this developed in Spanish merely by losing its final *-e*, yielding the modern *-ón*. In Basque, borrowed words with *-one* underwent the usual loss of intervocalic *n*, producing first *-oe* and then *-oi*. So, Romance words like **ratone* 'rat' and **razone* 'reason, right' have come into Castilian as *ratón* and *razón*, but into Basque as *arratoi* and *arrazoi*. Basque-speakers have therefore clearly concluded that Basque *-oi* is the normal equivalent of Spanish *-ón*, and so they continue to adjust new loans in *-ón* accordingly.

For further discussion, see Hualde (1993).

Chapter 4

Grammar

Since we have substantial connected texts only from the sixteenth century, and since those early texts are very largely congruent with the modern language in their grammar, the study of the history of Basque morphology and syntax has made little progress in comparison with the study of the phonology and the lexicon. Nevertheless, some conclusions can be drawn, and there is no shortage of speculative but interesting proposals, especially in the most recent literature. Here I shall summarize what we know, and discuss the most interesting proposals.

4.1 PRONOUNS, DEMONSTRATIVES AND THE ARTICLES

The personal pronouns *ni* 'I', *gu* 'we', *hi* 'you' and *zu* 'you' are clearly ancient. It is clear that *hi* was formerly singular and *zu* plural, but that *zu* has become an unmarked singular pronoun, with *hi* now restricted to certain special contexts. This is shown by the fact that *zu* takes plural absolutive agreement in finite verbs, exactly parallel to *gu* 'we'; moreover, the lexicographer Azkue reported, in the late nineteenth century, that *zu* was still in use as a plural pronoun in parts of Bizkaia. The modern plural pronoun *zuek* is a late creation, formed by adding a plural suffix to *zu*; in agreement, this new pronoun takes double plural marking. (On the agreement, see Chapter 2.) Accordingly, for the rest of this chapter, I shall treat *hi* as a singular form and *zu* as a plural form, with little discussion of the late creation *zuek*; this is convenient in historical work, but the reader should bear in mind that the modern language is different.

Some eastern varieties have created an additional second-person singular pronoun *xu* by palatalizing *zu*; this is intermediate in intimacy between *zu* and *hi*, and its origin clearly postdates the use of *zu* as a singular. A few western varieties have introduced a highly respectful second-person singular pronoun *berori* (*ber-* 'self' + *hori* 'that'), possibly on the model of Spanish, with its numerous respectful forms like *usted* 'you', from *vuestra merced* 'your grace'. See Alberdi (1995) for a survey of the historical development of these pronouns.

Third-person pronouns, which are generally absent, have been constructed in B and G by taking the intensive/reflexive stem *ber-* 'self' and adding to it the article: hence *bera* 'he, she', *berak* 'they' (some varieties of B have *eurak* for the plural; the formation of this is obscure). These formations are plainly recent.

The intensive personal pronouns have been constructed by adding a demonstrative to the absolute or genitive of the ordinary personal pronouns, with variable results: for example, *ni* 'I' gives *nihaur*, *neu* (both *ni* + *hau(r)* 'this') or *nerau* (*neure* 'my' + *hau(r)*)), while *zu* 'you' gives *zuhaur*, *zeu* (*hau(r)* 'this') or *zerori* (*hori* 'that').

The genitives of these intensive pronouns are of special significance; see section 4.14 below. They are also used to form the reflexive pronouns, by combining with *buru* 'head' plus the article, as explained in Chapter 2. The reflexives are everywhere the same, but we don't know how old they are.

The invariable reciprocal pronoun *elkar* ~ *elgar* ~ *alkar* 'each other' is thought to derived from **hark-har*, a combination of the ergative and the absolutive of the distal demonstrative stem *har-* (Michelena 1977a: 69; originally proposed by Uhlenbeck).

The interrogatives are all formed on two apparently ancient bases, *no-* and *ze-*. It is possible that the final *-r* appearing in *nor* 'who?' and *zer* 'what?' may be an ancient formative, perhaps an absolutive or a nominalizer, but we have no evidence. Most of the other interrogatives exhibit familiar case-endings or postpositions: *non* 'where?' has locative *-n*, *nora* 'whither?' has allative *-ra*, *nondik* 'whence?' has ablative *-tik* attached rather surprisingly to what looks like case-inflected *non*, *zergatik* 'why?' has the postposition *gatik* 'because of', *zertarako* has destinative *-rako* preceded by the morph *-ta-* discussed below. The form *zein* 'which?' is a specialized contraction of *zeren*, the genitive of *zer*. The form of *noiz* 'when?' is enigmatic. Some of these forms are probably of relatively recent origin; they certainly can't be older than the case-suffixes they contain.

The indefinites which are negative polarity items were originally formed by prefixing **e-* to the interrogatives; the origin of this prefix is unknown. This is the origin of forms like *ezer* 'anything'. The original **enor* 'anybody' underwent vowel raising in the west, and the new *i* palatalized the following *n*, protecting it from loss: hence western *iñor* 'anybody'. In the east, the intervocalic *n* was lost regularly, producing **ehor*; apparently by analogy with *nor*, an *n* was added to the beginning of this to produce the modern *nehor* 'anybody' – though R preserves *eŭr*. It follows that these indefinites were in the language when intervocalic *n* was lost. Some northern varieties have *deus* as a synonym for *ezer*; this is clearly a loan, and Michelena (1964b, 1965) proposes a Romance derivative of Latin GENUS 'kind'. From *zein* 'which?' is derived *ezein* 'any', which is now archaic.

The indefinites like *norbait* 'somebody' have an obvious origin. Originally, it seems, the interrogatives were also used as indefinites, and were marked in this function by the presence of the prefix *bait-* on the finite verb (see section 4.6). But sequences like **nor baitzen* 'it was somebody' were reanalysed as *norbait zen*, with the affix being transferred from the verb to the pronoun. An original **nork baitzuen* 'somebody had it' was therefore re-formed as the modern *norbaitek zuen*, with the case-ending moved to the end of the new pronoun.

The formation of the remaining group of indefinites is transparent, though of unknown antiquity. Reduplication of *zer* 'what?' gave *zer-edo-zer*, literally 'what-or-what', today often reduced to *zeozer* or *edozer*. The other pattern, like *zernahi* 'whatever you like', is formed with *nahi* 'desire' and looks to be a calque on Romance (cf. the identical use of *-quier* 'want' in Spanish).

There is little reason to doubt the antiquity of the three demonstratives, all of which show mysterious stem-alternations for which no explanation has yet been forthcoming: proximal *hau(r)*, oblique singular *hon-*, plural *haue-*; mesial *hori, horr-, ho(r)ie-*; distal *hura, har-, haie-*. It is clear that the distal demonstrative, whose singular oblique stem is *har-*, once had an absolutive singular **har* (see *elkar* 'above'). This survives today only in B, which has *a*. All other varieties have introduced a suppletive absolutive singular *hura*.

Many have speculated that the three-term deictic system might be the result of Romance influence, but there is no particular reason to believe this. However, in a classic paper, Irigoyen (1981b), after surveying a wealth of documentary and dialectal evidence, concludes that the attested three-term demonstrative system is descended from an earlier system with just two terms; his case is too lengthy to reproduce here, and the interested reader is invited to consult Irigoyen's work. In the same article, Irigoyen also proposes a source for the suppletive *hura*. Noting that some varieties have, in place of *hura*, a form *aura* or *aure* or *ore* (ergative *orrek*), and noting further that *haur* is used today as an introductory particle in Z rather like Latin ECCE, he concludes that *hura* derives from **haur-a*, that is from a combination of the proximal and distal stems.

In B (only), the oblique singular stems are found also in the plural, and, except in the absolutive, number is distinguished only by accent: *onėk, orrėk*, ergative singular, but *ónek, órrek*, ergative plural, and so on for the other forms. (Other varieties have something close to the standard forms *honek, horrek* (singular) but *hauek, ho(r)iek* (plural).)

The Pyrenean dialects have *kau(r), kori, kura* or *gau(r), gori, gura* for the demonstratives. There is no trace of such initial velars elsewhere, and these forms are mysterious. Michelena in several places concludes that the Pyrenean forms are conservative, and that all other varieties have lost the velars, but not everyone is convinced this is the right interpretation, and some would see the velars as representing some kind of reinforcing particle. Note that R, uniquely, also has the pronouns *ura* 'he, she' and *ori* 'you', which are clearly specializations of two of the demonstratives, with no initial velars.

The demonstratives always follow a head noun, though B has a pleonastic formation in which the demonstrative both precedes and follows: *au gizon au*, *ori gizon ori*, *a gizon a*.

B also has the curious forms *aorain* 'now' (common *orain*) and *aolan* 'thus' (common *holan*), in which the distal demonstrative appears to have been prefixed, and all varieties have *aurten* 'this year', in which *a* again appears to have been prefixed to *urte* 'year' plus locative *-n*.

It is perfectly clear that this distal demonstrative is the source of the modern 'definite article' (absolutive singular *-a*, absolutive plural *-ak*). Even today, there is generally no more than a suprasegmental distinction between, say, datives *gizon hari* 'to that man' and *gizonari* 'to the man'. The absolutive singular *gizona* 'the man' derives from *gizon *har*. The date of the emergence of the article is not known, but it is generally thought to be late. There is no trace of it in Aquitanian, and Picaud's twelfth-century word-list records some nouns with the article and others without. The best guess would be somewhere around the eighth to the tenth century, comparable to similar developments in Romance and Germanic languages. A key point is that the article, even though a bound morpheme, is attached only to a noun phrase, and not to a noun.

This *-a* is not the only article attested in Basque. Modern B and G have a proximate plural article *-ok*, all of whose oblique cases are formed with *-o-* in place of unmarked plural *-e-*; old L exhibits a proximate singular article *-or* ~ *-ori*; and a singular article *-o*, apparently with a stronger deictic force than *-a*, is well attested in medieval Navarre and is found today in Aulestia (Biz) (Irigoyen 1981b). Old B has usages like *ni bekatari au* 'I, the sinner', in which proximal *au* appears to be used much like an article. These articles too doubtless derive from the demonstrative stems, though the details are now difficult to unravel.

In modern Basque, number is distinguished only in NPs bearing the article or one of the three demonstratives; we may therefore assume that, at an earlier stage, number-marking in NPs was entirely confined to the demonstratives.

Sal exhibits a unique form of the article after a noun ending in *a*: for *alaba* 'daughter', for example, while B has the definite form *alabea* or *alabia* and other varieties have *alaba*, Sal has *alabara*. Here it appears that the *r* has been inserted to separate the vowels in hiatus, and the Sal form must be a late innovation.

A curiosity is that certain nouns traditionally do not take the article even when definite. These include at least *errege* 'king' and kinship terms. Traditionally, then, one says *erregek esan du* 'the king has said' and *aitonek esan du* 'Grandfather has said', rather than *erregeak* and *aitonak*. These may conceivably be survivals of the period when the article was not yet established, but more likely they result from the treatment of these words as proper names.

There is some regional variation in the vocalism of plural forms; for example, the ergative plural is -ak in the western half of the country (identical to the absolutive) but -ek in the eastern half, and the dative plural is similarly gizonai or gizonei. This kind of variation between a and e derives from an earlier *ae, which resolves to a in the west but e in the east. Thus, ergative plural (western) gizonak ~ (eastern) gizonek must reflect *gizonaek, a reconstruction supported by the observation that Z and R, in which the word-stress generally falls on the ancient antepenult, have final stress in plural endings like dative plural -en. There are two schools of thought on the origin of such forms. Some see the absolutive plural -k as deriving from earlier *-g, and assume that the case-endings were added directly to absolutive plurals like *gizonag, producing for example ergative plural *gizonagek, whence *gizonaek by loss of g. Others prefer to see all the plural forms as deriving directly from the corresponding case-inflected forms of the distal demonstrative, just as in the singular, and so the ergative plural would derive from something similar to the modern gizon haiek 'those men' (ergative). There appears to be a majority in favour of the first analysis, but I myself much prefer the second. In any case, whether from *-age- or from *haie-, -e has become the regular marker of plurality in all oblique case-forms in the eastern half of the country (and in the standard language), corresponding to singular -a and indefinite zero, while the western varieties frequently have -a in the plural as well.

Both these analyses still have to account for the form of the absolutive plural, and here the first view seems to have a problem, since the required *-ag has no obvious source, while the second view takes the universal -ak as nothing but a reduction of the absolutive plural haik of the distal demonstrative, well attested, though now replaced by haiek in much of the country and reduced to hek in much of the north.

In the modern varieties, the citation forms of nouns and adjectives are usually those with the article attached. Thus, asked for 'man' or 'red', most Basques will respond with gizona and gorria, rather than with gizon and gorri. The eastern dialect R is different: here gizon and gorri are indeed the citation forms.

The 'indefinite article' bat is, of course, a development of the numeral bat 'one'. Even today, the use of this article is largely confined to circumstances in which it means 'a certain', with the so-called definite article being used elsewhere: Semea dut/daukat 'I have a son' (just one), but Seme bat dut/daukat 'I have a certain son' (among others). Very recently, some Spanish Basques have begun to use bat as freely as Spanish un, continuing the marked southern trend towards calquing Spanish structures onto Basque sentences.

There is everywhere a sort of plural of bat; this is batzu(k) 'some, several'. The morph -*tzu* appears to be a kind of indefinite plural marker; in B (only), it is also found in *nortzuk*, *zertzuk* and *zeintzuk*, explicitly plural forms of *nor* 'who?', *zer* 'what?' and *zein* 'which?', and it can be added to numerals, as in *bitzuk* 'two groups' (*bi* 'two'). The B forms are perhaps more likely to be innovations than archaisms, given the zero evidence for them elsewhere.

The genitives of the three demonstratives yield items meaning 'so', as in 'so big (that)': *honen*, *horren*, *hain* (< **haren*). These in turn combine with *bat* 'one' to yield *honenbat* 'this much' and *horrenbat*, *hainbat* 'that much'. The demonstratives also take the manner suffix -*la(n)*: *honela* ~ *hola(n)* 'this way, like this', *horrela*, *hala(n)* 'that way, like that'.

4.2 THE CASES

There is no reason to doubt the antiquity of absolutive zero, ergative -*k*, dative -*i* or instrumental -*z*. Ergative -*k* is attested in the ninth-century Emilian Glosses. Aquitanian shows a dative -*ni*, perhaps the ancestor of modern -*i*. (The anomalous Z dative plural -*ér*, in the face of common -*ei* ~ -*ai*, presumably derives from **-eri*.) Instrumental -*z* is phonologically anomalous, since normally only affricates can occur word-finally, but seemingly this restriction does not apply to affixes.

Genitive -*en* is more problematic. The personal pronouns generally have -*e* (*gu* 'we', *gure* 'our' and so on), and we find -*e* instead of -*en* in certain complex forms like *horregatik* 'therefore' (< *horren* 'that' (Gen) + -*gatik* 'because') and *gizonarekin* 'with the man' (< **gizonare-kide(a)n* 'in the man's company'). Moreover, the item *are* 'even', as in *are gehiago* 'even more', is thought to represent an old genitive of the distal demonstrative *har-*. (And see also the archaic ablative -*(r)ean* below.) Michelena (1972b) suggests that -*e* might have been the original genitive ending, and that -*en* might be a later innovation. One or two others have suggested an ancient distinction between genitive singular -*e* and plural -*en*, but there is little evidence to support such a conjecture, beyond the intensive forms *bere* 'his/her own', *beren* 'their own', which are probably of late formation. The genitive forms of *ni* 'I' are anomalous. The most conservative form is *ene*, retained in the north, attested in old B, and still present as a fossilized exclamation in the south; this form is isolated and enigmatic, and it perhaps preserves a trace of some ancient morphological system very different from the attested one. (Dative *eni* 'to me', attested in Z and in old B, shows the same curious formation.) The more widespread *nere* is a reduction of *neure*, the intensive possessive. And *nire* is an analogical formation, formed on *ni* in a manner matching the other genitives like *hire* 'your', from *hi* 'you'.

Comitative -*ekin* is clearly late. It is composed of genitive -*e* plus the noun *kide* 'fellow, mate' (itself of no possible antiquity) plus locative -*n*; originally this case would have been an explicit postpositional phrase meaning 'in the company of': *gizonarekin* < **gizonare(n) kide(a)n*. The variant *-eki* possibly results from reanalysis of the sequence *-ekiko*, in which loss of *n* before the relational suffix *-ko* is regular. Northern *-ekila* appears to have been extended by means of the advertical suffix *-la*. B *-gaz*, with its anomalous plural *-kaz*, is mysterious; it looks more like an independent innovation than an archaism. It may be related to *-gan*, discussed below. We cannot tell if these modern comitatives have replaced an earlier formation; it is possible that instrumental *-z* once included the comitative among its functions, or even as its main function; the development of comitatives into instrumentals is a very familiar phenomenon in languages.

In all likelihood, the case-endings were originally suffixed directly to NPs unmarked for number, just as happens today with proper names, except when a demonstrative was present with its number-marking.

The local cases are very different from the others. With their numerous anomalies and idiosyncrasies, and with their unusual variation in space and over time, they look like late additions to the system, and they appear to have been stitched together out of bits and pieces of various origins. Still, a few conclusions can be drawn, with varying degrees of confidence.

Note first that definite singular NPs do not show the article *-a* in their local cases: ablative *etxetik* 'from the house', allative *etxera* 'to the house', and so on, not *etxeatik or *etxeara. This suggests that the local cases to some extent preserve the state of affairs just referred to: the addition of case-suffixes to NPs with no determiner. The locative at first glance looks different: *etxean* 'in the house'. But this *a* is most unlikely to be the article, since consonant-final stems show the unexpected locative singular ending *-ean*: *zuhaitzean* 'in the tree' (*zuhaitz* 'tree'). Such a form points strongly to a lost consonant: *zuhaitzeCan. Both Jacobsen (1977) and de Rijk (1981) have argued for original **-gan* here: *zuhaitzegan, and therefore also *etxegan, with the familiar loss of intervocalic *g*.

This **-gan* can readily be identified with the *-gan* which, in southern dialects, appears in the local cases of animate NPs: *gizona(ren)gan* 'in/on the man' (the genitive suffix is optional here). Jacobsen in fact argues that **-gan* was the original locative ending in all circumstances, with the more usual *-n* being a reduction of this. De Rijk disagrees, as do I. The problem is that, apart from animate NPs in southern dialects, this **-gan* is found nowhere but in the definite singular. Most tellingly, place names invariably take only *-n*: *Baiona-n* 'in Bayonne', *Zarautz-en* 'in Zarautz', the second with the inevitable *e* to break up an impermissible cluster. I therefore agree with de Rijk that *-n* is itself an ancient locative suffix, and that **-gan* must have another origin.

Now northern dialects form the local cases of animate NPs with the postposition *bait(a)-*, discussed below: *gizona(ren) baitan* 'in/on the man'. I therefore suggest that **-gan* is also a postposition in origin, and I would further suggest that it might be the same morpheme as the very common noun *gain* 'top', itself commonly used as a postposition for expressing senses like 'on top of'. I further speculate that, side by side with the original locative *-n*, this postposition came to be used to construct an alternative locative formation: **etxe gan* 'house top', and so on. Perhaps it originally had the more specific meaning of 'on top of' or 'on', but it must then have been generalized to expressing location in general.

Compare the behaviour of other postpositions. With animate NPs, spatial postpositions require the genitive: *gizonaren aurrean* 'in front of the man' (lit., 'at the man's front'). With inanimate NPs, however, the genitive is possible but not usual in the singular: *etxearen aurrean* or (much more usually) *etxe aurrean* 'in front of the house'. With locative **-gan*, we often find the genitive with animate NPs (*gizonarengan* 'in/on the man'), though this form can be reduced (*gizonagan*); with inanimate NPs, we find only **-gan*, with no genitive (**etxegan > etxean*).

Above I mentioned the divergent B comitative: *gizonagaz* 'with the man', *gizonakaz* 'with the men'. There is every reason to interpret these endings as also involving this postposition **-gan*. The extraordinary plural form *-kaz* points indisputably to such a postpositional origin involving full NPs in the absolutive: singular **gizona gaz > gizonagaz*, plural **gizonak gaz > gizonakaz*. I would suggest that this **gaz* represents **gan* with the instrumental ending *-z*; an original **gan-ez*, if present early enough to undergo the regular loss of intervocalic *n*, would have yielded **gaez > *gaiz*, whose reduction to *-gaz* would be unremarkable in B, in which the change *ai > a* is regular in final syllables even in lexical items.

In non-singular inanimate NPs, we do not find any trace of **gan*, but we find another peculiarity: the presence of *-ta-*. Thus, *mendi* 'mountain' has indefinite locative *menditan* (as in *zein menditan?* 'on which mountain(s)?') and plural locative *mendietan* 'in/on the mountains'. It has been believed for generations that the *-eta* in the plural is the same morph as the collective suffix *-eta* which is so common in place names (*Elorrieta*, from *elorri* 'hawthorn'). This in turn is suspected of being a loan from Latin -ETA, of similar meaning. Since I have already pointed out that the local cases do not involve the article in their formation, it seems natural to suppose that the number distinctions made possible by the article in the grammatical cases were extended to the local cases on a somewhat *ad hoc* basis. Thus, for example, while *mendi* 'mountain' was forming a singular locative **mendigan > mendian* as just described, the collective form *mendieta* (well attested as a toponym and a surname) was pressed into service by means of the old locative ending *-n* to create a distinct form *mendietan*, possibly strictly collective at first but soon reinterpreted as explicitly plural, in contrast to singular *mendian*. This is almost certainly the origin of the modern locative plural.

A complication is that plural *-eta* bears the accent in the western varieties with a pitch-accent: *-età*. Jacobsen (1975), as part of his belief that accented morphs continue former geminate vowels, posits **-eeta* as the source and derives this in turn from *-egeta*, with an overt plural marker. This is clearly incompatible with what I have said above, but I find it very hard to believe that the local cases could ever have contained the plural marker found in the grammatical cases, and I would prefer to find another explanation for the accent. In connection with this, I note that Hualde, in his studies of the history of the Basque accent (1992, 1995), is inclined to consider that vowel contraction has played no more than a minor part in the origin of the western pitch-accent.

That leaves us with the third form to account for, the indefinite *menditan*, but here a simple explanation is available. In the grammatical cases, the indefinite forms are simply those lacking the determiner, but, since the local cases never involved the determiner anyway, some other device had to be found to construct indefinite locatives to complete the new paradigm. Now, as we saw above, the almost invariable plural marker in the oblique cases is *-e-*. Since *-eta* happens to begin with *e*, I suggest that speakers simply reinterpreted the *e* of *-eta* as the plural marker, and removed it in order to obtain the indefinite forms like *menditan*.

In sum, then, this is how I see the modern locative case-forms developing: (1) before the introduction of the article and the number distinctions it brought with it, there was only an invariable locative marker *-n*; (2) an innovating locative construction was introduced involving the postposition **gan*, probably the same item as *gain* 'top'; (3) except with animate NPs, in which number was already marked by the presence of the article (plus the genitive), this new form was interpreted as strictly singular when the new number distinctions appeared in NPs bearing the article; (4) the locative in *-n* of the old collective suffix *-eta* was reinterpreted as a plural locative *-etan*; (5) the *e* of this plural was reanalysed as the usual oblique plural marker *-e-*, and was removed to obtain the indefinite locative *-tan*. Even though this account is largely speculative, for lack of early data, there is nothing in it that should raise any eyebrows.

Incidentally, many northern varieties have a contrast between *etxen* 'at home' and *etxean* 'in the house', with the first showing locative *-n* attached directly to the noun *etxe* 'house'. Since the first form appears to be confined to this one word, most specialists have preferred to invoke Romance influence, rather than seeing the word as an archaism (cf. Spanish *en casa* 'at home').

The other local cases have similar histories. Ablative *-tik* behaves just like locative *-n*, except that this time there is no need to posit anything parallel to **-gan* for most dialects: we have singular *menditik* 'from the mountain', plural *mendietatik* 'from the mountains' and indefinite *menditatik*, as in *zein menditatik?* 'from which mountain(s)?' Some varieties have ablative *-ti*, rather than *-tik*, and it has been suggested that *-tik* might represent a combination of an original *-ti* with the partitive *-ik*, though the unstressed nature of *-tik* in Z and R goes against this analysis. Moreover, many people have suggested that the partitive -*ik* might itself represent an ancient ablative ending, now supplanted in its central function by the innovating -*ti(k)*. This would be a rather familiar sort of development, since partitives are often derived from earlier ablatives. Indeed, the literature up to the eighteenth century contains a few examples of -*ik* apparently used with the value of an ablative, such as *ordurik ona* 'since then' (*ordu* 'then', *ona* 'hither') and *norik* 'from where?', and *arik* 'from there, from then' is still in use in B today. With place names, ablative -*ik* is particularly frequent in the peripheral dialects: old B *Flandesik* 'from Flanders', Z *Maulerik* 'from Maule', R *Aragorik* 'from Aragón'. Moreover, some northern varieties have, in place of indefinite and plural -*(e)tatik*, -*(e)tarik* instead, in which the final morph looks like partitive -*ik* rather than ablative -*tik*. Far more likely, though, this -*rik* simply results from dissimilation of the second of two /t/s.

Some of our earliest texts show ablative -*tika* and partitive -*ika*, and even today the combination of -*tik* or -*ik* with a following -*ko* produces -*tikako*, -*ikako* in many varieties. It thus seems likely that these longer forms are more conservative.

A complication is the existence of a totally different ablative case-ending -*(r)ean* in old B (also very scantily attested elsewhere). Here it is difficult not to see **gan* once again, this time attached to the archaic genitive **-(r)e* discussed above. It rather looks as though B took the use of the postposition **gan* much further than the other dialects: absolutive + **gan* > locative; genitive + **gan* > ablative; absolutive + **gan* + instrumental -*z* > comitative.

Yet another complication is the observation that our earliest text in B, the *Refranes y sentencias* of 1596, in which the ablative ending is -*(r)ean*, consistently uses the ending -*ti* to mean 'by way of, via', as in proverb 488: *zarra ta labea aoti berotu* 'heat up an old person and a furnace by way of the mouth' (*ao* 'mouth'). This observation calls into question the conclusion of Lafon (1968b: 1761) that ablative -*ti* is in origin the same morph as the -*ti* that forms adjectives, as in *beldurti* 'fearful', from *beldur* 'fear'. In modern Basque, 'via' is often expressed by the ablative ending -*tik*, which seemingly combines in one form two functions which were originally formally distinct.

The allative is similar again, but with yet another complication. The usual allative ending today is -*ra*: hence singular *mendira* 'to the mountain', plural *mendietara* 'to the mountains', indefinite *menditara*, as in *zein menditara?* 'to which mountain(s)?' However, instead of -*ra*, we find allative -*a* in three circumstances: with place names, with demonstratives and after -*gan* in animate NPs. Thus, 'to Zarautz' is *Zarautza* in most dialects and in our earliest texts; the *Zarautzera* of some varieties is almost certainly a recent innovation. The allatives of the demonstrative stems *hon*- 'this', *horr*- 'that' and *har*- 'that over there' are *hona*, *horra* and *hara*, respectively. And 'to the man' is *gizona(ren)gana*, not **-ganera*. Since place names nearly always occur in the local cases, it is hard to believe that -*a* can be other than ancient: recall Mańczak's 'eighth tendency', which asserts that place names retain archaic forms of local cases.

I therefore venture to suggest that -ra is an innovation which has largely displaced earlier -a. This innovation might have been favoured by the form *hara* 'thither', in which the r is part of the stem. But there is another factor favouring the replacement: the introduction of the article -a. Once the article existed, there was a potential ambiguity between, for example, the new absolutive singular *mendia*, with the article, and the traditional allative forms like *mendia, with allative *-a. Hence the introduction of r into the allative would have removed the ambiguity. Compare the absolutive of nouns in -a. A noun like *eliza* 'church' combines with the article to produce a definite NP *eliza* 'the church' in most varieties, with simple merger of the two vowels, though with a stress-shift in some eastern varieties. But Sal has the definite form *elizara*, in which an r has been inserted between the stem and the article (this form is attested in Picaud's twelfth-century glossary). There is therefore a clear parallel for the introduction of r into the allative to maintain a grammatical contrast. (A few eastern varieties have allative singular forms like *mendiara* 'to the mountain', in which the allative has apparently been added to a full NP with the determiner; there is no reason to suppose that such forms are anything but recent innovations.)

Since demonstratives and most place names cannot take the article, there was never any ambiguity with these, and the old allatives in -a have simply persisted.

Some northern dialects exhibit an extended allative ending -rat, which clearly derives from *-rada, as shown by the extensions of the allative discussed below. The source of the extra morph is unknown. And Z uniquely exhibits a strange collection of quite different-looking allative endings: -la, -lat, -alat, -ialat, -ilat. Here the t is clearly the same morph as in -rat. But the l is a puzzle. One obvious fact is that in Z, uniquely among the dialects, the otherwise categorical change of intervocalic l to r does not always occur. We might therefore surmise that Z -la represents a more conservative form of the widespread allative -ra (note that the allative ending -ra always follows a vowel). This idea, though, requires me to alter my scenario to a certain extent: if it is right, then the r of -ra is not merely a segment inserted to remove an ambiguity; instead, -ra < *-la must be a genuine morpheme of unknown origin.

De Rijk (1981: 94) proposes that some of these Z forms again involve *-gan. His idea is that the puzzling -lat was attached to -gan, producing, for example with *oihan* 'forest', *oihaneganlat > *oihanegalat > *oihanealat > oihanialat > oihanilat, the last two being attested forms. This seems very plausible.

The new morph -ta-, whose origin was discussed above, has crept into some local and/or instrumental case-forms of demonstratives and pronouns: *honetan* 'in this (one)', *zertaz* 'about what?', *zertan* 'in what?', *nitaz* 'about me', and so on. I see no reason to regard these as other than late developments. Note in particular that the demonstratives exhibit instrumental forms both with and without -*ta*-: *honez* ~ *honetaz*.

Three of the compound case-forms listed in Chapter 2 are obtained by adding extensions to the allative: the terminative -*raino* 'as far as, up to, until', the directional -*rantz* 'towards', and the destinative -*rako*(*tz*) 'for' (an inanimate NP). The first has a variant -*radino* in the varieties with allative -*rat*, but the origins of the extra morphs are generally mysterious, though see below for -*raino*.

Adverbs show a somewhat different set of local cases from NPs. Locative -*n* appears more or less normally in forms like *orain* 'now' (< Lat HORA 'hour'), *orduan* 'then' (< *ordu* 'hour'), *non* 'where?', *hemen* 'here' (< *hau* 'this'), and *han* '(over) there' (< *har*- 'that') (though curiously not in *hor* 'there' < *horr*- 'that'). But the ablative ending is -*danik*, as in *noizdanik* 'since when?' (*noiz* 'when?'), *betidanik* '(since) always' (*beti* 'always'), *gaurdanik* 'from now on' (*gaur* 'today') and *ihazdanik* 'since last year' (*ihaz* 'last year'). Moreover, our early texts show a number of adverbs with an allative in -*dara* and a corresponding terminative in -*daraino*, such as *oraidara*, *oraindaraino* 'until now' (*orai*(*n*) 'now') and *bihardara* 'until tomorrow' (*bihar* 'tomorrow').

These puzzling forms have been brilliantly explained by de Rijk (1992). De Rijk posits an ancient item **da*- 'present moment', which could take the usual local case-endings to produce **dan* 'now', **dara* 'until now' and **dandik* > **danik* 'from now'. Noting that Basque forms dvandva compounds readily, he further posits the earlier existence of dvandva compounds like **oraindan* 'now-now', i.e. 'right now', involving both words for 'now', with allative **oraindara* and ablative **oraindanik*. The disappearance of **dan* 'now' from the language in favour of the Latin loan *orain* left these forms isolated; speakers no longer recognized the presence of obsolete **da*(*n*), and therefore reanalysed -*dara* and -*danik* as allative and ablative endings suitable for time adverbs. De Rijk is able to show that the original state of affairs is still visible in some of our earliest texts. He also analyses *iadan* ~ *jadan* 'already' as another dvandva, this time with *ia* 'now, already' (< Lat IAM).

In the same paper, de Rijk points to the existence of a handful of forms like *egundo* and *oraindo*, both meaning 'still, yet'; these derive from *egun* 'today' and *orain* 'now', and must mean etymologically 'until today' and 'until now'. He therefore posits an archaic allative ending **-do*, whose presence is still detectable also in *bateo* 'together' (< **batedo* < *bat* 'one') and the pleonastic *artio* 'until' (< **artedo* < *arte* 'until').

De Rijk further proposes that this **-do* is present in the terminative morph -*ino* cited above. Citing the evidence of dialect variants, he reconstructs **-gain-do*, consisting of **-do* added to the noun *gain* 'top'. This form, reduced to -*giño*, is well attested in early and modern Bizkaian without a preceding allative, as in *oraingiño* 'until now' and *azken giño* 'until the end' (*azken* 'last'). Elsewhere, appearing variously as *-giño*, *-ino* or *-no*, it occurs only with a preceding allative; varieties with allative *-rat* have *-radino* or *-raano* (< *-radano*).

Finally, a word about northern *bait(a)-*, used to form the local cases of animate NPs, as in *gizona(ren) bait(h)an* 'in/on the man'. This same morph is often used in L also to mean 'house', as in *Aita bait(h)an dago* 'He's at his father's house.' This fact has led several commentators to suggest that 'house' was the original sense of *bait(a)-*, and that its use in locative NPs represents a generalization. This is possible, but no such word for 'house' is attested elsewhere in the language, the universal word for 'house' being *etxe*. It seems more likely, then, that the sense of 'house' represents a specialization of a general locative postposition. In any case, the origin of this postposition is unknown, and the astonishing declaration of Azkue (1923–1925) that it is a loan from Italian cannot be taken seriously.

4.3 POSTPOSITIONS AND GRAMMATICAL WORDS

The largest group of postpositions consists of spatial nouns like *gain* 'top', *alde* 'side' and *aurre* 'front'. These are case-inflected just like any other noun: there is no real difference between *gizonaren aurrean* 'in front of the man' (lit., 'at the man's front') and *gizonaren etxean* 'in the man's house'.

Sources can be identified for some of these. At least two are loans: *ondo* 'bottom, side', from a Romance derivative of Lat FUNDU 'bottom', and *inguru ~ ingiru* 'vicinity', from Lat IN GYRU 'around'. The item *atze* 'back' can be identified with *hatz* 'trace, track'; its final *e* derives from its frequent use in inflected forms like *atzean* 'behind', in which the *e* is required for phonological reasons. The same is true of *aurre* 'front', whose earlier form **aur* can be identified with the word *ahur* 'palm of the hand', found precisely in those eastern regions in which *aurre* is absent (Michelena 1971a).

The remaining postpositions are quite variable in their origins. Of the two meaning 'against, opposite to', *aurka* is merely *aurre* 'front' plus adverbial *-ka*, while *kontra* is an obvious loan (an unusual case of a preposition borrowed as a postposition). The three synonymous items *barne*, *barren* and *barru* 'interior' are all related: *barne* has been extracted from *barnean* 'inside', a syncopated form of *barrenean*, and *barren* in turn is probably *barru* plus an ending, probably the superlative *-en*. The postposition *kanpo* 'outside', with its very un-Basque form, must be a loan; Romance *campo* 'field' is usually suggested as the source. The item *buruz* 'about' is *buru* 'head' plus instrumental *-z*. The unusual *at* 'except' is a specialization of *ate* 'door'. The word *ondoren* 'after' is *ondo* again with an ending which appears to be genitive *-en*; its opposite *baino lehen* 'before' is a combination of *baino* 'than' with *lehen* 'first'. The item *gabe ~ baga* 'without' shows a metathesis, but we can't tell in which direction; the word has no known source, nor do a few others like *gero* 'after' and *zehar* 'across'.

The postposition *bezala* 'like, as' is clearly related in some fashion to *bezain* 'as . . . as' (B *baizen*). Lafon has proposed that they involve an element **bez-* combined with *hala* 'thus' and *hain* 'that much', both from the distal demonstrative. This **bez-* is perhaps to be identified with the *baiz-* that occurs in *baizik* 'but' (in 'not X but Y'), apparently with partitive *-ik*. Lafon sees as the source the word *bai*, today 'yes', but, he proposes, formerly 'this much, but no more'. All this is plausible, but not certain. These words may well be related to *baina(n)* 'but' and *baino* 'than' (and also the B equivalent of *baizik*). Now *baino* looks very much as though it contains the allative **-do* posited by de Rijk, especially since a variant *baindo* is attested in HN, and *bainan* conceivably contains the distributive suffix *-na(n)*, as in *bana(n)* 'one apiece, one at a time', from *bat* 'one', though this last idea is more speculative.

I therefore propose to accept Lafon's suggestion, and to see an ancient **bai*, roughly '(precisely this) amount', as the base of all these words, apparently with the instrumental *-z* attached in the first three cases. Such a stem yields a persuasive source for all these items, though the medial *n* of *baino* needs to be accounted for: perhaps, instead of **bai*, we should posit **bain* or **banĩ*?

The conjunction *eta* 'and' is widely thought to be a loan from Latin ET, but this etymology is far from secure. For *edo* and *ala*, both 'or', no source is known.

The word *bai* 'yes' is doubtless related to the affirmative morph *ba-*, as in *badator* 'he/she's coming', formerly 'he/she *is* coming'; *bai* may well be an ancient verb-form, along the lines of 'it is so', possibly involving the root *-di-* of the archaic verb **edin*. The word *baldin* 'if', which often reinforces *ba-*, has been much discussed; it has been variously analysed as **ba-* 'if' + *ahal* 'possible' + **edin*, the ancient verb which possibly meant 'become', as **ba-* + *ahal* + **dadien*, where the last is a finite form of the same verb, and as **ba-* + *ledin*, where the last is a conditional finite form of the same verb, still in use today. Michelena prefers the second; I incline towards the last.

The negative *ez* 'not, no' is invariable except in B, in which a variant *ze* is found in early texts when followed by a subjunctive or an imperative: *ce biarco echi* 'don't wait for tomorrow', in the *Refranes* of 1596. This *ze* survives today in at least one part of Bizkaia. Very speculatively, I might propose an ancient conditioned alternation **eza* ~ **eze*, with differing vowel loss. Again, it is not out of the question that we might be looking at ancient verb-forms here.

4.4 ADJECTIVES AND ADVERBS

Basque has a large and open class of adjectives, and these are generally quite distinct from nouns. This distinctness has been denied by one or two linguists, but wrongly so: in a syntagm N + Adj, the noun is indisputably the head (for example, its animacy determines the form of the local case-endings), while, in a syntagm N + N, the second noun is the head. But there are none the less a fair number of words which can behave indifferently as adjectives or nouns: *bero* 'hot' or 'heat', *ilun* 'dark' or 'darkness', *zikin* 'dirty' or 'filth', *hotz* 'cold' (adj.) or 'cold' (n.), *ezin* 'impossible' or 'impossibility', *argi* 'bright' or 'light', *ahal* 'possible' or 'ability', *gazte* 'young' or 'young person', *itzal* 'shady' or 'shade', *gose* 'hungry' or 'hunger', *ezti* 'sweet' or 'honey', and so on. This leads a number of vasconists to suspect that, at some ancient stage of the language, there was no distinction between adjectives and nouns. If so, this must have been at a very remote period, since the language has a number of word-forming suffixes, some of them seemingly ancient, which derive adjectives and only adjectives: *-din* 'resembling', *-zu* ~ *-tsu* 'full of', *-koi* 'fond of' and others.

Of the suffixes used in comparison, comparative *-ago*, superlative *-en* and excessive *-egi*, we have a plausible source only for the superlative, which is widely thought to represent a specialization of genitive *-en*, an analysis going back to Humboldt, though Humboldt saw *-en* specifically as a genitive plural ending. The other two are completely mysterious, as is *hobe*, the irregular comparative form of *on* 'good'.

Observe that comparative *-ago* is very occasionally attached to a noun, as in *gizonago* 'more of a man' (*gizon* 'man'). This has led one or two observers to suggest that adjectives and nouns are not distinguished even in modern Basque, a conclusion which can be emphatically rejected, for the reasons given above.

Adjectives are generally postposed in Basque, and this state of affairs is ancient: it is clearly represented in the Aquitanian names. The few exceptions are easily explained. Adjectives formed with the suffix *-dun* 'having', like *haurdun* 'pregnant' (*haur* 'child') and *bizardun* 'bearded' (*bizar* 'beard'), are in origin reduced relative clauses, since *-dun* is obviously nothing other than *duen* 'who has', the relative form of *du* 'has', and relative clauses are always preposed. Today these adjectives can be found both preposed and postposed. In contrast, adjectives in *-din*, probably originally 'resembling', are always postposed, even though this suffix too derives from a reduced relative form of the lost verb **edin*; formations in the now unproductive *-din*, however, are much older than those in *-dun*.

The adnominal modifiers in *-ko*, like *Lapurdiko* 'from Lapurdi' and *betiko* 'eternal' (*beti* 'always'), are not true adjectives, but *-ko* phrases, and these, like all complex modifiers, are always preposed in Basque.

The case of nationality adjectives is slightly more puzzling. These are usually preposed, though not invariably so, regardless of their formation; even borrowed adjectives like *frantses* 'French' are commonly preposed. The best guess is that many of these adjectives were originally nouns. This is certainly the case with some of them, like *euskal* 'Basque' (*Euskal Herria* 'the Basque Country'), which is merely the combining form of *euskara* 'Basque language'.

There is even less to be said about adverbs. The suffixes *-ki*, *-to* and *-ro*, which form adverbs of manner, are of unknown origin, as is the suffix *-ka*, which forms adverbs from N-bars. Interrogatives and demonstratives show a distinct suffix *-la(n)*: *holan* 'in this way', *hala(n)* 'in that way', *zelan*, *nola* 'how?'; this may be related to the complementizer *-la*.

The interrogative stem *no-* yields *non* ~ *nun* 'where?', with locative *-n*, and *noiz* 'when?', with an obscure final element. The demonstrative stems take locative *-n* to form adverbs of place, except in the mesial: *hemen* ~ *amen* 'here' (< **hau-en*), *hor* '(just) there', *han* (< **har-n*) 'over there'. The formation of the second is utterly mysterious. The interrogatives take the indefinite prefix **e-* to yield indefinite adverbs, with the same developments as in the indefinite pronouns: *iñoiz* ~ *nehoiz* 'ever' (< **e-noiz*), *iñon* ~ *nehon* ~ *nehun* 'anywhere' (< **e-non*), *iñola* ~ *ihula* ~ *eula* ~ *nehola* 'in any way' (< **e-nola*). For 'ever', northern varieties also have *sekula* (< SAECULA). As in other languages, some adverbs of time double as nouns, such as *egun*, both 'day' and 'today'. For this one, Michelena has suggested an ancient noun **egu* 'day', with *-n* then being the locative ending, and the form *egun* then being generalized to nominal status; this is possible, but far from certain. The word *gaur*, 'tonight' in the east but 'today' in the west, is from *gau* 'night' + *hau(r)* 'this'. See Chapter 5 for further discussion of the names of days.

The suffix *-ero* 'every', as in *astero* 'every week, weekly', is surely the same suffix as *-ro*; by chance, virtually every time noun allowing this suffix ends either in *e* or in a consonant which naturally requires the insertion of *e* before the suffix.

4.5 NON-FINITE VERB-FORMS

Virtually all ancient verbs show a prefix **e-* in all their non-finite forms; this appears today variously as *e-*, *i-*, *j-* or zero, in circumstances explained in Chapter 3. The function of this prefix is not known; it may conceivably be related to the prefix *e-* which forms indefinite pronouns, but it is hard to see a common value. In Trask (1995b) I argue that it originally derived a verbal noun from a verbal root.

This function is most visible in the simplest non-finite form, the so-called 'radical', which is merely the stem of the verb functioning as a free form (as in *ikus*, radical of *ikusi* 'see'); the radical survives today only in northern dialects, apart from a few fossilizations in the south (though see Azkue (1935) for a summary of western attestations). Among the various attested functions of the radical listed in Trask (1995b), a few are conspicuously nominal, such as its use with postpositions, as in *ikus arte* 'until seeing'. In the eastern dialect R (and in some varieties of Z?), the radical is used as the citation form of the verb. Most other speakers use the perfective participle for this purpose, though a few northerners use the gerund, probably as a self-conscious gloss of the French infinitive.

The majority of ancient verbs form their perfective participle by adding a suffix *-i* to the radical: *ikusi* 'see', *ekarri* 'bring', *ibili* 'go about', *jarri* 'sit down' and so on. It is noteworthy that an identical *-i* can also be used to derive participles from nouns and adjectives: *itzal* 'shade', *itzali* '(to) obscure'; *hauts* 'dust, powder', *hautsi* 'break'; *hatz* 'race, lineage', *hazi* 'bring up, rear'; *zorrotz* 'sharp', *zorrotzi* 'sharpen'; *igun* 'repugnance', *iguni* 'detest'; and a number of others. I assume we are looking at a single suffix in all these cases, and I take this as further evidence that radicals were verbal nouns. The source of this *-i* is not known, but it is notable that the language shows traces of an ancient adjective-forming suffix *-i*. The clearest case is *gatz* 'salt', *gazi* 'salty'. A number of others have been proposed, especially by Azkue (1923–1925: 41), who suggests that the colour adjectives *zuri* 'white' and *hori* 'yellow' may derive from *zur* 'wood' and *(h)or* 'dog'; he also proposes *gorri* 'red' from a hypothetical **gor* 'flesh'. Since perfective participles are conspicuously adjectival in nature, it may be that an ancient adjective-forming suffix was pressed into service to derive participles both from ordinary nouns and from verbal nouns, but here I confess I am stretching the evidence to the limit.

A smaller group of ancient verbs is represented by the highly anomalous class of verbs in *-n*, like *jakin* 'know', *jan* 'eat', *joan* 'go', *egin* 'do, make', *egon* 'stay, wait; be', *izan* 'be', *ukan* 'have', **edun* 'have', *eman* 'give' and *esan ~ erran* 'say'. These verbs exhibit a number of odd characteristics:

1 They lack an *-i* in the participle, which is identical to the radical.
2 They lose their final *-n* before the gerund suffix *-te* and the agent suffix *-le*. Southern dialects thus have *joate* 'going' and *joale* 'goer', *emate* 'giving' and *emale* 'giver', and so on, as though the stems were *joa-* and *ema-*. (Cf. *ikuste* 'seeing' and *ikusle* 'seer'.)
3 But northern varieties have an unexpected extra *ı* in the gerund and the agent noun: hence *joaite* and *joaile*, *emaite* and *emaile*, and so on, as though the stems were *joai-* and *emai-*.
4 The finite forms of these verbs, where they exist, take the relative marker *-en* after a vowel which is part of the stem: thus *daki* 'knows' has relative *dakien*, *dago* 'is' has *dagoen*, *du* 'has' has *duen* and so on. The form *da* 'is' forms western *dan* but eastern *den*, pointing clearly to earlier **daen*. This is extraordinary, since, apart from these verbs, we invariably find *-en* only after a consonant but *-n* after a vowel: *dakar* 'brings' and *dakarren*, *goaz* 'we go' and *goazen*, but *dugu* 'we have it' and *dugun*, *dakite* 'they know' and

dakiten, and so on. That is, these verbs behave as though there were a consonant present after that final vowel of the stem.

In Trask (1990) I propose an explanation for all this, one which has become widely accepted. I note that, in spite of the great frequency of *n* in Basque stems, including in final position, there are virtually no verbs of the -*i* class with stems ending in *n*. The only exceptions are those in which the *n* is preceded by *i*, as in *ipini* 'put' and *eskaini* 'offer'. I note further that intervocalic *n* was categorically lost in Basque, except that it sometimes survived as *ñ* after *i*. I therefore propose that these anomalous verbs were originally ordinary verbs of the -*i* class whose stems happened to end in *n*, and that this *n*, being intervocalic in the participle, was therefore lost. Thus, for example, the verb 'give' originally had radical *eman* and participle **emani*, just like any other verb, but the loss of *n* produced *eman* and *emai* – no asterisk here, because a participle *emai* is in fact attested in the *Refranes* of 1596 for this particular verb. (And the seventeenth-century writer Oihenart has *ikai* for *igan* 'go up'.)

The now-irregular relation between radical and participle led to a period of confusion, as a result of which *eman* was generalized to function as both radical and participle, while *emai* was confined to functioning as a stem in word-formation. This is the origin of the northern forms like *emaite* and *emaile*; southern varieties have undoubtedly regularized these odd-looking forms to *emate* and *emale*. (Note that the forms with *i* are attested in B: our earliest text in B, the *Refranes y sentencias* of 1596, exhibits a number of imperfective participles like *izaiten* 'being' (modern *izaten*) and *emaiten* 'giving' (modern *ematen*, B *emoten*). Indeed, Azkue (1935: 74) remarks that *emoile* 'donor', from *emon* 'give', the B variant of *eman*, was still in use in his day in the Bizkaian town of Orozko and in Roncal.)

Meanwhile, the finite forms of these verbs would have exhibited stem-final *n*, and hence they would have required the form -*en* of the relative suffix. But this *n*, being intervocalic, would also have been lost, producing the attested forms with -*en* after a vowel: thus, for example, original **dagon* 'is' would have had relative **dagonen* > *dagoen*, the modern form. In principle, final *n* should have remained in non-relative forms like **dagon*, but the combination of relative *dagoen* with the fact that final *n* is characteristic in Basque of both relative forms and past-tense forms (*e.g.*, *zegoen*, past tense of *dago*, < **zegonen*) induced the removal of this *n*, producing the modern forms like *dago*. With only a very modest amount of special pleading, then, this explanation accounts in a uniform manner for all the idiosyncrasies of these verbs, and it further explains why such a class of verbs should exist at all and why verbs of the -*i* class almost never have stems in *n*. Moreover, it does so by appealing only to one of the best-established and most pervasive phonological changes in the prehistory of Basque.

The participial formation in -*i* is no longer productive. For many centuries, the function of *-i* has been assumed by a new suffix *-tu*. This is of Latin origin: Basque borrowed verbs from Latin in the form of their perfective participles, such as *aditu* 'hear, understand' < AUDITU and *jostatu* 'play' < IUXTATU. Romance verbs have continued to be borrowed with the same suffix: *pentsatu* 'think' < Sp *pensar*, *sentitu* 'feel' < Sp *sentir*, *erreibindikatu* 'claim' < Sp *reivindicar*. In spite of occasional exceptions like *sentitu*, there has long been a marked tendency to generalize the form *-atu*, as in *bedeinkatu* 'bless' (< **benedikatu*), from Lat BENEDICERE, participle BENEDICTU, and *eskribatu* 'write' < Sp *escribir*. This new suffix is used to form participles of verbs from native materials, as in *aberastu* 'get rich' (replacing earlier *aberatsi*), from *aberats* 'rich', and *ilundu* 'get dark', from *ilun* 'dark'. As can be seen, verbs in *-tu* lack the prefix **e-*.

A handful of seemingly ancient verbs, all of them with monosyllabic stems, and all of them lacking the ancient prefix **e-*, are found everywhere with participles in *-tu*: *hartu* 'take', *sartu* 'enter', *galdu* 'lose', *saldu* 'sell', *kendu* 'remove', *lortu* 'achieve', *lotu* 'tie (up)', *bildu* 'gather, collect', *sortu* 'be born', *piztu* 'kindle, light', *heldu* 'ripen, mature; arrive'. Only a few of these have possible sources: *saldu* 'sell' is perhaps derived from *sari* 'price' (< **sali?*), and *piztu* 'kindle' is probably from *bizi* 'alive', with voicing assimilation. The verb *kendu* 'remove' is exceptionally attested as *ekendu* in LN, apparently with the prefix **e-*; this is mysterious.

In a few cases verbs in *-i* have been transferred into the *-tu* class: older *iratzarri* 'awaken' is now *iratzartu* in places (Leizarraga uses *iratzarri* only as an adjective 'awake'); older *ahantzi* 'forget', preserved in the north, is *anztu* in old B G and *aztu* today; older *bihurri* 'twist' is now *bihurtu* almost everywhere (though *bihurri* survives as an adjective meaning 'twisted'); common *itzali* 'obscure, eclipse' is *itzaldu* in places; *hautsi* 'break' is just as often *haustu*; older *irakurri* 'read' is *irakurtu* in some northern varieties. The word *neurri* is today only a noun meaning 'measure', but it is attested once in Axular as an adjective meaning 'which fits perfectly' (i.e., 'measured'), while the verb 'measure' is *neurtu*. The form *ezagun* is now everywhere an adjective 'familiar', while *ezagutu* is the verb meaning 'know' (a person). And even *izan* 'be' is *izandu* or *izatu* in a few central varieties.

A fair number of verbs are unusual in having no suffix at all in the participle. These verbs are heterogeneous, but several subclasses can be recognized. Verbs in *-o*, like *jo* 'hit', *eho* 'kill' and *ito* 'drown', exhibit many of the same peculiarities as verbs in *-n*, and they are undoubtedly verbs of the same type which have undergone some further phonological changes, now probably unrecoverable. In this connection, note that *igan* 'go up, ascend' has variants *igon* and *igo* in B and G, and *eman* 'give' appears as *emon* in B.

A few of these unsuffixed verbs derive from adjectives, like *hil* 'die, kill', derived from *hil* 'dead', and *busti* 'moisten', from *busti* 'moist' (this has a variant *bustitu*). A few are loans, like *gorde* 'keep' (cf. Sp *guardar*). Several are allatives of nouns, like *atera* 'go out' (from *atera* 'to the door', allative of *ate* 'door'). One or two are mysterious, like *erre* 'burn'.

But the most striking group of unsuffixed verbs is the group in *-ki*, like *ebaki* 'cut', *ideki* ~ *ireki* 'open', *eduki* 'contain, hold, have', *jaiki* 'get up' and *jalgi* 'go out'. These are discussed in section 4.8 below.

The gerund is clearly of later formation than the participle, since it exhibits significant regional variation in its formation. The two commonest suffixes used in forming gerunds are *-te* and *-tze*: *ikuste* 'seeing', *ekartze* ~ *ekarte* 'carrying', *hartze* 'taking' and so on. Eastern varieties of B use -(*k*)*eta*, as in *ikusketa* 'seeing' and *kantaeta* 'singing'. R has -*eta* ~ -*ta*, as in *bordalta* 'getting married'. Finally, old B apparently had a gerund ending -*zaite*.

Sources are available for most of these endings. First, *-te* probably derives from a specialization of the word-forming suffix *-te*, which forms nouns of duration, like *eurite* 'rainy spell' (*euri* 'rain'). Second, *-tze* is probably identical with the noun-forming suffix *-tze* ~ *-tza*, which has several functions, one of which is forming nouns of abundance, as in *jendetze* ~ *jendetza* 'crowd' (*jende* 'people'). Third, *-keta* is surely the same as the common noun-forming suffix *-keta*, which again has several functions but which very commonly forms nouns of activity, like *hizketa* 'conversation, speech' (*hitz* 'word') and *zezenketa* 'bull-running' (*zezen* 'bull'). R -(*e*)*ta* is very likely a variant of this last, which has a common variant -*eta*. The old B form is puzzling, but it appears to involve the suffix *-te*, and the preceding *i*, parallel to the northern gerund forms discussed above, strongly suggests that we are looking at an old *-te* gerund of an *-n* class verb, possibly *izan* 'be' or the widely accepted **ezan* 'do'.

In Trask (1995b), I conclude, therefore, that the modern gerunds are all late formations obtained by adding noun-forming suffixes mostly meaning 'duration', 'abundance' or 'activity' to verb-stems – that is, to radicals, again confirming that radicals are verbal nouns in origin. (In B, a variety in which the radical is long defunct, the suffix *-te* is often added instead to the participle, so that, for example, the verb *hartu* 'take', which forms gerund *hartze* elsewhere, forms *artute* in B.) These new formations would have been ordinary nouns at first, with no verbal properties, but they came to be reinterpreted as verb-forms, and hence acquired verbal characteristics, just like the gerund suffix *-ing* of English. For syntactic evidence confirming this conclusion, see section 4.19 below.

The imperfective participle everywhere derives from the gerund by the addition of locative *-n*: hence *ikusten* 'seeing', *hartzen* 'taking', and so on. This again is entirely parallel to the formation of the English imperfective participle: as is well known, the English gerund came to be used in locative constructions like *He is on writing a book*, and the locative preposition *on* was reduced to *a'* and then lost entirely, producing the modern forms like *He is writing a book*.

The form of the imperfective participle shows that the gerund could formerly occur without the article attached. From the earliest texts, however, we find the gerund occurring inevitably with the singular article *-a* firmly bound to it, and able also to take any case-ending. As a result, the gerund has an ordinary locative form, as in *ikustean* 'on seeing', contrasting with the imperfective participle, as in *ikusten* 'seeing'. An NP headed by a gerund can occupy any NP slot in a sentence; the gerund takes the ordinary case-marking, but still permits a full range of case-marked arguments and verbal adjuncts like adverbs.

The future participle is in every case derived from the combination of the perfective participle with a suffix *-en* or *-ko*. The first of these is undoubtedly the genitive *-en*; the second must be the familiar relational suffix *-ko*. In neither case is the motivation for the formation particularly clear, but it is doubtless significant that the future participle virtually never occurs outside of periphrastic verb-forms (except occasionally in a few early texts), and formations like *joanen naiz* and *ekarriko dut* must have had some significance along the lines of 'I am of going' and 'I have it of bringing'; Romance influence has often been invoked in explaining these formations.

Both the perfective participle and the gerund can take a full range of case-marked NPs representing NP arguments of those forms. In eastern varieties, the perfective participle can also take the partitive ending *-ik* to create a participle with an adverbial function: from *ikusi* 'see', we have *ikusirik* 'having seen' or 'having been seen' (recall that non-finite forms are unmarked for voice). A significant development in western varieties has been the creation of a new adverbial participle formed by adding to the perfective participle the suffix *-ta*, and hence the western equivalent of *ikusirik* is *ikusita* 'having (been) seen'. It is universally believed that this suffix derives from the conjunction *eta* 'and', which is routinely reduced to *ta* in western varieties after a vowel. Very commonly, though not invariably, this participle is reinforced by the postposition/adverb *gero* 'after', and hence we find *ikusita gero* 'having seen [it]' or 'having been seen'.

This new participle is extremely frequent in the west, and it has acquired a number of functions. Particularly striking is its use in forming an adnominal form of the participle, where, like other adverbials, it takes the adnominal suffix *-ko*. Thus, while an eastern Basque may express 'the book I bought' as *nik erosi liburua*, with the bare perfective participle *erosi* 'bought' and the argument *nik* 'I' (erg.), a westerner says *nik erositako liburua*, with the suffix sequence *-tako* attached to the participle.

It is convenient to discuss the agent-suffixes here. Basque has two such suffixes, both corresponding in function to English *-er*, as in *writer*: *-le* and *-tzaile*. Both are confined to use with transitive verbs, the rare attestations with intransitive verbs being sporadic and often idiosyncratic; Azkue (1923–1925: 78) considers the intransitive cases to be neologisms.

The suffix *-le* is clearly the older, and it is of unknown origin. This suffix is used with verbs of the *-i* class and the *-n* class: *ikusi* 'see', *ikusle* 'one who sees, onlooker'; *erosi* 'buy', *erosle* 'buyer, purchaser'; *irakatsi* 'teach', *ira-kasle* 'teacher'; *irakurri* 'read', *irakurle* 'reader'; *ebatsi* 'steal', Z *ebasle* 'thief' (most other dialects have only the unrelated *lapur* 'thief', but see below); *egin* 'do, make', *egile* 'doer, maker'; *entzun* 'hear, listen', *entzule* 'hearer, listener'; *edan* 'drink', *edale* 'drinker'. Most verbs in -*n* have an apparent variant -*ile*: *eman* ~ *emon* 'give', *emale* ~ *emaile* ~ *emoile* 'donor'; *esan* ~ *erran* 'say', *esale* ~ *erraile* 'sayer, narrator'. (See above for an explanation of this clearly secondary variant.) B has -*la*, reflecting the usual B lowering of final *e*. The key point here, I would suggest, is that the agent suffix is added to the radical of the verb, the form which I argued above was an ancient verbal noun.

The suffix -*tzaile* (B -*tzaila*) is added to all other verbs: *hil* 'kill', *hiltzaile* 'killer'; *ebaki* 'cut', *ebakitzaile* 'cutter, one who cuts'; *erre* 'smoke (tobacco)', *erretzaile* 'smoker'; *hartu* 'take', *hartzaile* 'taker'; *saldu* 'sell', *saltzaile* 'seller' (also 'traitor'); *garbitu* 'clean', *garbitzaile* 'cleaner'. One or two -*i* class verbs take -*tzaile*, when the addition of -*le* would produce an awkward cluster: *ipini* 'put', *ipintzaile* 'one who puts'; *erabili* 'use', *erabiltzaile* 'user'. Agent nouns derived with these suffixes normally denote human beings. There are, however, a few exceptions: *errun* 'lay (eggs)', LN *errule* '(egg-)layer', i.e., 'hen'. The eighteenth-century author Mogel extraordinarily uses *garbitzaile* 'cleaner' in the sense of '(barber's) razor', but such inanimate formations are not normal.

The suffix -*tzaile* is clearly compound in origin: the second element is -*le*, while the first is, in all likelihood, the noun-forming suffix -*tza*, which is known to derive from *-*zaha(e)*. Now, this suffix -*tza* ~ -*tze* is the same suffix which forms modern verbal nouns, and -*tzaile* in turn is overwhelmingly added to verbs which lack the ancient prefix *e*- and which hence lack the verbal noun which it derived. It looks, therefore, as if -*tzaile* must derive from the addition of -*le* to a verbal noun derived by means of the suffix -*tza*. So, while an ancient verbal noun like *ikus* 'seeing' (< *e-kus*) yields agent *ikusle*, a newer verbal noun like *saltze* 'selling' yields agent *saltzaile*. This line of reasoning once again confirms that the radical must be an ancient verbal noun.

The eastern and Pyrenean dialects exhibit two other agent suffixes: -*tale* and -*zale*, as in *erostale* 'buyer', (*h*)*ilzale* 'killer' and *ebastale* ~ *ebaszale* 'thief'. The first of these must derive from the verbal-noun-forming suffix -*ta* mentioned above as found in the Pyrenees, while the second either derives from -*le* added to an identified element or else merely represents an unusual extension in function of the common suffix -*zale* '(who is) fond of', as in *diruzale* 'avaricious; miser' (*diru* 'money'), though note also its unusual occurrence in *arrantzale* 'fisherman' (*arrain* 'fish').

4.6 FINITE VERB-FORMS: AGREEMENT AND PLURALITY

Finite verb-forms undoubtedly present the greatest difficulty of all in investigating the morphological history of the language. The periphrastic forms are generally of quite transparent formation, particularly the indicative ones, in which the use of the three participles is both semantically straightforward and parallel to similar constructions in Indo-European languages. The difficulties lie in the synthetic forms, whose morphological complexity is rather substantial.

I begin with the agreement-markers. In the first two persons, these are mostly, but not entirely, cognate with the corresponding free pronouns, from which they assuredly derive, possibly by cliticization; (M) and (F) mean 'male' and 'female', and *zu* is treated as plural, which it historically is. The agreement markers are listed in Table 4.1 alongside the corresponding personal pronouns; the curious Roncalese *-R*, as in *duR* 'I have it', was described by Bonaparte as 'between [d] and [r]'.

The three singular suffixes are justified by the behaviour of verb-forms to which further suffixes are added, such as the relative *-(e)n*: *dut* 'I have it', *dudan*; *duk* 'you (M) have it', *duan* (< *dugan*); *dun* 'you (F) have it', *dunan*. In the singular forms, it is only the prefixes which relate to the pronouns, while the suffixes appear to be unrelated. This may be a remnant of an ancient stem alternation in the pronouns, now otherwise lost. Martinet (1950, 1955) in fact posits a phoneme $*/^nd/$ for early Basque, with first-singular *n-* and *-d* reflecting different developments of this, but there is no support for such a proposal, and few have taken it seriously. The second singular is even worse, and Martinet's further suggestion of *$*k$*, with aspiration and lenition in initial position, is unsustainable. The contrasting male and female suffixes represent the sole occurrence of such sex-marking in Basque; this contrast is isolated and enigmatic. Jacobsen (1975) finds evidence for female *-naa* in some varieties, and reconstructs an original female *-na-ga*, with a morph *-na* preceding the ordinary suffix *-ga-*; his case is persuasive, but it doesn't help us to understand the origin of these mysterious forms. The singular agreement-markers are one of the great unsolved mysteries of Basque historical linguistics.

With the third person, things become more complex, and this topic has

Table 4.1 First- and second-person agreement-markers

	Pronoun	Prefix	Suffix
1Sg	ni	n-	-da- > -t (R -R)
2Sg	hi	h-	*-ga- > -a-, -k (M) -na- > -n (F)
1Pl	gu	g-	-gu
2Pl	zu	z-	-zu

generated a huge amount of confusion for a century. In general, Basque has
no third-person pronouns, and we might therefore expect little in the way of
overt agreement. In fact, that's exactly what we do find, but it has taken a
hundred years to realize this.

Recall from Chapter 2 that the absolutive (prefix) agreement slot is filled
by any of several different morphs when no first- or second-person
agreement-marker stands there: *d-*, *z-* (B zero), *l-*, *b-* or zero. Now, at least
since the days of Schuchardt, these morphs have accordingly been taken as
the third-person agreement-markers, and gallons of ink have been expended
in trying to find sources for them. Such distinguished vasconists as Schuchardt, Lafon and Jacobsen have proposed a battery of possible sources, many
of them invoking ghostly and otherwise unattested third-person pronouns
or demonstratives, such as the lost pronoun **do* proposed by Jacobsen
(1975). The problem is compounded further by the fact that the third-person
suffixes, where these exist at all, bear no relation in form to the prefixes;
moreover, in utter contrast to what happens with the first two persons, the
third person exhibits totally different suffixes for dative and ergative agreement. Specifically, the dative marker is normally *-o* in the singular, except
that B sometimes has *-a*, while the plural marker is usually *-e* but sometimes
-ote (= *-o* + plural *-te*). It is widely thought that *-o* and *-a* are derived from
the demonstrative stems, with the variation in B perhaps representing an
ancient contrast between proximal and distal datives. The ergative suffix,
however, is invariably zero, except that third plural is marked by *-te* (B *-e*).

We can begin by disposing of this last: though often described in the
literature as the 'third-plural agreement-marker', it is nothing of the sort.
Instead, it is merely a pluralizer, one of the several pluralizers whose presence is pervasive in finite verb-forms, and the third-person ergative suffix is
invariably zero. (Pluralizers are discussed further below.)

Now, as for the five prefixes, there is an obvious fact to be noted: each one
of them occurs only in certain tenses or moods. Broadly speaking, we find *d-*
in the present, *z-* or zero in the past, *l-* in the irrealis (remote conditional)
forms called 'hypothetical' by Basque grammarians, *b-* in the jussive (third-
person imperative) and zero in the imperative. The obvious conclusion was
drawn by no one until it was pointed out by Oregi Aranburu (1974) and,
independently, by Trask (1977): these prefixes are not agreement-markers at
all; instead, they are ancient markers of *verbal categories*.

It is difficult to understand why it has taken so long to realize this rather
obvious fact, but it is now universally accepted by specialists. The precise
mechanism by which these prefixes came to be confined to third-person
forms is not clear, and there have been various proposals. I myself favour the
view that the prefixes were formerly present in all finite forms but were lost
when first- and second-person prefixes came to be attached in front of them,
but see Gómez and Sainz (1995) for a summary of other possibilities.

Of course, we are still left with the problem of finding origins for these prefixes; this is discussed in the next section. For now, observe that this analysis of the prefixes, in addition to its other attractive features, accounts straightforwardly for a phenomenon which deeply troubled all the earlier investigators. Basque has a number of verbs which are syntactically intransitive but which for one historical reason or another require transitive morphology. The inflected forms of such verbs accordingly take ergative suffixes normally to mark their subjects. Now, according to the 'agreement-marker' view of the prefixes, the absolutive agreement slot (the prefix slot) should therefore be empty, since there is no absolutive NP in the sentence for the verb to agree with. And yet such verb-forms take the usual prefixes, according to verbal category: *Urak 100 gradotan diraki* 'Water boils at 100 degrees', *lo egin dut* 'I slept', in which the present-tense *d-* has absolutely nothing to agree with. Some earlier vasconists, notably Lafon (1975), tried desperately to identify a ghostly third-person NP at some level of representation, but the analysis defended here actually predicts such data: the tense-marker appears as usual, because there is no agreement-marker present to suppress it.

That leaves the dative suffixes to be accounted for. Several linguists have proposed that these derive from the demonstrative stems. In particular, singular *-o* would derive probably from proximal *hon-* 'this' (or conceivably from mesial *horr-* 'that', much less likely), while the singular *-a*, confined to B, would derive from distal *har-* 'that'. It may be that B retains traces of what was once a systematic distinction between proximal and distal datives, but the evidence from the earliest texts in B is not sufficient to underpin this idea. In the same way, plural *-e* would derive from *haie-*, the plural stem of the distal demonstrative. The variant *-ote* is transparently nothing but singular *-o* plus the pluralizer *-te*, and undoubtedly of late origin. Such a derivation from the demonstrative stems seems plausible to me, and I endorse it, but not all specialists are satisfied with it, though I know of no alternative suggestions apart from those invoking lost pronouns again.

As a rule, tripersonal agreement is possible in Basque only when the direct object is third person, as in *emango dizut* 'I'll give it to you'. If the direct object is first- or second-person, no suitable verb-form exists, and another construction must be used: *Eraman nau amarengana* 'She took me to her mother', with allative *amarengana* and no dative agreement.

There are, however, a very few attested exceptions. Most of these are found in the New Testament translation of Leizarraga in 1571, such as *gommendatzen cerauzquiotet* 'I recommend you to them'. (A complete catalogue of these is provided in Lafon (1944: I, 397–400).) Since this work is a translation, many have thought these odd forms were invented by the author purely to provide literal translations of his text – even though inventing complex verb-forms out of thin air is hardly the sort of move we would expect from a native speaker like Leizarraga. Moreover, the 1809 *Meditacioneac* of Martin Duhalde contains the single form *eman giotza* 'he has given us to him', and the auxiliary form *nako* 'he has me to him' was apparently current in L in the early years of the twentieth century. Further, Azkue (1923–1925: section 808) reports that two old women in Dima and in Zeanuri (Biz) had described as 'popular' such forms as *Ik ni aitari eroan nautsak* 'You have taken me to my father', *Zuk ni berari eroan neutsazu* 'You have taken me to him' and *Nik i berari eroan autsat* 'I have taken you to him.'

It is hard to know what to make of these sparse and scattered attestations. Since they can't all be explained by appeals to the exigencies of translation, there remain two possibilities: (1) such tripersonal forms were anciently normal, but have been lost, with only a few remnants surviving long enough to be attested here and there; (2) these forms are sporadic local innovations which have been created at various times and in various places, without ever becoming firmly established in the language. Failing the discovery of some substantial medieval texts, we will probably never know the truth.

There is a major divergence among varieties as to the presence or absence of agreement with indefinite NPs. While the details are complex, the general position is clear. Northern and eastern varieties do not normally show agreement with an indefinite NP, while the remaining varieties do. Thus, 'I have two books' is *Bi liburu dut* in the north and east (not *ditut*, with plural object agreement), but *Bi liburu dauzkat* (B *Liburu bi dauzkat*) elsewhere, with plural object agreement (not *daukat*). Similarly, 'There were few men' is *Gizon guti zen* in the north, with a singular verb, but *Gizon gutxi zeuden* in the south, with plural agreement. Since early texts in the west show traces of the absence of agreement, it seems safe to conclude that absence of such agreement is a conservative feature, and that agreement has spread from definite NPs to indefinite NPs in most varieties, a development which is familiar from other languages.

Particularly in eastern varieties, a few verbs, sometimes or always, idiosyncratically fail to show dative agreement even when an overt definite dative NP is present in the sentence: *Aitari obeditu dut* 'I obeyed [my] father', rather than the expected *Aitari obeditu diot*, with dative agreement, or *Aita obeditu dut*, with absolutive *aita*; both of these other forms also occur.

The pluralizers merit some discussion here. Apart from the auxiliary verbs, whose plural forms are highly irregular, the pluralizers mostly conform to a rather clear pattern, as least in their shape, if not always in their placement. An absolutive NP is pluralized by a suffix *-z*, occasionally extended to *-tza* or *-tzi*. An ergative NP is pluralized by *-te*, except in B, which invariably has *-e* instead. For the ergative pluralizers, Trask (1995b) proposes that both derive from *-de*. After a vowel, this *-de* would have been reduced to *-e*, while after a voiceless sibilant it would have been devoiced to *-te*. B has generalized the first form, while other dialects have generalized the second.

In fact, this *-de* is actually attested in one verb. The verb *egon* 'be' has the regular singular forms 1Sg *nago*, 2Sg *hago*, 3Sg *dago* 'everywhere'. B has the expected plural forms 1Pl *gagoz*, 2Pl *zagoz*, 3Pl *dagoz*, with the usual *-z* pluralizer for absolutives. But all other dialects have the irregular forms 1Pl *gaude*, 2Pl *zaude*, 3Pl *daude*, all from **gagode*, etc. For some reason, the transitive pluralizer *-de* has been introduced into this intransitive verb in most varieties.

Apart from the past-tense suffix, the ergative pluralizer always comes last in a verb-form, save only for a few anomalous local forms: *dakite* (B *dakie*) 'they know it' (cf. daki 'he/she knows it'), *dauzkate* 'they have them', *zeramakioten* 'they were taking it to him/her'. It is normally only used to pluralize a third-person ergative, the first- and second-persons plural being marked only by their distinctive personal affixes.

The absolutive pluralizer *-z* (and variants) is somewhat unpredictable in its placement. Most often, it comes at the end of the verbal root, preceding any dative or ergative markers or pluralizers and also the potential marker *-(te)ke* if this is present, but also sometimes preceding other morphs. This pluralizer usually occurs with all three persons. Examples: *gatoz* 'we're coming' (cf. *nator* 'I'm coming'), *dabiltza* 'they're going about' (*dabil* 'he/she's going about'), *gabilzke* 'we can go about' (*nabilke* 'I can go about'), *dauzkat* 'I have them' (*daukat* 'I have it'), *daramazkiote* 'they're taking them away from him/her' (*daramakiote* 'they're taking it away from him/her').

The verb *jakin* 'know' has the regular pluralizer in some regional forms, as in *dakitzat* 'I know them' (*dakit* 'I know it'). In many central varieties, however, and in the standard language, this verb has an anomalous pluralizer: *dakizkit* 'I know them'. This anomalous marker occasionally turns up elsewhere, and its origin is clear: it is a combination of *-z* with the dative flag *-ki*, discussed below. This sequence occurs regularly in a number of forms with dative markers (*doazkio* 'we go to him/her' vs. *noakio* 'I go to him/her'), and it has apparently been reanalysed as constituting a single pluralizer.

A further point is that the absolutive pluralizers are found in all three persons, while the ergative pluralizer is entirely confined to the third person. For example, we have *noa* 'I go' but *goaz* 'we go', *haukat* 'I have you' (intimate singular, old singular) but *zauzkat* 'I have you' (unmarked singular, old plural), *nakar* 'he brings me' but *gakartza* 'he brings us', *dakarkit* 'he brings it to me' but *dakarzkit* 'he brings them to me'; but we have *daukat* 'I have it' but *daukagu* 'we have it', *dauka* 'he has it' but *daukate* 'they have it'. In all likelihood, then, the absolutive pluralizer is older than the ergative one.

Past-tense forms show an interesting phenomenon. The standard language follows the eastern dialects and some northern varieties in distinguishing between singular *-nd-* and plural *-nt-*: *ninduen* 'he/she had me', *hinduen* 'he/she had you' (singular), but *gintuen* 'he/she had us', *zintuen* 'he/she had you' (old plural). Most varieties other than the eastern ones in fact have *-nd-* throughout: *nind-*, *hind-*, *gind-*, *zind-*. Since the eastern dialects alone fail to voice a plosive after *n*, it seems clear that, in a singular form like *ninduen*, we must be looking at the root *-du-* of the transitive auxiliary, while, in a plural form like *gintuen*, we must be faced with another absolutive pluralizer.

Nothing whatever is known of the origin of these pluralizers, but the contrast between absolute -z and ergative *-de is quite striking.

The verbs used as auxiliaries in constructing periphrastic forms are highly irregular in the way they mark plurality. The forms of *izan* 'be' are so irregular that a distinct pluralizer can hardly be identified at all, though a morph -r- is usually present: *naiz* 'I am', *gara* 'we are'; *da* 'he/she is', *dira* 'they are'. The verb **edin*, which provides suppletive forms for non-indicative auxiliaries, shows -z more or less regularly. With **edun*, the transitive auxiliary, we find an apparent pluralizer -it- which regularly precedes the root, unlike all other pluralizers, as in *ditu* 'he/she has them' (*du* 'he/she has it'), *gaitu* 'he/she has us' (*nau* 'he/she has me') and *nituen* 'I had them' (*nuen* 'I had it'). This morph also appears in the forms of the suppletive transitive auxiliary **ezan*: *nitzan* 'that I have them' (*nezan* 'that I have it'). All this is quite mysterious. Conceivably, we might be looking at fossilized traces of a very ancient state of affairs in which Basque verbs showed stem suppletion for singular and plural absolutive NPs, a system which is by no means rare in the languages of the world, but the evidence available is hardly sufficient to support such an interpretation – though note the enigmatic behaviour of *etzan* 'lie down': *datza* 'he/she lies down', *dautza* 'they lie down'.

Many varieties of B, uniquely, show -z instead of -it- as the pluralizer with **edun*: instead of the *du* 'he/she has it', *ditu* 'he/she has them', *gaitu* 'he/she has us' of other varieties, B has *dau, dauz, gauz* and so on. This is clearly a recent analogical development; older B texts share the forms found in the other dialects.

4.7 FINITE VERB-FORMS: TENSE AND MOOD

We saw above that the prefixes long regarded as 'third-person markers' are in fact fossilized markers of tense and mood. Present tense is marked by *da-* if no agreement prefix is present, and otherwise by -a- alone: *dago* 'he/she is', *nago* 'I am'. Past tense is likewise marked by *e-* in B and by *ze-* in other varieties when no agreement prefix is present, otherwise by -e-: B *egoan* 'he/she was', common *zegoen* ~ *zegoan*, but *nengoen* ~ *nengoan* 'I was'. (The extra nasal is discussed below.) Following the same pattern, we have *le-* in irrealis (remote conditional) forms, *be-* in the jussive (third-person imperative) and *e-* in the imperative. It can be seen that -a- appears to be the characteristic vowel of the present indicative, while -e- appears in all other tenses and moods.

Where do these prefixes come from? In all likelihood, these fossilized bits of morphology are so ancient that their origins are beyond investigation. Still, de Rijk (1992) has proposed that present-tense *da-* derives from the attachment to the verb of **da-* 'present moment', the same morph discussed above in section 4.2. And it is still possible, as first suggested by Schuchardt, that hypothetical *l-* is a residue of *ahal* 'ability', though I do not myself find this suggestion compelling, the more so since *ahal* has been reconstructed by Michelena as **anal*. But there is a near-consensus on past-tense *z-*. Almost everyone agrees that B zero is more conservative than the *z-* of the other dialects, and many are inclined to see the origin of this *z-* as lying in the exceedingly frequent forms *zen ~ zan* 'was' (< **zaen*) and *ziren ~ ziran* '(they) were' (< **ziraen*), found in all dialects, in which the tense prefix is zero and the *z-* is part of the stem of the verb *izan* 'be'. For jussive *b-* there have been few proposals, though one or two people have suggested *behar* 'necessity', which again I find unconvincing.

Uniquely, the past tense is invariably marked by a suffix *-(e)n*, which always follows all other morphs in a finite form: *nator* 'I'm coming', *nentorren* 'I was coming'. The origin of this suffix is unknown, and attempts to connect it with other suffixes involving *-n* have not been successful. Interestingly, when the complementizer *-(e)n* is added to a past-tense form, only one nasal appears: *nuen* 'I had it' plus *-(e)n* yields *nuen* 'which I had'. But then we would have expected an original **-enen* to yield *-en* by the loss of intervocalic *n*. A few eastern and western varieties have lost final *-n* in past-tense forms only, producing *nue* and *nuen* for the two forms just cited, but this loss is clearly secondary and late.

Past-tense forms with non–third-person absolutive prefixes contain an extra morph *n*, as in *ninduen* 'he/she had me', *nentorren* 'I was coming' (cf. *zuen* 'he/she had him/her', *nuen* 'I had him/her', *zetorren* 'he/she was coming'). The origin of this is completely unknown, and its distribution is not readily explicable by any obvious hypothesis.

All varieties exhibit a morph *-ke* in certain finite forms; this morph has a variant *-te* or (more usually) *-teke* which is entirely confined to the verb *izan* 'be'. These morphs chiefly occur in inflections which are explicitly marked for potential mood, though not exclusively so. Examples: *etor daiteke* 'he can come', *etor liteke* 'he would be able to come', *etor zitekeen* 'he would have been able to come', *egin dezake* 'he can do it', *egin lezake* 'he would be able to do it', *egin zezakeen* 'he would have been able to do it'. In some cases, the forms with *-ke* are best regarded as conditional, rather than as potential: *etorriko litzateke* 'he would come', *etorri(ko)* zatekeen 'he would have come', *egingo luke* 'he would do it', *egin(go) zukeen* 'he would have done it'. This *-ke* follows the verbal root but precedes any suffixed agreement-marker, and its origin is completely mysterious. Lafon's view, very plausible, is that *-ke* could anciently be attached to virtually any finite form to convey a sense of indefiniteness, possibility or probability, and that the modern distribution largely reflects a degree of fossilization of the affix in forms in which its presence was semantically natural; note that a number of conditional forms do not exist in isolation, but only with either a prefixed *ba-* 'if' or a suffixed *-ke*: *balu* 'if he/she had it', *luke* 'he/she would have it', but no attested **lu*, though conceivably such free forms did once exist.

In the past, the morph *-ke* had another function: it marked futurity. Corresponding to *noa* 'I'm going', *noake* meant 'I'm going to go', 'I'll go'; beside *ikusi dut* 'I've seen it', *ikusi duket* meant 'I'll see it', or perhaps 'I'll doubtless see it'. This 'archaic future' appears to represent an extension of potentiality to futurity; in effect, forms meaning 'I can do it' came to be used for 'I'll do it', in a way which is entirely understandable. Such forms are well attested in older literature throughout the country, perhaps especially in B, but they have been steadily losing out to the periphrastic future constructed with the present-tense auxiliary and the future participle, a development which is commonly explained as resulting from Romance influence. Azkue (1905) remarks that such forms were still just about alive in his day but that they were 'being used less and less'; today they are defunct everywhere except in Z and in part of LN. Curiously, in these varieties today, while the forms survive in speech, the meaning is not necessarily future: next to *etorri da* 'he has come', *etorri dateke* means, not 'he will come', but rather 'he has undoubtedly come (by now)', 'I expect he's come (by now)', 'he will surely have come (by now)'. See Azkue (1935) for a discussion of the archaic future, and Lafon (1970, 1972) for a detailed account of the suffix *-ke*.

Related is the use of *-ke* in the 'future imperative' found in some earlier varieties. The seventeenth-century Lapurdian writer Etxeberri of Ziburu makes frequent use of imperatives like *beguira çaqueçu* 'watch out for' (in the future), and similar forms are attested in B at a later date. The contrast between *begira zazu* 'watch out for' (now) and *begira zakezu* 'watch out for' (later) reinforces the conclusion that *-ke* had acquired the status of a simple future marker.

The prefix *ba-* is attached to a finite verb-form to express 'if'. This can be attached to any indicative form to express an open conditional: *naiz* 'I am', *banaiz* 'if I am', *nintzen* 'I was', *banintzen* 'if I was', and so on. It can also be attached to various conditional forms to express varying degrees of unreality: *etorriko banintz* 'if I came', *etortzen banintz* 'if I came', *etorri banintz* 'if I had come', *etor banadi* 'if I were to come', *etor benendi* 'if I had come'; the differences among these are not easy to gloss in English.

An identical prefix *ba-* may be labelled 'affirmative', though the affirmative sense of this affix is much reduced today. From our earliest texts, this *ba-* is distinguished from the conditional *ba-* in several respects. First, conditional *ba-* makes its clause subordinate, and hence incapable of taking the allocutive marking described below, while affirmative *ba-* has no such effect. Second, affirmative *ba-* can only be prefixed to a finite form which can stand without it, while conditional *ba-* can be found in forms which cannot stand alone, as in *banu* 'if I had it' (there is no **nu*). Third, conditional *ba-* can be accompanied by *ez* 'not', while affirmative *ba-*, unsurprisingly, cannot. Moreover, in the modern language, it is at best very unusual for affirmative *ba-* to be prefixed to the auxiliary in a periphrastic form, while conditional *ba-* occurs in such a position very commonly.

Still, out of context, a form like *badakit* can mean either 'I know it' or 'if I know it', and the conditional use is often reinforced by *baldin* 'if', whose origin is discussed in section 4.3. Most vasconists are satisfied that the two prefixes must share a common origin; cf. Spanish *si* 'if' and *sí* 'yes'.

In all likelihood, an affirmative form like *badakit* once meant 'I *do* know it', contrasting with *ez dakit* 'I don't know it'. Today, however, such affirmation is commonly expressed with *bai* 'yes': *bai dakit* 'I *do* know it', and affirmative *ba-* is now little more than an empty morph. In the south, it finds its chief use in occupying the preverbal slot when a synthetic verb-form would otherwise occupy sentence-initial position, something which is not permitted in Basque: hence 'I'm going' is *Banoa*, and never **Noa*. In the north, this *ba-* is used much more frequently: it is commonly inserted before almost any synthetic verb, but especially before a short one, so that, for example, 'He's in the house' is just as likely to be *Etxean bada* as *Etxean da*.

Northern varieties exhibit four prefixes in finite verbs and auxiliaries, only one of which is still alive today. The living one is *bait-* (variant *beit-*), which has several functions, united by the observation that the prefix always serves to convert its clause into a kind of weakly subordinated clause. One function is the creation of causal clauses: *Ez baitzuen paperik, ez dute sartzerat utzi* 'Since he didn't have any papers, they didn't let him in.' A second function is the formation of complement clauses: *Handia da eroriko hortan ez baitu burua hautsi* 'It's surprising that he didn't break his head in that fall.' A third is the construction of relative clauses which are either non-restrictive or merely extraposed: *Maule, Zuberoko hiriburua baita* . . . 'Maule, which is the capital of Zuberoa . . .'; *Gizon bat ikusi dut, ez baitzuen ilhe ondorik ere* 'I saw a man who didn't have a single hair [on his head].' A fourth use, and the only one in which *bait-* can occur on the only verb in the sentence, is in exclamations: *Damurik ez baitu atxeman!* 'Too bad he didn't find it!' The origin of this prefix is a complete mystery.

The other three prefixes are now archaic. The votive prefix *ai-* was prefixed to a conditional verb to express the sense of 'if only': *ainaki* 'if I had known', *ainu jakin* 'if I had known', *ainu ez ikusi* 'if only I hadn't seen him'. The origin of this too is unknown. The prescriptive prefix *albait-* (variant *albeit-*) was likewise attached to a conditional verb to express a prescription, a third-person imperative: *sar albeiledi* 'let him enter, he is to enter', *egin albaiteza* 'let him do it'. This looks very much like an extension of *bait-*, but the first element is obscure. It might be a reduced form of *ahal* 'ability', but it is not easy to see why this item should be involved in a command. Finally, a 'conditional potential' prefix *alba-* occurs in the early literature, as in *albadagik* 'if you can do it', from *dagik* 'you do it'. This is unquestionably a combination of *ahal* 'ability' and *ba-* 'if'.

4.8 DATIVE FLAGS

When a dative agreement-marker is present, it is almost invariably preceded by a flag. The most usual flags are -*ki* and -*i*, which Trask (1995b) derives from *-gi*, entirely parallel to the split of pluralizer *-de* into -*te* and -*e*. Occasionally we find -*k*, which probably derives from the same source, and very occasionally zero. B makes heavy use of a distinct flag -*ts*, which is also marginally attested in most other parts of the country. Attempts by Campión (1884: 609) and Schuchardt (1893: 44–45) to derive this last from -*ki* by palatalization are unsustainable; -*ts* clearly has a distinct origin.

So long as we confine ourselves to finite forms, these flags are simply mysterious. However, a crucial point is that identical morphs occur widely in non-finite forms. Moreover, many of the lexical verbs bearing these morphs are clearly related to other verbs lacking them. Here are some examples: verbs containing -*ts* regularly take the participial ending -*i*, and the -*ki* of the other dialects usually appears as -*gi* in B, and -*gi* is occasionally found also in eastern dialects: *egon* 'be', *egoki* 'fit, suit, correspond to'; *ikasi* 'learn', *irakatsi* 'teach' (< *e-ra-kas-ts-i*, where -*ra*- is the ancient causative morph); *ikusi* 'see', *erakutsi* 'show' (< *e-ra-kus-ts-i*). Lafitte (1979) suggests that *jakitu* 'eat carefully, savour' is related to *jan* 'eat', and that *jakin* 'know' might be from the same source (recall the Romance parallels involving 'taste' and 'know'). The verbs *jarki* 'oppose, resist' and *jarri* 'put' are possibly also related in the same way. Particularly interesting is the group related to *edun*: *edun* 'have', *eduki* 'contain, hold, have', *ukan* 'have' (< *edukan*), *eutsi* 'seize, grasp, hang on to' (< *edutsi*). Another interesting group consists of *epai* 'cut', *ebaki* (B *ebagi*) 'cut', whose stem is *eba-* in word-formation, *ebatsi* 'steal', *erabaki* (B *erabagi*) 'decide'. A few verbs show forms with and without these morphs with no difference in meaning: *jarrai(n)*, *jarraiki* 'follow'; *jali*, *jalgi* 'go out'. Schuchardt (1893: 46) suggests that *itsatsi* 'stick' and the synonymous *itxeki* ~ *etxeki* ~ *atxiki* may represent the same verb-stem with -*ts* in one case and -*ki* in the other, though it is perhaps more likely that these two are ancient compound verbs involving the same first element and different verbal components.

Two points are important. First, although there are a number of exceptions, there is a marked tendency for transitive verbs to take -*ts* and intransitive verbs to take -*ki*, as pointed out by Azkue (1891: 478.2–3; 632). In B, the same distribution is found with the dative flags in finite forms; other dialects mostly use only *-gi* with all verbs. Second, the addition of one of these morphs to a lexical verb usually increases its valency by one, and that additional argument is usually a dative NP. This is obvious with verbs like *egoki*, *irakatsi* and *erakutsi*. The verb *eutsi* oddly takes a dative object but no direct object. Even some of these verbs which take no dative today formerly did so; for example, *eduki* is well attested with a dative object in early texts: Schuchardt (1893: 46) cites from Haraneder's translation of the Gospel of

St Mark (early eighteenth century) the sentence *edukiko dio bere emazteari* 'he will hold [to] his wife', with a dative object which is not possible today. Further, Michelena (1954c) concludes that finite forms like *dauka*, now 'he/ she has it', with no dative object, were originally three-person forms, lit. 'he/ she has it to him/her', with dative flag *-k* and dative marker *-a*, today otherwise confined to B.

There are many more lexical verbs bearing similar-looking morphs which have no known corresponding simple verbs: *iguriki* 'wait for', *izeki* 'burn' (archaic), *ideki* ~ *ireki* 'open', *jaiki* 'get up', *irauntsi* 'say, tell', *erantsi* 'stick', *irautsi* 'persist with', *inotsi* 'flow', *jautsi* 'go down' and a number of others. The great majority of these verbs also take dative objects, and there is every reason to suppose that such verbs incorporate the same morphs and that the simple verbs from which they are derived merely dropped out of use too early to be recorded.

Now, it has long been agreed that these morphs appearing in non-finite forms are to be identified with the dative flags of identical form (Azkue 1891: 478.3, Schuchardt 1893: 34, Lafon 1944: 2: 14). We may therefore safely conclude that these two morphemes, one generally used with transitive verbs and the other with intransitive verbs, were anciently added to both finite and non-finite verb-forms in order to confer the ability to take an additional NP argument in the dative. It is probably impossible to decide whether they were added first to finite or to non-finite forms; I speculate that they might have appeared first in finite forms by the incorporation in the verbal complex of what were originally independent grammatical items, and that, since they immediately followed the verb-stem, they were reanalysed as constituting part of the stems of extended verbs of distinct meaning. That is, I propose a syntactic construction *FiniteVerb Flag+DativeNP developing to a single finite form incorporating both the flag and the dative marker, of the form *Prefixes–Root–Flag–Dative, and the sequence Root–Flag finally being taken as a new verb-stem.

A further complication is the presence in certain finite forms with dative-marking of an extra *i* preceding the verbal root: *egin dezake* 'he can do it', but *eman diezaioke* 'he can give it to him', in which the second form shows the expected dative flag *i* before the agreement marker *o* but also shows an additional *i* just after the initial *d*; *egin ezazu!* 'do it!', but *eman iezaiozu!* 'give it to him!'. Further, in a number of forms, this early *i* appears *instead* of the usual dative flag: *eman diezadake* 'he can give it to me' (not *eman d(i)ezaidake*); northern *eman ziezon* 'he gave it to him', instead of *eman zezaion* (standard *eman zion*). Indeed, such 'displacement' is the norm, except when the dative is third person, when we often find an *i* in both places.

Schuchardt (1923: 6) considers that such forms must result from a metathesis, with the *i* being attracted towards the beginning of the verb-form; this view is at first rejected by Lafon (1944: 394) but later accepted by him (1961: 156). Lafon draws attention to the possible parallel of the forms of *joan* 'go', whose past tense appears in the seventeenth-century writer Leizarraga both as *zohian* and *zioan*, both 'he went'. Not everyone considers this idea plausible, but no other suggestions have been put forward.

Be all this as it may, it can hardly be doubted that the history just sketched is correct in its essentials, and we can therefore get a glimpse of an important part of the development of the extraordinarily rich verbal morphology of Basque. We still, however, have little idea what the origin of these morphs might have been: if they were either adpositions or serial verbs, the order of elements is absolutely out of line with the postpositional and verb-final syntax of the language. Conceivably, therefore, we have here traces of an ancient stage when Basque was a VO language, as suggested by Trask (1977), who proposes SVO, and by Gómez (1994) and Gómez and Sainz (1995), who argue for an ancient VSO sentence structure comparable to that of ancient Celtic, in which the sentence-initial verb had to be preceded by a particle; see Russell (1995: 49–50). Since Basque is typologically extremely consistent, exhibiting virtually all of the properties typically found in consistent SOV languages, such suggestions apparently require us to believe that the morphology of finite verbs is very ancient indeed.

4.9 VOICE AND VALENCY

A number of Basque verbs are exclusively intransitive: *etorri* 'come', *ibili* 'go about', *jauzi* 'jump', *jaio* 'be born', *erori* 'fall down' and a number of others. This group includes a few verbs whose translation equivalents are transitive in English, such as *hasi* 'begin' and *saiatu* 'try' (which take a locative complement) and *jarrain* (and variants) 'follow' (which takes a dative complement). The verb *joan* 'go' is strictly intransitive in most varieties, but a few northern speakers can use it also as a transitive verb meaning 'take away'; other speakers require the causative *eraman* ~ *eroan* (< *eraoan*) in this sense. There is at least one dative-subject verb: *ahantzi* ~ *ahaztu* 'forget', whose syntax is illustrated by *Liburua ahantzi zait* 'I forgot the book', lit. 'The book forgot to me'. Note also two verbs meaning 'be pleasing to' (i.e., 'like'), *gustatu* (< Sp *gustar*) and *laket*(*u*) (< Lat PLACET), which are also construed as intransitives with dative arguments.

A sizeable number of verbs are syntactically intransitive (they cannot take direct objects) but none the less require full transitive morphology (ergative subjects, transitive auxiliaries, transitive agreement patterns). There has been much discussion of the origin of these verbs, which are somewhat unhappily termed 'deponents' by Lafitte (1944). A number of linguists, beginning with Levin (1983), have interpreted these verbs as 'unergatives': that is, such verbs are regarded as a semantically homogeneous group, those whose single argument is an underlying agent. Ordinary intransitive verbs are thus regarded as 'unaccusatives', with underlying patients.

I find this analysis untenable, since the class of 'deponent' verbs is decidedly heterogeneous semantically. The biggest group consists of compound verbs formed from a noun (or rarely another item) plus *egin* 'do', or occasionally *eman* 'give': *lo egin* 'sleep', *amets egin* 'dream', *eztul egin* 'cough', *bainu egin* 'take a bath', *nigar egin* 'weep', *galde egin* 'ask (a question)', *barre egin* 'smile, laugh', *usin egin* 'sneeze', *zurrunga egin* 'snore', *oihu egin* 'scream', *hotz egin* 'be cold' (of weather), *hitz egin* 'speak', *dardar egin* 'tremble', *porrot egin* 'collapse, fail', *uko egin* 'renounce, deny', *bekatu egin* 'sin', *haginka egin* 'chew', *hegaz egin* 'fly', *su eman* 'ignite, light', *musu eman* 'kiss' and hundreds of others. As can readily be seen from this small sample, it can hardly be maintained that such verbs regularly have agent subjects. Rather, the transitive morphology is induced by the formation, and such compound verbs can be readily constructed with both agent and non-agent subjects (though almost always with human subjects). Nor can it reasonably be maintained that strictly intransitive verbs like those meaning 'come', 'jump', 'go about', 'try' and 'start' have non-agent subjects. As far as I can see, the membership of the 'deponent' class is semantically arbitrary and merely the result of historical accidents.

There are also a few of these verbs which are not compound in form: *iraun* 'last', *iraki(n)* 'boil' (intr.), *kurritu* 'run', *usatu* 'get used to', *argitu* 'shine', *beilatu* 'sit up, keep a vigil', *dirdiratu* 'sparkle' and a number of others. The first two of these look like ancient causatives which have undergone a change of meaning; the rest are just unexpected, especially those which take inanimate subjects.

Furthermore, there are quite a few syntactically intransitive verbs which take intransitive morphology in the eastern dialects but transitive morphology in the west: *dantzatu* 'dance', *igan* ~ *igo(n)* 'go up, ascend' (allative complement), *afaldu* 'have dinner' (and all other meal verbs), *borrokatu* 'fight', *trabailatu* 'work', *solastatu* 'speak with', *jazarri* 'revolt', *jokatu* 'play games', *irten* ~ *erten* ~ *urten* 'go out' and others; see Oyharçabal (1992a) for a catalogue. And there are pairs of synonymous verbs exhibiting different behaviour: western *hitz egin*, *berba egin* 'speak' take transitive morphology, eastern *mintzatu* 'speak' takes intransitive. The picture that emerges is one of historical accident and regional preferences, rather than one of an underlying semantic basis.

Every single verb which takes a direct object is, of course, morphologically transitive; this includes a number of verbs with non-agent subjects, such as all verbs meaning 'have', 'hold', 'contain', 'possess' and 'own' (*Estherrek begi urdinak ditu/dauzka* 'Esther has blue eyes'), and perception verbs like those meaning 'know', 'recognize', 'love', 'hate', 'enjoy', 'see' and 'hear'.

A number of verbs can be used either intransitively or transitively with more or less predictable differences in meaning: *hil* 'die' and 'kill'; *esnatu* 'wake up' and 'awaken'; *itzuli* 'turn, turn over', 'return (go back)' and 'return (give back)'; *sartu* 'enter' and 'insert'; *kendu* 'get out of the way' and 'remove'; *mintzurratu* 'lose one's virginity' and 'deflower'.

The great majority of Basque verbs are best regarded as inherently transitive in syntax and hence also in morphology. However, with just a handful of exceptions, such as the verbs meaning 'have', every transitive verb in the language can be construed intransitively, in the construction called the *mediopassive*, as described in Chapter 2. The mediopassive cannot take an overt agent; the functional equivalent of the passive-with-agent is the participial construction also described in Chapter 2.

As explained in Chapter Two, all non-finite forms are inherently unmarked for voice; voice distinctions can only be expressed by means of auxiliaries.

Causatives can be formed in a variety of ways. A very few intransitive verbs can be construed transitively to form their own causatives, as with *hil* 'die' and 'kill' and *esnatu* 'wake up' and 'awaken'. (These are not instances of the mediopassive, since 'die' ≠ 'be killed' and 'wake up' ≠ 'be awakened'.) In one or two cases, the causative of an intransitive verb is arguably provided by a different lexical verb, as with *etorri* 'come' and *ekarri* 'bring'. At some ancient stage of the language, however, there was a productive causative prefix (!) of the form *-ra-*. The language still possesses a number of verb pairs related by this prefix: *ibili* 'be active' and *erabili* 'cause to move, use'; *joan* 'go' and *eraman* (B *eroan*) 'take away' (< *e-ra-oan); *ekarri* 'bring' and *erakarri* 'attract'; *jaiki* 'arise, get up' and *eraiki* 'raise, construct'; *ikusi* 'see' and *erakutsi* 'show'; *ikasi* 'learn' and *irakatsi* 'teach'; *izeki* 'burn' (now archaic) and *irazeki* 'set fire to'. In one or two cases the semantics has become rather strange, as with *jantzi* 'get dressed' and *erantzi* 'get undressed'; it is possible that an unrelated verb may have contaminated the second of these. This prefix has not been productive in historical times, though it was used by Sabino Arana to derive *eratorri* 'derive' from *etorri* 'come', one of his more elegant and successful creations. A few of the *-ra-*causatives, like *erabili*, are among the small number of verbs which can be conjugated synthetically, reflecting their great antiquity. As we saw above, there are quite a few verbs which look as if they are probably ancient *-ra-*causatives of simple verbs now lost.

In historical times, the function of *-ra-* has been taken over by a suffix *-erazi* ~ *-arazi* (B *-erazo* ~ *-arazo*). This suffix is highly productive: *joan* 'go', *joanarazi* 'make (someone) go'; *jan* 'eat', *janarazi* 'make (someone) eat, feed (animals)'; *ezagutu* 'know (a person)', *ezaguterazi* 'introduce'. This suffix is almost certainly an ancient lexical verb in origin, and is itself probably the *-ra-* causative of a simpler verb now lost. It is possible to see the replacement of the anomalous causative prefix by a postposed causative verb as another piece of evidence pointing to a very ancient VO sentence structure preserved in the verbal morphology.

Compound verbs in *egin*, unsurprisingly, form their causatives by replacing *egin* with its own causative *eragin*: *lo egin* 'sleep', *lo eragin* 'make (someone) sleep'. In B one occasionally finds *eragin* used to form causatives of simple verbs in place of *-arazo*.

4.10 THE AUXILIARIES

Generally speaking, there are four verbs commonly used as auxiliaries for constructing periphrastic forms. Intransitive verbs use the common verb *izan* 'be' to construct indicative forms and non-remote conditionals, and the otherwise unattested verb **edin*, sometimes glossed as 'become' for no good reason, to construct remote conditionals, potentials, subjunctives and imperatives. Transitive verbs use **edun* 'have' and **ezan*, usually glossed as 'do', in precisely the same way. B differs in using the common verb *egin* 'do, make' in place of **ezan*, but medieval and sixteenth-century texts in B show the presence of **ezan*, and B *egin* is therefore probably an innovation. Of these, both *izan* and **edun* are also used as ordinary main verbs (except that **edun* has been displaced in this function in western varieties by *eduki* 'have'), and these two verbs, of course, exhibit a wide range of synthetic (non-periphrastic) inflections when so used. The verb *egin* is everywhere used as a main verb, and our earliest texts show instances of synthetic forms of this verb, but today it is conjugated only periphrastically as a main verb.

The three verbs reconstructed as **edin*, **edun* and **ezan* are defective, in that they have only finite forms attested; the reconstructions depend on the observation that the roots appearing in finite forms are *-di-* (often reduced to *-i-*), *-du-* (often reduced to *-u-*) and *-za-*. Our sole certain attestation of **edun* is the participle *eun* recorded in Landucci's 1562 dictionary. A possible further, but doubtful, attestation of **edun* is the verbal noun *edutea* found in a single Bizkaian text from the eighteenth century. This form has been taken both as representing **edun* and as representing its derivative *eduki*, but Irigoyen (1971) notes that other and seemingly earlier copies of the same text show *ecutea* instead. He suggests that the obscure *ecutea* was probably unintelligible to later copyists, who therefore replaced it. If he is right, this *ecutea* might conceivably represent *ekun*, an attested variant of *ukan*, another derivative of **edun* which today serves as the participle and citation form of **edun* in the northern and eastern dialects.

The present-tense forms of *izan* are extremely irregular, and appear to show stem suppletion; the forms are listed in Table 4.2. The first two forms show the apparent stem *iza-* of *izan*, but the others seem to show a different stem.

The present-tense forms of **edun* are somewhat more regular, though they have developed differently in different regions. The reconstructed forms present few difficulties; these consist of present-tense prefix *da-*, the root *-du-* of **edun*, and the personal suffixes (zero for the third person, but the third-plural forms show the ergative pluralizer *-te* (B *-e*). The forms are listed in

Table 4.2 The present tense of *izan* 'be'

1Sg	*naiz* (variants *nax, naz, niz* by reduction)
2Sg	*haiz* (similar variants)
3Sg	*da*
1Pl	*gara* (variants *gera, gira, gire, gare*)
2Pl	*zara* (similar variants)
3Pl	*dira* (variant *dire*)

Table 4.3. (The forms labelled L are in fact found everywhere except in B and G, except that Z has fronted the *u* as usual: *düt*, etc.) The sequence **-adu-* was everywhere reduced to **-au-*. In B, this remains in the third person but is elsewhere levelled to *-o-*; third-plural **daue* has been strengthened to *dabe*. Elsewhere, **-au-* was raised to **-eu-*, which has been reduced to *-u-* in L (and in all other varieties) but to *-e-* in G, except in the third person, where we also find *-u-*. The singular endings **-da*, **-ga* and **-na* have everywhere lost their final *-a*, but this reappears when a suffix is added, as in relative *dudan, duan* (< **dugan*), *dunan*. (Some varieties have recently reanalysed these forms, so that B, for example, has for *dot* the relative form *doten*.)

Table 4.3 The present tense of **edun* 'have'

	L	G	B	
1Sg	dut	det	dot	*da-du-da
2SgM	duk	dek	dok	*da-du-ga
2SgF	dun	den	don	*da-du-na *or* *da-du-na-ga
3Sg	du	du	dau	*da-du
1Pl	dugu	degu	dogu	*da-du-gu
2Pl	duzu	dezu	dozu	*da-du-zu
3Pl	dute	dute	dabe	*da-du-te (B *da-du-e*)

For tripersonal forms of the auxiliary (transitive forms with a dative), there are significant regional differences. The eastern varieties show forms like *derauka ~ drauka ~ daroka* (rarely *doro ~ doo*) 'he/she has it to him/her'. Such forms are well attested in L and LN, and they are attested in G until the early eighteenth century, and in HN in the sixteenth century, suggesting that they are probably the most conservative forms. These forms have been variously interpreted as deriving from *eroan* 'take away', the causative of *joan* 'go' (van Eys 1873: xxi, 1879: 115), from *iraun* 'last', probably an ancient causative of *egon* 'stay, wait, be' (Bonaparte (1876: 12), or from **edun* with irregular phonological developments (Schuchardt 1893). The most plausible analysis, however, is probably that of Gómez and Sainz (1995: 240), who see the underlying verb as **eradun*, an otherwise unattested causative of **edun*. Central dialects show forms like *dio* (same gloss); these are present in our earliest texts and appear to have gained ground at the expense of the first group. They are generally thought to represent the usual transitive auxiliary *edun 'have' with extensive phonological reduction: perhaps *dio* < *dauio* < *da-du-gi-o*, more or less as proposed by Schuchardt (1893). (Some, however, have preferred to invoke a distinct verbal root *i-*, possibly attested also in the odd imperative forms meaning 'give', such as *i(n)dazu* 'give it to me' and *iguzu* 'give it to us' (see de Rijk 1985).) B, however, has a quite different set of forms, exemplified by *deutso* (same gloss). These show the dative flag *-ts-* in place of the *-gi-* used elsewhere, but the verbal root still appears to be *edun*. Such forms reflect the usual B preference for *-ts-* as a dative flag with transitive verbs, a preference which appears to be ancient in that variety. Equally, one could view these forms as involving the verb *eutsi* 'seize, grasp', itself derived from *edun* + *-ts-*, which takes a dative object (only).

There is one final group of distinctive forms: some eastern varieties have potential forms like *diro(ke)* 'he/she can V it', in place of common *dezake*, B *dai(ke)*. Gómez and Sainz (1995: 240) propose here an ancient *iron*, perhaps a causative of an unidentified verb. Like the B forms in *egin* (including *daike*), these forms may be late innovations, though for both this group and the tripersonal group cited above, Michelena (1964b) is inclined to see the variation as resulting from differing choices among competing forms all of which were available at an earlier stage of the language, possibly with some subtle difference in meaning.

4.11 THE ALLOCUTIVE FORMS

The allocutive forms are those in which a second-person marker is placed in the finite verb in order to mark the addressee even though the sentence contains no second-person argument: *naiz* 'I am' (unmarked), *nauk* 'I am' (allocutive, male addressee), *naun* 'I am' (allocutive, female addressee); *dago* 'he/she is' (unmarked), *diagok/-n* ~ *jagok/-n* ~ *zegok/-n* 'he/she is' (allocutive); *egin dut* 'I did it' (unmarked), *egin diat/dinat* 'I did it' (allocutive).

Though the precise forms used vary considerably from region to region, allocutivity is universal in Basque and has been so since our earliest texts. It is therefore probably rather old, though surely it is younger than the unmarked verb-forms upon which the allocutive versions are built. Allocutive forms are regularly used only when speaking to an interlocutor whom one addresses with the intimate singular pronoun *hi*, but then such forms are obligatory. Allocutive forms occur only in main clauses, and never in subordinate clauses of any kind.

Allocutive forms differ from the corresponding unmarked forms in several respects. First, the addressee is marked by a suffix *-ga* (male) or *-na* (female). With an intransitive verb, the addressee is marked like an ergative subject; with a transitive verb, the facts are more complex and more variable, though the addressee is not infrequently marked like a dative NP. The allocutive forms of *izan* 'be' are invariably formed with **edun* 'have'; those of **edun* are formed either with **edun* itself or with the reduced verbal root *-i-* typical of verb-forms showing dative agreement in central dialects. No other verb shows stem-suppletion in forming allocutives. In many, but not all, varieties an allocutive form exhibits a morph *-i-* preceding the verb root, just as occurs in unmarked forms showing dative agreement (see section 4.8): *nago* 'I am' (unmarked), *niagok ~ ñagok* 'I am' (allocutive).

Schuchardt (1893) sees the allocutive forms as ethic datives, a view largely supported by Gavel and Lacombe (1937), Lafon (1944) and Altube (1934). One difficulty with this interpretation is that, in allocutive intransitive forms, the addressee is generally coded like an ergative, not like a dative. Another is that ethic datives, in languages which have them, are usually optional, while the Basque allocutive is obligatory.

Allocutive forms are not usual when the addressee receives the unmarked pronoun *zu*, except in a few eastern varieties in which a set of allocutive forms used with the unmarked pronoun *zu* 'you' (and/or its palatalized variant *xu*) has developed quite recently.

There is, however, one other construction which needs to be considered here. Very many Basques normally express a copular sentence like 'I'm Bizkaian', not as the unmarked *Bizkaitarra naiz*, but as *Bizkaitarra nauzu*, which looks literally like 'You have me a Bizkaian'; similarly, 'Who are you?' is not *Nor zara?* but *Nor zaitut?*, seemingly 'Who do I have you?' These forms are termed 'implicational' by Basque grammarians, and many have seen the implicational forms as the source of allocutivity. However, as pointed out by Rebuschi (1984) and Alberdi (1995), there are major differences between implicational and allocutive forms. First, allocutivity occurs with both transitive and intransitive verbs, while implicational forms exist only for intransitive verbs. Second, allocutivity is confined to the marking of a singular addressee, while implicational forms can mark an NP of any person and number: *Gure baserritarra zintzoa da/duzue/dugu* 'Our farmer is honest' (*da* 'is', unmarked; *duzue* implicational, second-person plural; *dugu* implicational, first-person plural). Third, implicational forms are always optional and are more highly marked than the neutral forms, while allocutive forms are obligatory. Fourth, allocutive forms are confined to main clauses, while implicational forms can occur freely in subordinate clauses. Fifth, both allocutive and implicational marking can be present simultaneously: *Gure baserritarra zintzoa diagu* 'Our farmer is honest', with *diagu* showing allocutive *-a-* (second singular) and implicational *-gu* (first plural).

A further point of importance is that, in forms with first-person subjects, an allocutive form of *izan* 'be' is always identical to a non-allocutive form of **edun* 'have' marked for a second-person ergative, and an allocutive non-dative form of **edun* is always identical to a non-allocutive form of the same verb marked for a second-person dative: hence *nauk* 'I am' (allocutive) or 'you have me' (non-allocutive); *diat* 'I have it' (allocutive) or 'I have it to you' (non-allocutive). In the same way, each of the handful of other verbs with synthetic conjugations marks an allocutive with an ordinary second-person ergative agreement marker (if intransitive) or with an ordinary second-person dative marker (if transitive). In forms with third-person subjects, the same is true in the central dialects, and above all in G. In the peripheral dialects, however, this identity does not occur in past-tense and irrealis forms with third-person subjects: *zen* 'he/she was' (unmarked), *huen* 'you had him/her' (unmarked), but *zuan* (M), *zunan* (F) 'he/she was' (allocutive); *litzateke* 'he/she would be' (unmarked), *huke* 'you would have him/her' (unmarked), but *lukek* (M), *luken* (F) (allocutive). The significance of these facts is disputed. Rebuschi (1984) argues that the significant number of differences shows that allocutive forms must have been anciently distinct from all unmarked verb-forms, while Alberdi (1995) concludes that the greater number of identical forms indicates that the allocutive forms must have originated as a special function of non-allocutive forms with second-person markers, with the observed differences being therefore later innovations.

As for the 'displaced' *-i-* in allocutive forms like *niagok* 'I am', there is no more consensus than there is with the same phenomenon in dative agreement. Ros (1987) notes that the nineteenth-century Bizkaian writer Añibarro has unusual allocutive forms with a long vowel, such as *naagok* for unmarked *nago* 'I am'. He therefore proposes that such forms are conservative, and that the introduction of a glide [j] to break up the vowels in hiatus gave rise to (in this case) **najagok*, which he sees as the source of the modern dialectal variants like L *niagok*, HN *negok*, G *natxiok*, B *nai[ʒ]ok*, *najak*, Aezk *ñagok*, and so on, by varying phonological developments. Ros thus sees the troublesome *-i-* as the result of the morphologization of an originally expressive vowel-lengthening.

Alberdi (1995) rejects Ros's interpretation. He points out that allocutive forms with geminate vowels, while common in the writings of nineteenth-century Bizkaian authors, are entirely absent from the writings of earlier Bizkaian authors and from the work of authors from all other regions, suggesting strongly that the forms with geminate vowels are a late and localized innovation. Moreover, Añibarro's usage has, corresponding to unmarked *dago* 'he/she is', allocutive *jaagok*, which suggests an earlier **diaagok*, but hardly **dajagok*, as required by Ros.

The variation exhibited in L *niagok*, B *ñagok* 'I am' (allocutive) may result either from palatalization of original **niagok* or from depalatalization of earlier **ñagok*; the first view is more widely held, but Rudolf de Rijk (p.c.) has suggested that the second might be preferable, in line with the unpacking of palatal segments observed elsewhere in the central dialects (see section 3.8).

4.12 PERIPHRASTIC FORMS

Basque verbal morphology is overwhelmingly periphrastic, and has been so throughout the historical period. In the sixteenth century, there were about sixty verbs which had at least some synthetic forms, usually just the present and past indicative and sometimes also an imperative. Today there are no more than a dozen verbs which still have some synthetic forms in regular spoken use, though the Academy recognizes synthetic forms of about three dozen verbs for literary use.

A periphrastic form consists of a participle or the radical plus a finite auxiliary. Generally speaking, the combination of one of the participles – perfective, imperfective or future – with an auxiliary yields an indicative form, while the use of the radical produces a marked mood: conditional, subjunctive, potential or imperative. These marked forms also require a different auxiliary from the indicative forms: indicative *izan* (intransitive) and **edun* (transitive), but marked moods **edin* (intr.) and **ezan* (tr.) (B *egin*). Examples, with *sartu* 'enter' (intr.) and 'insert' (tr.): *sartu naiz* 'I entered', *sartuko naiz* 'I'm going to enter', but *sar naiteke* 'I can enter', *sar nadin* '(that) I enter', *sar hadi!* 'enter!'; *sartu dut* 'I inserted it', *sartuko dut* 'I'll insert it', but *sar dezaket* 'I can insert it', *sar dezadan* '(that) I insert it', *sar ezak!* 'insert it!'

The basis for these major differences in formation is not understood. It has, however, often been pointed out that the indicative forms look very much like forms of similar meaning and formation in the neighbouring Romance languages, and some scholars are inclined to see these forms as calques on Romance. If this view is correct, then the indicative forms are of late formation, and they must have displaced some earlier indicative forms, now lost; possibly these earlier indicative forms were not even periphrastic, and the synthetic forms which are now confined to the auxiliaries and to a handful of other verbs may represent the normal pattern for constructing indicative forms at an ancient stage of the language, one in which periphrastic forms existed only for the marked mood categories and were exclusively constructed with the radical (which, recall from above, I have argued was anciently a verbal noun). This idea is very appealing, but there is very little in the way of evidence to support it. One possible piece of evidence, though, is the observation that the synthetic forms of those verbs which have them have clearly narrowed their meaning. For example, the synthetic form *nentorren* is today explicitly imperfective: 'I was coming'. In the sixteenth century, however, this form could equally mean 'I came', a form which today must be expressed by the periphrastic form *etorri nintzen*, and similarly for other synthetic forms.

A complication is the existence in early northern Basque, and above all in the writer Leizarraga, of an indicative form constructed with the radical. Leizarraga contrasts the ordinary past-tense forms *sartu zen* 'he entered' and *sartu zuen* 'he inserted it' with intransitive *sar zedin* and transitive *sar zezan*, apparently with similar English glosses, even though the second set look like subjunctives. The contrast between the two sets appears to be one of aspect; the second set, variously called 'aorist' or 'narrative', appear from their contexts to express something like an event in a narrative sequence, while the first merely represent an ordinary punctual or perfective form. Rare outside of Leizarraga, and unknown since his time, the second set of forms is decidedly unusual, and may represent no more than an idiosyncratic development peculiar to a particular time and place.

Today the radical and the periphrastic forms involving it are fully alive in speech only in the northern varieties. In the south, some of these forms are now purely literary and have been replaced in speech by non-finite forms. For example, the subjunctive forms have been replaced by inflected forms of the gerund: where a northerner might say *Sar nadin esan dit* 'He told me to go in', with subjunctive *sar nadin*, a southerner says *Sartzeko esan dit*, with gerund *sartze* plus the suffix *-ko*. Where the periphrastic forms continue in use in the south, the radical has been replaced by the perfective participle, and so a southerner says, for example, *sartu hadi!* 'go in!', rather than *sar hadi!*

4.13 ASPECTUAL AND MODAL AUXILIARIES

The most widespread progressive (continuous) auxiliary is *ari izan* 'be . . .ing', which is a compound of *izan* 'be' with the item *ari*: *idazten du* 'he writes' (in general, habitually), but *idazten ari da* 'he is writing' (at the moment). The item *ari* hardly has any independent existence today, but it is attested in the literature in the sense of 'busy, hard at work'. This auxiliary can also be used without a verbal complement: *lanean ari da* 'he's working' (lit., 'he's busy at work'). In many varieties of B, the verb *ihardun ~ jardun* 'be busy' serves as the usual progressive auxiliary.

In the writing of the seventeenth-century author Axular, this same *ari* is the source of the verb *aritu*, which serves as an auxiliary marking habitual aspect and contrasting with *ari izan*. More commonly today, the habitual auxiliary is *ohi *edun*, a compound of the transitive auxiliary *edun* with *ohi* 'habit, custom'.

The synonymous nouns *nahi* and *gura*, both 'desire', form the compound verbs *nahi *edun* and *gura *edun*, 'want (to)'. Similarly, *behar* 'necessity' and *ahal* 'ability' form *behar *edun* 'need (to), must' and *ahal izan/*edun* 'be able (to), can'.

All such verbs lack the usual verbal distinction between perfective and imperfective participles, and hence they rely upon the auxiliary to bear any required tense-marking: *egin behar dut* 'I have to do it', *egin behar nuen* 'I had to do it'. The first elements can, however, take the future marker *-ko*, even though they are nouns (or adjectives) and not verbs: *egin beharko dut*

'I'll have to do it'. Prescriptivist writers have often condemned such future forms as illogical, demanding instead *egin behar izango dut*, with an extra participle to bear the future marker, but such coinages do not reflect normal usage.

4.14 LINSCHMANN'S LAW

The early northern literature written in what is known as *Classical Labourdin* (the Lapurdian of roughly 1600–1650) exhibits an important syntactic rule called *Linschmann's law* after the linguist who first identified it. This 'law' governs the distribution of the intensive, or 'strong', genitive forms and the unmarked, or 'weak', genitives: an intensive genitive is used always and only when the genitive NP is coreferential with another NP in the same simplex clause. Linschmann's law is categorical in the writings of the period. Here are some examples taken from Axular's *Gero* (1643); the spelling has been silently modernized.

Barka iatzagu$_j$tzu geure$_j$ zorrak, guk$_j$ [gure$_j$gana zordun diren]ei barkatzen derauztegu$_j$n bezala.
'Forgive us$_j$ our$_j$ debts, as we$_j$ forgive them to those [who have debts towards us$_j$].'

Here the first clause has the intensive genitive *geure* 'our', since this is coreferential with the indirect object *guri* 'to us', expressed here only by the agreement-marker in the auxiliary *iatzagutzu*, while the second clause has unmarked *gure* in *guregana* 'towards us', since it does not stand directly within the clause whose subject is *guk* 'we' but rather in the relative clause *guregana zordun diren* 'those who have debts towards us', in which it is coreferential with nothing.

Zeren [[[bere$_j$ barreneko] koleraren] suak] errai guztiak erratzen baiterau$_j$-tza . . .
'Because [the fire [of the anger [in his$_j$ heart]]] burns all his$_j$ entrails . . . '
(lit., 'burns all the entrails to him$_j$')

Here the intensive genitive *bere* is embedded within a -*ko* phrase which is in turn embedded within an NP in the genitive modifying *suak* 'the fire' (Erg), but it is still within the simplex clause containing the dative NP 'to him', though again this dative is expressed only by the agreement-marker in the auxiliary.

Iraungitzen da kolera ere [bat bederak$_j$ bere$_j$ falten gogoratzeaz].
'Anger too burns out, [with everyone$_j$ remembering his$_j$ offences].'

Here the intensive genitive *bere* 'his' stands within a non-finite clause in which it is coreferential with *bat bederak* 'each one' (Erg). As is usual in

Basque, non-finite clauses behave just like finite clauses in all respects save only in the absence of a finite verb (the verb *gogoratu* 'remember' occurs here in the gerund).

This rigorous system began to break up in Lapurdi some time after about 1650; in other parts of the country the full system is not attested even in our earliest texts. It seems reasonable to assume that the Lapurdian dialect was conservative in retaining what was formerly a universal syntactic character-istic of the language, but of course we cannot be sure. The manner in which the classical system broke up is complex and somewhat unexpected; the details are too intricate to summarize here, but they are painstakingly assembled by Rebuschi (1995). Oversimplifying somewhat, we may say that the intensive/unmarked distinction has been lost in the first two persons but retained in the third person, though the distribution of intensive and unmarked forms today is not quite what would be predicted by Linsch-mann's law.

4.15 THE COMPLEMENTIZERS

Basque has two suffixed complementizers, -(*e*)*n* and -(*e*)*la*. The first may be classed as [+WH], since it occurs in relative clauses and in embedded ques-tions. The second, which is [–WH], occurs in complement clauses. Each is attached to a finite verb or auxiliary. The historical form of an agreement suffix always surfaces when one of these suffixes is added; for example, *dut* 'I have it', which derives from **duda*, with first-singular -*da*, yields *dudan* and *dudala*, except in a few varieties in which the suffixed forms have been reshaped on the model of the unsuffixed auxiliary, as in those varieties of B in which *dot* 'I have it' yields *doten* and *dotela*. When one of these suffixes is added to a past-tense form, which in all cases already ends in -*n*, that -*n* is suppressed. Hence *nuen* 'I had it' yields *nuen* and *nuela*, the first often distin-guished from the simple form by its final accent: *nuén*.

It is widely thought that -(*e*)*la* is derived from -(*e*)*n* by the addition of a further morph -*la*, possibly cognate with the -*la* that forms adverbs of man-ner from demonstrative and interrogative stems, as in *hola* ~ *honela* 'thus, like this' (from *hon-* 'this') and *nola* 'how?' (from *no-*, interrogative stem). An original **-(e)n-la*, with its impermissible cluster, might have been assimilated to **-(e)lla*, yielding the attested -(*e*)*la* by regular phonological change. The adverbial origin of -(*e*)*la* is supported by the observation that this comple-mentizer can form a -*ko* phrase just like any adverbial: *dela* 'that he is', *delako* 'so-called'; *pozik zegoela* 'that she was happy', *pozik zegoelako ustean* 'in the belief that she was happy'.

The origin of -(*e*)*n* itself is disputed. Several early scholars were inclined to see it as a specialization of locative -*n*, a position which has few if any adherents today. Michelena in several places preferred to see the suffix as a specialization of genitive -*en*, since a relative clause occupies the same position within an NP as a genitive. But there are difficulties with this. For one thing, the complementizer is invariably added to a finite verb-form, something which is quite unexpected for a genitive case-suffix, which otherwise can only be attached to an NP. For another, the genitive ending is indisputably -*en*, while the complementizer is always -*n*. After a consonant, a position in which an *e* would be inserted automatically before another consonant, it makes no difference. But after a vowel the genitive always appears as -*ren*, while the complementizer is merely -*n*: *Ana* 'Ann', genitive *Anaren* 'Ann's', but finite *ikusi dugu* 'we saw it', suffixed *ikusi dugun* 'which we saw', never **ikusi duguren*. Thus, while a genitive origin cannot be ruled out, it does not seem to be obviously right, and the question must remain open.

Both -(*e*)*n* and -(*e*)*la* can take a large number of further suffixes to construct a range of subordinate clauses, chiefly adverbial clauses; these are mostly of transparent origin and they are too numerous to discuss here. A few involve obscure final elements, such as western -(*e*)*lako*, eastern -(*e*)*lakotz*, 'because'.

Certain types of adverbial clauses may or must take clause-initial particles: *zeren* 'because' (genitive of *zer* 'what?'), as in western *zeren ona dan*, eastern *zeren ona baita* 'because it's good' (*ona da* 'it's good') and *nahiz (eta)* 'although', as in *nahiz eta ona dan/den* 'although it's good'. Certain other types take clause-final affixes and/or postpositions, as in *ona danez/ denez gero* 'since it's good', in which the auxiliary *da* bears the complementizer -(*e*)*n* and the instrumental -*z*, which is followed by the postposition *gero* 'after'. In B, the sequence -*z gero* has been reanalysed as a single postposition *ezkero* 'since': *ona dan ezkero*.

4.16 THE SUFFIX -*ko*

A prominent characteristic of Basque syntax is the 'adnominal' or 'relational' suffix -*ko*, which turns almost any adverbial into a preposed adjectival modifier, as described in Chapter 2. In all likelihood, this suffix is an ancient feature of the language; certainly it has been syntactically central since our earliest texts.

After a vowel, the suffix has always appeared as -*ko*: *ate* 'door', *ateko giltza* 'the key to the door'. After a consonant, the modern language differs from the medieval records. Those records almost invariably show -*ko* as well after a consonant, as in the Navarrese phrases indicating place of origin: *Çumelzco*, *Eneriçco*, *Eulzco* and so on. On the other hand, medieval Navarrese shows a contrast between the adnominal *Larraingo* 'of/from Larrain' (a toponym) and the surname *Larraineco* 'of the threshing-floor' (*larrain* 'threshing-floor'), and the seventeenth-century writer Leizarraga has forms like *hurreneko* 'nearest', compared to the more widespread modern *hurrengo*.

When -*ko* is added (as it very frequently is) to an NP bearing the locative case-suffix -*n*, the historical facts are more complex. In the fifteenth-century song *The Burning of Mondragón*, the locative *barruan* 'in the interior' forms a *-ko* phrase *barruangoak*, exactly as expected. But this regular form has been everywhere displaced by an innovating form *barrukoak*, and similarly for all other locatives: today a locative like *mendian* 'on the mountain' yields only *mendiko* 'which is on the mountain', and the historically expected **mendiango* is nowhere attested. This cannot be the result of phonological change, and must represent a reformation. In some varieties, this new formation has even been extended to locatives like *hemen* 'here', *orain* 'now' and *orduan* 'then': in place of common (*h*)*emengo*, *oraingo* and *orduango*, some varieties have (*h*)*emeko*, *oraiko* and *orduko*.

4.17 THE QUESTION PARTICLES

There are three yes–no question particles, used in different parts of the country. G has *al*, which is undoubtedly derived from *ahal* 'ability': *Ona da* 'It's good', *Ona al da?* 'Is it good?' Formerly, and perhaps still today in some places, this same particle could mean 'possibly, perhaps': *Ona al da* 'Perhaps it's good'; this is probably the source of the interrogative function, in which *al* is almost always accompanied by rising intonation. Very similar is the northern *ot*(*h*)*e*, which forms yes–no questions with the sense of 'can it possibly be the case that . . . ?': *etorri da* 'he has come', *Etorri ote da jadanik?* 'Has he come already?', 'Can he have come already?' This too is used in statements with the sense of 'if by chance': *Hautemazu nehor heldu othe den* 'See if by chance somebody has arrived.' Again, the interrogative function is doubtless derived from the 'if by chance' sense, which is well attested south of the Pyrenees (B has *ete*). Finally, the unmarked northern question particle is *-a*, which is suffixed to the finite auxiliary, producing various phonological developments: *Ona da* 'it's good', *Ona daia?*, *Ona dea?* 'Is it good?' Oddly, this particle, whose origin is unknown, is usually accompanied by falling intonation. In some varieties, notably in B, there is no question particle, and yes–no questions are expressed solely by rising intonation. None of these particles ever appears in a question-word question.

The traditional Basque tag question is the invariable *ez da?*, lit. 'isn't it?', commonly interpreted as a reduction of *ez da egia?* 'isn't it true?' Today, however, many southern Basques use simply *ez?* 'no?' as the ordinary tag; this is undoubtedly a calque on Spanish.

4.18 PARTS OF SPEECH

Historically, Basque shows a very sharp distinction between verbal roots and all other lexical items. The roots which appear in the most ancient class of verbs, those with the prefix **e-* in their non-finite forms, seem to be exclusively verbal. Lexical verbs could be obtained from other parts of speech only by attaching a suffix, originally **-i* and later the Latin loan *-tu*, and such verbs did not take the prefix. Likewise, nouns and adjectives could be derived from verbs only by adding a suitable word-forming suffix to the *stem* of the verb (not the root), including the prefix, as was described in section 4.5.

In modern times the boundary between verbs and other items has become slightly less sharp, though it is far from lost. The main reason for this is that a number of adjectives have been converted into the participles of verbs without the addition of a suffix. Thus, the adjective *hil* 'dead' has given rise to the curious-looking verb *hil* 'die; kill'; *busti* 'moist' has yielded a verb *busti* 'moisten' (also *bustitu*, with more conservative morphology); and there are some others in this vein. Moreover, a somewhat larger group of adjectives and nouns occur in compound verbs with *izan* or **edun*; while these behave as ordinary compound verbs in many respects (that is, the verbal element alone bears all verbal morphology), they have the peculiarity that the future suffix is added directly to the adjective or noun. So, for example, *bizi* 'alive' forms a verb *bizi izan* 'live', whose future is *biziko da* 'he/she will live', rather than **bizi izango da*, and *behar* 'necessity' forms *behar *edun* 'need', whose future is *beharko dut* 'I'll need it', and not **behar izango dut*. (These non-existent forms have sometimes been recommended by prescriptivists, but they definitely do not represent normal usage at any period or in any place.) On the whole, though, verbs still constitute a noticeably distinct class of lexical items.

More interesting is the contrast between nouns and adjectives. In the modern language, this contrast is generally very sharp: a lexical item can only be one or the other. Thus, *gizon* 'man' is a noun and cannot possibly function as an adjective, while *handi* 'big' is an adjective and cannot possibly function as a noun. (Here I ignore as irrelevant the fact that any adjective phrase can be nominalized, as in *gorria* 'the red one'.) Furthermore, the numerous noun-forming suffixes of the language, like *-tza* and *-keta*, form nouns and only nouns, while the adjective-forming suffixes, like *-tsu* and *-kor*, form adjectives exclusively.

But there are exceptions, and they are ancient. A number of clearly old words can function equally as nouns or as adjectives: *hotz* 'cold' (adj.) or 'cold' (n.) (in the sense of 'low temperature'); *bero* 'hot' or 'heat'; *gazte* 'young' or 'young person'; *ilun* 'dark' or 'darkness'; *argi* 'bright' or 'light' (n.); *laket* 'pleasant' or 'pleasure' (a Latin loan); *goi* 'high' or 'height, elevation'; *haserre* 'angry' or 'anger'. There are perhaps two or three dozen of these, and many specialists believe that they must represent the relics of an earlier stage of the language in which nouns and adjectives were not regularly distinguished at all, in which the modern distinction may perhaps result from contact.

On the other hand, the use of an unaffixed adjective, noun or verb as an adverb is all but unattested. There exist one or two cases, such as the loan word *korrika*, which is a noun meaning 'race' and an adverb meaning '(while) running'; these are usually the result, as here, of adverbs being converted to nouns. Normally, though, an adverb related to another lexical item always bears a derivational suffix to show its status.

Beyond this, there is little that can be said about the history of the parts of speech.

4.19 THE GENITIVE WITH THE GERUND

As a general rule, the gerund in the modern language does what gerunds usually do: it converts an entire verb phrase or sentence into a noun phrase, which can then occupy any position in which an NP is normally possible; the gerund itself takes the usual case-marking for its role. At the same time, of course, the gerund can take both adverbials and NP arguments of its own, and these NP arguments are case-marked normally according to their role. In the example [*Zuk hori berehala egitea*] *nahi dut* 'I want you to do that immediately', the gerund *egitea* takes an ergative subject *zuk* 'you', an absolutive object *hori* 'that' and an adverb *berehala* 'immediately', and itself stands in the absolutive because it is the object of the transitive verb-form *nahi dut* 'I want'. Likewise, in [*Euskaraz ez jakiteak*] *kalte handia egin dio* 'Not knowing Basque has done her a great deal of harm', the gerund *jakitea* takes an instrumental complement *euskaraz* '(in) Basque', as is usual for the verb *jakin* 'know' when it means 'know a language', and it also takes the ordinary negative *ez* 'not', but this time the gerund itself stands in the ergative because it is the subject of a transitive verb.

In southern varieties, this behaviour of the gerund is exceptionless. In northern varieties, however, there is one glaring exception. In certain circumstances, and most obviously when the gerund of a transitive verb is used as the complement of a verb of motion, it takes its object, not in the absolutive as usual, but in the *genitive*. So, for example, to express 'I'm going to see my father', while a southerner says *Aita ikustera noa*, with *aita* 'father' in the absolutive, a northerner says *Aitaren ikustera noa*, with genitive *aitaren*. (The gerund here is *ikustea* 'seeing', which takes the allative case-ending *-ra* to express purpose.) The same thing happens with the object of an imperfective participle, which, recall, is historically only the gerund with a locative ending: *Arthoen jorratzen ari da* 'He's weeding the maize', in which *artho* 'maize' takes a genitive ending because it is the object of the imperfective participle *jorratzen* 'weeding'.

This construction is found in all northern texts, from the earliest to the most recent, and it is still current in northern speech today. South of the Pyrenees, however, it appears to be unattested. I interpret these facts as follows: the northern construction must be an archaism, the last trace of the period when the gerund had not yet become truly verbal and was still exhibiting nominal properties. Recall from section 4.5 that I maintain that the modern gerund started life as a verbal noun, a nominalized form of a verb-stem which was grammatically an ordinary noun with fully nominal properties, and that it must have acquired its verbal properties over time. Southern dialects have therefore gone all the way in reanalysing the gerund as fully verbal in all circumstances, while northern varieties have not yet done so.

Observe that this genitive is possible (indeed, obligatory) only with the direct object of a gerund, and in no other circumstances. This fact has not always been understood, because of apparent counterexamples like the following: *Aitaren jiteaz atsegin dut* 'I am happy at the arrival of my father', in which the genitive *aitaren* appears to be the subject of an intransitive gerund *jitea* 'arrival', from *jin* 'come', and *aitaren egite hori* 'that deed of father's', in which genitive *aitaren* appears to be the subject of a transitive gerund *egite* 'deed', from *egin* 'do'. But this is not so. In these examples, we are not looking at any gerunds at all, but only at ordinary verbal nouns which happen to be identical in form to the gerunds of the same verbs. Like other languages, Basque has several suffixes for deriving ordinary nouns (verbal nouns) from verb-stems, and among these are the suffixes also used to form gerunds. It is a simple matter to show that these examples are nouns, and not gerunds, because they plainly have nominal properties, while gerunds have only verbal properties. For example, we can say *aitaren egite izugarri horiek* 'those terrible deeds of father's', in which the noun *egite* 'deed' takes not only a genitive but also an adjective (*izugarri* 'terrible'), a demonstrative and a plural marker; a true gerund can do none of these things. For a discussion of this important distinction, see Abaitua and Trask (1987).

4.20 A SPECULATIVE SYNTHESIS

In this final section I shall try to bring together some of the most interesting points which have arisen in the present chapter and to integrate them into a coherent view of what Basque grammar might have been like some thousands of years ago, long before even the Aquitanian texts, and of how it might have developed into the modern language. I must stress that almost everything in this section is speculative, and that some of it is extremely speculative. The available evidence is quite inadequate for regarding most of my suggestions as anything more than interesting ideas, and this section is therefore best regarded as a basis for future discussion, and not as well-substantiated reconstruction.

To begin with, the evidence from verbal morphology suggests that much of that morphology was assembled at a time when sentence structure was very different from that of the modern language, which is exclusively verb-final and suffixing. The prefix *$*e$- in non-finite verb-forms, the archaic causative prefix *-ra-* and the fossilized tense/mood prefixes all seem to point to a language in which inflectional prefixes were the norm; if the causative morph derives from an originally distinct verb, this would be further evidence for VO order in the VP. Still further evidence is provided by the dative flags: whether these originated as prepositions or as serial verbs, they appear to preserve remnants of prepositional phrases or of VO syntagms eventually incorporated into the finite verb.

At this stage most of the modern case-suffixes would have been absent, and it is possible that all of them were absent. Apart from the unmarked absolutive, the oldest of the modern case-suffixes appear to be ergative -*k*, dative -*i*, instrumental -*z* and perhaps genitive -*e* or -*en* and locative -*n*; all of these might have arisen from postpositions at a later stage than the one being considered here. The unique genitive form *ene* 'my', from *ni* 'I', must preserve a trace of the ancient case-inflection.

NPs would have been unmarked for number, except that, at some stage, demonstratives acquired number-marking. In contrast, number appears to have been marked in finite verbs very early. Number-marking in verbs for absolutives is much older than that for ergatives: it is more pervasive than ergative number-marking, being found in all three persons, and it is much more complex and variable in form and position. Possibly there was stem-suppletion for number with absolutive NPs.

Person-agreement for first and second person was introduced later than absolutive number-marking, very possibly by cliticization of free pronouns. This process obliterated the tense/aspect prefixes whenever an agreement-marker was introduced into verb-initial position; the tense/aspect prefixes have survived otherwise down to the present day. The difference in form between prefixes and suffixes with first and second singular may reflect an ancient pronominal stem-suppletion now otherwise lost.

At some stage the language changed its word order to SOV and began acquiring all the usual typological characteristics of an SOV language. Post-positions accordingly came into use, replacing the earlier prepositions, if these existed. Most modern postpositions, apart perhaps from those under-lying the bound case-suffixes, are of transparent origin, and the majority of them are ordinary nouns which still survive as nouns in the language. The plural agreement for ergatives was perhaps introduced around this time; in any case, it was certainly later in origin than plural agreement for absolutives.

At one time, it is possible, indicative forms were exclusively synthetic, and the only periphrastic forms were those involving the radical.

A new set of non-finite forms was created, with the radical alone (a kind of verbal noun) surviving from the earlier system. First to be created was the perfective participle, obtained by attaching to the radical the suffix -*i*, prob-ably an adjective-forming suffix. After the Roman settlement, this -*i* was replaced by the new suffix -*tu*, borrowed from Latin. The future participle and the gerund were created much later, late enough that different forma-tions were preferred in different parts of the country. The gerund originated as a simple verbal noun and acquired its verbal characteristics only later; traces of its earlier nominal morphology can still be found today in the

French Basque varieties. Most recent of all is the imperfective participle, constructed from the new gerund by the addition of locative -*n*.

The new non-finite forms came to be widely used for a variety of purposes, including various types of non-finite adverbial clause. But they were also used to construct new periphrastic verb-forms, in which the inherited and very elaborate verbal morphology was increasingly confined to a small set of auxiliary verbs and to a few other common verbs. At the same time, a new set of finite subordinate clauses was introduced. Relative clauses were perhaps obtained by adding the genitive -*en* to finite clauses; like all genitives, these preceded their heads. Complement clauses were constructed in a manner which is not entirely clear, but which perhaps involved nominalized genitives. And a whole range of adverbial clauses was derived simply by adding familiar case-suffixes or postpositions to finite clauses.

For a long time, case-suffixes continued to be added directly to NPs unmarked for number, except when a demonstrative was present, and number-marking was accordingly still largely confined to finite verbs. At a very late stage, probably little more than a millennium ago, the distal demonstrative gave rise to the definite article, which became a bound morpheme. This introduced number contrasts for the first time into NPs lacking demonstratives. At first, the new number contrasts were confined to the grammatical cases and were absent from the local cases, into which the new article was not introduced. With time, however, the local cases, which are clearly of late formation, also acquired a full set of number distinctions by a combination of *ad hoc* devices and resegmentations, thus producing more or less the modern case-system. The comitative case is of very late origin.

That leaves the ergative morphology to be accounted for, and here even speculation becomes difficult. The change from VO to OV syntax, if it occurred, would probably have come about via the increased use of an originally marked construction, and that construction could have been a passive or a 'get'-construction. For example, an original canonical transitive like 'John hit Peter' might have been replaced by something along the lines of 'Peter got his hitting from John', a construction type well attested in the world's languages and one which often develops into a passive. So, using purely modern words and forms, we might hypothesize an ancient *Jon jo zuen Kepa* being replaced by a marked form *Kepa jo zuen Jon-ek* (which in fact is fully grammatical in modern Basque in the sense of 'It was Peter that John hit'); reanalysis of this as an unmarked form, followed by movement of the new subject to initial position, would have produced the modern *Jonek Kepa jo zuen*. Such a development would imply that the absolutive NP was once the subject of the innovating transitive construction, and hence a period of ergative syntax.

Chapter 5

Lexicon

5.1 THE SOURCES OF THE BASQUE VOCABULARY

It is never a simple task to estimate the size of the vocabulary of a language, and Basque is no exception. In addition to the thousands of lexical items found more or less throughout the Basque-speaking region, there are many thousands more which are used only in some part of that region, and some of these are very localized indeed, often being securely attested only in a single valley or even in a single town. Many hundreds of words found in our earliest Basque texts are now no longer in use, and an unknown number of these were assuredly deliberate coinages by particular writers which failed to catch on. A few apologists for the language have deliberately undertaken the coining of masses of neologisms, and some of these neologisms, particularly those constructed by Sabino Arana, maintain a kind of shadowy existence on the edge of the language, used self-consciously by a minority of enthusiasts but unknown to, or rejected by, everyone else. In recent years the language planners have produced a stream of specialist dictionaries containing tens of thousands of neologisms, some of which have already acquired some degree of currency while others remain confined to the pages of the dictionaries. The productive word-formation processes of the language permit transparent new formations to be derived at will: for example, I have never seen the word *belartasun* 'grasshood, quality of being grass', but I am confident that any Basque would understand the word at once. Finally, the coexistence of Basque with the more prestigious Spanish and French allows Basque-speakers to import virtually any Spanish or French word into Basque at will.

Azkue's great dictionary of 1905 contains an estimated 52,000 head words and perhaps double that number of senses, though a significant proportion of these entries are merely dialect variants of a single word. But Azkue deliberately excluded recent loans from Romance, which means that he excluded a large proportion of the everyday vocabulary. Aulestia's 1989 dictionary, which excludes localized dialect words as well as obvious loan words, contains about 48,000 head words, including many which have come into use since Azkue's time, and naturally it does not attempt to cover the horde of recently coined technical terms.

So far as I know, there have been no substantial studies to ascertain the number of words known or used by typical speakers or writers. There are, of course, dictionaries of the words used by particular writers. For example, Villasante's 1973 dictionary of the vocabulary used by Pedro de Axular in his 1643 book *Gero* runs to about 4,300 entries, including some proper names, but no one would suggest that this number represents anything like the author's entire vocabulary: even such everyday words as *behi* 'cow' and *ibai* 'river' happen not to occur in this book.

Nor have there been any studies of the proportion of Basque words derived from particular sources. Consequently, the best I can do here is to hazard a guess that the number of native Basque words (by which term I mean those lexical items which were certainly or probably in the language before the arrival of the Romans in the Basque Country) are now probably outnumbered in ordinary speech by words of Latin or Romance origin, though not by a large margin. Two thousand years of intense contact with Latin and Romance have had a profound effect upon the Basque lexicon, though not so profound as to have obliterated its distinctively non-Romance (and non-Indo-European) character.

Naturally, the native element in the Basque vocabulary is concentrated in certain semantic areas, and there are few surprises. The following areas consist largely or exclusively of native lexical items and morphemes:

all numerals below 1,000;
virtually all pronouns and grammatical words;
all inflectional affixes and about half of derivational affixes;
virtually all kinship terms, and words like 'man', 'woman', 'boy', 'girl' and
  'child';
the great majority of body-part names;
geographical features like 'sea', 'mountain', 'valley', 'plain', 'river';
natural phenomena like 'sun', 'moon', 'star', 'rain', 'snow', 'wind', 'storm',
  'ice';
familiar materials like 'water', 'stone', 'bone', 'wood', 'iron';
names of most indigenous animals, wild and domesticated;
the majority of names of indigenous plants and of long-established food
  plants;
many names of familiar implements like 'cart', 'wagon', 'wheel', 'knife',
  'pitchfork', 'hoe', 'sickle';
most common adjectives like 'big', 'old', 'black', 'red', 'hot', 'cold';
most common verbs like 'be', 'do', 'have', 'sleep', 'go', 'know', 'forget',
  'climb', 'fall', 'say', 'take', 'carry', 'die'.

Unsurprisingly, areas like religion, technology, government and the law are overwhelmingly dominated by loan words, and the same is true of seafaring: the maritime vocabulary of Basque contains very few native words, in spite of the long-established seafaring tradition of the Basques.

5.2 COMPOUNDS

Basque forms compounds very readily and has clearly done so for millennia. Compound nouns and compound verbs are very frequent; compound adjectives are less common. New compounds, especially nouns, can be formed with some freedom. As a general rule, the final element in a compound is its head, but there are exceptions. Older compounds typically show the phonological developments discussed in Chapter 3, as do some neologisms.

Compound nouns are typically N+N: *azalore* 'cauliflower' (*aza* 'cabbage' + *lore* 'flower'), *eskulan* 'handicraft' (*esku* 'hand' + *lan* 'work'), *gurpide* 'cartpath' (*gurdi* 'cart' + *bide* 'way'), *burugain* 'crown of the head' (*buru* 'head' + *gain* 'top'), *elizatxori* 'sparrow' (*eliza* 'church' + *txori* 'bird'), *ogibide* 'job, profession' (*ogi* 'bread' + *bide* 'way'), *giza-sorgin* 'sorcerer' (*gizon* 'man' + *sorgin* 'witch'), *logela* 'bedroom' (*lo* 'sleep' + *gela* 'room'), *burumuin* 'brain' (*buru* 'head' + *muin* 'pith'), *oinarri* 'foundation' (*oin* 'foot' + *harri* 'stone').

Dvandva (copulative) compounds are not rare, but are often plural: *aita-mak* 'parents' (*aita* 'father' + *ama* 'mother' + Pl), *hortz-haginak* 'teeth' (*hortz* 'incisor' + *hagin* 'molar' + Pl).

On occasion, an N+N compound contains the relational suffix *-ko*: *buru-komin* 'headache' (*buru* 'head' + *-ko* + *min* 'pain'), *etxeko jaun* 'master of the house' (*etxe* 'house' + *-ko* + *jaun* 'lord').

Also frequent is N+Adj, in which the noun is the head: *galgorri* 'species of wheat' (*gari* 'wheat' + *gorri* 'red'), *artatxiki* 'millet' (*arto* 'maize', but formerly 'millet' + *txiki* 'small'), *katamotz* 'lynx' (*katu* 'cat' + *motz* 'short'), *zainzuri* 'tendon; asparagus' (*zain* 'vein; root' + *zuri* 'white'). The participle of a verb may serve as an adjective: *emagaldu* 'prostitute' (*eme* 'female' + *galdu* 'lost'). Some of these are headless: *belarrimotz* 'foreigner, non-Basque' (*belarri* 'ear' + *motz* 'short'), *tripa(u)ndi* 'glutton' (*tripa* 'belly' + *ha(u)ndi* 'big').

By no means rare is V+N: *ezkondeiak* 'banns' (*ezkondu* 'get married' + *dei* 'call' + Pl), *ikusleku* 'vantage point' (*ikusi* 'see' + *leku* 'place'), *eginbide* 'procedure' (*egin* 'do' + *bide* 'way'), *jantzigela* 'dressing room' (*jantzi* 'get dressed' + *gela* 'room'), *bizimaila* 'standard of living' (*bizi izan* 'live' + *maila* 'level'), *janbehar* 'voracious appetite' (*jan* 'eat' + *behar* 'need').

A rare pattern is V+V: *janedan* 'food and drink' (*jan* 'eat' + *edan* 'drink'), *joanetorri* or *joan-jin* 'round trip, return trip' (*joan* 'go' + *etorri* 'come' or *jin* 'come').

Compound adjectives are of several types. With Adj+Adj: *gorrimotel* 'pink' (*gorri* 'red' + *motel* 'weak'). With N+Adj: *buruarin* 'foolish, empty-headed' (*buru* 'head' + *arin* 'light'), *ahobero* 'indiscreet' (*aho* 'mouth' + *bero* 'hot'), *larrugorri* 'naked' (*larru* 'skin' + *gorri* 'red'). With V+Adj: *ikustezin* 'invisible' (*ikusi* 'see' + *ezin* 'impossible'), *jaioberri* 'newborn' (*jaio* 'be born' + *berri* 'new'). With V+Postp: *ezkongabe* 'unmarried' (*ezkondu* 'get married' + *gabe* 'without'). Dvandva compounds exist: *zuribeltz* 'black-and-white' (*zuri* 'white' + *beltz* 'black'). An unusual pattern is *lokartu* 'become sleepy', which is *lo(a)k*, the ergative of *lo* 'sleep' plus *hartu* 'take'; *lokartuta nago* 'I'm sleepy' is etymologically 'I am taken by sleep'.

Compound verbs are exceedingly numerous. A compound verb consists of a simple lexical verb combined with another element, most usually a bare noun, less often an adjective or a suffixed noun. By far the most frequent simple verb employed is *egin* 'do, make'. Examples: *lo egin* 'sleep' (*lo* 'sleep'), *amets egin* 'dream' (*amets* 'dream'), *eztul egin* 'cough' (*eztul* 'cough'), *dantza egin* 'dance' (*dantza* 'dance'), *nigar egin* 'weep' (*nigar* 'tears'), *hitz egin* 'speak' (*hitz* 'word'), *zin egin* 'swear' (an oath) (*zin* 'oath'), *lan egin* 'work' (*lan* 'work'), *kalte egin* 'injure' (*kalte* 'injury'), *haginka egin* 'chew' (*hagin* 'molar' + *-ka* adv.), *hegaz egin* 'fly' (*hega* 'wing' + *-z* Instr). Much less frequent is *eman* 'give': *musu eman* 'kiss' (*musu* 'kiss'), *su eman* 'light, kindle' (*su* 'fire'), *hitz eman* 'promise' (*hitz* 'word'), *buru eman* 'confront, defy' (*buru* 'head'). A few compounds are formed with **edun*: *maite *edun* 'love' (*maite* 'beloved'), *gorroto *edun* 'hate' (*gorroto* 'hatred'), *atesegin *edun* 'like' (*atsegin* 'pleasure'), *behar *edun* 'need, have to, must' (*behar* 'necessity'), *ahal *edun* 'be able to, can' (*ahal* 'ability'), *nahi *edun* 'want' (*nahi* 'desire'), *damu *edun* 'regret' (*damu* 'regret'). One or two are formed with *izan* 'be': *bizi izan* 'live, dwell' (*bizi* 'alive'), *ari izan* 'be busy at, be . . .ing' (archaic *ari* 'busy, hard-working'), *laket izan* 'please' (*laket* 'pleasure'), *gauza izan* 'be useful' (*gauza* 'thing').

Also frequent are compounds formed with *-etsi* or *-eritzi*, both 'consider', only the second of which still exists today as an independent verb: *onetsi* or *oneritzi* 'approve of, accept' (*on* 'good'), *gaitzetsi* 'hate, condemn, disapprove of' and *gaitzeritzi* 'despise, detest' (*gaitz* 'bad'), archaic *oneritzi* 'love' (*on* 'good'), Z *jauretsi* 'adore' (*jaun* 'lord'), *gutietsi* 'undervalue' (*guti* 'not much'), *askietsi* 'be satisfied with' (*aski* 'enough'), *hobetsi* 'prefer' (*hobe* 'better'), *donetsi* 'sanctify' (*done* 'saint'), *sinetsi* (archaic *zinetsi*, *zin* 'truth, oath').

A handful of compounds involve other verbs: *onartu* 'accept' (*on* 'good' + *hartu* 'take'), *lokartu* 'fall asleep' (*lo* 'sleep' (+ Det) + Erg + *hartu* 'take'), *so egon* 'pay attention to' (*so* 'glance' + *egon* 'be'). These merge imperceptibly into forms best regarded as idioms rather than compound verbs: *lur jo* 'fail, collapse' (*lur* 'earth' + *jo* 'hit'), *larrua jo* 'copulate' (*larru* 'skin' + Det + *jo* 'hit'), *gogoan hartu* 'memorize' (*gogo* 'mind' + Det + Loc + *hartu* 'take'), *buru agertu* 'appear' (*buru* 'head' + *agertu* 'show'), *zaintiratu* 'sprain, twist' (*zain* 'nerve' + *tiratu* 'pull').

It is clear that a sizeable number of verbs which are not today regarded as compounds were compounds in origin; these verbs have often undergone complex and irregular phonological developments and they usually show an unusual degree of regional variation. The chief study of these verbs is Michelena (1977b). Examples, with the best available guesses at etymologies: *eguriki* 'wait for, expect' < *egun* 'day' + *eduki* 'hold'; *itxadon* 'wait for, expect' < *hitz* 'word + **edun* 'have'; *ihardun* 'be busy', *iharduki* 'converse' and *ihardetsi* 'reply', all < **inar-* (?) + **edun* 'have', *eduki* 'hold', *etsi* 'consider'; *eskaini* 'offer' < *esku* 'hand' + *ipini* 'put', *ohartu* 'notice' < *gogo* 'mind' + *hartu* 'take', *aurdiki* 'throw' < ?, *atzeman* 'seize, capture' < ? + *eman* 'give'. There are many of these, and their etymologies are often mysterious.

A few compounds exhibit unusual modes of formation. Examples: *eskuarki* 'usually' (*esku* 'hand' + *har-* 'take' + *-ki* adv.), *eztabaida* 'argument, dispute' (from *Ez da! Bai da!* 'No, it isn't! Yes, it is!').

5.3 DERIVATIVES

Basque is exceedingly rich in word-forming suffixes, and has clearly been so since ancient times, though word-forming prefixes are virtually unknown. As one would expect, we find ancient suffixes which have not been productive for centuries, together with others which have been productive for a very long time, and with still others which are of recent origin. Quite a few word-forming suffixes have been borrowed from Latin or Romance.

5.3.1 Word-forming suffixes

It is not possible here to provide an exhaustive list of all the many dozens of word-forming suffixes which have been identified together with an account of their behaviour, and I shall therefore content myself with providing some representative examples. More nearly comprehensive accounts can be found in Azkue (1923–1925) and in Múgica (1978).

As a general rule, any given suffix always produces the same part of speech. For example, *-tasun* ~ *-tarzun* '-ness' (as in *edertasun* 'beauty', from *eder* 'beautiful') and *-le* and *-tzaile*, both '-er' (as in *ikusle* 'one who sees, onlooker', from *ikusi* 'see', and *laguntzaile* 'assistant', from *lagundu* 'help') always produce nouns; *-tu* always produces (the participle of) a verb (as in *maitatu* 'love', from *maite* 'beloved'); *-tsu* ~ *-zu* 'full of' (as in *harritsu* 'stony', from *harri* 'stone') and *-garri* '-able, worthy of' (as in *ikusgarri* 'spectacular', from *ikusi* 'see') always produce adjectives; and *-ki* '-ly' always produces adverbs (of manner) (as in *gaizki* 'badly', from *gaitz* 'bad'). Naturally, since any adjective can be nominalized, an adjective-forming suffix may equally yield a noun, if the sense permits. For example, *-dun* 'having, who has' yields *euskaldun*, both 'Basque-speaking' (adj.) and 'Basque-speaker' (n.). Otherwise, the only exceptions are trivial ones. Note in particular that *-ka*, which normally derives adverbs, occasionally gives rise to nouns as well: the adverbs *hika* 'using the intimate pronoun' and *korrika* 'running' can also be used as nouns meaning 'use of the intimate pronoun' and 'race', respectively. Here we would have expected the nouns to be formed with -*keta*, the suffix which derives nouns of activity, and *hiketa* indeed also exists.

The part of speech to which a suffix can be added is not necessarily restricted to a single category. For example, the noun-forming suffix -*keta* can be added to a noun, as in *hizketa* 'conversation' (*hitz* 'word'), to an adjective, as in *berriketa* 'gossip' (*berri* 'new'), or to a verb, as in *salaketa* 'denunciation' (*salatu* 'denounce'), as well as to the pronoun *hi* 'you' in *hiketa*, just cited. Similarly, -*keria* 'fault, defect' can be added to an adjective, as in *zikinkeria* 'filth, depravity' (*zikin* 'dirty'), to a noun, as in *sorginkeria* 'witchcraft, sorcery' (*sorgin* 'witch'), or even to a postpositional phrase, as in *lotsagabekeria* 'shamelessness' (*lotsa* 'shame' + *gabe* 'without'); but this suffix appears never to go onto a verb.

Some other suffixes are much choosier. For example, the agent suffixes -*le* and -*tzaile* can be attached to nothing but verbs, the choice between them being predictable from the form of the verb. Likewise, the adjective-forming suffix -*tsu* ~ -*zu* 'full of' can be attached to nothing but nouns. Naturally, many such cases can be explained on semantic grounds.

A number of suffixes are clearly bimorphemic in origin. The common abstract-noun-forming suffix -*tarzun* ~ -*tasun* '-ness' consists of two elements, the first of which is apparently the equally common ethnonymic suffix -*tar* '(who is) from' (as in *Bizkaitar* 'Bizkaian') and the second of which seems to recur in the noun-forming suffix -*kizun* (as in *etorkizun* 'future', from *etorri* 'come'). The first element of -*kizun* may in turn be identical with the frequent concrete-noun-forming suffix -*ki* (as in *xahalki* 'veal', from *xahal* 'calf'). The two noun-forming suffixes -*kunde* (as in *sorkunde* 'conception', from *sortu* 'create; give birth to') and -*kuntza* (as in *hizkuntza* 'language', from *hitz* 'word') appear to share their first element; their second elements are very likely identical to the noun-forming suffix -*te* (as in *legorte* 'drought', from *legor* 'dry') and -*tza* (as in *jaiotza* 'birth', from *jaio* 'be born'), respectively. The suffix -*tza* itself is attested in 1025 as -*zaha*, and other evidence suggests a reconstruction *-*zahaa* or *-*zahae*, which may conceivably also be bimorphemic in origin.

Diminutive suffixes are numerous and frequent, and are attested from a very remote period; even the Aquitanian names appear to include a few of these. It is noteworthy that the earliest such suffixes, such as -*to*, -*ko* and -*no*, mostly fail to contain palatal consonants, though the Aquitanian suffix -*xo*, -*xso* may be an exception. The modern diminutive suffixes, in contrast, always contain palatal consonants, as in -*txo* ~ -*txu* and -*ño*; in all likelihood, these result from the expressive palatalization of some of the older diminutive suffixes.

Quite a number of the word-forming suffixes are borrowed from Latin or Romance. Chief among these is the enormously productive verb-forming suffix -*tu*, which derives from the Latin participial suffix -TU; it appears that

Basque borrowed so many Latin verbs containing this morph (such as *aditu* 'hear, understand', from AUDITU) that *-tu* became the productive verb-forming suffix, displacing the indigenous *-i* in this function. The very frequent professional suffix *-ari* (as in *pilotari* 'jai-alai player', from *pilota* 'jai-alai') is another such case: loans from Latin like *merkatu* 'market' (< MERCATU) and *merkatari* 'merchant' (< MERCATARIU) led to the establishment of *-ari* as a suffix in Basque. Among the numerous other borrowed suffixes are *-men* ~ *-mendu* (as in *barkamendu* 'forgiveness, pardon', from *barkatu* 'forgive, excuse') (< -MENTU), *-ezia* (as in *ahulezia* 'weakness', from *ahul* 'weak, feeble') (< a Rom development of -ITIA; cf. Sp *-eza*), *-tate* ~ *-dade* (as in *bakardade* 'solitude', from *bakar* 'alone') (< -TATE and its Rom continuations; cf. Sp *-dad*), *-zio* (as in *amorrazio* 'fury', from *amorro* 'fury') (< -TIO(NE)), *-ada* (as in *matxinada* '(a particular) revolt', from *Matxin* 'Martin') (< -ATA), and the very frequent *-tura* ~ *-ura* (as in *egitura* 'structure', from *egin* 'make') (< -TURA). There are, however, a number of others.

5.3.2 Pseudo-suffixes

I apply the term 'pseudo-suffixes' to a sizeable group of items which are mostly independent words which very frequently appear as final elements in compounds and which in this position have sometimes acquired distinctive senses or distinctive forms. Among these are *eme* 'female' and *ar* 'male' (as in *asteme* 'female donkey', from *asto* 'donkey', and *katar* 'tomcat', from *katu* 'cat'), *bitxi* 'pretty; jewel' (which has the special sense of 'god-' in kinship terms like *aitabitxi* 'godfather', from *aita* 'father'), *-kume* 'offspring' (as in *katakume* 'kitten', from *katu* 'cat'; this is the same morpheme as *ume* 'child'), *bide* 'road, way' (which sometimes has extended senses in word-formation, as in *galbide* 'danger', from *galdu* 'lose, get lost'), *buru* 'head' (which behaves similarly, as in *mahaiburu* 'presiding officer', from *mahai* 'table'), *begi* 'eye' (same again, as in *katenbegi* 'link of chain', from *katea* 'chain'). There are several dozen such items.

5.3.3 Prefixes

The few word-forming prefixes are almost exclusively loans or calques. There are two negative prefixes: *des-* (as in *desohore* 'dishonour', from *ohore* 'honour'), which is borrowed from Romance, and *ez-* (as in *ezjakin* 'ignorant', from the participle of *jakin* 'know'), which is a calque on Romance. There are likewise two prefixes meaning 're-, again': *er(re)-* ~ *arra-* (as in *arrapiztu* 'revive, resuscitate', from *piztu* 'kindle, ignite, animate'), a loan from Romance *re-*, and *ber-* ~ *bir-* (as in *berrogei* 'forty', from *hogei* 'twenty', and B *birramona* 'great-grandmother', from *amona* 'grandmother'). This last is attested in Sout as *bior-* and surely derives from *bihur* 'bent, twisted' (i.e. 'redoubled'). It too may well be a calque on Romance, but, if so, it is an old and deeply embedded one. Apart from some very recent neologisms, the only other word-forming prefixes found in Basque are the *e- which occurs in non-finite verb-forms (see section 4.5) and the seemingly functionless 'expressive' prefix ma- (see section 5.5).

5.3.4 Pseudo-prefixes

Once again, the language possesses a handful of items which are independent words but which very frequently appear as first elements in compounds and which in this position have acquired distinctive senses. Two of these are particularly common. First, baso 'woods', whose combining form is the regular basa-, commonly means 'wild' as a first element: basalore 'wildflower' (lore 'flower'), basurde 'wild boar' (urde 'pig'), basaran 'wild plum, sloe' (aran 'plum'), basahuntz 'deer' (ahuntz 'goat'). (The word otso 'wolf' is occasionally used in the same way, as in otsolizar 'mountain ash, rowan' (lizar 'ash')). Second, the word sasi 'bramble' occasionally has the same function, as in sasiarrosa 'wild rose' (arrosa 'rose'), but far more commonly this item, when a first element, means 'false, pseudo-, inferior', as in sasipoeta 'poetaster' (poeta 'poet') and sasiezkontza 'cohabitation' (ezkontza 'marriage'). Presumably the semantic development was something like 'bramble' > 'wild, uncultivated' > 'undisciplined, disorganized' > 'improper'.

5.3.5 Sex-marking

Sex-marking is not common in Basque, except by lexical means, as in gizon 'man' and emakume 'woman', behi 'cow' and zezen 'bull'. The adjectives eme 'female' (a loan from Gascon) and ar 'male' are sometimes attached to animal names when the distinction is thought necessary: katar 'tomcat', kateme 'female cat' (katu 'cat'), oilo 'hen', oilar 'cock, rooster'. The Romance loan -sa is very occasionally used as a female marker: jainko 'god', jainkosa 'goddess'; okin 'baker', okintsa 'female baker'. In most places alargun means both 'widow' and 'widower', but in some regions it is only 'widower', while 'widow' is alarguntsa. In one or two cases a diminutive suffix is used to mark a creature as female, as with urde 'hog', urdanda ~ urdanga 'sow', with the diminutive suffix -anda.

5.4 ANCIENT FORMATIVES

As one might expect, a number of Basque words appear to exhibit recurrent morphs, mostly final elements, whose meaning or function is now doubtful or opaque.

A rather clear case is -bil 'round', found in a number of formations like ukabil 'fist' (uko 'forearm'), ubil 'vortex' (ur 'water'), gurpil '(cart)wheel' (gurdi 'cart') and biribil ~ borobil 'round' (reduplicated). Almost equally clear is *bel 'black, dark', found in beltz 'black' (< *beletz), bele ~ bela 'crow, raven', harbel 'slate' (harri 'stone'), ubel 'purple, livid, dark' (ur 'water'), horbel 'fallen leaves' ((h)orri 'leaf'), goibel 'dark sky' (goi 'high place'), and very likely also in ezpel 'box tree' and gibel 'liver' and possibly also in belatz 'sparrowhawk', sabel 'stomach, belly' and ospel 'chilblain'. The form gibel, together with giharre 'lean meat', gizen 'fat, fatty meat', and perhaps giberri 'head of cattle', points to a possible *gi- 'meat'.

Lakarra (1995) suggests an ancient *-ger ~ *-ker 'bad' in oker 'twisted, crooked', oiher (same gloss), (p)uzker 'fart' (putz 'puff of air') and probably ezker 'left (hand)'; aker 'billygoat' may conceivably also contain this morph. Gorrochategui (1995) posits *-(d)ots, probably 'male', in bildots 'lamb' and ordots 'male pig, male animal'.

It may or may not be significant that the animal names ardi 'sheep', zaldi 'horse' and idi 'ox' all end in a morph -di. But it probably is significant that several tree names begin with a morph ez-: ezpel 'box tree', ezki 'poplar' (also applied to other trees), ezku 'linden, basswood' and ezkur 'acorn', but formerly also 'oak, tree'; note also ezpal ~ ezkal ~ ezkail 'chip of wood', B ezto 'log used for rolling' and Z ezkanda 'young oak'. Some have also seen a common morph ez- in ezti 'honey', ezko 'wax' and erle 'bee' (< *ez-le?).

Another possible morph is the sa(r)- found in tree names and related words: sahats 'willow', sabi 'tangled mass of tree roots', B sakuta, G sabiko, L LN sabuka 'elder tree', B sarbi, B G sabitegi, G sarasabi 'nursery for young trees', saraila ~ sarale 'hay', LN Z sarga 'branch', the first element of sarbagorri 'beetroot' (gorri 'red') and of B sarbegi 'small branches attached to a main branch' (begi 'eye') and possibly sagar 'apple'.

A final morph -ar is exceedingly frequent in nouns: adar 'horn', ilar 'pea', nigar 'tear', ondar 'remains; sand', bizar 'beard', bular 'breast', zatar 'rag', indar 'strength', izar 'star', behar 'necessity', abar 'branch', ibar 'water meadow, valley', gedar 'soot', sapar 'thicket' and a number of others. No one knows if this represents a single ancient morpheme.

But no one doubts the reality of the adjective-forming suffix -din, as in berdin 'same' (ber- 'self, same'), urdin 'blue', but formerly 'green, blue, grey' (ur 'water'?), gordin 'raw', B zardin 'wizened' (zahar 'old'?), and possibly B lotin 'wet ground' (lohi 'mud'?). This is undoubtedly a relative form of the defective verb *edin, now confined to forming non indicative intransitive auxiliaries (Michelena 1970b).

The putative 'body-part prefix' *be- is discussed in section 5.9.6 below.

5.5 SOUND SYMBOLISM

Sound symbolism is exceptionally important in Basque, and there are several classes of words to be distinguished, though the dividing lines are far from sharp. There is a good deal of regional variation here, although some of the words cited are found more or less throughout the country.

First, Basque has, of course, a number of nursery words, some of which have lost their nursery status. Among this last group are *titi* ~ *diti* 'breast, nipple', *txiz* 'urine', *kaka* 'excrement', *pot* 'kiss' and probably *ama* 'mother'. Retaining nursery status are *tutu* 'vulva', *tato* 'jump' (from *salto*, a loan from Spanish), *txitxi* 'meat, flesh', B *txitxo* 'dog', B *txotxo* 'child', HN LN *pan-pan* 'hit', *pipi* 'chicken, bird', LN 'baby', *pitxitxi* 'kitty', *mau-mau* 'eat' and hundreds of others. Some words, like *pitilin* and *txilina*, both 'penis', appear to be nursery words only for some speakers.

Second, there is naturally a large class of what may loosely be termed interjections. Examples: *ai!* 'oh!; ouch!' (with a wide variety of uses), *biz biz!* ~ *miz miz!* (used in calling a cat), *aida!* (used to encourage cattle to move), G *otx!* 'ouch!', B *eup!* (expressing mockery), with its remarkable final /p/, *txotxo!* 'hey!' (to a little boy), B *ujuju!* 'aha!', *uf!* 'whew!', B G *jo!* 'bloody hell!, Jesus!' (borrowed from Spanish and pronounced with a final glottal stop), *kaka zaharra!* 'shit!' (lit. 'old shit'), L LN *ortzi zuria!* 'bloody hell!' (lit. 'white sky'), and hundreds of others.

Third, Basque, like other languages, possesses a very large number of onomatopoeic words. These sometimes have extraordinary phonological characteristics. Here is a modest sample: B *dzast!* 'bang!', with its voiced laminal affricate, B Z *dzirt-dzart* (representing repeated blows), *krak!* 'crack!', *kosk!* 'crunch!'; 'thwack!', *taup* (sound of heartbeat), *murmur* 'murmur, whisper', G L LN *zurrunga* (sound of snoring or purring), *plast* and *zirrist* 'splash', *miau* 'meow', *au-au* 'bow-wow', *me* 'baa', *mu* 'moo', *pio* and *txio* 'cheep', *din-dan* 'ding-dong', *zart* 'bang, boom, snap', L LN Z *zanpa* 'crash, bang', *zapar* (the sound of heavy rain), B G *txintxin* 'clinking' (and by extension 'coins'), B G *zurrut* 'gulp', *pil-pil* (sound of boiling), L LN Z *burrunba* 'clatter', *gur-gur* 'growling' (of the stomach), *txirri-txirri* 'chirping' (of crickets) and hundreds of others.

Fourth, Basque has a large number of adverbs denoting particular sorts of actions or ways of doing things which are not strictly onomatopoeic. These are overwhelmingly reduplicated in form. A few are derived from ordinary lexical items, but most are not; instead, they appear to be coined out of thin air. Examples: *mara-mara* 'smoothly, steadily, continuously', *zapa-zapa* 'endlessly, on and on', *ttapa-ttapa* 'in small steps' (*tapa* 'step'), *zirti-zarta* 'decisively', *zirriki-zarraka* 'listlessly; awkwardly', *zurru-zurru* 'in gulps', B G *taka-taka*, L LN *triki-traka* 'toddling', *parra-parra* or *pirri-parra* 'profusely, copiously, lavishly, wastefully' and many others.

Fifth, Basque has a large number of adjectives in *m-* denoting physical or moral defects. Examples: *motel* 'weak, insipid', *matzer*, L *matxar* 'deformed, twisted, defective', B *mazkelo* 'clumsy', *mazkaro* 'blackened, dirty; having a mottled face (of an animal)', *makal* ~ *mazkal* ~ *maskal* 'weak, feeble, sick', L *mokor* 'perverse', *mozkor* ~ *moxkor* 'squat, stout, fat; drunk', R *mutzulu* 'wild, savage; unsociable', L *mazkor* 'empty' (as of a nut), Z *mixkiri* 'envious', B *motrotx* 'stocky, plump', *motzor* 'crude', B G *muker* 'unsociable;

arrogant; injudicious', B *mukur* 'clumsy, crude', G *mutxin* 'angry', *malmutz* 'fat, obese; tricky, shrewd', *makur* 'twisted, crooked', B G *mirrin* 'shrivelled, scraggly', *maltzur* 'dishonest' and so on. A few of these words are nouns, rather than adjectives: *moko* ~ *mosko* 'beak', *mutur* ~ *mustur* 'snout, extremity'. One or two of these may possibly be derived with the ancient 'expressive' prefix *ma-* from other words like *oker* 'twisted', but most appear to be coined *de novo*. Here, as elsewhere, the rarity of *m* in early Basque seems to have favoured its use in expressive coinages. A striking fact about these words is their irregular regional variation in form, and above all their tendency to occur both with and without medial sibilants: *makal* ~ *mazkal* ~ *maskal*, *moko* ~ *mosko* and so on. Perhaps more than anything else, such irregular variation points up the anomalous origin of these words.

Sixth, a handful of old words appear to show a mysterious prefix *ma-* which has no identifiable semantic value. We find doublets like *hegal* and *magal*, both 'wing', *udare* and *madari*, both 'pear', and *gako* and *mako*, both 'hook'. In all likelihood, this *ma-* merely represents an obsolete way of forming 'expressive' variants of lexical items.

Finally, Basque has an absolutely huge number of lexical items which I shall describe as phonaesthetic. By a 'phonaesthetic' word I mean one which has apparently been coined out of thin air purely because of its appealing sound. The majority of such words are readily identifiable, because they have a number of distinguishing characteristics, many of them shared with the words just discussed.

First, they often have unusual phonological characteristics: initial voiceless plosives, initial coronal plosives, initial clusters, odd internal clusters, final plosives, palatal consonants (especially *tx* or *x*, depending on region), and the nasal *m*. Second, they are usually at least three or four syllables long. Third, they are frequently reduplicated, sometimes totally but more often partially, and the second occurrence of a morph often shows initial *m*. Fourth, they often exhibit regional variation which is entirely different in nature from the usual regional variation in phonological forms. Fifth, particular words are frequently confined to certain areas of the country, and there are noticeable regional preferences in their formation. Sixth, a given word often exhibits a startling range of different meanings. Finally, they tend to be concentrated in certain areas of the lexicon: names of small creatures (especially insects and creepy-crawlies, but also crustaceans, reptiles, amphibians, fish and birds), types of activity, weather phenomena, names of noise-making instruments, physical characteristics, sexual terms.

Here is a representative but very modest list of this enormous group of words: *karramarro* 'crab', *zirimiri* 'drizzle', B *zarramarra* 'trash, rubbish', B *pirri-pirri* 'dysentery', *momorro* ~ *mamarro* ~ *mamurru* ~ *mozorro* ~ *zomorro* ~ *txomorro* 'bug, creepy-crawly', *koko* 'bug' (especially one that infests maize), *dunba* 'cowbell', B *txonbo*, B *dzanga*, L LN *pulunpa* 'dive', B G *tximeleta*, L *pinpilin* ~ *pinpirin* ~ *pinpilinpauxa* 'butterfly' (the L word also means 'garfish', 'bud', 'elegant' and 'pretentious', among other things), *txilina, txintxa, txintxarri* (and other forms) 'cowbell, sheep bell', *txalaparta* (a vernacular musical instrument consisting of a wooden plank struck with sticks; cf. *zalaparta* 'noise, ruckus'), *txintxirrin* 'baby's rattle', B *txitximur* 'pinch', *txorromorro* 'leapfrog', *kukur, tutur* 'crest (on a bird)', *aiko-maiko* 'pretext, excuse', *pipi* 'moth', *babazuza, kazkabar, txingor* 'hail', *txistmist ~ tximist ~ ximixt* 'lightning', *kilkir* 'cricket', *txirrita* 'grasshopper', B G *txirla* 'clam', *txingi-txingi, txikili-txakala* 'sexual intercourse', B G *txuringa* 'anal sphincter', *potxolo* (and many variants) 'chubby little thing; vulva', *zizare ~ txitxare* 'worm', *armiarma* (and many variants) 'spider', B G *txirri* 'golden plover', L LN Z *panpina* 'doll', L LN *panpoxa* 'pretty', *txor-txor* and *kalaka* 'chattering, jabbering', *handi-mandi* 'pompous, self-important' (*handi* 'big'), *ikusi-makusi ~ ikusi-mikusi* (a children's game resembling 'I spy', < *ikusi* 'see'), *zurrumurru ~ zurruburru* 'murmuring, whispering, gossip, rumour', *zirri-zarra* 'scribbling', B *txantxan* 'chatterbox' and hundreds of others.

This pervasive sound symbolism in Basque is a topic which has so far received nothing like the attention it deserves. The only point I would make here is that such words should not be employed, as they so often have been, in seeking possible cognates between Basque and other languages. There is no reason to suppose that such words are ancient; Basque-speakers have apparently felt free to coin them throughout the history of the language.

5.6 LOANS FROM LATIN AND ROMANCE

Two thousand years of intense contact with Latin and its Romance descendants have had a profound effect upon the vocabulary of Basque. This effect began very early: in spite of the minimal romanization of the Basque Country, it is clear from the phonological evidence discussed in Chapter 3 that at least some hundreds of Latin words passed into Basque at a time when the five short and five long vowels of Latin had not yet been reorganized into the seven-vowel system of early Romance, when the palatalization of velars before front vowels had not yet occurred, and when intervocalic voiceless plosives had not yet become voiced.

As one would expect, many of these early loans occur in the areas of law and administration, technology and higher culture generally; there are also some religious terms, even though the Basques did not accept Christianity until centuries later: *lege* 'law' < LEGE, *errege* 'king' < REGE, *liburu* 'book' < LIBRU, *diru* 'money' (Z *diharü*) < DENARIU 'denarius', *bake* 'peace' < PACE, *gela* 'room, chamber' < CELLA, *ohore* 'honour' < HONORE, *izpiritu* 'spirit' < SPIRITU, *mirakulu* 'miracle' < MIRACULU, *horma* 'wall' (archaic *borma*) < FORMA 'form', *magi(ñ)a* 'sheath, pod' < VAGINA, *aldare* 'altar' < ALTARE, *bedeinkatu* 'bless' < BENEDICERE, *madarikatu* 'curse' < MALEDICERE, *joko* 'game' < IOCU, *ingude* 'anvil' < INCUDE, B *zapatu* 'Saturday' < SABBATU 'Sabbath', *gisu* 'plaster' < GYPSU, *borondate* 'will' < VOLUNTATE, *errota* 'mill, wheel' < ROTA, *katea* 'chain' < CATENA, R *apario* Z *apaidü* 'meal' < APPARIU, B *abendu* 'December' < ADVENTU, *lukai(n)ka* 'type of pork sausage' < LUCANICA, *bike* 'pitch' < PICE, *sa(i)ndu* 'holy; saint' < SANCTU and many, many others.

The motivation for other early loans is less obvious, though no doubt the great prestige of Latin was an important factor: *mutil* 'boy' < PUTILLU, *(b)iku* 'fig' < FICU, *lore* 'flower' < FLORE, *lama* 'flame' < FLAMMA, *gorputz* 'body' < CORPUS, *gertu* 'sure; ready' < CERTU, *bortitz* 'strong' < FORTIS, *laket* 'it is pleasing' < PLACET, *aditu* 'hear, understand' < AUDIRE, *lau* 'flat' < PLANU, *katu* ~ *gatu* 'cat' < CATTU, *denbora* 'time' < TEMPORA 'times'. Loans like *bago* 'beech' (< FAGU), *gazta(i)ña* 'chestnut' (< CASTANEA) and *golde* 'plough' (< CULTER 'ploughshare') are decidedly surprising, but they have completely displaced any indigenous words.

Some early loans have undergone substantial shifts in meaning: *mo(e)ta* 'kind, sort, type' < MONETA 'coin' (but the early Spanish poet Berceo has *moneda* in the sense of 'kind, sort'), *okela* 'meat', but formerly also 'morsel' < BUCCELLA 'mouthful'. Others have undergone unexpected phonological developments: *puxika* 'bladder' < PESSICA, *muxika* 'peach' < PERSICA, B *bi(x)ao* 'siesta' < MERIDIANU.

On the whole, it is not easy to judge the date at which a particular word was borrowed. However, the later date of many loans can often be identified by the presence in the Basque words of phonological developments which are strictly peculiar to Romance, though this is not always easy. For example, the vocalism of *putzu* '(water) well' < PUTEU suggests an early borrowing, but the affrication of the plosive must reflect a Romance development (cf. Castilian *pozo*). Similarly, the palatal nasal in *gazta(i)ña* 'chestnut' < CASTANEA shows at least the beginning of the process that led to Castilian *castaña*. The participle *deitu* 'call' < DICTU 'said' perfectly displays the intermediate stage of the palatalization which led to Castilian *dicho*, and *zitu* 'harvest' is doubtless derived from a Romance intermediate of the general form **seito* from SECTU 'a cutting'. And *zeru* 'sky' must have been borrowed from a Romance form like **tselu*, from CAELU, in which the velar had already undergone palatalization and affrication before a front vowel (recall that such processes are unknown in the history of Basque).

On occasion a Latin loan has been renewed by a later loan from Romance. This, *errota* 'wheel' (< ROTA) has been largely displaced by *arroda*, showing the Romance intervocalic voicing of plosives. Earlier *dekuma* 'tithe' (< DECIMA or an unattested *DECUMA) has been displaced by *detxema*. Earlier *bakatu* 'pay' (< PACARE) has been displaced by *pagatu* (< Sp *pagar*).

Basque has never ceased to borrow words from its Romance neighbours, and naturally most of these loan words are taken from the immediately adjacent varieties of Romance: Castilian Spanish, Navarrese Spanish, Aragonese Spanish and Occitan (particularly Gascon). Basque was also in contact with Asturian Spanish, but there appear to have been few if any loans from that quarter. On the other hand, Basque was scarcely in contact with French before the French Revolution, and hence loans from French are almost all very recent, though these are now, of course, very numerous in the French Basque Country.

In some cases the direct Romance source of a word can be identified with some certainty. Thus, for example, *pintza* 'membrane' appears to derive from Aragonese *binza*, while *kuma* 'mane, horsehair' and French Basque *mulo* 'haystack' probably derive from Occitan *couma* ~ *coumo* and *moulou*, respectively, and *erraz* 'easy' almost certainly derives from Old Spanish *rahez*. In other cases, the precise source is uncertain, as with *musu* 'snout, face, mouth, lip, kiss' and the related *musin* 'snout, muzzle': the late Latin MŪSU 'muzzle' and its diminutives are widely represented in western Romance (Old Castilian *muso*, Old French *muse* ~ *musel*, Occitan *mus* ~ *musèu*, etc.), and it is difficult or impossible to trace the histories of the Basque words with confidence.

On occasion, the Romance source of a Basque word may be difficult or impossible to identify, even when the form of the word shows that it must be a loan. The word *gorotz(a)* ~ *korotz(a)* 'dung', which appears obscure, has been ingeniously derived by Corominas and Pascual (1980) from a Romance derivative of Latin CROCEA 'saffron-coloured', whose Old Spanish reflex *croça* was applied to a variety of yellowish garments and coverings, including to a covering of dung and straw placed over a haystack. Basque *alai* 'merry' may be related to Spanish *alhaja* 'gem, treasure'. French Basque *moto* 'head scarf, hairknot' (and other senses) may be derived from Occitan *moto* 'clod, ball'. The strange-looking word *perretxiko* 'small mushroom' may contain Romance *chico* 'small' attached to an unidentified first element. Basque *txarran* 'devil' is thought to represent *Txarran*, a Basque diminutive of the Spanish given name *Fernando*. Z *ülhañ* 'bird of prey' is conceivably a loan from Spanish *milano* 'kite', but the phonology is unusual. B *laru* 'yellow, jaundice' is almost universally believed to derive from Latin CLARU 'bright, clear'.

In recent decades, of course, developments in education, broadcasting and publication have ensured that most loans are now derived from standard Castilian and standard French, and this in turn has led to increasing divergences in the everyday vocabularies of Spanish Basques and French Basques. Thus, Spanish Basques have *juez* 'judge' (< Sp *juez*) and *kotxe* 'car' (< Sp *coche*), while French Basques have *juje* (< Fr *juge*) and *boitura* (< Fr *voiture*), and so on for thousands of other words. Such lexical divergence is in practice one of the more refractory problems in the development of a standard form of Basque, only weakly treatable by the coining of neologisms like *epailari* 'judge', from *epai* 'judgement'.

5.7 LOANS FROM OTHER SOURCES

A handful of Basque words have sometimes been suspected of being loans from pre-Indo-European languages, such as *gorosti* 'holly' (cf. Sardinian *colostri* 'holly'), *zakur* 'dog', *kukur* and *tutur*, both 'crest', and *muño* (and variants) 'hill'. There is, however, no indisputable case of such a loan. Most of the candidate words are also found in Romance and are therefore perhaps more likely to have been borrowed from Romance rather than directly from an earlier source. As Michelena was fond of pointing out, not all the pre-Indo-European elements in Basque are necessarily ancient in that language. Note also that *gorosti*, in spite of its appealing match with the Sardinian word, looks very much like a derivative involving the collective suffix *-di*, which is common in plant names.

Basque was indisputably in contact with Celtic, and possibly also with other Indo-European languages, for centuries before the arrival of the Romans in Spain and Gaul, and one might therefore expect to find a certain number of early Indo-European loans into Basque. In fact, only a very modest list of possible loans from earlier Indo-European languages exists, and not a single one of these is indisputable. The most plausible cases are *adar* 'horn, branch', *andere* 'lady', *aran* 'plum', *argi* 'light, bright', *gori* 'fiery', *hartz* 'bear', *landa* 'plain, prairie', *maite* 'beloved', *mando* 'mule' and *mendi* 'mountain'; these are discussed in Chapter 6. Given the undeniable presence of Indo-European toponyms and personal names in the Basque Country in the Roman period, this paucity and almost absence of loans from Indo-European is very surprising.

After the collapse of Roman power, the Basques were in contact for several centuries with two powerful Germanic neighbours, the Franks to the north and the Visigoths to the south. Nevertheless, there is not a single instance of an undeniable loan from these languages, though a very few candidates have been suggested. Chief among these is *ehun* 'one hundred'. The Gothic numeral for '100' is recorded as *ain hund*, which is known to have represented a pronunciation like [enhund], and this would have been borrowed into Basque as **enun*, yielding the attested *ehun* after the loss of intervocalic *n*. But it seems puzzling that the Basques, who had earlier borrowed *mila* 'one thousand' from Latin, should have borrowed the lower number later from Gothic, and the Germanic origin is not certain.

The Arab conquest of most of Spain resulted, of course, in large numbers of Arabic loans into Spanish, and a few of these have passed on into Basque, such as *alkate* 'mayor' (Cast *alcalde*), *almaiz* 'mortar' (Sp *almirez*), *azafrai* 'saffron' (Sp *azafrán*), *anega* 'a measure of grain' (Sp *fanega*), *erraz* 'easy' (Old Sp *rahez*) and *alkandora* 'shirt' (Old Sp *alcandor*). Particularly striking is *zainhori* 'carrot', from Castilian *zanahoria*, of Arabic origin, but folk-etymologized in Basque into *zain* 'root' plus *hori* 'yellow' plus the article *-a*. The word *atorra* 'shirt' cannot easily derive from Old Spanish *adorra*, and it appears to be borrowed directly from Arabic *ad-durraʔa*, with the usual Basque treatment of voiced geminates. The word *gutun ~ kutun*, now usually 'letter' (i.e., 'epistle'), but also attested as 'book', seems to derive directly from Arabic *kutub* 'books', since the word is not attested in Romance. Basque *arra* 'palm tree', formerly *arraa*, looks to be directly from Arabic *rāha* 'palm (of the hand)'.

A number of English words have been borrowed into Basque via Spanish or French: *gai ~ gay* 'gay' (homosexual), *hobby* 'hobby', *whisky* 'whiskey', *zoom* 'zoom (lens)', *footing* and *jogging*, both 'jogging', *bideo* 'video', *rock* 'rock (music)', *futbol ~ fubor* 'football' (soccer), *striptease* 'strip-tease', *fax* 'fax' and so on; these are both too obvious and far too numerous to enumerate. Such words are spelled and pronounced in whatever way speakers can manage, and there is considerable variation; naturally, these are strictly Romance loans, from the Basque point of view. One possible case of a loan directly from English is the common *porlan* 'cement'; this derives from the name *Portland* printed on the bags, and is for many speakers the ordinary word for 'cement', something which does not appear to be so for Spanish-speakers.

For a few possible words shared by Basque and ancient Iberian, see Chapter 6. Of evidence for loans from any other sources there is none. A few imaginative authors have been prepared to recognize loans into Basque from such implausible sources as Berber, Kartvelian, Ancient Egyptian and even Hurrian and Sumerian, but of course what they have seized upon is nothing more than chance resemblances, such as Basque *zazpi* 'seven' and *berri* 'new' and Coptic *šašf* 'seven' and *brre* 'new, young'.

5.8 NEOLOGISMS

It is clear that many Basque writers have introduced particular neologisms into their works for their own purposes, but these have nearly always been transparent formations constructed according to the ordinary rules of word-formation. There have, however, been several attempts at introducing large numbers of neologisms at one time. The first such occasion was the eccentric Basque dictionary published by Larramendi in 1745 and discussed briefly in Chapter 1. Larramendi's novel compounds were usually constructed in a technically correct manner, though many of them, like his *sutumpa* 'fire-bang' for 'artillery piece' certainly represent a style which is alien to the language, while many of his other formations seem to have been extracted from thin air. But Larramendi's efforts have had virtually no effect on the language: only very occasionally has any Basque writer attempted to make any use of his creations, and they remain museum pieces today.

Of somewhat greater consequence than Larramendi's fantasies are the coinages of Sabino Arana (1865–1903), whose highly eccentric approach to the language was described in Chapter 1. Apart from his absurd etymologizing, Arana also fancied himself as a language reformer, and he set about the task, necessary as it seemed to him, of coining hundreds of neologisms to replace the numerous Romance loans in Basque. To this end he arbitrarily deformed existing words to suit his own tastes, he invented new stems and suffixes *ad libitum*, and he rammed these together according to rules of his own devising, sometimes cheerfully applying phonological rules which he had no business applying. Only a handful of his mostly eccentric coinages have found a permanent place in the language, though quite a few others are still self-consciously used today by adherents of the PNV. Here are a few examples of Arana's technique.

Arana convinced himself that the language name *euskara* (*euskera* in his Bizkaian dialect) was derived from the word for 'sun', *eguzki*. In pursuit of this absurd etymology, he arbitrarily changed the name of the language to *euzkera*, and similarly for related words: *euzkeldun* for *euskaldun* 'Basque' and so on. The combining form *euskal*, as in *Euskal Herria* 'the Basque Country', he regarded as an altered form of *eguzkiko* 'of the sun', and so he rearranged *euskal* into *euzko*, whence the original name *Euzko Gudari* of the patriotic song sung by Basque soldiers in the Civil War. Noting that the indigenous *euskaldun* means, etymologically and in practice, 'Basque-speaker', he combined his *euzko* with the ethnonymic suffix *-tar* to produce *euzkotar* '(ethnic) Basque'; respelled as *euskotar*, this word finds some use today. Wanting a name for his proposed Basque political entity, he took this *euzko* and combined it with the word-forming suffix *-di* (see below), obtaining *Euzkadi*. (This name is still in use today, but its modern spelling is the more etymological *Euskadi*. Similarly, the official name of the Basque Autonomous Government is *Eusko Jaurlaritza*, with the same spelling change.)

The suffix *-di* just mentioned is common in Basque, but it normally only occurs attached to names of plants to form collective nouns: *pinu* 'pine', *pinudi* 'stand of pine trees'; *sagar* 'apple', *sagardi* 'apple orchard'; *haritz* 'oak', *harizti* 'oak grove', *elorri* 'hawthorn', *elordi* 'clump of hawthorn bushes' and so on. Arana, however, took a liking to this suffix and used it constantly in his creations. Apart from *Euzkadi*, he coined also *Euskaltzaindi(a)*, literally 'Basque-guardian-*di*', the Basque name of the Basque Language Academy, *ludi* 'planet Earth, world' (from *lur* 'earth'), and *izadi* 'nature' (from *izan* 'be'); the existing *gazteria* 'youth, young people', from *gazte* 'young' with a Romance suffix, he arbitrarily converted into *gaztedi*.

The common suffix *-ba* in kinship terms (see section 5.9.2) he fancifully interpreted as representing an ancient **aba* 'father', and this morph he used to coin such terms as *abizen* 'surname' (*izen* 'name'), *abenda* 'race' (*enda* 'lineage') and *aberri* 'fatherland' (*herri* 'land'); to this last he added *-zale* 'fond of' to obtain *abertzale* 'patriot'. These last two coinages have found a secure place in the language.

Seeking a genuine Basque word for 'write' to replace the various Romance loans, he came across the archaic word *iraatsi* 'carve', and altered this capriciously into *idatzi*, of which he liked the look better. This is another of the very few of his coinages which have taken root in the language, as it happens. The same cannot be said for some of Arana's derivatives of it, such as *idazti* 'book' and *idazki* 'document', use of which is confined to PNV stalwarts.

Noting that *irakurri* 'read' looks very much like an ancient causative in -*ra*-, he hypothesized a lost verb **ikurri*, upon which he conferred the meaning of 'signify'; from this he extracted a noun **ikur* 'sign'. In turn adding to this a mysterious suffix -*in* of his own devising, he obtained *ikurrin*, to which he assigned the meaning 'flag'. In fact, this has since become the name of the Basque flag specifically, though outside of Basque it is better known in the form *ikurriña*, with the article.

Arana took *lege* 'law', a loan from Latin, and deformed it into *lagi*; this he combined with *herri* 'country' to produce *laterri* 'state'. From *egin* 'make' and the noun-forming suffix -*ki* he somehow obtained *ingi* 'paper'; this in turn he combined with *hitz* 'word' and *barri*, the Bizkaian form of *berri* 'new', to obtain *izparringi* 'newspaper', a remarkable formation which is without parallel in the language. From *batu* 'unite' and *toki* 'place' he derived the ill-formed *batzoki* 'clubhouse', and from *gogo* 'soul, spirit' and -*zain* 'guardian' the equally ill-formed *gotzain* 'bishop'. On the other hand, the combination of *gudu* 'struggle, combat' with the professional suffix -*ari* yielded the well-formed *gudari* 'soldier', which has come to mean specifically 'Basque soldier'.

Some of Arana's coinages were of such tortured formation as to be unintelligible: *txadon* for 'church' (from *etxe* 'house' and *done* 'saint'), *gotzon* for 'angel' (from *gogo* 'soul' and *done*), *donoki* for 'heaven' (again from *done*) and so on. Only a very few matched the elegance of his *eratorri* 'derive', obtained from *etorri* 'come' by means of the ancient causative morph -*ra*-.

Arana's approach was that of the fanatical purist. Every one of his coinages was intended to replace an existing Basque word of Latin or Romance origin, sometimes one which had been in the language for thousands of years, like *lege* 'law', *zeru* 'sky', *errege* 'king' and *liburu* 'book'. After Arana's early death, this pointless and destructive purism was perpetuated by many of his followers in the PNV, who even down to our own day have continued to spatter their Basque with Arana's ugly and deformed monstrosities. We should honour Arana for his genuine achievements, and we will of course retain those few of his coinages which have found a real place in the language, but it would be best for all concerned if the great bulk of his wretched neologisms could be safely buried in a museum, where they belong.

The last two decades or so have seen the coining of neologisms on a grand scale: the Basque Language Academy has proposed a number of these; lexicographers like Xabier Kintana and Luix Mari Mujika have published general-purpose dictionaries containing thousands of their own neologisms;

the specialist organization UZEI has published a large number of technical dictionaries containing tens of thousands of new coinages; and many other individuals and organizations have chipped in with their own contributions. Naturally, the degree of acceptance of these new words varies considerably: while *euskalari* 'vasconist, specialist in the Basque language' is now universally used, *suomitar* 'Finn' has never left the pages of the dictionary in which it was proposed. Coinage has often been hasty and ill-considered. Consider, for example, the grammatical term 'node' (in a syntactic tree). The Spanish word for this is *nudo*, which in Spanish means all of 'node (in a tree)', 'knot (in wood)' and 'knot (in rope or string)'. Some Basque syntacticians have adopted the neologism *korapilo* for 'node', but this is the ordinary Basque word, not for anything botanical, but for 'knot (in rope or string)'; not only does this clumsy coinage miss the point of the arboreal metaphor, but *korapilo* is, by extension, an exceedingly common Basque word for 'problem', and hence its use for 'node' can easily lead to misunderstanding. The UZEI dictionary recommends the far more more sensible *adabegi*, which is the ordinary word for 'node (in a tree)' (*adar* 'branch' + *begi* 'eye'), but this word has so far found little use in linguistic work. (Not that the UZEI lexicographers are blameless: for 'voiceless', they propose *gor*, the ordinary word for 'deaf'; this is a clumsy calque on Spanish *sordo*, which means not only 'deaf' but also 'muffled' (hence its use for 'voiceless'), but the Basque word never means 'muffled', and something like *bozgabe* 'without voice' would seem to be preferable.)

In spite of the difficulties, a large number of modern neologisms have already found a secure place in the language. For example, the verb *hautetsi* 'choose' had already acquired the additional sense of 'elect' in the French Basque Country, and it has been used as a base for such derivatives as *hauteskunde* 'election', *hautesle* 'elector, voter' and *hautesleria* 'electorate', all of them now in regular use even in the south.

A major problem, though, has been that of finding Basque equivalents of the common European prefixes like *pre-*, *contra-*, *trans-*, *syn-*, *anti-*, *co-*, *super-*, *inter-* and *sub-*. Basque has no word-forming prefixes of its own, and it is far from obvious how these useful morphs should be rendered in Basque. Only in a few cases is an obvious solution available, as when 'postwar' is expressed as *gerra-ondoko* (*gerra* 'war' + *ondoan* 'after' + -*ko*), exactly parallel to indigenous formations like *afalondoko* 'after-dinner' (adj.), from *afari* 'dinner'. This policy of using the native postpositions to render prefixes can be successfully used in some other cases, as in *nazioarteko* 'international' (*artean* 'between') and *historiaurreko* 'prehistoric' (*aurrean* 'in front of'). But it doesn't always yield attractive results, especially with nouns. The noun 'prehistory' might logically be rendered as *historiaurre*, literally 'history-front', but many speakers find such formations very awkward and prefer the more radical solution provided by *aurrehistoria*, in which *aurre* 'front' is treated as a prefix, even though no such prefix had previously existed and even though the result has a decidedly anomalous form. Still others dislike both forms and simply borrow *prehistoriko* from Romance, though this way out is definitely frowned on by a large number of Basques. Only time will tell what solution will prevail, but a solution must certainly be found.

5.9 STRUCTURED PARTS OF THE LEXICON

5.9.1 Colour terms

Basque has the following colour terms which are, with the partial exception of the word for 'green', common to all varieties.

beltz (B *baltz*)	black
zuri (dimin. (*t*)*xuri*)	white
gorri	red
hori	yellow
urdin	blue
berde ~ *perde*	green

As we shall see in section 6.9, there is ancient evidence that the earliest form of *beltz* was **beletz*, probably from a stem **bel-*: cf. *bele* ~ *bela* 'raven, crow', *belatz* 'sparrowhawk' and B *harbel* 'slate' (*harri* 'stone': possibly 'dark stone'). There is little to be said about the next three items, except to note that Azkue (1923–1925: 46) proposes that all three might have been derived from nouns by the addition of the ancient adjective-forming suffix -*i*. The nouns he suggests are *zur* 'wood' (which has a tapped *r*), a hypothetical **gor* 'flesh', possibly supported by the existence of *gordin* 'raw', with the adjective-forming suffix -*din* 'resembling' (Azkue also adduces *gorputz* 'body', but this is a transparent loan from Latin *corpus*), and (*h*)*or* 'dog' (also with a tapped *r*). (In Azkue's account, the word for 'yellow' would originally have meant 'tawny'.) There appears to be no way of evaluating these proposals. Noteworthy is the existence in B and G of the word *gori* 'fiery, incandescent, red-hot'; this might be related somehow to *gorri*, but there is no parallel in Basque for such a derivational use of the *r/rr* contrast, and anyway there is good reason to believe that *gori* is a loan from Celtic (see Chapter 6).

With *urdin* things become more interesting. Though this word everywhere means 'blue' today, there is clear evidence that it formerly had a much broader scope. Throughout the Basque Country, *urdin* is the colour term applied to what we would call grey (not white) hair or beards, and it forms part of the compound *mutxurdin* 'old maid', literally 'grey-cunt'. Moreover, *gibelurdin* (literally, 'blue-back') is the name of a mushroom with a bright green underside. Therefore, as Michelena (1970b) remarks, it is easier to believe that *urdin* has narrowed its meaning than that the mushroom has changed its colour. Moreover, this term appears to have a transparent formation: it looks like a derivative of *ur* 'water' with the adjective-forming suffix *-din* 'resembling', an etymology which could hardly be more appropriate but is none the less not certain, though the widespread use of *urdin* as a noun meaning 'turbid water' (such as water disturbed by a storm) is encouraging. Lexically distinct, as so often, R alone has a different word for 'blue': *dundu*, a word which in Z just means 'dark' and which cannot possibly be ancient.

The word for 'green' is a conspicuous loan from Romance (Spanish *verde*, French *vert*, etc.), and is doubtless a late addition to the system which has usurped some of the former domain of *urdin*. A few French Basques use instead the word *musker*, which is also the name of a bright-green lizard and doubtless derived from the animal name. The Aranist neologism *orlegi* may also be encountered occasionally.

All modern varieties of Basque have a number of additional colour terms, most of which are simply borrowed from the local variety of Romance. For 'orange' we have *laranja*, from the name of the fruit. 'Pink' is *arrosa*, a Romance loan, though the compounds *gorrimotel* 'weak red' and *zurigorri* 'white-red' also find some use. For 'grey', the clearly ancient *arre* is widely used, though this word often means just 'drab, dun, dark', and the also ancient *nabar* finds some use for 'grey', though it more widely means 'multi-coloured', 'mottled' or 'drab'; otherwise, the Romance loan *gris* is the most usual word. For 'purple' or 'violet', the most widespread term is *ubel*, which also means both 'livid' and 'dark', and which appears to involve the ancient element **bel* 'dark', but some speakers have *more* ~ *mora*, a word which puzzles Azkue but which can hardly be other than Spanish *mora* 'blackberry', 'mulberry'. Finally, for 'brown' Basque follows its Romance neighbours in having no single equivalent to the English word: it uses various Romance loans such as *marroi* and *morosko* for various types of brown, though everywhere there exists also *beltzaran*, a compound of *beltz* 'black' with an uncertain second element (neither *aran* 'plum' nor *haran* 'valley' would seem to make any sense, nor is adjective–noun a possible pattern in Basque); this word is applied chiefly to dark or suntanned skin or to brown hair.

Other more specific colour terms exist, of course, such as B *beilegi* 'bright yellow', a derivative of *behi* 'cow', and B *laru* 'pale yellow' (< Lat CLARU 'clear'), but these additional terms do not constitute part of the basic colour terminology of the language.

5.9.2 Kinship terms

The kinship terminology of Basque is not particularly elaborate, though it does exhibit one or two features not typically found in western Europe. Only the most central terms are more or less universal in the language, while a much larger number of less central terms shows very considerable variation in space and time. The chief study of kinship terms is Michelena (1969a). First, here are the terms which are nearly universal:

mother   *ama*

This is probably of nursery origin, though an original *anba cannot be ruled out.

father   *aita*

Aquitanian *Atta-* possibly represents this word, which may result from the depalatalization of *atta, with a palatal plosive.

daughter   *alaba*

son   *seme* (*senbe < *seni 'boy' + *-be*)

sister (of a woman)   *ahizpa* (B *aizta*) (Sal *ainzpa*) (< *aniz-ba)

sister (of a man)   *arreba*

brother (of a woman)   *neba*

brother (of a man)   *anaia* (< *aNaea < ? *aNanea)

aunt   *izeba* (B *izeko*, Aezk *izo*), *tia* (< Sp)

uncle   *osaba*, *tio* (< Sp)

niece, nephew, grandson granddaughter   *iloba* ~ *lloba* ~ *loba* ~ *lioba*

wife   *emazte* (< *eme 'female' + *gazte* 'young') (some varieties use *and(e)re*, otherwise 'lady')

husband   *senar* (< *seni 'boy' + *ar* 'male' (?))

parents   *gurasoak* ~ *burasoak*, *aitamak* ~ *aitetamak* (*aita* 'father' + *ama* 'mother' + Pl)

child   *sehi* ~ *sein* (also 'boy, servant') < *seni; the element *SENI-* is abundantly attested in Aquitanian; *haur*, *ume* < *unbe, apparently attested in Aquitanian as *OMBE-*, *VMME-*

sibling   *haurride* (*haur* 'child' + *-ide* 'fellow') (this means 'brother' in some places)

relative   *ahaide* (< **ana-* + *-ide* 'fellow'), LN Z R *askazi*

The word *alaba* 'daughter' is frequently written *allaba* in the Classical Labourdin literature; no one knows why. In some regions, it is customary to address one's father as *aitajaun* (*jaun* 'sir, gentleman, lord') and one's mother as *amand(e)re* (*and(e)re* 'lady, madam'). The distinction between *neba* and *anaia* is made only in B; elsewhere, only *anaia* exists and is used in both functions. A few varieties distinguish *iloba* 'niece, nephew' from *lloba* 'grandchild', but this is not usual. Some varieties of B have *bi(r)loba* (*bir-* 'again') specifically for 'grandchild' (or sometimes for 'great-grandchild'), and some eastern varieties have *ilobaso* for 'grandchild' (see below for *-so*).

The frequency of the morph *-ba* in these terms has often excited comment, but rarely illumination. Sabino Arana's invention of an alleged *aba 'father' is a piece of pure fantasy which doesn't even make any sense, while Čirikba's (1985) proposed *ba 'son, child' is hardly an improvement. In my view, the most interesting point about -ba is its replacement by -ko in the Bizkaian form of the word for 'aunt'. This suggests that -ba might once have been a derivational or relational suffix parallel in some respects to -ko, but, whatever it was, it's probably too deeply buried for us to be able to recover its function now. (But izeko might also be from *izeba-ko.) The morph -ba also occurs in western asaba 'ancestor' (this means 'grandparent' or 'great-grandparent' in HN), and in G old L Sout aurba 'grandparent, ancestor', whose first element is probably aurre 'front'. Several of these words appear to be built on a stem *an-, of unknown significance.

The usual words for 'first cousin' are lehengusu for a male cousin and lehengusin for a female cousin; these consist of the word lehen 'first' added to loans from Romance which preserve the Romance sex distinction. Northern varieties derive from these by the addition of tipi 'small' words for 'second cousin': lehengusutipi and lehengusintipi. Most other varieties have for 'second cousin' a formation with bertze ~ beste 'other': bertzelengusu, -gusina, bestengusu -gusina and other variants. Straight Romance loans like kosin(o) are used for 'first cousin' in some varieties.

The words for 'grandmother' and 'grandfather' show regional variation. The most widespread word for 'grandmother' is amon(a) (literally, 'good-mother'), but northern varieties have ama(g)utxi ~ amatxi (gutxi 'small'), while B has amaso (with -so) or amama (literally, 'mother-mother'); the last term, in spite of its formation, is not confined to maternal grandmothers. Aezk has amiña and Sal has amato. For 'grandfather', we find an enormous number of local words: aiton(a) 'good-father', ait(a)ita 'father-father', aitaso (with -so), aitajaun 'father-lord', aitagoi(a) 'high-father', aita-nagusi 'chief-father', aitobe 'better-father' (?), aita(g)utxi ~ aitatxi (gutxi 'small'), aitatto (with a diminutive suffix), aitañi (with an unusual diminutive suffix). Aezk has the odd apitxi, apparently involving bitxi 'pretty'. Sal has aitaborze 'grandfather' and amaborze 'grandmother', apparently involving bertze 'other'.

For 'grandchild', we find iloba (and variants) in most places, the same word as for 'niece, nephew'. But L LN have arrahaur, literally 're-child', with a Romance prefix. B distinguishes bi(r)loba 'grandchild' from loba 'niece, nephew'.

The morph -so found in some of these words recurs in guraso ~ buraso 'parent', arbaso 'ancestor', 'great-grandfather', illobaso 'grandchild', 'great-niece, great-nephew' and alabaso 'granddaughter'. Azkue suggests that -so indicates the second generation ascending or descending, which fits some of the words but not all; Michelena (1969a) suggests that the affix indicates merely a greater distance. The word arbaso he derives from aurba 'great-grandfather', cited above.

In-laws are commonly denoted by adding -gi(n)arreba to another term: amagi(n)arreba, 'mother-in-law', aitagi(n)arreba 'father-in-law' and so on. Eastern varieties use -izun 'false' in the same way: amaizun 'mother-in-law'. However, we find common errein ~ erra(i)n for 'daughter-in-law' and eastern suhi ~ sui(n) (< *suni) for 'son-in-law'. For 'brother-in'law' and 'sister-in-law' some varieties use Romance loans like goñatu, goñata. Some varieties of B have auba ~ aube for 'mother-in-law'.

Godparents and godchildren are named in a variety of ways. Most frequently, bitxi 'pretty' is suffixed: aitabitxi 'godfather', alababitxi 'goddaughter', and so on. We also find ponteko 'of the font' used similarly: aitaponteko 'godfather', semeponteko 'godson' and so on. Western varieties also have aitabesoetako 'godfather' and amabesoetako 'godmother' (besoetako 'of the arms'). Eastern varieties further exhibit amatxi, amagutxi 'little mother' and amandere 'mother-lady' for 'godmother', and aitakide (-kide 'fellow'), aitagutxi 'little father' and aitader 'beautiful father' for 'godfather', as well as the Romance loans komai 'godmother' and konpai 'godfather'.

The most usual way of rendering English 'step-' or 'foster' is by preposing ugatz 'female breast': ugazama 'stepmother, foster mother', ugazanaia 'stepbrother, foster brother', ugazeme 'stepson, foster son' and so on. This same ugaz- is used for 'half-': ugazaurride 'half-brother' (aurride 'brother'), though in other regions we find suffixed erdi 'half' instead (haurriderdi 'half-brother') (in some places erdi is prefixed rather than suffixed). For 'foster' we also find orde 'stead' postposed: gurasorde 'foster parent', haurrorde 'foster child'. In a few regions -izun 'false' is used for 'step-' instead of for '-in-law'.

The following words are not strictly kinship terms:

man	gizon, attested in Aquitanian as CISON
woman	emakume < eme 'female' + -kume 'offspring' (this word, not attested in early texts, probably once meant 'girl' and does so today in Sal); R Aezk Sal emazte (= 'wife' elsewhere), emazteki (emazte + -ki NFS)
boy	mutil 'boy' < Lat PUTILLU (dimin. mutiko preferred in places)
girl	neska 'girl', whose diminutive neskato is attested in Aquitanian as NESCATO (dimin. neskato, neskako, neskaxe preferred in places)
gentleman	jaun, also 'sir', earlier 'lord'; possibly an ancient participle
lady	andere ~ andre ~ B andra 'lady' (also 'woman' in B), attested in Aquitanian as ANDERE
female	eme < Occ
male	ar
human	gizaki < gizon 'man' + -ki NFS
orphan	umezurtz, haurzurtz (ume, haur 'child')
widow(er)	alargun (eastern varieties distinguish alargun 'widower' from

alarguntsa 'widow') (Lafon has proposed **ez-lagun* 'no companion' as the source.)

old man   *agure* (< Lat AVULE), Sal *aitso*, *gizon zahar*

old woman *atso*, R *ematzar* (*eme* 'female' + *zar* 'old')

old maid   *neskazahar* ('old girl'), *mutxurdin* ('grey cunt')

bachelor   *mutilzahar* ('old boy'), *emaztegabe* ('without wife')

fiancée   *emaztegai* (*emazte* 'wife' + *-gai* 'destined for'), *ezkongai* (*ezkondu* 'get married')

fiancé   *senargai* (*senar* 'husband'), *ezkongai*

These last two are also the common words for 'girlfriend' and 'boyfriend' in much of the country, though the Spanish loans *nobia* and *nobio* are also widely used.

Also relevant here is western *ugazaba* 'boss', which appears to be from *ugatz* '(female) breast' + *asaba* 'ancestor'; this word must anciently have had a very different significance.

The universal *adiskide* 'friend' is derived by Lafon from **adinezkide*: *adin* 'age' + *-(e)z* Instr + *-kide* 'fellow', which looks plausible.

In earlier usage, kinship terms were treated like proper names and did not normally take the article: *izekok ekarri dau* 'Aunt brought it'.

See Michelena (1969a) for a study of kinship terms; Michelena is inclined to think that the ancient Basques traced kin relations only through the female line.

5.9.3 Numerals

Here are the first few Basque numerals. Note that several of them have distinctive forms in the northern (French Basque) dialects.

1   *bat*
2   *bi* (northern *biga* in isolation)
3   *hiru* (northern *hirur*)
4   *lau* (northern *laur*)
5   *bost* (eastern *bortz*)
6   *sei*
7   *zazpi*
8   *zortzi*
9   *bederatzi* (R *bedratzu*, Z *bede(r)atzü*)
10 *hamar*
11 *hamaika* ~ *hameka*
12 *hamabi*
13 *hamahiru(r)*
14 *hamalau(r)*
15 *hamabost* ~ *hamabortz*
16 *hamasei*

17   *hamazazpi*
18   *hemezortzi*
19   *hemeretzi*
20   *hogei* (northern *hogoi*)

It is most unusual for a native Basque word to end in a plosive, and *bat* is
clearly from earlier **bade* or **bada*, as suggested by the morph *bede-* in such
derivatives as (northern) *bedera* 'one apiece' and *bederatzi* 'nine'. The
numeral *bi*, in the French Basque Country alone, has a longer variant *biga*
(or *bida*) which is used in isolation: hence *biga* 'two' (as a noun phrase or as
an item in a counting sequence) but *bi etxe* 'two houses'; southerners use *bi*
everywhere. There is documentary evidence that the numeral for 'two' was
formerly postposed to its noun (as it still is today in B), and Michelena
(1977a: 413) suggests that postposed *-biga* was phonologically reduced to
*-bi(a), leading to the creation of *bi*. (Such reduction of the second element
of a compound is absolutely regular, and there are parallels for the generalization of such a reduced form to all positions; see section 3.19.2.) Northern
hirur and *laur* are clearly conservative, as shown by the universal occurrence
of forms like *hirurak* 'all three' and *laurak* 'all four', with plural *-ak* added to
the numeral. (Localized forms like *seirak* 'all six' and *zazpirak* 'all seven'
clearly represent analogical extension of this *r*: the most widespread forms
are *seiak* and *zazpiak*.) Eastern *bortz* is conservative; western *bost* represents
the frequent western development *rtz* > *st* (see Chapter 3). Naturally, *sei* has
often been suspected of being a loan word from Romance (Spanish *seis*,
etc.), but this seems impossible: all nearby Romance languages have a final
consonant in their word for 'six', and so a loan word should have taken a
form like **seis*. This is probably just a coincidence, especially since none of
the other numerals is borrowed. For *zazpi*, Michelena (1972b) has suggested,
how seriously I don't know, a derivation from **bortzaz-bi* 'two with five'.
Both *zortzi* and *bederatzi* seem to share a final element *-tzi*, of unknown
function. A few people have tried to read this as an ancient word for 'ten',
with **zor* then meaning 'two' and **bede-* being, as already suggested, 'one',
with the two numerals then being construed as 'two from ten' and 'one from
ten', respectively. All this, however, requires a great deal of special pleading:
a hypothetical **tzi* 'ten', later replaced; a hypothetical **zor* 'two', later
replaced; an embarrassing extra morph **-(e)ra-* in the word for 'nine' but not
in the word for 'eight'; an order of elements which is most un-Basque (the
rigorously head-final Basque expresses 'one from ten' literally as 'ten-from
one', not what is required by the hypothesis we are discussing). On the
whole, the case for recognizing an ancient **tzi* 'ten' seems far from convincing. Further, the eastern forms for 'nine' (Z *bede(r)atzü*, R *bedratzu*) exhibit
a final *-u* (or *-ü*, derived from **-u*); since there is no possible way of
deriving this *-u* from **-i*, Michelena (1954b) concludes that the word for
'nine' was originally **bederatzu*, and that the common *bederatzi* results from

interference from the unrelated *zortzi* 'eight', in a manner which is very familiar in other languages.

Most interesting of all the Basque numerals is the enigmatic *hamaika*. The first element is clearly *hamar* 'ten', but what of that puzzling second element? Michelena (1977a: 117) concludes, after examining the dialect variants (notably old B *amaeka*), that the earlier form of the final element was probably *-eka* rather than *-ika*, but this doesn't help to identify it. Of course, there has been no shortage of analysts who choose to interpret *hamaika* as literally 'ten-one', and hence to posit yet *another* 'lost' numeral, this time *ika* (or *eka*) 'one'. Again, there is not the slightest shred of independent support for such an interpretation, and, taking this proposal together with the last one, it is surely excessive to demand that the notoriously conservative Basque should have replaced both its numerals for 'one' and 'two', when these numerals are widely regarded as being among the lexical items most resistant to change in languages generally.

Anyway, it is impossible to maintain simultaneously an ancient Basque *ika* 'one' and *tzi* 'ten' without becoming incoherent. Anyone who tries is faced with the paradox that he must interpret *bederatzi* 'nine' as formed from the *old* word for 'ten' but the *new* word for 'one', while *hamaika* in contrast is formed with the *new* word for 'ten' but the *old* word for 'one'. This is probably ridiculous, and I suspect that the analysis of *hamaika* will forever escape us. With an only moderately light heart, however, I would like to point out that *hamaika*, aside from meaning 'eleven', is the word used everywhere in the Basque Country to denote an indefinitely large number: where we in English say *I told him a thousand times*, a Basque says literally 'eleven times'. Could *hamaika* therefore represent a fossilized relic of the time when the Basque counting system stopped at 'ten', so that *hamaika* just meant 'ten-something', in other words, 'lots'? In support of this, I note that Tovar (1959a: Ch. 15) has proposed that *hamar* 'ten' is related to *amai* 'end' in the same way as *ibar* 'water meadow' and *ibai* 'river', and *bizkar* 'ridge of mountains' and *Bizkai(a)* (the province name); this proposal is endorsed by Zytsar (1985). While by no means obviously correct, Tovar's intriguing proposal reinforces the idea that the Basque counting system once stopped at 'ten'. If so, then *hamaika* could be interpeted simply as *amai* plus -*ka*, the suffix which forms adverbs from nouns and pronouns; it would then have meant something like 'in conclusion'. Against this, however, is Michelena's conclusion that the final element was probably *-eka*, and also the suggestion of Michelena (1972c) that *amai* itself is probably derived from the verb *amaitu* 'finish', for which he proposes the etymology *hamabi-tu*, from *hamabi* 'twelve', citing as a parallel for this curious semantic development Castilian *adocenar(se)* 'become commonplace, become mediocre', from *docena* 'dozen'. (A more devastating objection to my suggestion, pointed out by Zabaltza (1995: 168), is that older texts in Basque clearly use *bortz* ~ *bost* 'five', rather than *hamaika*, to denote an indefinitely large number; see Perurena (1993: 146, 225).)

Michelena (1977a: 496) in fact derives *hamaika* from **hamar-bede-ka* 'ten-one-adv.', a proposal which has won some support.

(A note in passing: the nineteenth-century Basque linguist Inchauspé in fact also proposed **eka* 'one', on the basis of the levelled northern form *hameka*, and tried to link this to Sanskrit *éka-s* 'one' and Hebrew *ehad* 'one', suggesting that this might be the ancestral human word for 'one'.)

Of the later numerals, *hemezortzi* has apparently been influenced in form by the following *hemeretzi*, whose development from a presumed **hamar-bederatzi* shows considerable phonological reduction. The numeral *hogei* has no etymology. There have been various attempts at deriving it from Celtic, given the existence of Brythonic forms like Middle Welsh *ugeint*, Cornish *ugens* and Breton *ugent*, but the reconstructed Proto-Celtic **wi-kant-i* is a phonologically impossible source, and Michelena (1964b: 136–137) categorically rejects a Celtic origin. The northern variant *hogoi* is merely the result of vowel assimilation. The multiples *berrogei* 'forty' (Sout *biorrogei*), *hirurogei* 'sixty' and *laurogei* 'eighty' show transparent formation, with the first exhibiting the common first element *berr-* < **bihur-* 'twist, bend', i.e. 'double'. The numeral *ehun* 'one hundred' is interesting, since it looks so much like Germanic. As pointed out above, the recorded Gothic numeral for '100' is *ain hund*, which is known to represent a pronunciation [enhund]; such a form, if borrowed into Basque, would have given exactly the attested *ehun*, and hence several scholars have proposed that the Basque numeral is a loan from Visigothic. The problem is one of motivation: why should Basque-speakers have borrowed this one numeral from Visigothic at such a late date?

Save only for *lehen* 'first' with its numerous local variants, the Basque ordinals are constructed by adding the suffix *-garren* to the cardinal: *lehen*, *bigarren*, *hirugarren*, etc. (Note that 'twenty-first' is *hogeitabatgarren* and not **hogeitalehen*.) The origin of this suffix is unknown, but Lafitte has made the interesting suggestion that the ordinal suffix was originally merely the genitive suffix *-en*, but that the reduction of *biga* 'two' to *bi* converted the pair *biga/bigaren* into *bi/bigaren*, leading to the reanalysis of the morph *-garen* as an ordinal suffix later generalized to the other numerals. While appealing, this conjecture does not explain the replacement of *r* by *rr*, a process for which there is no parallel.

The word *bertze* ~ *beste* 'other' appears to mean 'second' in one or two formations, and may conceivably have been an ancient word for this. Attempts to link *bertze* to *berri* 'new', and even to *bi(ga)* 'two', have not so far found general support. The prefix *ber-* ~ *bir-* 're-, again' is clearly from *bihur* 'bend, twist', and is unlikely to be connected with any of the other items.

There are distinct words for the lower fractions: *erdi* 'half', *heren* 'third', *laurden* 'fourth', archaic *bosten* 'fifth' and also *hamarren* 'tenth'. All but the first apparently involve a suffix -*en*, possibly derived from the genitive, though some of the formations are more complex. Derivatives like *herene-gun* 'the day before yesterday' (lit. 'third day') suggest that these items were formerly ordinals.

Finally, *mila* ~ *milla* '1,000' is a simple loan from Latin MILIA, and all higher numerals, like *milioi* 'million', are Romance loans.

5.9.4 Names of days and related words

The Basque word for 'day' is *egun*, which exhibits the combining forms *egu-* and *egur-* (western *eguzki* 'sun' < *egun* + -*z-ki*; eastern *eki* 'sun' < *egun* + -*ki*; *eguerdi* 'noon' (*erdi* 'middle'); *eguraldi* 'weather' (*aldi* 'time, occasion')); this ancient and puzzling alternation is discussed in Chapter 3. 'Today' is also *egun* in eastern varieties and was formerly universal; western varieties have replaced this with *gaur*, from *gau* 'night' + *hau(r)* 'this', originally 'tonight', and still so in the east.

'Yesterday' is *atzo*, which some have tried to relate to *atze* 'back', from earlier **atz*, but the -*o* is inexplicable. 'The day before yesterday' is *herene-gun*, from *heren* 'third' (now only the fraction) plus *egun*. Some eastern varieties have a word for 'the day before the day before yesterday'; this is usually *laurdenegun* (*laurden* 'fourth', again only a fraction otherwise), though we also find *herenegunago* (*herenegun* + -*ago* 'more'). Some central varieties have *herenegundamu* (see below for -*damu*) or *herenegun-atzetik* (*atze* 'back, behind' + -*tik* 'from').

'Tomorrow' is *bihar*, and 'the day after tomorrow' is *etzi*. For 'the day after the day after tomorrow', the most widespread word is *etzidamu*, from *etzi* plus an element *damu* of unknown origin, often suspected of being an irregular alteration of *egun* 'day'. This word has numerous local variants: *etziluma*, *etzilimo*, *etzirimu*, *etziramu*, *etziridamu* and doubtless others. Severely localized alternative forms are *etziago* (-*ago* 'more') and *etziaste*; this last looks like containing *aste* 'week', but it has a variant *etziazte*, leading me to wonder if it might represent an alteration of **etziatze* (*atze* 'back').

A word for 'four days from now', *etzikaramu*, is uniquely attested in a sixtccnth century Bizkaian text, and both this and its variant *etzikaramon* are also attested in Bizkaian in the meaning 'the day after the day after tomorrow'; the final -*amon* ~ -*amu* is in all likelihood *egun* 'day'. Another word for 'four days from now', *etzikaramu-ostean* (*ostean* 'after') is attested in a work by a Bizkaian author who flourished around 1800.

'The next day' is *biharamon* ~ *biharamun*, from *bihar* 'tomorrow' + *egun* 'day'. There appears to be no word for 'the previous day'. 'Last night' is *barda* in the east, reduced in the west to *bart*. 'Tonight' is *gaur* in the east, as mentioned above; western varieties have no lexicalization for this and use phrases like *gaur gauean* 'today at night' or *gau honetan* 'on this night'. See Michelena (1972b) for a discussion of these words.

'Morning' is *goiz*, though some eastern varieties prefer extended forms like *goizalde* or *goizondo* (*alde* and *ondo*, both 'side'). 'Evening' is *arrats* (possibly from *arre* 'grey'?), and 'afternoon' is *arratsalde* (*alde* 'side'). 'Night' is *gau*. 'Noon' and 'midnight' are *eguerdi* and *gauerdi* (*erdi* 'middle').

The words for 'now' and 'then' are *orain* and *orduan*, respectively; these derive from Lat HORA 'hour' and Basque *ordu* 'hour' (itself from Latin) plus the locative ending. Recall from Chapter 4 that de Rijk has argued for an ancient **dan* 'now'. Landucci has for 'now' *orast* < Lat HORA EST, which is also the source of *arestian* 'just now', or possibly < HORA ISTA. Also from Latin are *ia* 'still, yet, already' (< IAM) and *maiz* 'often' (< MAGIS).

The word for 'week' is *aste*, a word of unknown origin which possibly contains the suffix *-te*, which expresses duration in a number of compounds (*eurite* 'rainy spell' < *euri* 'rain'; *gosete* 'famine' < *gose* 'hungry'; *frantseste* 'Peninsular War' < *frantses* 'French'; etc.).

The Basque names for the days of the week are as follows; the Bizkaian dialect is noticeably divergent:

Monday	*astelehen*, B *ilen*
Tuesday	*astearte*, B *martitzen*
Wednesday	*asteazken*, B *eguasten*
Thursday	*ortzegun* ~ *ostegun*, B *eguen*
Friday	*ortzirale* ~ *ortzilare* ~ *ostiral(a)*, B *bari(a)ku*, *egubakoitz*
Saturday	*larunbat*, B *zapatu*, R Z *neskanegun*, B (?) *egubakoitz*, LN *ebiakoitz*, LN Z *irakoitz*
Sunday	*igande*, B *domeka*

The major study of these names is Michelena (1971b), upon which my account is largely based, but see also Caro Baroja (1973: Ch. 6).

The first three names are compounds of *aste* with *lehen* 'first', *arte* 'interval, between' and *azken* 'last'. These transparent if unexpected formations have induced many commentators to suggest that the Basques anciently had a week of only three days, an arrangement which would seem to be highly inconvenient and which does not appear to be parallelled elsewhere. In connection with this, I find it significant that these forms are attested everywhere with unreduced *aste-*; nowhere do we find **asta-* or **ast-*, even before a vowel, which suggests to me that these names are of no great antiquity. B *ilen* and *martitzen* are calques on Romance: *il-* is 'month' (earlier 'moon'; see the next section), and the whole is a reduction of **il-egun* 'moon-day', while *martitz* is 'Mars' (apparently from the Latin genitive *Martis*), and the final element is possibly the genitive *-en* but more likely a reduction of *-egun*: hence **il-egun* 'moon-day' and **martitz-egun* 'Mars's-day'. Bizkaian *eguasten* is a compound of *egun* with an unidentified second element; a plausible surmise would be **egun-aste-egun* 'day-week-day' (see *eguen* below).

The name of Thursday has attracted an enormous amount of comment and speculation. Eastern *ortzegun* is conservative; western *ostegun* shows the familiar development of *rtz* > *st*. What is striking is that all varieties of Basque show a number of words involving an element *or(t)zi ~ ortze ~ osti*, all of which have meanings pertaining to 'sky', 'storm' or 'thunder'. Table 5.1 is a collection taken from Azkue's dictionary; items for which no provenance is given are widespread.

Table 5.1 The word *ortzi* 'sky'

ortzadar ~ orzadar ~ ostadar 'rainbow' (*adar* 'horn')
ortzantz 'thunder' (L LN) (second element obscure)
ortze 'storm' (Z)
hortzgorri 'red cloud' (LN Sal) (*gorri* 'red')
ortzi 'sky'; 'thunder' (LN); 'raincloud' (LN); 'daylight' (L LN)
ortzikara 'time when a storm is brewing' (L) (-(*k*)*ara* 'manner' ?)
ortziri 'thunder' (hapax)
ortzitsu 'stormy' (L) (-*tsu* 'full of')
ortzitu '(to) thunder' (LN)
or(t)zondo 'dawn' (LN Z R) (*ondo* 'after')
orz 'sky' (HN LN); 'cloud' (LN Sal)
orzaizki 'daylight', 'starlight' (LN) (second element obscure)
orzanz 'thunder' (LN Z); 'storm' (LN) (second element obscure)
orzargi 'daylight; dawn' (R) (*argi* 'light')
orzgorri 'red sky' (LN) (*gorri* 'red')
orzoski 'calm air' (hapax) (second element obscure, possibly a reduplication)
ostargi 'daylight' (B G HN L) (*argi* 'light')
ostarku 'rainbow' (B) (*arku* 'arc')
osti 'thunderclap' (B); 'storm' (G)
ostil 'rainbow' (G)
ostots 'thunder' (HN) (*hots* 'noise')
ostroi 'thunder' (B) (second element obscure)

To these I can add the exclamation *Ortzi zuria!* (*zuri* 'white'), roughly 'Bloody hell!', which I have heard in Lapurdi but never seen recorded. Now the first element of *ortzegun* appears transparently to be this widespread item *ortzi* 'sky, storm, thunder', and what has fascinated the observers is that this looks remarkably like a calque of the Latin name of Thursday, *Iovis dies* 'day of Jupiter'. Jupiter, of course, was a god of thunder, and it is well known that the Germanic peoples calqued the Roman name of Thursday with the name of their own thunder god: hence 'Thor's day', or 'Thursday', in English, and 'Thunder's day', or *Donnerstag*, in German. And from this follows the inference, drawn countless times and repeated as gospel in a number of popular books, that *Ortzi* must have been the name of the ancient Basque god of thunder or of the sky in general.

This inference gains support from the report of the twelfth-century French pilgrim Aimery Picaud that *Urcia* was the word for 'God' used by his Basque interlocutors. Note, however, that Picaud's is the *only* explicit testimony we have that this word was ever the name of a deity. Still, it *is* explicit, and the other items recorded by Picaud seem to be very accurate.

None the less, there are problems. For one thing, while Christianity came late to the Basque Country, it was almost certainly the religion of the people by the time Picaud came on the scene in the twelfth century, and hence it would seem surprising that the Basques should have been producing the name of a pre-Christian sky god when asked for their divine name. For another, Picaud records *Urcia* with the article, which is normal enough with a common noun but rather unexpected with a proper name.

There is perhaps a simple explanation available. Michelena (1964b: 51) suggests that, when Picaud asked for the name, he pointed to the heavens to try to clarify what he was asking for, and that the Basques, misunderstanding his intention, simply gave him their word for 'sky'. After all, *ortzi* is well attested in the meaning 'sky'.

This, of course, doesn't explain why the word *ortzi* should be present in the name of Thursday, but Michelena has another suggestion, somewhat unexpected. He proposes that the name of Thursday doesn't contain *ortzi* at all; instead, it is simply a compound from *bortz* ~ *bost* 'five': hence *bortz-egun* 'fifth day'. The loss of initial *b-* before *o*, recall, is so frequent in Basque as to be practically regular, though the word for 'five' itself happens to be the outstanding exception.

Against Michelena's proposal is the observation that no other day-name has such a formation. Moreover, we are left with the problem of the name of Friday: *ortzirale* and variants. This seems to contain the same first element plus an unidentified second element.

B *eguen* 'Thursday' (variants *eguun* and *eguaun*) appears to be from *egun-egun*, curiously 'day-day'. B *bari(a)ku* 'Friday' is confidently derived by Michelena from an original *abari-ba(gari)ko-egun* 'day without dinner' (*abari* 'dinner', B *bagarik* ~ *barik* 'without' + *-ko*): Friday is, after all, a fast day in Catholic countries. B *egubakoitz* is *egun* + *bakoitz* 'unique'.

The name of Saturday, *larunbat*, has attested variants *larenbat* and *laranbate*, and the *Refranes y sentencias* of 1596 cites the form *lauren bat*. As first pointed out by Vinson, this looks very much like a reduction of *laurden bat* 'one quarter': if Saturday is taken as completing the week, then each Saturday represents (approximately) one-quarter of a month. Michelena, however, is sceptical: he is inclined to see this name as derived somehow from *laur(en)-egun* 'fourth day', since, in the old Roman style of counting, Saturday is the fourth day after Wednesday, the *asteazken* of Basque. He notes, however, that the *laranbate* of the sixteenth-century author Leizarraga may well preserve a final vowel lost elsewhere, in which case this name might involve the suffix *-te*, which possibly occurs also in *igande* 'Sunday' (Z R *igante*), *aste* 'week', *urte* 'year' and *mende* 'century' (Z R *mente*).

The regional *egubakoitz* is again 'unique-day'; *ebiakoitz* is an alteration of this, as very likely is *irakoitz*.

Bizkaian *zapatu* is a loan from Latin SABBATU 'Sabbath', showing the interesting development of Latin -BB- to Basque -*p*- discussed in Chapter 3. The engaging eastern *neskanegun* is 'girls' day'.

The name of Sunday, *igande* (Z R *igante*) is troublesome. Somewhat reluctantly, Michelena considers the obvious derivation from *igan* 'ascend', since the Christian Ascension took place on a Sunday.

The Bizkaian *domeka* is a loan from Latin (DIES) DOMINICA '(day) of the Lord'.

5.9.5 Names of the months and the seasons

The major study is Caro Baroja (1973: Ch. 5), but Caro Baroja's linguistic work is sometimes suspect. The word for 'month' is *hilabete* (*bete* 'full'), while 'moon' is in most places (*h*)*ilargi* ~ *ilhargi* (*argi* 'light'). These suggest an earlier **iLa* or **iLe* 'moon', with a compound 'full moon' being specialized for 'month' and another compound 'moonlight' for 'moon'. Sal has for 'moon' *ilaski*, which is probably from **ilargi-zki* by contamination from *eguzki* 'sun'; the phonology here is regular. (Note that Azkue's cited *ilazki* is an error.) Eastern *argizagi* (? 'light-bottle' or ? 'chief light') and R *goikua* ('the one above') probably result from taboo. Most month names contain an element (*h*)*il*, apparently a reduction of **hilV* in which the final vowel was interpreted as the article. The word for 'year' is *urte*, which, like *aste* 'week', possibly contains the suffix -*te*. The most widespread word for 'century' is *mende*, a word of uncertain origin; also found is *ehunurte* (*ehun* '100' + *urte* 'year').

Month names vary significantly across the country: the same month can have different names, and the same name can be applied to different months. The attested names are given below; many of them are attested in early texts, though it does not follow that they are necessarily ancient:

January	*urtar(r)il*, B G *ilbeltz*, L (?) *beltzil*, Aezk Sal *izotzil*
February	*otsail*, B *zezeil*, Z *baranthail*
March	*martxo*, B G *epail*, (?) *jorrail*
April	*apiril, jorrail*, B (hapax) *ope*(*il*)
May	*maiatz, ostail, ostaro, orril*, B *lorail*
June	*ekain*, G *garagarril*, R Sal Aezk *garagartzaro*, B Z *bagil* *bagiril*, LN (?) *errearo*, Z (?) *arramaiatz*
July	*uztail*, B *garagarril*, LN R Sal Aezk *gari*(*i*)*l*
August	*abuztu, agorril*, B (hapax) *daguenil*
September	*irail*, LN L Z *buruil*, Sal Aezk *urri*, G *garoil*
October	*urril* ~ *urri, urrieta*, LN R Sal Aezk *azaro*, L (?) *bildil*
November	(*h*)*azaro, hazil*(*a*), Aezk *abendu*, Sal *lenabendu*, R *leinabentu*, old B *zemendi*(*a*)
December	*abendu* ~ *abendo*, B G *gabonil*, L LN Z *lotazil*, LN *neguil*, Aezk *bigarrenabendu*, R *bigarnabentu*, Sal *azkenabendu*

For January, *urtar(r)il* is from **urta-barr(i)-hil*: *urta-* is the combining form of *urte* 'year', *barr(i)* is a variant of *berri* 'new' and *hil* is 'month', and the whole means 'month of the new year'. B *ilbeltz* is **hil-beltz* 'black month', as is *beltzil*, with its odd order. Aezk Sal *izotzil* is 'ice-month'.

For February, *otsail* looks like **otso-il* 'wolf month', a name which has no explanation, and *zezeil* similarly looks like **zezen-il* 'bull-month'. The Z word is obscure.

For March, *martxo* is a loan from Romance, while *epail* looks to be from *epai* 'cut, prune'. The name *jorrail*, commonly applied to April, is given as 'March' by several early authors.

For April, *apiril* is a Romance loan; the popular variant *aberil* looks to have been contaminated by *abere* 'cattle'. The name *jorrail* is from *jorra* 'weeding'. The strange hapax *opeil*, attested once in the *Refranes y sentencias* of 1596, is of unknown derivation. Some have posited a connection with Latin OPE 'plenty', which seems a little implausible, but the alternative derivation from Basque *ope*, the name of a type of pastry, is not obviously appealing either. The same source also once cites *ope* for 'April', but this may perhaps just be an error.

For May, *maiatz* is a Romance loan, while *ostail*, *ostaro* and *orril* are all from *(h)osto* or *orri*, both 'leaf', and *lorail* is from *lore*, B *lora* 'flower'.

For June, *ekain* is uncertain, but is most likely from *eki* 'sun' plus *gain* 'top': June is when the sun is at its highest. This word is chiefly Low Navarrese, but it has been taken over as the standard word. The G R Sal Aezk words are from *garagar* 'barley', the last three with *-zaro* 'season'. The G word is the B name for 'July'. B *bag(ir)il* is mysterious: Azkue's suggested derivation from *baba* 'bean' does not look promising, nor does that from *bago* 'beech'. A derivation from B *ebagi* 'cut' looks linguistically acceptable, but what exactly is cut in June? The northern *errearo* is transparently from *erre* 'burn' plus *-aro* 'season'. The obscure *arramaiatz* is 'second May'.

For July, *uztail* appears to be straightforwardly, if unexpectedly, from *uzta* 'grain, harvest'. The B term is explained under June, while the eastern *gari-(i)l* is from *gari* 'wheat'.

For August, *abuztu* is a Romance loan, while *agorril* is from *agor* 'dry'. The hapax *daguenil* has been widely interpreted as **dagoen-il* '(the) month which is, the current month' (*dagoen* is the relative form of *dago* 'it is'), but Michelena prefers to see a derivation from **uda-goen-il*, where *uda* is 'summer' and *goen* is the superlative of *goi* 'high': hence 'month of highest summer'.

For September, *irail* is apparently from *ira* 'fern', while the northern *buruil* is from *buru* 'head', presumably (one supposes) from the prominence in this month of the heads of corn in the fields. The Pyrenean word is elsewhere 'October'. G *garoil* is from *garo* 'fern'.

For October, *urril* is mysterious: the often proposed derivation from *urre* 'gold' is conceivable but not obviously right. The northern variants *urri* and *urrieta* are also applied in places to September. The Pyrenean word is elsewhere November. The obscure *bildil* is apparently from *bildu* 'gather', i.e., 'harvest'.

For November, *(h)azaro* is from *hazi* 'planting seeds' plus *-aro* 'time': *azaro* is also in widespread use as a common noun meaning 'time for planting seeds'. The variant *hazil* is from the same source. The Aezk word is elsewhere 'December'; the other Pyrenean dialects have literally 'first *abendu*' here. Old B *zemendi(a)* is odd; Latin SEMEN 'seed' has been suggested as the source.

For December, *abendu* is a loan from Latin ADVENTU 'advent', while *gabonil* is literally 'Christmas-month' (*gabon*, literally 'good night' (< *gau on*), is 'Christmas' in Basque); *lotazil* is apparently a compound of *hazil* 'seeding', perhaps involving *loti* 'sound sleep', a derivative of *lo* 'sleep', and *neguil* is from *negu* 'winter'. The Pyrenean words are literally 'second *abendu*' and 'last *abendu*'.

The names of the seasons are as follows:

spring	*udaberri*, Aezk Sal *primad(e)ra*, R *bedatse*
summer	*uda*
autumn	*udazken*, Aezk *larrazken*, Sal *azaro*, R *urriet*
winter	*negu*

'Spring' is 'new summer'; the Aezk Sal word is a Romance loan; the R word is from *bedar* 'grass'. 'Autumn' is 'last summer'; the Aezk word is 'last pasture'; the Sal and R words are elsewhere the names of October or November.

There is a distinct word for 'last year' (*ihaz* ~ *igaz* ~ *iaz*); this is of unknown origin. 'This year' is *aurten*, formed from *urte* 'year' with locative *-n* and apparently with the distal demonstrative exceptionally preposed. All other time expressions of the type 'last ...', 'next ...' or 'this ...' are formed syntactically: *joan zen astean* 'last week' (lit. 'in the week that went'), *datorren urtean* 'next year' (lit. 'in the year that is coming'), *aste honetan* 'this week' (lit. 'in this week').

Basque folklore preserves substantial remnants of an event called *Olentzaro*, a festival associated with the winter solstice; Olentzaro is sometimes personified, usually as an ugly and deformed boy. The second element of the name is surely *-zaro* 'season', but the first element is obscure. However, since a variant *Onentzaro* is widely attested, many have concluded that the first element is simply *onen* 'best', and that the name corresponds directly to Spanish *Nochebuena* 'Christmas', literally 'good night'.

5.9.6 Body parts

The more frequent non-compound body-part names are generally native and seemingly ancient, though there are a few Romance loans, such as the words for 'leg' and 'cheek'. Compound names are in most cases not very ancient.

abdomen	*errai*
Adam's apple	*zintzursagar* (*zintzur* 'throat' + *sagar* 'apple'), *gorgoil*
ankle	*orkatila* ~ *txorkatila*, *aztalbeharri* (*aztal* 'thigh' + *beharri* 'ear'), *kabila*
anus	*ipurtzulo* (*ipurdi* 'buttocks' + *zulo* 'hole'), *uzki* (? (*p*)*utz* 'puff of air, fart' + -*ki* NFS)
appendix	*hestemutur* (*heste* 'intestine' + *mutur* 'extremity')
arm	*beso*
armpit	*besazpi* (*beso* 'arm' + *azpi* 'below'), *galtzarpe* (*galtzar* 'side of the body, chest, arm, (a derivative of the Romance loan *galtza*(*k*) 'trousers, shorts') + -*pe* 'below')
artery	*zain*
back	*bizkar*
backbone	*bizkar-hezur* (*bizkar* 'back' + *hezur* 'bone')
beard	*bizar*
belly	See **stomach**
bile, gall	*behaztun* ~ *behazun* ~ *beazuma*, *bedamin*
bladder	*puxika* ~ *bixika* (< Lat VESSICA)
blood	*odol*
body	*soin* (also 'torso' and formerly 'shoulder'), *gorputz* (< Lat CORPUS)
bone	*hezur* ~ B *azur* ~ R *enzur* (< *enazur)
brain	*garun*, *burumuin* (*buru* 'head' + *muin* 'inner part, marrow, pith'), *muin* (reduction of the preceding)
breast, chest	*bular*, *papo* ~ *papar*, *kolko* ~ *golko* (< Lat COLPU)

The first word looks ancient; the second cannot be. The last word strictly denotes the space between one's chest and one's clothes (or, in the case of a woman, the space between her breasts); it is commonly used with reference to carrying or hiding something in this location.

breast (female)	*bular*, *ugatz*, *diti* ~ *titi*
breath	*arnas*(*a*), *hats*
buttocks	*ipurdi*
calf	*berna* (< Lat PERNA 'ham'), *zangoaztal* (*zango* 'leg' + *aztal* 'heel'), *zangosagar* (*zango* + *sagar* 'apple')
cheek	*masaila* ~ *maxela* ~ *matraila* ~ *matela* (< Lat *MAXELLA 'jaw'), L *ahutz*

chest	See **breast**
chin	*kokots* ~ B *okotz* (also 'snout, muzzle' of an animal) (a derivative of *kokot* 'nape')
cleavage	*bulartarte* (*bular* 'breast' + *-tarte* 'between')
clitoris	*emazakil* (*eme* 'female' + *zakil* 'penis')
cranium	See **skull**
crotch	*hankarte* (*anka* 'leg' + *arte* 'between')
dandruff	*burukozahi, ezkabia, zolda*
ear	B G *belarri* ~ L LN Z *beharri* HN *begarri* ~ HN R Sal *bearri* (< **berarri*)

This word may be related to *behatu* 'look at, listen to'.

eardrum	*belarrimintz* (*belarri* 'ear' + *mintz* 'membrane')
earlobe	*belarrimami* (*belarri* 'ear' + *mami* 'fleshy part')
elbow	*ukondo* ~ G *ukalondo* ~ arch B *ukaondo* (< **ukarai* 'wrist' + *ondo* 'next to, below'), *besainko* (< *besain* 'whirling the arm', < *beso* 'arm')
eye	*begi*
eyebrow	*bepuru* (*begi* 'eye' + *buru* 'head'), *bekain* (*begi* + *gain* 'top')
eyelash	*betile* (*begi* 'eye' + *ile* 'hair')
eyelid	*betazal* (*begi* 'eye' + *azal* 'skin')
face	*aurpegi* (*aurre* 'front' + *begi* 'eye'), *musu* (< Rom), *begi(bi)tarte* (*begi* 'eye' + (*bi*)*tarte* 'between')
faeces	*kaka* (< Rom)

The word *gorotz* ~ *korotz* (probably < Lat CROCEA 'saffron-coloured') is in most areas applied only to animal dung. 'Turd' is *mokordo*.

fart	(*p*)*utz, puzkar* ~ *uzker, haize, sabelaize, tarratada*
finger	*hatz, er*(*h*)*i*

Some varieties have *behatz*, properly 'toe', presumably under the influence of Spanish, in which *dedo* means 'finger' or 'toe' indifferently. The compound *hatzamarrak* is widely used for 'fingers'; this is probably **hatz hamarrak* 'the ten fingers', though with an odd word order, whence *hatzamar* for 'finger' in some localities.

fingernail	*hatzazal* (*hatz* 'finger' + *azal* 'skin'), *hazkazal* (? variant of preceding), *hatzoskol* (*hatz* + *oskol* 'hard outer covering, shell'), *oskol*
fingertip	*eripunta* (*eri* 'finger' + *punta* 'point'), *erimami* (*eri* + *mami* 'fleshy part'), *erimoko, behatz-mutur* (*behatz* 'finger' + *mutur*), etc.

fist	*ukabil* (*uko* 'forearm' + *-bil* 'round')
foot	*oin*, L LN Z also *hanka*, *zango*, elsewhere 'leg'
forearm	*besaurre* (*beso* 'arm' + *aurre* 'front'), *uko* (archaic)
forehead	*bekoki* (*begi* 'eye' + ?, or a derivative of *beko*), (archaic) *beko* (< Rom), *belar*, *kopeta* ('top of the head' in places)
gall	See **bile**
gall bladder	*behazun-maskuri*, *behaztun-xixku*
groin	*iztai* (*izter* 'thigh' + *-egi* NFS), *izterrondo* (*izter* + *ondo* 'next to')
gums	*oi*, *haginoi* (*hagin* 'molar' + *oi*)
gut(s)	See **intestine**
hair	*ile* ~ B *ule* etc.

The startling range of dialect variants of this word might descend from either **iLe* or **uLe*. The word is also widely attested in the sense of 'wool', leading Uhlenbeck to suggest that it might be a loan word from Germanic (cf. Gothic *wulla* 'wool'). 'A single hair' is *bilo*, borrowed either from Lat VILLU 'hairlike projection' or from a cross of this word with PILU 'hair'.

hand	*esku*
head	*buru*
heart	*bihotz*
heel	*aztal*, *ostiko*, *orpo*, *oinburu* (*oin* 'foot' + *buru* 'head'), *zankarroi*
hip	*hankagain* (*hanka* 'leg' + *gain* 'top')
hymen	*emamintz* (*eme* 'female' + *mintz* 'membrane' (< Rom))
intestine	*hertze* ~ *heste*
joint	*giltza* (otherwise 'key'), *hezurgiltza* (*hezur* 'bone' + *giltza*)
kidney	*giltzurrin* ~ *giltzurrun* ~ B *guntzurrun* (? *giltza* 'joint, hip' + ?)
knee	*belaun*
knuckle	*koskor*
lap	*altzo*, *magal*
leg	*hanka* (< Rom; cf. Sp *anca* 'haunch'), *zango* ~ *zanko* (< Rom; see Corominas and Pascual (1980) under *zanca*), *berna* (< Lat PERNA 'calf')
lip	*ezpain*
liver	*gibel*
loins	*solomo* (< Rom; cf. Sp *lomos*)
lung	*birika* (archaic *biri*)
marrow	*mami* (< Rom), *muin* ~ *mun* ~ *fuin* ~ (*h*)*un* (< **bune*,

	possibly < Lat FUNE 'rope'), *barnemuin* (*barne* 'interior' + *muin*)
menstruation	*hilabeteak* (pl. of *hilabete* 'month'), *hilabeteko* (*hilabete* + *-ko*), *hileroko* (*hilero* 'every month' + *-ko*), *emalege* (*eme* 'female' + *lege* 'law')
moustache	*bibote* (< Sp *bigote*), *ezpaingaineko* (*ezpain* 'lip' + *gain* 'above' + *-ko*)
mouth	*aho* (B G *ago* ~ *abo* is secondary)
mucus	*muki* ~ *muku* (< Rom)
nape	*lepagain* (*lepo* 'neck' + *gain* 'top'), *lepondo* (*lepo* + *ondo* 'next to'), *kokot* (< Rom; cf. Occ *cogòt*, Sp *cogote*), *garondo* (*gara* 'high point' + *ondo* 'next to, below'), *garkola* ~ *garkhora* (*gara* + ? Sp *cola* 'tail'), *garkotxe* (*gara* + ? *kokot(s)* 'nape')

Azkue suggests that *gara* means specifically 'skull' in these formations; this is possible, but the word is not attested in this sense.

navel	*zilbor* ('belly' in places)
neck	*lepo*
nerve	*kirio, zain, nerbio* (< Sp)
nipple	*diti, ditimutur* (*diti* 'breast' + *mutur* 'extremity'), *ditiburu* (*diti* + *buru* 'head'), *ditipunta* (*diti* + *punta* 'point'), *bularmutur* (*bular* 'breast' + *mutur*)
nose	*sudur*
nostril	*sudurzulo* (*sudur* 'nose' + *zulo* 'hole'), *musuzulo* (*musu* 'face' + *zulo*)
oesophagus	*hestegorri* (*heste* 'intestine' + *gorri* 'red')
ovary	*arraulztegi* (*arraultza* 'egg' + *-tegi* 'place')
palate	*ahogain* (*aho* 'mouth' + *gain* 'top'), *ahozeru* (*aho* + *zeru* 'sky'), *ahosabai* (*aho* + *sabai* 'roof, ceiling')
palm	*eskubarne* ~ *eskubarru* (*esku* 'hand' + *barne* ~ *barru* 'interior'), *ahur* (< *aurre* 'front'), *zehe*
pancreas	*are*
pelvis	*azpilezur* (*azpil* 'platter' + *hezur* 'bone')
penis	*zakil, berga* (< Rom)

The second word is applied chiefly to animals.

phlegm	*gorro, karkaisa*
pubis	*sabelpe* (*sabel* 'belly' + *-pe* 'below')
pupil (of eye)	*begi-nini* (*begi* 'eye' + *nini* 'child')
rib	*saihets* (also 'side'), *saihetsezur* (*saihets* + *hezur* 'bone')
saliva	*listu* ~ *txistu, tu* ~ *ttu* (imitative), *xut* ~ *xux*
scrotum	*potrazal* (*potro* 'testicle' + *azal* 'skin')

semen	*hazi* (lit. 'seed')
shin	*hankezur* (*hanka* 'leg' + *hezur* 'bone')
shoulder	*sorbalda, besaburu* (*beso* 'arm' + *buru* 'head'), *besagain* (*beso* + *gain* 'top'), *soingain* (*soin* 'body' + *gain*), *bizkargain* (*bizkar* 'back' + *gain*), *soingiltza* (*soin* + *giltza* 'joint'), R (and archaic) *soin*, Aezk Sal *soinegi*
sinew	*zain*
skin	*azal, larru ~ narru* (also 'hide')
skull	*buruhezur* (*buru* 'head' + *hezur* 'bone'), *kasko ~ kaskar ~ kasket* (< Rom), *kaskezur* (*kasko* + *hezur*), *garezur* (*gara* 'high point' + *hezur*), LN *kali ~ kalo*, Aezk *kalabera*
sole	*oinazpi* (*oin* 'foot' + *azpi* 'under'), *zola* (< Rom; cf. Old Fr *sole*)
spleen	*bare* (also 'slug' (zool.))
stomach, belly	*sabel, tripa* (< Sp)
sweat	*izerdi*
temple	*loki*
tendon	*zain, zainzuri* (*zain* + *zuri* 'white')
testicle	*barrabil* (? + *-bil* 'round'), *potro* (< Rom)
thigh	*izter, aztal*
throat	*zintzur, eztarri*
thumb	*erpuru* (*eri* 'finger' + *buru* 'head'), *hatz*
toe	*behatz* (*behe* 'lower' + *hatz* 'finger')
tongue	*mihi ~ min* (< **mini* < **bini*), G *mingain* (*min* + *gain* 'top')
tooth	*hortz* (incisor), *hagin* (molar)

The word *hortz* is often used for 'tooth' in general, but 'teeth' is commonly rendered by the compound *hortz-haginak*.

torso	*soin* (also 'body')
trunk	*gorputzenbor* (*gorputz* 'body' + *enbor* '(tree)trunk'), *enbor*
umbilical cord	*zilborreste* (*zilbor* 'navel' + *heste* 'intestine')
urine	*gernu, txiza* (imitative), *piza ~ pixa* (imitative)
uvula	*gangaila ~ gargail*
vagina	*emagina* (*eme* 'female' + *magina* 'sheath'), *emabide* (*eme* + *bide* 'path'), *ematutu* (*eme* + *tutu* 'tube')
vein	*zain*
vulva	*alu, motz, emakuntza* (*eme* 'female' + *-kuntza* NFS), *potorro ~ potxor*, etc. (vulgar slang; < Rom), *tutu* ('tube'; nursery word)

Here *alu* is the most widespread word, while *motz* is somewhat archaic. Basque has a large number of regional terms in *pot- ~ pott- ~ potx-*, all of which are best regarded as coarse slang; see Etxezarreta (1983) for a catalogue. Similar words are found throughout Iberian Romance and Occitan (and even Italian), and the Basque words are undoubtedly derived from Romance. See Corominas and Pascual (1980) under *potra* for a discussion of the source.

waist   *gerri* ~ B *garri*
windpipe   *zintzurreste* (*zintzur* 'throat' + *heste* 'intestine')
wrist   *ukarai* (*uko* 'forearm' + *garai* 'high part'), *eskumutur* ~
               eskutur (*esku* 'hand' + *mutur* 'snout'), *besamutur* (*beso*
               'arm' + *mutur*)

In several publications, beginning with his 1927 article, Uhlenbeck pointed out the striking number of these terms which begin with *b*-, and especially with *be*-: *buru* 'head', *begi* 'eye', *belarri* 'ear', *bizar* 'beard', *bular* 'breast', *beso* 'arm', *bihotz* 'heart', *birika* 'lung', *bare* 'spleen', *bizkar* 'back', *behaztun* 'bile' and *belaun* 'knee'; to these we may add *mihi* ~ *min* 'tongue' (< **bini*). He defended the view that **b(e)-* was an ancient prefix attached to names of body parts, and others have seen this as an ancient dual prefix related to *bi(ga)* 'two'. This view was received cautiously but sympathetically by Michelena, in spite of the very great rarity of ancient prefixes in Basque. Michelena (1958) suggests that this **b(e)-* might in fact represent a fossilized attachment of *bere* 'his/her own', and might further have represented inalienable possession in general, rather than body parts specifically. I confess that I am rather sceptical about all of this. Only a small minority of body-part names begin with *b*-, and even fewer with *be*-. But *b*- is one of the commonest initial consonants in Basque. To take one crude but indicative measure, Azkue's 1905 dictionary, which excludes recent loans from Romance, lists seventy-four pages of words beginning with *b*-, more than for any other consonant except *z*-, and this makes no allowance for the very common development of original **b*- into *m*- in Basque (today the once non-existent *m*- is also one of the most frequent initial consonants in the language, with fifty-eight pages in Azkue). It seems to me, therefore, that the presence of a dozen or so words beginning with *b*-, alongside several dozen lacking *b*-, is an observation requiring no explanation. Indeed, even English, with its much larger set of initial consonants, has the body-part names *brain*, *brow*, *beard*, *breast*, *bosom*, *bust*, *back*, *belly*, *bowel*, *buttocks*, *bile*, *blood*, *bone* and, of course, *body*. Readers who do not share my scepticism should be aware, however, that it is completely out of order to assert, as several linguists have asserted, the existence of a 'body-part prefix **b(e)-*' as a fact: it is no more than a speculation enjoying some degree of plausibility.

5.9.7 Tools and implements

The notion that certain tool names in Basque are constructed from a stem meaning 'stone' was apparently first suggested by L. L. Bonaparte, but it has been independently proposed by the Basque philosopher Unamuno, by the Basque anthropologist Julio Caro Baroja and doubtless by others.

The evidence, ignoring obvious variants and derivatives, rests on just five words:

(*h*)*aizkora*	'axe'
(*h*)*aitzur*	'heavy hoe'
(*h*)*aizter* ~ *haiztur*	'shears'
(*h*)*aiztur*	'tongs, forceps'
aizto (R)	'knife'

(I ignore here one or two additional words which have sometimes been very dubiously tacked on, such as *azkon* 'dart', a word of unknown origin which is also widely found in Romance (e.g., Spanish *azcona*).) The suggestion is that all five of these words are based on the word (*h*)*aitz* 'rock, stone'. (In fact, this word means 'rock' only in part of the French Basque Country; elsewhere it means 'mountain with a bare rocky top, crag', but there are enough derivatives like (*h*)*aitzurdin* 'marble' (lit. 'bluestone') to show that 'stone' is probably the original meaning of (*h*)*aitz*.)

Is this a safe conclusion? First of all, the word (*h*)*aizkora* can be dismissed out of hand: it is a transparent loan word from Latin ASCIOLA 'axe', an etymology proposed decades ago by the Basque linguist Gorostiaga and accepted without reservation by Michelena and by most vasconists since. (The development of original intervocalic *-l-* into *-r-* is absolutely regular in Basque, and there are abundant parallels for the seemingly unexpected diphthong in the first syllable – or perhaps this word was contaminated by the other tool names.)

The other four cannot be dismissed as loan words: they appear to be ancient, and they appear to be built on the same stem. But is this stem the word for 'stone'? A complication is that the Roncalese dialect, which preserves ancient nasals better than other dialects, has the forms *aintzur* 'heavy hoe', *ainzter* 'shears', *ainztur* 'tongs' and *ainzto* 'knife', and some of these nasal forms also appear in other dialects. Michelena therefore reconstructs the first element in these tool names as **ani(t)z-* or **ane(t)z-* (an ancient intervocalic *n* is regularly lost in Basque, but sometimes shows up in the form exhibited by the Roncalese words).

The word (*h*)*aitz*, however, is *aitz* in Roncalese as elsewhere, and no such form as **(h)aintz* is attested for the meaning 'stone'. This, of course, does not prove that the tool names do not contain the word for 'stone', but it's certainly not encouraging: why should the nasal be lost in the simplest form of the word but retained in the derivatives, even when such retention leads to the presence of what is, in Basque terms, the very uncomfortable consonant cluster -*nzt*-, as in *ainzto*? Moreover, the transparent derivatives of (*h*)*aitz*, like the word for 'marble' cited above, show no trace of a nasal in any dialect, though of course they might simply be more recent formations than the tool names, and indeed Michelena (1964b: 138) cautiously suggests that the word *haitz* itself might derive from *anitz or *anetz.

On balance, then, it is not totally out of the question that *four* Basque tool names are derived from a word for 'stone', but such evidence as there is is not at all encouraging.

In any case, what could have been the motivation for such formations? Presumably the suggestion is that the tool names were coined at a time when the ancestral Basques were still using stone tools. Well, stone hoes and stone knives seem plausible enough, but I'm a little taken aback by the suggestion that the Basques might also have used stone shears and stone tongs. Stone tongs?

There are no other tool names of a relevant form. One or two overenthusiastic reports which I have seen attempt to introduce the word *hezur* 'bone' (ancient *enazur) into the discussion, but there are no Basque tool names remotely resembling this word.

Finally, what is the point of all this? Even if the Basques did construct a few tool names from the word for 'stone', what interesting conclusion can we draw? That the Basques have ancestors who used stone tools? Everybody has ancestors who used stone tools. That the Basques must have been in the modern Basque Country since the Stone Age? This is a shrieking *non sequitur*. If the Basques had migrated to western Europe from somewhere else in the first millennium BC, would they have changed all their tool names just to celebrate the event?

The vast majority of the names of tools and implements in Basque are loan words: *haizkora* 'axe', *mailu* 'hammer', *marteilu* 'sledgehammer', *zerra* 'saw', *tenaza* 'pliers', *marmita* 'cooking pot', *bahe* 'sieve', *pala* 'paddle' (e.g., for baking bread), *para* 'shovel, spade', *paru* 'pole', *sega* 'scythe', *errota* and *arroda*, both 'wheel', *zaku* 'bag, sack', *xako* 'leather bag for wine', *golde* 'plough' (< CULTER 'ploughshare', even though the plough is well attested in the region long before the Roman settlement), and probably *orga* 'cart, wagon' (< ORGANA; the Basque word is traditionally used as a *plurale tantum, orgak*). Some, however, are native: *sarde* 'pitchfork', *itze* 'nail', *giltza* 'key', *igitai* 'sickle', *gurdi* 'cart', *gurpil* 'wheel' (originally 'cartwheel' (< *gurdi* 'cart' + -*bil* 'round')), *laia* 'two-pronged fork for loosening soil', and the four items in (*h*)*ai*(*t*)*z*- cited above. A few compounds, like *haitzur-pikotx* 'pick-axe', are half native and half borrowed.

5.9.8 Compass points and hands

The names of the compass points show some regional variation. All of them are compounds involving the word *alde* 'side, region'; only the words for 'north' and 'south' can appear in compounds without this element. Most of these terms are derived from words having to do with winds or with the sun.

north   *iparralde* (in compounds *ipar*), *goialde, negualde*

The element *ipar*, common to all dialects, is mysterious, but Michelena (1957) has suggested that it might be a specialized variant of *ibar* 'valley' extracted from the compound *iparraize* 'north wind' (*haize* 'wind'), originally, perhaps, 'valley wind', i.e., 'wind from the valley'. There is a widespread variant *ifar(ralde)*. Western varieties have an alternative word *goialde*, from *goi* 'high place'; it is far from clear to me why the north should be regarded as high, since the land rises steadily in travelling from north to south in Bizkaia and Gipuzkoa. The form *negualde* (*negu* 'winter') is marginally attested in the French Basque Country. Azkue (1905) remarks that fishermen use *ipar* to denote the east, rather than the north.

south   *hegoalde*, in compounds *hego*

The word *hego* means 'south wind' as well as 'south', and *hegoalde* probably just meant originally 'where the south wind comes from'. Attempts at linking *hego* to *egun* 'day' have been quite unsuccessful.

east   *ekialde, eguzkialde, sortalde, iguzkibegi, ekhijalkigia*

The eastern form *ekialde* is a compound of eastern *eki* 'sun', while western *eguzkialde* is an identical compound with western *eguzki* 'sun'. The alternative *sortalde*, found throughout the country, is from *sortu* 'be born', but 'rise' when speaking of the sun; Azkue (1905) suggests that this word is more a literary coinage than a popular word. The word *iguzkibegi* is *iguzki* 'sun' + *begi* 'eye'; it is weakly attested in the French Basque Country. Harriet's dictionary cites a northern form *ekhijalkigia*, from *ekhi* 'sun' + *jalki* 'emerge', with a puzzling suffix.

west   *mendebalde, sartalde, itsasalde, ekhisargia*

The eastern form *mendebalde* is a compound of *mendebal*, the name of a wind blowing from the northwest, with the usual Basque haplology. This in turn is doubtless a loan from some Romance formation along the lines of French *vent d'aval* 'valley wind'; such formations are common in the Romance languages spoken in the Pyrenees. Western *sartalde* is from *sartu* 'go in', but 'set' when speaking of the sun. The word *itsasalde* is literally 'seacoast', and is so used everywhere, but the sense of 'west' is marginally attested in the French Basque Country. Finally, *ekhisargia* is a Z form, from *ekhi* 'sun' + *sar(tu)* 'enter, go in', plus the same puzzling suffix seen above.

The Basque words are far less frequent than their English equivalents; the names of local landmarks are generally preferred in giving directions. None of these words ever appears in place names, though there is one unusual surname containing *ipar*: *Iparragirre*, a compound of the common Basque surname *Agirre* which perhaps originally denoted a distinct branch of the widespread Agirre clan. In modern usage, the labels *Iparraldea* and *Hegoaldea* are commonly applied to the French and Spanish parts of the Basque Country, respectively.

The words for 'left' and 'right' are respectively *ezker* and *eskuin* ~ *eskubi* ~ *eskuma* ~ *eskoa*. The first word, which is found in Castilian and Portuguese, which are thought to have borrowed it from Basque, is obscure. It may contain the morph *-ker* (< *-ger*?) identified by Lakarra (1995) as occurring in a number of ancient formations and possibly meaning 'bad', in which case a derivation *esku-ger* 'bad hand' suggests itself, though the sibilant is wrong. The second word is generally regarded as deriving from *esku-on* 'good hand'.

5.9.9 Verbs of being and having

In all varieties of Basque the ordinary copular verb is the highly irregular *izan*. This verb is used both for equational sentences and for expressing class membership: hence, for example, *Bizkaiko hiriburua Bilbo da* 'The capital of Bizkaia is Bilbao' and *Bilbo hiri handia da* 'Bilbao is a big city.' Word order and pronouns are invoked when it is necessary to distinguish the two types of sentence: *Irakaslea naiz* 'I'm a teacher', but *Irakaslea ni naiz* or *Ni naiz irakaslea* 'I'm the teacher', 'The teacher is me.' (And, as we saw in Chapter 2, *izan* is also the verb used as the auxiliary in constructing the indicative periphrastic forms of intransitive verbs.)

In northern varieties, *izan* is commonly used in all circumstances, including with animate subjects and with locative complements. Thus, a northerner says *Aita etxean da* 'Father is in the house' and *Txindoki Gipuzkoan da* 'Txindoki (a mountain) is in Gipuzkoa.'

There is, however, a second copula: *egon*. Historically, this verb means 'wait' or 'remain', and still does so in the imperative: the inflected *Hago!* and *Zaude!* and the uninflected *Egon!* all mean 'Wait!' throughout the country. In northern varieties, this verb may be used as a copula in restricted circumstances: the subject must be animate, and the complement must be locative or comitative. Hence northerners may say *Aita etxean dago* 'Father is in the house' and *Zakurra etxean dago* 'The dog is in the house' (both with *egon*), but they can only say *Ene liburua etxean da* 'My book is in the house' (with *izan*).

In southern varieties, however, the use of *egon* has been greatly extended, apparently under the influence of Spanish, and this verb is now used in all circumstances in which Spanish uses its verb *estar*, while *izan* is used where

Spanish uses *ser*. Hence, in the south, *egon* is used to express all temporary states and conditions, and it is used with all locative complements. Thus southerners say *Moxkortuta dago* 'She's drunk', *Pozik nago* 'I'm happy', *Saldea hotza dago* 'The soup is cold', *Nere liburua etxean dago* 'My book is in the house', and *Txindoki Gipuzkoan dago* 'Txindoki is in Gipuzkoa.' All such sentences would require *izan* in the north (though occasionally with other minor differences). Somewhat surprisingly, southerners even say *Hil dago* 'He's dead', even though death is anything but a temporary condition; this is undoubtedly a calque on Spanish *Está muerto*. Interestingly, even though Spanish has *Está casada* for 'She's married', Basque seems to prefer *Ezkondua da*, though the speakers I have consulted agree that *Ezkondua dago* is also possible. This is the only case I have encountered in which southern Basque usage does not faithfully follow that of Spanish.

Something similar has happened with the verbs meaning 'have'. As we saw in Chapter 4, the oldest verb for 'have' is the defective -*du*-, attributed to a lost verb **edun*. This is everywhere the verb used as the auxiliary in constructing the indicative periphrastic forms of transitive verbs. Again, in northern varieties, it is also the verb ordinarily used in forming predications of possession: *Boitura berria dut* 'I have a new car', *Begi urdinak ditut* 'I have blue eyes' and so on. There is another verb, *eduki* (in the north, more usually *iduki*), which means 'hold', 'hold on to' or 'contain'. Thus, while *Liburua dut* (with **edun*) means 'I have a/the book' (i.e., I own it), *Liburua daukat* (with *eduki*) means 'I have the book in my hand', 'I'm holding the book.'

Southern varieties have again greatly extended the use of *eduki*, and again on the model of Castilian. In Castilian, the verb *haber*, descended from Latin HABERE 'have', is now entirely confined to use as an auxiliary in constructing periphrastic forms, and *tener*, from Latin TENERE 'hold', has become the ordinary verb for 'have'. Southern Basque follows this pattern exactly: southerners say *Kotxe berria daukat* 'I have a new car' and *Begi urdinak dauzkat* 'I have blue eyes.'

The use of these four verbs in southern Basque thus provides an outstanding example of the influence of Spanish grammar. Northern Basque has been subject to no such influence, since French does not make the lexical distinctions which Spanish makes.

Verbs meaning 'turn into', like *bihurtu*, take a predicate with no determiner: *Otso bihurtu zen* 'He turned into a wolf', not **Otsoa*.

5.9.10 Verbs of motion

Verbs of motion in Basque present a few interesting features. The commonest such verb is *joan* 'go', which can also mean 'go away' or 'leave'. This verb is used when a source or goal is implied or stated: *Etxera noa* 'I'm going home'; *Nora zoaz?* 'Where are you going?'; *Emaztea joan zait* 'My wife has left me.' The imperfective participle of this verb is the regular *joaten* in the south. In the north, it is either *joaiten*, showing the additional *i* explained in Chapter 4, or the quite extraordinary *johan*, a form which is inexplicable. Not only is *johan* morphologically without parallel, but the contrast between perfective *joan* and imperfective *johan* is phonologically anomalous: in the aspirating dialects, it is not normally possible to distinguish word-forms by the presence or absence of *h* between two non-high vowels. No explanation has ever been proposed for this mysterious behaviour.

There is a *-ra-* causative of *joan*, **eraoan*, which appears as *eroan* in B and as *eraman* in the other dialects, with the sense of 'take away', as in *Liburua eraman dut* 'I took the book away' (i.e., 'I went off with the book'). In at least one area of Lapurdi, however, *joan* can serve as its own transitive, and one can say *Liburua joan dut* 'I took the book away.' This is impossible in other varieties, in which *joan* is strictly intransitive.

For 'come', the most widespread verb is *etorri*, which is found throughout the country. This verb too is used when a source or a goal is stated or implied: *Haizea iparraldetik dator* 'The wind is coming from the north'; *Zatoz hona!* 'Come here!' Again, some northern varieties show an extraordinary imperfective participle: in place of the usual *etortzen*, they have *heldu*, which is otherwise the perfective participle of the verb meaning 'arrive'. In the east, there is a second, synonymous, verb, which appears as *jaugin* in LN but is irregularly contracted to *jin* elsewhere. (There is no doubt that these are the same verb, since no variety has both.) Neither *etorri* nor *jaugin ~ jin* can ever be used transitively, nor does either have a *-ra-* causative: the corresponding transitive verb is the unrelated *ekarri* 'bring'.

In Basque, the speaker is always the point of reference for these verbs, where relevant, and hence, where an English-speaker calling out to a companion says *I'm coming*, a Basque says *Ba noa*, literally 'I'm going.'

There is another exceedingly common verb of motion: *ibili*. This verb has no English equivalent in isolation; it may perhaps be glossed as 'go about', 'be active' or 'be doing', though it is a true lexical verb, rather than an auxiliary. It is usually used when no goal of motion is expressed or implied, and it is commonly used with some kind of adverbial complement expressing the particular kind of motion or activity: *igeri ibili* 'go swimming' (*igeri* 'swimming'); *zaldiz ibili* 'ride on horseback, go riding' (*zaldiz* 'on horseback'); *oihuka ibili* 'go about shouting' (*oihuka* 'shouting'); *potikoka ibili* 'crawl on all fours' (*potikoka* 'on all fours'). It also has a number of related meanings, such as 'act like', 'behave', 'run' (of a machine)', and especially 'fare': everywhere *Nola zabiltza?* or *Zelan zabiltza?* 'How are you doing?' is a common way of greeting someone, and *Amona nola dabil?* 'How's your grandmother?' represents the ordinary way of enquiring about someone else. In most varieties this verb is strictly intransitive, though again in a few northern varieties it can be construed transitively in the sense of 'bring along, take along'. It has a *-ra-* causative, *erabili*, which can mean 'put in motion', 'shake' (a liquid), or 'cultivate' (land), but this verb most commonly just means 'use', and it is the ordinary verb for expressing this meaning.

In general, Basque uses lexically distinct verbs to express going in, out, up or down. The verb *sartu* means 'go in, enter', while 'go out' is any of *jalgi* ~ *elki* (probably from **eelki*), *irten* ~ *urten*, or *atera* (derived from the allative of *ate* 'door'). For 'go up, ascend, climb', Basques use *igan* ~ *igo(n)*, and for 'go down', 'descend', *jaitsi* or *beheratu* (the last from the allative of *behe* 'below'). I might also mention *kendu*, which means 'remove oneself, get out of the way'. Some of these verbs can also be construed transitively: thus *sartu* 'insert, put in', *atera* 'carry out', *beheratu* 'carry down, bring down', *kendu* 'remove, subtract'. None of them has a *-ra-* causative except *igan*, whose causative *iragan* unexpectedly means 'pass, cross; happen; spend' (time).

All the verbs cited here take an ablative complement to express a source of motion and an allative complement to express a goal, except that *sartu* 'enter, insert' can (and most often does) take a locative complement to express a goal.

5.9.11 Animal names

It is perhaps stretching a point to treat animal names as a 'structured' part of the lexicon, but these words none the less offer enough points of interest to make them worth recording here. I list the words by the generic term; names for particular varieties are, with a few exceptions, discussed under the generic heading. Creatures which have not been indigenous to the Basque Country in recent times are, of course, not included, since all such names are recent loans from Romance, though I make an exception for 'turkey'. Naturally, it is impossible to record here every local form or variant ever recorded; I therefore confine myself to the most widespread terms and those others which are particularly interesting. Observe that a large number of names for insects and other small creatures, especially for 'creepy-crawlies', are clearly 'expressive' formations, as revealed by the high frequency of *m* and *tx* and of vowel assonance; I will not trouble to point these out individually.

anchovy	*antxoa* (< Italian), *bokarta*
animal	*abere* (< Lat HABERE), *animalia* (< Lat), *piztia* (related to *bizi* 'alive'), *kabale* (< Rom)
	Many varieties distinguish *abere* 'domesticated animal' from *piztia* 'wild animal'.
ant	*inurri* ~ *txingurri* ~ *txindurri* ~ *zinaurri* ~ *(t)xinaurri*
	These regional variants are probably all derived from a

single ancestor, possibly *zinaurri* itself, though there are other possibilities, such as **zinagurri*. The western form *inurri* suggests, however, an earlier **ina(g)urri*, in which case the initial *(t)x-* of the other forms would represent one of the rare cases of palatalization by prefixing this morph, and *zinaurri* would then be a back formation.

asp	*sugegorri* (*suge* 'snake' + *gorri* 'red')
avocet	*zangaluze* (*zango* 'leg' + *luze* 'long')
badger	*azkoi(n)* ~ *azkon* (< **azkoni*), *azkonar*

It has often been thought that *azkoin* might be a compound of *hartz* 'bear' with an unknown second element.

barnacle	*lanperna* (< Rom; cf. Fr *bernache*)
bass	*lupina*, *berrugeta* (this is the sea bass)
bat	*saguzahar* (*sagu* 'mouse' + *zahar* 'old'), *gauenara* (*gau* 'night' + *enara* 'swallow'), Sal *apoañari* (*apo* 'toad' + *enara* 'swallow')
bear	*hartz* (possibly < IE; see section 6.4)
bedbug	*tximitxa* ~ *imintxa*, *zumitz*
bee	*erle*

This word is found everywhere and is clearly of some antiquity, even though its medial *-rl-* cluster is found in very few other words. It may derive from **ezle*; cf. *ezti* 'honey', *ezko* 'wax'. 'Bumblebee' is *erlamando* (*erle* + *mando* 'mule'). 'Drone' is *erlalfer* (*alfer* 'useless').

bird	*(t)xori*

This universal word is a diminutive of *zori*, which is now the Basque word for 'luck'. Michelena (1955) considers that *zori* probably originally meant 'bird', but that it acquired a secondary sense of 'omen' from the common practice of taking the flight of birds as omens (cf. Old Sp *auçe* 'omen' < Lat AVICE 'bird'); the palatalized form consequently became specialized to denote the creature.

blackbird	*zozo* ~ *xoxo*
bream	*urkula* ('sea bream' is *besigu* < Sp *besugo*)
bull	*zezen* ('young bull' is *zekor*)
butterfly	*tximeleta* ~ *mitxeleta*, *kalapitxi*, *pinpirin*, *pinpilinpauxa*, *inguma*

This impressive collection of regional terms can hardly represent anything of any great antiquity; most of these terms appear to be strongly phonaesthetic in motivation. Western *tximeleta* is scarcely attested before 1900; it appears to be a metathesis of *mitxeleta*, which is possibly formed from *Mitxel* 'Michael'. The word *kalapitxi* contains *bitxi* 'pretty', while *inguma* also means 'incubus' (a phantom which possesses sleepers).

cat *katu* ~ *gatu* (< Lat CATTU)

'Wildcat' is *basakatu* (*basa-* 'wild').

caterpillar *mamarru* (also 'creepy-crawly')
centipede *ehunzango* (*ehun* '100' + *zango* 'leg'), *ehunoindun* (*ehun* + *oin* 'foot' + *-dun* 'having')
chaffinch *neguta* (*negu* 'winter' + ?), *txonta*, *elurtxori* (*elur* 'snow' + *txori* 'bird'), *pinpintxori*
chicken *oilasko*

'Hen' is *oilo* ~ *ollo*, while 'cock' is the derivative *oilar* (*ar* 'male'). The word *oilasko* itself is a derivative with the unusual suffix *-sko*. The source word *oilo* ~ *ollo* is probably a loan from the same Romance source as Spanish *pollo* 'chicken' (< Lat PULLU); an original *bollo* would have lost initial *b-* before *o*. 'Pullet' is *oilanda*, with a diminutive suffix. 'Chick' is *txita* (imitative).

chipmunk *urtxintxa* (= 'squirrel')
cicada *txirrita* (probably imitative), *txitxer*
clam *txirla*
cockroach *labazomorro*, *mamurio*
cod *bakailo* ~ *makailo* (< Sp *bacalao* or a related Romance form)
cormorant *potorro*, *ubarroi*
cow *behi*

'Calf' is *(t)xahal* (< *xanal*), *idisko* (*idi* 'ox' + *-sko* dimin.), *zekor*, *xexenko* (double dimin. of *zezen* 'bull') or *behikume* (*behi* + *-kume* 'offspring'). 'Heifer' is variously *behigai* (*-gai* 'destined to be'), *biriga*, or *bilarrozi*. A two-year-old cow is a *biga(i)* ~ *bigae* (< *bigana*, from Lat *BIMANA* 'two-year-old heifer', from BIMU 'two years old', possibly influenced by *biga* 'two'), while a cow of 3–12 months is *bigantxa* (dimin. of *bigana*). The generic *ganadu* (< Sp *ganado*) is applied to any bovine animal.

crab *karramarro*

'Sea crab' is *hammarratz* < *hamar* 'ten' + *hatz* 'leg'; 'spider crab' is *txangurro* ~ *txangurru*.

crane	*kurrilo* ~ *kurlo* ~ *kurri* ~ kurro (< Rom; cf. Sp *grulla*)
crayfish	*zigala, otarrainska* (*otarrain* 'lobster' + *-ska* dimin.)
cricket	*kilkir* (imitative), *lakasta*
crow, raven	*bele* ~ *bela* (related to *beltz* 'black'?), *belatzaga, belatxinga, erroi, oskilaso*
cuckoo	*kuku* (imitative)
cuttlefish	*pota* ~ *potta, txautxi*
deer	*orein, orkatz* (also 'Pyrenean chamois'), *basahuntz* (*basa-* 'wild' + *ahuntz* 'goat')
dog	*or, zakur* ~ *txakur*

Now confined to eastern dialects, *or* (rarely *hor*) is also attested in western dialects in early texts. The form *zakur*, in western varieties usually palatalized to *txakur*, is now the most usual or only word in most parts of the country. 'Puppy' is *pottolo* ~ *potxolo*, one of several names for young animals from Rom *pot-*.

dogfish	*mielga*
dolphin	*izurde* ~ *gizaurde* (*giza-* 'man' + *urde* 'pig'; Azkue's derivation from **iz-* 'water' can be rejected; see section 5.10.6)
donkey	*asto*

Many have tried to interpret this as a loan from Lat ASINU (cf. Sp *asno*), but the phonology would be unparalleled. Moreover, the Roncalese dialect, which preserves ancient clusters better than other dialects, has *arsto*. Azkue suggests a derivation from **harzto*, a diminutive in *-to* from *hartz* 'bear'; this is phonologically impeccable if semantically unexpected.

dove	See **pigeon**
dragonfly	*sorginorratz* (*sorgin* 'witch' + *orratz* 'needle'), *txitxiburduntzi* (appears to involve *burdun* 'iron')
duck	*ahate* (< Lat ANATE), B *paita*
eagle	*arrano*
eel	*aingira* (< Rom; cf. Sp *anguila*)
falcon	*aztore*
ferret	*hudo* ~ *uron* (< Rom; cf. Sp *hurón*)
finch	*txonta*
firefly	*ipurtargi* (*ipurdi* 'buttocks' + *argi* 'light'), *argihar* (*har* 'worm')
fish	*arrai(n)* (< **arrani*)

J. A. Lakarra has recently suggested (p.c.) that this word

might have originated as a perfective participle in *-i* (cf. Sp *pescado* 'fish', also a participle in origin).

flea   *kukuso*, *ardi* (B), *arkakuso* (B G)

The first is possibly a derivative of *koko* ~ *kuko* 'bug'. The last appears to be a compound of the first two.

fly   *euli* ('bluebottle' is *eltxar* (*euli* + *txar* 'bad'))
flycatcher   *eulitxori* (*euli* 'fly' + *txori* 'bird'), *otatxori*
fowl   *hegazti* (a neologism from *hegaz* 'winged')
fox   *azeri* ~ *azari* < **azenari* < Lat ASENARIU, a personal name

The surname *Aze(n)ari* is well attested in medieval documents; the modern surname *Aznar* has the same origin. Old B also had *luki* < Lat LUCIU, a personal name.

frog   *igel* ~ *ingel*

It has often been thought that this word is related to the noun and adjective *igeri* 'swimming', whose combining form is the expected *igel-*. This is very possibly correct, though the nature of the relationship is obscure. The derivation of *igeri* from *igel* by means of the ancient adjective-forming suffix *-i* would be morphologically straightforward, but a derivation in the opposite direction would seem to make more sense semantically. The variant *ingel* is mysterious. Oddly, in Z, *igel* is attested for 'locust'.

garfish   *akula*
genet   *katamuturluze* (*katu* 'cat' + *mutur* 'snout' + *luze* 'long')
goat   *ahuntz* (< **anu(n)tz*)

'Kid' is either the diminutive *ahuña* or *pit(t)ika*, and 'male goat' is *aker*. See *akelarre* in section 5.10.3.

goatsucker   *zata*
goldfinch   *gardantxilo*, *gardantxori*
goose   *antzar(e)* ~ *antzera* (< Lat ANSERE)
grasshopper   *oti*, *txirrita*, *matxinsalto* (< *Martin* 'Martin' + *salto* 'jump' (< Sp)), *saltamatxino* (likewise)

The word *txirrita* also denotes 'cicada' and 'locust'.

guinea pig   *akuri*, *kui*
gull   *antxeta*, *kaio*
hake   *legatz*
hare   *erbi*
hawk   *aztore*, *belatz* (< **bel* 'black' ?)

The first word is often specifically 'goshawk'. The commonest type of hawk in the Basque Country is the sparrowhawk, which is variously known as *gabirai*, *kabilara*, *mirumotz* (*miru* 'kite' + *motz* 'short'), *zapelaitz* or *belatz*.

hedgehog	*kirikiño*, *sagarroi* (< *sagu* 'mouse'?), *triku* (< Rom)
horse	*zaldi*, *zamari* (< Lat SAGMARIU 'packhorse')

'Mare' is *behor*. 'Colt' is *moxal* or *pottoka*, and 'filly' is *potro*, the last two being young-animal names from Rom *pot-*.

insect	*mamutz*, *zomorro* ~ *txamorro*, *momorro*, *koko* ~ *kuko*, *tximitx(a)*

The word *mamutz* is severely localized, but has now become the standard term; *zomorro* and *momorro* mean 'creepy-crawly' or 'bug', rather than 'insect' in the strict sense. The word *koko* also means 'bug' in general, but is particularly applied to a larva that infests maize.

kestrel	*zapelatz* (*zapo* 'toad' + *belatz* 'hawk')
kingfisher	*martinarrantzale* (< *Martin* 'Martin' + *arrantzale* 'fisherman')
kite	*miru* (< Lat MILUU)
leech	*izain*, *odoledale* (*odol* 'blood' + *edale* 'drinker')
limpet	*lapa* (< Sp)
lizard	*musker* (also 'green' in the north), *sugelindara* ~ *sugelandara* (*suge* 'snake' + ?)
lobster	*otarrain* (< *oti* 'grasshopper' (?) + *arrain* 'fish')
locust	*txirrita*, Z *igel*
louse	*zorri* ('nit' is *bartz* ~ *partz* < Rom)
lynx	*katamotz* (< *katu* 'cat' + *motz* 'short')
magpie	*mika* (< Lat PICA)
marmot	*musar*
marten	*martta* (< Rom)

'Pine marten' is *lepahori* (*lepo* 'neck' + *hori* 'yellow'); 'stone marten' is *fuina* (< Rom).

martin	*txirritxori* (*txirri* 'plover' + *txori* 'bird')
mite	*zeden*
mole	*sator* (*sagu* 'mouse' + ?), archaic *satsuri* (*sagu* + *zuri* 'white')
mosquito	*eltxo* (*euli* 'fly' + *-txo* dimin.)
moth	*sits* ~ *sats* (also 'ordure'), *pipi* ~ *bipi*, *zeden*
mouse	*sagu*

'Field mouse' is *saturdin* (*urdin* 'blue'), *satsuri* (*zuri* 'white', with sibilant harmony) or *sorosagu* (*soro* 'field').

mule	*mando* (pre-Roman, probably Celtic; see section 6.4)
mullet	*korkoin, lasun*
mussel	*muskuilu* (< Rom)
nightingale	*txindor, urretxindor* (*urre* 'gold'), *erresinul*
octopus	*olagarro* (? + *garro* 'tentacle')
otter	*ugabere* (*ur* 'water' + *abere* 'animal'), *udagara ~ igaraba* (irregular variants of the preceding), B *urtxakur* (< *ur* + *txakur* 'dog')
owl	*mozolo, hontz(a)*
ox	*idi*
oyster	*ostra* (< Sp)
partridge	*eper*
pheasant	*basoilanda* (*basa-* 'wild' + *oilanda* 'pullet'), *faisai* (< Rom)
pig	*urde, zerri ~ txerri*

The first word, now confined to derivatives in some parts of the country, is apparently older than the second. 'Sow' is *ahardi* or *urdanga*; 'boar' is *aketz*; 'wild boar' is *basurde* (*basa-* 'wild' + *urde*).

pigeon, dove	western *uso* < eastern *urzo*
plover	*txirri* (this is the golden plover)
polecat	*pitox(a) ~ pitotxa* (< Rom)
porpoise	*mazopa* (< Sp *marsopa*)
prawn	*otarrainska ~ otarraintxo* (diminutives of *otarrain* 'lobster')
rabbit	*untxi* (probably < Rom; cf. Lat CUNICULU), *koneju* (< Sp *conejo*)
rat	*arratoi(n)* (< Lat RATONE or a Rom reflex)
robin	*papogorri ~ papargorri* (*papo ~ papar* 'breast' + *gorri* 'red'), *txantxangorri*
salamander	*arrubi(o), arruge*
salmon	*izoki(n)* (< Rom *esocina*)
sardine	*sardina* (< Rom)
scorpion	*luhartz* (*lur* 'earth' + *hartz* 'bear'), B *lupu* (< *lur*?)
seal	*itsastxakur* (*itsaso* 'sea' + *txakur* 'dog')
sea lion	*itsasotso* (*itsaso* 'sea' + *otso* 'wolf')
sea urchin	*itsaslakatz* (*itsaso* 'sea' + *lakatz* 'burr')
shark	*marraxo, tiburoi* (< Sp *tiburón*)
sheep	*ardi*

'Ewe' is also *ardi*. 'Lamb' is either *bildots, arkume* (-*(k)ume* 'offspring'), *azuri ~ asuri ~ a(t)xuri* (? < *ardi* + *zuri* 'white') or *umerri* (*ume* 'offspring' + *berri* 'new'). 'Ram' is *ahari* < **anari*.

shrew	*satitsu* (*sagu* 'mouse' + *itsu* 'blind')

shrimp	*izkira*
slug	*bare* (also 'spleen'; originally 'squishy'?)
snail	*barraskilo* ~ *marraskilo* ~ *maskulo, barakurkuilo* ~ *barakuilo* (*bare* 'slug' + Rom; cf. Sp *caracol*)
snake	*suge, narrazt(ar)i* (< *narraz* 'dragging, trailing along the ground' + *-ti* NFS; eighteenth-century neologism), *herrestari* (< *herresta* 'drag' + *-ti*) (last two more properly 'reptile')

'Grass-snake' is *ziraun*.

sparrow	*elizatxori* (*eliza* 'church' + *txori* 'bird'), *aratxori* (? + *txori*), *etxetxori* (*etxe* 'house'), *txolarre* (*txori* + *arre* 'grey'), *pardel*
spider	*arm(i)arma* ~ *arbiama* ~ *armamio, marasma, marmara, lipu*

Nearly universal is *armiarma* and its variants; this word is vaguely reminiscent of the Romance words (Sp *araña*, Fr *araignée*, etc.), but it doesn't look like a loan, and is more likely a reduplicated formation. The northern *lipu* is a variant of *lupu*, which more commonly means either 'scorpion' or 'caterpillar'.

squid	*txibia, tximinoi, txipiroi* (< Rom; cf. Old Sp *xibia*, Sp *chipirón*)
squirrel	*urtxintx* ~ *urtxain(tx)* ~ *burtxintx* (*hur* 'nut' + *zain* 'guardian'?), G *katagorri* (*katu* 'cat' + *gorri* 'red')
starfish	*itsasizar* (*itsaso* 'sea' + *izar* 'star')
starling	*tordantxa* (< Rom + dimin. suffix)
stork	*zikoina* ~ *zinkun* (< Rom), *amiamoko*
swallow	*ainara* ~ *enara, elae* ~ *elai*

Michelena (1977a: 326) derives all of these from **eNala* ~ **eLana*, with an extraordinary double metathesis.

swan	*beltxarga*
swift	*txiritxori* (*txori* 'bird')
thrush	*birigarro* ~ *biligarro*
tick	*lapazorri* (*lapa* 'limpet' + *zorri* 'louse')
toad	*zapo* ~ *apo* ~ *sapo, txantxiku*

The more widespread first word is earliest attested as *zapo*. This is shared with Romance (Cast *sapo*, etc.), but the origin of the word is unknown.

tortoise	*dortoka* (< Rom)
trout	*amuarrain* (*amu* 'hook' + *arrain* 'fish'), *arrankari*
tuna	*atun* (< Sp)
turkey	*indioilo* (female), *indioilar* (male) (*indi* 'Indies', i.e. 'America', + *oilo* 'hen', *oilar* 'cock')

turtle	*dortoka* (< Rom)
vulture	*sai, arranobeltz* (*arrano* 'eagle' + *beltz* 'black'), *putre* (< Rom; cf. Sp *buitre*)
wasp	*liztor, erlabio* (*erle* 'bee' + ?), *baserle* (*basa-* 'wild' + *erle* 'bee'), *kurubio* ~ *kurlabio* (B)

In some places, the variants *leizor* ~ *listor* of the first mean specifically 'hornet'.

weasel	*erbinude* ~ *erbiunide* (*erbi* 'hare' + *iñude* ~ *unide* 'wet-nurse'), *ogigazta(e)* (*ogi* 'bread' + *gazta(e)* 'cheese', calque on Sp *paniqueso*), *satand(e)re* (*sagu* 'mouse' + *and(e)re* 'lady')
whale	*balea* (< Lat BALLAENA)
wildcat	*basakatu* (*basa-* 'wild' + *katu* 'cat')

This name strictly denotes a specific type of genet found in the Basque Country. The name *muxar*, a diminutive of *musar* 'marmot', is also locally given to a very small variety of wild cat.

wolf	*otso, arrama*

The universal *otso* is ancient, and is probably attested in Aquitanian (see section 6.9). It is common as a surname in both medieval and modern Basque: *Otxoa* (Spanish form *Ochoa*). The defunct southern dialect has *lupu*, a loan from Lat LUPU.

woodcock	*bekada* (< Rom)
woodlark	*pirripio*
woodpecker	*okil*
worm	*har* ~ *aar* (< *anar*), *zizare* ('earthworm'), *mamutz*

5.9.12 Tree and plant names

Like animal names, the names of trees and other plants are often of special interest in historical examinations, and so I present a list of the principal such names here. Names of food plants which have clearly been introduced into the Basque Country in historical times, such as potatoes, tomatoes and rice, are not included, since their names are invariably borrowed from Romance. Even so, it will be seen that a substantial proportion of these words are loans from Latin or Romance, or compounds which in most cases do not appear to be of any great antiquity. It is difficult to avoid the conclusion that a large number of ancient plant names must have been replaced by other words. A few words for parts of plants are also included. Note the several tree names with a first element *ez-*; the significance of this morph is unknown, though it may possibly be a reduced form of *haitz* 'oak, tree'. With fruit and nut trees, most often the name of the tree is derived by adding to the name of the fruit or nut the element *ondo*, which in isolation means 'base, foot, root of a tree': *sagar* 'apple', *sagarrondo* 'apple tree'. Instead of *ondo*, R uses *atze*, its own word for 'tree', and this can be attached to any tree name at all: *ezpel* 'box tree', *ezpelatze* 'box tree'.

aconite	*irabelar* (*ira* 'fern' + *belar* 'grass')
acorn	*ezkur* (also 'oak tree, tree') (probably **ez-* + ?), *zi* (< **zinV*)
alder	*haltz(a)* (related to such Rom forms as Sp *aliso*, but the nature of the relation is obscure)
alder buckthorn	*zumalakar* (*zume* 'osier' + *lakar* 'rough')
alfalfa	*argibelar* (*argi* 'light' + *belar* 'grass'), *frantzesbelar* (*frantzes* 'French')
almond	*almendra* (< Sp)
aloe	*zumintz*
amaranth	*almitz*, *sabi*
amber	*anbare* (< Rom; cf. Sp *ámbar*)
apple	*sagar* (fruit), *sagarrondo* (tree)

'Crab apple' is *sagarmakatz* (*sagar* + *makatz* 'wild').

artichoke	*orriburu* (*orri* 'leaf' + *buru* 'head'), *alkatxofa* (< Sp)
arum	*errebelar* (*erre* 'burn' + *belar* 'grass')
ash	*lizar* ~ *leizar*
asparagus	*zainzuri* (*zain* 'root(hair)' + *zuri* 'white'), *frantzesporru* (*frantzes* 'French' + *porru* 'leek')
aspen	*lertxun*, *orrikara* (*orri* 'leaf' + *ikara* 'tremble')
asphodel	*anbulu zuri* (*anbulu* 'daffodil' + *zuri* 'white')
barley	*garagar* (reduplication of *gari* 'wheat'?)
basswood	*ezku* (probably **ez-* + ?)
bean	*baba* (< Lat FABA)

'Kidney bean' is *babarruna* ~ *baberruna* (< Lat *FABA ROMANA); 'string bean' is *indibaba* ~ *indaba* ~ *inddaba* (*Indi* 'Indies', i.e. 'America' + *baba*; the sense is 'American bean').

beech	*bago* ~ *pago* ~ *fago* (< Lat FAGU), *fagondo* ~ *pagondo*

'Beechnut' is *bakaila* ~ *makaila* (< *bago* + ?).

beet(root)	*erremolatxa* (< Sp *remolacha*), *frantzesarbi* (*frantzes* 'French' + *arbi* 'turnip'), *sarbagorri* (hapax) (? + *gorri* 'red')

berry	*baia*
birch	*burki ~ urki ~* B *turki ~* old G *epurki* (possibly < IE)
blackberry	*marzusta ~ masusta ~ marzuza* (berry), *sasi* (plant) (earlier *zarzi*, akin to Sp *zarza*)
blackthorn	See **sloe**
box tree	*ezpel* (probably **ez-* + **-bel* 'dark')
bramble	*sasi* (< *zarzi*), *kapar, sastar* (< *sasi* + ?), *lahar*
branch	*adar, abar*

The first Basque word also means 'horn', and it bears a striking resemblance to Old Irish *adarc* 'horn', a word with no Indo-European etymology. This is a possible case of a pre-Indo-European substrate word.

briar	*txilar*
broom	*erraiz, isats*
brush	*txapar*
buckthorn	*karraskila*
bud	*pipil, begi* (= 'eye'), *ninika, ernamuin, kimu, kimetz, txerto, hozi, muskil*
bulrush	*urezpata* (*ur* 'water' + *ezpata* 'sword')
burdock	*lapa* (also 'limpet') (< Lat LAPPA), *lapabelar* (*belar* 'grass')
bush	*zuhaixka* (*zuhaitz* 'tree' + *-xka* dimin.), *mulu*
buttercup	*urrebotoi* (*urre* 'gold' + *botoi* 'button')
cabbage	*aza*(*k*) (always plural)
camomile	*idibegi* (*idi* 'ox' + *begi* 'eye'), *idibelar* (*belar* 'grass'), *kamamila* (< Sp)
cane	*kana* (< Lat CANNA), B G *ka(i)ñabera* (< Sp *cañavera*), *seska*
carrot	*zainhori* (*zain* 'root(hair)' + *hori* 'yellow', by folk-etymology < Sp *zanahoria*, of Arabic origin)
cauliflower	*azalore* (*aza* 'cabbage' + *lore* 'flower'), *azalili* (*lili* 'lily, flower')
cereal	See **grain**
cherry	*gerezi* (and variants) (< Lat CERESEA) (fruit), *gereziondo* (tree)
chestnut	*gaztaina* (< a Rom development of Lat CASTANEA) (nut), *gaztainondo* (tree)
chickpea	*garbantzu* (< Sp *garbanzo*), *txitxirio*
clary	*zauribelar* (*zauri* 'wound' + *belar* 'grass')
clover	*hirusta* (*hiru* 'three' + *-sta*), *sekulabelar* (*sekula* 'ever' + *belar* 'grass')

'Red clover' is *pagotxa*, apparently *pago* 'beech' + *-txa* dimin., though the motivation is obscure; Azkue and Michelena suggest that this is a loan from French or Occitan *farouch(e)*, presumably with a folk-etymology.

cork	*tortotx*
corn	See **grain** and **maize**
cranberry	*ahabi ~ abi ~ arabi*
cucumber	*kuia, kuiluze, pepino*
currant (black)	*andere beltx* (*andere* 'lady' + dimin. of *beltz* 'black'), *mahas-beltz* (*mahats* 'grape')
daffodil	*anbulu ~ anbulo, lilipa*
daisy	*bitxilore* (*bitxi* 'jewel' + *lore* 'flower')
dandelion	*sorginbelar* (*sorgin* 'witch' + *belar* 'grass'), *txikoribelar* (*txikori* 'chicory')
danewort	*ziaurriz ~ ziaurre*
dogwood	*zuhandor* (the first element might be *zur* 'wood', or, perhaps, *zuhain*, attested for 'tree', but the rest is obscure)
elder	*intsusa*

'Dwarf elder' is *zihaurre*.

elm	*zumar ~ zu(h)ar* (< **zunar*, possibly < *zur* 'wood' + an unidentified second element)
fern	*garo, ira ~ iratze* (-*tze* collective)
fig	*biku ~ piko ~ iko* (< Lat FICU) (fruit), *pikondo* (tree)
fir	*izai ~ izei* (< **izaCi*)
flax	*liho ~ linu* (< Lat LINU)
flower	*lore* (< Lat FLORE), *lili* (< Rom)
foxtail	*azeribuztan* (*azeri* 'fox' + *buztan* 'tail')
fungus	*onddo ~ onto* (< Lat FUNGU)
garlic	*baratxuri, berakatz*
gorse	*ote ~ ota*
grain (cereal)	*labore, zitu* (< Rom **seito* < Lat SECTU 'a cutting')
grain (kernel)	*ale, bihi, garau* (< Lat GRANU)
grapes	*mahats* (uncountable) (< **banats*)
grass	*belar ~ bedar* (< **berar*)

The word *belar* is used very frequently in forming compounds for naming a wide variety of small plants. The distinctive type of grass called 'brome (grass)' in English is *larraolo* (*larre* 'pasture, meadow' + *olo* 'oats').

hawthorn	*elorri, arantza, maspilondo, aspiltze*

The fruit of the hawthorn is *azpil ~ aspil ~ maspila*.

hazelnut	*hur* (also 'nut' in general)
heather	*inarra ~ ilar ~ txilar* (< **inar*), B *erika* (< Lat)

The B word is remarkable, since Lat ERICA has usually been regarded as exclusively a learnèd word.

holly   *gorosti*

This word seems to be related to Sardinian *golóstru ~ golóst(r)i ~ colostri* 'holly', suggesting that the original form of the Basque word might have been **goloztri*, whose development into *gorosti* would be unremarkable. Here we may have a rare instance of a pre-Roman substrate word surviving in Basque and in Romance, though the final *-ti* of the Basque word still looks very much like the common collective suffix *-di*.

ivy   *huntz ~ huntzadar* (*adar* 'branch')
juniper   *orre* (eastern), *ipuru* (western)
larch   *laritz* (< Lat LARIX), *zuzi*
leaf   *orri, osto* (< **orri-zto*)
leek   *porru* (< Lat PORRU)
lettuce   *uhaza* (*ur* 'water' + *aza* 'cabbage'), *letxu(a)* (< Sp *lechuga*)
lilac   *amatxilili* (*amatxi* 'godmother' + *lili* 'lily')
lily   *lili ~ lirio* (< Rom)
linden   *ezki ~ ezku* (probably **ez-* + ?)
maize   *arto* (earlier 'millet'; the name was transferred after maize supplanted millet as a major food crop)
maple   *astigar ~ aztigar ~ gaztigar, azkar*

Michelena (1977a: 253) suggests that the first is a compound of a substrate **kast-*, found in several European tree names, with the obscure but attested *ihar* 'maple'.

medlar   *mizpira ~ mizpila*
millet   *artatxiki, artaxehe* (*arto* 'maize', but formerly 'millet' + *txiki* 'small', *xehe* 'small')
moss   *goroldio*
mushroom   *perretxiko, txanpinoin* (< Sp), *ziza*
mustard   *ziape* (< Lat SENAPE)
nut   *hur* (also 'hazelnut')
oak   *haritz ~ haitz ~ (h)aritx* (also archaic *areitz ~ aretx*; *areitz* is probably the most conservative form) (formerly also 'tree'; see under **tree**)

'Holm oak' ('holly oak', 'evergreen oak') is *arte* or *zumel*, the second from *zur* 'wood' + *-bel* 'dark'. 'Gall oak' ('muricated oak') is *ametz* (possibly < something like **abentz*; a variant *amentx* is attested).

oats   *olo*
olive   *oliba* (< Rom)

onion	*tipula ~ kipula* (< Lat CEPULLA; the more widespread first form shows an unusual development of the Latin velar, and may perhaps represent a loan from the time at which Latin velars had just begun to be palatalized before front vowels)
osier	*zume* (*zur* 'wood' + *mehe* 'slender'), *mimen ~ mihimen* (< Lat VIMEN)
parsnip	*txiribi*
pea	*ilar ~ idar* (possibly < *irar)
peach	*muxika* (< Lat (MALA) persica), *melokotoi* (< Sp *melocotón*)
pear	*madari, udari ~ udare, muskil ~ muskin* (fruit), *madariondo, udareondo* (tree)

There is some evidence that *udari* formerly meant 'fruit' in general.

pepper	*biper ~ piper* (< Lat PIPER)
pine	*pinu* (< Lat PINU), R *ler* (an archaism?)
pine cone	*pinaburu* (*pinu* 'pine' + *buru* 'head')
pith	*muin* (and many variants) (< **bune ~ *(h)une*, possibly < Lat FUNE 'rope'), *mami* (< Rom)
plane tree	*albo*
plant	*landare* (< Rom), *zuhai(n), zugai ~ zumai* (< *zunai)
plantain	*zainbelar* (*zain* 'root(hair)' + *belar* 'grass')
plum	*aran*

There are various Romance and even Celtic words of similar form, but none of them provides a convincing source for *aran*.

pod	*leka* (< Lat THECA), *magi(ñ)a* (< Lat VAGINA)
poplar	*makal, ezki,* B *zuzun*
poppy	B *mitxoleta*
radish	*janarbi* (< *jan* 'eat' + *arbi* 'turnip')
raspberry	*masustagorri* (*masustu* 'blackberry' + *gorri* 'red')
reed, rush	*ihi* (< *ini)
root	*erro, sustrai ~ zustrai ~ zuzter(rai), orpo, erreboil,* R *izorro*
rose	*arrosa ~ larrosa* (< Lat ROSA or a Rom continuation)
rowan	*otsolizar* (*otso* 'wolf' + *lizar* 'ash')
rush	See **reed**
rye	*zikirio, zekale*
seaweed	*itsasbelar* (*itsaso* 'sea' + *belar* 'grass')
shrub	See **bush**

sloe	*basaran* (*basa-* 'wild' + *aran* 'plum')

The variant *patxaran* is the name of a favourite Basque alcoholic beverage, obtained by soaking anisette in sloes.

sorb tree	*udalatxondo* (*udalatx* 'sorb apple, serviceberry' + *ondo*)

In places the tree itself is called *udalatz*.

stem	*enbor, landarondo* (*landare* 'plant' + *ondo* 'root, tree')
strawberry	*marrubi* ~ *marubi* ~ *malubi* ~ *mailuki* ~ *mailug(a)i* ~ *malhuri* ~ *mag(a)uri* (and others), *arrega*

The word *marrubi* (the most widespread form) must surely derive from Lat MARRUBIU 'horehound', but it exhibits an extraordinary number and variety of local variants. Michelena concludes that the ancestral form must have been roughly *ma(u)CuCi*, in which one of the consonants was a liquid and the other was not.

sunflower	*eguzkilore* ~ *ekilore* (*eguzki* or *eki*, both 'sun', + *lore* 'flower')
teasel	*kardabera* (*kardu* 'thistle' or Sp *carda* 'teasel' + *bera* 'soft'), *txarrantxa*
thistle	*gardu* ~ *kardu* (< Lat CARDU)
tree	*zuhaitz* ~ *zugatz* (*zur* 'wood' + *haitz* 'oak', but formerly 'tree'), *arbol(a)* (< Sp *árbol*)

These are the usual words today, but a few other words occur locally, and the older language shows still others. The word *haritz* (and variants) now means just 'oak', but it formerly meant 'tree' in B. The word *zuhai(n)* (and variants) now means both 'plant' and 'hay, fodder', but it is also attested as meaning 'tree', both in this form and in the suffixed form *zuhaintze*. Another attested word is *zuhamu*, which may be a variant of the preceding. R has the curious *atze*, which is surely related to *-(a)tze*, commonly suffixed to tree names in the east, as in *gerezitze* 'cherry tree' and *ezpelatze* 'box tree'. Western dialects use *-ondo* in the same way: *gereziondo* 'cherry tree', *sagarrondo* 'apple tree'. Archaic B has *abe*, which seemingly appears in such derivatives as *abakondo* 'dried-out tree trunk' and *abar* 'branches', and also *ezkur*, today 'acorn'. Finally, Landucci's 1562 dictionary gives the hapax *errexal(a)*, thought to be a Romance loan.

trunk	*enbor*
turnip	*arbi, nabo*

walnut	*intzaur ~ intxaur* (? + *hur* 'nut') (nut), *intxaurrondo* (tree)
wheat	*gari* (probably < **gali*)
willow	*sahats ~ sarats ~ sagats* (< **saCats*)

The best guess is **sanats*, but this is not certain. Attempts at seeing this as a loan from Lat SALIX can be dismissed.

wood	*zur*
woodbine	*biurda ~ ziurda ~ birunga*
yew	*hagin*

5.9.13 Geographical features and natural phenomena

As expected, these words are mostly native and ancient, but there are a few surprises, such as some of the metal names. I can find no non-modern words for many celestial phenomena, such as 'meteor' and 'aurora'. Apart from Venus, the North Star and Ursa Major, there appears to be little trace of an indigenous tradition for naming planets, stars or constellations, which is surprising in a traditionally pastoral society.

afternoon	*arratsalde* (*arrats* 'evening' + *alde* 'side')
air	*aire* (< Rom) (some varieties do not distinguish this from *haize* 'wind')
ashes	*hauts, errauts* (*erre* 'burn')
beach	(*h*)*ondar* (also 'sand, residue'), (*h*)*ondartza* (*-tza* NFS), (*h*)*ondarreta* (*-eta* NFS), *hareatza* (*harea* 'sand')
bronze	*brontze* (< Rom)
cave	*haitzulo* (*haitz* 'rock' + *zulo* 'hole'), *haizpe* (*haitz* + *-pe* 'below'), *hartzulo* (*harri* 'rock' + *zulo*), *harpe* (*harri* + *-pe*), *le*(*i*)*ze* (also 'abyss'), *lurruspe* (*lur* 'earth' + ? + *-pe*), *koba* (< Rom), *kobazulo* (*koba* + *zulo*)
charcoal	*ikatz ~ inkatz*
cliff	See **precipice**
cloud	*hodei* (< **odeCe*)
copper	*kobre* (< Rom)
crag	*haitz* (? **anitz* or **anetz*)

This word also means 'rock, stone'.

darkness	*ilun* (and various suffixed forms of this)
day	*egun*
death	*herio, heriotza ~ heriotze*

Traditionally, *herio* is 'death' in the active sense, as in 'Death took him', while *heriotza* is 'death' in the passive sense, as in 'after his death'.

dew	*ihintz ~ intz (< *ini(n)tz)*
dusk	See **twilight**
dust	*hauts*
earth	*lur*
estuary	*ibaiondo* (*ibai* 'river' + *ondo* 'bottom')
evening	*arrats* (? < *arre* 'grey, dark')
evening star	*arratsizar* (*arrats* 'evening' + *izar* 'star')
field	*soro* (< Rom), *arlo*, *alor* (? < *ale* 'seed'), *zelai* (also 'plain'), *belardi* (also 'meadow') (*belar* 'grass' + NFS), *elge*

The words *soro* and *elge* are specifically 'field under cultivation', while *alor* is 'field prepared for sowing' (hence the likely etymology); *arlo* is more generally 'piece of land'.

fire	*su*
firewood	*egur*
flame	*gar*, *sugar* (*su* 'fire'), *lama* (< Lat)
fog	*lanbro*
ford	*ubide* (*ur* 'water' + *bide* 'path'), *ibi* (? variant of preceding), *ubehera* (*ur* + *behera* 'below'), *urmehe* (*ur* + *mehe* 'slender')
forest	*oihan*, *baso*

There is evidence that *baso* originally meant merely 'uncultivated or uninhabited land, wilderness'.

frost	*izotz* (probably *ihintz* 'dew' + *hotz* 'cold'), western *intzigar* (*ihintz* + *igar* 'dry')
gold	*urre*
gorge	*le(i)ze*, *amildegi* (**amil* 'gorge'? + *-tegi* 'place') and several similar derivatives of *amil-*
hail	*txingor*, *babazuza*, *kazkabar*
hill	*muino ~ muno* (< Rom **bunno*)
hillside	*aldapa*, *aldats* (< *alde* 'side')
ice	*izotz* (see **frost**)
icicle	*ziztor*, *zotzkandela* (*izotz* 'ice' + *kandela* 'candle')
iron	*burdin(a) ~ burduña ~ burnia* (< **burdina* or **burnina*)
island	*irla* (< Rom), *uharte* (*ur* 'water' + *arte* 'between')
lake	*zingira* (also 'swamp'), *aintzira* (also 'swamp'), *laku* (< Lat)

The Basque Country is virtually devoid of natural lakes, and the language does not commonly distinguish 'lake' from 'swamp, marsh, wet ground'.

land	*lur* (also 'earth')

The word *lehor* 'dry' is often used as a noun meaning 'dry land' (as opposed to the sea).

lead (metal)	*berun, plomo* (< Rom)
life	*bizi, bizitza*
light	*argi*
lightning	*tsismist* ~ *(t)ximist(a)* (and suffixed forms of this), *xasta*
meadow	*belardi* (*belar* 'grass' + -*di* collective for plants)
mercury	*zilar bizi* ('living silver')
metal	*metale* (< Lat or Rom)
midnight	*gauerdi* (*gau* 'night' + *erdi* 'middle')
Milky Way	*Frantses Bidea* ('the French Road'), *Santiobide* ('St James's Way')
mist	*laino*
moon	*(h)ilargi* (< **iLe* or **iLa* 'moon' + *argi* 'light')

Sal has the unique *ilaski*, which is probably < **ilargi-zki*, by analogy with *eguzki* 'sun'. 'Full moon' is *hilargibete* (*bete* 'full'); 'half moon' is *hilargierdi* (*erdi* 'half') or *hilerdi*; 'new moon' is *hilargiberri* (*berri* 'new').

morning	*goiz*
morning star	*goizizar* (*goiz* 'morning' + *izar* 'star')
mountain	*mendi*
mud	*lohi, lokatz* (? < *lohi*), *basa, istil*
night	*gau*
noon	*eguerdi* (*egun* 'day' + *erdi* 'middle')
North Star	*Artizar*
pasture	*larre*
path	*bide* (also 'road'), *bidexka* (*bide* + dimin.), *basabide* (*baso* 'wilderness' + *bide*)
peak	*gailur, tontor*
plain	*zelai, ordoki*
pool	*urmael* (*ur* 'water' + *ma(h)el* (archaic) 'pool')
precipice	*amildegi, erortoki* (*erori* 'fall' + *toki* 'place'), *jaustegi* (*jausi* 'fall' + -*tegi* 'place'), *malkor(tegi)*
rain	*euri*

There are various local words for particular types of rain, the best known being *zirimiri* 'drizzle'.

rainbow	*ortzadar* ~ *ostadar* (*ortzi* (see section 5.9.4) + *adar* 'horn')
ravine	*erreka*
ridge	*hegi*

river	*ibai, ugalde* (*ur* 'water' + *alde* 'side')

The word *ibai* is attested in 1741 in the definite form *hibaiea*, pointing to a stem **hibaie*, and an indefinite form *ibaia* is recorded in 1627. In all likelihood, the word was once longer and was a derivative of some sort, and indeed it is commonly regarded as a derivative of *ibar* 'water-meadow, valley'. L has *ibaso* 'river', and Pouvreau's seventeenth-century dictionary lists *ur ibaia* 'ford, fordable river', in which *ibai* is an adjective.

riverbank	*ibaiondo* (*ibai* 'river' + *ondo* 'side'), B *muna* (< Rom)
road	*bide*
sand	(*h*)*ondar* (also 'beach, residue'), *harea* (< Lat)
sea	*itsaso*
seacoast	*itsasalde* (*itsaso* 'sea' + *alde* 'side')
silver	*zilar ~ zillar ~ zirar ~ zidar* (< **zirar?*)

It is widely thought that this word is related to the Germanic and Balto-Slavonic words for 'silver', though some are sceptical of this.

sky	*zeru* (< a Rom development of Lat CAELU)

In all likelihood, the indigenous word was **ortzi*; see section 5.9.4.

slate	*lapitz* (< Lat LAPIS 'stone'), *harbel* (*harri* 'stone' + **bel* 'dark')
slope	See **hillside**
smoke	*ke* (Aezk *eke*, R *kei*)
snow	*elur ~ edur* (< **erur*)
soot	*kedar ~ gedar*
spring (of water)	*iturri*
star	*izar*
steam	*lurrin ~ lurrun, urlurrin* (*ur* 'water' + *lurrin*)
stone	*harri, haitz* (? < **anitz* or **anetz*)
storm	*ekaitz* (*egun* 'day' + *gaitz* 'bad'), *zurrunbilo, zirimola*
stormwind	*enbata* (coming from the sea)
stream	*erreka*
summit	*tontor* (expressive word or loan word)
sun	western *eguzki ~ iguzki ~* eastern *eki*, both < *egun* 'day' + -(*z*)*ki* NFS
sunrise	*arginabar* (*argi* 'light' + *nabar* 'grey'), *egunsenti* (*egun* 'day' + *senti* 'feel'), *argiurratze* (*argi* + *urratze* 'breaking'), *eguzkirtera* (*eguzki* 'sun' + *irtera* 'come out'),

	eguzkisorketa (*eguzki* + *sor-* 'be born' + *-keta* 'activity'), *goiznabar* (*goiz* 'morning' + *nabar*)
sunset	*ilunabar, ilunsenti, eguzkisarrera*
swamp	*baltsa, zingira, aintzira, istinga, fadura* (< Rom)
thunder	*trumoi, ostots, ihurtzuri*
tin	*eztainu* (< Lat)
twilight	*ilunabar* (*ilun* 'dark' + *nabar* 'grey'), *ilunseti* (*ilun* + *senti* 'dawn'), *ilunalde* (*ilun* + *alde* 'side'), B *iluntze* (*ilun* + *-tze* NFS)
Ursa Major	*Itohoin* (*idi* 'ox' + *ohoin* 'thief')
valley	*haran, ibar*
Venus	*Argizar* ~ *Artizar* (*argi* 'light, bright' + *izar* 'star')
water	*ur*
waterfall	*zurrunba, urjausi* (*ur* 'water' + *jauzi* 'leap')
weather	*eguraldi* (*egun* 'day' + *aldi* 'occasion')
well	*putzu* (< Rom), *pozo* (< Rom), *osin*

The word *osin* chiefly means 'deep place in a river', but it has several other localized meanings, apparently including 'well'.

wilderness	*eremu, mortu*

It seems likely that *baso*, now 'woods', formerly meant 'wilderness'.

wind	*haize*
wood (material)	*zur*
woods	*baso*
world	*mundu* (< Lat MUNDU)

5.9.14 Meals and food

There are several terms for 'meal': *otordu* (*ogi* 'bread' + *ordu* 'hour'), *jatordu* (*jan* 'eat' + *ordu*), *jataldi* (*jan* + *aldi* 'time, occasion'). R *apario* and Z *apaidü* derive from Latin *APPARIU. 'Breakfast' is *gosari* (*gose* 'hungry, hunger') and 'lunch' is *bazkari* (from earlier *barazkari*, possibly related to *barazki* 'vegetable'). 'Dinner' is *afari* ~ *apari* ~ *abari*, but the eastern dialects show more conservative forms: LN *auhari*, Z *aihári*, R *aigari*; all this points to an original **auhari*, preserved in LN, in which the first element is quite possibly *gau* 'night'. All three words show a suffix *-(k)ari*, of uncertain function. Schuchardt's attempts at deriving *afari* and *bazkari* from Latin **APPARIU and **PASCUARIU must be rejected as unsustainable.

The names of plants and animals which are eaten are included in the lists of plant and animal names above; the list below includes some further words not covered above.

bacon   *urdai* (probably a derivative of *urde* 'hog'), *urdaiki*, *urdai-giharre* (*giharre* 'lean part of meat'; *urdai* is sometimes applied more specifically to 'bacon fat')

beer   *garagardo* ~ *garagararno* (*garagar* 'barley' + *ardo* ~ *arno* 'wine')

blood pudding   *odolki* (*odol* 'blood' + *-ki* NFS)

bread   *ogi*

bun   See **roll**

butter   *gurin* ~ *guri* ~ *urin*

In older texts this word often means 'lard' or 'solid animal fat' (in general). In a few locations it means 'clotted cream' or 'juice' (of meat or vegetables).

cake   *tarta* (< Rom), *pastel(a)* (< Rom)

casserole   *kazolakada* (from *kazola* 'casserole (dish)' < Rom)

cheese   *gaztae* ~ *gaztai* ~ *gazta* ~ *gazna* (< **gaztane*)

This word is curiously similar to Latin CASEU, but it cannot be a direct loan. Most Basque cheeses are hard; a soft cheese resembling cottage cheese is *gaztanbera* (*bera* 'soft').

cider   *sagardo* (*sagar* 'apple' + *ardo* 'wine')

coffee   *kafe, akeita*

The second word is a northern term for an infusion of medicinal herbs; it was appropriated by the Aranistas to denote 'coffee', and this eccentric word still finds some limited use today.

cookie   *gaileta* (< Sp), *bixkotx* (< Rom)

cream   *esnegain* (*esne* 'milk' + *gain* 'top'), *esnemami* (*mami* 'best part' < Rom *m'ami*), *esnegurin* (*gurin* 'fat'), *esnetela*, B *kipur, gurin*

curd   *gatzatu* (also applied to a milk-based dessert)

dessert   *postre* (< Sp), *bazkalburuko* (*bazkari* 'lunch' + *buru* 'head' + *-ko*), *bazkalazkeneko* (*bazkari* + *azken* 'last' + *-ko*)

egg   *arraultza* ~ *arrautza* ~ *arraultze* ~ *arrauntza*

It is possible that this is a derivative of the verb *errun* 'lay' (eggs) with the noun-forming suffix *-(k)untza*.

fat   *gantz* ~ *gantzu, koipe, ziho* (<**zino*), *urin*

fruit   *fruita* ~ *fruitu* (< Rom)

ham   *urdaiazpiko* (*urdai* 'bacon' + *azpi* 'below' + *-ko*), *xingar, pernil*

juice	*zuku* (< Lat SUCCU), *zumo*, *ur* (= 'water')
lard	*gantz* ~ *gantzu*, *bilgor*
meat	*haragi*, *okela* (< Lat BUCCELLA 'mouthful, morsel', a sense recorded for the Basque word, whose meaning has developed 'morsel of food' > 'morsel of meat' > 'meat')

The word *haragi* is probably a derivative of ancient **har* 'flesh, meat'; cf. Z *aratsu* 'fleshy' (*-tsu* 'full of'), HN LN *aratxe* 'veal'. Names of individual meats are usually obtained by adding the concrete-noun-forming suffix *-ki* to the name of the animal: thus 'beef' is *idiki* (*idi* 'ox'), 'pork' is *urdeki* or *txerriki* (*urde* 'hog', *txerri* 'pig'), 'veal' is *txahalki* (*txahal* 'calf'), 'lamb' (meat) is *bildoski* (*bildots* 'lamb'), and 'chicken' (meat) is *oilaskoki* or *oilaki* (*oilasko* 'chicken', *oilo* 'hen').

milk	*esne* ~ *ezne* ~ HN *esene* (< **ezene*); cf. *zenbera* 'soft cheese' (*bera* 'soft')
mush	*ahi*
oatmeal	See **porridge**
oil	*koipe*, *olio* (< Rom)

The odd-looking first word is one of the very few seemingly ancient words with initial /k/.

omelette	*arrautzopil* (*arrautz* 'egg' + *opil* 'roll'), *tortila* (< Sp)
pastry	*pastel(a)* (< Rom)
pie	No real equivalent
porridge, oatmeal	*oloahi* (*olo* 'oats' + *ahi* 'mush')
roll, bun	*opil* (*ogi* 'bread' + *-bil* 'round')
salad	*entsalada* (< Rom)
salt	*gatz*
sandwich	*ogibitarteko* ~ *otarteko* (*ogi* 'bread' + (*bi*)*tarte* 'between' + *-ko*)
sausage	*saltxitxa*, *hestebete* (*heste* 'intestine' + *bete* 'full')

The name of the very popular spicy sausage *txorizo* is from Spanish *chorizo*; a larger version is *lukainka* (< Lat LUCANICA).

soup	*zuku* (< Lat SUCCU 'juice'), *zopa* (< Rom), *salda*

The last word is more properly 'broth'.

steak	*xerra* (from *zerra* 'slice')
stew	*eltzeko*, *lapikoko*, *marmitako*, *menestra* (< Sp)

The first three of these all derive from various words for 'cooking pot' + *-ko*.

vegetable	*barazki, eltzekari* (from *eltze* 'cooking-pot'), *ortuari* (*ortu* 'garden'), *lekari*
vinegar	*ozpin* (possibly ? + *min* 'bitter')
wine	*ardo* ~ B *ardao* ~ L LN *arno* ~ Z *ardú* (< **ardano*)

Red wine is described as *beltz* 'black'; rosé is *gorri* 'red'; white is *zuri* 'white'. A kind of green wine called *txakoli(n)* is widely drunk.

There are no indigenous words for spirits (hard liquor). A favourite tipple is *patxaran* (from *basaran* 'sloe'), made by soaking sloes in anisette. *Izarra* (*izar* 'star') is the trade name of a powerful herb-flavoured liqueur, based on Armagnac, manufactured in the French Basque Country; it somewhat resembles Chartreuse.

Cooking terms are few and not very specific. The most general verb is *egosi* 'cook (in liquid), boil'. The verb *erre* 'burn' is commonly used to render such English verbs as 'bake', 'grill' and 'roast'. The verb *iraki(n)* 'boil' is intransitive; its causative *irakierazi* is sometimes used for 'boil' (transitive). For 'toast' there are several verbs: *kiskaldu, (t)xigortu* and *errearindu* (*erre* 'burn' + *arin* 'light'). 'Fry' is the loan word *frijitu* ~ *prijitu* or *fritatu*.

'Kitchen' is *sukalde* (*su* 'fire' + *alde* 'side'), *sutondo* (*ondo* 'side'), L *ezkaratz*, B *eskatz*; 'cooking stove' is *sukalde* or *sutegi* (*-tegi* 'place'). 'Oven' is *labe* or its diminutive *labetxo*.

5.9.15 Occupations

The majority of these are of transparent formation and involve a suffix. This is most often the professional suffix *-ari* ~ *-kari* ~ *-lari*, but we also find *-zale*, which most often means 'fond of'. The suffixes *-le* and *-tzaile* are the ordinary agent suffixes attached to verbs. The suffix *-gin* is derived from the verb *egin* 'do, make' and means 'one who does/makes'; it has a variant *-gile* with the agent suffix *-le*. The suffix *-zai(n)* is the same item as the adjective *zai(n)* 'watchful, vigilant' < **zani*. Only a handful of these terms appear to be of any antiquity.

baker	*okin* (*ogi* 'bread' + *-gin*)
ball-player	*pilotari* (*pilota* 'ball' + *-ari*)
barber	*ileapaintzaile* (*ile* 'hair' + *apain-* 'beautify' + *-zaile*), *ilemozle* (*ile* + *moz-* 'cut' + *-le*), *bizargile* ~ *bizargin* (*bizar* 'beard' + *-gile, -gin*)
bard	*bertsolari* (*bertso* 'verse' < Rom + *-ari*), *koblakari* (*kobla* 'couplet' < Rom)

barman, barmaid	*tabernari* (*taberna* 'bar' < Rom + *-ari*), B *txiribogin* (*txiriboga* 'bar' + *-gin*)
basketmaker	*otargile, otargin, saskigile, otzaragile* (all from various words for 'basket' + *-gile* or *-gin*)
beekeeper	*erlazain* (*erle* 'bee' + *-zain*), *erlajaun* (*erle* + *jaun* 'gentleman'), *erladun* (*erle* + *-dun* 'who has')
blacksmith	*burdingile* (*burdina* 'iron' + *-gile*), *errementari, arotz*
brewer	*garagardogile* (*garagardo* 'beer' + *-gile*)
butcher	*harakin* (*haragi* 'meat' + *-gin*)
cabinetmaker	*zurgin* (*zur* 'wood' + *-gin*)
carpenter	*arotz, zurgin* (*zur* 'wood' + *-gin*)
cartwright	*orgagile, gurdigile* (*orga* and *gurdi*, both 'cart', + *-gile*)
cowherd	*betzain* (*behi* 'cow' + *-zain*)
doctor	*osagile, sendagile* (*osatu* and *sendatu*, both 'cure' + *-gile*)
dressmaker	See **tailor**
farmer	*nekazari, baserritar* (*baserri* 'farmhouse' + *-tar* ethnonymic suffix), *bordari* (*borda* 'farmhouse' + *-ari*), *laborari* (*labor* 'labour' + *-ari*), *lurlantzaile* (*lur* 'earth' + *landu* 'work' (tr.) + *-zaile* agent)
farrier	*ferratzaile* (first element < Rom)
fisherman	*arrantzale* (*arrain* 'fish' + *-zale*), *arraintzari* (*arraintza* 'fishing' + *-ari*)
forester	*oihartzain* (*oihan* 'forest' + *-zain*)
fortune-teller	*azti*
gardener	*baratzezain ~ baratzain* (*baratze* 'garden' + *-zain*), *ortuzain* (*ortu* 'garden')
grocer	*hornigile* (*hornitu* 'supply' < Rom + *-gile*), *hornitzaile, jakisaltzaile* (*jaki* 'food' + *saldu* 'sell' + *-zaile*)
hotelkeeper	*ostalari* (*ostatu* 'hotel' + *-ari*)
housewife	*etxekoand(e)re* (*etxe* 'house' + *-ko* + *and(e)re* 'lady')
hunter	*ehiztari ~ ihiztari* (*ehiza ~ ihiza* 'hunting' + *-ari*)
jeweller	*bitxigile* (*bitxi* 'jewel' + *-gile*)
judge	*epaile* (*epai* 'decision' + *-le*, irregular), *juje* (< Fr), *juez* (< Sp)
lawyer	*legegizon* (*lege* 'law' < Lat + *gizon* 'man'), *abogadu* (< Rom)
mason	*hormagin* (*horma* 'wall' < Lat + *-gin*)
merchant	*merkatari* (*merkatu* 'market' < Lat + *-ari*), *saltzaile* (*saldu* 'sell' + *-tzaile*), *salerosle* (*saldu* + *erosi* 'buy' + *-le*), *azokalari* (*azoka* 'market' + *-lari*)
midwife	*emagin* (*eme* 'female' + *-gin*), *erditzaile*

Larramendi has *amakide* (*ama* 'mother' + -*kide* 'fellow').

moneylender	*prestatzaile*
monk	*lekaide* (neologism), *fraide* (< Rom), *erlijioso* (< Sp)
muleteer	*mandaketari* (*mando* 'mule' + -*keta* activity + -*ari*)
musician	*musikari* (*musika* 'music' + -*ari*)
nun	*lekaime* (neologism), *serora* (< Rom), *moja* (< Rom)
nurse	*erizain* (*eri* 'ill' + -*zain*)
oxherd	*itzain* (*idi* 'ox' + -*zain*)
poet	*poeta*, *olerkari* (*olerki* 'poem', neologism, + -*ari*)
policeman	*polizia*, *goardia* (< Rom), *ertzain* (*herri* 'town' + -*zain*)
priest	*apaiz* ~ *apez* (< Lat ABBAS), B *abade* (< Sp)
prostitute	*emagaldu* (*eme* 'female' + *galdu* 'lost'), *ematxar* (*eme* + *txar* 'bad'), *maribidetako* (*mari* 'Mary' + *bide* 'road' + -*tako* 'of'), *maripurtzil* (*mari* + *purtzil* 'despicable'), *urdanga* (*urde* 'pig' + -*anga* dimin.), *puta* (< Rom)
quarryman	See **stonemason**
sailor	*itsasgizon* (*itsaso* 'sea' + *gizon* 'man'), *marinel* (< Rom)
shepherd	*artzai(n)* < **artzani* (< *ardi* 'sheep' + -*zai(n)*)
shopkeeper	*dendari* (*denda* 'shop' < Rom + -*ari*)
singer	*kantari* (*kanta* ~ *kantu* 'song' < Rom + -*ari*)
soldier	*soldadu* (< Rom), *gudari* ~ *gudulari* (*gudu* 'combat, struggle' + -*(l)ari*)

Since the Spanish Civil War, the word *gudari* has come to mean specifically 'Basque soldier'.

smuggler	*kontrabandista* (< Rom), *gaulangile* (*gau* 'night' + *lan* 'work' + -*gile*)
stonemason, quarryman	*hargin*, *harrigile* (*harri* 'stone' + -*gin*, -*gile*)
student	*ikasle* (*ikasi* 'study, learn' + -*le*, neologism), *estudiante* ~ *ixtudiant* (< Rom)
swineherd	*urdain* (*urde* 'hog' + -*zain*; irregular)
tailor	*joskile*, *joskin* (*josi* 'sew' + -*gile*, -*gin*), *jostun* (-*dun* 'who has'), *jantzigin* (*jantzi* 'clothing'), *jantzigile*
tanner	*larrugile* ~ *larrugin* (*larru* 'hide' + -*gile*, -*gin*)
teacher	*irakasle* (*irakatsi* 'teach' + -*le*)
weaver	*irule* (*irun* 'weave' + -*le*), *ehule* (*ehun* 'weave' + -*le*), *oihalgile* (*oihal* 'cloth' + -*gile*)
wet nurse	*inude* ~ *unide*, *amordeko* (*ama* 'mother' + *orde* 'stead' + -*ko*), B *aña*

whaler	*balenarrantzale* (*balea* 'whale' < Lat + *arrantzale* 'fisherman')
woodcutter	*haizkolari* (*haizkora* 'axe' < Lat + *-lari*)
worker	*langile* (*lan* 'work' + *-gile*)

The name of almost any profession is obtained by adding the suffix *-tza* to the name of its practitioner: *artzantza* 'sheep-herding', *nekazaritza* 'farming, agriculture' and so on.

5.10 INDIVIDUAL WORDS OF PARTICULAR INTEREST

5.10.1 The name of the language

The self-designation of the Basque language is *euskara* (B G *euskera*, L LN *eskuara*, Z *üská*); two sixteenth-century authors have *heuskara*. The etymology of this name is uncertain. Since the European designations for the Basques derive from the label *Vascones*, applied by the Romans to a people inhabiting the centre of the modern Basque Country, many scholars have assumed that Latin *vasc-* and Basque *eusk-* must represent the same stem, although the phonological difficulties involved are formidable, and the identification is rejected by most specialists today.

More interestingly, the Romans identified one of the important Aquitanian tribes as the *Ausci*, whose name is perpetuated in the modern French town of Auch (the form **Auscii*, cited in some works, is an error). (It may also be perpetuated in the curious Roncalese word *autx* 'Frenchman'.) Now the development of *au* into *eu*, though sporadic, is well attested in Basque, and hence it is tempting to assume that **ausk-* must have been the ancient self-designation of the Basque people, or of a significant number of them anyway, and that this stem has undergone the sporadic change to *eusk-*. In this view, the morph *-ara* would be the familiar suffix of the form *-(k)ara* or *-(k)era* which signifies 'way, manner', and hence 'to speak *euskara*' would originally have been, literally, 'to speak in the manner of the *Ausci*', 'to speak like the *Ausci*'. The origin of a language name as an adverb is, of course, a very common phenomenon: the Spanish name *vascuence* 'Basque (language)' has such an origin, as does the Turkish self-designation *Türkçe*, and the northern Basque *mintzaira* ~ *mintzara* 'language' is similarly derived from *mintzatu* 'speak' plus *-era*. This etymology is seductive, and it has been widely accepted.

However, a fascinating contrary view has been proposed and defended in recent years by the distinguished Basque philologist Alfonso Irigoyen. In two articles (1977a, 1990c), Irigoyen has pointed to the existence in Basque of a widespread and clearly ancient verb meaning 'say, tell'. Unusually, this verb is defective, and it has no attested non-finite forms, and hence no citation form; frequently the synonymous verb *esan* ~ *erran* is pressed into service as a citation form. The root is variable in form: outside of Bizkaian, the form is -io- when there is no indirect object and -io(t)s- when there is, but Bizkaian has -iño- and -iño(t)s-, respectively, with a variant -iñau(t)s- for the last. Hence, for example, 'he says' is *dio* (B *diño*), while 'he tells me' is *diost* (B *diñost* or *diñaust*).

Now it is well known that an ancient intervocalic *n*, otherwise uniformly lost, is frequently retained as *ñ* after the vowel *i*, and often also after an original *e* when this was earlier raised to *i*. This development is attested sporadically in all varieties: for example, Latin VAGINA 'sheath' is attested in Basque both as *magia* and as *magiña*; Z has *khatiña* for common *katea* 'chain' (< Lat CATENA); and so on (see Michelena 1977a: section 15.4). And it is particularly common in Bizkaian: for example, B has *iñes* 'flight' (< *ines(i)*), in the face of G HN *iges(i)*, L LN *ihes(i)*, Z *ihés*, R *ies(i)*, Sal *ies(i)*. Hence, assuming that the more widespread vocalism *o* in the forms of our defective verb represents a levelling of the more conservative B *au*, Irigoyen supposes that the earliest form of the verbal root must have been *-inau(t)s-*, and he therefore posits *enau(t)si* as the original participle of the verb 'say, tell', with the familiar element -*ts* indicating a verb which takes an indirect object (see Chapter 4).

So far, this is only an exercise in reconstructing a particular verb, but now Irigoyen introduces a stunning observation: the sixteenth-century Bizkaian Basque writer Garibay, in his *Compendio historial* of 1571, twice cites the name of the language as *enusquera*, and on the second occasion he explicitly opposes this name to *erdeera*, which he defines as the Basque name for a foreign language, especially Castilian. (In fact, *erdara* or *erdera* is everywhere the name given by Basques to the Romance speech of their neighbours; see below.) This odd-looking form has usually been dismissed as an error or an eccentricity, but Irigoyen proposes to take it at face value: the earliest form of the name of the language, he submits, is *enuskara* or *enuskera*, derived from the verb *enau(t)si* 'say' with the same adverbial suffix -(*k*)*ara* or -(*k*)*era* already identified (compare B G *siniskera* 'belief', from *sinitsi* 'believe'). Hence, in Irigoyen's analysis, the name of the language originally meant, literally, 'way of saying' or perhaps 'way of speaking'.

In his second article, Irigoyen defends his thesis by comparing the case of the widespread word for 'bark' (of a dog), which he reconstructs as *enausi* (possibly the same word as *enau(t)si*?) and which shows regional variants not unlike those for the language name. Astonishingly, Irigoyen's proposal has been received in deafening silence: very few linguists have accorded it even the most cautious approval. But this would seem to be a paradigm case of the old adage 'Look for Latin etymologies on the Tiber.' The form *enusquera* is securely attested, and Basque certainly has a verb of speaking whose ancient form must have been something rather similar to this. Why, then, should anyone want to reject such a straightforward analysis in favour of a speculative proposal involving the name given by the Romans to a people manifestly inhabiting a region which ceased to be Basque-speaking at an early date?

The combining form of *euskara* is *euskal*: *Euskal Herria* 'the Basque Country'. This suggests that the original form of the ending might have been *-ala*, rather than *-ara*, with the regular development of intervocalic *l* into *r*, but we cannot be certain about this, since inversion of this rule is well attested (see Chapter 3). In any case, this issue has no significant consequences for the etymologies considered above.

The word *euskaldun* means 'Basque-speaker, Basque'. It is derived by means of the common word-forming suffix *-dun* 'having, one who has', and hence means literally 'one who has *euskara*'. This is a rare instance of a people naming themselves after their language. Even today, this word is not commonly applied to any ethnic Basque, but only to a Basque-speaker, especially to a native speaker; where the distinction is necessary, *euskaldun zahar* 'old Basque' is applied to a native speaker, and *euskaldun berri* 'new Basque' to a person who has learned Basque as a second language.

(For the fanciful and unetymological forms in *euzk-*, such as *euzkera*, *euzkeldun*, *euzko*, and for the modern coinages like *Euskadi*, see the section on Sabino Arana in section 5.8.)

I mentioned above that *erdara* ~ *erdera* is the Basque name for a foreign language, applied by the Basques to the Spanish, French or Gascon speech of their neighbours. This word shows the same suffix as *euskara*, but the first element is obscure. Many have seen it as *erdi* 'half', interpreting *erdara* as 'half-language' (for example, Tovar 1959a: Ch. 13). There are, however, problems with this, since the combining form of *erdi* is normally *ert-*, not **erd-*, as in *ertain* 'middle-sized, medium, average'. Moreover, Irigoyen again points out, Garibay's form *erdeera* cannot be explained by *erdi*, but only by a form **erdV-*, where *V* might be any vowel except *i*, though preferably not *u*. One or two scholars have invoked the archaic verb *erdutu* 'come, arrive', but this is not obviously appealing. This *erdara* has a derivative *erdaldun* 'non-Basque-speaker, foreigner', formed just like *euskaldun*; both *erdara* and *erdaldun* are attested in medieval Navarre.

As for the Latin *Vascones*, an ingenious etymology has been proposed by Antonio Tovar (1949: 82–89). Tovar notes that the name *ba(r)scunes* is found inscribed on coins from an early period in the territory of the Vascones, and he reasons as follows. First, he identifies this *ba(r)scunes* with the name *Vascones*. Second, he interprets this as a typical Indo-European nominative plural in *-es* from a consonant-stem. Third, he takes the element *-con* ~ *-cun* to be an Indo-European suffix **-kon*. Finally, he interprets the apparent stem *ba(r)s-* as an *s*-extension of the well-known PIE root **bhar-* 'point, summit, top' (the source of English *bristle*, of Latin FASTIGIUM 'summit' and of other words). Hence he takes the whole as a purely Indo-European formation meaning roughly 'the high people', though he prefers to interpret this label as meaning 'the proud people', rather than the perhaps more obvious 'the mountain people'. This etymology has won considerable acceptance among specialists; it implies that Latin *Vascones* is merely an adaptation of the name given to the Basques by the earlier Indo-European peoples who inhabited part of the Basque Country.

5.10.2 The name of God

The enigmatic and speculative *Ortzi* was discussed above, in section 5.9.4, and will not be further considered here.

The most widespread word for 'God' in Basque is *Jaungoikoa*. This appears to be a transparent formation from *jaun* 'lord' and *goiko* 'who is on high', in other words 'heavenly', plus the article *-a*. But the order of elements is very un-Basque: a *-ko* phrase normally precedes its head, and we would have expected **Goikojauna*. It is possible that this odd formation merely results from a calque on some Romance phrase meaning 'the Lord in heaven', or the like. There exist a few parallels for this sort of calque, such as *zezensuzko* 'fiery bull' (Sp *toro de fuego*), again found in place of the expected **suzkozezen*; this is a papier-maché figure of a bull covered in fireworks, displayed at festivals. But there may be another explanation.

A second name for God is *Jainko*, which has an eastern variant *Jinko*. This name is found throughout the country and throughout the historical period; in the earliest texts it is often more frequent than *Jaungoikoa*. At least two proposals have been put forward to relate the two names: (1) *Jainko* is an irregular contraction of *Jaungoikoa*; (2) *Jainko* is in fact the earlier term, and *Jaungoikoa* is nothing more than a folk-etymology which attempts to rationalize the old name into something more obviously Christian, and this is the reason for the unusual formation. With the information at our disposal, it appears to be impossible to decide if either of these interpretations contains any truth, and it may be that the two names are simply unrelated. Notable, however, is the fact that *Jainko* contains a voiceless plosive after a nasal, an observation which suggests that this form cannot be of any great antiquity (recall from Chapter 3 that plosives were uniformly voiced in this position at some time in the post-Roman period, except in eastern dialects). These names, and the relation between them (if any) will surely remain mysterious in the absence of any new evidence.

Incidentally, the frequently made proposal that English *jingo* in *By jingo!* is derived from Basque *Jinko* is surely far too implausible to be taken seriously, in spite of the existence of Basque *Ala Jinko!* 'By God!'

5.10.3 Mythological creatures and terms from folklore

Like other peoples, the Basques possess a number of legends, myths and folktales. In fact, what we have today in this vein is probably only a remnant of what was earlier a much richer body of material, for it was only in the late nineteenth century that scholars (most of them amateurs) began to make systematic efforts to collect and record these stories. A few names and words occurring in these tales are particularly prominent, and some of them are recorded in earlier texts.

Chief among these is *akelarre*, which is conventionally regarded as the name of a witches' gathering (witches play an important part in Basque folklore). The precise significance of this term has been blurred by the imaginative embroiderings of Basque Romantics and perhaps also by the outraged attentions of the Church, but the akelarre is generally thought by enthusiasts to have been some kind of black mass or sabbat. The word appears to be a transparent derivative of *aker* 'he-goat' and *larre* 'meadow, pasture', and there is ample supporting evidence that he-goats were significant in some kind of pre-Christian religious ceremony, though little of this evidence appears to be of any great antiquity. Azkue, who was a priest as well as a linguist, is dismissive of the whole idea: he points out that *Akelarre* also happens to be the name of a plain in Navarre, between the village of Urdazubi and the mountain of Zugarramurdi, an area which has long been associated with witches, and implies that the name of the plain was transferred in the popular imagination into the name of the witches' supposed activity, and that the term therefore represents a late invention rather than a record of any historical practice.

Interestingly, one of the divine names recorded in Aquitanian (see Chapter 6) is *Aherbelste*, in which the second element appears to be *beltz* 'black' and the first has sometimes been interpreted as *aker*. This identification is, however, dismissed by Michelena, since there is no parallel for a development $h > k$ in Basque, though Gorrochategui (1995) is inclined to accept it.

The word for 'witch' is *sorgin*, a word whose etymology is deeply obscure. The second element looks very much like the familiar noun-forming suffix *-gin* 'one who makes', but the first element is troublesome. If it were *zori* 'omen, luck', we would have expected **zorgin* or even **zolgin*; if it were Latin SORTE 'chance, fate', we would have expected **zortagin*, or at best **zorkin*. In the east, we find R *beragile* ~ *beragin*, Z *belhagile* 'sorceror', literally 'maker of herbs'.

Among the most prominent figures in Basque folklore are the *Lamiak* or *Lamiñak*, usually portrayed as beautiful but malevolent women with animal feet who deceive, enchant and kill people, often especially young men. Though well developed in Basque legend, the Lamias are not exclusively Basque: various types of female monsters called Lamias are found throughout much of Europe and can be traced back at least to ancient Greek mythology. None the less, it seems faintly surprising that creatures of ancient Greek provenance should be so securely established in the Basque mountains. The widespread variant *lamiñak* is also puzzling, since the neighbouring Romance languages show no trace of a nasal in this word.

Another favourite character of folklore is *Basajaun*, the Old Man of the

Woods, frequently but not invariably portrayed as malicious. His name contains the common element *basa-* 'wild', the combining form of *baso* 'wilderness' and *jaun* 'lord, gentleman'. Interestingly, the name is never used with the article. Some versions give the Old Man a female companion, *Basandere*, but this is very likely a late accretion.

More shadowy but clearly of some importance is a mythical serpent, *Sugaar*, whose name is a compound of *suge* 'snake, serpent' and *ar* 'male'; this name too never takes the article. Casual observers have frequently confused this name with the unrelated word *sugar* 'flame', a compound of *su* 'fire' and *gar* 'flame'. The name of the monstrous sea-serpent *Herensuge* appears to mean, curiously, 'third snake'.

A positively enigmatic figure is that of *Mari*, apparently a semi-divine female figure who resides in several locations all of which have other associations with legend, such as on Anboto, the Bizkaian mountain which, like Zugarramurdi in the east, is strongly connected with witches in popular belief. Mari is apparently perceived as a largely benevolent figure, and of course the obvious explanation revolves around the figure of the Virgin Mary (Sp *María*). But the firm attachment to specific locations has led several scholars to suggest that what we have here may be a remembrance of one or more local divinities deriving from the pre-Christian period which have been somewhat vaguely wrapped in Christian garb. It has even been suggested that the name *Mari* itself may be pre-Christian, and that its resemblance to *María* may be coincidence, though this is perhaps pushing coincidence a little far.

5.10.4 Some political words

Sabino Arana's important coinages are described in section 5.8, including *Euskadi* 'Basque state', *ikurrin* 'Basque flag', *aberri* 'fatherland', *abertzale* 'patriot' and *gudari* 'Basque soldier'. Arana and his PNV also created the Basque national day, *Aberri Eguna* 'Fatherland Day', which is always celebrated on Easter Sunday.

The traditional name for the Basque Country is *Euskal Herria*, a label which is ethnic and geographical rather than political. The word *herri* means all of 'country, land', 'people, nation' and 'town', while *hiri* is more specifically 'town' or 'city'; this last clearly derives from **ili* and continues the element *Ili-* found in ancient toponyms.

The politically central word *askatu* 'liberate' is derived from Latin LAS-CARE 'untie, let go of' or a Romance development of it, and this is the only sense of the Basque word before the twentieth century, when it was pressed into service as a neologism for 'liberate'. From it are derived the noun *askatasun* 'liberty, freedom' and the back-formed adjective *aske* 'free'. All these words became prominent during the Basque struggle against the Franco dictatorship, and of course the noun appears in the name of the militant underground organization *Euskadi ta Askatasuna*, or *ETA* (the name means 'Basque Homeland and Liberty'), though for some reason the organization in its early days misspelled the word as **Azkatasuna*.

Popular accounts of the Basque Country often mention the slogan *Zazpiak Bat* 'The Seven Are One' (the reference is to the seven traditional Basque provinces) and describe it as 'ancient'. In fact, it dates only from around 1960, the period of rising Basque nationalist feeling. It is a modern reinterpretation of the phrase *Irurak Bat* 'The Three Are One', the slogan of the Real Sociedad Vascongada de Amigos del País, an important organization founded in 1766 to promote industry, commerce, agriculture and the arts in the three provinces of Bizkaia, Gipuzkoa and Araba.

Dominated in its early days by the PNV, with its Aranist leanings, the Basque Autonomous Government makes heavy use of Aranist neologisms in its official terminology. The Basque government calls itself *Eusko Jaurlaritza*, and the Basque president is the *lehendakari*, all of these being Aranist words recast in modern spelling.

Education has seen some important neologisms, most notably *ikastola* 'Basque-language school', formed from *ikasi* 'study, learn' and *-ola* 'place'.

5.10.5 Some cultural words

Undoubtedly the single best-known Basque artefact is the beret, the headgear which, even if it wasn't invented by the Basques, has become such a stereotype as almost to amount to a national emblem. In Spanish, the beret is called a *boina*, a word often thought to represent a Basque development of the same item which appears in English and French as *bonnet*. This word is little used in Basque (though some French Basques use *bonet*); instead, the Basque words are developments of the medieval Latin CAPELLA or CAPELLU 'head covering': southern *txapela*, northern *gapelu* ~ *kapelu*.

A traditional emblem everywhere in the country is the *lauburu*, a swastika with four rounded heads; the name is *lau* 'four' + *buru* 'head'. Nothing whatever is known of its origin.

The fundamental unit of traditional Basque society is the household, a large two-story stone house built in the distinctive Basque style with a shelter for animals on one side, and with some amount of land attached. This unit is called a *baserri* (*basa-* 'wild' + *herri* 'settlement') on the Spanish side, and a *borda* on the French side. (The second word originally meant 'hut, cabin', 'shepherd's summer quarters', and its extension to 'farmhouse' came about as a result of the frequent practice of developing summer pastures into farms during the population growth of the seventeenth and eighteenth centuries.) People who live in *baserriak* are *baserritarrak*, and there has long been a certain divide between them and the *kaletarrak* who live in town (*kale* 'street', from Spanish *calle*). The household is administered by the *etxekojaun* ('master of the house') and the *etxekoand(e)re* ('lady of the house'); these two have precisely delineated roles, and these roles are formally handed over, upon retirement, to the single child deemed most suitable and to that child's spouse. The child selected is usually the oldest son, but need not be. The household is never broken up, and other children must either marry into another household, remain as unmarried employees, or seek a living in the wider world – though the Napoleonic inheritance laws, forbidding this practice, wreaked havoc upon many households in the north.

Another central structure is the shepherd's hut, the seasonal shelter used by shepherds accompanying their flocks to mountain pastures in the summer. This has various names. One is *ola*, a word which also means 'forge, foundry' and, more generally, 'factory, place where something is done'; in toponyms and surnames it often seems to mean no more than 'place'. A second word is *borda*, which, in the French Basque Country, has come to mean 'farm, homestead', because of the eighteenth-century practice, at a time of growing population, of clearing new farms around existing huts. A third is *(t)xola*, of unknown origin but very likely a loan. A fourth is *etxola*, which looks very much like a derivative of *etxe* 'house', but this is probably just *txola* with contamination from *etxe*. The last and most recent term is *txabola*, which appears to be a loan from Old Spanish *javola* ~ *jaola* (modern *jaula*) 'cage, pen, cell', an etymology which amusingly makes the Basque word cognate with English *jail*.

Entertainment was traditionally provided by groups of singers and dancers, who performed (and still perform) on special occasions, most notably at *jaiak*, or festivals. Every city and town in the country has a *jai* once a year, and both folk groups and professional singers make the rounds of these festivals. Some Basque folk dances are very well known, such as the *aurresku*, the *ezpata-dantza* ('sword dance') and the *godalet dantza* ('wine-glass dance', in which a dancer wearing a paper horse which conceals his feet from him leaps onto and off a glass of wine without spilling any).

But the most striking musical entertainment is provided by the *bertsolari* competitions. A *bertsolari* (< *bertso* 'verse' + professional suffix) is a performer (always male) who is given a theme and who then must immediately compose and sing an original song upon that theme. Sometimes two *bertsolaris* meet head-to-head, each composing and singing a verse in turn, trying to get the upper hand. These performances are little short of miraculous. The winner of the competition, or of any Basque competition, is awarded a Basque beret, or *txapela*, as a result of which the word *txapeldun* 'one who has the beret' has become the ordinary word for 'champion', and *txapelketa* (-*keta* 'activity') is the ordinary word for 'contest, competition'.

Basque sports and games are usually rugged and occasionally boisterous. Traditional sports include wood-chopping contests (carried out by *haizkolariak*, from *haizkora* 'axe' < Lat ASCIOLA), weight-lifting, the tug-of-war (*sokatira* < *soka* 'rope' (< Lat) + *tira* 'pull' (< Sp)), walking with weights, and other things in this vein. Everyone has heard about the annual bull-running (*zezenketa* < *zezen* 'bull' + -*keta* 'activity') in Pamplona during the festival of San Fermín, during which young people run in front of loosed bulls. A somewhat safer version, common at festivals, is the *sokamutur* (*soka* 'rope' + *mutur* 'snout'), in which a bull is led on ropes by handlers through crowded streets.

But the Basque national game is *pilota* (< Sp *pelota* 'ball'), a game related to squash and played in several different versions. The most famous version is *cesta punta*, in which teams of two, each *pilotari* with a long wicker basket strapped to his arm, compete on an elongated court with three walls (there is no right-hand wall). The game has become popular in Latin America and in the United States, though outside the Basque Country it is somewhat curiously known as *jai alai* (*jai* 'festival' + *alai* 'merry'), a label never used in Basque but coined by the Basque Romantic writer Serafín Baroja in the late nineteenth century. Every village in the Basque Country has a municipal court, called a *frontón* in Spanish and a *pilota-leku* (*leku* 'place') in Basque; *pilotaris* are celebrities and often earn excellent money abroad.

5.10.6 The words in **iz-*

In his several publications, including his 1905 dictionary, Azkue argued for the recognition of a prehistoric element **iz*, with the meaning of 'water'. As evidence for this reconstruction, he pointed to the existence of a number of Basque words all beginning with a morph *iz-* and all having meanings apparently connected with water: *izurde* 'dolphin' (*urde* 'pig'), *izpazter* 'seacoast' (*bazter* 'edge'), *izotz* 'frost, ice' (*hotz* 'cold'), *izerdi* 'sweat' (*erdi* 'half'), *izokin* 'salmon', *Izaro*, the name of an island off Bermeo, and possibly one or two others. At first glance, this evidence looks reasonably persuasive. However, Azkue's case was vigorously attacked by Michelena in several places. Michelena points out that *izurde* could easily be from **gizurde*, in which the first element is *giza-*, the regular combining form of *gizon* 'man'. He notes as a parallel the place name attested in medieval texts as *Guiçayrudiaga* but modern *Izurdiaga*; to this we may add the observation that some northern varieties of Basque in fact have *giza-urde* as their word for 'dolphin'. Michelena goes on to point out that the first element in *izotz* could perfectly well be *ihintz ~ intz* 'dew', and that Azkue's alleged **izpazter* does not in fact exist, except as a place name *Izbazter*, modern *Ipazter*, in which *iz-* is most likely a reduction of **aiz-*, the combining form of *haitz* 'crag'. Moreover, *izokin* is a loan word from late Latin ESOCINA. Suddenly Azkue's case seems much less compelling, and few if any vasconists take Azkue's **iz-* seriously today, though seekers after remote comparisons never tire of invoking this ghost word in their comparisons.

5.10.7 The words in *gor-

Another of Azkue's pet speculations is the postulation of an ancient element *gor-, allegedly meaning 'flesh'. This he supports by pointing to the common adjectives gorri 'red' and gordin 'raw, crude', which look as if they might have been formed with the ancient adjective-forming elements -i and -din. (On occasion, he also adduces gorputz 'body', but this is an obvious loan from Latin CORPUS, and can be dismissed.) This speculation is perhaps more plausible than the preceding one, but note that Michelena (1970b) prefers to see gordin as derived from gor, today 'deaf' but well attested in an earlier sense of 'firm, hard, unyielding'.

5.11 PLACE NAMES

5.11.1 River names

The river names in the Basque Country have been very little studied, and at present we lack any survey of the attestations of river names in Roman and medieval documents. Consequently, all I can do here is to review the modern forms of these names.

There is a watershed running east to west across the country. North of it, the rivers in Bizkaia, Gipuzkoa, the northern tip of Navarre and the entire French Basque Country all flow into the Bay of Biscay; south of it, the rivers in Araba and in most of Navarre flow into the Ebro and hence ultimately into the Mediterranean. The most obvious point is that very few of the river names appear to be incontestably Basque in origin, even though nearly all of them exhibit unremarkably Basque phonological forms. This is particularly true of the larger rivers; the smaller streams more often have obviously Basque names, often names shared with significant towns lying upon them. It is convenient to consider first the rivers on the north side.

The northern boundary of the country is formed by the *Adour* (Bq *Atturri*), which was called the *Adur* by the Romans. This name looks Basque enough, but has no discernible source, and is possibly of Celtic origin. Of the major tributaries of this river on the Basque side, the *Maule* shares its name with the large town it passes through, while the *Biduze* (Fr *Bidouze*) and the *Errobi* (Fr *Nive*) both look tantalizingly Basque in form, but have no etymology. (Of course, *Errobi* could be taken as *erro bi* 'two roots', since it is known that the numeral *bi* was anciently postposed, but there is no obvious justification for such an etymology, since this river has multiple sources.) The smaller tributaries are the *Ardanabi*, the *Aran*, the *Lihuri*, the *Aphurra* and the *Aldude*, none of which has a clear Basque etymology, except possibly *Aran* (cf. *haran* 'valley'). The other main northern river, the *Sarrakaria* (Fr *Nivelle*) likewise has no etymology; its tributary, the *Sara*, shares its name with a town situated on it and is quite possibly Basque.

The Franco-Spanish frontier is formed by the *Bidasoa*, another opaque name, though it possibly shares its first element with *Biduze*, but the obvious *bide* 'road, way' does not seem appealing. Caro Baroja and others have proposed *Bide-Oiasso 'road to Oiartzun', but the formation is impossible: we would have expected *Oiasso-bide. Michelena (1956a) cautiously suggests a Latin *Via ad Oiasso, with the same meaning, noting that the name is always written in older texts as *Vidaso(a)*. In Gipuzkoa, we have the *Oiartzun* (Sp *Oyarzun*), which shares its name with a town. Now *oiartzun* happens to be the Basque word for 'echo', but this would seem to be a very odd way of naming a river, and coincidence seems likely. The name *Urumea* is as opaque as the others, except that, amusingly, it happens to be perfect Basque for 'the water child', but no one has ever suggested seriously that this might be the etymology. The name *Oria* is no more transparent; interestingly, the town at its mouth is called *Orio*, and the variation in vowels seems to me to suggest some kind of Indo-European influence. The Oria's tributary, the *Leitzaran*, simply takes its name from the valley it flows through, *Leitz* (Sp *Leniz*), pointing to an original Basque *Lenitz ((*h*)*aran* is simply 'valley').

Further west, the *Urola* shares its initial *ur-* with several other river names, and the obvious *ur* 'water' can hardly be ruled out here; *ola* is, of course, an exceedingly common final element in place names generally, though not otherwise in river names. And the river *Deba* (Sp *Deva*) has a name which is universally accepted as Celtic; the town at its mouth has the same name, and this name is found in formerly Celtic domains all over western Europe. Its tributaries the *Oñati* and the *Arantzazu* share their names with habitations; the first is probably Basque (*oin* 'foot') and the second certainly so (*arantza* 'thorn' + -*zu* 'full of').

Moving into Bizkaia, the name *Artibai* clearly contains *ibai* 'river'; the first element looks like *arte* 'between', a not implausible name for the river that roughly separates Bizkaia and Gipuzkoa and may anciently have separated the Caristii from the Varduli. The *Lea* and the *Oka* have mysterious names, while the *Butroe* (Sp *Butrón*) is transparently Indo-European, since the cluster *tr* cannot possibly occur in indigenous Basque words or names. On the other hand, the major river of Bizkaia, the *Ibaizabal*, has a name which could not be more Basque: it is *ibai* 'river' plus *zabal* 'wide'. This is one of the two rivers whose confluence forms the estuary of Bilbao, and it is striking that the only river with an undeniably Basque name is the most important river in the whole Basque heartland. Its two main tributaries, the *Indusi* and the *Arratia*, have names which look Basque enough, especially the second, but these also lack etymologies.

The other river forming the estuary, the *Nerbioi* (Sp *Nervión*) has a clearly non-Basque name; this name is very likely of Celtic origin. Several of the small streams flowing into the Nerbioi have names which are conspicuously Basque: *Altube* (*altu* 'height' < Lat + -*be* 'below'), *Arnauri* (? + *uri* 'town') and probably *Zeberio*. West of the Nerbioi, the river names are exclusively non-Basque, with the single exception of the *Izalde*, which at least looks convincingly Basque; *alde* means 'side', and the first element could be *haitz* 'peak', which is often reduced to *iz-* in initial position in toponyms. The name of the *Asua*, which also flows into the estuary, may be Basque but has no etymology.

South of the watershed the names are overwhelmingly non-Basque. The major river here is of course the *Ebro*, whose name is the Spanish development of *Iberus*, the name given to this river by the Romans; this name is of course the source of the name *Iberia*, applied to the whole peninsula. There have been repeated efforts to relate this name to the Basque *ibai* 'river', but there is no evidence for Basque speech in the Ebro valley in Roman times. A few scholars have tried to claim for the word *ibai* some kind of ancient pan-European existence by imputing it to an early 'Mediterranean' or 'Old European' substrate, but convincing evidence for such a suggestion has not been forthcoming.

The western tributaries of the Ebro are the *Baia* (Sp *Bayas*), the *Zadorra* and the *Ibaiuda* (Sp *Ayuda*), whose names look Basque enough, though they have no etymologies, apart perhaps from the presence of *ibai* in the last, and the *Odron*, which is certainly not Basque. Further east we have the *Ega* and its tributaries *Izkiz* and *Urederra*; only the last is clearly Basque (*ur* 'water' + *eder* 'beautiful' + Det). The *Arga* has tributaries *Salado*, *Arakil*, *Larraun*, *Arkil*, *Ultzama* and *Elortz*, of which only *Larraun* (? < *larre* 'pasture' + *on* 'good') and *Elortz* (= *elortza* < *elorri* 'hawthorn' + -*tza* Collective) look obviously Basque. The name of the *Aragón* is clearly not Basque. It has tributaries *Zidakos*, *Erro*, *Urrobi*, *Irati*, *Areta*, *Zatoia*, *Anduña*, *Zaraitzu* (Sp *Salazar*), *Ezka*, *Mintxate*, *Belagoa* and *Onsella*; several of these names look very Basque, but not one has a straightforward Basque etymology, though it is hard to believe that *Zaraitzu*, with its familiar suffix -*zu* 'full of', is not Basque, even though the first element is obscure.

5.11.2 Mountain names

Like the majority of place names in the Basque Country, mountain names have never been subjected to any systematic investigation, and we have no information on early references to mountains. Consequently, we have at present no way of knowing how long particular names have been in use. It is noteworthy, however, that the great majority of the names of the more prominent mountains show the phonological characteristics of native words, suggesting that they have been in use for many centuries. Only a handful of names, such as *Kalamua* and *Pardarri* (Gip), with their initial voiceless plosives, are unmistakably of more recent origin within Basque (though the second appears to contain the native word *harri* 'stone'). Far more typical are names like *Oitz*, *Intxorta* and *Lekanda* (Biz), *Ernio* (Gip), *Atxuria* (Lap) and *Zunbia* (Zub), which, even though they appear to have no Basque etymology, are phonologically indistinguishable from native words.

In fact, roughly half of the names of the more prominent mountains have names which are at least partly interpretable. Among these are the frequent formations involving *mendi* 'mountain', *haitz* 'crag' and its western variant *atx*, or *gain* ~ *gan* 'top'. Some examples: *Aizkorri* (Gip) (*haitz* + *gorri* 'red'), *Artzamendi* (Lap) (*artzan-*, combining form of *artzai(n)* 'shepherd'), *Zazpigaña* (Zub) (*zazpi* 'seven'), *Arbelaitz* (Gip) (*harbel* 'slate'), *Mendibeltza* (LNav) (*beltz* 'black'), *Iguzkimendi* (Lap) (*iguzki* 'sun'), *Murumendi* (Gip) (first element unidentifiable), *Udalatx* or *Udalaitz* (Biz) (*Udala* is the name of a village below the mountain but is not otherwise identifiable).

This is a topic which is crying out for investigation.

5.11.3 Province names

The names of the seven Basque provinces are largely of obscure origin, though a number of tantalizing clues exist.

The name of *Bizkaia* is universally thought to be a derivative of *bizkar* 'height in the mountains, summit' (and also 'back' as an anatomical term). The existence of derivatives like *bizkaitar* 'Bizkaian', showing the form *-tar* of the suffix which usually occurs after a consonant or a diphthong, and *bizkaiko* 'of or from Bizkaia' shows clearly that the name was originally **Bizkai*, and that the final *-a* must be the article. (Compare *Gipuzkoa* below.) A derivation of *Bizkai* from **bizkar-* plus a vowel-initial suffix would be entirely parallel to many other formations, such as *iztei* ~ *iztai* 'groin', from *izter* ~ *iztar* 'thigh' plus the noun-forming suffix *-e(g)i*. The word *bizkar* is clearly ancient, and an item *biscar* is attested in the ancient Iberian texts, which, although its significance is unknown, Michelena (1954a) is inclined to identify with the Basque word, presumably as a loan in one direction or the other. In fact, an identical element is found in several place names lying well outside the historical Basque Country, such as *Biscarosse*, *Biscarrosse* and *Biscarrués*, and the *Biscargitani* of ancient Spain belonged to a town called Βιοκαργις. There is also an ancient personal name *Arbiscar*. (Note also the R diminutive *bizkarxko* 'hill'.)

In the name of *Gipuzkoa*, in contrast, the final *-a* is organic: the derivatives are *gipuzkoar* 'Gipuzkoan', showing the variant *-ar* of the suffix which regularly appears after a vowel, and *gipuzkoako* 'of or from Gipuzkoa'. The final *-koa* is thought by many to be the ancient collective suffix *-(g)oa*, which suggests in turn that the stem *gipu(t)z-* might be an ethnic label; indeed, *giputz* is everywhere the word applied to a Gipuzkoan by a Basque from another province, but this usage is in all likelihood a recent formation derived from the province name.

With *Araba*, the Spanish form *Álava* is clearly more conservative, and the Basque form must derive regularly from an earlier **Alaba*, but the origin of the name is completely mysterious – though note that the *Alabanenses* are mentioned in Pliny.

The Basque name of Navarre shows considerable regional variation: beside the standard *Nafarroa*, we find also *Nafarra*, *Naparra* and *Nabarra*. The standard version reflects the form attested in our earliest documents, and again the presence of the collective suffix -*(g)oa* is suspected here; the other forms probably reflect Romance mediation. Many have seen this name as based on Romance *nabar* 'high plain'. The related word *nafar* 'person from Navarre' is attested early, from a time when *f* was otherwise almost non-existent in Basque. (The Navarri themselves are mentioned, in Latin, as early as the year 800.)

The name of *Lapurdi* clearly continues the ancient *Lapurdum*, the name of the Roman fort built on the site of Bayonne, and the name may well be of Basque origin, but no plausible etymology presents itself. (A derivation from *lapur* 'thief' has not been considered seriously by anyone.)

The small part of medieval Navarre extending north of the Pyrenees became a distinct unit only very late, as its name reflects. The French name *Basse Navarre* has both been calqued into Basque as *Nafarroa Beherea* (the official form) or *Benabarra* and borrowed directly as *Baxenabarra* (the local form).

Finally, *Zuberoa* once again possibly presents the collective suffix -*(g)oa*. In AD 635, a Frankish force led by Duke Arnebert was annihilated by the Basques at a certain 'Subola'; this is thought by many historians to represent an early form of the province name, in which case the intervocalic -*r*- would again derive from an original *-*l*-. The palatalized form *Xibero(a)* is used by the inhabitants.

5.11.4 Habitation names

Like all branches of Basque onomastics, the study of habitation names was initiated by Luchaire in the nineteenth century. After a long interval, Luchaire's work was continued in the twentieth century by Bähr and by Caro Baroja. Still, the amount of work done to date is disappointing. There have as yet been no comprehensive studies of habitation names in the Basque Country as a whole, though for the French Basque Country we do have Lemoine (1977) and, more recently, Orpustan (1990). In recent years the scholar who has been pursuing this subject most energetically is Alfonso Irigoyen; see in particular Irigoyen (1981a, 1985a, 1986, 1990a) and some of the essays in Irigoyen (1990b). Beyond this work, we have a few studies of individual names, a modest monograph on the subject by Michelena (1956b), chiefly devoted to phonology, and a number of useful remarks and observations scattered about in the general literature. Michelena's (1971a) paper includes some interesting remarks, and his (1973a) book on surnames also includes some useful information on toponyms. Echaide (1967) studies the names in -*oz*, and Agud (1973) attempts to divide the country into toponymic zones. Merino Urrutia (1978) is a valuable study of Basque toponyms in the Rioja and Burgos. Sasía (1966) is a somewhat overenthusiastic examination of possible Basque toponyms in the Encartaciones, the western zone of Bizkaia.

As was remarked in Chapter 1, the Greek geographers and the Roman historians noted a few place names in the country, some of them places founded by the Romans themselves. The Romans appear to have found few if any sizeable settlements in the Basque-speaking territory, and the Roman city of Pamplona is usually considered to have been the first city in what is now the Basque Country. Medieval documentation of place names is scattered but not entirely sparse. Particularly valuable is the *Reja de San Millán*, a record of the towns in Araba contributing goods to the monastery of San Millán and dated 1025; the archaic character of the names is very striking. See Michelena (1964a: 25–30) for an account.

Oddly, the toponyms and related ethnonyms recorded by the Romans in or near the Aquitanian-speaking territory include not one which is indisputably Aquitanian/Basque. Gorrochategui (1995) classifies the recorded names into three groups. The first are unmistakably or probably Celtic, such as *Lugdunum*, modern Saint-Bernard-de-Comminges. The second are probably Iberian. Here Gorrochategui places the several towns called *Calagurris* and also most of those in *ili-* and *ilu-*, such as *Iluro* (modern *Oloron*). He notes also the problematic *Iliberris* mentioned in Chapter 1 but is non-committal. The third are 'difficult to classify'. Among these are *Beneharnum* (modern Béarn), *Cocosates*, *Onobrisates* and *Sibuzates* (some read this as *Sibulates*), the last conceivably related to the modern Basque region of Zuberoa. One which is conceivably Aquitanian is the ethnonym *Tarbelli*, which might represent the same formation as Basque *harbel* 'slate', literally 'dark stone', given the possible Aquitanian development of *t-* > *h-* mentioned in Chapter 3.

A number of scholars have attempted to give the important city of Calagurris an Aquitanian/Basque etymology, pointing in particular to the resemblance of the final element to Basque *gorri* 'red'. Michelena has contemplated for the first element *garo* 'fern', whose combining form would be *gara-*; this word could easily derive from earlier **galo*. In support of this is the observation that the other two Basque words for 'fern', *ira* and its extension *iratze*, both figure in toponyms *Iragorri* and *Iratzagorri*; against it is the fact that *garo* is a severely localized word, found in only a part of Gipuzkoa. Another possibility would be *gara* 'height, elevation', well attested in toponyms, but the location of the city (modern Calahorra) in the Ebro valley, at the confluence of two rivers, is anything but encouraging. It is highly likely that, as most scholars believe, this city name is not Aquitanian/Basque at all, but Celtiberian or Iberian.

Generally speaking, the frequency of modern habitation names for which a Basque source is obvious or probable is highest in the eastern and central part of the country, declining noticeably towards the west and the south, reflecting what was said in Chapter 1 about the comparatively late spread of

Basque in these directions. Bizkaia in particular shows a high proportion of what are clearly Indo-European names of pre-Basque provenance, while much of Araba and Navarre is dominated by Romance names, and the Ebro valley today shows only a scant handful of Basque names, all of them confined to villages, though in medieval times there were clearly more Basque names there. To the north, Basque names stop rather abruptly once one crosses the border of the traditional three French Basque provinces, confirming that the Basque–Gascon linguistic frontier has been stable for a very long time.

Many places, especially sizeable ones, have distinct names in Basque and in French or Spanish. Sometimes the Romance name is merely an adaptation of the Basque one, or vice versa; sometimes the two names reflect differing phonological developments of the same medieval name; sometimes each name is a more-or-less literal translation of the other; sometimes the Basque and Romance names are totally unrelated.

As in all onomastic work, it is very treacherous to try to establish the etymologies of these names without careful scrutiny of such ancient and medieval documentation as we possess. Here are two excellent examples.

First, one of the best-known Basque toponyms is *Biarritz*, the name of the famous resort town on the coast of Lapurdi (the modern Basque form is *Miarritze*). At first glance, this looks like a combination of *bi* 'two' and *harri* 'stone', possibly with the common collective suffix *-tza*; a noun *arritza* 'stony place' is well attested south of the Pyrenees. Moreover, a visitor to Biarritz can actually see two large boulders sticking out of the water in the harbour. Such an etymology therefore looks very plausible, and it has been widely accepted. However, the earliest documentation of the name shows *Bearriz* (1170) and *Beiarriz* (1261). Here the final *-iz* looks very much like the patronymic suffix attached to a personal name **Beiar*. On investigation, Irigoyen (1990a: 71) finds a surname *Biar* attested in 1448 and an extension of this *Bearreta* in use as a surname, also in 1448, as well as a house name *Biar* in 1640. He therefore concludes that *Biarritz* is probably a patronymic derived in the usual fashion from a personal name **Beiar*, and that the popular etymology sketched above is wrong.

Second, the name of *Baiona* (Fr *Bayonne*), the chief city of the French Basque Country, looks transparent: it is surely from *ibai ona* 'the good river', with the common loss of an initial vowel (compare the nearby town of *Baigorri*, apparently from *ibai gorri* 'red river'). Moreover, Baiona is located at the mouth of a navigable river which, since Roman times, has been an important trade route. What could be simpler? But historical investigation once again changes the picture. Irigoyen (1990a: 39–54), in examining this toponym, begins by establishing the widespread existence in medieval Basque and Romance of a personal name *Baio*, derived from an attested Latin personal name *Baius*, and shows that this personal name occurs in other place names in and around the Basque Country, from

Gascony to Galicia. He therefore concludes that *Baiona* too contains this personal name. The second element, he is inclined to think, is probably indeed *on* 'good' plus the article *-a*, and he takes the source therefore as *Baio Ona, in which the adjective is an epithet applied to a certain person named *Baio*: Baio the Good. At the same time, he does not entirely rule out the possibility that this second element might in fact be a Latin *onna 'watercourse, spring', which is abundantly attested in toponyms in Gascony and which appears to derive from a substrate language.

Like other Basque names, toponyms are constructed exclusively from nominal and adjectival elements plus certain rather common affixes; verbal roots are unknown. A few suffixes are exceedingly frequent, notably *-aga* and *-eta* ~ *-keta*; the first of these appears to denote only 'place', while the second is usually interpreted as 'abundance of' and is thought by some to derive from Latin -ETA. Examples: *Urnieta* (Gip) (probably *Urdina* 'blue', a female personal name), *Arrigorriaga* (Biz) (*harri* 'stone' + *gorri* 'red'), *Ezpeleta* (Lap) (*ezpel* 'box tree'), *Zumarraga* (Gip) (*zumar* 'elm'), *Goizueta* (Nav) (earlier *Goizubieta*, from *goi* 'height' + *zubi* 'bridge'), *Olheta* (Lap) (*ola* 'forge, foundry'), *Areeta* (Biz) (Sp *Las Arenas*) (*harea* 'sand' < Lat ARENA), *Orreaga* (Nav) (Sp *Roncesvalles*) (*orre* 'juniper'), *Elgeta* (Gip) (*elge* 'cultivated field'). Also frequent are *-ti* and *-doi* ~ *-dui* ~ *-di*, both of which also appear to mean only 'place', and a suffix *-te*, of uncertain meaning.

There are two different elements which appear as *-ano* in official Spanish forms; one of these derives from Latin -ANU and appears in popular Basque as *-ao* or *-au* or (after *i*) as *-o*, reflecting the regular loss of intervocalic *n*, while the other appears in Basque as *-ano* and must derive from an indigenous element **-anno* (Michelena's **-aNo*); this is probably a diminutive suffix **-No* attached to a stem in *a*. Examples of the first: *Legutio* (Ara) (formerly *Legutiano*, Sp *Villareal de Álava*), *Galdakao* (Biz) (Sp *Galdácano*), *Abadiño* (Biz) (Sp *Abadiano*) (*abade* 'abbot'), *Otxandio* (Biz) (Sp *Ochandiano*), *Lazkao* (Biz) (Sp *Lazcano*), *Zeberio* (Biz) (Sp *Ceberio*, this time reflecting popular Basque speech, though the medieval spelling is *Ceberiano*), *Laudio* (Ara) (Sp *Llodio*, from ancient CLAUDIANU). Medieval documents show considerable fluctuation in spelling such names: *Zerio/Zeriano*, *Durandio/Durandiano* and so on. An example of the second is *Elkano* (Gip, Nav), attested in the Gipuzkoan case as *Helkanno* in 1025. Naturally, the loss of intervocalic *n* has occurred between other pairs of vowels, as in *Leioa* (Biz) (Sp *Lejona*) and *Lemoiz* (Biz) (Sp *Lemoniz*).

A final element *-iz* ~ *-itz* is rather frequent and is thought to represent a patronymic formation attached to a personal name: *Gaminiz* (Biz) (Sp *Plencia*), *Laukiz* (Biz), *Urduliz* (Biz), *Berriz* (Biz), and perhaps *Biarritz* (Lap), as explained above. In Bizkaia and Araba, the Indo-European endings *-aka* and *-ika* (rarely *-eka*) are very frequent and are almost always attached to initial elements which are not Basque; such names are doubtless of Indo-European origin: *Gernika* (Biz), *Mundaka* (Biz), *Sondika* (Biz), *Muxika*

(Biz), *Gatika* (Biz), *Ozeka* (Ara). Such names are not found in the eastern half of the country. A second final element *-ama* is also suspected of being of Indo-European origin: *Lezama* (Biz), *Zegama* (Gip), *Beizama* (Gip), *Arama* (Gip), *Ultzama* (Nav) (*U(t)çama* in medieval documents).

Two frequent elements, especially in medieval toponyms and house names, are *luku* and *zaldu*, both often attached to obviously Basque elements: *Lukumendi* (*mendi* 'mountain'), *Lukugarai* (*garai* 'high'), *Zalduburua* (*buru* 'head'), *Zalduzaharra* (*zahar* 'old') and many others. Orpustan (1994b) sees these items as continuing Latin LUCU and SALTU, both 'woods'. This makes the name *Oyhançaldua*, attested in 1319, rather interesting, since *oihan* is 'forest'. Also very interesting is the name *Aker zaltua* (1074), with the Latin gloss SALTUS IRCORUM, both meaning 'billy-goat woods'.

As was noted in Chapter 1, a final element *-oz* (Romance *-os*, *-ués*, etc.) is found throughout the area formerly occupied by Aquitanian and is indeed taken as the primary toponymic evidence for Aquitanian speech. This element is often thought to represent Basque *hotz* 'cold', but its great frequency suggests otherwise. Very frequent throughout the entire country, but especially in Navarre, is a final *-ain*, as in *Andoain* (Gip), *Antsoain* (Nav) and *Etulain* (Nav); this element is most often attached to a first element which is not Basque, very frequently to a personal name. Caro Baroja's attempt at deriving this from Latin -ANU runs into phonological difficulties, while a combination *-aren* of the article and the genitive suffix fits poorly with personal names, which should not take the article. Michelena (1973a) proposes *-ani*, the genitive of Latin -ANU, which is phonologically perfect. Bizkaian toponyms frequently show a final element *-o*, of unknown origin, as in *Elorrio* (*elorri* 'hawthorn'), *Erandio*, *Bakio*, *Amurrio* and a number of others. Other common final elements include adjectives like *zabal* 'wide', *luze* 'long', *on* 'good', *berri* 'new', *zahar* 'old' and *gorri* 'red', and the adjective-forming element *-zu* 'full of' appears in dozens of names. Some names contain the article *-a*.

The common derivational suffix *-(g)une* 'interval, space' apparently appears in a number of toponyms, variously as *-un* or as *-ue*, and possibly also as *-ume* and as *-une*: *Ataun* (Gip), *Unanue* (Nav, mountain), *Oiartzun* (Gip), *Donibane Lohitzune* (Lap) and many others. The variable retention of the *n* in this morph is anomalous and puzzling.

Among the nominal elements, particularly frequent are spatial nouns like *gara(i)* and *goi* 'high place', *behe* 'below', *gain* 'top', *arte* 'between', *alde* 'side' and *barne* 'interior'. Examples: *Azpeitia* and *Azkoitia* (Gip) (*haitz* 'peak' + *behe* and *goi* + *-ti*), *Azkaine* (Lap), (*haitz* 'peak' + *gain*), *Azkarate* (LNav) (*haitz* 'peak' + *gara* + *-te*), *Hazparne* (Lap) (*haitz* 'peak' + *barne*), *Lasarte* (Gip) (*lats* 'stream' + *arte*), *Axpe* (Biz) (*haitz* 'peak' + *behe*), *Bidarte* (Lap) (Fr *Bidart*) (*bide* 'road' + *arte*). Names of trees and shrubs are very frequent: *Elorrio* (Biz) (*elorri* 'hawthorn' + *-o*), *Zumarraga* (Gip) (*zumar* 'elm' + *-aga*), *Ezpeleta* (Lap) (*ezpel* 'box tree' + *-eta*), *Arteaga* (Biz) (*arte* 'holm oak' + -*aga*), *Lizarra* (Nav) (Sp *Estella*) (*lizar* 'ash tree'), *Phagola* (Zub) (*pago* 'beech' < Lat FAGU + *ola* 'place'), *Amezketa* (Gip) (*ametz* 'gall-oak' + -*keta*). Also common are geographical terms like *haran* and *ibar* 'valley', *mendi* 'mountain', *haitz* 'crag, peak', *zelai* 'plain', *larre* 'pasture' and *hondar* 'beach, sand'. Examples: *Aranguren* (Nav) (*haran* 'valley' + *guren* 'edge'), *Ondarroa* (Biz) (*hondar* 'sand' + *aho* 'mouth'), *Eibar* and *Elgoibar* (Gip) (*ibar* 'valley' with uncertain first elements), *Etxalar* (Nav) (*etxe* 'house' + *larre* 'pasture'), *Larrabetzu* (Biz) (*larre* 'pasture' + *behe* 'below' + -*zu* 'full of'), Naturally, *herri* 'village' and *hiri* ~ *uri* 'town' are very common, as are *etxe* 'house' and *eliza* 'church', *zubi* 'bridge' and especially *ola* 'forge, foundry; shepherd's hut', but in place names merely 'place where something is done' or just 'place'. Examples: *Zeanuri* (Biz) (*azeri* 'fox' < **azenari* + *uri* 'town'), *Basauri* (Biz) (*baso* 'woods' + *uri* 'town'), *Ziburu* (Lap) (Fr *Ciboure*) (*zubi* 'bridge' + *buru* 'head'), *Iruri* (Zub) (Fr *Trois-Villes*) (*hiru(r)* 'three' + *hiri* 'town'). Personal names are frequent but usually well disguised. The word *done* 'saint' (< Lat DOMINE) appears in the names of places derived from saints' names; the female counterpart *dona* is rare. Examples: *Donosti(a)* (Gip) (Sp *San Sebastián*), *Donapaleu* (LNav) (Fr *St Palais*), *Donibane-Lohitzune* (Lap) (Fr *St Jean de Luz*) (*lohitz* 'mud' + -*une* 'place'), *Donibane Garazi* (LNav) (Fr *St Jean Pied-de-Port*) (*garazi* 'grace'), *Doneztebe* (Nav) (Sp *Sanesteban*), *Donamaria* (Nav), *Donazaharre* (LNav) (Fr *St Jean-le-Vieux*) (*zahar* 'old').

Particularly interesting is the Basque name of Pamplona, *Iruñea*, attested in medieval documents as *Ironia, Ironie, Irunia*. The first element is assuredly *hiri* 'town', and the final element is certainly the article -*a*, but the middle element is puzzling. The favourite guess is *on* 'good', though a few scholars have argued instead for some kind of augmentative suffix. See Michelena (1958) for a discussion of this name.

Another interesting case is *Gasteiz*, the ancient Basque name of Vitoria (Ara). This is also attested in 1025 as *Gastehiz*, and Irigoyen (1981a), after a long and careful scrutiny of similar names all over the country, concludes that it derives from **Gartzeniz*, the patronymic in -*iz* of the common personal name which appears in modern Spanish as *García* but which is often *Gartze(a)* (and other variants) in the medieval period. The development **Gartzeniz > *Gartze(h)iz > Gasteiz* would be perfectly regular in Basque.

A striking case of folk-etymology is provided by *Ondarribia* (Gip). This is simply *ondar* 'sand' + *ibi* 'ford'. The Spanish name of the town is, however, *Fuenterrabía*, which is a folk-etymology based on a Romance reflex of Latin FONTE RAPIDE 'rapid spring'. Since the word for 'sand' is *hondar* in the north, this development very likely occurred at a time when [h] was still pronounced in the area of the town, which is just across the border with France.

The ordinary phonological processes of Basque operate normally in forming toponyms: for example, *Elosu* (Ara) is from *elorri* 'hawthorn' + -*zu* 'full of'.

Medieval records of toponyms often show voiceless plosives where the modern forms have voiced ones: *Gamboa* (Ara) is *Camboa* in 1025, and *Durango* (Biz) is *Turanko* in 1053. It is not clear whether such forms represent Basque pronunciations of the time or Romance ones, but note that a final element *-anco* (< Lat -ANICU) is common in Spanish place names in the area near the Basque Country.

A number of modern place names are clearly of non-Basque origin, such as *Placencia* (Gip), *Plencia* (Biz), *Tolosa* (Gip) and *Cambo* (Lap); some of these have entirely different names in Basque, such as *Soraluze* for Placencia and *Gaminiz* for Plencia. Place names like *Altube* and *Altuna*, involving a Romance descendant of Latin ALTU, must also have entered Basque late enough to escape the regular voicing of plosives after *l*.

On occasion we can identify the source of a toponym with some confidence. For example, *Pasajes* (Gip), earlier *Pasaje* (and modern Basque *Pasaia*), is clearly of Gascon origin, reflecting the substantial Gascon settlement in Gipuzkoa during the Kingdom of Navarre.

As noted in Chapter 3, toponyms not infrequently show the loss of an initial vowel, and names in the French Basque Country which would otherwise end in a consonant invariably acquire a final *e*.

Basque names for towns outside the Basque Country are often much more conservative than the Romance forms, such as *Bordele* 'Bordeaux', *Pabe* 'Pau' and *Akhize* 'Dax', the last representing Latin AQUIS rather directly.

5.12 SURNAMES

Basque surnames are highly distinctive and easily recognizable, and almost all of them are constructed according to a very small number of patterns. On the whole, Basque surnames can be accommodated within the phonological confines of Spanish with only minor adjustments (especially for the sibilants), but they can be put into French only with rather more drastic phonological modifications. Note also that the French preposition *de* is frequently found fused to Basque surnames as an initial *D-*, as in *Daguerre* and *Dagorret*.

The definitive treatment of Basque surnames is Michelena (1973a), an etymological dictionary of surnames arranged by elements; this work is both comprehensive and extremely reliable, and most of my discussion will be based on it. (Note that one or two other dictionaries of Basque surnames have been published by amateurs; these others are fanciful and unreliable in the extreme, and should not be treated as respectable sources of information.)

On both sides of the Pyrenees, surnames are used as is conventional in France and in Spain. Note in particular that Spanish Basques always have two surnames for official purposes: the father's first surname followed by the mother's first surname. The Basques typically take great interest in their surnames, and many individuals can reel off at least the eight surnames of their four grandparents. Note, too, that a Spanish Basque woman, following the usual Spanish custom, does not take her husband's surname on marriage. For the most part, ethnic Basques have distinctively Basque surnames, though of course it is not rare for a Basque to have a Spanish or French surname.

Particularly on the Spanish side, Basque surnames are well attested in medieval documents, though it is sometimes hard to be sure if the name accompanying a forename is a true family name or merely a sobriquet assigned to a particular individual. Many of these medieval surnames are still in use, though a few are both obsolete and of slightly unusual formation; these odd ones will be discussed below.

Linguistically, the first point to make about Basque surnames is that they are constructed entirely from nouns and adjectives (and less commonly numerals), plus a small set of affixes. They never involve verbal elements. (There are just two possible, and doubtful, exceptions to this statement, discussed below.) As a consequence, most surnames have the ordinary morphological structure of nouns, even though the majority of them have no independent existence as nouns in the language. Perhaps roughly half of surnames, like ordinary nouns, take the ordinary article -a, and not infrequently the same surname is attested both with and without the article, as with that most stereotypical of all Basque surnames, *Etxeberri(a)* 'new house'. A much smaller number of surnames consists of adjectives alone, such as *Gorri(a)* 'red' and *Zabala* 'wide', or of an adjective followed by a suffix, and it might be argued that surnames formed with the suffix -*zu* 'full of' should be regarded formally as adjectives, since this suffix otherwise forms adjectives. These are the only groups of surnames which are not straightforwardly classifiable as nouns.

Surnames are subject to the ordinary phonological processes of the language, and in particular they are usually (not always) subject to the rather distinctive processes applying in word-formation and discussed in Chapter 3. Finally, the loss of initial vowels, confined to proper names and also described in Chapter 3, is common in surnames but is still very far from being the norm.

The elements appearing in surnames are almost exclusively Basque, and are mostly items which have been in the language for millennia. A handful of very early loans from Latin and Romance also appear, but only very rarely do we encounter any elements borrowed from medieval Romance. The great majority of surnames are of transparent formation and meaning, though a not insignificant number contain elements which cannot be identified with certainty. An example is the **madina* which occurs in the names *Madinabeitia* and *Madinagoitia*, which is of unknown origin, even though the remaining elements in these names are perfectly transparent.

Moreover, the overwhelming majority of surnames are geographical: they describe or identify some location, presumably a location in which some ancestor of the name-bearer lived. There are some exceptions, however, mostly involving animal names or designations of office. In contrast to what happens in some other places, Basque surnames almost never represent occupations or professions, they never have the form of patronymics or metronymics (save only those names retaining the no-longer-transparent medieval patronymic -*iz*), and they rarely represent individual characteristics like size, colouring or origin (though some of those consisting only of adjectives may be of this type). Some surnames are identical to place names. In many such cases, the surname is clearly derived from the place name used as a geographical identifier, as with the common surname *Bilbao*. In other cases, though, it may be that the surname was formed independently of, but identically to, the place name: some people with the surname *Zumarraga* seem to have no connection with the town of that name in Gipuzkoa, and this surname is completely unremarkable in formation (*zumar* 'elm' plus the suffix -*aga*). Personal names may occur as elements in surnames, but usually only in the function of identifying the owner of some location, either with genitive -*en* or with -*tegi* 'place'.

The following patterns commonly occur in surnames: Noun, Adjective, Noun–Noun, Noun–*ko*–Noun, Noun–Adjective, Numeral–Noun. Each of these may be followed by a single suffix; only a few different suffixes occur. And, of course, the article -*a* may or may not be appended. A very few surnames exhibit longer patterns with more elements.

The suffixes which appear in surnames are largely the same ones appearing in place names and discussed in section 5.11.4: -*tza* ~ -*tze* 'abundance of', -*eta* ~ -*keta* 'abundance of', -*aga* 'place', -*di* ~ -*dui* ~ -*doi* 'place', -*ti* 'place', -*zu* 'full of'. Some of these, especially -*ti*, are also ordinary noun-forming suffixes, and are perhaps most often not to be regarded as immediate constituents of the surnames containing them. The suffix -*tu*, of unknown origin and function, is also common; attempts to connect this with the participle-forming suffix -*tu* look plausible only in one or two instances. Two other common suffixes are the genitive case-suffix -*en*, most often attached to personal names, and the suffix -*tegi* 'place', but, in surnames, usually 'house', attached both to personal names and to occupational names. A handful of others occur, uncommon and of unknown origin and function, such as -*da*, -*de* and -*te*. In the examples below, I shall take these suffixes for granted. Diminutive suffixes occur, but are always attached to personal names and are best not regarded as immediate constituents of the surname.

There follows a representative list of Basque surnames, organized by the structural types just cited. In general, I cite each surname in its canonical Basque spelling; I cite French or Spanish spellings only to give an idea of how these differ or when they are not obvious.

*Pattern **Noun***. While not rare, this pattern is not particularly common. *Otxoa* (Sp *Ochoa*) is from *otso* 'wolf'; this is one of the animal-name surnames in common use in the medieval period. Others of this type, now obsolete, include *Basaurde* 'wild boar', *Luki* 'fox' and *Artza* 'bear'. This last is often thought to be the origin of the Navarrese surname *García*, now found throughout Spain, but this etymology is not certain. *Oña* is from *oin* 'foot'; this odd-looking name is thought originally to have meant 'foot of the mountain'. *Mendi(a)* (Fr *Mendy*) is from *mendi* 'mountain'. *Lapitz(e)* is from *lapitz* 'slate'; the motivation is unknown. *Borda* is *borda* 'farmhouse'. *Aia* (Sp *Aya*) is usually thought to be from *ai* 'slope', even though this word is securely attested only in the work of the eighteenth-century Bizkaian author Añibarro. *Ganboa* (Sp *Gamboa*) or *Kanboa* (Sp *Camboa*) is troublesome: it might represent a development of Latin CAMPU 'field' not otherwise attested, but the name *Cambo* or *Gambo* is in several localities the name of a settlement associated with the presence of a mineral spring with alleged medicinal properties (including the well-known *Cambo-les-Bains* in Lapurdi), and this is probably a more obvious direct source, even though no such common noun is attested (though note the compound *kanbour* 'mineral water', literally 'Cambo water'). *Zu(g)atza* (Sp *Zu(g)aza*) is from *zugatz*, the western variant of *zuhaitz* 'tree'. The medieval surname *Umea* (*ume* 'child') is no longer in use.

*Pattern **Noun–Suffix***. This pattern is rather more frequent than the preceding. Very common are formations consisting of a personal name X plus the genitive suffix, meaning 'X's (place)'; these always take the article: *Mitxelena* 'Michael's', *Perurena* 'Peter's', *Juantorena* 'Johnny's' (with diminutive *-to*). Also in this group is *Harotzarena* and its variants, from *(h)arotz* 'smith'; note that this surname is geographical, not occupational. The suffix *-tegi*, here 'house', is frequent: *Lopetegi*, *Enekotegi*, *Mariategi*, all from personal names, *Arostegi* (*arotz* 'carpenter, blacksmith'), *Argindegi* (*hargin* 'stone-cutter'), *Amunategi* (*amuna* 'grandmother'). Also common are names in *-ti*, many of which are also independent nouns: *Barrutia* from *barruti* 'enclosure, district' (*barru* 'interior'), *Urrutia* from *urruti* 'distant place' (*urrun* 'distant'), *Goitia* from *goiti* 'height' (*goi* 'high place'). Among those in *-tza* are *Elortza* (Sp *Elorza*) from *elorri* 'hawthorn' and *Artatza* from *arte* 'holm-oak' The exceedingly common formations in *-eta* and its variant *-keta* include *Zuloeta*, from *zulo* 'hole' (possibly intended as 'cave' in this formation, since caves are common in the limestone mountains of the Basque Country), *Harrieta* ~ *Arrieta* (Fr *Harriet*), from *harri* 'stone', *Iztueta* ~ *Istueta* from *istun* 'channel', *Zubieta* from *zubi* 'bridge', *Amezketa* (Sp *Amezqueta*) from *ametz* 'gall-oak', *Larrazketa* (Fr *Larrasquet*) from *larratz* 'uncultivated land', *Bagoeta* ~ *Pagoeta* from *bago* ~ *pago* 'beech', *Elgeta* from *elge* 'cultivated field', and very many others; occasionally this suffix is added to a personal name, as in *Mikol(a)eta* from *Mikola* 'Nicholas'. Another frequent suffix is *-aga*: *Atxaga* (*atx* 'crag'; standard *haitz*), *Mendiaga* (*mendi* 'mountain'), *Lizarraga* ~ *Lei-zarraga* (Fr *Liçarrague* ~ *Leiçarrague*) (*lizar* ~ *leizar* 'ash tree').

Pattern **Adjective**.   There are not very many of these, and most of them are medieval surnames or sobriquets which have now vanished. Virtually all of them take the article. Examples: *Ona* from *on* 'good'; *Gorria* from *gorri* 'red'; *Zabala* (Sp *Zavala*) from *zabal* 'wide'; *Zaarra* from *zahar* 'old'; *Andia* from (*h*)*andi* 'big'; *Txipia* (Sp *Chipia*) from *txipi* 'small'; *Beltza* (Sp *Belza*) from *beltz* 'black'; *Zuri*(*a*) ~ *Txuri* (Sp *Churi*) from *zuri* 'white' and its diminutive *txuri*. Of these, only the very common *Zabala* remains in use today.

Pattern **Adjective–Suffix**.   These are not numerous and, with a couple of exceptions, they are uncommon. However, *zabal* 'wide' forms *Zabalaga*, *Zabaleta* and *Zabaltza* (Sp *Zabalza*), all rather common. From *gorri* 'red' we have *Gorriti*; from *agor* 'dry' comes *Agorreta* (Fr *Dagorret*).

Pattern **Noun–Noun**.   This is quite a common pattern, though the largest number of these are perhaps the ones in which the second noun is one expressing a spatial relation, notably *alde* and *ondo*, both 'side, beside', *arte* 'between' and *behe* ~ *bei* ~ *be* ~ *pe* 'below', but also *guren* 'edge, limit', *aurre* 'front, in front of' and others. Here are some examples:

With *alde* and *ondo* 'beside': *Uhalde* ~ *Ugalde* (*ur* 'water'), *Zubialde* (*zubi* 'bridge'), *Lizarralde* (*lizar* 'ash tree'), *Elizalde* and *Elizondo* (*eliza* 'church'), *Ibarrondo* (*ibar* 'valley'), *Larr*(*a*)*ondo* (*larre* 'pasture, meadow'), *Errekalde* ~ *Rekalde* (*erreka* 'stream').
With *arte* 'between': *Etxarte* (*etxe* 'house'), *Uharte* ~ *Ugarte* (Sp *Huarte*) (*ur* 'water'), *Iriarte* (*hiri* 'city').
With *behe* 'below' and its variants: *Altube* (*altu* 'height', from Romance), *Olabe* (*ola* 'forge, foundry'), *Iturbe* (*iturri* 'spring'), *Uribe* (*uri* 'town', western variant of *hiri*).
With *guren* 'edge': *Ibarguren* (*ibar* 'valley'), *Mendiguren* (*mendi* 'mountain'), *Ibaiguren* (*ibai* 'river').
With *aurre* 'front': *Bidaurre* (*bide* 'road').
With *gibel* 'behind': *Aizkibel* ((*h*)*aitz* 'crag'), *Etxagibel* (*etxe* 'house'), *Olagibel* (*ola* 'forge').
Without spatial nouns we find *Mendigarai* (*mendi* 'mountain' + *garai* 'elevation'), *Etxegarai* (*etxe* 'house'), *Errotaetxe* ~ *Rotaetxe* (*errota* 'mill', from Latin, + *etxe* 'house'), *Ibarruri* (*ibar* 'valley' + *uri* 'town'), *Mendiola* (*mendi* 'mountain' + *ola* 'forge'), *Loiola* (Sp *Loyola*) (*lohi* 'mud' + *ola* 'place'), *Bolibar* (Sp *Bolívar*) (*bolu* 'mill' < Lat MOLINU + *ibar* 'valley'), *Larramendi* (*larre* 'pasture' + *mendi* 'mountain'), *Garibai* (*garo* 'fern' + *ibai* 'river').

Pattern **Noun–Noun–Suffix**.   This is not particularly common. There are several seemingly whimsical surnames like *Astaburuaga* (*asto* 'donkey' + *buru* 'head') and the similar *Gizaburuaga* (*gizon* 'man'). The adjective *zabal* 'wide' finds some use as a noun in the sense of 'small (town) square', and it has this sense in *Zabalintxaurrieta* (*intxaur* 'walnut'). Another example is *Aldeiturriaga* (and variants) (*alde* 'side' + *iturri* 'spring').

*Pattern **Noun–ko–Noun***. This pattern yields a few very common surnames: *Goikoetxea* and *Garaikoetxea* (*goi* and *garai* 'high place' and *etxe* 'house'), *Bengoetxea* (*behen* 'furthest down'), *Urrutikoetxea* (*urruti* 'distance'), *Aurrekoetxea* (*aurre* 'front'). It is, at best, very rare for this pattern to be extended by a further suffix.

*Pattern **Noun–Adjective***. This is fairly common: *Baigorri* (*ibai* 'river' + *gorri* 'red'), *Etxeberri(a)* ~ *Etxebarri(a)* (*etxe* 'house' + *berri* ~ *barri* 'new'), *Etxenagusia* (*nagusi* 'chief, principal'), *Etxebeste* (*beste* 'other'), *Salazar* (*sala* 'house', of Romance origin, + *zahar* 'old'), *Mendiluze* (*mendi* 'mountain' + *luze* 'long'), *Gazteluzar* (*gaztelu* 'castle' + *zahar* 'old'). Another possible case is *Etxepare*, if this derives from *etxe* 'house' + a Romance *capale 'chief' (< CAPITALE) (Michelena 1968b: 518). The Spanish surname *Mendoza* is of Basque origin: *mendi* 'mountain' + *hotz* 'cold'.

*Pattern **Noun–Adjective–Suffix***. These mostly involve -*aga* and -*eta*: *Zubizarreta* (*zubi* 'bridge' + *zahar* 'old'), *Landagorrieta* (*landa* 'heath' + *gorri* 'red'), *Jauregizarraga* (*jauregi* 'palace' + *zahar* 'old'), *Gaztañazabaleta* (*gaztaña* 'chestnut' + *zabal* 'wide'), *Urberoaga* (*ur* 'water' + *bero* 'hot').

*Pattern **Numeral–Noun***. This is not particularly common. We have that shortest of all Basque surnames *Urbi* (*ur* 'water' + *bi* 'two'); the sense is 'confluence'. The surname *Irulegi* is possibly *hiru(r)* 'three' + (*h*)*egi* 'slope, place'.

*Pattern **Numeral–Noun–Suffix***. Many of these appear to be of whimsical origin: *Astobieta* and *Astobiaga* (*asto* 'donkey' + *bi* 'two'), *Azkonabieta* (*azkona* 'badger'), *Usabiaga* (*uso* 'pigeon'). Less remarkable are *Lausagarreta* (*lau* 'four' + *sagar* 'apple'), *Urbieta* (*ur* 'water' + *bi* 'two') and *Iruretxeta* (*hiru(r)* 'three' + *etxe* 'house').

Other patterns. A handful of surnames exhibit still other patterns: *Goikoetxeaundia* (*goi* 'high place' + -*ko* + *etxe* 'house' + (*h*)*a(u)ndi* 'big'), *Agirregomezkorta* (apparently the double surname *Aguirre Gómez* + *korta* 'court'). *Urbina* appears to be *Urbi* 'two waters', discussed above, with a further morpheme, possibly a diminutive. A very few surnames appear to derive from the participles of verbs, such as *Igartua*, from *igartu* 'dried up', and *Gazitua*, from *gazitu* 'salted'. The verb *ibeni* (and variants) 'put' seems to be present in a number of names, such as *Ibeniz* and *Ibañeta* ~ *Ibenieta*, but these names probably reflect more directly a noun derived from *ibeni*. These are perhaps the only traces of verbal elements in surnames.

In the medieval period, before surnames had become well established, individuals were often distinguished by sobriquets or by-names like *Ona* 'the Good', *Beltza* 'the Black' or *Otsoa* 'the Wolf', and these by-names are clearly the source of a number of attested surnames.

Also very common, especially among people of some standing, was the use of patronymics. The usual patronymic suffix was *-iz* ~ *-itz*, derived from the Latin genitive ending -IS. Among the numerous patronymics attested are *Enecoiz* (from the personal name *Eneko*), *Berascoiz* ~ *Erascoyz* (from *Berasko*), *Sanoiz* (from *Sanso*, with dissimilatory loss of the second sibilant), *Miqueleiz* (from *Mikele*) and *Ortiz* (from *Orti*, a Basque form of the Spanish name *Fortuni*), but there are many others. These formations appear to be direct continuations of the patronymics attested in Aquitanian: Aq *Enecon-is* = *Enecoiz*, with the usual loss of intervocalic /n/. In some regions, the patronymic suffix was palatalized after a vowel, yielding forms like *Enecoch* (= *Enekotx*) for *Enecoiz*.

For the common Spanish surname *García*, generally thought to be of Basque origin, see the next section.

Finally, I must mention yet another of Sabino Arana's interventions. For some reason, Arana decided that the Basques should write their names surname first, and to this end he advocated the use of the well-established ethnonymic suffix *-(t)ar* (*zarauztar* 'person from Zarautz', *donostiar* 'person from Donostia', etc.). Hence he wrote his own name *Arana'tar Sabin*, and this curious style was adopted by many of his supporters in the Basque Nationalist Party (PNV). Authors with PNV sympathies have therefore often signed themselves *Agirre'tar Iñigo, Altuna' tar Jesus, Lekuona'tar Manuel, Leizaola'tar Fermin* and so on. This custom has now largely died out. (In fact, this suffix normally appears as *-ar* after a vowel, and we would therefore have expected **Aranar* and so on.)

Very occasionally, one encounters a somewhat similar practice involving the relational suffix *-ko*. For example, the historical family name of the first Basque author was *Etxepare*, but, as with many French Basques, the French preposition *de* had fused to the name, producing *Detxepare*, or, with Romance spelling, *Dechepare* (the form used by the author himself). Others, however, have occasionally tried to render the French preposition by writing the author's name in Basque as *Bernard* (or *Beñat*) *Etxeparekoa*. All of these variant forms of the name are found in one place or another, and the variation can be quite confusing to a reader coming to Basque studies for the first time.

5.13 GIVEN NAMES

In the medieval period we find a large number of distinctively Basque given names, some of them of indigenous origin, others Basque renderings of

Latin and Romance given names. See Michelena and Irigaray (1955) for a survey of these.

Among the indigenous names are (female) *Urdina* 'Blue', *Usoa* 'Dove', *Ainara* (? 'Swallow'), *Idoia* (possibly from *idoi* 'pool, puddle'), (male) *Gabon* 'Christmas', *Umea* 'Child', *Xabier* (probably from *Etxaberri* 'new house', with Romance mediation to account for the vocalism), *Enneco* (sense unknown; possibly from *ene* 'my'). One of these medieval names, *Xabier*, has in fact established itself in Spanish (in the form *Javier*) and in other languages (English *Xavier*). The name *Enneco* (modern *Eneko*) has been taken into Spanish as *Iñigo*. Kinship terms like *umea* 'child' were much favoured as personal names, as were formations like *Emazteona* (*emazte* 'wife' + *on* 'good' + -*a* article). The male given name *Beraxa* (*beratz* 'gentle, kindly') appears to continue the Aquitanian name *Berhaxis*. The Navarrese personal name *Aceari Umea* (1167) is striking: it can be interpreted either as 'the child of the fox' or less literally as 'the child of (a man called) *Azeari*'.

Among the medieval given names of Romance origin are *Berasko* (Sp *Velasco*), *Bazkoare* (*Pascual*), *Domiku* (*Domingo*) and its female counterpart *Domeka*, *Dota* ~ *Tota* (*Toda*), *Edrigu* (*Rodrigo*), *Estebe* ~ *Eztebe* (*Esteban*), *Garindo* (*Galindo*), *Jakobe* ~ *Jakue* (*Jacobo*), *Jurgi* ~ *Jurtzi* (*Jorge*), *Onsalu* (*Gonzalo*), *Orti* (*Fortún*), *Sostie* ~ *Sastie* (*Sebastián*), and *Mari(a)* (*María*). Certain names, such as *Bikendi* (*Vicente*) and *Laurendi* (*Lorenzo*), have forms showing that they must have been borrowed from Latin very early. The common medieval name *Sanso* (= modern *Sancho*) often appears in Basque as *Anso*, showing dissimilatory loss of the first sibilant. The name *Diaoz* (*Diego*) shows an unexplained final sibilant, while *Baladi* (*Blas*) shows an unexplained plosive.

The diminutive suffix -*co* occurred only in male names: *Enneco*, *Bellaco*, *Vitaco* and so on. The well-attested name *Juanicote* appears to show an extended diminutive. In contrast, the diminutive suffixes -*ca* and -*nda* were confined to female names: *Onneca*, *Urraca*, *Ochanda* and so on. Otherwise, overt sex-marking was found only in names of Romance origin, as in male *Semeno* (Sp *Jimeno*) and female *Semena* and male names often ended in -*a*: *Belagga*, *Garsea* and so on.

Medieval documents show a female suffix -*iza*, which has vanished from the modern language: *Lopeiza* (female equivalent of *Lope*), *Martitza* (of *Martie* 'Martin'), *Ochoiza* (of *Ochoa* 'the Wolf'), and so on.

The following examples illustrate a very frequent medieval pattern for forming diminutives, for both male and female names: *Txana* for *Ana*, *Txelena* for *Elena*, *Txatalin* for *Katalin*, *Txadalen* for *Madalen*, *Txekolas* for *Nicolás*, *Txerran* for *Hernando*, *Txorgori* for *Gregorio*, *Txeru* for *Peru* (= *Pedro*), and so on. A few diminutives show somewhat different patterns, such as *Mitxel* for *Miguel* and northern *Manex* or *Ganex* (from *Ioannes*) for *Jean*.

The widespread Spanish surname *García* derives from a personal name

Gartzia ~ *Gartzea* (and other variants) which occurs very widely in the medieval Basque Country, above all in Navarre, where it was the name of several kings, and is generally thought to be of Basque origin. However, it has no obvious Basque etymology. Many people have seen it as a derivative of *hartz* 'bear', but this etymology is far from obviously correct; it is reported without comment by Michelena (1973a), but flatly rejected as unsustainable by Irigoyen (1981a).

The majority of the medieval given names have dropped out of use and been replaced in more recent times by other names. The modern given names in Basque may be conveniently divided into four classes, not all of them equally frequent.

To begin with, all Basques have for centuries been given ordinary Spanish or French forenames; this was until recently required by law in Spain and France. Hence the official given names of all individuals have been things like *José María* and *María Carmen* in Spain and things like *Daniel* and *Françoise* in France. Only since the end of the Franco period have the Spanish Basques won the right to refrain from conferring such names, and the French Basques only since 1993.

Second, many of these French and Spanish names have acquired distinctively Basque forms which are frequently used by their owners for everyday purposes, even though the owners may sign themselves with the official forms; some of these are continuations of medieval forms while others are innovations. Thus, for example, French *Bernard* has the Basque form *Bernat*, with a diminutive *Beñat*, *François* 'Francis' or 'Frank' is *Pantxo*, *Pierre* 'Peter' may be any of *Piarres*, *Betri* or *Betti*, *Dominique* is *Xomin*, *Françoise* 'Frances' is Basque *Pantxika*, *Catherine* is *Kattalin*, and *Marie* is the phonologically unusual *Mayi*; Spanish *José María* 'Joseph Mary' is *Joxe Mari* or *Txema*, *Domingo* 'Dominic' is *Txomin*, *Francisco* 'Francis' or 'Frank' is *Patxi*, *Santiago* 'Saint James' is *Xanti*, *Pedro* 'Peter' is *Peru* or its diminutive *Pello*, *Manuel* 'Emmanuel' is *Imanol*, and *Ignacio* 'Ignace' is *Iñaki*.

Note that *Txomin* and *Txema* are rare survivals of the medieval pattern of diminutive formation. A few more of these survive in the north, where one can still encounter individuals called *Ttotte* or *Tote* (*Joseph*) or *Xiber* (*Gilbert*), not to mention *Manex*.

María Teresa is *Maite* (*maite* 'beloved', merely from the coincidental resemblance in form), and *Concepción* 'conception' is *Kontxi* (this one is merely a Basque spelling of the usual Spanish diminutive). The common Spanish practice of naming women after manifestations of the Virgin has produced a number of Basque forms: thus *María del Mar* 'Mary of the Sea' is *Itxaso* (*itsaso* 'sea'), while *María de Aránzazu* 'Mary of Arantzazu' (a place in the Basque Country) has yielded the exceedingly common name *Arantza* or *Arantxa* (literally 'thorn'), now found elsewhere in Spain, and *María de Itziar* (another place name) has yielded *Itziar*. Occasionally the Basque version is no more than a minor adjustment of the Spanish form to conform to Basque phonology and/or orthography, as when Spanish *Alfonso* 'Alphonse' becomes *Alfontso* in Basque.

The modern forms of these common European names are often different from the medieval ones. For example, *Martín* and *Miguel* are often *Martie* and *Mikele* in medieval documents, but the modern forms are *Martin* (diminutive *Matxin*) and *Mikel*.

Third, a certain number of Basque given names attested in medieval documents have recently been revived, particularly on the Spanish side; among the most popular of these are the female names *Idoia* and *Ainara*.

Finally, a very large number of Basque given names are neologisms. One or two of these were created before the 1890s, notably the male name *Aitor*. This was introduced by the early nineteenth-century French Basque Romantic Augustin Chaho, who noted that the Basques traditionally referred to themselves as *aitoren semeak*, apparently 'sons of Aitor', and who consequently invented the myth of Aitor, the shepherd who was supposed to be the ancestor of the Basques. In fact, philologists are satisfied that the phrase is nothing more than a dissimilation of *aitonen semeak* 'sons of good fathers'. Inevitably, however, most of the neologisms came from the pen of that inveterate tinkerer with the language, Sabino Arana. Just as he was determined to stamp out Romance words in Basque, he set out also to replace the Romance given names with 'genuine' Basque equivalents. To this end he devised a long list of Basque versions of common Spanish names. These names were largely fanciful, being guided by no principle beyond Arana's own decision that male names should end in *-a*, female names in *-e*. Some of his coinages were rough translations from Spanish, while others were whimsical alterations of Germanic or Semitic equivalents.

Here are some of his coinages. For Spanish *Luis* 'Louis', he invented *Koldobika* (abbreviated to *Koldo*), based on Germanic *Chlodwig*, the source of the name. For *Pedro* 'Peter', he devised *Kepa*, apparently from Aramaic *Cephas*, which, like Greek *Petros*, means 'stone'. For *María* 'Mary', he took the more-or-less Hebrew version *Miriam* and produced Basque *Miren*. Spanish *Jorge* 'George' came out as *Gorka*, while *José* 'Joseph' emerged as *Joseba*. Spanish *Nieves* 'Snows' became *Edurne* (*edur* 'snow'), *Ascensión* 'Ascension' became *Igone* (*igo(n)* 'ascend'), *Natividad* 'Nativity' became *Jaione* (*jaio* 'be born'), *Juana* 'Joan' became *Jone*, *Jesusa* (a Spanish female form of 'Jesus') became *Jexone*, and *Anunciación* 'Annunciation' became *Agurtzane* (*agurtza* 'greeting'). All these names have become very widespread in the Spanish Basque Country, and may occasionally even be found on the French side. For example, the Basque linguist Luis Michelena, who was certainly no enthusiast for Arana's excesses, was known to his friends as Koldo, and always signed himself Koldo Mitxelena when writing in Basque.

5.14 HOUSE NAMES

A Basque farmhouse (*baserri* or *borda*) always has a name. This name is usually conferred, not by the inhabitants, but by the people of the neighbourhood. A man's surname may be unknown to his neighbours, but his house name is always known, and is regularly used for identification. Thus, Yvan Labéguerie of Milafranga (Lapurdi) is addressed by the men of the village as *Bakoitza* ('unique'), the name of his family house, and Alejandro Barrutia of Elorrio (Bizkaia) is referred to by the people in town as *Alejandro Patxi Errege* (his house has the curious name *Patxi Errege* 'King Frank', discussed below). The great Basque writer Pedro de Axular was actually born Pedro Daguerre Azpilcueta, but *Axular* was the name of the house he was born in (it still stands today in the village of Urdazubi, Navarre), and he chose to sign himself with his house name. Even tombstones often bear the house name of the deceased.

A house name is so well known that it can be used as a postal address, even though the name is never written on the house. (Visitors to the French Basque Country will observe obviously modern houses with cloying names inscribed across their fronts, such as *Gure Ametsa* 'Our Dream' or *Gure Kaiola* 'Our Retreat', but these, of course, are not inhabited by Basques, but by wealthy Parisians.) Basque houses are often centuries old, and so are their names, which are sometimes recorded in old official documents. House names do not normally change, but I know of one case in which this has happened.

A certain *baserri* in Elorrio (Bizkaia) was formerly known as *Ibarguren* ('edge of the valley'), a name recorded on official maps. Early in the twentieth century it was inhabited by one Francisco Barrutia, whose shrewd business dealings made him the wealthiest man in town. His doubtless envious neighbours gave him the ironic nickname *Patxi Errege* 'King Frank' (*Patxi* is the Basque equivalent of *Francisco*), and this nickname eventually became transferred to the house, which ever since has been known to the town as *Patxi Errege*.

It is an astounding fact that no one has ever undertaken a systematic study of house names. Consequently, we know next to nothing about the principles of house naming, or even whether any principles exist. Here I can do no more than present a representative list of house names with comments; those listed below are all names of houses in the vicinity of Elorrio (Bizkaia) and have been collected by Esther Barrutia and Alejandro Barrutia. Since these names have been collected orally, and since the Bizkaian dialect does not distinguish /s/ and /z/, I am sometimes uncertain as to the correct spelling of a name. Note that the common suffix -*ko* 'which is in/at/ of' often appears in names as -*ku*, especially before a following -*a*, and note that the determiner -*a* is frequently present. Only in a very few cases do I have information on the location of a house, but, in each such case, that location is consistent with the name.

Agarrekoa   An unidentified element **agar* or **agarre* + -*ko*.

Agarreko Erdikoa   The preceding plus *erdiko* 'which is in the middle': lit. 'central *Agarreko*'.

Agarreko Gainekoa   The same again with *gaineko* 'which is in the high place': lit. 'upper *Agarreko*'.

Aidesokua   This is probably better *Aidezokua*, from *aide* 'air' + *zoko* 'corner': 'airy corner'.

Aixea   This is merely 'wind': *aixe* is the Bizkaian form of *haize* 'wind'.

Aiztikua   The first element is obscure. Bizkaian *aizta* 'sister (of a woman)' (standard *ahizpa*) seems implausible, and the formation would be highly anomalous. More likely is *haitz* 'crag, rock' + -*di* or -*ti* NFS, though we would have expected **Axtikua* as the result of this.

Aldezokua   From *alde* 'side' + *zoko* 'corner': 'side corner'.

Amillakua   The first element is probably the **amil(l)(a)* 'cliff, precipice' which is not attested as an independent word but which appears with various suffixes in exactly this sense. It would be desirable to find out if this house is indeed near a cliff.

Amordikua   Here Bizkaian *amorde* 'stepmother' (*ama* 'mother' + *orde* 'stead') cannot be ruled out, but it seems implausible to me.

Anagoitia   The female name *Ana* 'Ann' seems highly implausible, and I cannot identify the first element. Otherwise, *goi* 'high place' + -*ti* NFS.

Angioerroetxauna   The first element is *angio* 'fenced-off pasture', while the second looks like *erro*, usually 'root' but attested in Bizkaian in several other senses, including 'sunbeam'. The third is *etxe* 'house', and the final element is most likely *on* 'good'. I have little idea what all this is supposed to mean.

Ardantza   This is *ardantza* 'vineyard' (*ardao* 'wine' + -*tza* NFS).

Arregi   From *harri* 'rock' + -*egi* 'place': 'rocky place'.

Arrialde   From *harri* 'rock' + *alde* 'side': 'rock-side'.

Arrokua   Far more likely than *harro* 'proud' is Bizkaian *arro* 'gully, ravine': probably this house is located near a ravine.

Arzubialde   This is *harri* 'stone' + *zubi* 'bridge' + *alde* 'side': 'beside the stone bridge'.

Atxerua   The first element is probably *atx*, the Bizkaian form of *haitz* 'crag, rock', but the rest seems uninterpretable: neither *zeru* 'sky' nor *ero* 'foolish' is at all appealing.

Atzekoa   This is from *atze* 'back, space behind': 'the one in back'.

Azarkua   Obscure. The first element might be *azari* 'fox' (standard *azeri*), but there is no parallel for such a formation.

Azkarrakolea   The first element is *azkar* 'maple', but the rest is obscure.

Azkarratxo   Also from *azkar* 'maple' plus a diminutive suffix.

Azkarratxona   Same as the preceding plus a genitive suffix.

Azpotxa   Perhaps better *Aspotxa*, from *haspo* 'bellows' + a diminutive suffix, but the motivation is obscure.

Azulena   Here we have the surname *Azula* + the genitive plural *-en*: hence, 'the Azulas' (place)'.

Bazterretxea   A compound of *bazter* 'edge' + *etxe* 'house': 'edge house'.

Bulungarai   From *garai* 'high' plus an unidentified first element.

Elizalde   This is *eliza* 'church' + *alde* 'side': 'beside the church'. I am given to understand that this house is indeed located next to a church.

Elizondo   This is *eliza* 'church' + *ondo* 'side': also 'beside the church'.

Errandona   From *Herrando*, a Basque form of the given name *Fernando*, probably with a genitive suffix.

Errementarikua   From *errementari* 'blacksmith'.

Er(r)osalde   An obscure first element + *alde* 'side'.

Errotakua   The first element is *errota* 'mill' (< Lat ROTA).

Estakazulu   The second element is *zulo* 'hole'; for the first, B *eztaka* 'splinter' makes little sense.

Etxegorri   This is *etxe* 'house' + *gorri* 'red': 'red house'.

Galartza Barri   From the surname *Galartza*, itself derived from *galar* 'dead wood' + *barri* 'new'.

Ganboa   From the identical surname.

Giputzena   An interesting case. It's *giputz* 'person from Gipuzkoa' + the genitive plural *-en*: hence 'the Gipuzkoans' (place)'.

Goikoetxe   This is *goiko*, a *-ko* derivative of *goi* 'high place', + *etxe* 'house': hence 'house in the high place'.

Ibarguren   This is *ibar* 'valley' + *guren* 'edge': 'edge of the valley'. The house in question is indeed at the very end of town and halfway up the mountain at the head of the valley.

Ibergarai   Apparently *ibar* 'valley' + *garai* 'high'.

Iparrandikua   From *ipar* 'north' + *handi* 'big' + *-ko*.

Iparranikua   Probably a variant of the preceding.

Isasikua   The first element is *isasi*, commonly 'broom' (the plant), though also 'arum lily' in B.

Leibar   From *ibar* 'valley' with an unknown first element.

Liorreta   Probably *lehor* 'dry' + *-eta*.

Lope   Apparently just the Spanish personal name *Lope* (which is a common element in Basque surnames), though just remotely conceivable is a derivation from *lohi* 'mud' + *-pe* 'below'.

Munitxa   This looks like B *muni* 'riverbank, slope' + a diminutive suffix.

Muturtukoa   This looks for all the world like a derivative of *muturtu* 'annoyed'.

Olaldekua   From *ola* 'forge' + *alde* 'side' + *-ko*: 'beside the forge'.

Otalakua   The first element is Bizkaian *ota* 'gorse, furze' (common *ote*). The second is puzzling: *laku* 'lake' seems implausible, and anyway this Latin loan does not appear to be used in Bizkaian. Possibly an alteration of *leku* 'place'?

Otzekua   From *hotz* 'cold' + *-ko*?

Otzeta   From *hotz* 'cold' + *-eta*.

Otzeta Gorua   The first word is the same as the preceding, but the second is mysterious. The common B *goru* 'distaff' makes no sense at all. A possibility would be *goroa* 'crown' (< Lat CORONA), but I am not aware that this eastern word is even attested in Bizkaia.

Patxi Errege   'King Frank', explained above.

Pedro Lapur   Another strange one: it's Sp *Pedro* 'Peter' + *lapur* 'thief': 'Peter the Thief'.

Teietxe   The second element is *etxe* 'house', an item which is in fact not at all common in house names; the first is obscure.

Torrekua   The first element is *torre* 'tower', a loan from Spanish.

Ugalde   A compound of *ur* 'water' + *alde* 'side': 'waterside'.

Zabalaikua   Both *zabal* 'wide' and *-ko* are obvious, but not the medial part.

Zabalko Azpikua   The first word is *zabal* 'wide' plus *-ko* and is very likely a house name itself; the second is *azpi* 'below' plus *-ko* again; the whole means 'below Zabalko'.

Ziarsolo   This looks like *zehar* 'across' + *solo* 'field': 'cross-field'.

Zuburruti   This looks like *zur* 'wood' + *burruti* 'enclosure'.

5.15 THE SWADESH WORD-LIST

Since lexical items vary from place to place, no single list can be given for the entire language. Here I present the most widespread words, ignoring severely localized items. The list of 200 items is taken from Gudschinsky (1956). At the end I append a few other words sometimes included in other versions of the list.

1	all	*guz(t)i, den*
2	and	*eta*
3	animal	*abere* (usually domesticated), *pizti* (often wild) (*bizi* 'alive'), *animalia*
4	ashes	*hauts, errauts*
5	at	*-n*
6	back	*bizkar* (anat.), *atze, gibel* 'space behind'
7	bad	*tzar ~ txar*
8	bark	*azal*
9	because	*zeren, -lako(tz), bait-*
10	belly	*sabel*
11	big	*handi ~ aundi*
12	bird	*(t)xori*
13	bite	*horzkatu, haginkatu, haginka egin*
14	black	*beltz*
15	blood	*odol*
16	blow (v.)	*putz egin, haizeman*

17	bone	*hezur*
18	breathe	*arnasa hartu*
19	burn	*erre*
20	child	*haur, ume*
21	cloud	*hodei*
22	cold	*hotz*
23	come	*etorri, jaugin ~ jin*
24	count	*kontatu, zenbatu*
25	cut (v.)	*ebaki, moztu*
26	day	*egun*
27	die	*hil*
28	dig	*zulatu*
29	dirty	*zikin*
30	dog	*zakur ~ txakur, or*
31	drink	*edan*
32	dry	*eihar ~ igar, lehor, agor, ziku*
33	dull	*motz ~ amotz, kamuts*
34	dust	*hauts*
35	ear	*belarri ~ beharri ~ begarri*
36	earth	*lur*
37	eat	*jan*
38	egg	*arraultza ~ arrauntza*
39	eye	*begi*
40	fall (v.)	*erori, jausi*
41	far	*urrun*
42	fat/grease	*gantz, koipe, ziho*
43	father	*aita*
44	fear (v.)	*beldur izan*
45	feather	*luma*
46	few	*guti ~ gutti ~ gutxi*
47	fight (v.)	*borrokatu*
48	fire	*su*
49	fish	*arrai(n)*
50	five	*bortz ~ bost*
51	float	*urgaindu, flotatu*
52	flow	*jario, isuri*
53	flower	*lore*
54	fly (v.)	*hegaz egin*
55	fog	*laino, lanbro*
56	foot	*oin*
57	four	*laur ~ lau*
58	freeze	*izoztu*
59	fruit	*fruitu*
60	give	*eman*

61	good	*on*
62	grass	*belar ~ bedar*
63	green	*berde*
64	guts	*hertze ~ heste*
65	hair	*ile*
66	hand	*esku*
67	he	No equivalent
68	head	*buru*
69	hear	*entzun*
70	heart	*bihotz*
71	heavy	*astun*
72	here	*hemen*
73	hit	*jo*
74	hold/take	*eduki, eutsi* ('hold'), *hartu* ('take')
75	how	*nola, zelan*
76	hunt	*ehiztatu*
77	husband	*senar*
78	I	*ni*
79	ice	*izotz*
80	if	*ba-*
81	in	*-n*
82	kill	*hil*
83	know	*jakin* (a fact), *ezagutu* (a person)
84	lake	*zingira, laku*
85	laugh (v.)	*barre egin, irri egin*
86	leaf	*orri, osto*
87	left (side)	*ezker*
88	leg	*zango, hanka*
89	lie (down)	*etzan ~ etzun*
90	live (v.)	*bizi izan*
91	liver	*gibel*
92	long	*luze*
93	louse	*zorri*
94	man/male	*gizon* (man), *ar* (male)
95	many	*anitz, asko*
96	meat/flesh	*haragi, okela*
97	mother	*ama*
98	mountain	*mendi*
99	mouth	*aho*
100	name	*izen*
101	narrow	*estu, mehar*
102	near	*hurbil* (adj.), *ondoan, inguruan* (postp.)
103	neck	*lepo*
104	new	*berri*

105	night	*gau*
106	nose	*sudur*
107	not	*ez*
108	old	*zahar*
109	one	*bat*
110	other	*bertze ~ beste*
111	person	*pertsona*
112	play (v.)	*jokatu, jostatu*
113	pull	*tiratu*
114	push	*bultzatu, saka egin*
115	rain	*euri*
116	red	*gorri*
117	right (correct)	*zuzen*
118	right (side)	*eskuin*
119	river	*ibai, uhalde*
120	road	*bide*
121	root	*erro, sustrai*
122	rope	*soka, lokarri*
123	rotten	*ustel*
124	rub	*igortzi, ferekatu*
125	salt	*gatz*
126	sand	*harea, hondar*
127	say	*erran ~ esan*
128	scratch	*hazkatu, hatz egin*
129	sea	*itsaso*
130	see	*ikusi*
131	seed	*bihi, garau*
132	sew	*josi*
133	sharp	*zorrotz*
134	short	*labur, motz*
135	sing	*kantatu*
136	sit (down)	*eseri, jarri*
137	skin	*azal*
138	sky	*zeru*
139	sleep (v.)	*lo egin*
140	small	*tipi ~ ttipi ~ txiki*
141	smell (v.)	*usaindu*
142	smoke	*ke*
143	smooth	*leun, lau*
144	snake	*suge*
145	snow	*elur*
146	some	*batzu(k), zenbait*
147	spit (v.)	*txistu egin, listu egin, ttu egin*
148	split	*erdibitu, ezpaldu*

149 squeeze	*hertsi(tu), trinkatu, eskuztatu*
150 stab/pierce	*sasta(ka)tu, barrundu*
151 stand (up)	*zutitu, jaiki ~ jeiki*
152 star	*izar*
153 stick (n.)	*makila*
154 stone	*harri*
155 straight	*zuzen*
156 suck	*esoski, xurgatu*
157 sun	*eguzki ~ eki*
158 swell (v.)	*handitu*
159 swim	*igeri egin*
160 tail	*buztan*
161 that	*hori* (mesial), *hura* (distal)
162 there	*hor* (mesial), *han* (distal)
163 they	No equivalent
164 thick	*lodi*
165 thin	*argal, mehe, mehar*
166 think	*pentsatu* ('ponder'), *uste ukan* ('opine')
167 this	*haur ~ hau*
168 thou	*hi* (intimate), *zu* (unmarked)
169 three	*hirur ~ hiru*
170 throw	*bota, egotzi, iraitzi, (j)aurtiki*
171 tie	*lotu*
172 tongue	*mihi ~ min*
173 tooth	*hortz* ('incisor'), *hagin* ('molar')
174 tree	*zuhaitz, arbola*
175 turn	*itzuli*
176 two	*biga ~ bi*
177 vomit (v.)	*oka egin, goitikatu, bota*
178 walk	No equivalent. Use *oinez* 'on foot' plus motion verb.
179 warm	*bero* ('hot'), *epel* ('lukewarm')
180 wash	*ikuzi, garbitu*
181 water	*ur*
182 we	*gu*
183 wet	*busti*
184 what	*zer*
185 when	*noiz*
186 where	*non*
187 white	*zuri*
188 who	*nor*
189 wide	*zabal*
190 wife	*emazte*
191 wind	*haize*
192 wing	*hegal*

193	wipe	*igurtzi, ferekatu*
194	with	*-ekin*
195	woman	*emakume*
196	woods	*oihan, baso*
197	worm	*har*
198	ye	*zuek*
199	year	*urte*
200	yellow	*hori*

Additional items:

201	breast	*bular* (all senses), *diti, ugatz* (female)
202	claw	*atzapar*
203	clothing	*jantzi, soineko*
204	cook	*egosi*
205	dance (v.)	*dantzatu, dantza egin*
206	eight	*zortzi*
207	full	*bete*
208	horn	*adar*
209	hundred	*ehun*
210	knee	*belaun*
211	moon	*ilargi*
212	round	*biribil ~ borobil*
213	seven	*zazpi*
214	shoot (v.)	*tiro egin* (intr.), *tiratu* (tr.)
215	sister	*ahizpa* (of woman), *arreba* (of man)
216	spear (n.)	*burtzi*
217	ten	*hamar*
218	twenty	*hogei*
219	work (v.)	*lan egin*

Chapter 6

Connections with other languages

6.1 PRELIMINARIES

As the only non-Indo-European language in western Europe, Basque has inevitably attracted a great deal of attention from linguists hoping to find some relatives for it somewhere, or, failing that, at least to turn up evidence of ancient contact between Basque and something else. Connections (mostly genetic) have been proposed at least with ancient Iberian, with ancient Aquitanian, with Indo-European (especially Celtic, Latin, Greek, Slavonic and Sanskrit), with Pictish, with the Berber languages of North Africa, with ancient Egyptian, with a wide range of Sudanic and sub-Saharan languages of Africa, with Semitic, with Etruscan, with Minoan, with Sumerian, with Uralic (especially Finnish), with Burushaski, with Dravidian, with the Munda languages of India, with the Yeniseian and Chukchi-Kamchatkan languages of Siberia, with Sino-Tibetan, with Eskimo, with the Na-Dene languages of North America, and above all with the Caucasian languages, North and South, and this list is anything but exhaustive. This vast body of work ranges from the sober and well informed through the increasingly fanciful and incompetent to the downright preposterous, with a rather strong bias towards the preposterous end of the scale.

In particular, a very large proportion of this work consists of nothing more than some random observations along the following lines: 'Look, I've got a few Basque words here that look quite a bit like some words in Bongo-Bongo.' For example, all of the work by Schuchardt and others attempting to relate Basque to Berber and to other African languages is of exactly this calibre, and indeed it is difficult to find any proposals which rise above this level.

In a book aimed at professional linguists, it should hardly be necessary to point out that this kind of observation is completely worthless. Unfortunately, my experience is that it *is* necessary to point this fact out again and again. Every language has thousands of meanings to provide forms for, and only a modest number of speech sounds to combine in order to obtain those forms, and hence, given sufficient material, similarities of form and meaning can be found between any two languages whatever, or, more easily still, between any two groups of languages. Finding such similarities in a particular case, therefore, means *absolutely nothing* – or at least it means only that the laws of probability are not taking the day off. Later in this chapter, I shall document this assertion for any readers who are sceptical of it. For the moment, I cite only an utterly typical example: the comparison of regional Basque *umerri* 'lamb' with Akkadian *immeru* 'lamb' – but the Basque word means 'new offspring of an animal' in LN, and it can hardly be other than a compound of *ume* 'offspring' and *berri* 'new'.

There have been a few attempts at elaborating this crude approach by the introduction of lexicostatistics. Now, when lexicostatistics is applied to languages whose genetic relationship is established, and whose cognates are already identified, it can perhaps be useful in determining the degree of linguistic separation between particular members of the family. But, when it is applied to languages of unknown affinity, with no established cognates, it is a waste of time. Thus, for example, when Tovar (1980: 196) tells us that lexicostatistical studies with the Swadesh word-list yield a 10 per cent match between Basque and Berber and a 7.5 per cent match between Basque and Kartvelian, all he means is that these numbers represent the proportion of random similarities by which he is prepared to be impressed. Ten random similarities in a hundred words is still ten random similarities, and dignifying the result with polysyllabic labels and with numbers expressed to several decimal points does nothing to strengthen the case.

Nevertheless, Tovar *et al.* (1961), Echenique (1987: 25–28) and Mukarovsky (1981c) solemnly calculate lexicostatistical percentages of 'cognates' between Basque on the one hand and Northeast Caucasian, Northwest Caucasian, Kartvelian, Berber, Finnish and the Mande languages of Africa on the other, and in some cases they go so far as to calculate 'dates of separation' – 8,000 years ago for Basque and Berber, apparently. This is the height of silliness.

Furthermore, almost all the attempts at comparing Basque with something else involve large numbers of Basque items which have no business being included: obvious loan words, transparent compounds and derivatives of late formation, onomatopoeic items and other phonaesthetic formations, obscure and localized words of doubtful provenance, regional variants of transparently secondary form, nursery words and even modern neologisms. Basque words are often cited wrongly or glossed wrongly, and not infrequently non-existent words are adduced as evidence. Basque segments and sequences of any form and length are routinely chopped off and discarded when they fail to match, leading Michelena (1950b) to complain of one such malefactor that he apparently believes that Basque words are characterized by 'spontaneous generation'. Deletions, epentheses, metatheses, coalescences, unmotivated alternations, all are invoked without hesitation whenever they will make a dubious matchup look better.

Finally, there are, of course, the 'great decipherments' – the dramatic announcements by unknown scholars, working in total isolation from other specialists, that the long undeciphered inscriptions in Pictish, or Etruscan, or Minoan, or Iberian, have suddenly proved to be written in Basque. In fact, so far as I am aware, the Indus Valley script and the Easter Island inscriptions are the only remaining undeciphered texts which have not yet been painfully rendered by some deluded toiler into what he fancifully regards as a version of Basque. Readers will not be surprised to learn that the 'Basque' which emerges from these improbable enterprises is invariably lacking in any recognizable Basque grammatical structure, or indeed in *any* grammatical structure, and moreover tends to exhibit such unexpected characteristics as nineteenth-century neologisms, loan words from Occitan and word-initial suffixes, not to mention descriptions of such intriguing artefacts as nets for holding water. I would not bother to discuss these lunacies at all, were it not for the absolutely incredible fact that some of them have actually been taken seriously by professional linguists of impeccable reputation.

So numerous are the proposals to relate Basque to something else that it is hardly possible even to list them all here, let alone to discuss them all. I shall therefore confine my attention to the following cases: (a) all those which are serious enough to merit a response, (b) all those recent proposals which have attracted favourable attention, whether deservedly or not, and (c) a representative sample of the rest, including the ones which have been pursued most thoroughly. I exclude almost all proposals based on nothing more than a list of six or eight supposed 'cognates' linking Basque to this or that improbable relative, and I exclude also the marginally more substantial work on relating Basque to Uralic, or more precisely to Finnish, an idea which was popular in the early years of this century but which has proved to be so unrewarding that it has been quietly dropped. (See the very brief Uhlenbeck (1912) for the best-known suggestion along these lines.) Nor do I treat the outstandingly eccentric attempts at relating Basque to Etruscan (Ellis 1886, Esandi 1946).

In examining these proposals, it will be convenient to bear in mind some of the most important results from Chapter 3 on the historical phonology of Basque. Briefly:

No native Basque lexical item of any period (except for imitative items of no great antiquity) can begin with any of *p-, t-, d-* or *r-*.

Virtually no native Basque lexical item of any antiquity can begin with *k-*.

No native Basque lexical item in the period before the Roman invasion could contain *m*.

No native Basque lexical item of any period can begin with any consonant cluster at all.

Except in the eastern dialects, no native Basque lexical item of any antiquity can contain any of the clusters *np, nt, nk, lp, lt* or *lk*.

The palatal segments are always secondary: they could not occur anciently in lexical items.

The reader is advised to remember these findings, since they immediately rule out of court a large number of the cognates and etymologies which have been proposed in the work we shall examine here.

In closing this section, I note that López García (1985b) has recently proposed that Basque, or rather a remote ancestor of Basque, might have originated as a creole. This is possible, of course, but a remote creole origin is always possible for any language family, and such a suggestion is beyond the scope of this book.

6.2 AFRICAN LANGUAGES

I begin with one of the most venerable of all proposals: that Basque is related to some of the languages of Africa. An African connection has been pursued since at least the late nineteenth century, for no particular reason, perhaps, except that North Africa is closer to the Basque Country than some other non-Indo-European-speaking parts of the world. Though a startling number of African languages and families have been invoked in these enterprises (not excluding Khoisan!), the favourite candidate has always been Afro-Asiatic, and most particularly Berber, the African language geographically closest to Basque.

A Basque–Berber connection was defended by Georg von der Gabelentz (1894) and by Hugo Schuchardt in several publications, most notably in his articles of 1913 and 1914–1917 (though Schuchardt never hesitated to compare individual Basque words with words in over a dozen diverse African languages). But the doyen of this line of investigation is the Austrian linguist Hans Mukarovsky, who has published several substantial attempts at identifying cognates (Mukarovsky 1963–1964, 1969, 1981a, 1981b); the last of these argues for a link between Basque and the Afro-Asiatic languages generally.

Like so much other work considered in this chapter, Mukarovsky's is riddled with serious errors. Among the Basque items compared with Berber are the transparent loan words *lili* 'flower, lily', *matel* 'cheek', *eme* 'female, sweet', *tirria* 'rancour' and eastern *barraiatu* 'scatter, disperse', all of which have secure sources in Latin or Romance, and for the last he openly dismisses the obvious Romance etymology (Gascon *barreia* 'empty out, scatter', and related words throughout the Iberian Peninsula), *papo* 'breast', whose form shows that it cannot conceivably be either native or ancient, the non-existent **aba* 'father', a flight of fancy coined by Sabino Arana in the nineteenth century, a non-existent 'causative' suffix **-zi*, the nursery word *mama* 'potable liquid', the onomatopoeic word *tu* 'spit, saliva' and the interjection *mix-mix* ~ *mox-mox*, a noise used to call a cat, wrongly glossed as 'cat' and solemnly compared with a Berber name for the animal. Basque *oskol* 'bark, rind' is wrongly glossed as 'fingernail' to get a match, and *naba* 'large plain near mountains' is likewise wrongly glossed as 'slope' to get a match. The strictly L word *xixku* 'container, scabbard, pincushion, pod' is cited only as 'pod' and matched with a Berber word for 'pulses'. Mukarovsky fails to realize that *ukabil* 'fist' is a transparent compound of *uko* 'forearm' and *-bil* 'round', that *emazte* 'wife' is a compound of *eme* 'female' (a loan from Occitan) and *gazte* 'young', and that *tzar* 'bad' is a specialized development of *zahar* 'old'. For *euri* 'rain', he deliberately chooses the severely localized and transparently secondary form *ebri* in order to get a match. The Basque genitive ending *-en* is wrongly cited as *-n* and compared with a Berber preposition *n*, which apparently links noun phrases. For *belaun* 'knee', he selects for comparison *belaurika-* 'kneel down', in which *belaun* exhibits the usual combining form of old *n*-stems and *-(i)ka* is merely an adverbial suffix commonly found in derived verbs, merely to conjure up a match of sorts with Semitic words like Akkadian *birku* 'knee'.

Very often the Berber words adduced are specifically Tuareg and not pan-Berber. In his (1981b) paper, he compares the Basque words with miscellaneous words from assorted Afro-Asiatic languages, words which have not themselves been shown to be cognate and probably are not. He does not hesitate to match a Basque word with something attested in a *single* Afro-Asiatic language, as when he matches Basque *ibai* 'river' with *aba*, a word for 'river' found in the Cushitic language Bedauye. Basque *izen* 'name' is matched with Berber *isəm* 'name', which is a loan from Arabic *ism* (Jamal OuHalla, p.c.). Basque *ni* 'I' is cited as *nik*, with the ergative case-suffix *-k*, in order to improve the match with Berber *nik(ki)* 'I'. And so it goes. Even when a native Basque word is cited correctly, the comparisons are far from overwhelming: Basque *bide* 'road' and Tuareg *a-bareqqa* 'path, road'; Basque *gibel* 'liver' and Semitic *k-b-d* 'liver'; Basque *bilo* 'hair' (a loan word) and Cushitic words in *ball-* meaning 'feather'; Basque *-(e)n*, a +WH complementizer, and Berber *-n*, a nominalizer of finite verbs; Basque *biribil* 'round' (a reduplication of *bil-*) and Egyptian *b n n t* 'ball' and Galla *bururi* 'round'.

I see nothing here that any reasonable person could regard as evidence of any kind of link between Basque and Afro-Asiatic. The sole potentially interesting point uncovered is the very rough match between Basque *-ga* and *-na* (or *-naga*) and Berber *-k* and *-m*, in both cases respectively the male and female suffixes of the second-person singular in the verb, a comparison taken seriously by Tovar (1966). But this match is supported by nothing else at all, and is best dismissed as an apparent coincidence.

The Basque–Berber parallels have also been briefly considered by James Anderson (1973: 67, 1988: 109). Though apparently intrigued, Anderson very sensibly dismisses the matchups as insignificant: he concludes that they represent nothing more than chance resemblances, with possibly one or two ancient loans in one direction or the other. Very many other linguists, however, have been considerably less level-headed in their evaluation of such similarities. According to Bengtson (1994b), Aron Dolgopolsky is now defending the Basque–Afro-Asiatic link, but I have seen no work by Dolgopolsky. Unusually, Giacomino (1895) tries to link Basque, not to Berber, but to its distant relative ancient Egyptian.

Mukarovsky (1981c) rejects the universally held view that the Mande languages of west Africa, and also the single language Fula, belong to the vast Niger-Congo family and maintains instead that they are related to Basque (and of course also to Afro-Asiatic). These ideas he supports with some two dozen putative Basque–Mande cognates and about seventeen matches involving Basque and Fula. Even this modest data set contains a number of errors. The obvious Romance loan *kolko* 'breast' is matched with Mande **kwan-* ~ **kwar-* 'breast'; the transparently bimorphemic *eguzki* 'sun' (from *egun* 'day') is matched with a few miscellaneous words in particular languages, like Susu *koge* 'sun' and Samo *woso* 'sun', and the Basque word's eastern variant *ek(h)i* is matched with a completely different set of Mande words, most of them meaning 'moon', such as Numu *kahi*; the eastern Basque word *aketz* 'male animal, boar' is wrongly glossed as 'male' and matched with various Mande words for 'man, male', such as Kono *kai* ~ *ke*; Basque *ibili* 'go about, be active' is wrongly glossed as 'march' and matched with various Mande words for 'run', such as Bambara *boli*; Basque *toka*, an adverb derived from *to*, an interjection used in calling out to a man or a male animal, is wrongly glossed 'thou' and matched with various Mande words for 'name', such as Mandinka *to*; Basque *bi(ga)* 'two' is confused with the unrelated *bigae* (and variants) 'two-year-old heifer' (a loan from Latin *BIMANA, well attested in Romance) and matched with Fula *wiige*, plural *big-i*, unglossed but apparently 'heifer'; for the universal Basque *bare* 'spleen; slug', Mukarovsky extracts the very severely localized sense of 'liver' and compares this with Fula *ber-nde* 'heart'.

Nor can it be said that the remaining comparisons are striking: Basque *belaun* 'knee' and Mande words like *kumbalin*, *khimbi* and *kpuo*; Basque *odol* 'blood' and Mande words like *dyelo* and *woli*; Basque *(h)or* 'dog' and Mande words like *wulo* and *gbane*; Basque *gau* 'night' and Mande words like *su* and *gun*; Basque *su* 'fire' and Fula *sum-a* 'burn'; Basque *txori* 'bird' and Fula *son-ⁿdu*, plural *tyol-li*; and so on. Again, this is not the sort of thing that any reasonable linguist would regard as evidence for anything: it is a modest collection of miscellaneous resemblances, and very vague resemblances at that.

Proposed links with other African languages, while numerous, have not so far been defended in any detail.

An amusing footnote is the demonstration of Zyhlarz (1932) that there is just as much evidence linking German to Afro-Asiatic languages as there is linking Basque.

6.3 THE 'OLD EUROPEAN' SUBSTRATE

Europe had been inhabited for tens of thousands of years before the arrival of the Indo-European languages, and there is no doubt that these languages obliterated a number of earlier languages spoken throughout the continent. With only a few scanty exceptions here and there, we have no direct evidence of these earlier languages, but we do perhaps have some indirect evidence. Linguists have long suspected that the vocabulary, the grammatical features and even the phonological developments characteristic of particular Indo-European languages might reflect the influence of speakers of the indigenous population upon whom Indo-European speech was imposed. For example, the verb-initial sentence structure, the vigesimal number system and the distinctive consonant mutations of the Celtic languages have all been at times attributed to the influence of an unknown indigenous population. Such 'substrate' theories have proved to be of enduring popularity, even though our almost total lack of information about the nature of the pre-IE languages necessarily renders substrate theories little better than sheer speculation in most cases.

Many of those who have embraced substrate explanations for seemingly non-IE features of Indo-European languages have tended to posit a single substrate language, or at most a single group of closely related languages, extending over a vast area of the continent in prehistoric times. Depending on the particular scale envisaged, these hypothetical substrates have been variously referred to in the literature by such labels as 'Mediterranean' or 'Old European'. Apparently non-IE lexical items, often especially place names, in a large expanse of IE-speaking territory have very frequently been attributed to just such a source. And more than a few linguists, of course, have been eager to find in Basque, the sole surviving pre-IE language of western Europe, direct evidence of their posited substrate language.

In fact, there seems very little reason, *a priori*, to expect Basque to be a representative example of what was once a more or less monolithic linguistic unity stretching across Europe. The idea that the invading Indo-Europeans would have encountered a linguistically homogeneous Europe seems implausible in the extreme. Far more probably, what the Indo-Europeans found was a patchwork of languages, large and small, some related, some not, resulting from previous millennia of settlement, displacement and language shift, just like anywhere else. Consider, for example, the linguistic position in the pre-Roman Iberian Peninsula. When the Romans arrived, they found an ancestral form of Basque in the north, the seemingly unrelated Iberian in the east and south (see below), various Indo-European languages (at least Greek and Celtic, and quite possibly others), the Semitic language Punic, the mysterious Tartessian language, which was apparently related to nothing else at all (see Anderson 1988: Ch. 5), and very probably yet other languages of which nothing is recorded. It takes an enormous leap of faith to believe that this kind of diversity was unknown in Europe before the arrival of the Indo-Europeans. Consequently, any attempt to identify in Basque those mysterious elements which turn up in plant names in the Alps, tool names in Sardinia or place names on the Danube must be undertaken more in hope than in confidence.

Nevertheless, such efforts have not been wanting. In particular, a number of romanists, most of them Italian, have, during the last seventy years or so, advanced many dozens of proposals identifying some word or name in a Romance language with something in Basque; see Echenique (1987: 21–22) for a list of references. The doyen of such scholars, however, is indubitably the German linguist Johannes Hubschmid, who has argued that Basque is the last remnant of two large language families which had occupied western Europe before Indo-European: a 'Euro-African' family and a 'Hispano-Caucasic' family (Hubschmid 1953, 1955), many words from which can still be found in modern European languages, especially in Romance. Further, in a long series of publications culminating in three books (Hubschmid 1960, 1963, 1965), he has attempted a critical review of the whole history of the 'Old European' substrate question, as well as adding many further proposals of his own. In his 1965 book, he lists the 'Basque' words proposed in Romance, rejects most of them as implausible, and finishes with a modest list of only thirteen apparently pre-Indo-European words which, in his view, can probably be identified with words in Basque and hence imputed to an ancient substrate.

Unfortunately, even Hubschmid's final list, modest though it is, suffers from very severe difficulties. In particular, the majority of his words have phonological forms which would have been impossible in the Pre-Basque of 2,000 years ago: *tutur* and *kukur*, both 'crest', *kosko* 'acorn cap', *pentoka* 'little hill', *muga* 'boundary' and so on. Word-initial *p-*, *t-* and *k-* and word-medial *-nt-* are all clear evidence that these words must have entered Basque in post-Roman times, while word-initial *m-* must indicate either a loan word, an original **b-* or an 'expressive' formation of no great antiquity. Of course, it is still conceivable that some of these are pre-IE words which have somehow found their way into Basque, but they can hardly have been present there millennia ago, and so Basque can provide no independent evidence bearing on the question. Note that Michelena (1967: 322) stresses the point that pre-IE words found in Basque are not necessarily ancient within that language.

More recently, the German linguist Theo Vennemann has proposed to identify Basque with Old European on the basis of river names (Vennemann 1994a). Extending and modifying earlier work by Hans Krahe, Vennemann begins by noting that a very large number of river names in Europe north of the Alps show, in their earliest attested or reconstructible forms, such a strong family resemblance that they must all derive from a single language. Here is a sample of Krahe's data, arranged to show off the obvious patterns:

Ava	Aura	Aula	Auma	Avantia
Ara	—	Arla	Arma	Arantia
Ala	Alara	—	Alma	Alantia
Sala	Salara	—	Salma	Salantia

That is, the river names are constructed from a modest set of roots each of which can be followed by any of an identifiable set of suffixes, or sequences of such suffixes. Vennemann analyses all such names as consisting of an initial root, an optional 'determinative' (a single consonant), one or more derivational suffixes, and a final -a; he therefore concludes that the language which provided the river names must have been strongly agglutinating and more or less exclusively suffixing, and that therefore it could not, as Krahe had always maintained, have been an Indo-European language.

Vennemann goes on to examine the phonotactics of this language and to reconstruct a minimal phoneme system for it ('minimal', of course, because the river names have reached us only after centuries or millennia of being filtered through Indo-European languages, and hence any additional segments not found in those languages might simply have been lost). The system which he reconstructs for his 'Old European' is as follows:

$$i \quad e \quad a \quad o \quad u$$

$$p \quad t \quad k$$
$$b \quad d \quad g$$

$$s$$
$$m \quad n$$
$$l$$
$$r$$

This, of course, is not a very distinctive system: it consists merely of those unmarked segments which are found in the majority of the world's languages. Nevertheless, Vennemann somewhat optimistically compares this system with the system reconstructed for Pre-Basque (which he calls 'Old Basque'). Unfortunately, his presentation of Michelena's reconstruction is seriously inaccurate: it omits the fortis nasal and lateral **N** and **L**; it fails to note the fortis/lenis contrasts proposed by Michelena and appears to present a voicing contrast explicitly denied by Michelena; and it takes no account of the extensive neutralizations and defective distributions posited by Michelena. (Later in the article, Vennemann does briefly draw attention to some of these facts, though his account is confused, but he appears never to take them into account in his analysis.)

Vennemann then points to two characteristics of his river names: the very high frequency of initial *a-* and the near omnipresence of the final *-a*. These characteristics, of course, are also found in Basque. As we saw in Chapter 3, word-initial *a-* is astoundingly frequent in Basque, and moreover the Basque article *-a* is almost invariably attached to nouns cited in isolation. Vennemann therefore proposes that his 'Old European', the language of the river names, was an ancestral form of Basque.

But there are very serious difficulties with this interpretation. First, as we saw in Chapter 4, the Basque article *-a* has an obvious source entirely within Basque, as a specialization of the distal demonstrative stem *(h)a(r)-*; this article is even today not bound to nouns in the eastern dialects in the way that it is elsewhere, and hence the creation of the article, in all probability, took place in post-Roman times: millennia too late for Vennemann's purposes. Second, none of the roots or suffixes listed by Vennemann for Old European looks like anything in Basque, save (inevitably!) for the root **Is-*, which Vennemann of course wants to identify with Azkue's putative Basque root **iz-* 'water', discussed and dismissed as a phantasm in Chapter 5. Third, a sizeable number of the roots identified by Vennemann have forms which would have been impossible in Pre-Basque: *Drava-*, *Kara-*, *Pala-*, and others with impermissible initial plosives; *Vara-*, *Visa-* and many others with initial *v-* (identified by Vennemann as a non-syllabic allophone of /u/); and a large number of roots with initial clusters of two and even three consonants. Of course, none of these objections is necessarily fatal to Vennemann's position, but they are far from helpful, and I would suggest that what Vennemann has identified is, at best, an agglutinating language that looks very little like Basque. In any case, Schmid (1987) has recently pointed out that a number of the morphs found in these old hydronyms can be straightforwardly identified with Indo-European morphemes.

In further publications (1993, 1994b, 1995), Vennemann has attempted to find Basque (or more precisely 'Vasconic') sources for a wide range of European toponyms, personal names and common nouns. One of these is the city name *München*, for which a satisfactory Germanic etymology has long been available. This he wants to connect with Basque *muino* ~ *muno* 'hill' or the related B *muna* 'slope, riverbank'. But this word cannot be indigenous in Basque, at least not in this form, and in fact it is confidently traced by Corominas and Pascual (1980) to a Romance **bunno*, well attested outside of Basque. This word is problematic, but it is scarcely likely to be Basque in origin, and the same is true of many other items invoked by Vennemann.

A rather novel approach to the question of Basque and Old European is adopted by Adams (1980). What Adams does is to compare a sample of apparently pre-Indo-European river names with a sample of Basque words extracted from a dictionary, in order to see if there is any kind of match in terms of length and syllable structure. This is an interesting idea, but unfortunately the author chooses the K section of the dictionary for his sample of Basque, and, as we saw in Chapter 3, native Basque words of any antiquity do not begin with voiceless plosives, and hence the sample is hardly likely to be representative of Pre-Basque. And, just to make things worse, recall from Chapter 5 that the majority of river names in the Basque Country itself appear to be of non-Basque origin.

Finally, I note that V. Bertoldi, cited in Michelena (1961–1962), has suggested that the final morph -*ar* which is so common in both Basque and ancient Iberian might represent an ancient 'Mediterranean' plural suffix. The Basque words he has in mind are those like *adar* 'horn', *ilar* 'pea', *nigar* 'tear', *ondar* 'remains; sand', *bizar* 'beard', *bular* 'breast', *zatar* 'rag', *indar* 'strength', *izar* 'star', *behar* 'necessity', *abar* 'branch', *ibar* 'water meadow, valley', *gedar* 'soot' and *sapar* 'thicket'. Such words are indeed numerous, and an original plural sense is by no means out of the question for many of them, but Bertoldi's idea, plausible though it may be, remains an unsubstantiated conjecture.

6.4 INDO-EUROPEAN

Given the vast amount of information we have on the various Indo-European languages, given the degree to which the history of the family has been reconstructed, all the way back to Proto-Indo-European, and given the defiantly non-Indo-European character of Basque, a connection between Basque and Indo-European would seem to be *a priori* one of the most implausible suggestions that could possibly be made. None the less, suggestions along these lines *have* been made: the nineteenth-century Basque Romantic writer Chaho, whose linguistic endeavours are in most respects best forgotten, argued for a Basque-IE connection (Chaho 1824); the amateur Basque linguist Darricarrère amazingly tried to maintain that Basque *was* an IE language (Darricarrère 1885, 1903, 1912); and, rather more surprisingly, Unamuno carefully explored the possibility of some kind of relation between Basque and the IE family. And throughout the last two centuries there have been confused attempts to link Basque specifically with Celtic, with Latin, with Slavonic and even with Sanskrit. Most of those who have argued for a Basque-IE link, however, have proposed only ancient contact, or at best some kind of ancient *Sprachbund*, rather than a highly implausible genetic link. Of course, it can hardly be denied that Basque was in contact with Indo-European languages, or at least with Celtic, before the Roman period: we know that Gaul was divided between Basque and Celtic (see section 6.9 below), that Indo-European personal names were common in much of the Basque Country (see Chapter 1), and that place names of certain or probable Indo-European origin are found in much of the Basque

Country (see Chapter 5). Aside from the place names, however, it is by no means easy to find clear evidence of contact in the Basque vocabulary.

To begin with, there are a very few Basque words of seemingly ancient provenance which bear enough resemblance to words in ancient Indo-European languages (often especially Celtic) to suggest that they might be either ancient loans from IE to Basque or loans into both from some unknown source. Here are the ones which have been most often cited; my discussion is largely based upon Michelena (1964b: section 5) and Gorrochategui (1987).

Bq *adar* 'horn, branch' : Old Irish *adarc* 'horn'

The Irish word appears to have no IE etymology, and may represent a loan from an unknown language.

Bq *andere* 'lady' : Old Irish *ander* 'young woman', etc.

The same word appears in the Brythonic languages, where it generally denotes a young animal of some sort. The Basque word is clearly ancient, since it is attested in Aquitanian (see section 6.9). Many scholars have been prepared to accept a common origin for the Basque and Celtic words, but the loan, if it is one, could equally have been in either direction, or into both from an unidentified source. Note also that Gorrochategui (1995) has recently proposed that both Aq *Andere* (female name) and Aq *Andossus* (male name) contain a stem *and-* with female and male suffixes *-ere* and *-oss*, respectively.

Bq *angi(o)* 'fenced-off pasture' : Old Irish *aingid* 'protect'

This rather far-fetched comparison has attracted no support from either vasconists or Indo-Europeanists.

Bq *aran* 'plum' : Aragonese Romance *arañón* 'plum', etc.; Irish *áirne* 'plum', etc.

A difficulty is that the Romance forms point to an original *agraniō*, while the Celtic forms require an original *agrinja*.

Bq *argi* 'light; bright' : PIE *arg-* or *Aerg-* 'shine'

The PIE root is attested in Latin, Greek, Germanic and Hittite, at least, for example in Latin ARGENTUM 'silver', Greek *argyros* 'silver', Latin ARGUERE 'make clear' and Greek *argillos* 'white clay'. It is by no means out of the question that the Basque word might be related, but a difficulty is that no Indo-European language appears to show a form *argi, and it is therefore difficult to see how the Basque word could have been taken from any Indo-European source.

Bq *arto* 'maize', but originally 'millet' : Greek *artos* 'bread'

The Greek word has often been described as being of unknown origin, but

Buck (1949) suggests a derivation from *ar-* 'prepare'. In the absence of any relevant forms in the intervening languages, this resemblance looks like nothing more than a coincidence.

Bq (western) *bost* 'five' : Celtic **bost-* 'palm (of the hand)'

This one can be rejected out of hand, since western Basque *bost* is transparently derived from *bortz*, retained in the east, by the usual development of *rtz* to *st* (see Chapter 3).

Bq *gari* 'wheat' and *garagar* 'barley' : PIE **ghers-* 'bristle'

It is generally agreed that the two Basque words are related, the second being apparently a reduplicated form of the first. The connection with PIE is based upon the existence of the Latin reflex HORDEUM 'barley', together with the presence in a number of Near Eastern and even south Asian languages of words for various cereals, grasses and even beans of the general form *gVr-* or *gVrgVr-*. It is difficult to take this evidence seriously. While the PIE root is well attested in Europe, Latin alone has developed a relevant meaning, and the words from Semitic, Caucasian and Dravidian are surely far too remote to be connected with the Basque words in the absence of any suitable words in the intervening territory. Moreover, there is clear evidence that Basque *gari* derives from earlier **gali*, by the regular phonological development: all compounds of *gari* show the combining form *gal-*, as in *galarri* 'grist stone', *galbahe* 'sieve', *galburu* 'head of wheat' and *galeper* (a type of quail).

Bq *gezi* 'dart' : Celtic **gaiso-*

Opinion is deeply divided on this item. The problem is that the diphthong *ai* would normally have been retained in Basque (Michelena 1977a: 104), and hence proponents of a Celtic origin are obliged to posit a monophthongization which is natural enough but which is not normal in Basque. Michelena (1952) therefore concludes that the word must have entered Basque via Romance mediation.

Bq *gori* 'fiery, burning' : Middle Irish *gorim* 'hot', Breton *gor* 'blaze', etc.

The Celtic words are regularly derived from PIE **g^{w}hero-* 'hot', with the uniquely Celtic development of **g^{w}h-* into *g-*. This looks like a plausible case of a loan from Celtic, which would make the Basque word cognate with English *warm*, from the same IE etymon.

Bq *haitz* 'stone, crag' : Latin AES 'copper, bronze', Skt *áyas-* 'iron, metal', etc.

A PIE root **ayos-* is widely attested as denoting one metal or another, but never 'stone'; the Basque word, in contrast, denotes only stone and never any kind of metal. It is therefore difficult to see why this comparison has attracted so much attention.

Bq *hartz* 'bear' : PIE **rkso-* or **rkto-* 'bear'

The suggestion here is usually that the Basque word might be a loan from the supposed Celtic **artos* (Old Irish *art*, etc.). This is one of the most interesting proposals, and one that continues to enjoy a certain amount of support, though Gorrochategui (1987) is inclined to see the word as deriving from a much earlier Indo-European source, such as **arksos* or **arktos*, rather than a specifically Celtic one, since the Celtic form is a phonologically awkward source for the Basque word.

Bq *hogei* 'twenty' : Middle Welsh *ugeint* 'twenty', etc.

This match was discussed and dismissed in Chapter 5.

Bq *izoki(n)* 'salmon' : Celtic ?

The earliest attested form of the Basque word is *izokina*, and a Celtic origin has frequently been suggested on the basis of forms like Old Irish *éo* (Gen *iach*) and Gallo-Latin *esox*. But the comparative evidence from Celtic requires a Proto-Celtic form in **-āko*, which could not have served as a source for the Basque word. It is far more likely that the Basque word is a loan from late Latin ESOCINA. (Interestingly, Asturian Spanish has *esguín* 'baby salmon', considered by Coromina and Pascual (1980) to be a loan from Basque.)

Bq (eastern) *iratze* 'fern' : Irish *raith* 'fern' (< **ratis*), etc.

This can be dismissed out of hand, since *ira* is the western word for 'fern', and *-tze* is a common suffix in plant names.

Bq *landa* 'plain, prairie' : Celtic **landa*

The word is widespread in western Romance, but is thought to be a loan from Celtic. The Basque word is found throughout the country and occurs in several place names, suggesting that it is ancient in Basque. Gorrochategui (1987) prefers to see the Basque word as a loan from Celtic.

Bq *maite* 'beloved' : Old Irish *maith* 'good'

Gorrochategui (1987), following Michelena, is inclined to see the Basque word as a loan from Celtic.

Bq *mando* 'mule' : IE **mand-* 'horse, mule', etc.

A stem **mand-* 'horse, mule' is widely attested in the ancient Indo-European languages of Europe, with 'mule' being specifically Celtic. Gallo-Romance in fact shows a word *mannus* 'pony', from **mandos*, but this Romance form cannot be the direct source of the Basque word, and a Celtic origin seems more likely.

Bq *mendi* 'mountain' : Latin MONS, MONT- 'mountain', Welsh *mynydd* 'mountain' (< Proto-Celtic **moni'jo*)

The IE words are traced to a PIE root *men- 'project', with a supposed extended form *mn-ti-, leading to *menti-. A major difficulty is that the eastern dialects of Basque do not show the expected *menti, and hence, if this is a loan from Indo-European, it must have undergone a very ancient voicing of the plosive, distinct from the voicing which occurred in all but the eastern dialects of Basque in post-Roman times.

Bq *saldu* 'sell' : Proto-Germanic *saljan

The stem *sal-* bears a striking resemblance to the Germanic word (which is, of course, the source of English *sell*), but *saljan is explicitly Germanic, not Indo-European, and we are perhaps more likely to be looking at a coincidence than at a Germanic loan.

Bq *zilar* 'silver' : Proto-Germanic *silubra- 'silver'

The Germanic word, the source of English *silver*, is apparently found only in Germanic and Balto-Slavonic and has no IE etymology. Watkins (1969) traces it to Akkadian *sarpu* 'refined silver'. Few doubt that the Basque word has a common origin with the Germanic one, but the history is obscure, and the Basque–Germanic connection is expressly rejected by Agud and Tovar (1988–   ). Interestingly, a form *silubhra* is attested in Celtiberian.

Bq *zitu* 'grain; harvest; vintage' : Greek *sîtos* 'grain'

Even though the Greek word is of unknown origin, this resemblance has been interpreted as representing remnants of an ancient European word of wide distribution. However, the central meaning of the Basque word appears to be 'harvest' or 'fruits of the harvest', and the Basque word can be straightforwardly derived from a Romance development of Latin sectum 'a cutting' along the lines of *seito (Michelena 1977a: 106).

Bq *zulo* ~ *zilo* 'hole' : Celtic *sīlon

The problems here are first that *zulo* is unquestionably the more conservative form of the Basque word and second that an ancient intervocalic *l* would, of course, give *r* in modern Basque, and hence the comparison seems ill-founded.

In sum, then, the evidence for pre-Latin Indo-European loans in Basque is scanty to the point of non-existence. There is probably not a single undeniable instance of such a loan: only a small handful of candidates has been identified, and every one of them is problematic for one reason or another, with the possible exception of *mando* 'mule'. These results are in striking contrast to what we find elsewhere: no one doubts the clear cases of Indo-European loans in Finno-Ugrian languages, for example, or of ancient Celtic loans in Germanic. The absence of early Indo-European loans in Basque is surprising, perhaps even mysterious.

Michelena (1964b: 54–55) suggests that many ancient loans may simply have been displaced from Basque by later loans from Latin and Romance, and that others may have been remodelled under Latin influence (for example, Basque might have borrowed the Celtic word for 'king' as something like *errigV- but later altered this to the attested errege after contact with Latin REGE). These are perhaps plausible speculations, but they are speculations none the less.

Moreover, it is noteworthy that Basque appears to show no trace of any ancient grammatical influence from Indo-European. Such prominent features of Indo-European grammar as verbal prefixes, relative pronouns and subordinating conjunctions are generally absent from Basque, and the few instances which are found are clearly of late origin and derived from Romance influence. As usual, negative evidence proves nothing, but, if there was ancient contact on any scale, it is still slightly surprising to find no grammatical evidence at all.

There has, however, been one serious attempt to demonstrate a shared grammatical feature involving an ancestral form of Basque and some early variety of Indo-European, possibly Proto-Indo-European itself. This attempt has been made by the eminent Indo-Europeanist Antonio Tovar in a series of publications (Tovar 1954b, 1959a: Ch. 5, 1970). The essence of his claim is that the Basque relational suffix -ko, discussed in Chapter 2, is so similar in its behaviour to the word-forming suffix *-ko reconstructed for PIE that the two must be derived from a single common source. Tovar therefore concludes that PIE and Proto-Basque were members of an ancient European linguistic area which was sufficiently cohesive to allow linguistic elements, even bound morphemes, of whatever origin to diffuse into the various constituent languages. The morph -ko he takes to be one such element. His case is interesting enough to merit some discussion.

To begin with, it should be stressed that Tovar, in all of his considerable historical work, promoted the notion of what he called a 'proto-historical relationship' among languages. By this term he meant something less than a genetic relationship but something more than mere contact, and apparently even something more than a Sprachbund. It is not exactly clear just what Tovar had in mind, and other historical linguists have often found the whole concept rather dubious. Here I shall ignore this puzzling construct and simply concentrate on the evidence involving the suffix -ko.

All of Tovar's writings take the description of PIE *-ko for granted, but it will be convenient to provide a summary of the IE morph here. The handbooks from which the description below is taken are Brugmann (1891), Hirt (1927) and Pokorny (1959); some use is also made of Watkins (1969). These sources are in substantial agreement about PIE *-ko.

According to all these sources, PIE possessed a suffix of the form *-ko, whose reflexes are attested in all branches of the Indo-European family except Hittite. Very occasionally, this suffix was attached directly to a verbal root (that is, it was 'primary', in the terminology of nineteenth-century Indo-Europeanists), but much more usually it appeared attached to a nominal stem ('secondary' use). On rare occasions it was suffixed to an adverb. Its function in primary use is completely obscure (Brugmann 1891: 253), but otherwise it normally derived adjectives, or nouns based on adjectives, with a meaning along the lines of 'related to, belonging to'. Examples of this suffix include Greek *thēkē* 'receptacle' (< PIE **dhē-* 'put'; cf. Greek *títhēmi* 'put'); Latin RECIPROCUS 'reciprocal' (< **re-ko-pro-ko*, where **re* and **pro* are adverbs); Sanskrit *dvi-ka* 'consisting of two' (< *dvi* 'two'); Latin ŪNI-CU-S 'unique' (< ŪNUS 'one'); Sanskrit *síndhu-ka-s* 'coming from the Indus' (*síndhu-s*); Greek *Liby-kó-s* 'Libyan' (< *Liby-s* 'Libya'); Greek *physi-kó-s* 'natural' (< *phýsi-s* 'nature'); Latin CĪVI-CU-S 'civic' (< CĪVI-S 'city').

The addition of **-ko* to stems ending in a vowel, especially *i* (as in *physikós* and CĪVICUS above), was so common that a reanalysis apparently took place, resulting in several new suffixes of the form **-Vko*, and above all **-iko*. This suffix, which is widely attested in Indo-Iranian, Greek, Italic and Celtic, is again used to derive adjectives from nouns. Examples of its use include Sanskrit *āhn-ika-s* 'daily' (< *áhan-* 'day'); Greek *hipp-ikó-s* 'equine' (< *hippo-s* 'horse'); Greek *ethn-ikó-s* 'national' (< *ethno-s* 'nation'); Latin BELL-ICU-S 'warlike' (< BELL-UM 'war').

In some cases PIE **-ko* was added to nouns or adjectives without changing the part of speech, producing a derivative meaning, roughly, 'similar to, like'; this pattern was often used to form diminutives, sometimes with the addition of further diminutive suffixes. In a number of instances the derivative replaced the original word completely. Examples include Sanskrit *mus-ká-s* 'testicle' (< *mūs-* 'mouse'); Latin MŪS-CU-LU-S 'muscle' (< MŪS 'mouse'); Sanskrit *ajakā* 'little goat' (< *ajá-s* 'he-goat'); Sanskrit *sana-ká-s* 'former, old' and Latin SENEX 'old', both < **sene-ko-*, probably 'oldish', < **seno-* 'old'.

Finally, PIE also exhibits a suffix **-sko*, which is perhaps a compound suffix **-s* + **-ko*. This suffix is much less common than the others. An example is Greek *dískos* 'quoit' (< **dik-sko-s* < *dikein* 'throw'). This suffix also, as a result of frequent additions to stems ending in *i*, developed a variant **-isko*, which became highly productive in several branches, above all in Germanic. Examples include Old High German *diutisc* 'German'; OHG *frencisc* 'Frankish'; Gothic *mannisk-s* 'human'; Gothic *gudisk-s* 'divine'; and the whole range of English words in *-ish*.

This is the suffix which Tovar wants to identify with the Basque suffix *-ko*. It will be convenient to summarize here the properties of PIE **-ko*:

1 It is a derivational suffix.
2 It is attached to nouns (rarely to other parts of speech).
3 It derives adjectives or nouns based on adjectives.

4 It bears the meaning 'related to', 'belonging to' or 'similar to'.
5 It has a specialized use in forming diminutives.

I turn now to Basque -ko, whose major function was described in Chapter 2. Briefly:

1 It is not a derivational suffix, but a syntactic element which can be added freely to any constituent of an appropriate type.
2 It is attached to adverbials, regardless of their internal structure.
3 It derives adjectival modifiers which behave quite differently from lexical adjectives.
4 It has no semantic content, but only a syntactic function.

On the face of it, then, Basque -ko does not look much like PIE *-ko. However, matters are complicated by the fact that Basque -ko has some additional functions, rather different from its principal function. First, -ko can also be added to an N-bar to derive an adjectival modifier which, like the more usual type of -ko phrase, precedes its head. This is only possible with certain types of N-bar: generally, the N-bar must consist of more than a single word, and it must express one of only a small range of possible attributes. Here are some examples:

(a) *hiru urteko umea*
   three year-*ko* child-Det
   'a three-year-old child'
(b) *hortz biko haitzurra*
   tooth two-*ko* hoe-Det
   a two-pronged hoe'
(c) *bihotz oneko neska*
   heart good-*ko* girl-Det
   'a good-hearted girl'
(d) *beso ederreko pilotaria*
   arm lovely-*ko* pilota-player-Det
   'a pilota player with a great arm'

There is no possibility of interpreting these as instances of the more usual behaviour of -ko: first, they have no source (one cannot say in Basque *'a child who is in three years' or *'a girl who is in a good heart'); and, second, the forms are wrong (derivation from adverbials would yield the incorrect forms *hiru urtetako umea and *hortz bitako haitzurra). The presence of the numeral or adjective is obligatory: one cannot say *bihotzeko neska to express 'a girl with a heart' or *hortzeko haitzurra to express 'a hoe with prongs'. And the semantic restrictions are severe, if not altogether clear: one cannot say *begi urdineko neska for 'a blue-eyed girl' or *kotxe gorriko mutila for 'a boy with a red car'. (These meanings are expressed by using the suffix -dun 'having' in place of -ko: begi urdindun neska, kotxe gorridun mutila.) While somewhat puzzling, and certainly different from the canonical use of -ko, this use of the suffix is still a long way from the behaviour of the IE affix.

Very different from the canonical use of -ko, however, is its use as a derivational affix. The suffix can be added to a noun or to a numeral to produce a derivative which is also a noun. This cannot be done freely, and indeed the word-forming suffix is unproductive or only weakly productive. The meanings of the derivatives are generally unpredictable, though those formed from body parts often denote either a blow to the appropriate part of the anatomy or clothing or jewellery for that part. Examples include *gerriko* 'girdle' (*gerri* 'waist'), *zortziko* (a particular dance for eight people) (*zortzi* 'eight'), *marmitako* 'stew' (*marmita* 'stewpot'), *ipurdiko* 'smack on the arse' (*ipurdi* 'buttocks') and *belarritako* 'earring' (*belarri* 'ear'). Here the behaviour of *-ko* is altogether more reminiscent of PIE *-*ko*, but there is still a difference: these derivatives are nouns, not adjectives.

There is, however, a further point to be made about derivational *-ko*: it forms diminutives and, much more rarely, augmentatives: *mandako* 'small mule' (*mando* 'mule'), *zezenko* 'small bull' (*zezen* 'bull'), *mutiko* 'boy', but formerly 'little boy' (*mutil* 'boy'), *zatiko* 'big piece' (*zati* 'piece'). This use of *-ko* is no longer productive, but its frequency in medieval documents suggests that it was still highly productive at the time. (Note also, in section 6.9 below, the apparent presence of this suffix in Aquitanian.) However, the compound diminutive suffix *-sko* and its palatalized variant *-xko*, which are still very frequent today, probably represent reinforced versions of diminutive *-ko*.

Here we finally have something resembling a convergence between the Basque and IE suffixes: both form diminutives. Unfortunately, diminutive formation appears to be something of a secondary development for PIE *-*ko*, and it is very marginal indeed for Basque *-ko* in historical times, though it was probably more central in the prehistoric period.

So what should we make of Tovar's proposal? Well, there are serious difficulties. It would appear that this proposal requires an ancestor of Basque to have been in contact, not merely with a western IE language, but with PIE itself, or something very close to it. But this is a problem: while there is as yet no consensus on the location of the Indo-European homeland, everybody agrees that it must have been very far from the Basque Country. Most specialists prefer a homeland in Russia or the Ukraine, while a minority argue for the Balkans, Anatolia or even the Middle East. Only one proposal, supported today by virtually no one, puts it as close as northern Europe. Hence the necessary transmission of a bound morpheme between PIE and Proto-Basque would have required some very intense contact spanning the entire European continent some thousands of years ago. We have no evidence for such contact, but then we effectively have no evidence of anything for such a remote period beyond the obvious spread of the Indo-European languages across Europe. My best guess, then, is that Tovar's proposal must remain at best an implausible conjecture, at least until someone turns up more extensive evidence for an ancient *Sprachbund* involving Proto-Basque and PIE.

In fact, there has recently been an attempt to provide just such evidence, in the form of Roslyn Frank's 1980 book *En torno a un mito: el euskara y el indoeuropeo*. This purports to be an attempt to demonstrate the existence of some further morphemes shared by Basque and some early form of Indo-European. However, the value of this work can be quickly gauged by reading the author's very first page, on which she declares openly that she intends to pay no attention at all to the orthodox standards of work in historical linguistics, our 'sacred rules', as she calls them. Instead, she proposes to regard her investigations as nothing more than an amusing little game to be played by rules of her own devising. She is as good as her word.

The book treats only three items: Basque *haitz* 'stone', *jo* 'hit' and *su* 'fire', for each of which she attempts to demonstrate some kind of presence in Indo-European. I shall deal very briefly with each in turn.

For *haitz*, she accepts without reservation the 'stone-tool' conjecture discussed in Chapter 5, apparently not excluding the Latin loan *haizkora* 'axe'. She then proceeds to enumerate a list of words in various languages having something to do with tools or stone, including (among others) Spanish *azcona* 'dart', *hacha* 'axe', *azada* 'hoe', English *axe*, *adze*, *hammer*, and Sanskrit *aśman* 'stone'. All of these except the first have secure etymologies from various sources. In the end, what she demonstrates is that a few tool names and words for 'stone' in various languages look vaguely like Basque *haitz*. Few readers will find this conclusion stunning, or even interesting.

Her treatment of *jo* is altogether more colourful, since she wants to relate this to Basque *joko* 'game'. This is a challenge, since *jo* is clearly an indigenous word, while *joko* is a transparent loan from Latin IOCU. Her point of attack is the etymology of Latin JOCUS itself. All authorities agree that the Latin word is derived from **yok-o*, a suffixed form of the *o*-grade of the PIE root **yek-* 'speak'. Brushing this view aside, however, the author argues that the Latin word is in fact a compound of Basque *jo* and the suffix *-ko* discussed above. (Strictly, she does not claim that the Latin word is borrowed from Basque, but that it is constructed from ancient European morphemes which have survived in Basque.) Other difficulties aside, she ignores several awkward facts: (1) the Basque word *jo* is not a single morpheme, but a participle derived from a verbal root; (2) Basque *j-* is in every case derived from **e-* (see Chapter 3); (3) the existence of the northern combining form *joi-* implies that the ancestral form of *jo* must have been something like **eoni*; (4) Basque *-ko* never derives nouns from verbal stems or roots, and PIE **-ko* does so only very rarely (curiously, Frank makes only one brief passing mention of Tovar's 1954b paper, and doesn't cite his later work at all). But these are not important considerations for the author: Latin JOCUS *looks* like modern Basque *jo* plus *-ko*, and so *jo* plus *-ko* it must be. End of discussion.

Finally, she begins her discussion of Basque *su* by attempting to analyse Latin FOCUS 'hearth', of unknown origin, as a compound of Basque *su* and, of course, *-ko*, an analysis whose phonological difficulties alone are insurmountable. She goes on to compare *su* with Indo-European words for 'sun' (such as Latin SŌL) and for 'sweat' (such as Spanish *sudor*, which she tries to analyse as the alleged (but ungrammatical) Basque *su da 'it is fire'). And she concludes by citing a reported root *su-* 'fire' from the Dravidian languages. Aware that the Dravidian languages are conspicuously non-Indo-European, she observes lamely, if perhaps none too accurately, that these languages provided 'the background in which Sanskrit developed', and hence that something or other pretty damned significant must be going on here.

I expect that few linguists will find the author's 'game' entertaining.

Finally, before leaving Indo-European, I cannot resist mentioning here what is arguably, in the face of some exceedingly fierce competition (see below), the funniest attempt of all time at demonstrating a genetic connection for Basque. This is the attempt (1960) by the Catalan cleric, Monsignor Antoni Griera, bishop of Bergen, to demonstrate that Basque is not merely an Indo-European language but a *Romance* language, descended from Latin just like Spanish and French. In pursuit of this improbable goal, Griera proposes to derive every single word of Basque, without exception, from Latin, even including a few Basque words which do not actually exist. Wielding an approach to etymology which owes nothing to phonology or to semantics, the author sensationally derives Basque *gizon* 'man' from Latin BISON 'wild ox', *andere* 'lady' from CAPRA 'goat', *seme* 'son' from SIMIUS 'ape', and *alaba* 'daughter' from PAVA 'peahen', leading Michelena, in his 1960 review, to comment that Griera seems to believe that the ancient Basques were 'tenants of Noah's Ark', and of the ground floor, at that. In a splendid revival of the ancient *lucus a non lucendo* technique, Griera derives Basque *gau* 'night' from Latin DIURNUS 'of the day', though he spoils this a bit by mistranslating *gau* as 'day'. The author's uncertain command of Basque is, however, magisterial in comparison with his grasp of Latin: among the 'Latin' sources which he cites are such engaging confections as *merda-mamma, spera-care, per-en-ad, genitus-lacte-bal* and *vercia-troncho-el*.

It would be nice to be able to report that Griera's efforts constitute an exceptional piece of light relief among the more sober efforts at finding a relative for Basque, but, as will shortly become clear, this is far from being the case.

6.5 IBERIAN

The ancient Iberian language is recorded in a number of inscriptions, on stone, on metal tablets and on coins, found in eastern and southern Spain and southern France and dating from about the sixth to the first centuries BC. A few of these are inscribed in the Greek alphabet, but most are written in an indigenous script which long remained undeciphered. A handful of Iberian personal names are found in Latin texts.

Even though the Iberian texts are confined to an area which is not known ever to have been Basque-speaking, scholars have suspected for centuries that they might conceal a language related to Basque, and possibly even ancestral to Basque.

Something along these lines was suggested as early as 1587 by the Basque apologist Andrés de Poça (or Poza) (*ca.* 1530–1595), born in Orduña (Bizkaia), in his book *De la antigua lengua, poblaciones y comarcas de las Españas*. Poça, far more clear-headed than most of the apologists who followed him, was among the first to declare in print that Spanish, French, Italian and even Rumanian were modern forms of Latin. He argued that ancient languages could not disappear without trace, and suggested that fragments of ancient Basque speech could be found, especially in the form of place names and personal names, all over Spain; though his etymologies were rarely correct, his appreciation of the importance of ancient data was wholly modern. He did not, however, go so far as to identify Iberian explicitly with Basque.

His remarkably advanced ideas were adopted with enthusiasm, if with much less understanding, by the Basque apologists who followed him, but it was only in 1728 that Larramendi, whom we met in Chapter 1, proposed explicitly, in his *La antigüedad y universalidad del Bascuenze en España*, that Iberian was an ancestral form of Basque. Larramendi's suggestion was embraced by succeeding apologists, most notably by Pablo Pedro Astarloa, who passed it on to Wilhelm von Humboldt. Humboldt in turn publicized the proposal in his 1821 book *Prüfung der Untersuchungen über die Urbewohner Hispaniens vermittelst der Vaskischen Sprache*, as a consequence of which he is widely, if not very accurately, credited with having originated the idea.

Though well received, the proposal could not be seriously investigated so long as the Iberian script remained undeciphered, a step which was facilitated by the publication by Emil Hübner of the known Iberian texts in 1893. The necessary decipherment proceeded slowly and uncertainly, but a century after Humboldt Hugo Schuchardt, a supporter of the Basque–Iberian relation, ventured a reconstruction of the Iberian nominal declension in his 1908 book *Die iberische Deklination*, in which he tried to identify the Iberian case-endings with the Basque ones (or more precisely with his reconstructions of the Basque ones). Here is a summary of Schuchardt's comparison:

	Iberian		*Basque*	
Case	*Singular*	*Plural*	*Singular*	*Plural*
Inert	—	c	—	k
Agent	c	?	k	kek
Recipient	i ~ e	ce(a)i	i	ki
Instrument	š ~ s	ciš	z	kez
Possessive	n ~ m	cen	n	ken
Adjectival	co	—	ko	—

Impressive though this might appear at first, it can be dismissed. For one thing, progress in deciphering the Iberian script quickly revealed that the readings used by Schuchardt were seriously in error. For another, many of the 'Iberian' texts published by Hübner and used by Schuchardt were later found to represent an entirely different language, the Indo-European language now known as Celtiberian. Finally, five of the ten forms reconstructed by Schuchardt for Basque are unsustainable (see Chapter 4). (A bibliography of Schuchardt's scattered writings on Basque and Iberian is given by Georges Lacombe in *RIEV* 7: 210–216 (1927).)

In the first half of the twentieth century, several linguists turned their attention to the Basque–Iberian question. Among these were the Basque-born German scholar Gerhard Bähr, who concluded that the evidence for such a connection was so scanty that the Basque–Iberian hypothesis could not be maintained, and the Spanish linguist Pío Beltrán, who made very considerable progress in deciphering the Iberian script, and who supported a Basque–Iberian link.

Towards the middle of the century, the Spanish linguist Manuel Gómez Moreno finally arrived at a decipherment of the Iberian script which is now generally accepted; after partial solutions in 1925 and 1943, the definitive version was published as Gómez Moreno (1949). The script is mixed syllabic–alphabetic, with single syllabic characters used for CV sequences in which the C is a plosive, and alphabetic characters used for all other consonants and vowels. The script is defective in failing to distinguish voiced and voiceless plosives, even though these apparently contrasted in the language, and in having no unambiguous way of representing word-final plosives, which were not rare. One sign, Y, remains uninterpreted: this rare sign has a highly defective distribution, appearing chiefly in the common ending -*Yi* and in the stem *Ybar-*, which surprisingly seems to correspond to Latin Vmar-. It is variously thought to have represented either some kind of nasal or a rounded vowel. In many, but not in all, of the inscriptions (in both Greek and indigenous scripts), the text is broken up by marks into what are presumably words (though no one is certain about this, and some such sequences appear far too long to be single words).

Here are two examples of Iberian texts. The first is a transcription of the Alcoy lead tablet, perhaps the most famous of all the Iberian texts; written in the Greek alphabet, it was discovered near the village of Alcoy, not far from Alicante, and it is usually dated to the sixth century BC. The symbols *s* and *ş* are used for the two contrasting sibilants, while *r* and *r'* are used for the two contrasting rhotics; the symbol *?* stands for a mysterious character which is not a regular part of the system.

> rike or'ti garokan dadula bask
> buistiner' bagarok sss? turlbai

lurs legusegik başerokeiunbaida
urke başbidirbar'tin irike başer
okar' tebind belagasikaur işbin
ai aşgandiş tagişgarok binike
bin salir' kidei gaibigait

iunştir salir'g başirtir şabari
dar bir'inar gurs boistingisdid
şesgersduran şeşdirgadedin
şeraikala naltinge bidudedin ildu
niraenai bekor şebagediran

And here is a transcription of a lead tablet recently discovered in Los Villares (near Valencia). This is written in the indigenous script, though the enigmatic **Y** happens not to occur in it; the obliques are in the original, while the symbol *?* represents an unreadable character, and square brackets [ ] represent a portion of the tablet which is broken off, leaving a line incomplete.

bilosiunteşalir [ ]
ega ga ////////// elerte
ba şalirbosita şalibos
ngantobanteinbeletene
iboeganteşalirga //////////
dibandebaşalibosendenbilos
ştentiste ar'abagi bobaitinba
ganegaşalir ga /////////
ba iuntibilose

[ ]tinba bar'er şalir
[ ]ita şalirbos eter'ai
?ar'agar'er bobaitinba
[ ]ir duntibarte bobaitinba
şalirga //////////////////

After the decipherment, both Antonio Tovar and Luis Michelena quickly turned their attention to the Iberian texts, now readable at the phonological level. At first glance, the position seemed encouraging in some respects. For one thing, the phonological system of Iberian appeared strikingly similar to that of Basque and more especially to that reconstructed for Pre-Basque: five vowels; a preponderance of voiced plosives (especially *b* and *g*); two contrasting sibilants; two contrasting rhotics; no word-initial rhotics; the near-absence of *m*; the almost total absence of *p*; few and simple consonant clusters (including no initial clusters and virtually no clusters beginning with plosives). Moreover, there were a number of recurrent morphs which strongly resembled words and affixes in Basque (I say 'morphs' because there is no certain way of identifying morpheme boundaries). For example, there are Iberian sequences which strikingly resemble the Basque words *bizkar* 'back; height in mountains', *bihotz* 'heart', *beltz* 'black', *bihur* 'twisted', *argi* 'light, bright', *ilun* 'dark', *lagun* 'companion' and *nabar* 'dark, mottled', though it must be stressed that the meanings of the Iberian morphs are totally unknown, and in any case we would surely expect a few similar-looking morphs between languages with such similar phonological systems. (But note that ⟨h⟩ is absent from Iberian.) Further, the formation of personal names looks generally similar to the Aquitanian pattern, and an occasional Iberian personal name looks strikingly Basque, such as *M. Iunius Iaurbeles*, in which *Iaur-* looks like the familiar combining form *jaur-* of Basque *jaun* 'lord' and *-beles* looks like *beltz* 'black'. (On the other hand, most stems end in a consonant, which is not remotely true of Basque, and many end in a plosive, something which is unknown in Basque.) Moreover, the common morphs *-ko*, *-en* and *-tar* are reminiscent of the Basque relational suffix *-ko*, the Basque genitive suffix *-en* and the Basque ethnonymic suffix *-tar*. On occasion, Iberian *-tar* does indeed appear to be unmistakably ethnonymic in function, as in *Saitabietar* 'people of Saitabie' (Latin Saetabenses), but Michelena (1964b: 94) concludes that the Iberian suffix does not really resemble the Basque suffix on the whole. Iberian *-en* does not behave much like the Basque genitive, and its interpretation as a genitive requires some charity (Michelena 1976). Strikingly, though, we find what looks like an alternation linking the sequences *-ildun/iltu-/iltur-*, closely parallel to the ancient and puzzling alternations in Basque of the type *egun/egu-/egur-* 'day', discussed in Chapter 3. A summary of Basque–Iberian resemblances is given in Tovar (1961: 62ff.), while Michelena (1955) discusses possible Basque–Iberian cognates.

Nevertheless, in a series of publications (1949, 1951, 1954a, 1959a, 1959b, 1961), Tovar was able to demonstrate that these resemblances were entirely superficial, that Iberian really did not look much like Basque, and (most importantly) that Basque was of no assistance whatever in reading the Iberian texts. Exactly the same conclusions were reached independently by Michelena (1955, 1958, 1973b, 1976, 1979), though both scholars at least allowed that the phonological resemblances and possible shared morphs might point to an ancient Iberian *Sprachbund* including Iberian and Basque, especially since there is some evidence for shared elements in personal names; Michelena suggests an 'onomastic pool' from which both Basques and Iberians drew their names. But the main conclusion of both scholars is quite clear: there is no significant evidence to relate Iberian to Basque, and the Iberian texts remain uninterpretable. Iberian might be a distant relative of Basque, but it is not a close relative, and it is certainly not an ancestral form of Basque. To this conclusion I should add that Iberian was in all likelihood in contact with the Aquitanian ancestor of Basque (see below) in a region lying between the Ebro and the Pyrenees, very roughly modern

Aragón, and hence a few loan words in one direction or the other are to be expected. (See Map 1 in Tovar (1959b) or Map 1 in Echenique (1987).)

In the 1940s, the Basque scholar Julio Caro Baroja attempted a scrutiny of the Basque–Iberian question; his articles, now collected as Caro Baroja (1979), are painstaking and reliable but somewhat out of date.

In 1988 the American linguist James Anderson returned to the question. In Chapter 8 of his book, he makes determined and even heroic efforts to identify pieces of Iberian with something in Basque, even going so far as to compare Iberian *geitesnaura* with Basque *gaitzerauntsi* 'scandalmongering' and *gaitzerran* 'speak ill of, malign' (both transparent compounds of *gaitz* 'bad', with *erauntsi* 'speaking' and *erran* 'say'), and Iberian *geietisia* with Basque *izigaitz* 'intrepid, brave' (another transparent compound, this time of *izi* ~ *izu* 'fear, trembling' and -*gaitz* 'difficult', 'in . . . able'). He also tries to relate the first part of Iberian *gaisurargetan* to Basque *gaitzuru* 'measure of grain' (about 4.5 litres), but this is merely an eastern variant of the more usual *gaitzeru*, which is surely a loan from Romance. Anderson's comparison is nothing if not enthusiastic, though it unfortunately contains an extraordinary number of errors in the citation and glossing of Basque forms, as well as several other transparent loan words from Romance. In the end, though, while he reaches no explicit conclusion, he apparently considers that no parallels of any significance can be drawn between Basque and Iberian, and he does not question the thoroughgoing negative conclusions of Tovar and Michelena.

These negative conclusions thus remained unchallenged for more than two decades, until very recently, when the Spanish linguist Juan Luis Román del Cerro dramatically announced that he had achieved a complete reading of the Iberian texts in terms of Basque and that he had moreover found Iberian to be virtually indistinguishable from Basque (Román del Cerro 1993). Given the profoundly negative conclusions of the earlier specialists, Román del Cerro's claims are entirely unexpected, even astounding. They have, however, been very favourably received in some quarters, and some linguists appear to believe that the author has proved his case. Like all other vasconists, I fail to share this enthusiastic opinion. Let us briefly examine Román del Cerro's work.

The author's procedure is to chop up the Iberian texts into pieces which seem good to him, and then to try to find a Basque identification for each of his pieces. He next tries to interpret the resulting sequence of Basque elements in a coherent manner. Here is a representative example, involving the sequence STARIENMÜ, which is repeated in one Iberian text (Ü is his reading of Y). This the author segments arbitrarily as follows: ST/ARI/EN/ MÜ. Now he looks for Basque matches.

His morph ST he identifies with the Basque suffix -*zto*. Yes, I did say 'suffix': Basque -*zto* is a word-forming suffix, found only in the Bizkaian dialect, which forms adjectives from nouns, as in *zorrizto* 'lousy' from *zorri* 'louse'. This is a compound suffix composed of the instrumental -z and an unidentified second element; it is rare and unproductive, and all attested examples of it (there are fewer than a dozen) are clearly pejorative in meaning, like the one cited. Román del Cerro appears not to be troubled by the signal innovation of analysing a word as beginning with a suffix, and a compound suffix at that, nor is he disturbed by positing a 'Basque' word which begins with a consonant cluster which is absolutely unattested at all stages of Basque (pre-Basque, recall, had *no* initial clusters, and Basques cannot pronounce initial *st-* even today).

The second element ARI he identifies with Basque *hari* 'fibre, thread', a word whose antiquity is not in doubt. The third morph EN he identifies with the Basque genitive suffix -*en*, which is fine except that -*en* is quite possibly an innovation replacing the earlier -*e* (see Chapter 4).

Finally, MÜ the author proposes to identify as Basque *muin* 'pith, marrow'. There are, however, massive difficulties with this. For one thing, no word could begin with *m* in Pre-Basque, because there was no /m/ in the language. For another, the extraordinary range of dialect variants of this word (*muña, hun, un, gun, uña, fuin*) would seem to point to an original *fune; certainly nothing like *mu would be possible. Schuchardt suggests that this is a loan word from Latin FUNE 'rope', which is phonologically perfect if semantically a bit difficult (though note that the Basque word also means 'spinal cord').

These matches yield the following reading of STARIENMÜ:

-zto hari -en muin
-y   thread's pith

This does not look at all encouraging, but now Román del Cerro introduces the next aspect of his technique: he alters the meanings of the Basque elements in a capricious manner to obtain something suitable for his purposes. The derivational suffix -*zto* he chooses to interpret as an adjective meaning 'rich, abundant', even though the Basque suffix (quite apart from *being* a suffix) means nothing of the sort, and in spite of the fact that no Basque adjective can precede its head. The equally unhelpful *hari* he interprets as 'vein of ore', even though the Basque word has no such meaning. (Doubtless he is influenced here by the existence of Spanish *filón* 'vein of ore', a derivative of Latin FILU 'thread', but no such semantic development is attested in Basque.) The genitive case-suffix -*en* is not really what he needs either, so he arbitrarily reads it as an *ablative* suffix meaning 'from', a meaning which the Basque suffix never has. (But, of course, the Spanish preposition *de* functions as a marker of both genitive and ablative, so perhaps that makes it all right.) But it is the treatment of *muin* which reveals the author's technique most clearly. While its central meaning is 'pith' or 'marrow', this word has an extended meaning of 'the most important part of something, without the details': Basques speak of the *muin* of something in the same way that English-speakers speak of the 'meat' of something. Consulting his Basque–Spanish dictionary, the author therefore finds a series of glosses with the general sense of 'summary, abstract'. Now one of the Spanish words for 'abstract' happens to be *extracto*. But, in such fields as chemistry and mining (and Román del Cerro is *very* keen on mining: he seems to regard the Iberian texts as so many treatises on mining technology), the same word can also mean 'extract' – that is, a small mass of material separated from a larger mass. Given the established utility of Spanish in overcoming these little epigraphical hiccups, the author does not hesitate, therefore, to conclude that 'extract' is precisely the sense intended here – in spite of the fact that Basque *muin* does not remotely have such a meaning.

Putting all these inspirations together, the author comes out with

'rich vein-of-ore from extract'

and concludes triumphantly that STARIENMÜ means, in his version of Basque/Iberian, 'extract from the rich vein of ore'.

Lest the reader suspect that I have unfairly targeted an exceptionally dubious example, let us look at one more of Román del Cerro's readings: that of BASEROKEIUNBAIDA (from the Alcoy tablet), which he proposes to segment as BASER/OKE/IUN/BAIDA. The morph BASER he identifies with Basque *matzer* 'deformed, defective', one of a number of localized adjectives in *m-* denoting various kinds of defects, all of them surely of late formation. For his OKE he adduces Basque (*k*)*ok*(*a*) 'vomit, indigestion, disgust', a phonaesthetic formation if ever there was one. The morph IUN he identifies with *una* 'small channel', an exceedingly obscure word attested only in the speech of the Bizkaian town of Orozko; this word is so limited in its distribution that even Azkue, a native speaker of Bizkaian who provided particularly extensive coverage of that dialect in his dictionary, failed to record it, and there is certainly no reason to attribute any antiquity to this word, nor an earlier form resembling **iun*. Finally, BAIDA is for Román del Cerro Basque *baida* 'bay' (a curved inlet of the sea). This word exists only in a small area of Bizkaia, and the author is untroubled by, or more likely unaware of, the fact that this a transparent loan from Romance, of the same origin as Spanish *bahía*, French *baie* (whence English *bay*) and other Romance cognates; the Romance origin of the Basque word is regarded by Corominas and Pascual (1980) as too obvious to be worth discussing.

And here is the result:

matzer   oka   una   baida
deformed indigestion small-channel bay

Again this is disappointing, and again the author is ready with some creative interpretation. He arbitrarily alters the meaning of *matzer* to 'twisted', of *oka* to 'be full of, be filled with', of *una* to 'channel' and of *baida* to 'inlet', and gets 'twisted be-full-of channel inlet'

which he, with a little more work, interprets as 'the inlet of the twisted channel', in which the 'be-full-of' is apparently dropped as inconvenient, while a little judicious syntax is quietly introduced without licence from the text.

These are not atypical examples: they are absolutely representative of Román del Cerro's work, and they are moreover two of the examples which the author himself singles out as displaying the success of his approach particularly well.

One might reasonably ask what sort of grammatical structure is exhibited by the 'Iberian' that comes out of Román del Cerro's manipulations. The answer is: none at all. In Román del Cerro's 'Iberian', there are no parts of speech: any morph can function indifferently as noun, verb or adjective, without affixation or modification, as required by the analyst. There are also no words: words are 'undefined in Iberian', and there is no recognizable structure in terms of roots, stems or affixes. There is no fixed order of elements: morphs can come in any order at all, without restriction, and, as a consequence, the morph sequences must sometimes be read 'in the direct sense' (forwards) but at other times 'in the inverse sense' (backwards). There is no limit on the length of morph sequences: sometimes they're longer, sometimes they're shorter. That's just the way it is. Nor are any of these statements merely my own assessment of Román del Cerro's work: every one of them is explicitly asserted by the author himself.

Román del Cerro's 'Iberian', then, is a language with no parts of speech, no words, no fixed order of elements, no syntax, no morphology apart from one or two case-suffixes, no restrictions on the length of sequences, no restrictions on anything. In short, it is a 'language' with no grammar at all, let alone with any trace of the abundant grammatical characteristics of Basque. I find it exceedingly difficult to believe that any reader could take this sort of thing seriously, but some linguists have none the less done so.

It is clear what the author has done. He has carved up his Iberian texts into bite-sized pieces and then leafed through one or two large Basque dictionaries, looking for entries which bear some kind of resemblance to his pieces. For this purpose, *any* entry will do. It matters not at all that the entry is an obscure dialect word of no great antiquity, or that it is plainly a regional variant of a more widespread form that is not convenient, or that it is an obvious loan from Latin or Romance. If he can find it in the dictionary, he is happy to project it thousands of years into the past, without any attempt to find out something about the history of the word or affix he has discovered.

Here are a few more of Román del Cerro's supposedly prehistoric Basque words. He finds the onomatopoeic item *karrak* 'crack!' and uses it to read his KAR as a verb meaning 'split'. He finds the word *ede* 'tanner's pit' (attested in a *single* locality), confuses this with the unrelated verb *edeki* 'open, remove', a variant of the more usual *ideki* ~ *ireki*, and reads his EDE as 'remove', 'ditch' or 'cave', as it suits him. He finds *bahe* 'sieve', a transparent loan from Romance, and uses it to explain his BA as a verb meaning 'sift'. He finds *tilet* 'punctuation mark', a very recent loan from Romance, and identifies this with his TILE. In the same vein, he finds *kulatz* 'full stop, period' and invokes it to interpret his KULES as 'mark' – but *kulatz* is a modern neologism. He finds *trikatu* 'stop, pause' and assigns this to his DIRGA, apparently unaware that this is a loan from the ancestor of Occitan *trigar* 'delay, be late, be slow', and equally unaware that no ancient Basque word can begin with *t-*, let alone with a consonant cluster. He finds the nursery word *tato* 'jump', a childish form of the loan word *salto*, and matches this with his DADU. He somehow manages to cite a number of non-existent Basque words, including an alleged **ain* 'offspring' and **abe* 'fate, destiny'. Other words he just cites or glosses wrongly: he gives **iunz* for 'dew' (the correct form is *ihintz* ~ *intz* < **ini(n)tz*) and **erre* for 'ravine' (correct *erreka*), and he glosses *heldu* as 'sprout' (of plants) when in fact it means 'ripen, mature'. I could go on in this vein for some time, but I shall content myself with just one more example, my particular favourite. Looking for a match for his AI, he can find nothing better than Basque *aiaia*. This is strictly a nursery word meaning '(a) walk'; it is explicitly identified as a nursery word by Azkue, who correctly glosses it with Spanish *paseo* '(a) walk'. But, not only does Román del Cerro ignore the comment, he misreads the gloss, and solemnly puts into his book the translation *el paso* 'pass, passage', which suits his purposes better. Not only does the author not know much about Basque, it seems he even has a little trouble reading his own language.

Apart from such fanciful stuff, the once-popular Basque–Iberian thesis is now dead, although it continues to attract wistful glances. For example, Oroz Arizcuren (1981) argues that the apparent lexical similarities derive from a substrate influence of Basque upon Iberian, though for this he appears to require a substantially greater geographical extension of Basque than we have any evidence for, including a sizeable expanse of the Mediterranean coast. More surprisingly, the distinguished Catalan etymologist Juan Corominas has recently been invoking Basque with some freedom in seeking sources for troublesome place names in the formerly Iberian-speaking part of Spain. For example, he proposes for *Begur* on the Costa Brava the Basque etymology **beko-uri* 'forehead-town', even though the un-Basque-looking *beko* is almost certainly a loan from Romance and even though *uri* is a specifically Bizkaian (western) variant of the otherwise universal *(h)iri*, which moreover clearly continues Pre-Basque **ili*. While I have great respect for Corominas, I am deeply puzzled by these manoeuvres, and I know of no vasconists who would be happy with them.

A footnote: there is a venerable tradition of perceiving Iberian as an

African language, most likely an Afro-Asiatic language, intrusive into Spain. It should be noted that there is zero evidence for such a view: Iberian looks nothing like any known African language, and it conspicuously fails to exhibit any trace of the internal inflection which is so typical of the North African languages like Berber.

I close with a passage from Michelena (1964b: 61): 'And this [our utter inability to make the slightest sense of Iberian in terms of Basque], whatever the non-specialists may say, could scarcely happen if Iberian were an ancient form of Basque or even a close relative of it' (my translation).

6.6 MINOAN

Ever since their discovery a century ago by Sir Arthur Evans, the Minoan Linear A texts of ancient Crete have exercised a magnetic pull upon linguistic scholars. Though the related Linear B script of Mycenean Greece was successfully deciphered by Michael Ventris in the 1950s, Linear A remains mysterious today. This is not for lack of effort: work on Linear A has been prolonged and intense, and indeed several 'decipherments' have been offered, each of them, of course, completely different from all of the others, and none of them having won any support.

It was doubtless inevitable that someone would try to read the Linear A texts as Basque, and precisely that was attempted by the British scholar F. G. Gordon, in his book *Through Basque to Minoan*, published in 1931 by the prestigious Oxford University Press. Like so many of those who have 'discovered' Basque in unexpected places, Gordon seems to have known little about Basque: his statements about it are frequently very surprising, and the one example of a Basque sentence which he offers in his brief introduction is ungrammatical.

Linear A is a syllabary with about seventy-five characters; in some texts the syllabic characters are accompanied by logograms ('pictograms') apparently providing a clue to the meaning, as happens regularly in the later Linear B texts. Gordon, however, takes a very surprising view of the script: he regards each syllabic character as representing a complete word, like a logogram. This, of course, immediately gives him a 'language' with an exceedingly small number of words, a result which seems to have caused him no discomfort. Moreover, he very frequently, in his interpretations, allows a word boundary to fall *in the middle of a single character*: for example, the sign which he reads as *bizal* and identifies as Basque *bizar* 'beard' can be used not only to represent the meaning 'beard' but also to represent the syllable *-biz* at the end of a preceding word followed by the syllable *al-* at the beginning of the next. This is an inspired piece of legerdemain the like of which I have never seen elsewhere.

In the several texts for which he offers readings, there occur a total of seventy-eight characters (a mixture of syllabic characters and true logograms). For six of these he can find no suitable Basque word, though he still provides translations. All of the other seventy-two signs are identified with individual words of Basque, or rather of what Gordon imagines to be Basque. Of these, no fewer than thirty-four are absolutely non-existent in Basque, and are merely inventions of the author's, while a further seventeen have the form of real Basque words but do not, however, have the meanings that Gordon assigns to them. Many of the imaginary words are compounds, which the author justifies on the ground that they are 'correctly constructed', but most of them are nothing of the sort. For example, he invents a word *edukardo, allegedly 'wine-holder', from eduki 'contain' and ardo 'wine', but compounds of this form, parallel to English words like scarecrow and pickpocket, are absolutely unknown in Basque, which permits only the type parallel to English wine-holder. Other inventions are even less convincing: Gordon invents a word *oi, allegedly 'flower', which he justifies by interpreting the real Basque word oihan 'forest' as a compound of *oi and han 'there', a bizarre type of compound of which he is particularly fond. He takes Basque betiko 'for ever' as meaning 'vase', estugarri 'bond' as 'cord', su 'fire' as 'oven', ollo 'hen' as 'bird', the verb atz egin 'scratch' (from (h)atz 'finger') as 'engraver's tool'. But the pièce de résistance is surely his treatment of the sign he reads as khallu. Finding this correctly glossed in a dictionary as corteza de tocino, he delightedly translates this as 'boarskin', a meaning which suits his heroic and elevated purposes. In fact, it means 'bacon rind'!

Vocabulary aside, it cannot be said that syntax plays a large part in Gordon's view of things. All of his readings consist of phrases loosely strung together, with no connecting grammar. With only a couple of exceptions, all the 'Basque' verbs appearing in his readings stand in the form of the perfective participle, the form which he finds entered in dictionaries. It seems that the Basques of Crete, in great contrast to our own Basques, did not bother to inflect their verbs, and Gordon simply supplies whatever tenses, auxiliaries or agreement markers appear to him to be required.

Finally, it has to be said that Gordon's interpretations of the Minoan texts are beyond the merely fanciful. He reads all the texts as instances of poetry, and a rather lofty form of poetry at that. Here, for example, is his reading for the first text he considers, identified only as B.M. First, a literal gloss:

> In/with a coffin/grave a spider mouth thread-holding, a flesh fly
> Head round, flower skin, holdwine tapperling:
> Take, drinker, care, mouth-with embracing a grave/coffin,
> Wine drinking – twice ohé! Dead he has spun round.
> Wine-cup walking, measure keeping, threaded, the thirsty one dead has spun
>   round.

And now the author's rendering into English:

> A spider in a web, holding thread in its mouth; a flesh-fly, round-headed, flower-

skinned, the little wine-jar tapper. Take care, drinker, embracing a tomb with the mouth, drinking wine – alas! alas! He has spun round, dead!

This is apparently a poem about a crafty spider which has trapped an unwary fly sipping from a container of wine. As the author genially remarks, 'After all, a composition of this kind is only what might be expected from the Minoan genius.'

Not content with deciphering the Linear A inscriptions, Gordon applies his method as well to the Phaistos disc, that unique and enigmatic artefact whose die-stamped characters some scholars have suggested might not represent an attempt at writing at all. It is no more resistant to the application of 'Basque' than the Linear A texts:

> The lordling skimming the girdle-tracks; the lord clenching the fist, bruising the skin with delight, hewing at the flower of the teeth, smiting with cestus, driving home; the lord walking on wings the breathless path, the star-smiter, the foaming gulf of waters, dogfish smiter on the creeping flower; the lord, smiter of the horse-hide (*or* the surface of the rock), the dog climbing the path, the dog emptying with the foot the water-pitchers, climbing the circling path, parching the wine-skin, the tall jars, the high-stemmed vessel, climbing the circling path, the solitary rocks; the lord clasping to the breast the pillars; the dog holding and seizing the pitchers.

This is certainly picturesque, if not so easy to follow (as I remarked above, syntax is not a prominent feature of Gordon's interpretations). It is not at all clear why this fellow is smiting dogfish on the flowers, or just what that dog is up to with the water-pitchers. The author's annotations, extensive though they are, provide little illumination: for example, he explains that the sign he has chosen to gloss here as 'water-pitcher' is actually the sign which he otherwise reads as 'net', which would seem to suggest that the Minoan genius had not entirely got the hang of the principles of water storage. Baseball fans will, however, be delighted to find our lord, whoever he is, described as a 'smiter of the horse-hide': apparently we are dealing here with a kind of prehistoric Babe Ruth.

I do not think that Gordon's interpretation of Minoan as Basque is one of the monuments upon which the reputation of the Oxford University Press has been built.

6.7 PICTISH

The Pictish inscriptions of Scotland are among the most puzzling and frustrating linguistic monuments in Europe. Few in number, mostly brief, often badly weathered, and, when readable, often consisting of long repetitions of the same character, these largely indecipherable inscriptions are thought to date from the eighth and ninth centuries; they are labelled 'Pictish' merely because the Romans, and later the Anglo-Saxons, applied the name *Picti* to an unidentified people who inhabited Scotland in their day. Most of the inscriptions are in the Celtic Ogam alphabet, though two are in the Roman alphabet. Since the work of Jackson (1955), it has been generally agreed that the inscriptions represent two distinct languages, one of them assuredly Celtic ('Celtic Pictish') and the other of unknown affiliation ('Pictish' proper), though this conclusion has recently been challenged by Katherine Forsyth (p.c.), who prefers to see only a single (Celtic) Pictish.

It was suggested by Sir John Rhŷs (1892–1893) that Pictish, as a seemingly pre–Indo-European language, might be related to Basque. Rhŷs later withdrew this suggestion, however, and the Pictish specialists who have followed him have generally taken no interest in it. This is hardly surprising, since the Pictish which emerges from the inscriptions looks very little like Basque, and Basque has proved to be of no use in deciphering them.

In 1968, however, the French-Catalan scholar Henri Guiter dramatically announced that he had succeeded in deciphering almost the entire Pictish corpus in terms of Basque, and indeed that he had found Pictish to be virtually indistinguishable from Basque. Like the majority of such dramatic announcements, this one has been universally rejected. Pictish specialists dismiss it out of hand, and vasconists have been no more impressed. Guiter's interpretation suffers from a number of apparently fatal shortcomings:

1 The values assigned to the Ogam letters are completely at odds with those accepted by all Pictish specialists. On occasion, Guiter even reads a single character as two syllables, something otherwise as alien to the Ogam alphabet as to any other.

2 Some of the inscriptions for which Guiter claims a complete decipherment are, according to the Pictish specialist Oliver Padel, so badly weathered as to be unreadable. Guiter seems to have supplied a generous amount of imagination in reading these texts.

3 In most respects, the individual words and word-forms in Guiter's 'Basque' are identical with those of twentieth-century Basque. Guiter would apparently have us believe that the ancient Picts, separated by more than a thousand miles and by more than a millennium from their continental cousins, were effectively speaking twentieth-century Basque. This is absurd: Basque is conservative, admittedly, but it's not *that* conservative.

4 On a larger scale, however, Guiter's 'Basque' readings suffer from a distinct lack of Basque syntax, or perhaps of any syntax. Words and short phrases are loosely strung together, with no syntactic links, and crucial affixes, required to make the 'Basque' text coherent, are absent.

5 Finally, Guiter's 'Basque' readings are, to put it mildly, somewhat fanciful. Here, for example, is Guiter's reading of a set of three inscriptions from Brodie (Moray), which incidentally are described by Padel (1972) as 'worn to the point of being nearly indecipherable':

I, Idarrako, depart. He departs, melancholy, so let him have need of tears. On the

place where he lies, the supply of earth that he bears has burned   him. He is
asleep beneath the snow. Arise! He has a stream of moans.

(translated from French by Price 1984: 25)

This is not at all the sort of thing that we find in Dark Age inscriptions that
we can read with confidence, but it is very much the sort of thing we find in
other instances of 'decipherments' of indecipherable texts by scholars who
decide in advance what they intend to find and then proceed to find it.

6.8 CAUCASIAN

There are some thirty-eight Caucasian languages, all of them concentrated
in an area about half the size of France, lying between the Black Sea and the
Caspian Sea. Four genetic groupings are recognized: Northeast, North-
central, Northwest and Southern (or Kartvelian). Many specialists are satisfied that the Northeast and North-central groups are probably related, and
some are increasingly confident that all three northern groups are remotely
related within a larger family, though this has yet to be demonstrated to
general satisfaction. So far, however, there appears to be no evidence linking
the northern languages to the Kartvelian group, which includes the best-
known and earliest-attested Caucasian language, Georgian.

Attempts at linking Basque genetically to some or all of the Caucasian
languages have been underway for nearly a century, and the volume of work
in this area probably exceeds all other work on Basque genetic connections
put together. This is not because of any great success in these investigations,
but only because of typological similarities. Basque shares its ergative morphology and its elaborate system of verbal agreement in varying measure
with most of the Caucasian languages, and the common presence of these
non–Indo-European characteristics has been enough to persuade any
number of linguists that there *must* be a connection there to be discovered –
a dangerous assumption, of course, since typological resemblances have
rarely proved to be of much assistance in identifying genetic relations.

On the whole, the work on Basque and Caucasian has been considerably
more sober and careful than most of the other work I discuss in this chapter.
It was begun in a small way by Schuchardt, who was chiefly interested in
finding a North African connection for Basque, but he occasionally, as in
Schuchardt (1913), cited some Caucasian parallels. The Dutch linguist C. C.
Uhlenbeck pursued the Basque–Caucasian connection throughout his
career, for example in Uhlenbeck (1923a, 1924, 1940–1941, 1946, 1947). The
Italian linguist Alfredo Trombetti produced an entire book (1925) claiming
a long list of Basque–Caucasian cognates. The Russian linguist Nikolai
Marr, in the days when his work was becoming decidedly eccentric, published several articles comparing Basque and Caucasian. The French Caucasianist Georges Dumézil devoted a chapter of his 1933 book on North

Caucasian languages to citing a number of supposed cognates with Basque. The French vasconist René Lafon produced a long series of papers arguing for a Basque–Caucasian genetic link and proposing some dozens of cognates (Lafon 1933, 1944 (appendix to vol. 1), 1948, 1951, 1952a, 1952b, 1957, 1967, 1968a). The Norwegian Caucasianist Hans Vogt pursued the question in two papers and proposed a modest list of cognates (Vogt 1942, 1955), though his conclusions are more negative than otherwise. Finally, the German linguist Karl Bouda, the most enthusiastic of all the proponents of a Basque–Caucasian link, after surveying the entire earlier literature and devising some further comparisons of his own, put the seal on the whole enterprise by presenting nearly 500 putative cognates in a series of papers (Bouda 1948, 1949, 1951, 1952).

Though most of these investigations are mercifully free of the kind of fantasizing that characterizes so much of the work I have discussed above, the blunt fact is that they do not measure up to the standards normally expected in establishing genetic relationships. With the partial exception of Lafon (1948), which at least attempts (unconvincingly) to identify some systematic correspondences between Basque and Georgian sibilants, all of this work remains at the level which I condemned at the beginning of this chapter: the investigators achieve nothing, and indeed attempt nothing, beyond compiling lists of Basque words and morphemes which bear some kind of resemblance to words and morphemes in one Caucasian language or another. But, with some thirty-eight highly divergent languages to play with, they could hardly fail to find such resemblances, particularly since the Caucasian 'cognates' they cite are in nearly all cases merely items found in some particular language, items which cannot be shown to have existed in any version of Proto-Caucasian.

Here are a few representative examples selected from this work. Basque -tzu, a plural marker found in a few pronouns, is matched with the Abkhaz plural suffix -c"a; the Basque relative-clause-forming suffix -n is matched with the particle ni in Mingrelian, which, among other functions, can mark relative clauses; Basque haragi 'meat' is matched with Cherkess lə 'meat'; Basque hotz 'cold' is matched with Abkhaz s" 'freeze'; Basque etxe 'house' is matched with Lak ča 'hut'; Basque larri 'anxious' is matched with Avar λerize 'be afraid'; Basque ezpel 'box tree' is matched with Georgian bza and Mingrelian bzakali 'box tree' (these two Kartvelian languages are closely related); Basque oso 'whole, sound' is matched with Avar čago 'alive'; Basque ahari 'ram' is matched with Chechen εaχar, Ingush häχar, and Batsbi aχrab 'small lamb' (these three Northeast Caucasian languages are closely related). And so it goes, for item after item, page after page, article after article.

All of this work was done before Michelena's elucidation of the phonological history of Basque, and hence the Basque forms cited are not infrequently words which could not have been of the same form 2,000 years ago.

Among these cases are *bihi* 'grain' (< **bini*), *hezur* 'bone' (< **enazur*), *ahant-zi* 'forget' (< **ana(n)tzi*), *jin* 'come' (< *jaugin*), *zain* 'watchful' (< **zani*) and the definite article *-a* (< **har*), but there are many others. There are even some Romance loans included in the Basque items cited, such as *bahe* 'sieve' and *zango* 'leg'. And, of course, many of these investigators do not hesitate to segment away any arbitrary part of a Basque word which they find inconvenient in seeking a match.

Nevertheless, this body of work was received with enthusiasm in some quarters. The Spanish linguist Antonio Tovar apparently accepted the proposed Basque–Caucasian unity without hesitation in his various works on Basque (Tovar 1950, 1959a), and it is not difficult to find other linguists who take a similarly favourable view. But the proposal also encountered some formidable opposition in the person of Luis Michelena.

Now Michelena was in no way hostile to the idea of a Basque–Caucasian genetic link. Quite the contrary: by his own admission, he would dearly have loved to find some relatives for Basque, and he took a keen interest in all such work. He even contributed to a lexicostatistical study of Basque and Caucasian (Tovar *et al* 1961), and, in his (1950b) article, he went so far as to point out a Basque–Georgian parallel which had been overlooked. None the less, he had a very clear understanding of what could be counted as evidence, and he did not find such evidence here.

In two reviews of Bouda's work (1950b, 1953), Michelena roasts the German linguist for playing fast and loose with the Basque data – in particular, for arbitrarily segmenting Basque words in order to extract the portions he wants to match, while airily dismissing the remaining material as ancient 'prefixes' or 'suffixes'. In his (1964b) book, he complains that the Basque/Caucasian proposals rest on nothing more than random similarities, that they mostly display a shocking ignorance of Basque, and that they have succeeded in shedding no light at all on the prehistory of Basque. And, in an article published in 1968a, by which time the work on Basque and Caucasian had largely dried up, Michelena reviews the whole body of such work. Though politely phrased, as always, this review is scathing, even devastating. In his considered opinion, no evidence of any significance at all can be extracted from this long list of publications. All those carefully compiled lists of putative cognates amount, in Michelena's view, to nothing more than lists of random similarities between Basque and one or another Caucasian language. Michelena is confident that an equally impressive list of 'cognates' could be found between Basque and any sample of thirty-odd Indo-European languages, if anyone were willing to go to the trouble of looking for them. He finds nothing resembling systematic correspondences: the rule seems to be that any Basque segment can be matched with any remotely similar Caucasian segment, at the whim of the author. Even the grammatical parallels offered mostly involve very short morphs of simple form, such as *-a*, *-n*, *-k* or *-ra*, of the sort that one might expect to find in profusion in any highly inflected language, and these parallels never involve systematic alternations.

Michelena closes his review by suggesting that the linguists whose work he is surveying had started by simply *assuming* that Basque and Caucasian must be related, and that they had therefore proceeded merely to collect possible confirming instances, without attempting any sort of scrutiny of their work. Michelena's assessment, I am confident, must be accepted by anyone who takes historical linguistics seriously.

Michelena's review effectively dismissed the entire Basque–Caucasian enterprise as something close to a total waste of effort, and for nearly two decades hardly anyone seems to have pursued the matter further, except that some of Lafon's Basque–Kartvelian work was republished in Russian as Lafon (1976).

Since the 1980s, however, the Polish linguist Jan Braun has again been pursuing a possible Basque–Kartvelian genetic link in a series of papers (Braun 1981, 1985, 1994). Braun's work is in some respects more sober than most such work: he attaches priority to identifying systematic correspondences, and he sometimes takes advantage of Michelena's reconstructions of particular words. But the correspondences he adduces rarely extend to more than a single segment in a word, a typical example being Old Georgian *rcqwa* 'irrigate' and Basque *iturri* 'spring, fountain' to illustrate the correspondence Old Georgian *c* : Basque *t*. Moreover, most of the time he totally ignores Michelena's reconstruction and uses for comparison such obvious loan words and late formations as *mutur* 'snout', *potzo* 'mastiff', *tini* 'summit', *patar* 'rugged slope', *korotz* 'dung', *matxar* 'hollow', *kantal* 'boulder' and *kurlabio* 'wasp', none of which can possibly be of any antiquity and some of which have transparent Romance sources. He also has a habit of inventing some rather fanciful reconstructions to make unsuccessful comparisons work better, as when he reconstructs *orre* 'juniper' as *ose, or *orri* 'leaf' as *ortzi, or *luze* 'long' as *lurtze, or *osin* 'deep place in a river' as *iswin. Finally, he makes heavy use of expressive formations, such as *zomorro* and *momorro*, both 'creepy-crawly', *koko* 'bug, larva' and *marmara* 'spider'. I regret that I am unable to see in Braun's work anything more than a fistful of exceedingly vague chance resemblances.

Braun's work seems to have attracted little attention, but the same is not true of the next item. In 1985, the Caucasian linguist V. A. Čirikba returned to the issue with a ten-page paper proposing a total of some ninety cognate words and grammatical morphemes between Basque and various North Caucasian languages (he excludes Kartvelian). It is difficult to tell whether Čirikba considers that he is presenting new work, or a summary of the earlier work, or a combination of both. On the one hand, he mentions the names of Bouda, Lafon, Trombetti, Dumézil and Uhlenbeck, and he certainly repeats a large number of their proposed cognates. On the other hand, he cites no work by any of these scholars except for the irrelevant Uhlenbeck

(1927) and the even more irrelevant Lafon (1976), he speaks in his brief introduction of the importance for his purposes of recent work in the reconstruction of North Caucasian proto-languages, and he presents a number of putative cognates which I have not seen elsewhere.

Čirikba's paper has attracted a certain amount of favourable comment from linguists who are apparently not familiar with the earlier work or with Michelena's dismissal of it. That being so, it is perhaps in order to provide a brief review of the paper here (a point-by-point critique is provided in Trask (1995c)).

Of Čirikba's ninety proposed cognates, forty-five, or exactly half, are merely repetitions of proposals made by Uhlenbeck, Dumézil, Lafon and Bouda, and dismissed by Michelena. The remaining forty-five appear to be new, but virtually every one of the new 'cognates' suffers from serious problems of one sort or another. Some of his 'Basque' words simply do not exist, and are either inventions of the author's or out-and-out blunders: thus his alleged 'plural suffix' *-ar, his *beri 'this same', his *ilu 'move', his *giz 'man, person', his *ba 'son, child', his *kilte 'key', his *zartzu and *ziri, both 'sharp', and his *xor 'dog'. He cites Basque kolko as meaning 'woman's breast'; in fact, it means 'the space between one's chest and one's clothing' and also 'bay, gulf', and it is a transparent loan from Latin COLPU, and hence cognate with English gulf. He cites Basque aditu 'understand', a loan from Latin AUDITU, Basque busti 'moist', a loan from Occitan musti and cognate with English moist, and Basque gela 'room, chamber', a loan from Latin CELLA. He even (and this is almost beyond belief) cites an alleged Basque abets 'voice' and compares it with Abkhaz, but this is merely a garbled version of abesti 'song', a somewhat lunatic late-nineteenth-century neologism coined by Sabino Arana; the real Basque word for 'voice' is ahots, a compound of aho 'mouth' and hots 'sound'.

Čirikba compares Basque gurpil 'wheel' and inguru 'around', which he assumes are related, to Caucasian roots of the form gʷVr- 'ring', but gurpil is a compound of gurdi 'cart, wagon' with -bil, in which it is the second element that carries the notion of 'roundness', while inguru is merely a loan from Latin IN GYRU. He compares Basque belarri 'ear' with Caucasian words of the form lV-, airily removing an alleged 'body-part prefix' *be-, but belarri is assuredly a dissimilation of earlier *berarri, and the 'body-part prefix' is not removed when he compares Basque beso 'arm' to Caucasian forms, because there he needs the b- to get his match. He mistranslates Basque magal 'lap' as 'belly', assumes that potzo 'mastiff' is the same word as otso 'wolf' (they are unrelated), and picks out the obscure and severely localized dialect variant maguri 'strawberry' for comparison and ignores the far more widespread but apparently less convenient form marrubi, a loan from Latin MARRUBIU 'horehound'. In order to obtain matches, he happily obliterates the first syllable of bizkar 'back', the first syllable of handi 'big', the last syllable of lagun 'companion' and the first and the last syllable of *belaun* 'knee'. He describes Basque *mara-mara* as an adjective meaning 'abundant'; in fact, it is a phonaesthetic adverb meaning 'steadily, continuously', and its form shows that it cannot be of any great antiquity. He compares Basque *jin* 'come' with Abkhaz -*i*-, even though *jin* is merely a contraction of the synonymous *jaugin*. He cites western Basque *igar* 'dry', ignoring the more conservative eastern form *eihar*, which is not convenient. He cites Basque *txiki* 'small' without realizing that it is derived from an earlier (attested) *tipi*, which does not suit his purposes. He cites Basque *ze* 'small' and its palatalized form *txe* as though they were unrelated, and compares them with different Caucasian words which happen to resemble each one separately, and he is unaware that this word derives from earlier *zene, which destroys both matches. His treatment of the three demonstratives is a monument to confusion: he tangles up their forms, he mistranslates one of them and he treats a case-ending as part of a stem.

Finally, Čirikba's work, like all the rest, fails to identify even a single systematic correspondence. His very brief summary of some of the consonant matchups required by his proposals serves only to emphasize that each Basque consonant is matched with a wide range of consonants in any given Caucasian language, with no discernible pattern.

In short, then, Čirikba's paper is in no way an advance on the earlier work, and in fact the extraordinary number of errors which it contains renders it greatly inferior to that earlier work, which at least managed to cite and gloss Basque words correctly. There are no grounds for taking it seriously, and still today there is *no evidence at all* for a genetic link between Basque and any of the Caucasian languages. The not infrequent statements in the literature to the effect that 'Basque cannot be separated from the Caucasian languages' constitute so many fantasies. (The recent survey by Chicobava and Sturua (1980) expresses no more than a hope that links may eventually be found.)

Indeed, there are reasons to suspect that the Caucasian languages (especially the northern ones) are *a priori* most implausible candidates for being relatives of Basque. For one thing, Basque has a very modest consonant system, and, as we saw in Chapter 3, the consonant system of Pre-Basque was even more impoverished, consisting of no more than sixteen consonants and possibly of as few as eight. Some North Caucasian languages, in complete contrast, have the largest inventories of consonants on the planet. The recently extinct Ubykh had no fewer than eighty consonants, while many others exhibit between fifty and seventy. Nor is work in reconstruction obviously simplifying this picture: according to Catford (1991: 265), a recent reconstruction of the Proto-Lezgian subgroup of Northeast Caucasian posits the startling total of 101 consonants, while the first attempt at reconstructing Proto-North-Caucasian has provisionally set up the astounding total of 180 consonants. Hence it would appear that *any* attempt to relate Basque to North Caucasian would have to assume either that the Caucasian

languages have undergone a comparatively recent explosion of their consonant systems or that Basque has undergone a catastrophic meltdown of its
system on a scale not parallelled elsewhere. Even the dramatic reduction of
the Proto-Indo-European obstruent system exhibited by Tocharian, often
singled out as the most profound system collapse ever discovered, was not of
this magnitude, and was moreover accompanied by the introduction of
some new consonants.

Finally, I should note that the American linguist John Bengtson has
recently revived the Basque–North-Caucasian idea again, but Bengtson's
objective is to place both Basque and North Caucasian into a much larger
grouping, and so I shall defer discussion of his work until section 6.10.

6.9 AQUITANIAN

Here we come at last to the one and only proposal which has borne fruit.
According to Julius Caesar, while most of Gaul was occupied in his day by
Celts, the southwestern part was inhabited by a people whom he calls the
Aquitani (or Aquitanians) and whom he describes as entirely distinct from
their Celtic neighbours. The Aquitanian language is attested in the form of
about 400 personal names and seventy names of divinities, embedded in
Latin texts. These texts are mostly votive and funerary inscriptions, but there
are also a few of a literary nature. There are no connected texts in Aquitanian, but most of the names are compound in form or contain derivational
suffixes, and some of them exhibit what appear to be indigenous case-
endings in place of Latin ones. Given the nature of most of the texts, it is
unsurprising that they frequently stress the sex, age and parentage of a
named individual, a fact which is highly convenient.

That the Aquitanian fragments might reveal a language related to Basque
was suspected by generations of vasconists and romanists, many of whom
pointed to this or that tempting resemblance, and the close relation, or even
identity, of Basque and Aquitanian was openly maintained by some, beginning perhaps with Luchaire (1877). A list of the Aquitanian names then
known was compiled and published by Seymour Ricci (1903). But it was
only with the publication of Luis Michelena's long monograph (1954a),
surveying and cataloguing the entire corpus of Aquitanian material, that it
became possible to weigh up the evidence. Briefly, what Michelena found
was this: (1) of the forty or so stems and affixes which are sufficiently frequent to be isolated with some confidence, more than half appear to be
transparently Basque or can at least be plausibly identified with elements in
Basque; (2) so far as can be determined from the apparently somewhat
defective Roman alphabet in which the texts are written, the phonological
system of Aquitanian is strikingly similar to what is independently reconstructed for Pre-Basque (see Chapter 3); and (3) the pattern of word-
formation in Aquitanian is identical to that in Basque. One or two

additional texts have turned up since 1954, notably the Lerga stele discovered in 1960, and these additional materials confirm Michelena's findings.

This is not the place to repeat Michelena's findings in detail (a convenient brief sample of annotated Aquitanian texts is provided in the first chapter of Michelena's 1964a book), but I shall at least illustrate these findings. Michelena's work has recently been confirmed and extended by Gorrochategui (1984, 1995).

The very frequent elements indicating sex, age and parentage are often identical with Basque:

Aquitanian	*Basque*
Andere, Andre-	*and(e)re* 'lady'
Cis(s)on	*gizon* 'man'
Nescato	*neskato* 'young girl'
Sembe-	*seme* 'son' (< **senbe*)
Seni-	*sehi, sein* 'boy, child' (< **seni*)

All of these elements occur uniformly in the names of individuals of the appropriate sex, and they do not merely resemble Basque words: they are identical to Basque words. Moreover, the use of such relationship terms in personal names is very well documented in Basque: such names as *Sein*, *Andere*, *Aita* 'father', *Ama* 'mother' and *Annaya* (*anaia* 'brother') are amply attested as personal names in the medieval Basque Country, and *Arreba* 'sister (of a man)' and *Osaba* 'uncle' were in use as surnames until recently. Interestingly, both *Min(n)aya* (= *Mi anaia*) and *Miecha* (= *Mi aita*) are used frequently as honorifics in the great medieval Spanish epic *Cantar de Mio Cid*.

Other Aquitanian morphs are hardly less transparent, or at least have plausible readings in Basque:

Aquitanian	*Basque*
And-	*handi* 'big'
Arixo	*haritz* 'oak'
Artehe	*arte* 'holm oak'
Atta-	*aita* 'father' (?)
Belex, -belex, -bel(e)s	*beltz* 'black' (cf. *bele* 'crow, raven')
Berhax-	*beratz* 'soft, benign'
-berri	*berri* 'new'
Bihox-, Bihos-	*bihotz* 'heart'
Bon-, -bon(n)	*on* 'good'
Bors-	*bortz* 'five'
-co(n), -cco(n)	*-ko* (ancient dimin. suffix, still productive in medieval times)
-en(n)	*-en* (genitive case-ending)
-gori, -cor(r)i	*gorri* 'red'

Aquitanian	Basque
Hars-	hartz 'bear'
Heraus-	herauts 'boar'
Ilun(n)-	ilun 'dark' (< *iLun) (?)
Laur-	lau(r) 'four'
Lohi-	(archaic) lohi 'body'
Osson, Oxson, -oss(o)-, -ox(o)-	otso 'wolf'
Sahar	zahar 'old'
-tar(r)	-tar (ethnonymic suffix)
-to(n), -tton(n)	-to (dimin. suffix)
Vmme-	ume 'child'
-xo, -xso	-txo (dimin. suffix)

A few of these items deserve comment. The frequency of -belex as a final element leads Michelena to suggest that modern beltz 'black' was originally *beletz, and that the second vowel was lost in this position (note Aq -bels), with the reduced variant being later generalized to the free form. (See further under beltz in Chapter 5.) The Basque word beratz 'soft, benign' is well attested as a personal name Beraxa in the medieval period. The identification of Aq bon(n)- with Basque on 'good' implies that this word must have undergone the very common loss of initial b- before o, described in Chapter 3, and reinforces speculations about a connection between the Basque word and Latin BONUS. The absence of a double l in Aq Ilun(n)- is troubling, since we would have expected *Illun(n)-, but see below. The occurrence of what appear to be the numerals for 'four' and 'five' in such personal names as Laurco is entirely parallel to the Roman practice of giving names like Quintus and Sextus.

Please note that this is not just another modest list of random similarities. It is true that a smaller number of common elements and a larger number of infrequent ones cannot be plausibly identified with anything in modern Basque, but the proportion of common elements for which a Basque identification can be given is above 50 per cent, a figure not remotely approached by any of the other investigations discussed in this chapter. Moreover, the Aquitanian elements do not merely exhibit a vague resemblance to Basque forms: within the limits of the orthography, they are identical to Basque forms, and, where relevant, they are identical to the forms independently reconstructed for Pre-Basque.

A further point is that the phonological system represented in the Aquitanian texts appears strikingly similar to that reconstructed for Pre-Basque. We may note the following points:

1 The letter p is very rare: with only a handful of exceptions, it is found only as a positional variant of b. (Recall from Chapter 3 that /p/ seems to have been rare in Pre-Basque.)

2 In intervocalic position, the geminates tt, cc, nn and rr are all at least as

common as the corresponding simplex consonants, though *ll* is unexpectedly rare. (Recall that Pre-Basque had contrasting 'fortis' and 'lenis' consonants in this position, and that the fortis consonants appear to have been phonetically long.)

3 With only a couple of exceptions (*Monsus*, *Vmar-*), the nasal *m* is absent except before *b* (as in *Sembe-*). (Recall that Pre-Basque had no /m/, though [m] was (and is today) the pronunciation of /n/ before /b/, and that modern *m-* and *-m-* derive from earlier **b-* and **-nb-*, respectively.)

4 Word-initial *r* is absolutely unattested.

5 The aspirate *h* is very frequent, not only word-initially and between vowels, but also following *r, l, n* and rarely *t*. This is almost exactly the distribution of *h* in the modern dialects which retain the aspiration.

6 The unsystematic fluctuation among *s, ss, x* and *xs* strongly suggests that Aquitanian had more contrasting sibilants than could be accommodated in the Roman alphabet (Latin had only a single sibilant /s/). It appears that the otherwise unneeded *x* was pressed into service to deal with some of the Aquitanian sibilants, but that no consistent system of transcription was achieved. (Recall that Pre-Basque was rich in sibilants, having at least *s z ts tz*, and possibly also *x tx*.)

7 Consonant clusters do not occur word-initially, with the single exception of *Britexanossi*, which is possibly an error. Word-medially, clusters are either of the form nasal or liquid plus plosive or sibilant, or of the form sibilant plus plosive, except for *rl*: exactly the clusters which we find in Basque at all periods. Specifically, we find *mb, nt* (only at morpheme boundaries), *nd, nc* (only at boundaries), *ng, ns, nx(s), ld* (once), *lc* (doubtful), *lg, ls, rp* (once), *rb, rt, rd, rc, rg, rs, rl, sp, st, sc, xp, xt* (?), *xc*. Clusters of plosive plus liquid are absent, just as in Basque. A handful of three-consonant clusters occur: *nbr* (once), *ndr* (once), *rsp, rst, lst, lsc*. Most of these are attested in modern Basque, and it is known that such clusters were much commoner in the language a few centuries ago.

Given the limitations imposed by the use of the Roman alphabet, it would be difficult to imagine how Aquitanian could be phonologically more similar than it is to Michelena's reconstructed Pre-Basque.

The structure of the names is generally quite transparent: each name consists of a single stem, or a sequence of two stems, or either of these followed by a suffix. The names are thus very similar in formation to modern Basque surnames. Examples: *Belex, Bombelex, Belexconis* (Gen), *Belexeia, Andere, Anderex(s)o, Bihoxus, Bihoscinnis* (Gen), *Cisson, Cissonbonnis* (Gen), *Seniponnis* (Gen), *Senitennis* (?) (Gen), *Senicco*.

Some stems occur exclusively in male names: *Andoss-, Atta-* (cf. Bq *aita* 'father'), *Cisson* (cf. *gizon* 'man'), *Hanna-* (cf. *anaia* 'brother' < **anna-*), *Sembe-* (cf. *seme* 'son' < **senbe*), *Seni-* (cf. *sehi* ~ *sein* 'boy' < **seni*), *Hars-* (cf. *hartz* 'bear'), *Oxson* (cf. *otso* 'wolf'), *Bors-* (cf. *bortz* 'five'), *Bihox-* (cf. *bihotz* 'heart'), *Berhax-* (cf. *berhatz* 'benign'), *Enne-*. Others occur exclusively in female names: *Andere* (cf. *andere* 'lady'), *Edun(n)-*, *Er(h)e-*, *Hahan(n)-*, *Hauten-*, *Nescato* (cf. *nescato* 'young girl'), *Silex-*. Still others occur in names of both sexes but take a suffix to mark sex: *Belex-* (cf. *beltz* 'black' < **beletz*), male *Belex-co*, female *Belex-eia*; *Laur-* (cf. *laur* 'four'), male *Laur-co*, female *Laur-eia*; *Neure*, male *Neuri* (Dat), female *Neure-seni* (Dat)

Gorrochategui (1995: 42) makes the interesting suggestion that the male stem *Andoss-* and the female name *Andere* represent a common element **And-*, with a male suffix *-oss* and a female suffix *-ere*. This *-oss* he is inclined to identify with the word-forming element *-ots* found in several Basque animal names, such as *ordots* 'boar; male animal' and *bildots* 'lamb'. He goes on to note that *Andoss-* is documented three times as the epithet of a deity and hence to propose that *Andoss-* was the Aquitanian word for 'lord', parallel to *Andere* 'lady' (still so today). This is a very persuasive interpretation, and it fits in well with the observation that *jaun*, the modern Basque word for 'lord', looks like an old verbal participle converted to a noun.

As noted in Chapter 1, the divine name *Ilurberrixo deo* occurs rather frequently, and appears to be the name of a particularly important deity. The first element might be identical to Basque *ilun* 'dark(ness)' < **iLun*?), with the usual combining form of *n*-stems, while the second can hardly be other than *berri* 'new'.

The identifiable case-endings are somewhat puzzling. We apparently have genitives *-(n)is*, *-(n)i* and datives *-(n)i*, *-(n)o*, *-e*. Not all of these can be explained as Latin, particularly the surprising dative *-e* and the puzzling *n* which appears frequently, but not invariably, in all the other suffixes.

However, the frequent genitives in *-(n)is* merit a further observation, first pointed out by Caro Baroja (1945). Early medieval texts from the Basque Country frequently cite the genitives of personal names, and these commonly look just like the Aquitanian genitives: *Belascones* from *Belasco*, *Galindonis* from *Galindo*, *Garseanis* from *Garsea*, *Enneconis* from *Enneco*, *Furtunionis* from *Furtunio*, *Scemenonis* from *Scemeno* and *Belascotenes* from *Belascot(e)*. And these genitives in turn, after the regular Basque loss of intervocalic *n*, provide straightforward sources for the frequent medieval Basque patronymics in *-iz*: *Berascoiz*, *Garindoiz*, *En(n)ecoyz*, *Semeroyz* and so on. Moreover, the less common type of Aquitanian genitive illustrated in *Halscotarris* likewise provides a model for the medieval patronymic *Ahoçtarriç*.

The conclusion seems inescapable: Aquitanian is so closely related to Basque that we can, for practical purposes, regard it as being the more-or-less direct ancestor of Basque. It follows that an ancestral form of Basque was spoken in a large area of southwestern Gaul, as well as (as we know from other evidence) throughout the greater part of the Pyrenees and, most likely, in at least the east and north of the modern Basque Country.

In 1960 a funerary stele was discovered at Lerga, in south-central Navarre, just west of the river Aragón, containing a brief inscription in the Roman alphabet; the stele dates from the second or third century AD. The text is partly in Latin and partly in an indigenous language. It reads as follows:

VM.ME.SA.HARFI
NAR.HVN.GE.SI.A.BI
SVN.HA.RI.FI.LIO
ANN. XXV.T.P.S.S.

Michelena (1961–1962) demonstrates, by appealing to the frequency of the letter H, that the indigenous language cannot be Iberian, and must be Aquitanian. Ignoring the date in the last line, he reads the text as follows:

'Umme Sahar fi[lius] Narhungesi Abisunhari filio'

Now *Umme Sahar* is a personal name, and it transparently consists of Basque *ume* 'child' and *zahar* 'old', both of which are abundantly attested in Basque personal names in the medieval period. Since *ume* is generally thought to be derived from earlier **unbe*, also seemingly attested as *Ombe-* in Aquitanian, it is likely that the *umme* occurring here represents an intermediate stage of development. The other names Michelena takes as *Narhunges* and *Abisunhar*, with the Latin case-ending -*i* attached. The first of these appears to be constructed from a stem *Narhun-*, which is also found in the Aquitanian personal name *Narhonsus*, with a suffix -*ges*, which also occurs in the Aquitanian name *Enneges*. The other name is less transparent, though phonologically similar to other Aquitanian names; the element -*sunhar* could well represent Basque *zunhar* 'elm', the most conservative of several forms of the word, but no other example is known of a tree name featuring in a Basque personal name. Invoking the maxim 'prefer the obvious to the ingenious', Michelena therefore concludes that this stele provides firm evidence that Aquitanian was spoken south of the Pyrenees in Roman times, in the territory of the Vascones, if perhaps only in a small part of Navarre; the text also, of course, demonstrates that the aspiration *h* was anciently present in the ancestral Basque of Navarre, the region from which the aspiration is thought to have disappeared earlier than elsewhere.

6.10 BASQUE AND THE SUPER-FAMILIES

On various occasions one linguist or another has put forward a startlingly ambitious proposal to link genetically some languages or families which have usually been regarded as unrelated, sometimes even languages spoken on different continents. Among the more prominent proponents of such long-range comparisons have been Alfredo Trombetti, Edward Sapir, Morris Swadesh and Joseph Greenberg. Their proposals, and the controversies which they have engendered, are summarized in Ruhlen (1991) and in several of the papers in Ruhlen (1994). A few of these proposals have included

Basque. Trombetti, for example, stressed the Basque–Caucasian and Basque–Afro-Asiatic connections discussed above, though he also proposed connections between Basque and various languages of southern Asia, Siberia and western North America (Trombetti 1902–1903, 1925). Swadesh, in his 1960 paper, compared Basque with most of the languages on the planet, while in his 1971 book he asserted a genetic unity between Basque and the Na-Dene languages of North America, though on the basis of no evidence at all. On the whole, all such proposals, whether involving Basque or not, have been greeted with something approaching universal condemnation, and they have been taken seriously by almost no one.

In recent years, however, there has been growing interest in examining the possibility of linguistic super-families, vast agglomerations of existing families and language isolates spanning two or three continents. Among the most publicized of these conjectural groupings are Nostratic, Eurasiatic, Austric, Amerind and Dene-Caucasian. Not all of these proposals are equally well supported. At one extreme, the proponents of Nostratic have invested decades in painstaking reconstruction of the conventional kind, and they have published moderately substantial accounts of their 'Proto-Nostratic' and of the phonological developments posited in the various daughter languages they recognize. At the other extreme, nothing whatever has so far been published about Joseph Greenberg's Eurasiatic construct, beyond its putative membership, though we are told that Greenberg's evidence is at an advanced stage of preparation.

On the whole, Basque has attracted surprisingly little attention in these enterprises: the Nostraticists have shown no interest in it, and apparently it will not be included in Greenberg's Eurasiatic. Dene-Caucasian, however, is another matter. This sprawling construct, extending from Anatolia through east Asia, Siberia, Canada and the southwestern United States, has chiefly been developed by linguists in and from the former Soviet Union, and until recently little had been published except in Russian – though the papers collected in Shevoroshkin (1991) and Ruhlen (1994) have begun to change the picture. There is as yet no canonical position on the membership of this putative super-family, but the accounts I have seen present a curious picture of a collection of leftovers from all the other super-families. Beginning with a nucleus of Sino-Tibetan, the proponents have added North Caucasian (though not South Caucasian, already included in Nostratic), Yeniseian (but not the other Siberian languages, already attached to Eurasiatic), Na-Dene (but not the other North American languages, already assigned to Eurasiatic or to Amerind), and a bagful of isolates: Hattic, Hurrian, Urartian, Sumerian, Etruscan, Iberian (!), Burushaski and Nahali.

This enthusiastic hoovering up of isolates was no doubt bound to get to Basque eventually, and this has now happened: John Bengtson and Merritt Ruhlen, at least, now propose to include Basque in the Dene-Caucasian construct (Bengtson 1991a, 1991b, 1991c, 1991d, 1991e, 1991f, 1993, 1994a,

1994b, 1995a, 1995b; Ruhlen 1991, 1992, 1995; Bengtson and Ruhlen 1994; Starostin and Ruhlen 1994), and Vaćlav Blažek (1995) supports the proposal far more cautiously. In fact, Bengtson and Ruhlen (1994: 288) go so far as to assert that Basque may be 'confidently' added to the Dene-Caucasian family. This is a surprising assertion, since the evidence so far adduced by Bengtson, Ruhlen and others is, as I shall try to show, scarcely more substantial than the zero evidence provided by Swadesh for his Basque–Na-Dene proposal. Among their 'evidence', the authors cite Čirikba's flawed (1985) attempt to relate Basque to North Caucasian, discussed and dismissed as worthless in section 6.8 above (though Bengtson (1993: 3) describes it as 'a giant step forward'), but they also put forward a number of proposed Basque cognates with various other languages assigned to Dene-Caucasian, including North Caucasian, Yeniseian and Burushaski. Here I shall examine their work in such detail as space permits. A point-by-point critique can be found in Trask 1995c. Note also that a Basque–Burushaski link has been defended by Berger (1960).

To begin with, like so much of the work discussed above, this work is based on no methodology more sophisticated than trawling through modern bilingual dictionaries in search of entries that appear to match something in one or more of the other languages involved, with no attention to the status or provenance of the items extracted and no attention to what is known of their histories. Further, it is characterized by a very large number of errors in citing the Basque data.

A number of the 'Basque' items cited do not exist: the alleged *gor 'meat', *zaki 'bone', *zaro 'night', *zartzu 'sharp', *bergi 'eye', *min- 'put', *abets 'voice', *kala 'castle', *-tzi 'ten', *oz 'sky'; these arise from various misunderstandings, and oz- in fact is merely the combining form of ortzi 'sky', which is compared to a *different* Burushaski word from that compared with the non-existent *oz. Some items are glossed wrongly: bortz 'five' is glossed as 'hand' so that it may be compared with words meaning 'paw, gammon, thigh' in the other languages; zamar 'sheepskin jacket' is glossed as 'lock of wool' and matched with a word meaning 'eyebrow'; haur 'this' is extracted from the intensive pronouns like nihaur 'I myself' and glossed as 'self' to get a match; atal 'segment' is glossed as 'limb' to get a match; iztai 'groin' is glossed as 'anus'; the inflectional morph -ta- is wrongly glossed as a 'locative case-ending'; and, most entertainingly of all, maño, a variant of mañddo, a diminutive of 'mule; sterile', is glossed as 'masculine' to make a match go through, apparently because Spanish macho, used to gloss the word in a bilingual dictionary, has both meanings.

A very large number of the Basque words cited as evidence are transparent loan words from Latin and Romance: lapa 'burdock', kokot(s) 'nape; chin', azeri 'fox', toska 'kaolin', xahu 'clean', zuku 'soup', pintza 'membrane', patasa 'bottle', biga(e) 'two-year-old heifer', busti 'wet', zango 'leg', korotz 'dung', agure 'old man', kolko 'bosom', moko 'beak', kurlo 'crane', *akain* 'tick', *kuma* 'mane', *musu* 'face, mouth, snout, kiss', *musin* 'snout', *phau* 'stake, pole', *kaiku* 'wooden bowl', *horma* 'ice', *kasko* 'head, skull', *matel* 'cheek', *ganga* 'palate', *mulo* 'pile', and a number of others; particularly engaging is the extraction of *santan* from the French Basque phrase *sekulan santan* 'never in a hundred years' so that it can be solemnly compared with Caucasian, Burushaski, Yeniseian and even Sumerian – but it is, of course, a borrowing of French *cent ans* '100 years'.

Indeed, sometimes the words cited are not even Basque at all, but Spanish, as with *marrano* 'pig' and *becerro* 'bullock'. Apparently the investigators are hoping that these Spanish words will prove to be of Basque origin – a vain hope, as it happens.

Phonaesthetic coinages and nursery words are invoked with complete freedom if they afford matches with something. Western *tximeleta* 'butterfly', which is not even attested before the twentieth century, is projected thousands of years into the past, as is L *pinpirin* 'butterfly'; the phonaesthetic *mara-mara* 'continuously' is misglossed as 'abundant' and matched with something in Abkhaz; the nursery word *mama* 'potable liquid' (and also 'breast') and the conspicuously imitative *tu* 'spit, saliva' are treated on the same footing as lexical items because, unsurprisingly, they readily match things in the other languages.

To a greater degree than any preceding seekers after relatives for Basque, these investigators do not hesitate to segment their Basque words in any matter they find convenient, cheerfully throwing away any bits that don't match their chosen comparanda – and there are lots of such bits. Transparent compounds and derivatives are, as a result, grossly mis-segmented without exception: *emakume* 'woman, girl' (< *eme* 'female' (a loan) + *-kume* 'offspring') is chopped into gibberish plus *-kume* to get a match of sorts with Burushaski *quma* 'concubine'; *ukondo* 'elbow' (< *uko* 'forearm' + *ondo* 'bottom' (a loan)) is sliced into *u-* + *-kondo* to match Yeniseian **gid* 'elbow'; *aberats* 'rich' (< *abere* 'cattle' (a loan) + a suffix) is analysed as *a-* plus *-berats* to get a match; *ukabil* 'fist' (*uko* 'forearm' + *-bil* 'round') is pared down to *-kab-* to make something fit; *berezi* 'separate' (< *berez* 'by itself', from *ber-* 'self', + *-i* VFS) is taken as *ber-* plus gibberish to match Burushaski *bAr-* 'thresh'; *alderatu* 'separate' (< *aldera* 'to the side', from *alde* 'side', + *-tu* VFS) is assumed to contain a morpheme *aldera-* in order to match some words meaning 'tear down'; *eskubarne* 'palm' (*esku* 'hand' + *barne* 'interior') is analysed as built on a stem *bar-* 'palm' plus some inconsequential junk to get some sort of match with a Caucasian word; western *intzigar* 'hard frost', which to the innocent eye looks like a compound of *intz* 'dew' and *igar* 'dry', is carved up so as to leave a hypothetical root *-tzig-* 'frost', which looks like something in Caucasian – and on and on it goes in this vein. The single finest example is *makutsik* 'in one's shirtsleeves' (< *mauka* 'sleeve' (a loan) + *huts* 'bare' + *-ik* adverbial), which is ripped into a root *-kuts-* 'sleeve' plus some rubbish to provide a match with something in Caucasian.

On the other hand, obvious morpheme boundaries are ignored when *that* is required to make something fit. Thus, B *urtxakur* 'otter', a transparent and obviously modern compound of *ur* 'water' and *txakur* 'dog', is treated as monomorphemic and compared with a Yeniseian **täχAr* 'otter', and the same is done with *uxuri* 'urine', a compound of *ur* 'water' and *xuri* 'white'. The word *umoi* 'womb; cradle', a transparent compound of *ume* 'child' and *ohe* 'bed', is cited in its Z form *hümoi* to get the aspiration and then compared with a Burushaski word for 'bowels'.

Naturally, words lacking any obvious structure are chopped up just as enthusiastically if doing so will provide a match. The authors happily remove and dispose of the initial vowels of *adar* 'branch', *adin* 'age', *ahuñe* 'kid', *agor* 'dry', *ametz* 'gall oak', *arraultza* 'egg', *egur* 'firewood', *euli* 'fly', *igel* 'frog', *itoi* 'drop', *itsaso* 'sea', *odol* 'blood', *ohoin* 'thief', *uhin* 'wave', *uzki* 'anus' and many, many others. They chop off the first syllables of *belarri* 'ear', *bihotz* 'heart', *handi* 'big', *haitz* 'rock', *hegal* 'wing' and very many other words, the first two syllables of *behaz(t)un* 'bile', the last syllable of *bular* 'breast', *kurlo* 'crane', *lorratz* 'track, scent', and the first and the last elements of *bizkar* 'back', *ihintz* 'dew', *intzigar* 'frost', *jin* 'come' (!), and *elur* 'snow', among many, many others.

Inevitably, the known phonological history of Basque is never taken into account: words are cited in their modern forms when we are certain that they had very different forms 2,000 years ago. So, for example, *mihi* 'tongue' is matched with a Caucasian **mēlc'i*, but the Basque word derives from **bini*. Basque *sasi* 'bramble' is matched with Yeniseian **seʔs* 'larch', even though the word derives from (attested) *zarzi*. The verb *jin* 'come' is treated as ancient in form when in fact it is a contraction of the synonymous *jaugin*. The unetymological Basque aspiration is frequently treated as continuing an earlier segment to make something match better – but on occasion it is quietly dropped when its presence is not so convenient. Nor are fanciful reconstructions wanting. Basque *bi* 'two', which assuredly derives from (attested) *biga*, is instead reconstructed as **Gʷi* in order to make it look like a Caucasian numeral. And *azkoin* (and variants) 'badger', which obviously derives from **azkone*, is cited in the non-existent form **ha(r)zkoin* in order to make the first syllable look like *hartz* 'bear', after which the morph *-koin* is arbitrarily extracted and declared unilaterally to be an otherwise unknown Basque word for 'dog', so that it can be compared with a Yeniseian word for 'wolverine'. Basque *sahats* (and variants) 'willow', from **sanats*, is arbitrarily reconstructed as **sakats*, in defiance of everything that is known about the phonological prehistory of the language, in order to make it look a bit more like Burushaski *šAsk* 'willow', after which a few metatheses and deletions are dreamt up to provide an 'etymology'.

Sometimes the investigators manage to combine several errors in one word. For example, they cite *bepuru* 'eyebrow' (< *begi* 'eye' + *buru* 'head'), misgloss this as 'eyelash', chop off the first syllable, extract an alleged root

-*puru*, assign to this the meaning 'hair', and then proceed to compare it with words for 'hair', 'mane', 'eyelash' and 'down' in the other languages. Another example is *zuhain* 'hay, fodder', which is cited only in the unusual and obscure sense of 'tree' and which has its first syllable detached and thrown away in order to get some kind of match for things like Burushaski *kuna* 'rod, pole' – ignoring the fact that the Basque word clearly derives from earlier **zunai*. Yet another is *arroda* 'wheel', a loan from Romance (Occitan *roda*), which is cited in a severely localized metathesized form *adorra*, after which the final vowel is removed (apparently by mistake) and the initial vowel is removed (deliberately) to get something that looks like a Caucasian **t'wirV* 'wheel'.

In three consecutive paragraphs in a single article, one of the authors compares Basque *egun* 'day' with one set of words in the other languages, compares its derivative *eguzki* 'sun' with a completely different set of words, and then compares the last word's variant *eki* with a *third* different set of words. The unrelated *ihintz* 'dew' and *uhin* 'wave' are assumed to be built on a putative root **-hin-* 'water', which is extracted and compared freely, but the first word is assuredly from **ini(n)tz*, while the second is a mere variant of *uhain*, almost certainly a compound of *ur* 'water' and *gain* 'top'.

To be fair, Bengtson, at least, does try to identify some systematic correspondences in some of his comparisons, but these correspondences are manifestly anything but systematic: in practice, any segment is matched with any vaguely similar segment in another language, and, of course, any segments which stubbornly refuse to match are simply dropped. Bengtson also attempts to justify some of his exceedingly frequent removals of initial segments and syllables on the ground that they must be fossilized noun-class prefixes comparable to those found in some of the other languages, but he is completely unable to identify any kind of semantic basis for his removals, and they remain arbitrary manoeuvres.

In short, then, the attempt to link Basque to the putative Dene-Caucasian family is a conspicuous failure. If any evidence of such a connection existed, these authors would surely have found it, but they have come up with nothing but a long catalogue of errors and misunderstandings and a few vague and arbitrary resemblances.

This outcome is anything but surprising. Given the spectacular failure of every attempt to relate Basque to anything at all, apart from Aquitanian, few vasconists are likely to be galvanized by the news that Basque is related, not to European languages, but to Tibetan, Ket, Burushaski, Tlingit and Apache.

6.11 BASQUE AND 'PROTO-WORLD'

Before I close this chapter, it is perhaps in order to say a few words about Basque and the 'Proto-World' hypothesis. This hypothesis consists of the claim that remnants of the single ancestral language of all humankind can still be identified in the languages of the world, and it has recently been defended in various publications by Ruhlen, Bengtson, Vitaly Shevoroshkin and Vaćlav Blažek. It would be an understatement to say that this hypothesis has not been well received by the community of linguists, but that is not my concern here.

The most substantial presentation of evidence for Proto-World (PW) of which I am aware is Bengtson and Ruhlen (1994), which posits twenty-seven Proto-World etymologies, for eight of which the authors adduce putative cognates from Basque. These are as follows; all segmentations and annotations are theirs:

PW	Basque
ČUN(G)A 'nose; to smell'	*su-dur* 'nose', *sun-da* 'smell'
KATI 'bone'	*gar-khotx(e)* 'nape' (*gara* = 'skull')
KUAN 'dog'	*haz-koin* 'badger' (lit. 'bear-dog')
MANA 'stay (in a place)'	*min* 'to place, set up, settle'
MENA 'to think (about)'	*mun* 'medulla', *munak* 'brains'
PAR 'to fly'	*pinpirin* 'butterfly' (< **pir-pir-*)
PUTI 'vulva'	*poto-rro* 'pubis, vulva'
TSUKA 'hair'	*zam-ar(r)* 'lock of wool, shock of hair'

There are a number of difficulties with these citations. The words for 'nose' and 'smell' (the second actually means 'stench', rather than 'smell' in general) have been arbitrarily segmented by the authors, and there is no reason within Basque to suppose that the two words are related, though of course they might be, at some considerable remove. The word for 'nape' is undoubtedly a compound of some sort, but the authors' analysis of it cannot be accepted at face value. For one thing, no such word as **gara* 'skull' is attested; this is one of Azkue's little inventions against which I warned the reader in Chapter 1, and *gara* means nothing more than 'height, high part'. More importantly, the alleged **khotx(e)* 'bone' is unsubstantiated: no such word or element is found anywhere, and once again I must point out that ancient Basque words do not begin with voiceless plosives. It is far more likely that *-khotx(e)* here merely represents the Romance word for 'nape' (Occitan *cogòt*, Castilian *cogote*, etc.), which is also borrowed into Basque as *kokot(e)* ~ *kokots*: a formation like **gar-kokots* would have undergone the inevitable Basque haplology to yield **garkots*, whence the palatalized form *garkotx*. Further, the cited form for 'nape' is less widespread than the alternative *garkola* ~ *garkhora*, which shows the same first element but seemingly a different second element – most likely, Spanish *cola* 'tail'. Finally, the semantics suggested here are very odd: why should the nape of the neck, which is anything but a bone, be denoted by a compound meaning 'skull-bone'?

The word for 'badger' is cited as *hazkoin, but this is an error: the word is *azkoin ~ azko ~ azkon(a) ~ azkuin ~ asko* in the dialects with the aspiration, save only for the variant *hazku ~ harzkũ*, found only in Zuberoan, the dialect which is known to have extended the aspiration to initial position in words which did not historically have it. Moreover, as pointed out above, no such word as *koin 'dog' is attested anywhere in Basque: this is a pure invention of the authors, and yet another impossible form with an initial voiceless plosive. Anyway, the dialect variants point clearly to an original *azkone, or possibly *arzkone (Michelena 1964b: 193). Bengtson and Ruhlen are not the first to see the first element as representing *hartz* 'bear', but the second element is simply unidentifiable; see Agud and Tovar (1988–   ) for a survey of proposed etymologies for this word.

The alleged Basque *min 'place, set up, settle' does not in fact exist, and is yet another invention of the authors: no Basque verb could even have such a form. I would guess that what they have in mind is the verb *imiñi* 'put' (it doesn't mean 'settle'), which is an uncommon variant of the more usual *ipini* ~ *ibeni* (and other variants). The first and last vowels of *ipini* are unquestionably affixes, but the earliest form of the root must have contained a plosive (*-pin- or *-ben-, perhaps); the *m* merely results from the familiar Basque process of nasal assimilation (see Chapter 3), and a connection with the putative *MANO is too far-fetched to be taken seriously.

Things get worse with Basque *mun*. This is a very severely localized variant of the word whose most widespread form is *muin*. As was pointed out in section 6.8, the several variant forms of this word point clearly to an original *bune ~ *fune ~ *(h)une, which is not what Bengtson and Ruhlen require; moreover, these forms are exactly what we would expect to find if the Basque word were a loan from Latin FUNE 'rope', as suggested by Schuchardt a century ago. In any case, the central meaning of this word is 'pith, marrow, inner part'. Its use in the sense of 'brain' is again severely localized; more commonly, 'brain' is the compound *burumuin* (*buru* 'head'). Apart from this compound, the word has no connection with thinking.

The citation of Basque *pinpirin* 'butterfly' as representing PW *PAR 'fly' I find extraordinary. To begin with, this is merely one of a range of quite different regional words for 'butterfly', and one confined to the Lapurdian dialect of the French Basque Country. (The word means 'elegant' and 'favourite' as well as 'butterfly'.) Further, I must point out yet again that *no* native Basque word of any period begins with *p*, except for phonaesthetic items. And that's exactly what this word appears to be: compare the words *pinpa* 'bounce', *pinpoil* 'somersault' and also 'bubbling', *pinpi-panpa* (and also *panpa*) 'smack!, bang!', *panpina* 'child's doll', *panpalina* 'small bell', *panpotsa* 'throbbing' and *pinpili-panpala* 'favourite' (all from the same dialect) and *pinpin* (a certain finger game played by children) (from an adjoining dialect). It is clear that phonaesthetic formations involving the morphs *pin-* and *pan-* are highly favoured in this area, and there is little reason to regard the word for 'butterfly' as any different from the others: given the frequency of *pin-* in such formations, Bengtson and Ruhlen's proposed **pir-* ('with dissimilation') represents nothing but special pleading. Anyway, flight is hardly the most conspicuous characteristic of butterflies, and butterflies are hardly likely to be the creatures singled out above all others as the quintessential flying creatures.

Basque *potorro*, an obvious loan from Romance, was discussed and dismissed above.

Finally, the authors' *zamar*, which they gloss as 'lock of wool, shock of hair', in fact means nothing of the sort. It means 'sheepskin cloak', of the type traditionally worn by Basque shepherds as a raincoat, but *specifically one from which the wool has been removed*, and in some places it also means '(sheared) sheepskin' in general. This word is of unknown origin, but, once again, that medial *m* cannot be original. Finally, since the authors seem eager to get rid of that troublesome final *r*, I might point out that a derivation from Latin SABANU 'covering' cannot be ruled out (compare Basque *zamau* 'tablecloth', taken directly from the Latin word).

I leave it to the reader to decide whether the Basque data adduced by Bengtson and Ruhlen lend any support to their Proto-World hypothesis.

6.12 SUMMARY

In spite of the fragmentary nature of our Aquitanian materials, the evidence relating Basque to Aquitanian is very impressive, and probably all vasconists now accept that Basque is more or less directly descended from Aquitanian. However, *all* other attempts at relating Basque to anything at all must be dismissed as total failures. Not one of them has turned up the smallest shreds of what could be taken with a straight face as evidence, in spite of ceaseless assertions to the contrary.

With the sole exception of a small part of the work on Basque and Caucasian (notably the work of the distinguished vasconist René Lafon), all the innumerable claims of genetic links have been made by scholars who appear to have known little or nothing about Basque, and in particular about the history of Basque. Almost all of these investigators seem to have proceeded merely by extracting words and affixes incomprehendingly from modern dictionaries of the language. As a result, their 'evidence' consists largely of a mish-mash of preposterous citations. Items are cited which could not possibly have been in the language even 2,000 years ago, or which could not have had a relevant form at that time. Some of them are obvious loans from Latin or Romance, while others are transparent formations within Basque; a few are even modern neologisms. For reasons which I do not pretend to understand, Basque words are constantly cited wrongly or glossed wrongly, and more than a few of the 'Basque' words adduced are entirely non-existent. Not infrequently, localized dialect variants are adduced when more widespread and clearly more conservative forms do not lend themselves to establishing the required match. Quite a few of the citations involve obscure and severely localized words to which no great antiquity can be assigned. Basque words are regularly ripped apart into arbitrary pieces, in order to extract some morph which the investigator wants to match. And, with the conspicuously unsuccessful exceptions of some of Lafon's work on Kartvelian and some of Bengtson's work on 'Macro-Caucasian', not one of these innumerable proposals so much as attempts to identify any systematic correspondences, and it is impossible to extract anything resembling systematic correspondences from any of this work: all we ever see is arbitrary resemblances, without rhyme or reason.

Once all these impossible and objectionable 'cognates' are stripped away, we are left in every case with nothing but a handful of Basque words that look a bit like some words in another language. And I am at a loss to understand why some linguists become so excited when they find two dozen Basque words that look like two dozen words in Berber or Sumerian. I am at a loss to understand why Schuchardt (1913) thought it was worth publishing the list of 105 Basque words which, in his view, resembled words in one or another of more than a dozen languages of northern and eastern Africa, languages which themselves are not all related. I am at a loss to understand why people still turn up at conferences waving these dreary word-lists. Rather than argue against all these proposals, however, I shall simply provide what I hope will be taken as a *reductio ad absurdum* of this whole approach, in the form of an equally impressive list of similarities between Basque and Hungarian. I have chosen Hungarian merely because, to my knowledge, no one has ever previously tried to relate it specifically to Basque (at least in print – I believe there have been a few unpublished proposals), because I happen to have a large Hungarian–English dictionary handy, and because I do not suffer from the inconvenient handicap of knowing anything about the history of Hungarian. My list of sixty-five Basque–Hungarian resemblances is rather longer than some of those I have seen presented in defence of other proposed links, but it took me somewhat less than four hours to assemble.

Basque		*Hungarian*	
-a	Def article	a	Def article
aita	father	atya	father
-ak	Noun plural	-ak	Noun plural
alde	side	oldal	side
ama	mother	anya	mother
arau	proportion	arány	proportion
asko	many	sok	many
ate	door	ajtó	door
atze	back	hát	back

Basque		Hungarian	
az(ti)	fortune-teller	jós	fortune-teller
baba	bean	bab	bean
bake	peace	béke	peace
balea	whale	bálna	whale
bereter	priest	barát	monk, friar
(ber)un	lead (metal) (cf. *bera* 'soft')	ón	lead (metal)
burki	birch	bükk	beech
edari	beverage (< *edali*)	ital	beverage
egiaz	truthfully	igaz(i)	true, real
ele	word, conversation	(ny)elv	language
-(e)n	in, on	-(e)n	in, on
ene	my (Gen. -*e*)	én	I
eros(i)	buy	áros	seller
erreka	stream, watercourse	árok	ditch, trench
gaztaiña	chestnut	gesztenye	chestnut
hara	thither	arra	thither
hegi	ridge	hegy	hill
hes(te)	gut, intestine	has	belly
(hi)guin	repugnance	gúny	sneer, mockery
hil	die	hal(ni)	die
hiru	three	három	three
hobe	better	jobb	better
huts	empty	üres	empty
iduri	form, appearance	idom	form, shape
*iz	water	víz	water
izerdi	sweat	izza(dék)	sweat
jan	eat	en(ni)	eat
jaus(i)	fall, drop	es(ni)	fall, drop
joan	go	jarni	go, walk, move
kal(te)	injury, harm	kár	injury, harm
kohat	bellows (of a forge)	kohó	forge
kontu	care, attention	gond	care, attention
lagun	inhabitant, friend	lakos	inhabitant
lama	flame	láng	flame
lapur	thief	lopó	thief
lasai	calm, relaxed	lassu	slow, gentle
liño	flax	len	flax
lo	sleep	álom	sleep
mugitu	move	mozgat	move
nagusi	chief, principal	nagy	big, great
oge (B, G)	bed	ágy	bed
oka	vomiting	okád(ás)	vomiting

Basque		*Hungarian*	
ortu	garden	kert	garden
ostroi	thunder	ostrom	storm
otzara	basket	kosár	basket
pare	pair, couple	pár	pair, couple
-ra	to (motion)	-ra	to (motion)
soinu	music, sound	zene	music
txiki	small	kicsi	little (with metathesis)
*-tzi	ten	tíz	ten
uda	summer	üde	fresh, blooming
(ul)ertu	understand	érte(ni)	understand
ur	water	ár	flood, current
zaku	bag, sack	zsák	bag, sack
zamar	trash, filth	zavar	mess, confusion
zoko	corner, nook	zug	corner, nook

With another twenty hours of work, I am confident I could extend my list very considerably, but I am unwilling to give up that much time in order to make a point. But sixty-five matchups is still good going by the standards of such work. Of course, the alert or well-informed reader may notice that I have cheated a bit here and there. I have sometimes segmented away morphs that I couldn't match, but in this I am conforming entirely to the procedure adopted by all other advocates of this technique. Moreover, the majority of my bracketed morphs are indisputably separate morphemes, though the rest are just arbitrary manoeuvres on my part. I have cited two of the non-existent Basque morphs discussed in Chapter 5, but here again I am in no way out of line with established practice in these enterprises. I have gratuitously invoked a metathesis to make one matchup work, but other such practitioners have rarely declined a good metathesis, if it suited their purposes. In some cases I have suppressed my knowledge of the history of Basque, which would immediately rule out a number of my matches, but few of the previous practitioners of this technique have distinguished themselves by their knowledge of Basque: almost all have worked exclusively with modern-day forms extracted incomprehendingly from dictionaries, just as I have done here with my Hungarian items. Naturally, I have not made the slightest attempt to identify systematic correspondences between the two languages, since such attempts are invariably regarded as unsporting by the advocates of the more full-blooded approach I am adopting here. Finally, I have slipped in one deliberate error. The Hungarian word glossed as 'storm' does not, in fact, mean 'thunderstorm' or anything of the sort: it only means 'assault' as in 'take a place by storm'. But, if my list contains only one howler, I am performing above par: most other such lists of any length which I have seen contain several blunders, and some of them, as we have seen, contain dozens.

Any reader who suspects that I am being unfair, or that I have somehow cooked the books, or who (heaven forbid) finds himself persuaded that I have actually turned up something important, is invited to try the same exercise with any language that he knows well and any other arbitrary language for which a good bilingual dictionary is available. Try Welsh and Thai, or Norwegian and Zulu, or Quechua and Japanese – the result will always be the same.

The words of Michelena (1973c: 141) are just as valid today as when he wrote them in commenting upon the etymological excesses of Humboldt:

> The old aphorism *qui nimis probat, nihil probat* has been too often forgotten: need we recall the names, so different from each other in other respects, of Trombetti and Swadesh? A method which, in comparative linguistics, is powerful enough to demonstrate anything at all only succeeds, in the end, in demonstrating nothing of value.
>
> (my translation)

Not one of the proposals in the literature is in any way more impressive than this joke demonstration of a Basque–Hungarian relationship. Moreover, not one of them has succeeded in shedding even the tiniest amount of light on the prehistory of Basque. Except that we have now identified the immediate ancestor of the language, Basque remains today as genetically isolated as it was a hundred years ago.

6.13 THE ALLEGED INFLUENCE UPON CASTILIAN SPANISH

For generations there has been a persistent view in some Romance circles that Castilian Spanish, the form of Iberian Romance which, because of the political power of Castile, has come to be the prestige standard variety of Spanish, might have originated as a form of Latin or Romance spoken by individuals whose mother tongue was Basque. As we shall see, the evidence for such a view is effectively zero, but the idea is persistent: even now, articles continue to appear claiming to explain this or that development in Castilian in terms of Basque influence. Here I shall examine these various claims from three points of view: vocabulary, grammar and phonology.

Most familiarly, if also least significantly, there have long been attempts to identify a number of Spanish words which have no Latin etymology as being of Basque origin. In most such cases, the evidence for a Basque origin is exceedingly sparse. What follows is a representative list of such words, including all the ones which are particularly interesting or which have been cited especially frequently. A few of the words are peculiar to Castilian; most are found throughout the Iberian Peninsula; a few are even attested in much of western Romance. In this section I rely heavily upon Corominas and Pascual (1980), the standard etymological dictionary of Spanish, though I take issue with them on a few points concerning Basque. Where no gloss is provided for a Basque word, it is identical in meaning to the Castilian word.

Cast *anchoa* 'anchovy' : Bq *antxu*

This word, widely diffused throughout western Europe (including in English), can be confidently traced back to Genoese Italian *anciōa*, ultimately of Greek origin; the word was carried to Mediterranean ports by Genoese sailors, and hence entered Castilian via Catalan *anxova*. The Basque word is borrowed from the same Italian source, but probably not via Castilian.

Cast *azcona* 'dart' : Bq *azkon* 'dart, javelin'

Found throughout the Iberian Peninsula in several variant forms, this word is of unknown origin. The Basque *azkon* is only feebly attested, but Aymeric Picaud's twelfth-century word-list records *aucona* in the same sense, which muddies the waters considerably. A number of romanists have expressed conflicting opinions about the source of the word; Corominas and Pascual provide a survey which drags in the Basque tool-names in *haitz-* and eventually descends into some far-fetched speculations involving the language name *euskara*. All that can be concluded is that a Basque origin for *azcona* cannot be entirely ruled out, but does not seem especially probable.

Cast *becerro* 'two-year-old bull' : Bq *behi* 'cow'

The word *becerro* is found throughout the Iberian Peninsula, together with the possibly related *bicerra* 'mountain goat'. The Basque word *behi* is a most implausible etymon. Larramendi's dictionary cites *bicerra* as a Basque word for 'mountain goat', but the word is attested nowhere else, and Larramendi is not a trustworthy source. Corominas and Pascual dismiss the Basque connection, and conclude that the Spanish words are probably derived from an unattested suffixed form of Latin IBEX.

Cast *bizarro* 'gallant, brave' : Bq *bizar* 'beard'

This popular but implausible etymology is destroyed by the existence in Old Italian of *bizzarro* with a similar meaning to that of the Spanish word.

Cast *boina* 'Basque beret' : Bq ?

It is striking that this most stereotypical Basque artefact is universally known in Basque by the term *txapel(a)* (var. *gapelu*), of transparent Romance origin, while Castilian uses the curious word *boina*, which hardly looks like a Romance word and is widely thought to be of Basque origin. Corominas and Pascual are inclined to believe that *boina* is probably a Basque development of Vulgar Latin ABONNIS, and hence related to Spanish *bonete* and French (and English) *bonnet*; this seems plausible enough. Even if the Castilian word is borrowed from Basque, the loan appears to be a recent one.

Cast *cachorro* 'puppy' : Bq *txakur* 'dog'

There is nothing in favour of this speculative etymology. First, Basque *txakur*, in the dialects adjoining Castile, most emphatically does not mean 'puppy' or even 'small dog': it just means 'dog'. This is the expressive form of *zakur*, which in the west now means 'large dog' (some eastern varieties retain *txakur* for 'small dog' and *zakur* for 'dog'). Second, the proposal requires a dramatic metathesis of a sort which is rarely found in Castilian. Third, the existence of such seemingly related words as *cachondo* 'in heat' (of a bitch) and the fish names *cachuelo* and *cachucho*, not to mention *cacho*, the name of a fish with, it is said, a dog-like appearance, points to the existence of an original but unattested Romance **cacho* as the source of *cachorro*.

Cast *cazurro* 'rude, unsociable, malicious' : Bq ?

Castilian *cazurro*, found elsewhere in the Peninsula, is of unknown and possibly pre-Latin origin. There have been several rather wild attempts to give it a Basque etymology: *zakur* 'dog', *zuhur* 'discreet, prudent' (< **zunur*), *gezur* '(a) lie'. All of these can be dismissed out of hand.

Cast *chamorro* 'close-cropped' : Bq *samur* 'tender, soft, delicate' or Bq *txamorro* 'grub (of an insect), bug or worm that lives underground'

The word *chamorro* occurs widely in the Peninsula, and is well attested in medieval texts as a term of derision applied by Castilians to Portuguese and by Catalans to everybody else; its origin is unknown and deeply controversial. The two Basque words, which do not appear to be related, have both been invoked frequently to explain the Spanish word; the second is phonologically perfect, but of exceedingly limited distribution; the first is ancient and widespread, and its well-attested expressive form *xamur* is phonologically acceptable, but the semantics requires a certain amount of ingenuity. Such ingenuity has not been lacking: see Corominas and Pascual for a long and exasperated survey of the issue. In the end, nothing can be established, but *chamorro* is arguably one of the more plausible candidates for a Basque origin. (Curiously, the indigenous language of the Pacific island of Guam is Chamorro, a name apparently bestowed by Spanish settlers.)

Cast *chaparro* 'small bushy oak shrub' : Bq *txapar*

The Basque word is the expressive form of *sapar* 'thicket, scrub, hedge', and the common origin of the Basque and Castilian words is probably not doubted by anyone. Almost certainly we are looking at a pre-Latin word here, but it does not follow that it was taken into Castilian from Basque.

Cast *guija, guijarro* 'pebble' : Bq *egi* 'corner, edge'

The earliest attested form of the first Spanish word is *aguija*, and there have been several attempts to derive the Spanish words from Basque *egi* (with the article *egia*) or from an unattested compound **egi-harri* (*harri* 'stone').

These attempts are not obviously convincing, and Corominas and Pascual prefer a derivation from late Latin (PETRA) AQUILEA 'sharp stone'.

Cast *izquierdo* 'left' : Bq *ezker*

Widely attested throughout the Peninsula and in the south of France, the Romance word is indisputably of the same origin as Basque *ezker*. For once, almost all authorities accept without hesitation that the word is of Basque origin. Of course, its wide distribution across an area in which Basque is not known ever to have been spoken means that we must accept a steady diffusion of the word from the Basque Country throughout southwestern Romania, and, as a consequence, one or two scholars have diffidently suggested that the word might actually have been borrowed into Basque from Romance, but few have listened to them. If there is one genuine ancient Basque word in Spanish, this appears to be it.

Cast *laya* 'a certain agricultural implement' : Bq *laia*

This word, denoting a large two-pronged fork used for loosening soil, is widespread in western Romance. It occurs throughout the Spanish Basque Country and in part of the French Basque Country, and it has no Romance etymology. Scholars from Schuchardt to Corominas and Pascual have suggested that the word is Basque in origin, and this conclusion appears plausible, though by no means certain.

Cast *mogote* 'isolated mound' : Bq *moko* 'peak', *muga* 'boundary', etc.

These words are part of a vast and messy complex of words in Basque and in western Romance. Forms exist in *mok-*, *muk-*, *mog-*, *mug-*, *bog-*, *bueg-* and so on, with a variety of meanings centring on 'mound', 'peak', 'stone', 'boundary stone' and 'boundary', among others. None of them appears to have a Latin etymology, but it is far from clear which of them are related. A specific proposal is that Castilian *mogote* might derive from a Basque *moko-ti*, which is not attested but which would be an unremarkable derivative of *moko*. Basque *muga* is also commonly taken as the source of a range of similar words in Romance. However, both *moko* and *muga*, with their initial *m-*, cannot directly represent ancient forms: if these words existed at all in Pre-Basque, their forms must have been *boko* and *buga*, and the development of *b-* to *m-* in the absence of a following *n* would be a little unusual. It seems clear that the Romance words must derive from some indigenous language, but there is no compelling case for identifying that language as Basque. It is at least equally likely that Basque itself has taken these words from the same (unidentified) source as Romance, or perhaps directly from Romance.

Cast *nava* 'broad plain' : Bq *naba* 'broad plain in or near mountains'

The word *nava* is found throughout the Iberian Peninsula and also in several other parts of Romania, including the eastern Alps. Therefore, though the word is surely derived from some pre-Latin source, it can hardly be of explicitly Basque origin, and Basque *naba* is probably borrowed from Romance. Some have seen this word as the base of the name of *Navarra*, which is possible but not certain.

Cast *parra* 'trained grapevine' : Bq ?

Once again, this word is found throughout the Peninsula and also in Occitan. No such word is attested in Basque, however, and a Basque origin is exceedingly improbable, if only because native Basque words never have initial /p/. Most scholars prefer to posit a Germanic or a Celtic source for the word.

Cast *perro* 'dog' : Bq ?

This word, unique to Castilian, has attracted an extraordinary amount of scholarly attention, with no consensus so far. Once again, no such word exists in Basque, and the initial /p/ makes a Basque origin scarcely plausible. Corominas and Pascual, after surveying the proposals, opt for an imitative origin.

Cast *pizarra* 'slate' : Bq ?

This word, attested no earlier than 1475, has for centuries been regarded as a loan from Basque, but the proposals have been various and none seems completely convincing. The word *pizarra* in fact exists in Basque, but, with its initial /p/, this is surely a borrowing from Castilian. Larramendi proposes, and Schuchardt accepts, a compound of *pitzatu* '(to) crack' and *harri* 'stone', but the verb *pitzatu* is a localized word in Basque and is itself probably a loan, possibly (as Schuchardt himself admits) from an unattested Latin *FISSARE. The most widespread Basque word for 'slate' is *lapitz*, a borrowing from Latin LAPIS 'stone' or from its derivative LAPIDEUS 'made of stone' (most romanists prefer the second, but Michelena prefers the first, which is exactly parallelled by *gorputz* 'body' from Latin CORPUS). Perhaps the most appealing suggestion is that of Corominas and Pascual, who propose an unattested Basque compound *lapitz-arri*, literally 'slate-stone', with the initial *la-* interpreted as the Spanish article. Though unknown, such a compound would be completely unremarkable in Basque. Again, the best we can say is that a Basque origin is not completely ruled out, but is not obviously correct.

Cast *sapo* 'toad' : Bq *apo*

Castilian shares this word only with Portuguese. The Basque word appears variously as *zapo*, *apo* or *sapo*, of which *zapo* seems to be the earliest form. Basque *sapo* is recent, and almost certainly due to Castilian influence. The form *apo* may also result from a mishearing of Castilian *los sapos* as *los apos*. It has frequently been thought that Castilian *sapo* is a loan from Basque *zapo*. This is not impossible, but a complication is the well-attested use of *zapo* in Basque as a generic term for 'creepy-crawly', with various other specializations besides 'toad', such as 'firefly'. Corominas and Pascual show little interest in a Basque origin for the Castilian word, and provide instead an extraordinarily wide-ranging discussion of possibly related European words ranging as far as ancient Greek *sēps* 'poisonous snake, lizard'.

Cast *sarna* 'scabies, mange' : Bq *sarra* 'rust, slag'

Corominas and Pascual provide a breathtaking survey of words, in languages ranging from Africa all across Europe as far as Estonian, Latvian and Mordvin, with a similar form and with meanings like 'skin disease', 'sawdust', 'waste', 'rubbish', 'excrement'. These numerous forms provide such a labyrinth that it is difficult to see how any sensible conclusions can be drawn at all.

Cast *sarrio* 'Pyrenean chamois' : Bq ?

This widespread word is of pre-Latin origin, but the attempts to provide it with a Basque etymology have been unconvincing. Most proposals have centred on Basque *izar* 'star', on the assumption, often asserted but unsubstantiated, that this word could formerly also mean 'height'.

Cast *sarro* 'incrustation, deposit' : Bq *sarra* 'rust, slag'

This word, peculiar to Castilian and Portuguese, is entangled with the complex of words alluded to under *sarna*, and its history is no clearer.

Cast *vega* 'water meadow, fertile land beside a river' : Bq *ibaiko* (?) riverbank

Found in Castilian, Portuguese and Sardinian, *vega* is attested in early texts as *vajka* and *vayca*, and hence scholars assume a pre-Latin *baika* as its source. The most strenuous attempts have been made to relate it somehow to Basque *ibai* 'river', which, given the Sardinian evidence, is assumed to represent a widespread pre-Latin word. But the difficulties are severe. First, a derivation from *ibai* requires some kind of suffix. Many have proposed a Basque *ibaiko*, with the common relational suffix -*ko*, meaning something like 'riverbank' or 'land beside the river'. But no such word is attested in Basque, though the formation would be unremarkable enough. Second, the suffix required would appear to be *-ka*, not -*ko*, but no such suffix of a relevant meaning or function is known in Basque, and proposals that *-ka* might have been an ancient variant of -*ko* are supported by no evidence. Third, a derivation involving *ibai* would require loss of the initial *i-*; attempts by Corominas and Pascual (among others) to point to parallels like the place-name *Baigorri*, from *ibai gorri* 'red river', founder on the fact that such loss of initial vowels is almost exclusively confined in Basque to proper names, as explained in Chapter 3. Fourth, Basque has a perfectly good word of its own, *ibar*, with (originally) the same meaning as *vega*, and it is not obvious why Romance speakers should have borrowed a putative word with a different meaning when one with the desired meaning was available. (It is clear that Basque *ibai* and *ibar* are related somehow, since they show the same pattern as *Bizkaia* and *bizkar* 'ridge of mountains', but the nature of the word-formation process involved is obscure.)

Cast *zarza* 'blackberry, bramble' : Bq *sasi*

This connection has only rarely been cited in the literature, but it is perhaps one of the most convincing cases. The word *sasi* is cited by the early Basque writer Oihenart as *çarci* (= *zarzi*), and a development from *zarzi* to **zasi* would be quite regular (see Chapter 3), as would a development of **zasi* to the attested *sasi* by sibilant harmony. Corominas and Pascual consider that the Castilian word is indisputably related to the Basque one, and they point out that similar (though not identical) words for 'blackberry' and related meanings are found throughout the Iberian Peninsula and in Occitan.

Cast *zorro, zorra* 'fox' : Bq ?

This is undoubtedly the most celebrated of all the Castilian words imputed to a Basque origin. Confined to Castilian and Portuguese, and attested in this sense no earlier than 1475, *zorro* certainly looks Basque enough, but the word is completely unknown in Basque. It has been suggested that *zorro* might be an ancient Basque word now displaced by the innovating *azeri* (see Chapter 5), and attempts have further been made to relate the Spanish word to any of several Basque etyma; the most popular of these has been *zuhur* 'discreet, prudent' (< **zunur*), apparently under the erroneous perception that the Basque word means 'cunning, astute'. All such attempts founder on the simple facts that the Spanish word is first attested far from the Basque Country and that it is undeniably attested in the earliest texts with a *voiced* sibilant, which seems to make a Basque origin impossible, and Corominas and Pascual suggest a Romance origin.

In sum, then, the attempts to derive elements of the Castilian vocabulary from Basque are unconvincing in the extreme. Few of them have been based upon anything more than the recognition of a problem, a Romance word with no etymology, and a vague hope that Basque might provide some kind of explanation. No more than two or three of the words in my list are even plausibly of Basque origin, and I have included all of the most promising cases. The effect of Basque upon the Castilian lexicon has been virtually nil.

There have also been a few attempts to argue that some of the distinctive characteristics of Castilian grammar are evidence for an early Basque influence upon the language, for example Montgomery (1977), Lekuona (1982) and Berrondo (1980). The most prominent advocate of this view, however, has been the Spanish linguist Angel López García, who has defended his position in a series of publications, but most notably in López García (1985a). His case is feeble, and is demolished point by point by Trask and Wright (1988). Here I shall content myself with the briefest of summaries.

López García collects some fourteen grammatical characteristics of Castilian which he says can be most satisfactorily interpreted as features borrowed from Basque. Many of these, it should be noted, are not peculiar to Castilian, but are found widely in the Romance languages of the Iberian Peninsula, and a few are also prominent in non-Iberian Romance, none of which is encouraging for his case. Far more devastating, though, is the blunt fact that, of López García's fourteen features, twelve are absolutely unattested in Basque and one is present in Spanish Basque dialects only as a calque from Spanish. The only feature in his list which Basque genuinely shares with Castilian is the presence of ethic datives, but ethic datives are so common in the languages of the world as hardly to require a substrate explanation. (Interestingly, the one Basque form López García cites in this section does not contain an ethic dative.)

The author tries to get round this seemingly insuperable obstacle by the curious device of citing features of Basque grammar which are *different* from Castilian but which, he argues, can be interpreted as bearing some kind of resemblance to the Castilian facts – in most cases, a very vague resemblance. Moreover, his appeals to Basque in several cases involve serious misunderstandings of the facts. For example, he attempts to trace the presence of the Castilian 'neuter article' *lo*, used with nominalized adjectives, to Basque. But Basque has nothing of the sort, and his case rests on nothing more substantial than the banal observation that a Basque noun phrase which contains an indefinite determiner does not also take the definite determiner -*a*. His attempt at finding a Basque source for the preposition sequences of Castilian is supported merely by the hopelessly confused descriptions of so-called 'superdeclension' explained in Chapter 2: Basque *never* allows sequences of case-endings or postpositions – though English and some other European languages, just like Spanish, do allow sequences of prepositions. His claim that the Castilian use of the infinitive as a nominal is parallelled in Basque rests upon a serious confusion among three entirely different Basque constructions: the perfective participle, the gerund and the headless (but finite!) relative clause, only the second of which even remotely resembles the Castilian infinitive. He even tries to uncover a Basque source for the famous 'personal *a*' of Castilian, in which an animate direct object is preceded by the preposition *a*, just like an indirect object, but Basque has nothing remotely similar, and is indeed somewhat unusual among languages for the rigour with which it distinguishes direct objects from indirect objects (the few exceptions to this statement are all recent consequences of the influence of Spanish or French syntax). Nor are his remaining points any more convincing. Neither López García nor anyone else has yet uncovered the slightest shred of evidence that Basque has ever had any effect upon the grammar of Castilian.

We turn now to phonology, where several arguments have been adduced. First, many observers have pointed to the fact that the Castilian phoneme system is rather similar to that of Basque. In particular, Castilian, unusually among Romance languages, has developed the five-vowel system /i e a o u/, identical to the vowel system of Basque, and it is suggested that this development represents the habit of Basque-speakers of pronouncing Romance with their own five vowels. But exactly this system is by some way the most frequent vowel system in the languages of the world: it is so frequent that typologists have dubbed it the 'canonical' vowel system. Hence there is nothing here to be explained. Of course, the two additional vowels /ɛ/ and /ɔ/ of the antecedent seven-vowel Romance system were removed from Castilian by diphthongization to /ie/ and /ue/, but a similar diphthongization occurred elsewhere in Romance, notably in Italian, in which a Basque substrate is out of the question. A few people, such as Anderson (1988: Ch. 9), have further pointed to some similarities between the consonant systems of Old Spanish and of Basque (three voiceless sibilants, two rhotics, palatal lateral and nasal), but nearly all of these characteristics are or were widely found in western Romance, and there seems to be little mileage in attempting to invoke a Basque substrate to explain them.

A second argument involves the Old Spanish merger of /v/ and /b/. This appears to have happened early, especially in the north, and Alonso (1962) argues that it must have resulted from Basque influence, since Basque has never had a /v/ and since Basques routinely render Romance /v/ with their own /b/ in loans. This sounds plausible, but there are severe difficulties. First, it is known that Old Spanish /b/, like the other voiced plosives, was realized as a plosive only in limited circumstances; in most circumstances it was realized as a voiced continuant [β], and the phonetic distance between [v] and [β] would have been perilously small, making a merger so likely that no external explanation is required. Second, if the /v/–/b/ merger was really due to a Basque inability to pronounce [v], and not to internal factors, why did /f/ not likewise merge with /p/ in Castilian? (It didn't, but see below for another argument involving /f/.) Third, and most damningly, the /v/–/b/ merger was not confined to Castilian: it occurred also in Gascon and in some other varieties of Occitan, in Galician, in most varieties of Portuguese and in most varieties of Catalan. Since Basque influence cannot remotely be invoked throughout these areas, it is surely pointless to argue that the merger was the result of Basque influence in Castilian alone but the result of other factors everywhere else.

A third argument concerns the devoicing of fricatives. Old Castilian, like all other varieties of western Romance, possessed contrasting sets of voiced and voiceless fricatives. Around the sixteenth century, however, the voiced fricatives were categorically devoiced and merged unconditionally with the voiceless ones in standard Spanish; this change had probably occurred several centuries earlier in the north. (This development did not affect the earlier /v/, which had already merged with /b/ by this time.) Since Basque has only voiceless fricatives, the proposal is that the devoicing was a result of Basque substrate or adstrate influence, and exactly this view is put forward by Martinet (1955, 1981) and by Jungemann (1955). But there are serious difficulties with this view. For one thing, the devoicing of fricatives is a natural change, since voiceless fricatives are far commoner than voiced ones (Ladefoged and Maddieson 1996: 176), and hence devoicing of fricatives hardly calls for an explanation. For another, the Castilian change was accompanied by the reduction of all but one of the existing affricates to fricatives (Penny 1991: 86–87), something which has never happened in Basque, in which all the original affricates survive today. Most importantly, though, fricative devoicing was not confined to Castilian: it occurred also in Galician and in the Valencian variety of Catalan, languages for which Basque influence can hardly be invoked, and also in two or three other small areas of the Peninsula (Echenique 1987: 93).

A possible fourth argument is the observation that Castilian shares with Basque the characteristic that the plosives /b d g/ are pronounced as approximants between vowels and in certain other positions; there is abundant evidence that this pronunciation is ancient in Basque, but no reason to believe that it was found in Latin, and hence the Castilian pronunciation must be an innovation, possibly resulting from Basque substrate influence. In fact, I am not aware that this argument has ever been explicitly defended, but, in any case, this type of pronunciation is found in most of the Iberian Peninsula (for example, throughout Catalan), and again a specifically Basque substrate seems out of the question; very likely what we have here is an ancient areal feature of the Peninsula and nothing more.

The final argument involves the most famous of all claims for Basque influence on Castilian. Briefly, at some time before the medieval period, the word-initial [f-] of Latin developed into [h-] in Castilian; when Castilian became the prestige variety of Spain, this new [h-] spread throughout much of the Peninsula; more recently, the [h-] has been lost in most areas, though it survives in parts of southern Spain and in parts of the Americas. The date of the change [f-] > [h-] is very difficult to determine, because scribes continued to write ⟨f⟩ long after the pronunciation had become [h]. But countless scholars have seen this change as evidence of Basque influence.

The argument goes as follows. As we know, Pre-Basque had no /f/. Hence, when Basque-speakers adopted Romance speech, they could not pronounce the [f], and so they replaced it with [h], the nearest approximation they could muster.

Though always controversial, this account has proved to be deeply seductive, and even some of the most distinguished and critical hispanists have embraced it, including Menéndez Pidal and von Wartburg; others, such as

Meyer-Lübke, have vigorously opposed it. The controversy is astonishing, since even a moderate amount of consideration is sufficient to show that the substrate explanation is impossible. Perhaps the most comprehensive demolition of the substrate theory is that of Izzo (1977); this article should have been the final word on the subject, but clearly there are still some diehards holding out. In my account below, I largely summarize Izzo's more detailed arguments.

The evidence against the substrate idea is simply overwhelming. Consider the following points:

1 There is not a single piece of independent evidence that Basque was ever spoken in the territory that became Old Castile, except for the temporary spread of the language into parts of Burgos in the fifth century and for the influx of Basque settlers from Navarre in the time of King Sancho the Great, nor is there any evidence that any significant numbers of Basques in the Peninsula adopted Romance speech in the late Roman period or in the early medieval period. Basque place names, for example, are scarce or nonexistent south of the Ebro and west of Bizkaia, and are at best very rare in the Encartaciones, the western territory added to Bizkaia in the thirteenth century, at the expense of its Asturian neighbours.

2 Though word-initial Latin [f-] became [h-] in most cases, it failed to do so before the diphthong /ue/ and before /r/, where [f-] remained: hence, for example, Latin FACERE yields Castilian *hacer* 'do'; Latin FICU yields Castilian *higo* 'fig'; and Latin FORNU yields Castilian *horno* 'oven'; while Latin FORTE yields Castilian *fuerte* 'strong'; Latin FONTE yields Castilian *fuente* 'spring'; and Latin FRONTE yields Castilian *frente* 'forehead'. Proponents of the substrate view are therefore seemingly obliged to argue that the Basques could pronounce [f-] without difficulty before /ue/ or /r/, but not otherwise, which is absurd. The labial element in /ue/ might conceivably be invoked to explain the retention of [f-] before that diphthong, but no such way out is available before /r/. Attempts at invoking 'dialect mixing', the historical linguist's beloved cure-all for every phonological problem, fail, because the retention of [f-] is so highly regular.

3 A Basque substrate explanation of [f-] > [h-] would seem to require that this change must have occurred very early. Yet, as Meyer-Lübke (1935) argues, there is clear evidence that it occurred quite late, long after Romance speech was well established in Castile. This evidence consists of the treatment of loan words in Castilian. From the fifth to the eighth century the Visigothic kingdom was the major power in northern Spain, and Castilian borrowed a number of words from Visigothic, which had both [f-] and [h-]. Visigothic [h-], without exception, appears in Castilian as zero: for example, Gothic *hilms* > Old Sp *elmo* 'elm', and Gothic *hanka* > Old Sp *anca* 'haunch'. But the few loan words with [f-] all show Castilian [h-]: for example, Gothic **fat* > Old Sp *hato* 'clothing', while the Gothic

personal name *Friþunands* > Cast. *Hernando*. Hence the aspiration of [f-] must have occurred after the period of Visigothic influence – that is, hardly earlier than the eighth century, much too late for a Basque substrate to play a part. In contrast, the Arabic loanwords borrowed into Castilian from the eighth century onward show a complex picture, with Arabic [f-] sometimes appearing as [h-] and sometimes (more usually) as [f-], suggesting that the change took place in Castilian soon after the beginning of the period of Arabic influence, with the earliest loans borrowed in time to participate in the aspiration of [f-]. Later still, when Castilian began to borrow words from Old French, the [f-] and the [h-] of that language were both retained unchanged, showing that [h-] was now present in Castilian and that the change of [f-] to [h-] was complete.

4 When Latin and Romance words with [f-] were borrowed into Basque, that [f-] was regularly represented by Basque [b-], and not by [h-], except in the case of clusters, in which [f-] was sometimes simply dropped. Thus, Latin FRONTE yields Basque *boronde* 'forehead' (compare the Castilian development of this word above); Latin FORTIS yields Basque *bortitz* 'force'; Latin FICU yields Basque *biko* ~ *iku* 'fig'; Latin FAGU yields Basque *bago* 'beech'; Latin FAVA yields Basque *baba* 'bean'; Latin FLAMMA yields Basque *lama* 'flame'; Latin FLORE yields Basque *lore* 'flower'. Only in a few instances was the initial consonant lost entirely, and usually only before /o/, but the sporadic loss of initial [b-] before /o/ is well attested in Basque, and requires no independent explanation: Latin FUNGU yields Basque *onddo* 'fungus'; Latin FUNDU yields Basque *ondo* 'bottom'. This development is confirmed by the case of Latin FORMA, which yields modern Basque *(h)orma* 'wall; ice', but some of the earliest texts have *borma*. Hence the 'accent' imputed by the substrate theory requires a treatment of Romance [f-] which is entirely at odds with the observed treatment of Latin and Romance words in Basque itself.

5 Though the change of [f-] to [h-] is confined to Castile within the Iberian Peninsula, it is well attested elsewhere in Romania. The same change is found in Gascon, next to the French Basque Country, which might look at first like support for the substrate proposal. However, this change is also found in part of eastern Sardinia, in much of Calabria in southern Italy, in two small areas in northern Italy, and in Arumanian (a dialect of Rumanian). Since there were no Basques in Italy or the Balkans, a proponent of the substrate theory is faced with an impossible choice: either he must posit a string of unidentified substrate languages stretching across Europe, all of them lacking [f-], which is preposterous, or he must accept that [f-] > [h-] is a frequent and spontaneous change in Romance which requires no substrate to explain it, in which case he destroys his own position.

6 If the aspiration of [f-] was genuinely the result of a Basque accent in Romance, then we might reasonably expect to see this development in the one place in which there is no doubt that Romance speech was

superimposed upon a predominantly Basque-speaking population: the Kingdom of Navarre. The territory of Navarre was itself overwhelmingly Basque-speaking until recent times, and the kingdom included the entire Basque-speaking region within its borders until the thirteenth century. Romance in Navarre was very much a superstrate language introduced for administrative purposes, and hence here, if anywhere, we might expect to see Basque speech habits showing up in Romance. But there is no evidence of this, and in particular the aspiration of [f-] never occurred in Navarre: Latin [f-] was preserved there until Navarrese Romance itself finally gave way to the spread of the more prestigious Castilian.

7 We have already seen that the aspiration of [f-], imputed by the substrate enthusiasts to Basque, represents a development which never occurred in Basque itself. But things are very much worse than this for the proponents of the Basque substrate. Basque has a number of distinctive phonological characteristics of its own which it does not share with Castilian; it underwent, sometime before the twelfth century, certain striking phonological developments which did not affect Castilian; and it fails to show any trace of the most important phonological developments which did occur in Castilian. Here is a brief summary of the chief phonological differences between the two languages:

(a) Intervocalic voiceless plosives and fricatives were uniformly voiced in Castilian, but remained voiceless in Basque.

(b) Intervocalic *n* was lost in Basque, but remained in Castilian.

(c) Intervocalic *l* became *r* in Basque, but remained in Castilian.

(d) Voiceless plosives were voiced after a nasal or /l/ in Basque, but remained voiceless in Castilian.

(e) The word-initial voiceless plosives of Latin remained voiceless in Castilian, but became voiced in Basque.

(f) Latin velars were palatalized and spirantized before front vowels in Castilian, but remained velar in Basque.

(g) Latin word-initial consonant clusters were invariably broken up in Basque, either by insertion of a vowel or by loss of a consonant; the same clusters were preserved in Castilian.

(h) Basque invariably inserted a prothetic vowel before a word-initial rhotic; Castilian did not.

(i) Latin short *e* and *o* were diphthongized in Castilian, but not in Basque.

(j) Basque merged Latin *i* with *ī*, *e* with *ē*, *a* with *ā*, *o* with *ō*, and *u* with *ū*; Castilian merged *i* with *ē*, *u* with *ō*, and *a* with *ā*, while keeping the other four Latin vowels separate.

It would, of course, be unreasonable to reject the Basque substrate idea merely because Castilian did not behave identically to Basque. But it is not unreasonable at all to expect that, if Castilian really did originate as a version of Romance spoken by Basques, at least *some* of the phonological characteristics of Basque might be evidenced in Castilian. Yet there is no such evidence.

This mass of evidence against the Basque substrate interpretation of the aspiration of [f-] in Castilian is overwhelming and monolithic. A defender of the substrate idea is apparently obliged to argue as follows: sometime between the eighth and tenth centuries, an unidentified but sizeable group of Basques, who otherwise have left no trace of their existence, adopted Romance speech somewhere in Castile; they carried over into their new language no trace of their native speech habits except for a certain difficulty with [f-], which they could mysteriously pronounce in some circumstances but not in others; and they then treated the problematic instances of [f-] in a manner completely different from the way in which they treated [f-] in their own language. This is a preposterous assembly of special pleading, and it still doesn't explain the aspiration of [f-] in areas far from the Basque Country or its failure to occur in Navarre. I do not see how anyone can still take the Basque substrate idea seriously. (But people do. Purely for its enter-tainment value, I can't resist pointing out that Salvador (1982) has recently revived the Basque substrate idea in a novel 'geological' form: his argument is that the Basques suffered from such a deficiency of fluoride in their drink-ing water that all their teeth fell out, leaving them unable to pronounce [f] – except, of course, before /ue/ and /r/. This interpretation goes straight to the heart of the matter, but the author is sadly unable to explain what happened to the water supply in the Middle Ages, when Basque itself acquired its /f/. A pioneering fluoridation programme, perhaps?)

The evidence for interpreting Castilian as a variety of Romance largely created by Basque-speakers, then, is so slender as to be insignificant. Not one of the various arguments is even moderately persuasive.

A Basque substrate has also at times been invoked to account for some of the distinctive characteristics of American Spanish. I will not pursue this question here; the interested reader can find a summary, with references, in Echenique (1987: 97–100).

Naturally, Basque *has* had an effect upon the Spanish spoken in the Basque Country; Zarate (1976) gives a comprehensive examination of the Basque-influenced Spanish spoken in the region of Bizkaia called Txorierri, near Bilbao.

Finally, I note that, in contrast to the Castilian case, there is a small but genuine body of evidence for Basque substrate influence upon some other neighbouring varieties of Romance. Gascon, Navarrese Romance and Rio-jan Romance all contain a few indisputable loans from Basque – though not all these loans are necessarily early. Gascon readily forms compound verbs of a type common in Basque but rare in Romance: *coulou-mudà* 'change colour', *cap-herrà* 'tip an extremity (with metal)', *capplegà* 'lower one's head', *cot-poudà* 'break one's neck', and many others. More interestingly, adjoining Romance varieties share certain phonological developments with Basque (Echenique 1987: 45, 84–86): word-initial plosives were voiced in Aragonese, Navarrese and Riojan; plosives were voiced after /n/ in Riojan; a prothetic vowel was added before initial /r/ in Gascon; and intervocalic /n/ was lost in Gascon. All these developments have occasionally attracted comment (see especially Allières 1992 for Gascon), but so far, it seems, few people have tried to argue that Gascon, Aragonese, Navarrese or Riojan Romance is the result of Latin in the mouths of Basques – even though, in the cases of Gascon and Navarrese, at least, the *a priori* case might seem rather stronger than for Castilian. See Pellegrini (1980) for a review.

References

ABBREVIATIONS

ASJU	*Anuario del Seminario de Filología Vasca 'Julio de Urquijo'*
FLV	*Fontes Linguae Vasconum*
BRSVAP	*Boletín de la Real Sociedad Vascongada de Amigos del País*
BSL	*Bulletin de la Société Linguistique de Paris*
RIEV	*Revista Internacional de los Estudios Vascos*

Note: Unless otherwise indicated, all page references in the text to the works of Luis Michelena are to the reprinted versions.
The cities which are called *Bilbao* and *San Sebastián* in Spanish are called *Bilbo* and *Donostia* in Basque. Books published in Spanish cite the place of publication in the Spanish form, while those published in Basque use the Basque form. The entries below follow the form used on the title page in each case.

Abaitua, Joseba and R. L. Trask. 1987. 'Accusativity in Basque: reply to Bossong'. *Linguistics* 25: 395–401.
Adams, Breandán. 1980. 'Place-names from pre-Celtic languages in Ireland and Britain'. *Nomina* 4: 46–63.
Agud, Manuel. 1973. 'Áreas toponímicas en el País Vasco'. *ASJU* 7: 37–57.
Agud, Manuel and Antonio Tovar. 1988– . *Materiales para un diccionario etimológico de la lengua vasca*. Published in fascicles in *ASJU* XXII(1)– . Also published in separate fascicles.
Alberdi, Jabier. 1995. 'The development of the Basque system of terms of address and the allocutive conjugation'. In Hualde *et al* (1995), pp. 275–293.
Allières, Jacques. 1979. *Manuel pratique de basque*. Paris: A. & J. Picard.
—— 1992. 'Gascón y euskera: afinidades e interrelaciones lingüísticas'. *ASJU* 26: 801–812.
Alonso, Dámaso. 1962. *La fragmentación fonética peninsular*. Published as *Enciclopedia Lingüística hispánica*, vol. 1 (supplement). Madrid: CSIC.
Altube, Severo [writing as Altube'tar Seber]. 1929. *Erderismos*. Published in fascicles in *Euskera* X: nos 1–4. Facsimile edition in one volume 1975, with an introduction by Luis Villasante, Bilbao: Indauchu.
—— 1932. *El acento vasco*. Bermeo.
—— 1934. 'Observaciones al tratado de "Morfología Vasca" de Don R. M. de Azkue'. Bermeo: Gaubeka. Repr. as Appendix to the 1969 edition of Azkue (1923–1925), vol. III, pp. 159–231.

Anderson, James M. 1973. *Structural Aspects of Language Change*. London: Longman.

—— 1988. *Ancient Languages of the Hispanic Peninsula*. Lanham, MD: University Press of America.

Anderson, Stephen 1976. 'On the notion of subject in ergative languages'. In Charles N. Li (ed.), *Subject and Topic*, pp. 1–24. New York: Academic Press.

Añibarro, Pedro de. 1820. *Gramática bascongada*. Published (1969), Luis Villasante (ed.), as vol. 3 of *ASJU*.

Arbelaiz, Juan José. 1978. *Las etimologías vascas en la obra de Luis Michelena*. Tolosa: Kardaberaz.

Arco, Ricardo del. 1993. 'Ordenanzas inéditas dictadas por el concejo de Huesca (1284 a 1456)'. *Revista de Archivos, Bibliotecas y Museos* 29: 112–126, 427–452.

Arejita, Adolfo. 1978. *Euskal Joskera* [*Basque Syntax*]. Durango: Leopoldo Zugaza.

Arocena, Fausto. 1948. 'El topónimo *Guipúzcoa*: ensayo de interpretación'. *BRSVAP* 4: 279–284.

Astarloa, Pablo Pedro. 1803. *Apología de la Lengua Vascongada o ensayo crítico filosófico de su perfección y antigüedad sobre todas las que se conocen*. Madrid.

—— 1883. *Discursos filosóficos sobre la lengua primitiva o Gramática y análisis razonada de la Euskera o Bascuence*. Bilbao.

Aulestia, Gorka. 1989. *Basque-English Dictionary*. Reno, NV: University of Nevada Press.

Azkue, Resurrección María de. 1891. *Gramática eúskara*. Bilbao.

—— 1905. *Diccionario vasco–español–francés*. Bilbao. Repr. 1969, Bilbao: La Gran Enciclopedia Vasca, with an addendum by Lino Aquesolo. Repr. 1984, Bilbao, with an introduction by Luis Michelena [= Michelena 1970a].

—— 1923–1925. *Morfología vasca*. Published in fascicles in the journal *Euskera*. Repr. 1969, Bilbao: La Gran Enciclopedia Vasca, 3 vols, with appendices.

—— 1935. 'Evolución de la lengua vasca'. *Euskera* 16: 57–133.

Bähr, Gerhard. 1931. 'De toponimia vasca'. *RIEV* XXII: 143–145.

—— 1935. *Los nombres de parentesco en vascuence*. Bermeo.

—— 1948. *Baskisch und Iberisch*. Bayonne. Separata of *Eusko-Jakintza*.

Bakker, Peter. 1987. 'A Basque nautical pidgin: a missing link in the history of *fu*'. *Journal of Pidgin and Creole Languages* 2: 1–30.

Barandiarán, I. 1973. *Guipúzcoa en la Edad Antigua: Protohistoria y romanización*. San Sebastián.

Barandiarán, J. M. de. 1934. *El hombre primitivo en el País Vasco*. San Sebastián. Revised edn (1953), *El hombre prehistórico en el País Vasco*. Buenos Aires.

Bengtson, John D. 1990. 'An end to splendid isolation: the Macro-Caucasian phylum'. *Mother Tongue* 10 [no page numbers].

—— 1991a. 'Notes on Sino-Caucasian'. In Shevoroshkin (1991), pp. 67–129.

—— 1991b. 'Some Macro-Caucasian etymologies'. In Shevoroshkin (1991), pp. 130–141.

—— 1991c. 'Macro-Caucasian phonology (part I)'. In Shevoroshkin (1991), pp. 142–161.

—— 1991d. 'Macro-Caucasian: a historical linguistic hypothesis'. In Shevoroshkin (1991), pp. 162–170.

—— 1991e. 'Some Sino-Caucasian etymologies'. In Shevoroshkin (1991), p. 172.

—— 1991f. 'Macro-Caucasian again'. *Mother Tongue* 13: 19–26.

—— 1993. 'The Macro-Caucasian hypothesis'. *Dhumbadji!* 1(2): 13–16.

—— 1994a. 'Comment on Colarusso 1994'. *Mother Tongue* 22: 13–16.

—— 1994b. 'On the genetic classification of Basque'. *Mother Tongue* 22: 31–36.

—— 1995a. 'Is Basque isolated?' *Dhumbadji!* 2(2): 33–44.

—— 1995b. 'Basque: an orphan forever? A response to Trask'. *Mother Tongue* 1 (new series): 84–103.

Bengtson, John D. and Merritt Ruhlen. 1994. 'Global etymologies'. In Ruhlen (1994), pp. 277–336.

Berger, Helmut. 1960. 'Bericht über sprachliche und volkskundliche Forschungen im Hunzatal'. *Anthropos* 55: 657–664.

Berrondo, P. 1980. 'Don Kijote Mantxa'ko (oarpen batzuk)' [Don Quixote de la Mancha (some observations)]. In [no editor] *Lekuona'tar Manuel Jaunaren Omenezko Odazki-Bilduma*, vol. I, pp. 73–80. San Sebastián.

Bertranpetit, J. and Luigi Luca Cavalli-Sforza. 1991. 'A genetic reconstruction of the history of the population of the Iberian Peninsula'. *Annals of Human Genetics* 55: 51–67.

Bilbao, Jon. 1970– . *Eusko Bibliographia: Dictionary of Basque Bibliography*. 8 vols. San Sebastián: Auñamendi.

Blažek, Vaćlav. 1995. 'Towards the position of Basque: a reply to Trask's critique of the Dene–Caucasian hypothesis'. *Mother Tongue* 1 (new series): 104–110.

Bonaparte, Prince Louis Lucien. 1869a. *Le Verbe basque en tableaux*. London.

—— 1869b. *Deux Cartes des sept provinces basques*. London.

—— 1876. *Observations sur le basque de Fontarabie, Irun, etc.* Paris.

Bouda, Karl. 1948. 'Baskisch und Kaukasisch'. *Zeitschrift für Phonetik* 2: 182–202; 336–352.

—— 1949. *Baskisch-Kaukasische Etymologien*. Heidelberg: Carl Winter.

—— 1951. 'L'euskaro-caucasique'. In *Homenaje a D. Julio de Urquijo*, vol. III, pp. 207–232. San Sebastián: Real Sociedad Vascongada de Amigos del País.

—— 1952. 'Neue baskisch-kaukasische Etymologien'. *Acta Salmanticensia Filosofia y Letras* 5(4): 3–16.

Braun, Jan. 1981. 'Euscaro-Caucasica'. In Euskaltzaindia (1981), pp. 213–219.

—— 1985. 'Africadas de las lenguas kartvélicas y sus correspondencias regulares en el vasco: observaciones adicionales'. In Melena (1985), vol. 2, pp. 875–879.

—— 1994. 'Nombres de los insectos en las lenguas kartvélicas y en el vasco'. In Orpustan (1994a), pp. 87–92.

Brugmann, Karl. 1891. *A Comparative Grammar of the Indo-Germanic Languages*, trans. R. S. Conway and W. H. D. Rouse, vol. 2. London: Kegan Paul, Trench Trübner.

Buck, Carl D. 1949. *A Dictionary of Selected Synonyms in the Principal Indo-European Languages*. Chicago: University of Chicago Press.

Campión, Arturo. 1884. *Gramática de los cuatro dialectos literarios de la lengua euskara*. Tolosa.

Caro Baroja, Julio. 1943. *Los pueblos del norte de la Península Ibérica*. Madrid.

—— 1945. *Materiales para una historia de la lengua vasca en su relación con la latina*. Salamanca.

—— 1958. *Los vascos*, 2nd edn. Madrid.

—— 1973. *Estudios vascos*. San Sebastián: Txertoa.

—— 1979. *Sobre la lengua vasca (y el vasco-iberismo)*. Estudios Vascos IX. San Sebastián: Txertoa.

Castro Guisasola, F. 1944. *El enigma del vascuence ante las lenguas indoeuropeas*. Madrid: Consejo Superior de Investigaciones Científicas (Supplements of *Revista de Filología Española*, 30).

Catford, J. C. 1991. 'The classification of Caucasian languages'. In Sydney M. Lamb and E. Douglas Mitchell (eds), *Sprung from Some Common Source: Investigations into the Prehistory of Languages*, pp. 232–268. Stanford: Stanford University Press.

Cavalli-Sforza, Luigi Luca. 1988. 'The Basque population and ancient migrations in Europe'. *Munibe (Antropología y Arqueología)*, Suplemento 6, 129–137.

Cavalli-Sforza, Luigi Luca, Paolo Menozzi and Alberto Piazza. 1994. *The History and Geography of Human Genes*. Princeton: Princeton University Press.

Chaho, Joseph Augustin. 1824. 'Comparaison du basque avec le sanscrit'. *Journal de la Société Asiatique* XVI.

Chicobava, Arnold and Natela Sturua. 1980. 'On Euscaro-Caucasian linguistic relations: evidence of the system of languages and their history'. In Euskaltzaindia (1981), pp. 459–464.

Čirikba, Vjačeslav. A. 1985. 'Baskskij i severokavkazskie jazyki' ['Basque and the North Caucasian languages']. In B. B. Piotrovskij (ed.), *Drevnjaja Anatolija [Ancient Anatolia]*, pp. 95–105. Moscow: Nauka.

Clark, Robert P. 1979. *The Basques: the Franco Years and Beyond*. Reno: University of Nevada Press.

Collins, Roger. 1986. *The Basques*. Oxford: Basil Blackwell.

Corominas, Juan. 1960. 'La toponymie préromane et la survivance du basque jusqu'au bas moyen age'. *Kongressberichte*, Sixth International Congress of Onomastic Sciences, vol. I, pp. 105–146.

—— 1965. *Estudis de toponímia catalana*, vol. I. Barcelona.

—— 1975. 'Les plombs sorothaptiques d'Arles'. *Zeitschrift für Romanische Philologie* 91: 1–53.

Corominas, Juan and José A. Pascual. 1980. *Diccionario crítico etimológico castellano e hispánico*. Madrid: Gredos.

Darricarrère, Jean Baptiste. 1885. *La Langue basque et les idioms aryens*. Barcelonnette.

—— 1903. 'La théorie des racins communes aux langues indo-européennes et à l'idiome basque'. *Bulletin de Biarritz-Association* VIII: 136–144.

—— 1912. 'La langue basque est une langue indo-européenne'. *Bulletin de la Société des Sciences, Lettres, et Arts de Bayonne* 33: 116–119.

Deen, N. G. H. 1937. *Glossaria duo Vasco-Islandica*. Amsterdam.

Douglass, William A., Richard W. Etulain and William H. Jacobsen, Jr (eds). 1977. *Anglo-American Contributions to Basque Studies: Essays in Honor of Jon Bilbao*. Reno: Desert Research Institute Publications on the Social Sciences, no. 13.

Dumézil, Georges. 1933. *Introduction à la grammaire comparée des langues caucasiennes du nord*. Paris: Bibliothèque de l'Institut Français de Léningrad, vol. XIV. Ch. V: 'Caucasien du nord et basque', pp. 123–149.

Echaide, Ana María. 1967. 'Topónimos en -oz en el País Vasco español'. *País Vasco* 28: 11–14.

Echenique Elizondo, María Teresa. 1987. *Historia lingüística vasco-románica*, 2nd edn. Madrid: Paraninfo.

Eguzkitza, Andolin. 1986. 'Topics in the syntax of Basque and Romance'. Unpublished PhD dissertation, UCLA.

Ellis, Robert. 1886. *Sources of the Basque and Etruscan Languages*. London: Trübner.

Esandi, Nicolás. 1946. *Vascuence y etrusco: origen de los lenguajes de Italia. Documentos prehistóricos. Estudio comparativo*. Buenos Aires: Universidad de Buenos Aires.

Estornés Lasa, Bernardo. 1960–1961. *Geografía histórica de la lengua vasca*, 2 vols. Zarauz: Auñamendi.

Etxezarreta, Ramon. 1983. *Hiztegi erotikoa [Erotic Dictionary]*. Donostia: Hordago.

Euskaltzaindia. 1979. *Euskal Aditz Batua [The Unified Basque Verb]*. (Txillardegi, ed.) San Sebastián: Euskaltzaindia.

—— 1981. *IKER-1: Euskalarien Nazioarteko Jardunaldiak* [*Proceedings of the International Congress of Vasconists*]. Bilbo: Euskaltzaindia.

—— 1983. *IKER-2: Piarres Lafitte-ri omenaldia* [*A Festschrift for Pierre Lafitte*]. Bilbo: Euskaltzaindia.

—— 1985– . *Euskal gramatika: lehen urratsak* [*Basque Grammar: the First Steps*]. Vol. 1 1985; vol. 2 1987; vol. 3 1990. Bilbo: Euskaltzaindia.

Eys, W[illem] J. van. 1873. *Dictionnaire basque–français*. Paris.

—— 1879. *Grammaire comparée des dialectes basques*. Paris.

—— 1883. *The Basque Language: Outlines of Basque Grammar*. London: Trübner.

Frank, Roslyn M. 1980. *En torno a un mito: el euskara y el indoeuropeo*. Donostia: Hordago.

Gabelentz, Georg von der. 1894. *Die Verwandtschaft des Baskischen mit den Berbersprachen Nord-Afrikas*. Braunschweig.

Gamillscheg, Ernst. 1950. *Romanen und Basken*. Mainz: Akademie der Wissenschaften und der Literatur in Mainz.

Garibay. 1571. *Compendio Historial*. Madrid.

Gavel, Henri. 1920. *Eléments de phonétique basque*. Paris. Repr. 1921 as vol. 21 of *RIEV*.

—— 1929. *Grammaire basque*, vol. I. Bayonne: Courrier.

Gavel, Henri and Georges Lacombe. 1937. *Grammaire basque*, vol. II: *Le Verbe*. Bayonne: La Presse [only the first eighty pages ever published].

Giacomino, C. 1895. 'Delle relazioni tra il Basco e l'Egizio'. *Supplementi periodici all'Archivio Glottologico Italiano* II: 15–96.

Gifford, Douglas J. 1964. 'An early White Paternoster in Basque?'. *Bulletin of Hispanic Studies* XLI: 209–222.

Gifford, Douglas J. and Luis Michelena. 1958. 'Notas sobre un antiguo texto vasco (Biblioteca de la Catedral de Pamplona, Cód. 7, f. 142 v)'. *Príncipe de Viana* 19: 167–170.

Goenaga, Patxi. 1980. *Gramatika bideetan* [*On the Paths of Grammar*], 2nd edn. Donostia: Erein.

Gómez-Ibáñez, Daniel Alexander. 1975. *The Western Pyrenees*. Oxford: Clarendon Press.

Gómez Moreno, Manuel. 1925. 'Sobre los iberos y su lengua'. In [no editor], *Homenaje ofrecido a Menéndez Pidal*, vol. III, pp. 475–499.

—— 1943. 'La escritura ibérica'. *Boletín de la Real Academia de la Historia* CXII: 251–274.

—— 1949. *Misceláneas (dispersa, emendata, inedita). Excerpta: La escritura ibérica y su lenguaje*, pp. 257–218. Madrid: Consejo Superior de Investigaciones Científicas.

Gómez, Ricardo. 1994. 'Euskal aditz morfologia eta hitzordena: VSO-tik SOV-ra?' ['Basque verbal morphology and word order: from VSO to SOV?'] In Orpustan (1994a), pp. 93–114.

Gómez, Ricardo and Koldo Sainz. 1995. 'On the origin of the finite forms of the Basque verb'. In Hualde *et al.* (1995), pp. 235–273.

Gordon, F. G. 1931. *Through Basque to Minoan*. Oxford: Oxford University Press.

Gorrochategui, Joaquín. 1984. *Estudio sobre la onomástica indígena de Aquitania*. Bilbao: Universidad del País Vasco.

—— 1987. 'Vasco-Celtica'. *ASJU* XXI(3): 951–959.

—— 1995. 'Basque and its neighbors in antiquity'. In Hualde *et al.* (1995), pp. 31–63.

Griera, Antoni. 1960. *Vocabulario vasco: ensayo de una interpretación de la lengua vasca*. Privately published.

Grundt, Alice W. 1977. 'The inflectional accent in Basque and Indo-European'. In

Kenneth Whistler *et al.* (eds), *Papers from the Third Annual Meeting of the Berkeley Linguistics Society*, pp. 637–643. Berkeley: Berkeley Linguistics Society.

—— 1980. 'Tonal accents in Basque and Greek'. In Elizabeth M. Traugott *et al.* (eds), *Papers from the Fourth Annual Conference on Historical Linguistics*, pp. 321–379. Amsterdam: John Benjamins.

Gudschinsky, Sarah C. 1956. 'The ABC's of lexicostatistics (glottochronology)'. *Word* 12: 175–220.

Guiter, Henri. 1968. 'La langue des Pictes'. *BRSVAP* 24: 281–321.

Haritschelhar, Jean. 1969. *Le Poète souletin Pierre Topet-Etchahun (1786–1862): contribution à l'étude de la poésie populaire basque du XIXe siècle.* Bayonne.

Heath, Jeffrey. 1974. 'Some related transformations in Basque'. In Michael W. La Galy, Robert A. Fox and Anthony Bruck (eds), *Papers from the Tenth Regional Meeting of the Chicago Linguistic Society*, pp. 248–258. Chicago: University of Chicago Press.

Hirt, Heinrich. 1927. *Indogermanische Grammatik.* Heidelberg: Carl Winter.

Holmer, Nils M. 1950. 'Las relaciones vasco-celtas desde el punto de vista lingüístico'. *BRSVAP* 6: 399–415.

Hualde, José Ignacio. 1991. *Basque Phonology.* London: Routledge.

—— 1992. 'On the historical origin of Basque accentuation'. *Diachronica* 10: 13–50.

—— 1993. 'Phonologically unmotivated changes in language contact: Spanish borrowings in Basque'. *Folia Linguistica* XXVII: 1–25.

—— 1995. 'Reconstructing the ancient Basque accentual system: hypothesis and evidence'. In Hualde *et al* (1995), pp. 171–188.

Hualde, José Ignacio, Joseba A. Lakarra and R. L. Trask (eds). 1995. *Towards a History of the Basque Language.* Amsterdam: John Benjamins.

Hübner, Emil. 1893. *Monumenta Linguae Ibericae.* Berlin: Georg Reim.

Hubschmid, Johannes. 1953. 'Hispano-Baskisches'. *Boletim de Filologia* 14: 1–26.

—— 1955. 'Vülgarlateinisches Dorngestrüpp und baskischaltwest-europäische Etymologien'. *Orbis* 4: 214–229.

—— 1960. *Mediterrane Substrate mit besondere Berücksichtigung des Baskischen und der westöstlichen Sprachbeziehung.* Bern: Francke.

—— 1963. *Thesaurus praeromanicus*, vol. 1. Bern: Francke.

—— 1965. *Thesaurus praeromanicus*, vol. 2: *Probleme der baskischen Lautlehre und baskisch-vorromanische Etymologien.* Bern: Francke.

Humboldt, Wilhelm von. 1821. *Prüfung der Untersuchungen über die Urbewohner Hispaniens vermittelst der Vaskischen Sprache.* Spanish translation by F. Echebarria (1959), *Primitivos pobladores de España y lengua vasca*, Madrid.

Hurch, Bernhard. 1991. 'Sobre la reconstrucción del euskera. Observaciones a Trask'. In Lakarra (1991), vol. 2, pp. 607–613.

Inchauspe, Manuel. 1858. *Le Verbe basque.* Bayonne/Paris: Benjamin Duprat. Facsimile edn 1979, Donostia: Hordago.

Irigoyen, Alfonso. 1971. 'Estudio de un texto arcaico del vizcaíno antiguo'. In [no editor], *I Semana de Antropología Vasca*, pp. 455–474. Bilbao: La Gran Enciclopedia Vasca.

—— 1977. 'Geure hizkuntzari euskaldunok deritzagun izenaz' [On the name by which we Basques call our language]. *Euskera* XXII: 513–538.

—— 1981a. *Sobre el topónimo* Gasteiz *y su entorno antroponímico.* Bilbao: Universidad de Deusto.

—— 1981b. 'Haur ola zirola: elementos deícticos en lengua vasca'. In Euskaltzaindia (1981), pp. 365–404.

—— 1985a. *Las lenguas de los vizcaínos: antroponimia y toponimia medievales.* Bilbao: Universidad de Deusto.

—— 1985b. *De re philologica linguae uasconicae*. Bilbao: Universidad de Deusto.
—— 1985c. *En torno a la evolución y desarrollo del sistema verbal vasco*. Bilbao: Universidad de Deusto.
—— 1986. *En torno a la toponimia vasca y circumpirenaica*. Bilbao: Universidad de Deusto.
—— 1987. *De re philologica linguae uasconicae II*. Bilbao: Universidad de Deusto.
—— 1990a. *Sobre toponimia del País Vasco norpirenaico*. Bilbao: Universidad de Deusto.
—— 1990b. *De re philologica linguae uasconicae III*. Bilbao: Universidad de Deusto.
—— 1990c. 'Etimología del nombre vasco del vascuence y las vocales nasales vascas descritas por Garibay'. In Irigoyen (1990b), pp. 1–13.
Ithurry, Jean. 1894–1907. *Grammaire basque*. Published in fascicles in *Eskualduna*. Repr. in one vol. (1920), Bayonne: Foltzer. Repr. (1979), San Sebastián: Ediciones Vascas.
Izzo, Herbert J. 1977. 'Pre-Latin languages and sound changes in Romance: the case of Old Spanish /h-/'. In M. P. Hagiwara (ed.), *Studies in Romance Linguistics*, pp. 227–253. Rowley, MA: Newbury House.
Jackson, Kenneth H. 1955. 'The Pictish language'. In F. T. Wainwright (ed.), *The Problem of the Picts*, pp. 129–166. Edinburgh: Nelson.
Jacobsen, William H., Jr. 1971. 'Rule reordering in Vizcayan Basque vowel harmony'. Unpublished ms. University of Nevada at Reno.
—— 1975. 'Historical implications of the western Basque tonal accent'. Unpublished ms. University of Navada at Reno.
—— 1977. 'The Basque locative suffix'. In Douglass *et al.* (1977), pp. 163–168.
Jelinek, Eloise. 1984. 'Empty categories, case, and configurationality'. *Natural Language and Linguistic Theory* 2: 39–76.
Jungemann, Fredrick H. 1955. *La teoría del sustrato y los dialectos hispano-romances y gascones*. Madrid.
King, Alan R. 1994. *The Basque Language: a Practical Introduction*. Reno: University of Nevada Press.
King, Alan R. and Begotxu Olaizola Elordi. 1996. *Colloquial Basque*. London: Routledge.
Kintana, Xabier. 1977. *Euskal hiztegi modernoa [A Modern Basque Dictionary]*, 2nd edn. Bilbao: CINSA.
—— 1980. *Hiztegia 80*. Bilbo: ELKAR.
—— 1981. 'Euskal eta Kartveliar izen batzuren kidetasunaz' ['On the affinity between some Basque and Kartvelian nouns']. In Euskaltzaindia (1981), pp. 261–267.
Klimov, G. A. 1977. *Tipologija jazykov aktivnogo stroja [The Typology of Languages with an Active Structure]*. Moscow: Nauka.
Lacarra, José María. 1957. *Vasconia medieval: historia y filología*. San Sebastián.
—— 1972a. 'La romanización del País Vasco'. *Estudios de Deusto* 20: 209–393.
—— 1972b. *Historia política del reino de Navarra*, vol. I. Pamplona.
Ladefoged, Peter and Ian Maddieson. 1996. *The Sounds of the World's Languages*. Oxford: Basil Blackwell.
Lafitte, Pierre. 1944. *Grammaire basque (navarro-labourdin littéraire)*. Bayonne. 2nd edn 1962. 3rd edn 1979, Donostia: ELKAR, with appendices.
—— 1979. 'L'expression de l'aspect en basque'. Appendix to Lafitte (1944), 3rd edn. No page numbers.
Lafon, René. 1933. 'Basque et langues kartvèles: à propos des postpositions basques formées au moyen de -*gan*'. *RIEV* 24: 150–172.
—— 1944. *Le Système du verbe basque au XVIe siècle*, 2 vols. Bordeaux. Repr. 1980, San Sebastián: ELKAR. Vol. 1: Appendice: 'Quelques correspondances morphologiques entre le basque et les langues caucasiques', pp. 527–535.

—— 1948. 'Correspondances basques-caucasiques'. *Eusko-Jakintza* 2: 359–370.
—— 1950–1951. 'Les origines de la langue basque'. *Conférences de l'Institut de Linguistique de l'Université de Paris* 10: 59–81.
—— 1951. 'Concordances morphologiques entre le basque et les langues caucasiques', part 1. *Word* 7: 227–244.
—— 1952a. 'Le basque et les langues caucasiques (suite et fin)'. *Word* 8: 80–94.
—— 1952b. 'Etudes basques et caucasiques'. *Acta Salmanticensia Filosofía y Letras* 5(2): 5–91.
—— 1957. 'Le géorgien et le basque sont-ils des langues parentes?' *Bedi Kartlisa*, nos 26–27 (November).
—— 1961. 'Sur les formes verbales basques qui contiennent un indice datif'. *BSL* 56: 139–162.
—— 1967. 'Le linguistique basque et caucasique'. *Revue de l'Enseignement Supérieur* (Paris) 3–4: 56–66.
—— 1968a. 'Pour la comparaison du basque et des langues caucasiques. I. Les indices de personne dans la conjugaison basque'. *Bedi Kartlisa* 28: 13–26.
—— 1968b. 'Basque'. In Thomas A. Sebeok (ed.), *Current Trends in Linguistics*, vol. 9, pp. 1744–1792. Original French version published (1973) as *Le Langage basque*, separata of *Bulletin du Musée Basque* (Bayonne), no. 60.
—— 1970. 'Le suffixe -*ke*, -*te* dans la conjugaison basque'. *BSL* 65: 184–212.
—— 1972. 'Le suffixe -*ke*, -*te* dans la conjugaison basque (suite et fin)'. *BSL* 67: 239–265.
—— 1975. 'Indices personnels n'exprimant rien de déterminé dans les verbes basques'. In [no editor], *Mélanges linguistiques offerts à Emile Benveniste*, pp. 331–337. Paris: Société de Linguistique de Paris.
—— 1976. *Baskskij jazyk i basksko-kavkazskaja gipoteza* [*The Basque Language and the Basque–Caucasian Hypothesis*]. Tbilisi.
Lakarra, Joseba A. (ed.) 1991. *Memoriae L. Mitxelena Magistri Sacrum*, 2 vols. San Sebastián: *ASJU,* Gehigarriak XIV, Diputación Foral de Gipuzkoa.
—— 1995. 'Reconstructing the Pre-Proto-Basque root'. In Hualde *et al.* (1995), pp. 189–206.
Landucci, Niccolò. 1958 [1562]. *Dictionarium linguae Cantabricae.* Manuel Agud and Luis Michelena (eds) San Sebastián: Publicaciones del Seminario de Filología Vasca 'Julio de Urquijo'. [Introduction by Luis Michelena repr. in Michelena (1988a), vol. II, pp. 762–782.]
Larramendi, Manuel de. 1728. *De la antigüedad y universalidad del Bascuenze en España; de sus perfecciones y ventajas sobre otras muchas lenguas. Demostración previa al Arte que se dará a luz desta lengua.* Salamanca.
—— 1729. *El imposible vencido: arte de la lengua bascongada.* Salamanca. Facsimile edn published 1979, Donostia: Hordago.
—— 1745. *Diccionario trilingüe del Castellano, Bascuence y Latín*, 2 vols. San Sebastián.
Larrasquet, Jean. 1928. *Recherches expérimentales sur l'évolution des vélaires dans le basque souletin & Action de l'accent dans l'évolution des consonnes étudiée dans le basque souletin.* Paris: Vrin.
—— 1934. *Le Basque souletin nord-oriental.* Paris: Maisonneuve.
—— 1939. *Le Basque de la Basse-Soule orientale. Collection Linguistique*, 46. Paris: Société de Linguistique de Paris.
Leizarraga, Joannes. 1571. *Jesus Christ gure jaunaren testamentu berria* [*The New Testament of Our Lord Jesus Christ*]. Rochellan. Facsimile edn (1979), Donostia: Hordago.
Lekuona, Manuel de. 1982. 'Euskerismos en el castellano antiguo (en el fuero de

Sepúlveda)'. *Eusko-Ikaskuntza/Sociedad de Estudios Vascos, Cuadernos de sección Hizkuntza eta Literatura* 1: 13–30.

Lemoine, Jacques. 1977. *Toponymie du Pays Basque français et des Pays de l'Adour.* Paris.

Levin, Beth. 1983. 'On the nature of ergativity'. Unpublished PhD dissertation, MIT.

Lhande, Pierre. 1926. *Dictionnaire basque–français.* Paris: Gabriel Beauchesne.

Löpelmann, Martin. 1968. *Etymologisches Wörterbuch der Baskischen Sprache.* Berlin: De Gruyter.

López García, Ángel. 1985a. 'Algunas concordancias gramaticales entre el castellano y el euskera'. In *Philologica Hispaniensia in Honorem M. Alvar*, vol. II, pp. 391–405. Madrid: Gredos.

—— 1985b. 'Una hipótesis tipológica relativa a la lengua vasca'. In Melena (1985), vol. 2, pp. 849–857.

Luchaire, Achille. 1874. *Les Noms de lieu en Pays basques.* Pau.

—— 1877. *Les Origines linguistiques de l'Aquitaine.* Pau.

—— 1879. *Etudes sur les idiomes pyrénéens de la région française.* Paris.

Marineus Siculus, Lucius. 1533. *De las cosas memorables de España.* Alcalá de Henares.

Martinet, André. 1950. 'De la sonorisation des occlusives initiales en basque'. *Word* 6: 224–233.

—— 1955. *Economie des changements phonétiques: traité de phonologie diachronique.* Berne.

—— 1962. 'Le sujet comme fonction linguistique et l'analyse syntaxique du basque'. *BSL* LVII: 73–82.

—— 1981. 'La phonologie synchronique et diachronique du basque'. In Euskaltzaindia (1981), pp. 59–74.

Meillet, Antoine. 1925. *La Méthode comparative en linguistique historique.* Oslo. Repr. 1966. Paris: Champion.

Melena, José L. (ed.) 1985. *Symbolae Ludovico Mitxelena Septuagenario Oblatae.* 2 vols. Vitoria-Gasteiz: Instituto de Ciencias de la Antigüedad, Universidad del País Vasco.

Menendez Pidal, Ramón. 1942. *Toponimia prerrománica hispana.* Madrid: Gredos.

—— 1950. *Orígenes del español: estado lingüístico de la Península Ibérica hasta el siglo XI*, 3rd edn. Madrid.

Merino Urrutia, José J. 1978. *La lengua vasca en la Rioja y Burgos*, 3rd edn. Logroño: Servicio de Cultura de la Excma. Diputación Provincial.

Meyer-Lübke, Wilhelm. 1935. 'Lat. *F.* im Baskischen, Span., Gaskogn. *h* aus Lat. *F.*' *Archiv für das Studium der neuren Sprachen* 166: 50–68.

Michelena, Luis. 1949. 'Notas de gramática histórica vasca'. In [no editor] *Homenaje a D. Julio de Urquijo e Ybarra*, vol. II, pp. 483–487. San Sebastián. Repr. in Michelena (1988a), vol. 1, pp. 445–447.

—— 1950a. 'Notas etimológicas vascas'. *Emerita* 18: 467–481. Repr. in Michelena (1988a), vol. 1, pp. 458–466.

—— 1950b. 'De etimología vasca'. *Emerita* XVIII: 193–203. Repr. in Michelena (1988a), vol. 1, pp. 439–444.

—— 1950c. 'De fonética vasca: la aspiración intervocálica'. *BRSVAP* VI: 443–459. Repr. in Michelena (1988a), vol. 1, pp. 190–202.

—— 1951. 'De fonética vasca I. La distribución de las oclusivas aspiradas y no aspiradas'. *BRSVAP* 7: 539–549. Repr. in Michelena (1988a), vol. 1, pp. 212–219.

—— 1952 Review of Tovar (1949). *Emerita* XX: 545–552. Repr. in Michelena (1988a), vol. 1, pp. 85–90.

—— 1953. Review of Bouda (1952). *BRSVAP* 9: 141–144.

—— 1954a. 'De onomástica aquitana'. *Pirineos* 10: 409–458. Repr. in Michelena (1985), pp. 409–445.

—— 1954b. 'La posición fonética del dialecto vasco del Roncal'. *Via Domitia* I: 123–157. Repr. in Michelena (1988a), vol. 1, pp. 273–297.

—— 1954c. 'Nota sobre algunos pasajes de los *Refranes y sentencias* de 1596'. *ASJU* 1: 25–33. Repr. in Michelena (1988a), vol. 2, pp. 792–798.

—— 1955. 'Cuestiones relacionadas con la escritura ibérica'. *Emerita* XXIII: 265–284. Repr. in Michelena (1985), pp. 357–370.

—— 1956a. 'Guipúzcoa en la época romana'. *BRSVAP* 12: 69–74. Repr. in Michelena (1988a), vol. 1, pp. 138–155.

—— 1956b. 'Introducción fonética a la onomástica vasca'. *Emerita* 24: 167–186; 331–352. Repr. in Michelena (1988a), vol. 2, pp. 555–580.

—— 1957. 'Las antiguas consonantes vascas'. In [no editor], *Miscelánea homenaje a A. Martinet*, vol. I, pp. 113–157. Universidad de La Laguna. Repr. in Michelena (1988a), vol. 1, pp. 166–189. English translation by R. L. Trask, 'The ancient Basque consonants', in Hualde *et al.* (1995), pp. 101–136.

—— 1957–1958. 'A propos de l'accent basque'. *BSL* 53: 204–233. Repr. in Michelena (1988a), vol. 1, pp. 220–239.

—— 1958. 'Hispánico antiguo y vasco'. *Archivum* 8: 33–67. Repr. in Michelena (1988a), vol. 1, pp. 99–106.

—— 1959. Review of M. L. Wagner, *Dizionario etimologico sardo*. *Word* 15: 523–527.

—— 1960. Review of Griera (1960). *BRSVAP* XVI: 384–387. Repr. in Michelena (1985), pp. 329–333.

—— 1961–1962. 'Los nombres indígenas de la inscripción hispano-romano de Lerga (Navarra)'. *Príncipe de Viana* 22: 65–74. Repr. in Michelena (1985), pp. 446–457.

—— 1964a. *Textos arcaicos vascos*. Madrid: Ediciones Minotauro.

—— 1964b. *Sobre el pasado de la lengua vasca*. San Sebastián: Auñamendi. Repr. in Michelena (1988a), vol. 1, pp. 1–73.

—— 1965. 'Vasco-románica'. *Revista de Filología Española* 48: 105–119. Repr. in Michelena (1985), pp. 268–281.

—— 1966. 'Azkue lexicógrafo'. In Luis Michelena, Julio Caro Baroja and Antonio Tovar, *Don Resurrección María de Azkue*, pp. 14–37. Bilbao. Repr. in Michelena (1988a), vol. 1, pp. 373–384.

—— 1967. Review of Hubschmid (1965). *Zeitschrift für romanische Philologie* 83: 602–609. Repr. in Michelena (1985), pp. 321–328.

—— 1968a. 'L'euskaro-caucasien'. In André Martinet (ed.), *Le Langage*, pp. 1414–1437. Paris: Editions Gallimard, Encyclopédie de la Pléiade 25. Repr. in Michelena (1985), pp. 458–475.

—— 1968b. 'Aitonen, aitoren seme "noble hidalgo"'. *BRSVAP* XXIV: 3–18. Repr. in Michelena (1988a), vol. 2, pp. 516–527.

—— 1969a. 'Sobre algunos nombres vascos de parentesco'. *FLV* 1: 113–132. Repr. in Michelena (1988a), vol. 2, pp. 492–508.

—— 1969b. 'Notas lingüísticas a *Colección Diplomática de Irache*'. *FLV* 1: 1–59. Repr. in Michelena (1987), pp. 87–140.

—— 1970a. *Estudio sobre las fuentes del diccionario de Azkue*. Bilbao: Publicaciones del Centro de Estudios Históricos de Vizcaya (Real Sociedad Vascongada de Amigos del País). Repr. as Introduction to the 1984 edition of Azkue (1905).

—— 1970b. 'Nombre y verbo en la etimología vasca'. *FLV* 2: 67–93. Repr. in Michelena (1987), pp. 283–309.

—— 1971a. 'Toponimia, léxico y gramática'. *FLV* 3: 241–267. Repr. in Michelena (1987), pp. 141–167.

—— 1971b. [writing as Koldo Mitxelena]. 'Egunak ta egun izenak' ['Days and names of days']. *Munibe* 23: 583–591. Repr. in Michelena (1987), pp. 269–282. Also reprinted in Michelena (1988b), pp. 93–110.

—— 1971c. 'Descubrimiento y redescubrimiento en textos vascos'. *FLV* 3: 149–169. Repr. in Michelena (1988a), vol. 2, pp. 713–728.

—— 1972a. 'A note on Old Labourdin accentuation'. *ASJU* 6: 110–120.

—— 1972b. 'Etimología y transformación'. In [no editor], *Homenaje a Antonio Tovar*, pp. 305–317. Madrid: Gredos. Repr. in Michelena (1985), pp. 296–308.

—— 1972c. 'Léxico vasco y etimología'. In [no editor], *Beiträge zur Romanistik und allgemeinen Sprachwissenschaft: Festschrift Wilhelm Giese*, pp. 79–95. Hamburg. Repr. in Michelena (1987), pp. 337–348.

—— 1973a. *Apellidos vascos*, 3rd edn [1st edn 1953]. San Sebastián: Txertoa.

—— 1973b. 'Sobre la posición lingüística del ibérico'. *Archivo Español de Arqueología* (Homenaje a don Pío Beltrán) VII: 147–153. Repr. in Michelena (1985), pp. 334–340.

—— 1973c. 'Guillaume de Humboldt et la langue basque'. *Lingua e Stile* VIII: 107–125. Repr. in L. Heilmann (ed.) (1976), *Wilhelm von Humboldt nella cultura contemporanea*, pp. 113–131. Bologna: Il Mulino. Also repr. in Michelena (1985), pp. 126–142.

—— 1976. 'Ibérico -en'. In *Actas del I Coloquio sobre lenguas y culturas prerromanas de la Península Ibérica*, pp. 353–361. Salamanca. Repr. in Michelena (1985), pp. 379–387.

—— 1977a. *Fonética histórica vasca*, 2nd expanded edn [1st edn 1961; 3rd edn 1985]. San Sebastián: Publicaciones del Seminario de Filología Vasca 'Julio de Urquijo' de la Excma. Diputación de Guipúzcoa.

—— 1977b. 'Notas sobre compuestos verbales vascos'. *Revista de Dialectología y Tradiciones Populares* XXXIII: 245–271. Repr. in Michelena (1985), pp. 311–335.

—— 1979. 'La langue ibère'. In *Actas del II Coloquio sobre lenguas y culturas prerromanas de la Península Ibérica*, pp. 23–39. Salamanca. Repr. in Michelena (1985), pp. 341–356.

—— 1983. [writing as Koldo Mitxelena]. 'Iruñea'. In Euskaltzaindia (1983), pp. 445–451. Repr. in Michelena (1987), pp. 187–193.

—— 1985. *Lengua e historia*. Madrid: Paraninfo.

—— 1987. *Palabras y textos*. Vitoria.

—— (ed.) 1987– . *Orotariko Euskal Hiztegia/Diccionario General Vasco*. Bilbao: Euskaltzaindia.

—— 1988a. *Sobre historia de la lengua vasca*, 2 vols, ed. J. A. Lakarra, Donostia/San Sebastián: Anejos del *ASJU* 10.

—— 1988b. [writing as Koldo Mitxelena]. *Euskal idazlan guztiak* [*Complete Writings in Basque*]. Donostia.

Michelena, Luis and A. Rodríguez Herrero. 1959. 'Los cantares de la quema de Mondragón (1448)'. *BRSVAP* 15: 371–381. Repr. in Michelena (1988a), vol. 2, pp. 741–747.

Michelena, Luis and Ángel Irigaray. 1955. 'Nombres vascos de persona'. *ASJU* 2: 107–127. Repr. in *BRSVAP* XI: 405–425. Also repr. in Michelena (1988a), vol. 2, pp. 581–594.

Michelena, Luis, Antonio Tovar and Enrique Otte. 1981. 'Nuevo y más extenso texto arcaico vasco: de una carta del primer obispo de México, Fray Juan de Zumárraga'. *Euskera* XXVI: 5–14. Repr. in Michelena (1988a), vol. 2, pp. 748–755.

Montgomery, T. 1977. 'Basque models for some syntactic traits of the *Poema de Mio Cid*'. *Bulletin of Hispanic Studies* 54: 95–99.

Moutard, Nicole. 1975a. 'Etude phonologique sur les dialectes basques (I)'. *FLV* VII(19): 5–42.

—— 1975b. 'Etude phonologique sur les dialectes basques (II)'. *FLV* VII(20): 141–189.

—— 1976. 'Etude phonologique sur les dialectes basques (III)'. *FLV* VIII(22): 9–54.

Múgica: see Mujika.

Mujika, Luix M. 1977. *Diccionario general y técnico/Hiztegi orokor-teknikoa*. 2 vols Bilbao: Ediciones Vascas.

—— [writing as Luis María Múgica]. 1978. *Origen y desarrollo de la sufijación euskérica*. Bilbao: Ediciones Vascas.

—— 1982. *Hitz konposatu eta eratorrien morfo-fonetika* [*The Morphophonetics of Compound and Derived Words*]. Bilbao: Ediciones Vascas.

Mukarovsky, Hans G. 1963–1964. 'Baskisch und Berberisch'. *Wiener Zeitschrift für die Kunde des Morgenlandes* 59/60: 52–94.

—— 1969. 'Baskische-berberische Entsprechungen'. *Wiener Zeitschrift für die Kunde des Morgenlandes* 62: 32–51.

—— 1981a. 'Einige hamitosemitische und baskische Wortstämme'. *Berliner afrikanistische Vorträge* (Serie A: Afrika) 28: 103–118.

—— 1981b. 'Common Hamito-Semitic and Basque with examples for a proto-phoneme /+B/'. In Euskaltzaindia (1981), pp. 189–198.

—— 1981c. 'Outline of a lexicostatistical study of Basque and the Mande languages, with a note on Fula'. In Euskaltzaindia (1981), pp. 199–219.

Navarro Tomás, T. 1923. 'Observaciones fonéticas sobre el vascuence de Guernica'. *Tercer Congreso de Estudios Vascos*, pp. 49–56.

—— 1925. 'Pronunciación guipuzcoana'. In [no editor], *Homenaje a Menéndez Pidal*, vol. III, pp. 593–653.

Nichols, Johanna. 1992. *Linguistic Diversity in Space and Time*. Chicago: University of Chicago Press.

Oregi Aranburu, Josu. 1974. 'Euskal-aditzaz zenbait gogoeta' [Some thoughts on the Basque verb]. *FLV* 17: 265–283.

Oroz Arizcuren, Francisco J. 1981. 'La relación entre el vasco y el ibérico desde el punto de vista de la teoria del sustrato'. In Euskaltzaindia (1981), pp. 241–255.

Orpustan, Jean-Baptiste. 1990. *Toponymie basque: noms des pays, communes, hameaux et quartiers historiques de Labourd, Basse-Navarre et Soule*. Bordeaux.

—— (ed.) 1994a. *La Langue basque parmi les autres*. Saint Etienne de Baïgorry: Editions Izpegi.

—— 1994b. 'De quelques latinismes de l'ancienne toponymie basque: *luku, zaldu*, etc.' In Orpustan (1994a), pp. 43–58.

Ortiz de Urbina, Jon. 1989. *Some Parameters in the Grammar of Basque*. Dordrecht: Foris.

Otte, Enrique. 1979. 'Juan de Zumárraga, vasco'. In [no editor], *Les Cultures ibériques en devenir: essais publiés en hommage à la mémoire de Marcel Bataillon (1895–1977)*, pp. 486–496. Paris: Fondation Singer Polignac.

Oyharçabal, Beñat. 1992a. 'Structural case and inherent case marking: ergaccusativity in Basque'. In Joseba A. Lakarra and Jon Ortiz de Urbina (eds), *Syntactic Theory and Basque Syntax*, pp. 309–342. Supplement 27 of *ASJU*. Donostia and San Sebastián: Diputación Foral de Gipuzkoa.

—— 1992b. 'Les travaux de grammaire basque avant Larramendi (1729)'. *Euskalaritzaren historiaz I: XVI-XIX mendeak*, pp. 91–105. Supplement 15 of *ASJU*. Donostia and San Sebastián: Diputación de Guipúzcoa.

Padel, Oliver J. 1972. 'Inscriptions of Pictland'. Unpublished M.Litt. thesis, University of Edinburgh. Cited in Price (1984).

Payne, Stanley G. 1975. *Basque Nationalism*. Reno: University of Nevada Press.

Pellegrini, Giovanni Battista. 1980. 'Substrata'. In Rebecca Posner and John N. Green (eds), *Trends in Romance Linguistics and Philology*, vol. 1: *Romance Comparative and Historical Linguistics*. Mouton: The Hague, pp. 43–73.

Penny, Ralph. 1991. *A History of the Spanish Language*. Cambridge: Cambridge University Press.

Perurena, Patziku. 1992. *Koloreak euskal usarioan* [*The Colours in Basque Usage*]. Donostia: Erein.

—— 1993. *Euskarak sorgindutako numeroak* [*The Numerals Bewitched by Basque*]. Donostia: Saiakera.

Poça, Andrés de. 1587. *De la antigua lengua, poblaciones y comarcas de las Españas, en que de paso se tocan algunas cosas de la Cantabria*. Bilbao. New edn (1959), ed. A. Rodríguez Herrero. Madrid.

Pokorny, Julius. 1959. *Indogermanisches etymologisches Wörterbuch*. Bern and Munich: Francke.

Price, Glanville. 1984. *The Languages of Britain*. London: Edward Arnold. Ch. 2: 'Pictish', pp. 20–27.

Rebuschi, Georges. 1978. 'Cas et fonction sujet en basque'. *Verbum* (Nancy) 1: 69–98.

—— 1983. 'Autour du parfait et du passif basque'. In Euskaltzaindia (1983), pp. 545–558.

—— 1983/1984. 'Réforme et planification en basque: une expérience en cours'. In István Fodor and Claude Hagège (eds), *Language Reform: History and Future*, vol. 3, pp. 119–138. Hamburg: Buske.

—— 1984. *Structure de l'énoncé en basque*. Paris: SELAF.

—— 1985a. 'Niveaux de représentation et non-configurationalité: remarques sur les anaphors et les variables du basque'. *Sigma* 9: 109–144.

—— 1985b. 'Positions, configurations et classes syntaxiques: aspects de la construction de la phrase simple en basque'. *Euskera* 30(1): 117–128.

—— 1985c. 'Théorie du liage et langues non-configurationelles: quelques données du basque navarro-labourdin'. *Euskera* 30(2): 389–433.

—— 1986. 'Diathèse et (non-)configurationalité: l'exemple du basque'. *Actances* 2: 175–207.

—— 1989. 'Is there a VP in Basque?' In László Marácz and Pieter Muysken (eds), *Configurationality: the Typology of Asymmetries*, pp. 85–116. Dordrecht: Foris.

—— 1995. 'Weak and strong genitive pronouns in northern Basque: a diachronic perspective'. In Hualde *et al.* (1995), pp. 313–356.

Rhŷs, John. 1892–1893. 'The inscriptions and language of the northern Picts'. *Proceedings of the Society of Antiquaries of Scotland* 26: 263–351. 'Addenda and corrigenda', *ibid.*, pp. 411–412.

Ricci, Seymour. 1903. 'Notes d'onomastique pyrénéenne'. *Revue Celtique* 24: 71ff.

Rijk, Rudolph P. G. de. 1969. 'Is Basque an S.O.V. language?' *FLV* 1(3): 319–351.

—— 1970. 'Vowel interaction in Bizcayan Basque'. *FLV* II(5): 149–167.

—— 1972. 'Relative clauses in Basque: a guided tour'. In Paul M. Peranteau, Judith N. Levi and Gloria C. Phares (eds), *The Chicago Which Hunt: Papers from the Relative Clause Festival*, pp. 115–135. Chicago: Chicago Linguistic Society.

—— 1981. 'Euskal morfologiaren zenbait gorabehera' ['Some problems in Basque morphology']. In [no editor], *Euskal linguistika eta literature: bide berriak* [*Basque Linguistics and Literature: New Roads*], pp. 83–101. Bilbo: Deustuko Unibertsitatea.

—— 1985. 'Un verbe méconnu'. In Melena (1985), vol. 2, pp. 921–935.

—— 1992. '"Nunc" vasconice'. *ASJU* 26: 695–724. Condensed English translation in Hualde *et al.* (1995), pp. 295–311.

Rohlfs, Gerhard. 1933. 'La influencia latina en la lengua y cultura vasca'. *RIEV* 24: 323–348.

—— 1935. *Le Gascon: études de philologie pyrénéenne*. *Zeitschrift für Romanische Philologie* Beiheft 85. 2nd edn 1970; 3rd edn 1980. Tübingen and Pau.

—— 1952. 'Sur une couche préromane dans la toponymie de Gascogne et de l'Espagne du nord'. *Revista de Filología Española* 36: 209–256.

Román del Cerro, Juan L. 1993. *El origen ibérico de la lengua vasca*. Madrid: Aguaclara.

Ros, Ander. 1987. 'Aditz morfologia historikarako ohar kritikoak: alokuzioa' [Critical notes on the historical morphology of the verb: allocutivity]. *Enseiucarrean* 2: 5–54.

Rotaetxe, Karmele. 1978. *Estudio estructural del euskara de Ondárroa*. Durango: Leopoldo Zugaza.

Ruhlen, Merritt. 1991. *A Guide to the World's Languages*, 2nd edn. London: Edward Arnold.

—— 1992. 'An overview of genetic classification'. In John A. Hawkins and Murray Gell-Mann (eds), *The Evolution of Human Languages*, pp. 159–189. Redwood City, CA: Addison-Wesley. Proceedings Volume XI, Sante Fe Institute Studies in the Science of Complexity. Repr. as Chapter 1 of Ruhlen (1994), pp. 9–38.

—— 1994. *On the Origin of Languages: Studies in Linguistic Taxonomy*. Stanford: Stanford University Press.

—— 1995. 'Comments on R. L. Trask's critique: is Basque an isolate?' *Mother Tongue* 1 (new series): 149–156.

Ruhlen, Merritt and John Bengtson. 1994. 'Global etymologies'. In Merritt Ruhlen, *On the Origin of Languages*, pp. 277–336. Stanford: Stanford University Press.

Russell, Paul. 1995. *An Introduction to the Celtic Languages*. London: Longman.

Salaburu, Pello. 1986. 'Uztarduraren teoria' ['The binding theory']. In Patxi Goenaga (ed.), *Euskal sintaxiaren zenbait arazo* [*Some Problems in Basque Syntax*]. Vitoria: Universidad del País Vasco/Euskal Herriko Unibertsitatea.

Saltarelli, Mario. 1988. *Basque*. London: Croom Helm.

Salvador Caja, Gregorio. 1982. 'Hipótesis geológica sobre la evolución *f- > h-*'. In Francisco Marcos Marín (ed.), *Introducción plural a gramática histórica*, pp. 11–21. Madrid: Cincel.

Sarasola, Ibon. 1984– . *Hauta-lanerako euskal hiztegia* [*A Basque Dictionary of Selected Works*]. Published in fascicles. Donostia: Gipuzkoako Aurrezki Kutxa Probintziala.

Sasía, J. M. 1966. *Toponimia euskérica de las Encartaciones de Vizcaya*. Bilbao.

Saussure, Ferdinand de. 1916. *Cours de linguistique générale*, ed. Charles Bally, Albert Sechehaye and Albert Riedlinger, Lausanne: Payot. English translation *Course in General Linguistics* by Wade Baskin, 1966. New York: McGraw-Hill.

Schmid, Wolfgang P. 1987. ' "Indo-European" – "Old European" (On the reexamination of two linguistic terms)'. In Susan Nacev Skomal and Edgar C. Polomé (eds), *Proto-Indo-European: the Archaeology of a Linguistic Problem: Studies in Honor of Marija Gimbutas*, pp. 322–338. Washington, DC: Institute for the Study of Man.

Schmoll, U. 1959. *Die Sprachen der vorkeltischen Indogermanen Hispaniens und das Keltiberische*. Wiesbaden.

Schuchardt, Hugo. 1887. 'Romano-baskisches'. *Zeitschrift für Romanische Philologie* 11: 474ff.

—— 1893. 'Baskische Studien I: Über die Entstehung der Bezugsformen des baskischen Zeitworts'. *Denkschriften der kaiserlichen Akademie der Wissenschaften, Philosophisch-Historische Classe* (Vienna) 42: 1–82.

—— 1906. *Baskisch und Romanisch. Zeitschrift für Romanische Philologie*, Supplement 6. Spanish translation (1957–1960) 'Vascuence y romance'. *BRSVAP* 13: 463–467, 15: 181–205, 16: 239–263.

—— 1908. 'Die iberische Deklination'. *Sitzungsberichte der Wiener Akademie der Wissenschaften* CLVII: 1–90. Also published as a book, *Die iberische Deklination*, Vienna: A. Holder.

—— 1913. 'Baskisch-hamitische Wortvergleichungen'. *RIEV* 7: 289–340.

—— 1914–1917. 'Baskisch und Hamitisch'. *RIEV* 8: 76ff.

—— 1922. *Zur Kenntnis des Baskischen von Sara (Labourd)*. Berlin: Abhandlungen der Preussischen Akademie der Wissenschaften, Phil.-hist. Klasse.

—— 1923. *Primitiae linguae vasconum: Einführung ins Baskische*. Halle and Saale: Max Niemeyer. 2nd edn 1968, ed. Antonio Tovar, Tübingen: Max Niemeyer.

—— 1925. *Das Baskisch und die Sprachwissenschaft*. Vienna.

Schulten, A. 1927. 'Las referencias sobre los Vascones hasta el año 800 después de J.C.'. *RIEV* 18: 225–240.

Shevoroshkin, Vitaly (ed.). 1991. *Dene-Sino-Caucasian Languages*. Bochum: Brockmeyer.

Starostin, Sergei A. and Merritt Ruhlen. 1994. 'Proto-Yeniseian reconstructions, with extra-Yeniseian comparisons'. In Ruhlen (1994), pp. 70–92.

Stempf, Victor. 1889. *Besitzt die baskische Sprache ein transitives Zeitwort, oder nicht?* French translation *La Langue basque possède-t-elle, oui ou non, un verbe transitif?* Bordeaux.

Swadesh, Morris. 1960. 'On interhemispheric linguistic connections'. In Stanley Diamond (ed.), *Culture in History: Essays in Honor of Paul Radin*, pp. 894–924. New York: Columbia University Press.

—— 1971. *The Origin and Diversification of Languages*, ed. Joel Sherzer, London: Routledge & Kegan Paul.

Tovar, Antonio. 1949. *Estudios sobre las primitivas lenguas hispánicas*. Buenos Aires: Universidad de Buenos Aires.

—— 1950. *La lengua vasca*. San Sebastián: Biblioteca Vascongada de Amigos del País. 2nd edn (1954).

—— 1951. 'Léxico de las inscripciones ibéricas (celtibérico e ibérico)'. In *Estudios dedicados a Menéndez Pidal*, vol. II, pp. 273–323.

—— 1954a. 'Sobre el planteamiento del problema vasco-ibérico'. *Archivum* IV: 220–231.

—— 1954b. 'El sufijo -*ko*: indoeuropeo y circumindoeuropeo'. *Archivio Glottologico Italiano* 39: 56–64.

—— 1959a. *El euskera y sus parientes*. Madrid: Ediciones Minotauro.

—— 1959b. 'Lenguas prerromanas no indoeuropeas: testimonios antiguos'. *Enciclopedia lingüística hispánica*, vol. I, pp. 5–26. Madrid.

—— 1961. *The Ancient Languages of Spain and Portugal*. New York: S. F. Vanni.

—— 1966. 'El vascuence y África'. *BRSVAP* 22: 303–306.

—— 1970. 'The Basque language and the Indo-European spread to the west'. In G. Cardona, H. Hoenigswald and A. Senn (eds), *Indo-European and Indo-Europeans*, pp. 267–278. Philadelphia: University of Pennsylvania Press.

—— 1980. *Mitología e ideología sobre la lengua vasca*. Madrid: Alianza.

Tovar, Antonio, Luis Michelena, Karl Bouda, René Lafon, W. Vycichl and Morris Swadesh. 1961. 'El método léxico-estadístico y su aplicación a las relaciones de vascuence'. *BRSVAP* 17: 249–281.

Trask, R. L. 1977. 'Historical syntax and Basque verbal morphology: two hypotheses'. In Douglass *et al.* (1977), pp. 203–217.

—— 1985. 'On the reconstruction of pre-Basque phonology'. In Melena (1985), vol. 2, pp. 885–891.

—— 1989. 'Why the Basque transitive verb is not passive'. University of Sussex Cognitive Science Research Reports 137.

—— 1990. 'The -n class of verbs in Basque'. Transactions of the Philological Society 88: 111–128.

—— 1994–1995. 'Basque: the search for relatives'. Dhumbadji! 2(1): 3–54, 2(2): 3–18.

—— 1995a. 'Origin and relatives of the Basque language: review of the evidence'. In Hualde et al. (1995), pp. 65–99.

—— 1995b. 'On the history of the non-finite verb-forms in Basque'. In Hualde et al. (1995), pp. 207–234.

—— 1995c. 'Basque and Dene-Caucasian: a critique from the Basque side'. Mother Tongue 1 (new series): 3–82. [Followed by critical discussion by twelve commentators (pp. 83–171) and by a response from the author (pp. 172–201).]

Trask, R. L. and Roger Wright. 1988. 'El "vascorrománico"'. Verba: Anuario Galego de Filoloxía 15: 361–373.

Trombetti, Alfredo. 1902–1903. 'Delle relazioni delle lingue caucasiche con le lingue camito-semitiche e con altri gruppi linguistici'. Giornalle della Società Asiatica Italiana XV, XVI.

—— 1925. Origini della lingua basca. Bologna: Memorie della R. Accademia delle Scienze dell' Istituto di Bologna.

Ugalde, Martín de. 1979. Unamuno y el Vascuence. Bilbao: Ediciones Vascas.

Uhlenbeck, C. C. 1909–10. 'Contribution à une phonétique comparative des dialectes basques'. RIEV 3: 465–503; 4: 65–118.

—— 1912. 'Basque et ouralo-altaïque'. RIEV 412–414.

—— 1916. 'Het passieve Karakter van het Verbum transitivum of van het Verbum actionis in Taalen van Nord-Amerika'. Verslagen en Mededeelingen der Koninklijke Akademie van Wetenschappen (Amsterdam). Afd. Letterkunde 5(2): 187–216. French translation (1922), 'Le caractère passif du verbe transitif ou du verbe d'action dans certaines langues de l'Amérique du Nord'. RIEV 13: 399–419.

—— 1923a. Over een mogelijke verwantschap van het Baskisch met de palaeo-kaukasische talen. Amsterdam.

—— 1923b. Zur vergleichenden Lautlehre der baskischen Dialekte. Amsterdam: Verhandelingen der koninklijke Akademie van Wetenschappen te Amsterdam.

—— 1924. 'De la possibilité d'une parenté entre le basque et les langues caucasiques'. RIEV XV: 565–588.

—— 1927. 'Die mit b- anlautenden Körperteilnamen des Baskischen'. In Festschrift Meinhof, pp. 351–357. Hamburg. Spanish translation (1949), 'Los nombres vascos de miembros de cuerpo que comienzan con b-'. Eusko-Jakintza 3: 105–111.

—— 1940–1941. 'Vorlateinische indogermanische Anklänge im Baskischen'. Anthropos 35–36: 202ff.

—— 1946. Gestaafde en vermeende affiniteiten van het Baskisch. Amsterdam. French translation (1947), 'Affinités prouvées et présumées de la langue basque', Revue d'Etudes Basques I: 171ff.

—— 1947. 'La langue basque et la linguistique générale'. Lingua 1: 59–76.

Unamuno, Miguel de 1916 [1902]. 'La cuestión del Vascuence'. In M. de Unamuno, Ensayos, vol. III, pp. 191–237. Madrid: Residencia de Estudiantes.

Untermann, Jürgen. 1961. Sprachräume und Sprachbewegungen im vorromoschen Hispanian. Wiesbaden.

Urquijo, Julio. 1925. '¿Cuál es el primer texto vasco impreso conocido?' RIEV 16: 477ff.

Valle Lersundi, F. del. 1933—1934. 'Una forma del femenino y el valor de la letra ch como diminutivo en los nombres de los guipuzcoanos de los siglos XV y XVI'. RIEV XXIV: 176–181, XXV: 192–194.

Vennemann, Theo. 1993. 'Zur Erklärung bayerischer Gewässer-und Siedlungsnamen'. *Sprachwissenschaft* 18: 425–483.

—— 1994a. 'Linguistic reconstruction in the context of European prehistory'. *Transactions of the Philological Society* 92(2): 215–284.

—— 1994b. 'Der Name der Landeshauptstadt München'. *Literatur in Bayern* September: 2–7.

—— 1995. 'Etymologische Beziehungen im alten Europa'. *Der Ginkgo Baum: Germanistisches Jahrbuch für Nordeuropa* 13: 39–115.

Villasante, Luis. 1973. *Axular-en Hiztegia*. Oinati: JAKIN.

—— 1979. *Historia de la literatura vasca*. Aránzazu: Editorial Aránzazu.

Vinson, Julien. 1891. *Bibliographie de la langue basque*.

—— 1898. *Complément et supplément*.

Vogt, Hans. 1942. 'La parenté des langues caucasiques'. *Norsk Tidskrift for Sprogvidenskap* 9: 321–338.

—— 1955. 'Le basque et les langues caucasiques'. *BSL* 51: 121–147.

Watkins, Calvert. 1969. 'Indo-European roots'. Appendix to *The American Heritage Dictionary of the English Language*, pp. 1505–1550. Boston: American Heritage and Houghton-Mifflin.

Ybarra. 1955. 'Lo romano en Vizcaya'. *Zumárraga* 4: 11–43.

Zabaltza, Xabier. 1995. 'Comments on R. L. Trask's article "Basque and Dene-Caucasian: a critique from the Basque side"'. *Mother Tongue* 1 (new series): 165–171.

Zarate, Mikel. 1976. *Influencias del vascuence en la lengua castellana*. Bilbao: La Gran Enciclopedia Vasca.

Zyhlarz, E. 1932. 'Zur angeblichen Verwandtschaft des Baskischen mit afrikanischen Sprachen'. *Prehistorische Zeitschrift* XXIII, fascicles 1/2. Spanish translation (1934), 'El vasco y el camítico'. *RIEV* 25: 240–244.

Zytsar, Yu. Vl. 1985. 'Los numerales del vascuence'. In Euskaltzandia (1983), pp. 709–729.

Index